Developing Interoperable and Federated Cloud Architecture

Gabor Kecskemeti
University of Miskolc, Hungary

Attila Kertesz
University of Szeged, Hungary

Zsolt Nemeth
MTA SZTAKI, Hungary

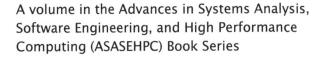
A volume in the Advances in Systems Analysis, Software Engineering, and High Performance Computing (ASASEHPC) Book Series

Information Science REFERENCE
An Imprint of IGI Global

Published in the United States of America by
    Information Science Reference (an imprint of IGI Global)
    701 E. Chocolate Avenue
    Hershey PA, USA 17033
    Tel: 717-533-8845
    Fax: 717-533-8661
    E-mail: cust@igi-global.com
    Web site: http://www.igi-global.com

Library of Congress Cataloging-in-Publication Data

Names: Kecskemeti, Gabor, 1981- editor. | Kertesz, Attila, 1980- editor. |
  Nemeth, Zsolt, 1971- editor.
Title: Developing interoperable and federated cloud architecture / Gabor
  Kecskemeti, Attila Kertesz, and Zsolt Nemeth, editors.
Description: Hershey, PA : Information Science Reference, 2016. | Includes
  bibliographical references and index.
Identifiers: LCCN 2015051296| ISBN 9781522501534 (hardcover) | ISBN
  9781522501541 (ebook)
Subjects: LCSH: Cloud computing. | Computer network architectures.
Classification: LCC QA76.585 .D488 2016 | DDC 004.67/82--dc23 LC record available at http://lccn.loc.gov/2015051296

This book is published in the IGI Global book series Advances in Systems Analysis, Software Engineering, and High Performance Computing (ASASEHPC) (ISSN: 2327-3453; eISSN: 2327-3461)

British Cataloguing in Publication Data
A Cataloguing in Publication record for this book is available from the British Library.

For electronic access to this publication, please contact: eresources@igi-global.com.

Advances in Systems Analysis, Software Engineering, and High Performance Computing (ASASEHPC) Book Series

Vijayan Sugumaran
Oakland University, USA

ISSN: 2327-3453
EISSN: 2327-3461

MISSION

The theory and practice of computing applications and distributed systems has emerged as one of the key areas of research driving innovations in business, engineering, and science. The fields of software engineering, systems analysis, and high performance computing offer a wide range of applications and solutions in solving computational problems for any modern organization.

The **Advances in Systems Analysis, Software Engineering, and High Performance Computing (ASASEHPC) Book Series** brings together research in the areas of distributed computing, systems and software engineering, high performance computing, and service science. This collection of publications is useful for academics, researchers, and practitioners seeking the latest practices and knowledge in this field.

COVERAGE

- Human-Computer Interaction
- Computer System Analysis
- Network Management
- Parallel Architectures
- Computer Graphics
- Storage Systems
- Enterprise Information Systems
- Computer Networking
- Software Engineering
- Performance Modelling

IGI Global is currently accepting manuscripts for publication within this series. To submit a proposal for a volume in this series, please contact our Acquisition Editors at Acquisitions@igi-global.com or visit: http://www.igi-global.com/publish/.

Titles in this Series

For a list of additional titles in this series, please visit: www.igi-global.com

Managing Big Data in Cloud Computing Environments
Zongmin Ma (Nanjing University of Aeronautics and Astronautics, China)
Information Science Reference • copyright 2016 • 314pp • H/C (ISBN: 9781466698345) • US $195.00 (our price)

Emerging Innovations in Agile Software Development
Imran Ghani (Universiti Teknologi Malaysia, Malaysia) Dayang Norhayati Abang Jawawi (Universiti Teknologi Malaysia, Malaysia) Siva Dorairaj (Software Education, New Zealand) and Ahmed Sidky (ICAgile, USA)
Information Science Reference • copyright 2016 • 323pp • H/C (ISBN: 9781466698581) • US $205.00 (our price)

Modern Software Engineering Methodologies for Mobile and Cloud Environments
António Miguel Rosado da Cruz (Instituto Politécnico de Viana do Castelo, Portugal) and Sara Paiva (Instituto Politécnico de Viana do Castelo, Portugal)
Information Science Reference • copyright 2016 • 355pp • H/C (ISBN: 9781466699168) • US $210.00 (our price)

Emerging Research Surrounding Power Consumption and Performance Issues in Utility Computing
Ganesh Chandra Deka (Regional Vocational Training Institute (RVTI) for Women, India) G.M. Siddesh (M S Ramaiah Institute of Technology, Bangalore, India) K. G. Srinivasa (M S Ramaiah Institute of Technology, Bangalore, India) and L.M. Patnaik (IISc, Bangalore, India)
Information Science Reference • copyright 2016 • 460pp • H/C (ISBN: 9781466688537) • US $215.00 (our price)

Advanced Research on Cloud Computing Design and Applications
Shadi Aljawarneh (Jordan University of Science and Technology, Jordan)
Information Science Reference • copyright 2015 • 388pp • H/C (ISBN: 9781466686762) • US $205.00 (our price)

Handbook of Research on Computational Simulation and Modeling in Engineering
Francisco Miranda (Instituto Politécnico de Viana do Castelo and CIDMA of University of Aveiro, Portugal) and Carlos Abreu (Instituto Politécnico de Viana do Castelo, Portugal)
Engineering Science Reference • copyright 2016 • 824pp • H/C (ISBN: 9781466688230) • US $420.00 (our price)

Intelligent Applications for Heterogeneous System Modeling and Design
Kandarpa Kumar Sarma (Gauhati University, India) Manash Pratim Sarma (Gauhati University, India) and Mousmita Sarma (SpeecHWareNet (I) Pvt. Ltd, India)
Information Science Reference • copyright 2015 • 407pp • H/C (ISBN: 9781466684935) • US $255.00 (our price)

www.igi-global.com

701 E. Chocolate Ave., Hershey, PA 17033
Order online at www.igi-global.com or call 717-533-8845 x100
To place a standing order for titles released in this series, contact: cust@igi-global.com
Mon-Fri 8:00 am - 5:00 pm (est) or fax 24 hours a day 717-533-8661

Editorial Advisory Board

Table of Contents

Detailed Table of Contents

Section 1
Foundations

    Marcio R. M. Assis, University of Campinas, Brazil
    Luiz Fernando Bittencourt, University of Campinas, Brazil
    Rafael Tolosana-Calasanz, Universidad of Zaragoza, Spain
    Craig A. Lee, The Aerospace Corporation, USA

With the maturation of the Cloud Computing, the eyes of the scientific community and specialized commercial institutions have turned to research related to the use of multiple clouds. The main reason for this interest is the limitations that many cloud providers individually face to meet all the inherent characteristics of this paradigm. Therefore, using multiple cloud organizations opens the opportunity for the providers to consume resources with more attractive prices, increase the resilience as well as to monetize their own idle resources. When considering customers, problems as interruption of services, lack of interoperability that lead to lock-in and loss of quality of services due to locality are presented as limiting to the adoption of Cloud Computing. This chapter presents an introduction to conceptual characterization of Cloud Federation. Moreover, it presents the challenges in implementing federation architectures, requirements for the development of this type of organization and the relevant architecture proposals.

    Szilvia Varadi, University of Szeged, Hungary

Cloud Computing is a diverse research area that encompasses many aspects of sharing software and hardware solutions, including computing and storage resources, application runtimes or complex application functionalities. In the supply of any goods and services, the law gives certain rights that protect the consumer and provider, which also applies for Cloud Computing. This new technology also moves functions and responsibilities away from local ownership and management to a third-party provided service, and raises several legal issues, such as data protection, which require this service to comply with necessary regulation. In this chapter the author investigates the revised legislation of the European Union resulting in the General Data Protection Regulation, which will be used to set up the new European Data Protection Framework. The author gathers and summarizes the most relevant changes this regulation brings to the field of Clouds, and draws relations to the previous legislation called the Data Protection Directive currently in force.

Chapter 3

Manoj V. Thomas, National Institute of Technology Karnataka, India
K. Chandrasekaran, National Institute of Technology Karnataka, India

Nowadays, the issue of identity and access management (IAM) has become an important research topic in cloud computing. In the distributed computing environments like cloud computing, effective authentication and authorization are essential to make sure that unauthorized users do not access the resources, thereby ensuring the confidentiality, integrity, and availability of information hosted in the cloud environment. In this chapter, the authors discuss the issue of identity and access management in cloud computing, analyzing the work carried out by others in the area. Also, various issues in the current IAM scenario in cloud computing, such as authentication, authorization, access control models, identity life cycle management, cloud identity-as-a-service, federated identity management and also, the identity and access management in the inter-cloud environment are discussed. The authors conclude this chapter discussing a few research issues in the area of identity and access management in the cloud and inter-cloud environments.

Chapter 4

Tamas Pflanzner, University of Szeged, Hungary
Roland Tornyai, University of Szeged, Hungary
Ákos Zoltán Gorácz, University of Szeged, Hungary
Attila Kertesz, University of Szeged, Hungary

Cloud Computing has opened new ways of flexible resource provisions for businesses migrating IT applications and data to the cloud to respond to new demands from customers. Recently, many businesses plan to take advantage of the flexible resource provision. Cloud Federations envisage a distributed, heterogeneous environment consisting of various cloud infrastructures by aggregating different IaaS provider capabilities coming from both the commercial and academic area. Recent solutions hide the diversity of multiple clouds and form a unified federation on top of them. Many approaches follow recent trends in cloud application development, and offer federation capabilities at the platform level, thus creating Platform-as-a-Service solutions. In this chapter the authors investigate capabilities of PaaS solutions and present a classification of these tools: what levels of developer experience they offer, what types of APIs, developer tools they support and what web GUIs they provide. Developer experience is measured by creating and executing sample applications with these PaaS tools.

Section 2
Practice and Experience

Chapter 5

Chetan Jaiswal, University of Missouri Kansas City, USA
Vijay Kumar, University of Missouri Kansas City, USA

Legacy database systems manage transactions under a concurrency control and a recovery protocol. The underlying operating system creates transaction execution platform and the database executes transactions concurrently. When the database system fails then the recovery manager applies "Undo" and/or "Redo" operations (depending upon the recovery protocol) to achieve the consistent state of the database. The recovery manager performs these set of operations as required by transaction execution platform. The availability of "Virtual" machines on cloud has given us an architecture that makes it possible to eliminate the effect of system or transaction failure by always taking the database to the next consistent state. We present a novel scheme of eliminating the effect of such failure by applying transaction "roll-forward" which resumes its execution from the point of failure. We refer to our system as AAP (Always Ahead Processing). Our work enables cloud providers to offer transactional HA-DBMS as an option that too with multiple data sources not necessarily relational.

Chapter 6

Ioan Petri, Cardiff University, UK
Javier Diaz-Montes, Rutgers University, USA
Mengsong Zou, Rutgers University, USA
Ali Reza Zamani, Rutgers University, USA
Thomas H Beach, Cardiff School of Engineering, UK
Omer F. Rana, Cardiff University, UK
Manish Parashar, Rutgers University, USA
Yacine Rezgui, Cardiff University, UK

Cloud computing has emerged as attractive platform for computing data intensive applications. However, efficient computation of this kind of workloads requires understanding how to store, process, and analyse large volumes of data in a timely manner. Many "smart cities" applications, for instance, identify how data from building sensors can be combined together to support applications such as emergency response, energy management, etc. Enabling sensor data to be transmitted to a cloud environment for processing provides a number of benefits, such as scalability and on-demand provisioning of computational resources. In this chapter, we propose the use of a multi-layer cloud infrastructure that distributes processing over sensing nodes, multiple intermediate/gateways nodes, and large data centres. Our solution aims at utilising the pervasive computational capabilities located at the edge of the infrastructure and along the data path to reduce data movement to large data centres located "deep" into the infrastructure and perform a more efficient use of computing and network resources.

ENTICE is an H2020 European project aiming to research and create a novel Virtual Machine (VM) repository and operational environment for federated Cloud infrastructures to: (i) simplify the creation of lightweight and highly optimised VM images tuned for functional descriptions of applications; (ii) automatically decompose and distribute VM images based on multi-objective optimisation (performance, economic costs, storage size, and QoS needs) and a knowledge base and reasoning infrastructure to meet application runtime requirements; and (iii) elastically auto-scale applications on Cloud resources based on their fluctuating load with optimised VM interoperability across Cloud infrastructures and without provider lock-in, in order to finally fulfil the promises that virtualization technology has failed to deliver so far. In this chapter, we give an inside view into the ENTICE project architecture. Based on stakeholders that interact with ENTICE, we describe the different functionalities of the different components and services and how they interact with each other.

Many e-science initiatives are currently investigating the use of cloud computing to support all kinds of scientific activities. The objective of this chapter is to describe the architecture and the deployment of the EUBrazilCC federated e-infrastructure, a Research & Development project that aims at providing a user-centric test bench enabling European and Brazilian research communities to test the deployment and execution of scientific applications on a federated intercontinental e-infrastructure. This e-infrastructure exploits existing resources that consist of virtualized data centers, supercomputers, and even opportunistically exploited desktops spread over a transatlantic geographic area. These heterogeneous resources are federated with the aid of appropriate middleware that provide the necessary features to achieve the established challenging goals. In order to elicit the requirements and validate the resulting infrastructure, three complex scientific applications have been implemented, which are also presented here.

Chapter 9

Bruno Veloso, Instituto Superior de Engenharia do Porto, Portugal
Fernando Meireles, Instituto Superior de Engenharia do Porto, Portugal
Benedita Malheiro, Instituto Superior de Engenharia do Porto, Portugal
Juan Carlos Burguillo, Universidade de Vigo, Spain

This paper presents the CloudAnchor brokerage platform for the transaction of single provider as well as federated Infrastructure as a Service (IaaS) resources. The platform, which is a layered Multi-Agent System (MAS), provides multiple services, including (consumer or provider) business registration and deregistration, provider coalition creation and termination, provider lookup and invitation and negotiation services regarding brokerage, coalitions and resources. Providers, consumers and virtual providers, representing provider coalitions, are modelled by dedicated agents within the platform. The main goal of the platform is to negotiate and establish Service Level Agreements (SLA). In particular, the platform contemplates the establishment of brokerage SLA – bSLA – between the platform and each provider or consumer, coalition SLA – cSLA – between the members of a coalition of providers and resource SLA – rSLA – between a consumer and a provider. Federated resources are detained and negotiated by virtual providers on behalf of the corresponding coalitions of providers.

Chapter 10

Javier Prades, Technical University of Valencia, Spain
Fernando Campos, Technical University of Valencia, Spain
Carlos Reaño, Technical University of Valencia, Spain
Federico Silla, Technical University of Valencia, Spain

Current data centers leverage virtual machines (VMs) in order to efficiently use hardware resources. VMs allow reducing equipment acquisition costs as well as decreasing overall energy consumption. However, although VMs have noticeably evolved to make a smart use of the underlying hardware, the use of GPUs (Graphics Processing Units) for General Purpose computing (GPGPU) is still not efficiently supported. This concern might be addressed by remote GPU virtualization solutions, which may provide VMs with GPUs located in a remote node, detached from the host where the VMs are being executed. This chapter presents an in-depth analysis about how to provide GPU access to applications running inside VMs. This analysis is complemented with experimental results which show that the use of remote GPU virtualization is an effective mechanism to provide GPU access to applications with negligible overheads. Finally, the approach is presented in the context of cloud federations for providing GPGPU as a Service.

Chapter 11

Cloud Computing (CC) offers simple and cost effective outsourcing in dynamic service environments and allows the construction of service-based applications extensible with the latest achievements of diverse research areas. CC is built using dedicated and reliable resources and provides uniform seemingly unlimited capacities. Volunteer Computing (VC) on the other hand uses volatile, heterogeneous and unreliable resources. This chapter per the authors makes an attempt starting from a definition for Cloud Computing to identify the required steps and formulate a definition for what can be considered as the next evolutionary stage for Volunteer Computing: Volunteer Clouds (VCl). There are many idiosyncrasies of VC to overcome (e.g., volatility, heterogeneity, reliability, responsiveness, scalability, etc.). Heterogeneity exists in VC at different levels. The vision of CC promises to provide a homogeneous environment. The goal of this chapter per the authors is to identify methods and propose solutions that tackle the heterogeneities and thus, make a step towards Volunteer Clouds.

Preface

BACKGROUND

Infrastructure as a Service (IaaS) cloud systems allow the dynamic creation, destruction and management of Virtual Machines (VM) on virtualized clusters. IaaS clouds provide a high-level of abstraction to the end user that allows the creation of on-demand services through a pay as you go infrastructure combined with elasticity. The increasing range of choices and availability of IaaS toolkits has also allowed creation of cloud solutions and frameworks suitable for private deployment and practical use even on smaller scales. As a result, many academic infrastructure service providers have started transitions to add cloud resources to their previously existing campus and shared grid deployments. To complete such solutions, they should also support the unification of multiple cloud and/or cloud and grid solutions in a seamless, preferably interoperable way. Hybrid, community or multi-clouds may utilize more than one cloud systems, which are also called cloud federations. The management of such federations raises several challenges and opens issues that require significant research work to be done in this area.

The Positioning of the Book

The more widespread cloud computing technologies are, the more likely people will face the interoperability issues when several cloud infrastructures must be used in parallel. This book is well suited to the practitioners who utilize cloud infrastructures and would like to avoid lock in issues or to increase the reliability of their virtual infrastructures. On the other hand, with the rise of private cloud infrastructures, hybrid clouds, cloud bursting technologies and partial outsourcing, the solutions offered in this book aid the private infrastructure providers to help efficiently deal with temporal under-provisioning situations.

Whom Is This Book Intended For?

This book provides a dedicated forum for sharing the latest results, exchanging ideas and experiences, presenting new research, development and deployment efforts in developing and running interoperable, federated IaaS cloud systems. It is aimed at defining the current state, determining further goals and presenting architectures and service frameworks to achieve highly interoperable federated cloud infrastructures. It presents solutions to interoperability and efficient management challenges faced by current and future infrastructure clouds, with a specific focus on cloud federation aimed at readers with specific interest in topics not addressed elsewhere such as federation policies, energy awareness, federation use cases, legal aspects of federation, scheduling and interoperability.

OVERVIEW OF THE SUBMISSIONS AND THE ACCEPTED CHAPTERS

The 'Call for chapter proposals' for the book was launched in winter 2014/15 and resulted 22 submissions, which were of good quality and generally relevant to the theme of the special issue. The chapter proposals, submitted chapters and their subsequent revisions were reviewed both by the experts in the field and by the guest editors - this procedure guaranteed that each paper received at least 2-3 reviews. After the initial selection process, the chapters were sent for one further revision round. Finally, we have selected the 8 strongest chapters (giving us a 36% acceptance rate). These chapters represent three major research areas, requirements and solutions for creating federated cloud infrastructures. These chapters are organized into two major sections. The first section overviews the theoretical background and provides an analysis of current research on cloud federations and multi-clouds, in general. The second section is more technical and provides in-depth details of particular topics. To strengthen the sections, we have also invited 3 additional papers. One on the legal aspects of the topic, how European data protection laws affect cloud federations. The second additional paper presents a H2020 funded European research project (called ENTICE) and presents how it envisions altering the current federated cloud landscape with a novel view on virtual machine image delivery techniques. Finally, the third additional paper presents the aspect of volunteer clouds to conclude the book with an interesting outlook for potential future practices. In the followings we provide a short overview of the selected papers.

Chapter 1, is titled "Cloud Federations: Requirements, Properties, and Architectures", and presents a generic view on Cloud Federations. It summarizes the inherent characteristics of this paradigm and the limitations many cloud providers face. The chapter argues that multiple cloud organizations open the opportunity for the providers to utilize resources with more attractive prices, increase the resilience and monetize their own idle resources. When considering customers, problems such as interruption of services, lack of interoperability that lead to lock-in and loss of quality of services due to locality are presented as limiting factors to the adoption of Cloud Computing. The chapter presents an introduction to the conceptual characterization of Cloud Federation solutions, and highlights the challenges of implementing federated architectures, the requirements for the development of this type of organization and the relevant proposed architectures.

Chapter 2, "Regulating European Clouds - The New European Data Protection Framework" is one of the additional papers that introduces legal aspects of federated cloud computing. In the supply of any goods and services, the law gives certain rights that protect the consumer and provider, and this also applies for Cloud Computing services. This new technology moves functions and responsibilities away from local ownership and management to a service provided by third-parties and raises several legal issues, such as data protection, which require the service to comply with certain regulation. This chapter overviews and analyses the revised legislation of the European Union resulting in the General Data Protection Regulation, which will be used to set up the new European Data Protection Framework. The author gathers and summarizes the most relevant changes this regulation brings to the field of Clouds and relate them to the antecedent legislation called the Data Protection Directive currently in force.

Following, Chapter 3, "Identity and Access Management in the Cloud Computing Environments" explores the issue of identity and access management that became an important research topic in cloud computing recently Since cloud infrastructures and even more, federated cloud infrastructures may collect and provide an enormous quantity and quality of resources, their access must be controlled and effective authentication and authorization are essential to make sure that unauthorized users cannot access the resources, thereby ensuring the validity, confidentiality, integrity, and availability of information hosted in the cloud environment. This chapter discusses the identity and access management by analyzing the work carried out in this area. Also, various issues in the current identity and access management practices in cloud computing, such as authentication, authorization, access control models, identity life cycle management, cloud identity-as-a-service, federated identity management and also, the identity and access management in the inter-cloud environment are presented.

Chapter 4, "Characterizing PaaS Solutions enabling Cloud Federations" gives an outlook at realizing interoperale cloud services at a higher level above IaaS. Recently many businesses migrate their IT applications and data to the Cloud to take advantage of the flexible resource provisioning that can bring benefits to businesses by responding quickly to new demands from customers. Recent solutions hide the diversity of multiple utilized clouds and form a unified federation on top of them. Many approaches follow recent trends in cloud application development, and offer federation capabilities at the platform level thus, creating Platform-as-a-Service solutions. This chapter overviews the capabilities of these approaches: what levels of developer experience they offer, how they follow recent trends in cloud application development, what types of APIs, developer tools they support and what web GUIs they provide.

Subsequently, Chapter 5, "Highly Available Fault-Tolerant Cloud Database Services" presents a different aspect of utilizing the virtual machines in the cloud. Legacy database systems manage transactions under a concurrency control and a recovery protocol. The underlying operating system creates a transaction execution platform and the database executes transactions concurrently. The availability of virtual machines in clouds however, makes it possible to eliminate the effect of system or transaction failure by always taking the database to the next consistent state. This chapter presents a novel scheme of eliminating such failures by applying transaction "roll-forward" which resumes the execution from the point of failure.

Chapter 6, "Distributed Multi-Cloud Based Building Data Analytics" sets the focus on data storage and data movement in a scenario where computation is dispersed and also defines a hierarchical view of the processing capabilities. The efficient computation of data intensive applications requires understanding how to store, process, and analyze large volumes of data in a timely manner. Many smart city applications, for instance, identify how data from building sensors can be combined together to support applications such as emergency response, energy management, etc. Enabling sensor data to be transmitted to a cloud environment for processing provides a number of benefits, such as scalability and on-demand provisioning of computational resources. This chapter proposes the use of a multi-layer cloud infrastructure that distributes processing over sensing nodes, multiple intermediate / gateway nodes, and large data centres. The presented solution aims at utilizing the pervasive computational capabilities located at the edge of the infrastructure and along the data path to reduce data movement to large data centres located deep into the infrastructure and perform a more efficient use of computing and network resources.

Next, Chapter 7, "dEcentralised repositories for traNsparent and efficienT vIrtual maChine opErations: Architecture of the ENTICE Project " is another additional paper that presents the aims and approaches of a major project on federated clouds. ENTICE is an H2020 European project aimed at creating a novel Virtual Machine (VM) repository and operational environment for federated Cloud infrastructures. The operational environment in focus is envisioned to simplify the creation of lightweight and highly optimized VM images tuned for functional descriptions of applications. Furthermore, it also automatically decomposes and distributes VM images based on multi-objective optimization to meet application runtime requirements, and enables the elastic scaling of applications on Cloud resources, based on their fluctuating load, by optimized VM interoperability across Cloud infrastructures. This chapter gives an inside view into the ENTICE project architecture. Based on stakeholders that interact with ENTICE, it also describes the different functionalities of the various components and services and how they interact with each other.

Chapter 8, "EUBrazilCC Federated Cloud: A Transatlantic Multi-Cloud Infrastructure" is another overview of a major project on creating an intercontinental federated cloud. This chapter describes the architecture and the deployment of the EUBrazilCC federated e-infrastructure, a Research & Development project that aims at providing a user-centric test bench enabling European and Brazilian research communities to test the deployment and execution of scientific applications on a federated intercontinental e-infrastructure. This e-infrastructure exploits existing resources that consist of virtualized data centers, supercomputers, and even opportunistically exploited desktops spread over a transatlantic geographic area. These heterogeneous resources are federated with the aid of appropriate middleware that provides the necessary features to achieve the established challenges. In order to elicit the requirements and validate the resulting infrastructure, three complex scientific applications have been implemented, which are also presented.

Chapter 9, "Federated IaaS Resource Brokerage" is more towards the in-depth insights and analyses of technical realizationsof Service Level Agreements. It presents the CloudAnchor brokerage platform for dealing with both individual providers as well as federated Infrastructure as a Service (IaaS) resources. The platform, which is a layered Multi-Agent System (MAS), provides multiple services including (consumer or provider) business registration and deregistration, provider coalition creation and termination, provider lookup and invitation and negotiation services regarding brokerage, coalitions and resources. Providers, consumers and virtual providers, representing provider coalitions, are modelled by dedicated agents within the platform. The main goal of the platform is to negotiate and establish Service Level Agreements (SLA). In particular, the platform supports multiple notions of SLA and contemplates the establishment of 'brokerage SLA' between the platform and each provider or consumer, 'coalition SLA' between the members of a coalition of providers and 'resource SLA' between a consumer and a provider. Federated resources are detained and negotiated by virtual providers on behalf of the corresponding coalitions of providers.

Chapter 10,"GPGPU as a Service: Providing GPU-Acceleration Services to Federated Cloud Systems" adds further technical challenges and solutions for enhancing cloud federations by advanced computing resources. Current data centers leverage virtual machines in order to efficiently use hardware resources. VMs allow reducing equipment acquisition costs as well as decreasing overall energy consumption. However, although VMs have noticeably evolved to make a smart use of the underlying hardware, the use of GPUs (Graphics Processing Units) for General Purpose computing (GPGPU) is still not efficiently supported. This concern might be addressed by remote GPU virtualization solutions, which may provide VMs with GPUs located in a remote node, detached from the host where the VMs are being executed. This chapter presents an in-depth analysis of providing GPU access to applications running inside VMs. This analysis is complemented with experimental results which show that the use of remote GPU virtualization is an effective mechanism to provide GPU access to applications with negligible overheads. Finally, the approach is presented in the context of cloud federations for providing GPGPU as a Service.

Chapter 11, "Volunteer Clouds: From Volunteer Computing to Interconnected Infrastructures" concludes the book and gives an outlook to potential future directions of realizing federated clouds. Volunteer Computing (VC) is an established and known paradigm that uses volatile, heterogeneous and unreliable resources. This chapter makes an attempt, starting from a definition for Cloud Computing, to identify the required steps and formulate a definition for what can be considered as the next evolutionary stage of Volunteer Computing: Volunteer Clouds (VCl). There are many idiosyncrasies of VC to overcome (e.g., volatility, heterogeneity, reliability, responsiveness, scalability, etc.) for example, heterogeneity exists in VC at different levels whereas the vision of cloud computing promises to provide a homogeneous environment. The chapter identifies methods and proposes solutions that tackle the heterogenity and thus, make a step towards Volunteer Clouds.

Section 1
Foundations

Chapter 1
Cloud Federations:
Requirements, Properties, and Architectures

Marcio R. M. Assis
University of Campinas, Brazil

Rafael Tolosana-Calasanz
Universidad of Zaragoza, Spain

Luiz Fernando Bittencourt
University of Campinas, Brazil

Craig A. Lee
The Aerospace Corporation, USA

ABSTRACT

With the maturation of the Cloud Computing, the eyes of the scientific community and specialized commercial institutions have turned to research related to the use of multiple clouds. The main reason for this interest is the limitations that many cloud providers individually face to meet all the inherent characteristics of this paradigm. Therefore, using multiple cloud organizations opens the opportunity for the providers to consume resources with more attractive prices, increase the resilience as well as to monetize their own idle resources. When considering customers, problems as interruption of services, lack of interoperability that lead to lock-in and loss of quality of services due to locality are presented as limiting to the adoption of Cloud Computing. This chapter presents an introduction to conceptual characterization of Cloud Federation. Moreover, it presents the challenges in implementing federation architectures, requirements for the development of this type of organization and the relevant architecture proposals.

INTRODUCTION

Cloud Computing (Mell & Grance, 2011) has emerged as a *vedette* in information technology in the 21st century, presenting a paradigm shift on how computing capacity is acquired by consumers. In this paradigm, computing resources of various kinds are offered as a service in the form of utilities, where users pay according to their necessity for computing power. Computing services in clouds can be offered at three different levels, according to the computing object being offered: (i) Infrastructure as a Service (IaaS), offered to infrastructure management clients; (ii) Platform as a Service, offered to application

DOI: 10.4018/978-1-5225-0153-4.ch001

development clients; and (iii) Software as a Service (SaaS), offered to the application's final users. The most prominent characteristic that makes cloud computing attractive is the elasticity, which allows management of computing power, increasing or decreasing it, according to the workload. For cloud clients, elasticity allows cost reduction and avoidance of upfront investments in computing infrastructure. On the other hand, providing elasticity is a challenging technical issue that must be tackled by cloud providers.

Elasticity provisioning is inherent to the amount of physical resources (e.g., CPU) that each cloud provider has on its datacenter(s). Therefore, resource exhaustion can compromise service offering to cloud clients, as well as hamper the quality of services already running, especially in small- and medium-sized cloud providers. Other limiting factors of monolithic clouds (where a provider is a single, isolated, domain) include the business continuity problems in case of unexpected faults that cause service disruption (Toosi, Calheiros, & Buyya, 2014; Grozev & Buyya, 2012); the challenging issues related to lack of geographical dispersion, which can affect quality of service; and lack of interoperability with other providers (Grozev & Buyya, 2012; Assis, Bittencourt, & Tolosana-Calasanz, 2014). In face of such limitations, a need for evolution of this technology arises, where solutions of multiple clouds started to be designed and deployed.

Along with the multiple clouds solutions recently proposed, such as Multi-Clouds (Kurze et al., 2011; Grozev & Buyya, 2012; Toosi et al., 2014) and Sky-Computing (Keahey, Tsugawa, Matsunaga, & Fortes, 2009), the Cloud Federation can be highlighted as a voluntary association of clouds subject to a federative contract that defines the behavior (duties and penalties) of participating entities. In this chapter we define and discuss properties, opportunities, challenges, current research state and development of Cloud Federations.

The remainder of this chapter is organized as follows: the Background section presents the characteristics of Cloud Computing in detail. The definition of Cloud Federation, the motivations to the emergence of this kind of association, the open challenges in Federations, and the identified characteristics are presented in Cloud Federations: Motivations and Challenges section. The Cloud Federations Properties section describes the properties identified in cloud federations. In Architectural Specifications, Blueprint and Existing System section, some of the main federation architectures available in the literature are presented, followed by the concluding section.

BACKGROUND

This section aims to provide insight for understanding the rest of the document. It presents the Cloud Computing paradigm, exploring its main properties, delivery and deployment models, as well as covering their characteristics and key elements.

Cloud Computing

The term Cloud Computing has frequently been used as a synonym for technological advancement. However, there is not a uniform understanding of its meaning, which is mainly due to the overloading of multiple related concepts behind the term Cloud.

As quoted in the compilation of cloud-related work performed by Vaquero et al. (Vaquero, Rodero-Merino, Caceres, & Lindner, 2008), some authors as Watson et al. (Watson, Lord, Gibson, Periorellis, & Pitsilis, 2008) and Geelan et al. (Geelan et al., 2008) define Cloud Computing as a novel computing

Figure 1. Three-layer model of Cloud Computing

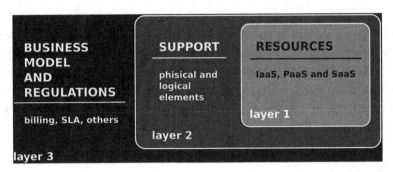

paradigm providing resources through a new business model, which allows the reduction of capital used to purchase resources (Zhang, Cheng, & Boutaba, 2010). Antonopoulos and Lee (Antonopoulos & Gillam, 2010) describe Cloud Computing as the natural evolution of existing technologies offered on a new business model in which consumers only pay for usage resources of interest. In another seminal work, the technical report produced by the UC Berkley Adaptive Distributed Systems Laboratory (Armbrust et al., 2009) states that Cloud Computing refers to the applications offered as a service (SLA@SOI, 2011) over the Internet and all hardware and software used to provide the services. The institute National Institute of Standards and Technology (NIST) (Mell & Grance, 2011) describes Cloud Computing as a model to conveniently activate a set of computational resources that can be rapidly provisioned and released with minimal effort or interaction.

Synthesizing the definitions above, Cloud Computing can be described as a set of several existing technologies working in a symbiosis to provide computing resources to interested parties on a new paradigm of computing utility and marketing, where customers sometimes pay for usage according to restrictions and duties defined in a contract. This description allows Cloud Computing to be organized in a three-layer model, as shown in Figure 1. At the first layer are the resources for the provisioning in the form of services; at the second layer there are physical and logical elements that enable the operation of the cloud; and at the peripheral layer the business model and items that regulate how services will be offered and charged can be found.

Cloud Computing Paradigm Properties

Although Cloud Computing shares characteristics with previous types of distributed systems, there is a number of properties for Cloud Computing that differentiate it from previous paradigms.

Physical Resource Sharing

Recent advances in virtualization technologies have enabled an efficient sharing, or multi-tenancy, of physical resources (i.e. networking communications, processors, memory, and storage) among various users (Zhang et al., 2010). Virtualization is a critical aspect in Cloud Computing as it supports the on-demand computation by allowing stakeholders to adjust customized resources to the run-time requirements. This is made considering the isolation between consumers (the resources allocated to a consumer cannot be accessed by others without authorization), and it offers consumers control over the acquired virtualized resources (Foster, Zhao, Raicu, & Lu, 2008).

Elasticity

Elasticity is the ability of a system to adapt to workload changes by on-demand provisioning and de-provisioning of resources, such that at each point in time the available resources match the current demand as closely as possible (Herbst, Kounev, & Reussner, 2013). As discussed by Herbst et al. in (Herbst et al., 2013), elasticity differs from scalability in which the latter is the ability of the system to sustain increasing workloads by making use of additional resources at run-time and without requiring human intervention.

Self-Provisioning

Self-provisioning is the property that allows Cloud consumers to manage contracted resources in an affordable and agile way, reducing bureaucracy and increasing the dynamism of use. This is accomplished mostly often by means of a dashboard, which makes the interface more user-friendly to the environment. This dashboard enables consumers to perform management and monitoring tasks such as instantiation and consumption of resources agreed in the Service Level Agreement (SLA), as well as reporting without requiring previous, advanced knowledge in administration of these types of activities.

Business Model

The marketing model in this technology differs from conservative systems that determine a fixed monthly fee for consumption of a quantity of resources within a time period (month, year etc.). Called pay-as-you-go (Mell & Grance, 2009; Foster et al., 2008), this model is to charge only what the customer consumes. For the values to be charged, metrics are used to account the amount of resources consumed (e.g. processing cycles/hour), and basic values (Zhang et al., 2010) by unit use (e.g. the value of a processing cycle). Both items are specified and pre-agreed in the SLA.

Delivery Models

In Cloud Computing, resources are offered in the form of services (Gang & Mingchuan, 2014). There is no explicit limitation on the type of resource that can be offered as a service within this paradigm, ant it is common to find in the literature (Banerjee et al., 2011; Armbrust et al., 2009) the term Everything as a Service (XaaS). Within this universe of features, the ones that act on resources can also be found and may also be available as services, such as high availability and monitoring (Al-Hazmi, Campowsky, & Magedanz, 2012).

There is a canonical organization of services in Cloud Computing (Zhang et al., 2010). This organization consists of three distinct delivery models that are now a reference to all the services offered in this computing model. It is possible to characterize these classes by the target audience (infrastructure manager, developer, and end user) of their services. Considering this relationship we have: i) Infrastructure as a Service (IaaS) – focuses on providing resources such as processor, storage or communication networks, ii) Platform as a Service (PaaS) – focuses on mapping applications onto the infrastructure, and iii) Software as a Service (SaaS) – focuses on end-users and providing them with applications. Figure 2 organizes these three models of service. These service models were originally used to denote how much of the system stack is "owned" by the provider and the user, as illustrated in Figure 3.

Figure 2. Canonical organization of cloud delivery services

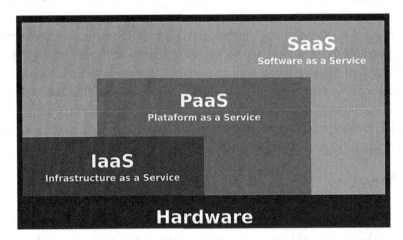

Figure 3. System stack ownership in cloud delivery service

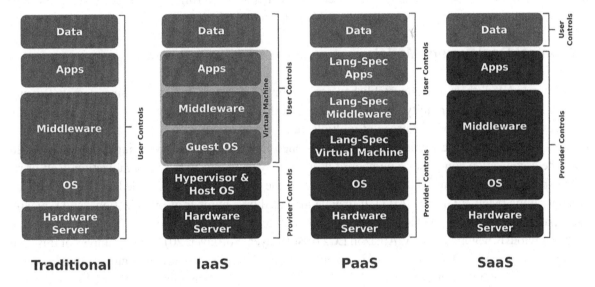

Infrastructure as a Service

Infrastructure as a Service (Bhardwaj, Jain, & Jain, 2010) is the basis of Cloud Computing. It is the delivery of computing infrastructure assets that can be offered (processors, storage areas, etc.) as a service to customers. These assets are made available through virtual partitions of physical resources (some exceptions (Campbell et al., 2009) do not use virtualization). However, customers see these partitions as completely isolated and independent resources. There are several IaaS providers available in the market. Amazon stood out for popularizing Cloud Computing to the general public and has a portfolio of IaaS products, including EC2 (EC2, 2015). Microsoft also offers infrastructure as a service through Microsoft Azure (Azure, 2015). Adding to them, Google and Rackspace companies that, respectively, provide Google Compute Engine (Google Compute Engine, 2015) and the Rackspace Open Cloud (Rackspace, 2015). A study by Li et al. (Li, Yang, Kandula, & Zhang, 2010) compares the features and functionalities of the leading IaaS providers that were available in 2010.

Platform as a Service

Platform as a Service (Tolosana-Calasanz, Bañares, & Colom, 2015) abstracts the underlying computing infrastructure and provides the developer with a language interface, so that both the program logic and the SLAs can be specified. It is of paramount importance that such specifications are infrastructure-agnostic, that is, without referring to specific details of a particular infrastructure. PaaS aims at application developing and subsequent deployment. Hence, it typically provides a complete set of tools and programming models and interfaces for processing the logic and automatically deploying and executing them into de underlying infrastructures (Tolosana-Calasanz et al., 2015).

Software as a Service

The Software as a Service model provides software applications as a service, thereby end-users do not have to install them in their computers, but they can access them through the network. This delivery model allows end-users to pay for the usage of the software and save costs of management and maintenance of hardware. On the other hand, SaaS providers can also benefit by offering the same software instance to a multiple clients, adopting the so-called SaaS Multi-tenancy architecture.

Canonical Deployment Models

According to NIST, there are four established deployment models for Cloud computing, namely Private, Public, Hybrid, and Community clouds. Moreover, both Hybrid and Community clouds can actually involve the interconnection and usage of multiple cloud infrastructures.

In a *Private cloud*, the infrastructure is provisioned for exclusive use by a single organization. In turn, the organization comprises a number of users. It may be managed by the organization itself or by a third-party (Mell & Grance, 2011). In *Public clouds*, the infrastructure is provided for open use by the general public (Mell & Grance, 2011). It may be managed by a number of organizations, and typically users pay per the usage, while the provider agrees to enforce the Quality of Service (QoS) in accordance with a previously negotiated SLA. Amazon EC2 or SoftLayer (Softlayer, 2015) are examples of this type of deployment model. A *Hybrid cloud* is a composition of two or more distinct cloud infrastructures (i.e. private, community, or public) that remain unique entities, but are bound together by standardized or proprietary technology that enables data and application portability (e.g., cloud bursting for load balancing between clouds) (Mell & Grance, 2011). Finally, *a Community cloud* is a collaborative effort among several organizations from a specific community with common concerns (security, compliance, jurisdiction, etc.). The organizations share their infrastructures among the users (Mell & Grance, 2011).

CLOUD FEDERATIONS: MOTIVATIONS AND CHALLENGES

The study of Cloud Federations is a relatively new topic in the broader Cloud Computing subject. Therefore, some concepts are new and diffuse. One of the pioneers in research in this area is Dr. Rajkumar Buyya in his work with Grozev (Grozev & Buyya, 2012), which discussed aspects of the formalization of various concepts related to multiple cloud organizations. The same authors addressed Cloud Federations as a voluntary grouping of different clouds that work together to exchange resources[1] when needed.

In another study, Buyya et al. (Buyya, Ranjan, & Calheiros, 2010) report that a Cloud Federation must have at least three characteristics in order to be effective: to be able to dynamically expand or resize the present resources to meet the demand that may arise; operate as part of a market directed to loan resources; and, finally, deliver reliable services to customers, with effective costs and respecting QoS predetermined by a contract.

In works by Manno et al. (Manno, Smari, & Spalazzi, 2012) and Celesti et al. (Celeti et al., 2010), a Cloud Federation is described as a geographically dispersed community, where several heterogeneous and autonomous clouds cooperate sharing computer resources to achieve a common goal described in a contract. This agreement also defines the economic and technical aspects of the federation: charging model, quality of service, policies, use restrictions and penalties that may arise when the restrictions are violated. Manno et al. (Manno et al., 2012) also report that every cloud belonging to a federation is interpreted as an independent domain, with autonomy over their native computing assets and the free will to, at any time, leave the community.

Govil et al. (Chaurasiya, Srinivasan, Thyagarajan, Govil, & Das, 2012) argue that this organization arose from the union of service providers to make more resources available for their clients, and thereby to reduce problems related to non-compliance with SLAs. From the point of view of the authors, clouds organized in associations provide several advantages, among which: i) performance guarantee – through the use of resources "borrowed" from other clouds, the performance of services can be maintained; ii) guaranteed availability – the diversity of locations where clouds infrastructure are located allows the migration of services from areas that may be affected by outages (Amazon, 2011, 2012), maintaining the availability of consumer services; iii) convenience – the federation provides convenience for consumers in relation to contracted services, and they may see their various services in a unified manner; and iv) dynamic distribution of workload – due to geographical dispersion, it is possible to redirect workloads to clouds closer to customers.

This work uses a synthesis of the above definitions, also exploiting the fact that there is no impediment for specialized clouds from the same institution to constitute a federation. We propose the following definition:

Cloud Federation is a multiple cloud organization with a voluntary character. It should have a maximum geographical dispersion, a well-defined marketing system, and be regulated in terms of the Federative Agreement that determines the behavior of heterogeneous and autonomous clouds. This organization has to be able to provide effective resource scalability, ensure the performance of services, perform a dynamic allocation of resources present in the environment, and honor end-to-end SLA to consumers.

In the remainder of this section, we list the main reasons to the emergence of federations and challenges identified by several authors to design a final architecture of a Cloud Federation. Based on this, are describes so the functional and usage properties that must be present in this organization.

Motivation

As discussed above, individual cloud providers cannot achieve certain properties from Cloud Computing paradigm. Even some multiple clouds solutions, such as Hybrid Clouds (Bittencourt & Madeira, 2011; Mell & Grance, 2009), are not able to meet all identified needs. This section aims to describe four major limitations that are presented as reasons for the emergence of Cloud Federations.

Resource Provisioning

The predicted amount of physical resources needed to support the applications is subject to variable behavior. This dynamicity is one of the main difficulties faced by resource management in this environment. There are two conservative approaches (Toosi, Calheiros, Thulasiram, & Buyya, 2011) used by providers to handle variable resource consumption: oversizing, or overprovisioning, and undersizing, or underprovisioning. In oversizing, the environment allocates beforehand a significant amount of resources to handle peak workload. Since demand can be variable, there may be a waste of resources most of the time (light gray area in Figure 4a) because many resources will be idle unnecessarily consuming energy (Armbrust et al., 2009). The second approach underestimates consumption, pre-allocating resources according to the average usage over time, thus not considering potential unexpected variations in the workload. In undersizing (Figure 4b) there is less waste of computational resources, but peak demand for resources can lead to degradation of service until the extra resources can be reactively allocated. This lack of prompt provisioning can lead to eminent losses that go beyond economic performance, such as loss of confidence in the service provision or in the provider itself.

One of the objectives in Cloud Computing is to dynamically solve (proactively or reactively) the resource provisioning problem (Zhang et al., 2010), offering the property called elasticity. However, the elasticity is performed on physical assets which in turn are finite. Small and medium providers are more sensitive because they have fewer assets, which can cause resource contention to new requests and hamper elasticity (Toosi et al., 2014). Providing mechanisms to mitigate this limitation is one of the motivations of the Cloud Federation (Hassan, Abdullah-Al-Wadud, & Fortino, 2015). Clouds organized in associations can offer their idle resources and/or request additional resources as needed to other members of the organization (Gomes, Vo, & Kowalczyk, 2012), which transcends the limits of local physical resources. Being governed by a contract, this sharing behaves obeying certain pre-established rules. Solutions such as the categorization of supply/resource consumption by clouds within the federation are proposed by Kecskemeti et al. (Kecskemeti et al., 2012; Marosi, Kecskemeti, Kert´esz, & Kacsuk, 2011). Gomes et al. (Gomes et al., 2012) propose the use of economic tools to provide context to resource sharing. Other authors (Mihailescu & Teo, 2010; Flake, Tacken, & Zoth, 2012) dynamically define resource prices to regulate supply and demand within the federation and the use of policies (Petri et al., 2014) to define sharing (Rochwerger et al., 2009). A reputation system can also be used to moderate sharing on multiple cloud organizations, especially in Cloud Federation. Hassan, Abdullah-Al-Wadud and Fortino (2015)

Figure 4. Chart depicting the variation from resource allocation to meet variable demands in workload: (a) represents oversizing of resources and (b), undersizing

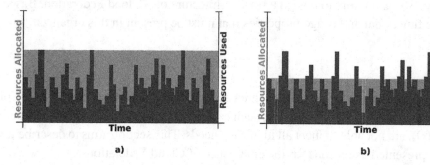

interpret the provisioning of resources as a financial incentive problem, and they proposed a dynamic distribution mechanism of the profit earned in the federation to cloud providers.

Regional Workloads

The worldwide network of computers named as Internet is scattered globally. Services such as social networks and search engines run over it, benefitting from its reachability to aggregate the largest number of potential customers. In this scenario, the quality of services is affected by technical factors (e.g. latency) and usage factors, such as those based on consumer culture of certain regions. Popular services that have global range (users worldwide) are subject to local workload variations determined by regional events (in addition to the global ones). For example, the famous day of discounts in the US department stores, called Black Friday, can generate a significant increase in workload in the search services (e.g. Google) coming from the American consumers, while having little or no impact in the rest of the world. Another example is the possibility that some social networks offer to users to construct small applications (Buyya et al., 2010). Therefore, some may become very popular and used in specific regions, so it is better to have those applications running geographically close to users.

Due to technical factors (e.g. network latency), this phenomenon can lead to loss of quality in provisioning for services that do not have infrastructure close to consumers. Some providers use other strategies, such as the Amazon CloudFront (Amazon, 2014), which uses Points of Interest (PoI) distributed across the globe to assist the demand for regional workloads with low latency without the need to maintain their own infrastructure scattered. These POIs are implemented in leased data centers in a similar behavior to an organization of multiple clouds. Services such as Content Delivery Networks (CDNs) (Pathan, Buyya, & Vakali, 2008; Canali, Cardellini, Colajanni, & Lancellotti, 2008) also offer a similar solution to POIs, bringing the application closer to consumers.

Cloud Federations are designed taking geographic dispersion into account. This dispersion and other goals, such as resilience to natural disasters (Aoyama & Sakai, 2011) and costs mitigation (Le et al., 2011), focus on tackling with the regional workloads. As the federation is a well-behaved organization, defined in terms of a contract, the location of each cloud that composes the federation is known, which makes it possible to redirect workloads to partner clouds closer to regions of interest.

Economic Barriers

The services market forces institutions within the same niche to implement techniques and properties that differentiate them from others, pursuing a competitive advantage (Buyya, Pandey, & Vecchiola, 2012). Service providers, due to lack of standards, implement their own storage and operating mechanisms, as well as interfaces and access protocols. Such characteristic increases the data migration cost from one provider to another, limiting the freedom of customers by the lack of portability and creating a phenomenon called "lock-in" (Armbrust et al., 2009; Ardagna et al., 2012; Petcu, 2011; Petri et al., 2014). This is clear in the case where, due to economic opportunities offered by other providers, a customer cannot migrate her services because the cost to perform the conversion between data types is so high that migration becomes inviable (Kurze et al., 2011).

It is possible to discuss the lock-in phenomenon from the perspective of customers and that of the service providers. For customers, it is extremely important to mitigate the lock-in, since it forces them to come under the tutelage of a single provider technology and, therefore, be exposed to the costs and directions that such provider thinks as appropriate. Moreover, this phenomenon contributes to increased caution of many institutions in adopting Cloud Computing. On the other hand, for the service providers the lock-in can be attractive, since the data implementation schemes, techniques, and standards themselves may create advantage over competitors (Toosi et al., 2014).

Kurze et al. (Kurze et al., 2011) describe a situation related to the lock-in that triggers another economic phenomenon in the context of isolated clouds. In this situation, an institution can establish a contract with a cloud provider to develop applications related to it. Hence, this institution needs to make an investment in technical knowledge and technological directives for that infrastructure in order to enable the development of the application. However, during the establishment of the contract not all aspects of the relationship institution-provider are raised. Given this situation, the provider can take advantage benefiting from previous investments made by the institution in relation to the technological direction for the development of its applications. In order to avoid such a scenario, interested parties may come into hold-up situations, generating underinvestment and consequently inefficient results for both sides.

Two properties inherent to the Cloud Federation enable stakeholders to mitigate the exposed economic barriers. Volunteering and Federation Level Agreement (FLA) enable the maintenance of interoperability within the organization. These properties lead the members of the federation to be willing to participate in the organization and to submit to pre-established interoperability standards.

Legal Issues

In the Cloud Computing paradigm, customer data can be stored in or travel to a location far from the user – a customer in Africa may be using a cloud allocated in the US, for example. After the terrorist attacks that occurred on the fateful 11 September 2011, several countries have imposed strict laws related to break of data confidentiality in their territory. The United States approved the US Patriot Act (Us Patriotic Act, 2001) and began to monitor cloud providers infrastructure located in its territory, as denounced the US National Security Agency (NSA, 2015) former contractor Edward Snowden. The possibility of monitoring and break of confidentiality motivated providers to migrate to countries where laws were milder in order to keep their business and to protect consumer data (Buyya, Broberg, & Goscinski, 2011).

On the customer side, some institutions, especially government entities, are subject to laws restricting the use of commercial Cloud Computing providers (Jeffery & Neidecker-Lutz, 2010) due to the characteristics presented in the previous paragraph. In Brazil, for instance, these features restrict the use of public clouds because the law prevents the Brazilian government data from leaving the country.

In federations, localities where data is or will travel can be defined in advance. This behavior can be used to overcome legal restrictions faced by some institutions. Returning to the case of Brazil, it would be possible to create a federation containing countries in Mercosul (Mercosur, 2015), where the data storage and traffic from Brazilian government would be limited to those clouds located within national boundaries.

Open Challenges

Several authors, as Toosi et al. (Toosi et al., 2014) describe a set of challenges inherent to the establishment of multiple cloud organizations. This section discusses these challenges, focusing solely on Cloud Federations.

Interoperability

Interoperability (Bernstein et al., 2009; Assis et al., 2014), the ability for systems to interact with each other, is a crucial aspect for forming a Cloud Federation. It involves the development of interaction protocols and interfaces that must be known in advance for all the interacting parties. The formation of a federation is possible only with the presence of such a property, as the federation is formed by a set of heterogeneous domains that can exchange information, resources, and services. According to Toosi et al. (Toosi et al., 2014) and Chen and Doumengts (Chen & Doumeingts, 2003), interoperability in multiple cloud organizations such as federations, can be implemented by using ontologies, brokers, or interfaces, which in Computing Cloud paradigm are exposed in most cases in the form of Application Programming Interfaces (APIs).

Ontologies (Manno et al., 2012) are representations of knowledge that can be used to provide interoperability without the need to explicitly implement the technologies used by delegating this responsibility to local contexts of the participants of the federation. Brokers (Kurze et al., 2011; Buyya et al., 2010; Villegas et al., 2012; Makkes et al., 2013; Marosi et al., 2011), in this context, are responsible for the intermediation of interactions between customers and providers, performing the translation of messages originating in and destined to providers. This mitigates the need of a single communication language/protocol, allowing the diversity within the federation. The interfaces provide a direct and controlled way of communication between different entities. Standard interfaces make the process of improvement and introduction of new features faster if compared to other approaches, because in most cases there is an exclusive working group to develop standard interfaces.

As to the limitations that make interoperability an open challenge, brokers add an extra layer in the composition of the federation, since all interactions with the environment are made through it. This type of interaction mechanism generates an overhead, being also a Single Point of Failure (SPOF). Therefore, if no replication strategy is implemented and the broker fails, the whole environment can stop working. On the other hand, the standard interfaces, even if bypassing the problems faced by brokers, are more difficult to be adopted by providers (Rochwerger et al., 2009), who are mostly interested in maintaining their own interfaces that reflect the implementation of various technologies (Petcu, Craciun, & Rak, 2011). Among the initiatives to implement standard interfaces, the Open Cloud Computing Interface (OCCI) (Nyr´een, Edmonds, Papaspyrou, & Metsch, 2011) is focused on remote management services (IaaS, PaaS and SaaS). The Distributed Management Task Force (DMTF, 2015) is an organization that also works for publication of standards and interface specifications in the cloud context, such as Cloud Management Working Group (CMWG) and the Cloud Infrastructure Management interface (CIMI) (CIMI, 2012), which respectively describe patterns of interaction between customers and providers, and IaaS resources management.

Portability is also important in the context of interoperability. In Federations of Clouds, constant migration of applications and customer data must be supported by other elements of the organization. In order to generate the portability of applications, it is necessary to list the types of services requested and the granularity of the elements that support the applications: Containers – e.g. LXC (LXC, 2015), Docker (Docker, 2015) –, virtual machines etc. Another element that enhances the difficulties of portability refers to the origin and destination domain. Items such as the local network settings and security constraints present in each domain can hamper migration between clouds. In his work about Sky Computing, Keahey et al. (Keahey et al., 2009) attack the problem of migration of virtual machines, highlighting that the main limitations to this migration are the diversity of VMs representation formats, which can cause incompatibility during the change of context, which they are subject to. The authors propose the use of Virtual Appliances and context descriptors (e.g. metadata) to mitigate such difficulties. As an initiative to migration problems, the DMTF keeps the Open Virtualization Format (OVF, 2015), which describes how to package software to run in virtual environments.

Federated Identity Management

Identities management (IdMs) are entities present in the domain of a cloud provider (Toosi et al., 2014; Celesti, Tusa, Villari, & Puliafito, 2010; Dreo, Golling, Hommel, & Tietze, 2013). IdMs are responsible for the authentication process, and to enable the authorization process for access to resources. On multiple cloud organizations, such as federations, IdMs may need prepared to treat visitors (customers) that were not originally registered in their user base. This treatment consists in authentication to the visitor and to allow him access to resources of interest with certain policies that state the scope of access. In some multiple cloud organizations, the complexity to allow these actions is accentuated (Toosi et al., 2014) due to different IdMs implementations and standards of the authentication information representation. For example, X.509 certificates – RFC 4158 (RFC 4158, 2015) and RFC 5280 (RFC 5280, 2015) – and the Security Assertion Markup Language (SAML, 2015) depend on the local context and may compromise interoperability. The Organization for the Advancements of Structure Information Standard (OASIS) maintains a working group to standardize identity management in Cloud Computing. As a result, this group published the Identity in the Cloud Use Cases (OASIS, 2012), presenting use cases that describe the identity management between clouds.

As described in (Toosi et al., 2014), federated identity management can enable Single Sign-On (SSO) whereby after a single authentication, a user can gain access to multiple systems. Different approaches are possible for the implementation of SSO: global user and identity provides (Makkes et al., 2013). The first approach is the simplest: the existence of a standard user registered in all user bases of the clouds in the federation, and any action related to the consumption of a foreign resource[2] is performed by this user. Although this approach is the simplest to implement, using a single user can add a single point of security failure, since with the acquisition of authentication properties of this user, a malicious user has access to all clouds in the federation. The use of global users also introduces difficulties in tracing the origin of the consumer of foreign resources, and encumbers the process of accounting and charging the use of foreign resources between clouds.

Another approach is to delegate authentication to Identity Provides (IdPs) (Celesti, Tusa, Villari, & Puliafito, 2011). IdPs are specialized institutions in IdM and can be public or private. Public IdPs are open to all interested parties, implement open authentication standard protocols – OpenID (OpenID, 2015), Oauth (Oauth, 2015) etc. –, and are a solution to normalize the authentication process in environments such as Cloud Federations. This normalization is achieved by the delegation of the authentication process by the federation to the selected IdP. However, IdPs may also be focus of malicious attacks, since they are centralized and with sensitive information. Moreover, they can result in an increase in cost to the authentication process, as well as introduce authentication lock-in, because the authentication data will be delegated to a service provider that in turn can direct its own policies. A second model is targeted to specific clients, which have a well-defined niche, such as those formed by commercial institutions that do not expect their databases to be exposed, or by classes of workers within a certain niche with compatible trade relations. In addition to the lock-in, private external IdPs add to the federation a non-negligible cost.

Services Management

Service management comprises the discovery and mapping of services offered by the clouds in the federation and the presentation thereof to stakeholders. Manno et al. (Manno, Smari, & Spalazzi, 2012) reported that in a federative environment is essential to have a mechanism for service discovery, which should allow internal or external entities to request the availability and types of service provided. Also, it should be considered that each Cloud Federation is independent and have control of their own resources, therefore some clouds from a federation may be not interested in publishing all the services they offer. Toosi et al. (Toosi et al., 2014) report that there is a lack of publishing methods and standards designed for multiple cloud organizations. This arises from the heterogeneity of publishing methods and the lack of expressiveness of these methods. However, in environments such as federations, where the clouds are well behaved considering the methods they implement (because they are subject to an FLA), it is possible to mitigate these problems. Thus, the question shifts from implementation methods to choosing the most efficient of them, because all the clouds will be subject to the chosen method.

Data communication that occurs outside of a single domain can be a bottleneck, since exchange of messages among multiple clouds mainly uses shared/untrusted networks with high latency, e.g. the Internet. Some solutions, such as the use of repositories and catalogs, are presented as centralized approaches where clouds proactively or reactively perform the publication of the resources made available to interested parties, as in a planned approach in publishing protocol of the Service Oriented Architecture (SOA) (The Open Group, 2009).

Contract Maintenance

Among domains, the contract between the federation and the clouds that compose it is the main item that distinguishes this organization from other multiple clouds. Extending the initial concept of the FLA defined by Toosi et al. (Toosi et al., 2011), such document actually acts as an internal SLA, stipulating how clouds should behave in the environment. The FLA should describe the mode of provisioning of resources from the clouds to the federation, that is, if every cloud reserves a fixed amount of resources to the environment or if the resources are dynamically offered without pre-fixed quantities. This contract should also define items that determine the quality of the use of the offered resources. This is necessary because clouds are heterogeneous, and each one has a certain amount and types of computing assets, in most cases diverse, and different procedures to access them.

As within SLAs, penalties should also be contained in the FLA. These penalties can occur if the clouds do not comply with contract items such as the provision of predetermined features. These penalties may reflect the orchestration held in the federation. Clouds with penalties history can be discarded in the feature selection process and, if penalties are recurrent, such clouds can even be disassociated from the federation. Bernsmed et al. (Bernsmed, Jaatun, Meland, & Undheim, 2011) state that the SLA must present mechanisms to the user describing criteria for security items, i.e., introducing the concept of Quality of Protection (QoP), which can also be extended to the Federation Level Agreement.

There are few studies about contracts in the Federations of Clouds, as there is a lack of research in this area in monolithic Cloud Computing environments. As a result of this gap, the contracts are not yet mature (Cloud Standards Customer Council Workgroup, 2012) to express the Service Level Specifications (service delivery restrictions, QoS, and penalties) (Bernsmed et al., 2011) at the time of translation of textual description (semantics) to logical description that can be interpreted automatically within the environment. Some initiatives, such as Patel et al. (Patel, Ranabahu, & Sheth, 2009), propose the utilization of specifications created for other contexts, such as WS-Agreement (Andrieux et al., 2005) and Web Service Level Agreement (WSLA) (Keller & Ludwig, 2003) implemented in representative languages – (JavaScript Object Notation (JSON, 2015) and eXtensible Markup Language (XML, 2015) –, to manage SLAs in clouds. Such initiatives can be adapted to perform the translation and representation of the FLA at a level that the federation is able to understand and execute. Another challenge is to maintain a rigorous policing (Emeakaroha et al., 2012) of the FLA. This policing is only possible through efficient capture of items of interest by the monitoring system of the federation. Comuzzi et al. (Comuzzi, Kotsokalis, Spanoudakis, & Yahyapour, 2009) propose an architecture for SLA monitoring in monolithic clouds that can be used to monitor FLAs.

Providers Behavior

As described by Toosi et al. (Toosi et al., 2011), each cloud from the providers that form a federation are autonomous and can have a customer portfolio that has nothing in common with the others. Attending these customers can restrict the provision of computational resources that each cloud can provision to the federation. Moreover, apart from institutions with scientific focus, the associations may be established by private institutions aimed at maximizing the profitability by selling their idle resources and using foreign resources that are offered at more attractive prices for the internal members of the organization (Toosi et al., 2011). Maximizing profitability may lead some clouds to only request resources, and not offer them to the federation.

Finding ways to avoid this problem leads to the analysis of some challenges, particularly service management. The supply management of resources by constituent clouds is critical in organizations such as federations, since mismanagement can result in environmental degradation. In this context, three scenarios arise which show the main behaviors that require uplifting the association of regulatory mechanisms.

The first scenario is related to setting in the FLA some explicit limits for the provision of resources from each Cloud Federation. The definition of such limits can lead to problems such as resource idleness; thereby the respective clouds of origin mostly supply the amount of workload. For example, suppose that in a hypothetical Cloud Federation each clouds must provide 25% of their resources to the organization, but each cloud is operating at 70% of its capacity. If a cloud cannot have its own management policy to freely turn off its resources because of the FLA, this cloud would have 25% idleness of computing assets. This may generate unnecessary expenses (power, cooling, maintenance) and consequently a lack of interest in using this type of organization. Furthermore, in certain situations to meet its own consumers' workloads, some clouds may be required to request resources from the federation to meet the local workload demand even if it has idle resources in their organizations. These resources could not be used directly as they are reserved to the federation. This problem is described in the example where a cloud belonging to a federation has 30% of its local resources reserved to the federation environment, and at some point it faces a sudden increase in workload that consumes 80% of its assets. In this situation, the cloud will be required to request to the federation more resources even though it has sufficient resources to meet the demand within its own domain.

A second scenario considers the extinction of such a explicit designation of a minimum amount of resources to be offered for the federation. This strategy alleviates the idle problem from the previous scenario, but can provide the possibility of some of the clouds not to offer resources proportionally to the environment, consuming much more than it offers. When there is no explicit determination in the FLA of the resources that every cloud should offer to the federation, a cloud with a high number of customers could demand an increasing amount of resources from the federation to serve them taking advantage of economic factors (attractive prices, for example) or technical factors (specialized resources, optimized communication channels etc.). Due to its high workload, this cloud could deny the supply of resources to any request from the federation. The recurrence of this behavior from a cloud provider could make it undesirable in the environment, contributing to the de-characterization of the organization, since strict consumption has similar behavior to Hybrid Clouds, for example, and not a Cloud Federation.

Another scenario, which is in the scope of resource management in the federation, refers to the administration of clouds life cycle in the organization. In order to try to mitigate problems related to the withholding of resources, a federation should be able to delete or quarantine[3] clouds that do not honor the basic principles of supply and demand of resources.

There are no works in the current literature that clearly specify methods for the acquisition or exclusion of clouds within the federation environment, as well as the management of available resources. This management ends up being done manually through relationships between institutions. Such methods can cause waste of human resources and loss of resources when clouds are excluded. In the latter, the amount of resources lost is directly linked to the temporality of detection of those clouds that are only consuming and are not contributing to the environment.

Monitoring

The monitoring in a distributed environment, such as the Cloud Federation, is extremely important because it will provide information for the maintenance of the organization. As described by Toosi et al. (Toosi et al., 2014), in environments such as federations, diversity of components (e.g. the Orchestrator) and features (elasticity, high availability, etc.) may increase the complexity and the need to maintain a monitoring system. In federations, monitoring can be divided into two distinct groups considering the object of interest (Al-Hazmi et al., 2012): monitoring the federation and monitoring applications. The monitoring of the federation, as the Lattice (Clayman et al., 2010), should be able to check the status and the alignment of each cloud to the FLA, as well as the components that are part of the federation infrastructure (communication channel, resources utilization etc.) with maximum temporality (Flake et al., 2012) and with minimal impact on the communication network. For the federation infrastructure elements this task is trivial from the point of view of tools and implementation, but it becomes difficult when the clouds belonging to the organization are considered. Providers are independent and heterogeneous and may have systems to monitor their own infrastructure, so it is necessary the monitoring of the federation to be able to perform communication and the exchange of information between the various monitoring systems that can coexist in the environment. Faced with this challenge, some solutions can be implemented, such as the development of interfaces for interoperability to perform data exchange between different monitoring systems, and the implementation of an appropriate mechanism to communicate with the most popular proprietary monitoring tools – HP Openview (HP, 2015) for example – or free monitoring tools–Ganglia (Ganglia, 2015), Nagios (Nagios, 2015), Zabbix (Zabbix, 2015)–with low level intrusion. A more restrictive approach can also be assumed, creating a compatibility matrix in the FLA with monitoring systems supported by the federation.

When considering applications in the environment, especially those implemented in multi-tier, the monitoring of the properties related to them can be offered to customers as a service – Monitoring as a Service (MaaS). AlHazmi et al. proposed the BonFIRE (Al-Hazmi et al., 2012), which provides global monitoring of the federation and also offers MaaS to interested parties. MaaS can use the federation monitoring information to tracking of resource utilization by customers and their applications. Seo, Kim, Cui, Seo & Lee (2015) proposed a solution based on aggregation to assist administrators in monitoring resources and services used by users in a federated environment. As SLAs may be binding between customers and certain clouds of the organization (transparent federation) or directly to the federation, the two modes of supplying Monitoring as a Service must be considered. In the first way, the customer does not know the existence of the federation and hires the services of the specific provider. Considering MaaS, in this scenario, the provider, through the FLA, knows the details of the global monitoring system which in turn can be used to trace the execution of the customer application and if it will use other service providers from the federation. The second way comprises the establishment of a contract between the customer and the Cloud Federation, where the Monitoring as a Service can be delegated directly to a central component of the federation and not to the clouds that compose it, which should be a global monitoring system.

Three characteristics directly impact in the efficiency and effectiveness of monitoring systems in a federation: temporality, diversity, and scalability. The first two influences on the amount of messages generated in the network: decreasing the time window to obtain information and increasing the diversity of components and monitoring systems in the network generates more messages to the shared federation network. Such messages can be influenced by network latency as well as contribute to the increase of this latency. Solutions such as implementing more efficient protocols (pooling or publishing), segmented networks only for monitoring and calculation periods, or collection/publication of data can be useful in this context. About scalability, in an environment such as the one considered in this work, association and disassociation of clouds belonging to the federation are expected to occur. Thus, the global monitoring system must be able to efficiently scale according to the fluctuation of these occurrences. If this is not possible, the monitoring system may use outdated information, which can compromise other systems that depend on this information, such as scheduling or orchestration of components that need to know the actual state of the Cloud Federation, as for example when building dynamic workflows[4]. From the point of view of MaaS, there may also be fluctuations in relation to systems that each cloud uses within its domains to monitor their environments. Both the global monitoring and the MaaS should be able to provide support to new monitoring system when necessary. Solutions based on the Advanced Message Queuing Protocol (AMQP) (Godfrey, Ingham, & Schloming, 2012) – Apache Qpid (Qpid, 2015), zeroMQ (zeroMQ) etc. – can be used to automate the insertion of new monitoring systems within the federation.

Business Model

In an organization of multiple clouds as the federation, it is possible to create new marketing models as well as to adapt existing models used in other contexts. The framework proposed by Buyya et al. (Buyya et al., 2010) uses a market-oriented model (Buyya, Yeo, & Venugopal, 2009; Petri et al., 2015) as resource trading system in the Federation. In this marketing model, a central entity acts as a point of concentration and through the supply and demand of the federation's resources in terms of a product market. Another marketing model is the offering of specialized resources by certain providers within the federation. In this model, some clouds within the federation are specialized in certain types of resources, and thus the customers can hire differentiated resources to run their applications or parts thereof. Among the benefits of this model, are: the high degree of specialization of certain resources, resources differentiated costs, explicit separation of responsibilities, and improvement of customer experience by optimizing the operation of their applications. Moreover, in this model, applications should be prepared (as a TIER model, for example) to use segmented features on more than one cloud.

Considering only the customers, it is also possible to abstract the Cloud Federation from the commercial context and use it only as an improved infrastructure provider for elasticity and geographical dispersion to the interested parties. Thus, customers could use the marketing model of monolithic clouds and negotiate directly with them as in a decentralized architecture. In this approach customers are unaware that the cloud they interact is part of a federation, and the clouds would hold negotiations with others transparently to the allocation of foreign resources, if they are necessary. Thus, only clouds in the organization would benefit from the lucrative aspect of the federation, offering their idle resources and obtaining resources with more attractive prices as compared to the public cloud model, as exemplified by Petri et al. (Petri et al., 2014). Similarly to a resource market model, it is also possible in a centralized architecture to make the supply and demand concentration, omitting the party responsible by the auction.

In the contract present in the federation, it should be specified the marketing of services model, i.e., charging and service models, of the services offered by the clouds. In SLAs between customers and providers, the business model should be described because it directly impacts on how resources in the federation are hired and charged with customers. In the FLA, the business model specification influences how orchestration systems perform their tasks, such as resource allocation and accounting of consumption.

The monetary value of the resources contained in the clouds are subject to market variations and the costs of the infrastructure maintenance and management where they are allocated, as well as variable according to utility and local supplies prices (electricity, water for cooling etc.). Given these two regulators, it is necessary to define economic criteria regarding price fluctuations within the federative environment because large variations may impact the integrity of the Cloud Federation. This is clear in two extremes, when a particular provider A has a high maintenance cost of its own cloud and dilutes this value in the final price of the offered resources, while another provider B has a very low supplies cost due to a privileged location, and can reduce resource prices. In this scenario, and considering a business model, there would be a very high demand from the federation clients for resources offered by B and lower demand for resources available in A, which consequently unbalances the federation.

Obtaining an embracing business model in all contexts as well as polices for the availability and prices of resources within the federation remains an open challenge.

Orchestration

In multiple cloud organizations, orchestration consists in receiving an application and distributing it over the environment considering pre-established criteria by customers and/or providers. Performing this distribution includes the selection and allocation of the best service providers available that meet customer/application needs. Moreover, from the providers' point of view, they want to optimize the use of resources and reduce costs of their own infrastructure (Toosi et al., 2014). In organizations like Cloud Federations, factors such as diversity of quality of services, price of resources, geographic dispersion and network latency between providers directly impact the selection and allocation of services required by customers. Toosi et al. (Toosi et al., 2014) mention that it is necessary to implement automatic methods for deploying applications that optimize the various dynamic factors to which federations are exposed, as the latency and throughput in data transfers, in addition to considering constants like legal and security constraints. Le et al. (Le et al., 2011) propose a solution where through policies; workloads are migrated from region to region within the federation, according to the cost of use (cost of energy, cooling etc.).

The orchestration is associated with other properties of the Cloud Federation, mainly related to aspects of interaction (centralized or peer-to-peer) and visibility (translucent and transparent) to the customer. In federations, translucent centralized selection of services and resources can be performed directly by customers or automatically by the organization through a set of criteria established in the SLA. Concentrator service offerings, as the market model, enable customers to analyze the providers who fulfill their momentary needs. Customers then become responsible for the selection and distribution of their applications over the chosen providers. In another federation architecture, a service of the organization itself performs this task automatically. Regarding the automatic process, there are solutions that use monitoring to perform data collection and analysis on which providers can meet SLAs required by customers (Cuomo et al., 2013).

In the orchestration topic, the Topology and Orchestration Specification for Cloud Application (TOSCA) (TOSCA, 2013) is an OASIS working group focused on developing a document called Server Template, which describes the topologies and deployment procedures, implementation, and management services. This document can be used to soften the orchestration task in federations, where the support of Server Template abstracts cloud providers and the technologies used for the implementation and execution of services.

Use Cases

Clouds Federation associations can be utilized in different situations. This flexibility is one of the characteristics that make them attractive when compared with other Inter-Clouds organizations. Among the scenarios that federations can be used, we highlight the following ones:

- **To Increase the Profitability of Cloud Providers:** federations can be used to increase the profitability of cloud providers (Gori, Guilart, & Torres, 2010). In this situation providers can obtain resources with more attractive prices, as well as market their own idle resources to the other members of the federation, thus increasing revenue.
- **To Maintain the Resilience of Services:** Aoyama and Sakai (2011) apply the federation of clouds to implement a monitoring system and responses to natural disasters. Benefiting from the geographic distribution of the cloud that a federation provides, disrupted services from locations affected by disasters are supplied by other providers in non-affected locations.
- **To Avoid Lock-In:** a cloud federation allows customers to migrate to other providers when convenient with minimal financial impact and technical difficulty.
- **To Lower the Cost to Customers:** through federation that are directed to the resource market (Buyya et al., 2010), customers can select the resources and services that best suit their needs with the cost they are prepared to pay.
- **To Process Hard Problems:** applications that require enhanced computing capacity can use the cloud federations to scatter application components through various providers, with the same SLA, to improve response time.

CLOUD FEDERATIONS PROPERTIES

There exist a variety of definitions related to concepts and their semantics in Cloud Computing. Many concepts are defined more than once, which impairs their understanding and can hamper attractiveness of this technology for the general user. This lack of definition is also true to organization of clouds as the Cloud Federations. Based on concepts learnt and extracted from the state-of-art research on Cloud Federation, such as the proposal by Toosi et al. (Toosi et al., 2014) for generic multiple cloud organizations, this section aims at describing properties specifically from Cloud Federations, separating them into *Functional Properties* and *Usage Properties*, detailed below.

Functional Properties

In this work, functional properties proposed in GICTF 2010 (GICT, 2010) are highlighted. They are presented in Table 1, and are detailed in the next sections.

Authentication

In Cloud Federations, there is a frequent consumption of foreign resources, i.e., resources from other participants in the federation. In order to enable such a utilization of foreign resources, users need to obtain access credentials to the relevant foreign domains, which usually do not have his/her authentication information. In this context, some solutions are highlighted in section *Global Identity Management: Global User and IdPs*.

Commercialization

Federation models must foresee how services will be commercialized with their peers. This kind of organization supports the adoption of a fixed commercial model, defined as a contract, or provides free choice to the federated providers. In this first mode (fixed), there is a consensus among organization

Table 1. Functional properties related to Cloud Federations derived from those defined for multiple clouds and presented in GICTF 2010

FUNCTIONAL PROPERTIES
Authentication – authentication mechanisms for users of organizations participating in the federation.
Contracts – support for service contracts as well as environment contracts (rules to participate in the federation).
Commercialization Model – commercialization model of services in the federation.
Integrity – integrity maintenance regarding resource offer and demand.
Interoperability – data exchange among clouds in the federation.
Monitoring – environment monitoring, including offered services and contracts.
Object – what is the object of commercialization.
Provisioning – resources provisioning, considering consumers and federation environment requirements.
Service Management – management of services offered in the environment.

members on how commercialization is performed, since it is defined in the FLA. This commercialization can be marked-driven, where providers publish their offers in a central entity, and consumers interact with this entity to check prices and post proposals/requests. In this scenario, the auctioneer may or may not be present, who is responsible for matching offers and proposals. When no auctioneer is present, the client himself verifies prices and providers that better fits his needs. In the second mode (free choice), providers have the autonomy to decide their own commercialization model, different (or not) from the other participants in the federation. In this case, the federation acts more as an extension of each provider's infrastructure. The RESERVOIR proposal, described in the next section, utilizes this model.

Contracts

SLAs are contracts between providers and consumers that act as a guarantee of service fulfillment to the users (Buyya et al., 2012). These contracts contain technical and administrative details regarding contracted services. The technical details section of the contract, called Service Level Specification (SLS), describes the quality of service, penalties for violations of contract terms, and how services are delivered to consumers.

In Cloud Federations, in addition to customers SLAs, there is also the federation level agreement, which regulates and maintains the integrity of the federation. Details of functional and usage properties are described in this document, which serves as a basis for the federation activities.

Integrity

Integrity is the functional property that describes the consistency of the environment in what regards offer and demand of resources by providers in the federation. As mentioned earlier, environments where no such regulation mechanism exists are prone to suffer from lack of resources and, at the end of the day, the federation can have its purpose questioned by its participants. This situation can be illustrated in the scenario where a provider offers low-cost resources, but other providers only take advantage of those resources without offering their own share of services.

In order to maintain the federative organization characterization, a management process is needed by the providers. This process can be executed manually by a designated federation administrative board, or by an automatic process that triggers administrative actions/sanctions when anomalies are detected. In both cases, indicators that help in observing cloud participants performance within the FLA are needed to back up administrative decisions. Common indicators are rankings, rewards, and reputation. Ranking uses a score to classify providers according to the relation offer/demand; reward systems is an incentive mechanism to enhance resource offering, which in general attaches resource offering with advantages when using foreign resources; and reputation considers a history of a provider to generate an index that reflects its behavior in the federation.

Interoperability

In a distributed heterogeneous system, interoperability mechanisms are of paramount importance to perform data exchange between different domains. According to solutions presented in section *Cloud Federations: Open Challenges: Interoperability*, there are three strategies to achieve interoperability in a federation: broker, ontology, and standard interfaces. The first one can be easier to implement, but introduces a new layer into the federation. The second is at a conceptual level, and delegates the implementation mechanisms to third parties. Lastly, the standard interfaces can provide better performance, reducing overheads, but may be harder to implement in commercial federations.

Monitoring

As highlighted in section *Cloud Federations: Open Challenges: Monitoring*, two types of monitoring can co-exist: global and MaaS. Global monitoring is focused on the maintenance of the federative organization, while MaaS aims at providing consumers with information to track contracted services. MaaS can rely of global monitoring services in order to reduce implementation efforts.

Objects

The marketing object is the smallest unity of service that a service provider can offer. This object will pass through the federation when resource consumption is needed. Thus, migration mechanisms must be taken into account. This objects can be organized into delivery models: Infrastructure, Platform, and Software as a Service.

Infrastructure as a Service (IaaS) clouds can offer physical resources (bare metal), virtual machines, virtual appliances, and containers. Platform as a Service (PaaS) development frameworks and tools can be delivered through virtual machines as well as using their packing/distribution methods, such as the cartridges utilized in the OpenShift solution. In the Software as a Service class (SaaS), the commercialized service is the access to that specific software.

Provisioning

Provisioning consists of the distribution of application coordinators (or part of them) to consumers through federation providers. This provisioning considers the installation and migration of application components and can be performed in two modes: automatically or manually. In the automatic way, an entity within the federation chooses the best providers for application installation or migration, according to SLA requirements. This can also be done manually, where a system operator performs provider selection and application installation.

Service Management

Service management is responsible for discovery and publishing of services offered by the federation members. Service discovery can be performed by the federation through pooling mechanisms, where consults to the federated clouds are performed regularly. The pooling frequency must be defined to reduce network traffic, but also to capture the dynamicity of the federation.

Service management is also responsible for publishing services throughout the federation members. This service publication can be done by any federation component after running a service discovery, resulting into an indirect publication. If the provider who offers the service publishes it, then we have a direct publication.

Table 2. Six main usage properties of a federation: visibility, interaction, centric, volunteer, practice niche and expansion

USAGE PROPERTIES
Centric – the focus of the Cloud Federation.
Expansion – the way federations expand on in relation to the services offered.
Interaction – the interaction architecture within the federation.
Practice Niche – acting area of the federation.
Visibility – the way customers see and use the Cloud Federation.
Volunteer – voluntary level of clouds contained in the organization.

Usage Properties

In this section, the properties that must be present in federations related to environmental usage from the customers' perspective are presented. Table 2 lists six properties that were highlighted in the literature.

Centric

Recently, proposed approaches in Cloud Federation (next section) have the focus on implementation and usability in certain elements of their respective architectures. This feature is called centric and in this work four centrics were identified: customer, business, provider and service. In the first, all the architecture and federation support mechanisms are designed prioritizing the customers leaving the others in the background actors. Business Centric makes the federation focuses on monetization thus federations focused on eScience not fit into this classification. In the Provider Centric the use of resources and services providers are maximized in detriment of other authors. Finally, in Service Centric the types of services and their specialities are treated as references to the architecture. Architectures with this focus may be prepared to offer homogeneous services considering IaaS, PaaS, and SaaS or heterogeneous, differentiated by diversity and specialty in certain features.

Expansion

Expansion property reflects how a federation uses the resources and services available in the environment. This property is based on the work by Celesti et al. (Celeti et al., 2010), which describes the possibility of expanding a Cloud Federation horizontally and vertically (in addition to those expanding in both modes – hybrid), and working of Bermbach et al. (Bermbach, Kurze, & Tai, 2013). The horizontal federations expand in relation to the same class of service (IaaS, PaaS and SaaS). When considering IaaS, the expansion can be used to provide redundancy and parallelism. When the class is SaaS the expansion can be used to improve the Quality of Experience (QoE) of use or encourage independence from providers (e.g. mitigate the lock-in). The vertical expansion uses all service classes in the environment. In this scenario a SaaS service can use the infrastructure of other federation providers, for example. Finally, the hybrid federations perform horizontal and vertical expansion in accordance with the interest of both customers and providers.

Interaction Architecture

In the Federations of Clouds the interaction of customers (providers of clients) with the organization can be performed centrally (Manno et al., 2012; Buyya et al., 2010) through a single access point, or decentralized (Petri et al., 2014), where every cloud belonging to the federation is a gateway. In centralized interaction architecture, a common approach is to use brokers to mediate the interaction of stakeholders with the rest of the organization. In the decentralized architecture (peer-to-peer), where users interact directly with the clouds, standards or ontologies are often used.

In both architectures actors that interact with the federation are the providers and customers. Considering this last, as the visibility property is inherent to them, the relationship visibility and interaction architecture affects how customers interact with the organization. In transparent federation customers are unaware of the existence of the Cloud Federation, so they interact indirectly with the federation through those providers with whom they have contact. However, providers that are part of the organization are aware of the existence of the federation and interact directly with it. In the translucent federation customers interact directly with the organization because they are aware of their existence, whether organized centrally or decentralized.

Practice Niche

Federations of Clouds operate in different niches, among them stand out from the commercial and non-commercial. In the first group, private, public or hybrid clouds with commercial nature can be found, where the clouds intend to use the organization to increase their respective revenue by selling idle resources as well as to acquire foreign resources with more attractive prices and conditions. As for the non-commercial associations, those where there is no explicit monetary profitability within the organization can be found. In this group, government federations are formed to mitigate, among other factors, legal restrictions, whereas scientific federations consists of research institutions that aim at sharing of computational resources for research.

Visibility

The visibility of the federations is a usage property that determines how customers interpret the organization. It is possible to view the federations translucently as an organization of multiple clouds that can be seen by the user, or transparently as an independent monolithic cloud. In the first mode (translucent), customers explicitly use the benefits of the infrastructure of the federations (e.g. real elasticity) and the economic potential they provide with knowledge of the federation components, such as in a services market. In transparent mode, customers interact with the elements of the federation as a monolithic cloud, whereas cloud components interact among themselves, without user knowledge, to make use of the benefits that the federation infrastructure offers.

Volunteer

Organizations like the federations proposed by Grozev and Buyya (Grozev & Buyya, 2012) must be voluntary, i.e. all the elements involved must have some level of knowledge that they are part of the organization (Assis & Bittencourt, 2015). Moreover, clouds should be able to leave the federation as soon as they want, according to the established agreement (i.e. the FLA). Volunteer is an abstract property and its exposition can vary from solution to solution, as illustrated by the architectures presented in next section. This abstraction makes it difficult to, at a first sight, identify when an architecture has this voluntary characteristic or not.

Finally, in order to highlight and summarize the properties described above and in order to foster their readability and understanding, we provide a diagram, depicted in Figure 5, which covers both the functional and usage properties.

ARCHITECTURAL SPECIFICATIONS, BLUEPRINTS, AND EXISTING SYSTEMS

Recently, several architectures have been proposed aiming at the creation and formalization of cloud federations. This section presents prominent architectures published in the literature representing the state of art of federation models.

Contrail

The Contrail (Contrail, 2015) project was a European Union funded project executed from 2010 to 2014. Contrail was designed to support the integration of a number of independent clouds, forming an integrated federation, a combination of a number of independent clouds into one integrated federated cloud (Harsh et al., 2011; Copolla et al., 2012). The main objective of Contrail was to bring different cloud providers under the umbrella of a true federation, where users have the option to deploy services of multiple providers transparently and homogeneously. In order to achieve such an objective, a Contrail federation manages users identities, coordinates application deployment and the SLA management conducted by single cloud providers. Unique API, billing and monitoring capabilities were provided regardless of the nature of the heterogeneous infrastructures of the federation. Moreover, a Contrail federation is said to be horizontal and vertical. Horizontal, as different IaaS providers (for instance, both public and private

Figure 5. Functional and usage properties of Cloud Federations

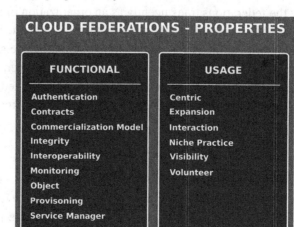

clouds) can become part of the federation. Whereas, vertical integration is achieved by developing both the Infrastructure- and the Platform-as-a-Service architectural tiers.

mOSAIC

The Open-source API and Platform for Multiple Clouds (mOSAIC) is also a European initiative that tried to solve the challenges of cloud federations (executed from 2010 to 2013). The focus os mOSAIC was to offer a solution for application portability and interoperability across multiple clouds (Petcu et al., 2013). The emphasis of mOSAIC was on data intensive applications, though other objectives also include governance and security. The system architecture was designed with a language- and vendor-agnostic application-programming interface for accessing multiple clouds homogenously. In order to enforce the SLA of applications, it also incorporates user-centric service level agreements, a cloud ontology, and mechanisms for dynamic negotiation of resources based on multi-agent technologies and semantic data processing.

IEEE P2302

Cloud Federation has many areas that can benefit from standardization. Hence, the IEEE initiated the P2302 Standard for Intercloud Interoperability and Federation project. (P2302, 2015) The initial goal for this effort was to define topologies, functions, and governance for interoperability among Cloud Federations. To facilitate the development of a deeper understanding of practical federation challenges and approaches, the IEEE Intercloud Testbed project was concomitantly started. (Intercloud Testbed, 2015). From the many federation challenges, the IEEE Intercloud Testbed has focused on federated network communications management (Bernstein & Vij, 2104). Possible federated relationships are identified through a signaling protocol. Once this is established, a bearer network can be set up. This architecture leverages software-defined networks and virtual private networks through an Intercloud Federation API.

OpenStack Keystone

OpenStack is a large, open source software project that is creating a suite of services for Cloud Computing (OpenStack, 2015). The core services include computing (Nova), object storage (Swift), image storage (Glance), and identity (Keystone). To support the business models of cloud-bursting (Hybrid Clouds) and cloud brokering, the Keystone team has been developing critical capabilities for federation management. Concerning federated identity management, Keystone has implemented an attribute mapping capability whereby identity credentials from different identity providers can be mapped to attributes that are locally understood (Chadwick et al., 2013). Keystone has also added two calls to the API whereby trusted Identity Providers and trusted Service Providers can be explicitly specified. This is called "federating in" and "federating out", respectively. While this relies on trust relationships to be managed by cloud administrators out-of-band, it nonetheless enables fundamental pair-wise federation management. Such federations can be symmetric or asymmetric. In a symmetric federation, users from both sites can use the other's resources. In an asymmetric federation, as in a Hybrid Cloud scenario, users from only one site can use the other's resources.

Massachusetts Open Cloud

Notably the Massachusetts Open Cloud project (MOC, 2015) is deploying this capability to manage a collaborative federation initially among Boston University, Harvard, UMass Amherst, MIT and Northeastern University. Users from different institutions will be able to instantiate VMs at one site that can access storage containers at a different site, in support of "big data" science projects. Ultimately, though, the goal is to achieve an Open Cloud eXchange (OCX) where cloud consumers can discover and use resources from multiple providers (Bestravros & Krieger, 2014).

EGI

The European Grid Infrastructure (EGI) is also deploying a set of federated cloud resources (Sipos et al. 2013). While EGI and grid community originally endeavored to deploy a global infrastructure to support "big science", EGI is deploying these cloud resources for all the same reasons as industry, e.g., ease of access to elastic compute resources. EGI can act as a cloud broker for resources from many of the member nations. Users can also instantiate VMs with the traditional grid software stack to support legacy grid applications. It is important to realize, however, that federation was central to the original grid concept. Hence, EGI is able to leverage many existing tools and capabilities to support Cloud Federation. For example, core EGI services for service discovery, monitoring and accounting using standards developed in the Open Grid Forum are all applicable. The Virtual Organization (VO) concept was also developed in grid computing as a way to manage federations. VO membership was managed by obtaining a PKI proxy certificate that augmented a user's identity with VO-specific attributes used to manage authorizations within a VO. This existing VO capability has been integrated with the OpenStack Keystone service (Garcia & Puel, 2013).

Broker Multi-Clouds

In the work by Kurze et al. (Kurze et al., 2011) the authors described and discussed various concepts (redundancy, migration etc.) as well as scenarios related to the use of multiple clouds associations to supply mainly emerging economic problems of Cloud Computing paradigm such as Lock-in and Hold-up. The main contribution was the presentation of a centralized reference architecture based on open source cloud management systems and multi-cloud libraries (Kurze et al., 2011; Grozev & Buyya, 2012; Toosi et al., 2014), where it is highlighted a federal layer represented by a broker. This broker is assigned to perform actions on the resources of multiple domains and is located between the business logic and computing assets contained in the fields it has visibility.

Oriented to Computing Service

The architecture proposed by Buyya et al. (Buyya et al., 2010) focused on IaaS services. The authors were motivated mainly by two challenges of the inherent heterogeneity of both the quantity and the types of services that run on Clouds: the prediction of workload variability and the contracted QoS. It is a centralized federation approach that indirectly interacts with customers through a Broker. One of the highlights of this proposal is the business model called driven market (Buyya et al., 2012). In this model the clouds composing the federation publish their services and their values in a component responsible for offering it to the interested parties. One can also offer bids for services in a scenario similar to an auction.

Oriented to Service Layer

Villegas et al. (Villegas et al., 2012) explore the canonical services of Cloud Computing and the interrelationships between them to model a federation centered in service layers. The highlight of this architecture is the isolation between layers of services and the restriction of expansion between clouds in the federation being restricted to layers at the same level. These two properties allow the existence of heterogeneous clouds regarding computing assets, business models, and types of layers. The proposal provides two feature request modes that are selected at runtime: Delegation and Federation. The first performs the request and allocation of resources to subsequent layers of the cloud (IaaS – PaaS). The Federation is the act of requesting the allocation of resources between the same layers of different clouds. To accomplish this task, the authors highlight the difficulty of the definition and adoption of protocols and policies for interoperability between layers of clouds to expose or to share services during the composition of federation. The choice between performing a Delegation or Federation, as stated previously, is a process that must be done in real time during a request. It is complex and involves cost analysis and availability of resources within the clouds themselves. Besides the architecture, the authors describe the flow of information and processing requirements between the same cloud layers.

RESERVOIR

RESERVOIR (Rochwerger et al., 2009) is a project funded by the European Commission (EC, 2015) and sponsored by the Seventh Framework Programme (FP7, 2015). This architecture was developed with the aim of providing a federal environment for SaaS offering service providers. Its model was focused on loosely coupling and in the absence in the literature of support to Business Service Management[5] (BSM). The functional requirements set by the proposal include the fast and automatic installation of applications and services, dynamic elasticity, automated continuous optimization, and independence virtualization technologies. This organization is "well behaved" as it keeps the same arrangement of the layered components in the federation elements. Consequently, interoperability is maximized because the structural elements are known and communicate over a set of protocols optimized for this purpose. Moreover, RESERVOIR does not have an FLA, since the clouds of the federation already behave following certain rules defined at the implementation level. Another feature is that every cloud has autonomy to choose its marketing model (fixed price per use period or pay-per-use, for example). These features provide the federation sites freedom to adapt to different scenarios and niches (commercial and non-commercial).

Federated Cloud Framework Architecture

Manno et al. (Manno et al., 2012) use semantics to model a federation called Federated Cloud Framework Architecture (FCFA) aiming at IaaS level. The authors use ontology to provide interoperability between distinct and autonomous clouds. The representation language chosen to describe the ontology was the Web Ontology Language (OWL, 2015), which has been used in the implementation of semantic aspects of Web 2.0[6]. The proposal focuses on the utilization of the federation as an execution environment for distributed and complex applications, treating resources as the main feature of a cloud. Around the resources are ontologies used to provide interoperability between different technologies and environments. The FCFA treats the Cloud Federation from the aspect of infrastructure, linking components with the physical elements, and a semantic level related to dynamic operation where there are three actors and four ontologies. The actors and their ontologies are: virtual environments – hNode Ontology, physical server – hNode Ontology, datacenter – Cloud Ontology and Federation – Federation Ontology.

Inter-Cloud Federation Framework

Inter-Cloud Federation Framework architecture (ICFF) is part of an Inter-Cloud framework proposed by Makkes et al. (Makkes et al., 2013). The main objective of this proposal is the creation of a set of solutions capable of performing centralized allocation and coordination of distributed services to appear to the user as single set of services. The ICFF provides a federated environment of heterogeneous clouds, also adds to the organization features that are not allocated in clouds but in other administrative domains providing the implementation and migration of legacy applications. The component responsible for providing interoperability within the ICFF is the Gateway, which performs the translation of requests, protocols, and data formats between clouds that participate in the federation. In addition to the Gateway, there are also components in the architecture capable of providing security features: identification and trust management; and those related to the services themselves: discovery, record, and brokerage services.

Federated Cloud Management

Marosi et al. (Marosi et al., 2011) propose a service-oriented architecture for Federation of IaaS Clouds. Services are made available as Virtual Appliances (VAs) (Sapuntzakis et al., 2003), which meet the requests and are initially available in a central repository called FCM Repository. For the VAs to be effectively used, they must be locally present, so their replication by local repositories is necessary. The replication of VAs contained in the FCM Repository to local repositories is performed thought the segmentation of the VA of interest into small pieces and reconstruction of the Virtual Appliance in the local destination repository. Two classes of Brokers perform all actions within the federation: Generic Meta-Broker, performing the interface with consumers and with other Brokers of the environment; and the Cloud Brokers who are responsible for managing the virtual machine instances of a VA provider located in a specific cloud.

CometCloud Federation

The federation proposed by Petri et al. (Petri et al., 2014) has a fully decentralized profile and focuses in providers' revenue maximization by outsourcing tasks. Petri et al. used the CometCloud as the infrastructure to implement a federation using a Master-Workers methodology. This autonomic computing engine (Huebscher & McCann, 2008) implemented over Comet (Li & Parashar, 2007) supports the integration of public and private clouds by generating spaces (sharing and manager) and also a set of services that assists building of multiple clouds environments, e.g. service discovery. In the CometCloud Federation, each cloud present in the organization interacts directly with one or more clouds without performing broadcast or using a centralized entity. The authors formalize a service execution as a set of tasks that could be outsourced. To decide between outsourcing a task or running it in-house, the architecture uses policy sets: the time to conclude the task, local computing power, and the cost to run it locally.

SUMMARY OF APPROACHES

In order to foster a deeper understanding of the concepts described previously on Cloud Federations, we propose the following summary and comparison of the existing Cloud Federation systems and how they addressed the functional properties described in Section III. Based on such functional properties, a Cloud Federation can accommodate or adopt multiple uses for any of the usage properties also from Section III, with the only constraints imposed by the functionality implemented. For instance, any of the Cloud Federation systems can implement policies to prioritize any participating actor (namely, customer, business, provider or service) of the centric property. Moreover, regarding the expansion of a Federation, it can be accomplished in a number of ways depending on the functional mechanisms adopted, the approaches that decided to adopt a broker-based interoperability can perhaps be more flexible than purely standard-based interoperability approaches, as the former can expand on vertically and horizontally easier.

As it can be seen in Table 3, all of the approaches adopted automated provisioning of resources and this requires specifications to express contracts (SLAs) and monitoring mechanisms for supervising the state of resources as well. Authentication is also a mandatory requirement for accessing the federations, most of the approaches adopted them or referred to consolidated authentication / security policies and mechanisms. Regarding the interoperability approach, it seems that the broker is the most adopted one, as it provides with certain degrees of isolation between consumers and providers and, therefore, more flexibility (less coupling) in the interactions. Nevertheless, the broker is also enhanced in many cases by means of standardization and ontologies for describing the services / resources available. On the other hand, many of the existing approaches are dealing with IaaS, PaaS and SaaS. Finally, the integrity property, as defined above, is the one that opens more research challenges and opportunities. It aims at regulating the behavior of cloud providers in the federation and it establishes and regulates the consumption and provision of resources by the participants. OpenStack / keystone with their Virtual Organization (VO) concept is the only system, to be best of our knowledge, that worked in defining the role played by each participant and the rules that govern the offering / consumption of resources. However, this concept of VO, as discussed within the ICFF project in (Makkes et al. 2013), comes from Grid computing and may need to be adapted to the Cloud Computing domain.

EMERGING PRACTICAL APPLICATIONS OF CLOUD FEDERATION

While much of the concepts defined and work cited here may be more research-oriented, the fact that cloud federation has such tremendous potential to enable large-scale collaborations among institutions, corporation and even governments means that there are definite emerging practical applications of cloud federation. The importance of cloud federation has been recognized by NIST as "Requirement 5: Frameworks to Support Federated Community Clouds", in the NIST US Government Cloud Computing Technology Roadmap (NIST, 2011). The NIST cloud deployment models are widely accepted definitions, but both *hybrid* and *community* clouds are fundamental examples where federation management is necessary to be done in a secure manner.

Table 3. Functional properties

Federation Approach	Authentication		Contracts	Comm. Model	Integrity
Contrail	N/A initially, certificates eventually		Cloud SLAs (SLA@SOI)	Market-driven	N/A
mOSAIC	Keystone		User-centric SLAs (Cloud SLAs)	Market-driven	N/A
OpenStack	X509 certificates: Global Identities		Virtual Organization + Cloud SLAs	Market-driven	VOs as a FLA
RESERVOIR	Certificates		No global SLA, rules for each service (Cloud SLAs).	Free-choice	N/A
FCFA	Federated Id Management: 3rd party IDP		Cloud SLAs + Federated Contract	Market-driven	N/A
ICFF	N/A initially, certificates eventually		Cloud SLAs (SLA@SOI)	Market-driven	N/A
FCM	Keystone		User-centric SLAs (Cloud SLAs)	Market-driven	N/A
CometCloud	X509 certificates: Global Identities		Virtual Organization + Cloud SLAs	Market-driven	N/A
Federation Approach	Broker	Monitoring	Object	Provisioning	Service Mngmnt.
Contrail	Broker + ontology	✓	IaaS, PaaS, SaaS	Automatic	✓
mOSAIC	Broker	✓	PaaS	Automatic	✓
OpenStack	Standards	✓	IaaS, PaaS, SaaS	Automatic	✓
RESERVOIR	Broker + ontology	✓	IaaS	Automatic	✓
FCFA	Broker	✓	IaaS	Automatic	✓
ICFF	Broker	✓	IaaS, PaaS, SaaS	Automatic	✓
CommetCloud	Broker	✓	IaaS	Automatic	✓

Federation can be managed at any level in the system stack. As we have noted above, the OpenStack Keystone project is building out basic support for cloud federation whereby multiple OpenStack deployments can peer to one another at the IaaS level (OpenStack, 2015). That is to say, different deployments can offer resources, e.g., compute and storage, to users within the federation. This is being done to support the hybrid cloud business model where one cloud can cloud-burst into another. Offering resources from a provider to a consumer is a form of *asymmetric* federation. The OpenStack corporate sponsors that are major contributors to the Keystone project clearly view this as enabling a cloud marketplace.

As a fully commercialized example of IaaS federation, Cisco offers the Cisco *Intercloud Fabric* that can establish a hybrid cloud between private and public clouds (Cisco, 2015). This provides an environment where consistent network configurations and security policies can be enforced. The hybrid resources can be managed by either the consuming enterprise IT department or the public Service Provider. Enterprises can use the fabric to access different cloud service providers. Likewise, service providers can use the fabric to make their resources available to consumers. Regardless of who's managing the environment, users see a uniform set of resources and workloads.

Besides enabling a marketplace for cloud infrastructure services, federation can enable a marketplace for business-level services at the SaaS-level. Here, one corporation can contract with a commercial SaaS provider for web-based services. As an example, the training courses in many businesses are provided by external organizations. These can be offered as SaaS-level services where the consuming organization acts as the Identity Provider to the SaaS-level Service Provider. Employees log into web-based training exercises that have been customized for their corporation using their corporate identity credentials. These corporate identity credentials are then validated by the SaaS-provider with the home organization. Again, this is an example of an asymmetric federation to sell commercial services.

Such commercial SaaS-level federations are supported by tooling from corporations such as PingIdentity (PingIdentity, 2015). PingIdentity's PingFederate tool enables federated identity management for SaaS-level access using established standards, such as OpenID Connect, OAuth and SAML. The actual integration of user services with secure communication is enabled by PingAccess. We note that other corporations such as Amazon Web Services, Microsoft, F5, and CA Technologies, all support different forms of SaaS federation.

Clearly these systems do not support federation in the most general sense, but rather these corporations are tailoring the use of federation technologies to build an economically viable marketplace. As use of federation technology widens, we can expect to see broader and more general uses. As an important precedent, the Interoperable Global Trust Federation (IGTF) is an operational organization that is critical to enabling the global collaboration of "big science" groups (IGTF, 2015). IGTF essentially defines standards for the operation of PKI Certificate Authorities (CAs). Once an institution demonstrates that it's CAs are compliant, other institutions will trust certificates signed by their CA. While this was originally developed to support the sharing of data from the high-energy sensors at CERN, it is now used by a wide variety of science user groups, including chemistry, biology, and environmental monitoring, on five continents. While IGTF provides trust management in a very specific context, it nonetheless demonstrates the possibilities of global-scale federations.

CONCLUSION

The Cloud Computing paradigm has emerged as an answer to pursue computing as a utility. However, as its adoption and usage are widespread, a number of difficulties and limitations arise. Such limitations are related to the idea of *unlimited* computation on-demand, which can be constrained in cases where the amount of available resources is exhausted (e.g. a small- or medium-sized Cloud provider with heavy workload conditions). The solution for clients in order to overcome such limitations is the capability of interacting with multiple Cloud providers simultaneously. However, due to the lack of standardized methodological approaches and mechanisms, Clouds have been built as monolithic systems, where Cloud providers act as single and isolated domains. In this paper, we review the literature and existing Cloud technologies with different purposes and profiles in order to present a survey of the existing organizations involving multiple Clouds and Federation of Clouds. For each organization, its architectural blueprints were described and the potential applications and current limitations were discussed for each organization, as well as the research challenges and opportunities. A number of different organizations were proposed integrating various methods and techniques of associations. This chapter is suitable as a reference material for researchers interested in the topic to guide their research.

ACKNOWLEDGMENT

This work was co-financed by the Industry and Innovation Department of the Aragonese Government and European Social Funds (COSMOS research group, ref. T93); and by the Spanish Ministry of Economy under the program "Programa de I+D+i Estatal de Investigación, Desarrollo e Innovación Orientada a los Retos de la Sociedad", project id TIN2013-40809-R. Also, M.R.M.A would like to thank CAPES and L.F.B. would like to thank CNPq for the financial support.

REFERENCES

P2302 interoperability and federation (SIIF). (2015). *P2302*. Retrieved from https://standards.ieee.org/develop/project/2302.html

Al-Hazmi, Y., Campowsky, K., & Magedanz, T. (2012). A monitoring system for federated clouds. *Proceedings of 1st International Conference on Cloud Networking (CLOUDNET)*, Paris, France: IEEE.

Amazon AWS Cloudfront. (2014). *Amazon*. Retrieved from http://aws.amazon.com/cloudfront/

Amazon EC2. (2015). Retrieved from http://aws.amazon.com/ec2/

Andrieux, A., Czajkowski, K., Dan, A., Keahey, K., Ludwig, H., Nakata, T., . . . Xu, M. (2005). *Web services agreement specification (WS-Agreement)* (Tech. Rep.). Global Grid Forum, Grid Resource Allocation Agreement Protocol (GRAAP) WG.

Antonopoulos, N., & Gillam, L. (2010). *Cloud computing: principles, systems and applications*. London, UK: Springer Publishing Company, Incorporated. doi:10.1007/978-1-84996-241-4

Aoyama, T., & Sakai, H. (2011). Inter-cloud computing. *Business & Information Systems Engineering*, *3*(3), 173–177. doi:10.1007/s12599-011-0158-4

Apache Qpid. (2015). *Qpid*. Retrieved from https://qpid.apache.org/

Ardagna, D., di Nitto, E., Mohagheghi, P., Mosser, S., Ballagny, C., D'Andria, F., & Sheridan, C. et al. (2012). Modaclouds: A model-driven approach for the design and execution of applications on multiple clouds. *Proceedings of Workshop on Modeling in Software Engineering (MiSE) in Internation Conference on Software Engineering (ICSE)*, Zurich, Switzerland (pp. 50-56). doi:10.1109/MISE.2012.6226014

Armbrust, M., Fox, A., Griffith, R., Joseph, A. D., Katz, R. H., Konwinski, A., ... Zaharia, M. (2009). *Above the clouds: A Berkeley view of cloud computing* (Tech. Rep. No. UCB/EECS-2009-28). EECS Department, University of California, Berkeley.

Assis, M. R. M., & Bittencourt, L. F. (2015). An Analysis of the Voluntary Aspect in Cloud Federations. *Proceedings of the 4rd International Workshop on Clouds and (eScience) Applications Management (CLOUDAM 2015)*. Limassol, Cyprus.

Assis, M. R. M., Bittencourt, L. F., & Tolosana-Calasanz, R. (2014). Cloud federation: Characterisation and conceptual model. *Proceedings of 3rd International Workshop on Clouds and (eScience) Applications Management (CLOUDAM 2014)*. London, UK.

Banerjee, P., Friedrich, R., Bash, C., Goldsack, P., Huberman, B., Manley, J., & Veitch, A. et al. (2011). Everything as a service: Powering the new information economy. *Computer, 44*(3), 36–43. doi:10.1109/MC.2011.67

Bermbach, D., Kurze, T., & Tai, S. (2013). Cloud federation: Effects of federated compute resources on quality of service and cost. *Proceedings of the IEEE International Conference on Cloud Engineering (IC2E),* San Francisco, California, USA (pp. 31–37). IEEE Computer Society. doi:10.1109/IC2E.2013.24

Bernsmed, K., Jaatun, M. G., Meland, P. H., & Undheim, A. (2011). Security SLAs for federated cloud services. *Proceedings of IEEE International Conference on Availability, Reliability and Security (ARES),* Vienna: Austria (pp. 202-209). IEEE Computer Society.

Bernstein, D., Ludvigson, E., Sankar, K., Diamond, S., & Morrow, M. (2009). Blueprint for the intercloud - protocols and formats for cloud computing interoperability. *Proceedings of the Fourth International Conference on Internet and Web Applications and Services (ICIW),* Washington, DC, USA. IEEE Computer Society. doi:10.1109/ICIW.2009.55

Bernstein, D., & Vij, D. (2104) Intercloud federation using via semantic resource federation API and dynamic SDN Provisioning. *Proceedings of International Conference and Workshop on the Network of the Future (NOF),* Paris, France (pp.1–8). IEEE Computer Society.

Bestavros, A., & Krieger, O. (2014). Toward an open cloud marketplace: Vision and first steps. *IEEE Internet Computing, 18*(1), 72–77. doi:10.1109/MIC.2014.17

Bhardwaj, S., Jain, L., & Jain, S. (2010). Cloud computing: A study of infrastructure as a service (IaaS). *International Journal of Engineering and Information Technology, 2*(1), 60–63.

Bittencourt, L. F., & Madeira, E. R. M. (2011). HCOC: A cost optimization algorithm for workflow scheduling in hybrid clouds. *Journal of Internet Services and Applications, 2*(3), 207–227. doi:10.1007/s13174-011-0032-0

Buyya, R., Broberg, J., & Goscinski, A. M. (2011). *Cloud computing principles and paradigms. Hoboken.* New Jersey, USA: John Wiley & Sons, Inc. doi:10.1002/9780470940105

Buyya, R., Pandey, S., & Vecchiola, C. (2012). Market-oriented cloud computing and the cloudbus toolkit. In S. Azad & H. Zomaya (Eds.), *Large Scale Network-Centric Distributed Systems.* Wiley-IEEE Press.

Buyya, R., Ranjan, R., & Calheiros, R. N. (2010). Intercloud: Utility-oriented federation of cloud computing environments for scaling of application services. *Proceedings of the 10th International Conference on Algorithms and Architectures for Parallel Processing,* Busan, Korea (Vol. part I pp. 13–31). Springer-Verlag Berlin, Heidelberg. doi:10.1007/978-3-642-13119-6_2

Buyya, R., Yeo, C. S., & Venugopal, S. (2009). Market-oriented cloud computing: Vision, hype, and reality of delivering computing as the 5th utility. *Proceedings of the 2009 9th IEEE/ACM International Symposium on Cluster Computing and the Grid (CCGRID),* Shanghai, China (p. 1). IEEE Computer Society. doi:10.1109/CCGRID.2009.97

Calheiros, R. N., Toosi, A. N., Vecchiola, C., & Buyya, R. (2012, October). A coordinator for scaling elastic applications across multiple clouds. *Future Generation Computer Systems*, *28*(8), 1350–1362. doi:10.1016/j.future.2012.03.010

Campbell, R., Gupta, I., Heath, M., Ko, S. Y., Kozuch, M., Kunze, M., & Soh, Y. C. et al. (2009). Open CIRRUS™ cloud computing testbed: Federated data centers for open source systems and services research. *Proceedings of the 2009 Conference on Hot Topics in Cloud Computing (HotCloud)*, San Diego, CA, USA. USENIX Association.

Canali, C., Cardellini, V., Colajanni, M., & Lancellotti, R. (2008). Content delivery and management. In R. Buyya, M. Pathan, & A. Vakali (Eds.), *Content Delivery Networks* (Vol. 9, pp. 105–126). Springer Berlin Heidelberg. doi:10.1007/978-3-540-77887-5_4

Celesti, A., Tusa, F., Villari, M., & Puliafito, A. (2010). Security and cloud computing: Intercloud identity management infrastructure. In S. Reddy (Ed.), *Enabling Technologies: Infrastructures for Collaborative Enterprises (WETICE)* (pp. 263–265). IEEE Computer Society. doi:10.1109/WETICE.2010.49

Celesti, A., Tusa, F., Villari, M., & Puliafito, A. (2011). Evaluating a distributed identity provider trusted network with delegated authentications for cloud federation. *Proceedings of the 2th International Conference on Cloud Computing, Grids and Virtualization (CLOUD COMPUTING 2011)*, Rome, Italy (pp. 79–85). International Academy, Research, and Industry Association.

Chadwick, D. K., Siu, K., Lee, C., Fouillat, Y., & Germonville, D. (2013). Adding Federated Identity Management to OpenStack. *Journal of Grid Computing*, *12*(1), 3–27. doi:10.1007/s10723-013-9283-2

Chaurasiya, V. K., Srinivasan, K., Thyagarajan, K., Govil, S. B., & Das, S. (2012). An approach to identify the optimal cloud in cloud federation. *International Journal of Cloud Computing and Services Science*, *1*(1), 35–44.

Chen, D., & Doumeingts, G. (2003). European initiatives to develop interoperability of enterprise applications - basic concepts, framework and roadmap. *Annual Reviews in Control*, *27*(2), 153–162. doi:10.1016/j.arcontrol.2003.09.001

Cisco Intercloud Fabric: Hybrid Cloud with Choice, Consistency, Control and Compliance. (2015). *Cisco*. Retrieved from http://www.cisco.com/c/en/us/td/docs/solutions/Hybrid_Cloud/Intercloud/Intercloud_Fabric.pdf

Clayman, S., Galis, A., Chapman, C., Toffetti, G., Rodero-Merino, L., Vaquero, L. M., & Rochwerger, B. (2010). Monitoring service clouds in the future internet. In G. Tselentis, A. Galis, A. Gavras, S. Krco, & T. Zahariadis et al. (Eds.), *Towards the Future Internet - Emerging Trends from European Research*, Amsterdam, Netherlands (pp. 115–126). IOS Press.

Cloud infrastructure management interface (CIMI) model and restful http based protocol an interface for managing cloud infrastructure (Standard No. DSP0263). (2012). *Distributed Management Task Force*.

Comuzzi, M., Kotsokalis, C., Spanoudakis, G., & Yahyapour, R. (2009). Establishing and monitoring SLAs in complex service based systems. *Proceedings of the IEEE International Conference of Web services (ICWS)*, Miami, FL, USA (pp. 783–790). IEEE Computer Society. doi:10.1109/ICWS.2009.47

Cuomo, A., Modica, G., Distefano, S., Puliafito, A., Rak, M., Tomarchio, O., & Villano, U. et al. (2013). An SLA-based broker for cloud infrastructures. *Journal of Grid Computing, 11*(1), 1–25. doi:10.1007/s10723-012-9241-4

Distributed management task force. (2015). *DMTF*. Retrieved from http://www.dmtf.org/

Docker: open platform for developers and sysadmins of distributed applications. (2015). *Docker*. Retrieved from http://www.docker.com/

Dreo, G., Golling, M., Hommel, W., & Tietze, F. (2013). ICEMAN: An architecture for secure federated inter-cloud identity management. *Proceedings of the IFIP/IEEE International Symposium on Integrated Network Management (IM),* Ghent, Belgium (p. 1207–1210).

Emeakaroha, V. C., Netto, M. A., Calheiros, R. N., Brandic, I., Buyya, R., & De Rose, C. A. F. (2012). Towards autonomic detection of SLA violations in cloud infrastructures. *Future Generation Computer Systems, 28*(7), 1017–1029. doi:10.1016/j.future.2011.08.018

European Commission. (2015). Retrieved from http://ec.europa.eu/index/

Flake, S., Tacken, J., & Zoth, C. (2012). Real-time rating and charging in federated cloud environments. *Proceedings of the IEEE 17th Conference of Emerging Technologies Factory Automation (ETFA),* Krakón, Poland (pp. 1–6). IEEE Computer Society. doi:10.1109/ETFA.2012.6489791

Foster, I., Zhao, Y., Raicu, I., & Lu, S. (2008). Cloud computing and grid computing 360-degree compared. *Proceedings of the Grid Computing Environments Workshop (GCE),* Austin, TX (pp. 1–10). USA: IEEE Computer Society. doi:10.1109/GCE.2008.4738445

Gang, L., & Mingchuan, W. (2014). Everything-as-a-service platform for on-demand virtual enterprises. *Information Systems Frontiers, 16*(3), 435–452. doi:10.1007/s10796-012-9351-3

Ganglia monitoring system. (2015). *Ganglia*. Retrieved from http/ganglia.sourceforge.net/

Garcia, A. L. C., & Puel, M. (2013). Identity Federation with VOMS in Cloud Infrastructures. *Proceedings of the 5th IEEE International Conference on Cloud Computing Technology and Science (CLOUDCOM),* Bristol, UK (pp. 42–48). IEEE Computer Society. doi:10.1109/CloudCom.2013.13

Geelan, J., Klems, M., Cohen, R., Kaplan, J., Gourlay, D., Gaw, P., . . . Berger, I. W. (2008). *Twenty-one experts define cloud computing*. Retrieved from http://virtualization.sys-con.com/node/612375

Godfrey, R., Ingham, D., & Schloming, R. (2012). *OASIS advanced message queuing protocol (AMQP) version 1.0*. Retrieved from http://docs.oasis-open.org/amqp/core/v1.0/os/amqp-core-complete-v1.0-os.pdf

Goiri, I., Guitart, J., & Torres, J. (2010). Characterizing cloud federation for enhancing providers' profit. *Proceedings of the 3rd International Conference on Cloud Computing (CLOUD),* Miami, FL, USA (pp. 123–130). IEEE Computer Society. doi:10.1109/CLOUD.2010.32

Gomes, E. R., Vo, Q. B., & Kowalczyk, R. (2012). Pure exchange markets for resource sharing in federated clouds. *Concurrency and Computation, 24*(9), 977–991. doi:10.1002/cpe.1659

Google apps for works. (2015). *Google Apps*. Retrieved from https://www.google.com/intx/pt-BR/work/apps/business/

Google Compute Engine. (2015). *Google.* Retrieved from https://cloud.google.com/products/compute-engine/

Grozev, N., & Buyya, R. (2012). Inter-Cloud Architectures and Application Brokering: Taxonomy and Survey. ACM Computing Surveys, 47(1), 7:1–7:47.

Harsh, P., Jegou, Y., Cascella, R. G., & Morin, C. (2011, October 26-28). Contrail virtual execution platform challenges in being part of a cloud federation - (invited paper). In Abramowicz, W., Llorente, I. M., Surridge, M., Zisman, A., and Vayssière, J., (Eds.), *Towards a Service-Based Internet – Proceedings of the 4th European Conference, ServiceWave 2011,* Poznan, Poland, LNCS (V*ol. 6994,* pp. 50–61). Springer.

Hassan, M. M., Abdullah-Al-Wadud, M., & Fortino, G. (2015). A socially optimal resource and revenue sharing mechanism in cloud federations. *Proceedings of the 19th IEEE International Conference on Computer Supported Cooperative Work in Design (CSCWD),* Calabria, Italy (pp. 620–625). IEEE Computer Society. doi:10.1109/CSCWD.2015.7231029

Herbst, N. R., Kounev, S., & Reussner, R. (2013). Elasticity in cloud computing: What it is, and what it is not. *Proceedings of the 10th International Conference on Autonomic Computing (ICAC),* San Jose, CA, USA (pp. 23–27). USENIX.

HP Openview. (2015). *HP.* Retrieved http://www.hp.com/

Huebscher, M. C., & McCann, J. A. (2008). A survey of autonomic computing—degrees, models, and applications. *ACM Computing Surveys, 40*(3), 7. doi:10.1145/1380584.1380585

An open, global, cloud interoperability project. (2015). Intercloud Testbed. Retrieved from http://www.intercloudtestbed.org

Interoperable Global Trust Federation. (2015). Retrieved from http://www.igtf.net

Jeffery, K., & Neidecker-Lutz, B. (Eds.), (2010). The future of cloud computing: Opportunities for European cloud computing beyond 2010 (Tech. Rep). European Commission, Information Society and Media.

Javascript object notation. (2015). *JSON.* Retrieved from http://www.json.org/

Keahey, K., Tsugawa, M., Matsunaga, A., & Fortes, J. (2009). Sky computing. *IEEE Internet Computing, 13*(5), 43–51. doi:10.1109/MIC.2009.94

Kecskemeti, G., Kertesz, A., Marosi, A., & Kacsuk, P. (2012). Interoperable Resource Management for Establishing Federated Clouds. In M. Villari, I. Brandic, & F. Tusa (Eds.), *Achieving Federated and Self-Manageable Cloud Infrastructures: Theory and Practice* (pp. 18–35). Hershey, PA, USA: Business Science Reference. doi:10.4018/978-1-4666-1631-8.ch002

Keller, A., & Ludwig, H. (2003). The WSLA framework: Specifying and monitoring service level agreements for web services. *Network and System Management, 11*(1), 57–81. doi:10.1023/A:1022445108617

Kurze, T., Klems, M., Bermbach, D., Lenk, A., Tai, S., & Kunze, M. (2011). Cloud federation. *Proceedings of the 2nd International Conference on Cloud Computing, Grids, and Virtualization (Cloud Computing 2011),* Rome, Italy (pp. 32–38). International Academy, Research, and Industry Association.

Le, K., Bianchini, R., Zhang, J., Jaluria, Y., Meng, J., & Nguyen, T. D. (2011). Reducing electricity cost through virtual machine placement in high performance computing clouds. *Proceedings of 2011 International Conference for High Performance Computing, Networking, Storage and Analysis,* Seattle, Washington (pp. 22:1–22:12). ACM. doi:10.1145/2063384.2063413

Li, A., Yang, X., Kandula, S., & Zhang, M. (2010). CloudCmp: Comparing public cloud providers. *Proceedings of the 10th ACM SIGCOMM Conference on Internet Measurement,* Melbourne, Australia (pp. 1–14). ACM.

Li, Z., & Parashar, M. (2007). A computational infrastructure for grid-based asynchronous parallel applications. *Proceedings of the 16th International Symposium on High Performance Distributed Computing,* Monterey, California, USA (pp. 229– 230). ACM. doi:10.1145/1272366.1272404

LXC. (2015). *Linux container.* Retrivied from https://linuxcontainer.org/

Makkes, M. X., Ngo, C., Demchenko, Y., Stijkers, R., Meijer, R., & Laat, C. d. (2013). Defining intercloud federation framework for multi-provider cloud services integration. *Proceeding of the 4th International Conference on Cloud Computing, Grids, and Virtualization (CLOUD COMPUTING 2013),* Valencia, Spain (pp. 185–190). International Academy, Research, and Industry Association.

Manno, G., Smari, W. W., & Spalazzi, L. (2012). FCFA: A semantic-based federated cloud framework architecture. *Proceedings of the International Conference on High Performance Computing & Simulation (HPCS),* Madrid, Spain (p. 42-52). IEEE Computer Society. doi:10.1109/HPCSim.2012.6266889

Marosi, A., Kecskemeti, G., Kertesz, A., & Kacsuk, P. (2011). FCM: An architecture for integrating iaas cloud systems. *Proceedings of the 2th International Conference on Cloud Computing, Grids, and Virtualization (CLOUD COMPUTING 2011),* Rome, Italy (pp. 7–12). International Academy, Research, and Industry Association.

Marshall, P., Keahey, K., & Freeman, T. (2010). Elastic site: Using clouds to elastically extend site resources. *Proceedings of the 10th IEEE/ACM International Conference on Cluster, Cloud and Grid Computing (CCGrid),* Washington, DC, USA (pp. 43–52). IEEE Computer Society. doi:10.1109/CCGRID.2010.80

Mell, P., & Grance, T. (2011). *The NIST definition of cloud computing (Technical Report). National Institute of Standards and Technology.*

Mercosur. (2015). Retrieved from http://www.mercosur.int/

Microsoft Azure cloud computing platform and services. (2015). *Azure.* Retrieved from https://azure.microsoft.com/

Mihailescu, M., & Teo, Y. M. (2010). Dynamic resource pricing on federated clouds. *Proceedings of the 10th IEEE/ACEM International Conference on Cluster, Cloud and Grid Computing (CCGrid),* Washington, DC, USA (pp. 513–517). IEEE Computer Society.

Massachusetts open cloud. (2015). *MOC.* Retrieved from http://www.bu.edu/hic/research/massachusetts-open-cloud

National security agency. (2015). Retrieved from https://www.google.com/intx/pt-BR/work/apps/business/

NIST US Government Cloud Computing Technology Roadmap. (2011) *NIST*. Retrieved from http://www.nist.gov/itl/cloud/upload/SP_500_293_volumeI-2.pdf

Nyréen, R., Edmonds, A., Papaspyrou, A., & Metsch, T. (2011). O*pen cloud computing interface (OCCI) – core*. Retrieved from http://www.ogf.org/documents/GFD

Identity in the cloud use cases version 1.0. (2012). *OASIS*. Retrieved from http://docs.oasis-open.org/id-cloud/IDCloudusecases/v1.0/cn01/IDCloud-usecases-v1.0-cn01.pdf

Open computing infrastructure for elastic service. (2015). *Contrail*. Retrieved from http://www.contrail-project.eu/

Open standard for authorization. (2015). *oAuth*. Retrieved from http://oauth.net/

OpenId. (2015). Retrieved from http://openid.net/

OpenStack. (2015). Retrieved from http://www.openstack.org/

Open virtualization format. (2015). *OVF*. Retrieved from http://www.dmtf.org/standards/ovf

Web ontology language. (2015). *OWL*. Retrieved from http://www.w3.org/TR/owl-ref/

Patel, P., Ranabahu, A., & Sheth, A. (2009). Service level agreement in cloud computing. *Proceedings of the Conference on Object Oriented Programming Systems Languages and Applications (OOPSLA)*, Orlando, FL, USA.

Pathan, M., Buyya, R., & Vakali, A. (2008). Content delivery networks: State of the art, insights, and imperatives. In R. Buyya, M. Pathan, & A. Vakali (Eds.), *Content Delivery Networks* (Vol. 9, pp. 3–32). Springer Berlin Heidelberg. doi:10.1007/978-3-540-77887-5_1

Petcu, D. (2011). Portability and interoperability between clouds: Challenges and case study. *Proceedings of the 4th European Conference on Towards a Service-based Internet,* Poznan, Poland (pp. 62–74). Springer Berlin Heidelberg. doi:10.1007/978-3-642-24755-2_6

Petcu, D., Craciun, C., & Rak, M. (2011). Towards a cross platform cloud API. *Proceedings of the International Conference on Cloud Computing and Services Science (CLOSER),* Noordwijkerhout, The Netherlands (pp. 166–169).

Petcu, D., Di Martino, B., Venticinque, S., Rak, M., Máhr, T., Lopez, G. E., & Stankovski, V. et al. (2013). Experiences in building a mOSAIC of clouds. *Journal of Cloud Computing*, 2(1), 1–22.

Petri, I., Beach, T., Zou, M., Montes, J., Rana, O., & Parashar, M. (2014). Exploring models and mechanisms for exchanging resources in a federated cloud. *Proceedings of the IEEE International Conference on Cloud Engineering (IC2E)*, Boston, Massachusetts (pp. 215–224). USA: IEEE Computer Society. doi:10.1109/IC2E.2014.9

Petri, I., Montes, J. D., Zou, M., Beach, T., Rana, O. F., & Parashar, M. (2015). Market models for federated clouds. *IEEE Transactions on Cloud Computing*, 3(3), 398–410. doi:10.1109/TCC.2015.2415792

PingIdentity. (2015). *Ping Identity*. Retrieved from http://www.pingidentity.com

Practical guide to cloud service level agreements version 1.0 (Tech. Rep.). (2012Cloud Standards Customer Council Workgroup. CSCC.

Rackspace open cloud. (2015). *Rackspace.* Retrieved from http://www.rackspace.com/cloud/

Rebai, S., Hadji, M., & Zeghlache, D. (2015). Improving profit through cloud federation. *Proceedings of the 12th Annual IEEE Consumer Communications and Networking Conference (CCNC),* Las Vegas, Nevada, USA (pp. 732–739). IEEE Computer Society. doi:10.1109/CCNC.2015.7158069

Reference architecture for an SLA management framework (Standard). (2011). EU FP7 project SLA@SOI.

RFC 4158. (2015). *Request for comment.* Retrieved from http://tools.ietf.org/html/rfc4158

RFC 5280. (2015). *Request for comment.* Retrieved from http://tools.ietf.org/html/rfc5280

Rochwerger, B., Breitgand, D., Levy, E., Galis, A., Nagin, K., Llorente, I. M., & Galán, F. et al. (2009). The RESERVOIR model and architecture for open federated cloud computing. *IBM Journal of Research and Development, 53*(4), 535–545. doi:10.1147/JRD.2009.5429058

Sapuntzakis, C., Brumley, D., Chandra, R., Zeldovich, N., Chow, J., Lam, M. S., & Rosenblum, M. (2003). Virtual appliances for deploying and maintaining software. *Proceedings of the 17th USENIX Conference on System Administration,* Berkeley, CA, USA (pp. 181–194). USENIX Association.

Seo, S., Kim, M., Cui, Y., Seo, S., & Lee, H. (2015). SFA-based cloud federation monitoring system for integrating physical resources. *Proceedings of the International Conference on Big Data and Smart Computing (BIGCOMP)* Jeju Island, Korea (pp. 55–58). IEEE Computer Society. doi:10.1109/35021B IGCOMP.2015.7072851

Seventh framework programmer. (2015). Retrieved from http://ec.europa.eu/research/fp7/index/

Sipos, G., Turilli, M., Newhouse, S., & Kacsuk, P. (2013, April). A European Federated Cloud: Innovative distributed computing solutions by EGI. Proceedings of the EGU General Assembly Conference Abstracts (Vol. 15, p. 8690).

Softlayer cloud built to perform. (2015). *Softlayer.* Retrieved from http://www.softlayer.com/

Summary of the Amazon EC2 and Amazon RDS service disruption. (2011). *Amazon.* Retrieved from http://aws.amazon.com/message/65648/

Summary of the aws service event in the US east region. (2012). *Amazon.* Retrieved from http://aws.amazon.com/message/67457/

The enterprise-class monitoring solution for everyone. (2015). *Zabbix.* Retrieved from http://www.zabbix.com/

SOA source book. (2009). *The Open Group.* Retrieved from http://books.google.com.br/books?id=SbZfhkdqbagC

Thomas, M. V., Dhole, A., & Chandrasekaran, K. (2015). Single sign-on in cloud federation using cloudsim. *International Journal of Computer Network and Information Security, 7*(6), 50–58. doi:10.5815/ijcnis.2015.06.06

Tolosana-Calasanz, R., Bañares, J. A., & Colom, J.-M. (2015). On autonomic platform-as-a-service: Characterisation and conceptual model. *Proceedings of the Agent and Multi-Agent Systems: Technologies and Applications – 9th KES International Conference (KES-AMSTA),* Sorrento, Italy (Vol.. 38. pp. 217–226).

Toosi, A. N., Calheiros, R. N., & Buyya, R. (2014, May). Interconnected cloud computing environments: Challenges, taxonomy and survey. *ACM Computing Surveys*, 47(1), 7:1–7:47.

Toosi, A. N., Calheiros, R. N., Thulasiram, R. K., & Buyya, R. (2011). Resource provisioning policies to increase IaaS provider's profit in a federated cloud environment. *Proceedings of the 13th IEEE International Conference on High Performance Computing and Communications (HPCC),* Washington, DC, USA (pp. 279–287). IEEE Computer Society.

Topology and orchestration specification for cloud applications (TOSCA) version 1.0. (2013). *TOSCA*. Retrieved from http://docs.oasis-open.org/tosca/TOSCA/v1.0/os/TOSCA-v1.0-os.pdf

US Patriotic Act. (2001). Retrieved from http://www.gpo.gov/fdsys/pkg/PLAW-107publ56/pdf/PLAW-107publ56.pdf

Use cases and functional requirements for inter-cloud computing (Tech. Rep.). (2010). Global Inter-Cloud Technology Forum.

Vaquero, L. M., Rodero-Merino, L., Caceres, J., & Lindner, M. (2008, December). A break in the clouds: Towards a cloud definition. *SIGCOMM Computer Communication Review*, 39(1), 50–55. doi:10.1145/1496091.1496100

Villegas, D., Bobroff, N., Rodero, I., Delgado, J., Liu, Y., Devarakonda, A., & Parashar, M. et al. (2012). Cloud federation in a layered service model. *Journal of Computer and System Sciences*, 78(5), 1330–1344. doi:10.1016/j.jcss.2011.12.017

Watson, P., Lord, P., Gibson, F., Periorellis, P., & Pitsilis, G. (2008). Cloud computing for e-science with CARMEN. *Proceedings of the 2nd IBERIAN Grid Infrastructure Conference,* Porto, Portugal (pp. 3–14). NETBIBLO.

Extensible markup language. XML. (2015). Retrieved from http://www.w3.org/standards/xml/

ZeroMQ enterprise messaging broker. (2015). *ZeroMQ*. Retrieved from http://zeromq.org/

Zhang, Q., Cheng, L., & Boutaba, R. (2010). Cloud computing: State-of-the-art and research challenges. *Journal of Internet Services and Applications*, 1(1), 7–18. doi:10.1007/s13174-010-0007-6

ENDNOTES

1   The term resource is associated with the assets used by customer service.

2   Resources from other providers which are marketed to interested parties.

3   Quarantine this context means a trial period where the suspicion cloud is monitored more closely to determine whether it will return or not to be part of the federation. In this period, the consumption of the resources from the federation may be restricted.

4   In this context, workflow is a sequence of procedures for the execution of workloads considering the application characteristics.

5   Business methodology that aligns the management of information technology companies with their strategic business goals.

6   Term popularized by O'Reilly Media Company designating a second generation of communities and services based on the Web as a platform.

Chapter 2
Regulating European Clouds:
The New European Data Protection Framework

Szilvia Varadi
University of Szeged, Hungary

ABSTRACT

Cloud Computing is a diverse research area that encompasses many aspects of sharing software and hardware solutions, including computing and storage resources, application runtimes or complex application functionalities. In the supply of any goods and services, the law gives certain rights that protect the consumer and provider, which also applies for Cloud Computing. This new technology also moves functions and responsibilities away from local ownership and management to a third-party provided service, and raises several legal issues, such as data protection, which require this service to comply with necessary regulation. In this chapter the author investigates the revised legislation of the European Union resulting in the General Data Protection Regulation, which will be used to set up the new European Data Protection Framework. The author gathers and summarizes the most relevant changes this regulation brings to the field of Clouds, and draws relations to the previous legislation called the Data Protection Directive currently in force.

INTRODUCTION

Cloud Computing allows the outsourcing of computational power, data storage and other capabilities to a remote third-party (Buyya et al., 2009). In the supply of any goods and services, the law gives certain rights that protect the consumer and provider, which also applies for Cloud Computing: it is subject to legal requirements and constraints to ensure Cloud services are accurately described and provided to customers with guarantees on quality and fitness-for-purpose.

As a result of the pace of technical and economic progress in this field, it was important to determine the compliance of common Cloud Computing usage patterns with legal constraints and requirements. In a former work (Kertesz et al., 2014) the authors provided a method for and the results of an evalua-

DOI: 10.4018/978-1-5225-0153-4.ch002

tion of commonly-observed Cloud federation use cases against the law applying to Cloud Computing. To point out where legal problems may arise, they summarized the national laws of major countries related to data protection, then they revealed relevant use cases for Cloud Federations (Marosi et al., 2011) and assessed them against evaluation criteria derived from legislation for the data processing of end-user details and materials, including the roles and responsibilities necessary for legal compliance. To clarify and exemplify legal compliance in the identified usage patterns, they considered the Data Protection Directive (Directive 95/46/EC, 1995, DPD) of the European Union, which is a commonly accepted and influential directive in the field of data processing legislation. In this former evaluation of data management in Cloud Federations against legal requirements the authors have chosen to perform the investigation exclusively using requirements from data protection law. Data protection covers the dynamic provisioning and processing of data in Cloud environments – intrinsic to the operation of all Clouds – and the field covers the majority of currently available Cloud Computing characteristics and functions, including cases where (Section 4 of OPTIMIS, 2010):

- The infrastructure used to store and process a costumer's data is shared with other customers (i.e., multi-tenancy);
- The Cloud provider's servers are located in several jurisdictions;
- Data is transferred from one location (also called as establishment) to another depending on where resources are available;
- The Cloud service provider decides the location of the data, service and security standards instead of the customer;
- IT resources are not dedicated to a customer but instead are dynamically provisioned.

Data protection legislation is fundamental to Cloud Computing as the consumer looses a degree of control over personal artifacts when they are submitted to the provider for storage and possible processing. To protect the consumer against the provider misusing their data, data processing legislation has been developed to ensure that the fundamental right to privacy is maintained. The distributed nature of Cloud Computing, i.e. Cloud services are available from anywhere in the world, makes is difficult to analyze every country's data protection laws for common Cloud usage evaluation criteria. Therefore it is important to know how the corresponding legislation affects the behavior of Cloud providers.

In this chapter the author investigates the revised European legislation resulting in the General Data Protection Regulation (General Data Protection Regulation, 2012, GDPR), which will be used to set up the new European Data Protection Framework. Then the author gathers and summarizes the most relevant changes this regulation brings to the field of Clouds, and draws relations to the previous legislation called the Data Protection Directive currently in force.

The remainder of this chapter is as follows: Section 2 introduces the current legislation of data protection applicable to Clouds. Section 3 summarizes the EU Data Protection Directive discussing the relevant roles to be determined by Cloud stakeholders. Section 4 contains the legislation changes relevant for Cloud Federations set out in the new General Data Protection Regulation currently under consideration by the EU Parliament. Finally, Section 5 concludes the chapter.

CURRENT LEGISLATION OF DATA PROTECTION IN CLOUDS

International Approaches

According to a report (Greenleaf, 2012) the first influential national legislation was the Swedish law in 1973, since than there has been a major technological development in computer science, and the emergence of cloud computing has contributed to the escalation of national legislations; as a result 89 countries have data protection laws nowadays. These national laws determine separate legal jurisdictions, which are generally the countries themselves. But there are some exceptions: there could be special administrative regions within a country, which belong to different jurisdictions (such as Hong Kong and Macao in China). In the United States of America there is no comprehensive data protection law, since there are no authorities having such power, and its states can regulate data protection separately. Regarding federated laws, the Privacy Act of 1974 regulates the collection, maintenance, use and dissemination of personal information by federal agencies, but it cannot be applied to non-US citizens, and it contains outdated guidelines that cannot cope with novel technological solutions. Such controversial and uncovered issues could be solved by litigations and case law development (justice.gov, 2012). In order to handle cross-border situations, the U.S. uses international agreements. For example the Safe Harbor Framework has been created to enhance U.S.-EU cooperation by providing streamlined means for U.S. organizations to fulfill the adequate level criteria for data protection of the EU (export.gov, 2012). On the other hand there are some international organizations which defined guidelines for harmonizing national laws of data protection. For example the OECD's (Organisation for Economic Cooperation and Development) privacy Guidelines in 1981; the APEC's (Asia-Pacific Economic Cooperation) Privacy Framework in 2005; the Data Protection Convention of the Council of Europe in 1981; and finally the European Union's data protection Directive of 1995, which has been the most influential international instrument. Although it is an EU directive, "countries that wish to engage in data transactions with EU Member States are indirectly required to provide an adequate level of protection" and "the Directive has had a far greater global impact than thus far acknowledged", making it an "effective mechanism to raise the level of data protection worldwide" (Birnhack, 2008). In the following section the author discusses the EU DPD in detail.

Data Protection Directive of the European Union

EU Data Protection Directive (Directive 95/46/EC, 1995) is a directive adopted by the European Union designed to protect the privacy and protection of all personal data collected for or about citizens of the EU, especially as it relates to processing, using, or exchanging such data (Whatis.com, 2008). All 28 EU Member States are reported to have enacted their own data protection legislation that transposes the directive into internal law, Canada, Australia and Argentina have implemented legislation that complies with the DPD, Switzerland has partially implemented legislation and the USA has voluntary registration to the "Safe Harbor" program to ensure private companies who sign up adhere to the rules set out in the DPD (Whittaker, 2011).

The DPD is a commonly accepted and influential directive in the field of data processing legislation. It was produced in 1995, before Cloud Computing was developed, but can be applied to Cloud Computing as it describes how the protection of the processing of personal data and the free movement of such data should be achieved in a technology-neutral way. The DPD can be summarized as having elements concerned with the responsibilities of two actors involved in data exchanges and restrictions on the free movement of data between them based on their location.

The requirements of the DPD are expressed as two technology-neutral actors or roles that have certain responsibilities that must be carried out in order to fulfill the Directive. These roles, the data controller and data processor, are naturally equivalent to service consumer and service provider roles found distributed computing. According to the Article 2 of DPD a data controller is the natural or legal person which determines the means of the processing of personal data, whilst a data processor is a natural or legal person which processes data on behalf of the controller. However, following these definitions, a special case arises: if the processing entity plays a role in determining the purposes or the means of processing, it is a controller rather than a processor.

Finally, although not a specific role, third parties are defined in Article 2 of DPD as "any natural or legal person, public authority, agency or any other body other than the data subject, controller, processor and the persons who are authorized to process the data". This definition is further clarified in (Data Protection Working Party, Feb. 2010) by stating that such a third party has no specific legitimacy or authorization to process the personal data, therefore it is not involved in the controller-to-subject relationship.

The DPD was designed to allow the free-flow of data between EU Member States. However, this Directive also gives the opportunity to third countries to participate in free-flow activities, if deemed to implement "adequate level" of data protection (Article 25 of DPD). This condition means that a third country has to provide at least the same level of protection as the national provisions of the Member States. Once this condition is fulfilled, they can interoperate with other providers within the EU with no barriers.

In a previous work, the authors chose the EU Data Protection Directive as legislation to evaluate the identified Cloud Computing use cases, since this directive was a widely-used and adopted set of rules governing Cloud Computing fundamentals. The DPD also introduces a set of responsibilities for the roles of data controller and processor. These duties could be used to form evaluation criteria to assess Cloud Computing use cases. The directive is also discussed in much detail with respect to Cloud Computing in (OPTIMIS, 2010), and provides a set of criteria that the roles must meet.

According to these sources, the data controller must:

- Be responsible for compliance with data protection law.
- Comply with the general principles (e.g., legitimate processing) laid down in Article 6 of DPD.
- Be responsible for the choices governing the design and operation of the processing carried out.
- Give consent for processing to be carried out (explicit or implied, orally or in writing).
- Be liable for data protection violations.

The data processor, meanwhile, must:

- Be responsible for compliance with data protection law.
- Process data according to the mandate and the instructions given by the controller.
- Be an agent of the controller.
- Be a separate legal entity to the controller.

These roles are strengthened if:

- The controller gives detailed instructions to the processor.
- The controller monitors the processor for the status of the processing.
- Relevant expertise can be shown to be present in either party (e.g., the processor is a specialist in it).
- A written contract exists between the controller and processor.
- The controller is able to exercise full and sole control at any time while the data processing takes place.
- The controller is informed of the main elements of the processing structure.

In the digital age, data is routinely transferred between countries both inside and outside the EU. We can see that not all countries provide the same level of protection for personal data. Binding corporate rules are one tool that can be used to adequately protect personal data, when it is transferred or processed outside the EU. Businesses can adopt these rules voluntarily and they can be used for transfers of data between companies that are part of the same corporate group. Currently, in order to be approved, binding corporate rules must be verified by at least three data protection authorities. This situation was also identified by Wong (Wong, 2011), who gathered related steps of the Article 29 Working Party to revise the EU directive. This Working Party was set up under the DPD and it has advisory status and acts independently.

In a previous work of the author (Kertesz et al. 2014), they discussed six cases where legal issues may arise due to private data processing at multiple jurisdictions resulting from utilizing data center establishments at different geographical locations. Considering European Cloud federations, the Article 4 of the current DPD states that the location of the data controller's establishment determines the national law applicable for data processing. (The DPD also applies to the EEA and EFTA countries according to (EEA Joint Committee, 2000)). In such cases, in general, an adequate level of data protection should be provided according to the EU DPD. They found that new developments in legislation regulation applying to Cloud Computing were still needed. This fact served as a motivation for the author to investigate the new European regulation, and gather the relevant changes it will bring to Cloud Federations.

THE REVISED EUROPEAN LEGISLATION: GENERAL DATA PROTECTION REGULATION

The currently effective European DPD is basically appropriate for determining the law applicable for data management in Cloud services, when the data controller and processor roles are well identified. What is more problematic for companies is to apply the identified law at a European scale, because the Member States implemented the DPD rules in different ways. This fact has also been recognized by the European Commission. In our opinion, instead of taking sanctions, it decided to perform a reform of the data protection rules using the principle of subsidiarity. Based on this principle the European Union can introduce a unified legislation for data protection to be applied by all Member States. This reform will also give the opportunity for the Commission to replace the flexible directive with a strictly applicable regulation.

The European Commission first initiated a public consultation in 2011 (Commission, 2011), in the framework of their Digital Agenda for Europe (DAE) launched in May 2010, to find the requirements, barriers and opportunities for the provisioning and use of Cloud Computing which is highlighted in the Agenda (COM 0245, 2010). As a result, the European Cloud Computing strategy was published in 2012 by the Commission (CCS, 2012). In this strategy the Commission aimed at enabling and facilitating faster adoption of cloud computing throughout all sectors of the economy in order to boost the productivity, growth and jobs. On the basis of an analysis of the overall policy, regulatory and technology landscapes and a wide consultation of stakeholders, undertaken to identify what needs to be done to achieve that goal, the European Commission endorsed a communication on "Unleashing the Potential of Cloud Computing in Europe" (COM 529, 2012). This document set out the most important and urgent additional actions. It represents a political commitment of the Commission and serves as a call on all stakeholders to participate in the implementation of these actions. The strategy includes three key actions: Standards and Certification, Contract terms and Conditions, and European Cloud Partnership. The development of model contract terms was planned to cover issues such as: data preservation, disclosure and integrity, data location and transfer, ownership of the data, and direct and indirect liability change of service by cloud providers and subcontracting. This document shows that the Commission now regards cloud computing primarily as an internal market issue with the intention to turn the EU's high standards of data protection and security into a virtue for Europe. Europe could become the world's leading trusted cloud region, although the Commission's Cloud Computing Strategy does not require the localization of cloud services or proposes to set-up a dedicated "European Super-Cloud".

The European Commission also set up a European Cloud Partnership (ECP) program in 2012 to create a common framework for cloud computing across Europe (Kroes, 2012), by bringing together industry expects and public sector users to work on common procurement requirements for cloud computing in an open and fully transparent way. The steering board of the new European Cloud Partnership has met 20 November 2012 in Brussels, kicking off the process to build an EU Digital Single Market for cloud computing.

The economic and social integration resulting from the functioning of the internal market has led to a substantial increase in cross-border data flows. The exchange of data between public and private, economic and social actors across the Union increased. Also the scale of data sharing and collecting has increased spectacularly. Technology allows both private companies and public authorities to make use of personal data on an unprecedented scale in order to pursue their activities. Individuals increasingly make personal information available publicly and globally. Technology has transformed both the economy and social life, and requires to further facilitate the free flow of data within the Union and the transfer to third countries and international organizations, while ensuring a high level of the protection of personal data.

The EU found that these developments require building a strong and more coherent data protection framework. In order to ensure consistent and high level of protection of individuals and to remove the obstacles to flows of personal data, the level of protection of the rights and freedoms of individuals with regard to the processing of such data should be equivalent in all Member States.

The protection of individuals should be technologically neutral and not depend on the techniques used, otherwise this would create a serious risk of circumvention. The current DPD remains sound as far as its objectives and principles are concerned, but it has not prevented fragmentation in the way personal data protection is implemented across the Union, legal uncertainty and a widespread public perception that there are significant risks associated notably with online activity. This is why it is time to build a stronger and more coherent data protection framework in the EU, backed by strong enforcement that will allow the digital economy to develop across the internal market, put individuals in control of their own data and reinforce legal and practical certainty for economic operators and public authorities. According to the Commission the lack of trust makes consumers hesitate to buy online and adopt new services. This risk could slow down the development of innovative uses of new technologies. Personal data protection therefore plays a central role in the Digital Agenda for Europe.

The European Commission is currently in the process of reforming the European data protection rules, where the main objectives are: to modernize the EU legal system for the protection of personal data, in particular to meet the challenges resulting from globalization and the use of new technologies; to strengthen users' influence on their personal data, and at the same time to reduce administrative formalities to ensure a free flow of personal data within the EU and beyond; to improve the clarity and coherence of the EU rules for personal data protection and achieve a consistent and effective implementation and application of the fundamental right to the protection of personal data in all areas of the Union's activities (COM 09, 2012).

To achieve these above mentioned goals, the Commission has two legislative proposals according to a press release of the European Commission (EC Press release, 2012): a Regulation (COM 11, 2012) setting out a general EU framework for data protection and which will replace the currently effective DPD, and a Directive (COM 10, 2012) on protecting personal data processed for the purposes of prevention, detection, investigation or prosecution of criminal offences and related judicial activities.

Personal data is increasingly being transferred across borders – both virtual and geographical – and stored on servers in multiple countries both within and outside the EU. The globalised nature of data-flows calls for strengthening the individuals' data-protection rights internationally. This requires strong principles for protecting individuals' data, aimed at easing the flow of personal data across borders while still ensuring a high and consistent level of protection without loopholes or unnecessary complexity. In these legal documents the Commission proposes the following key changes:

- A single set of rules on data protection across the EU to avoid unnecessary administrative requirements.
- It places increased responsibility and accountability for the companies processing personal data (e.g. they must notify the national supervisory authority of serious data breaches within 24 hours).
- It promotes a single national data protection authority in each EU country that people can refer to, even when their data is processed by a company based outside the EU. These authorities will be empowered to fine companies that violate EU data protection rules.
- It strengthens the right to data portability by enabling easier access to users' personal data, and easier data migration among service providers.
- It introduces the "right to be forgotten" to enable the deletion of user data upon request, when there are no legitimate grounds for retaining it.
- It explicitly states that EU rules must be applied for data processing outside the EU by companies that are active in the EU market.

The Commission's proposals have been sent to the European Parliament and the Council of the European Union (sometimes just called the Council, and sometimes still referred to as the Council of Ministers) for discussion. The Committee on the Internal Market and Consumer Protection (IMCO, 2012) and the Committee on Legal Affairs of the European Parliament (JURI, 2012) proposed some amendments in the text of the regulation. The Council of the European Union has also stated that further examination of the text of the proposed regulation is still needed (Council, 2012). The new legislation will take effect two years after they have been adopted by Parliament and the Council. The proposals are now at the European Parliament.

According to the impact assessment of the Commission (Impact Assessment, 2012), the acceptation and then the implementation of the proposals will lead inter alia to considerable improvements regarding legal certainty for data controllers and citizens, reduction of administrative burden, consistency of data protection enforcement in the Union, the effective possibility of individuals to exercise their data protection rights to the protection of personal data within the EU and the efficiency of data protection supervision and enforcement.

The legal bases to the new data protection framework (to be determined by the GDPR) are the following:

Article 16(1) of Treaty on the Functioning of the European Union (TFEU), as introduced by the Lisbon Treaty, establishes the principle that everyone has the right to the protection of personal data concerning him or her. Moreover, Article 16(2) TFEU introduced a specific legal basis for the adoption of rules on the protection of personal data. Article 8 of the Charter of Fundamental Rights of the EU enshrines protection of personal data as a fundamental right.

According to the Commission, the protection of individuals should apply to processing of personal data by both automated and manual means, if the data are contained or are intended to be contained in a filing system. The proposed Regulation should not apply to processing of personal data by a natural person, which are exclusively personal or domestic, such as correspondence and the holding of addresses, and without any gainful interest or without any connection with a professional or commercial activity. The exemption should also not apply to controllers or processors which provide the means for processing personal data for such personal or domestic activities.

In the following the relevant Articles of the GDPR are summarized. The Preamble (30) of the Regulation states the quality of the data, which means that the data should be adequate, relevant and limited to the minimum necessary for the purposes for which the data are processed. The period for which the data are stored is limited to a strict minimum. In order to ensure that the data are not kept longer than necessary, time limits should be established by the controller for erasure or for a periodic review. Personal data should only be processed if the purpose of the processing could not be fulfilled by other means. It shall ensure, that inaccurate personal data are rectified or deleted.

Article 4 of the Regulation contains definitions of terms. Some definitions are taken over from DPD, others are modified, complemented with additional elements, or newly introduced ("genetic data," "biometric data," "data concerning health," "main establishment," "representative," "enterprise," "group of undertakings," "binding corporate rules," etc.).

In the definition of the "controller" the additional element is that the controller determines also the conditions of the processing of personal data.

In the definition of consent, the criterion "explicit" is added to avoid confusing parallelism with "unambiguous" consent and in order to have one single and consistent definition of consent, ensuring the awareness of the data subject that, and to what, he or she gives consent either by a statement or by a clear affirmative action.

Article 5 sets out the principles relating to personal data processing, which correspond to those in Article 6 of DPD. The new elements are in particular the transparency principle, the clarification of the data minimization principle and the establishment of a comprehensive responsibility and liability of the controller.

Article 6 of the Regulation contains, based on Article 7 of DPD, the criteria for lawful processing, which are the following:

- The data subject has given consent to the processing of their personal data for one or more specific purposes;
- Processing is necessary for the performance of a contract in which the data subject is party or in order to take steps at the request of the data subject prior to entering into a contract;
- Processing is necessary for compliance with a legal obligation of the controller;
- Processing is necessary in order to protect the vital interests of the data subject;
- Processing is necessary for the performance of a task carried out in the public interest or in the exercise of official authority vested in the controller;
- Processing is necessary for the purposes of the legitimate interests pursued by a controller, except where such interests are overridden by the interests or fundamental rights and freedoms of the data subject which require protection of personal data, in particular where the data subject is a child. This shall not apply to processing carried out by public authorities in the performance of their tasks.

As it can be seen, in order for personal data processing to be lawful, it has to be on the basis of the consent of the data subject. Article 7 contains the conditions for consent, so the data subject shall have the right to withdraw his or her consent at any time. In this case, the lawfulness of the former processing based on consent should not be affected by the withdrawal of consent. Consent shall not provide a legal basis for the processing, where there is a significant imbalance between the position of the data subject and the controller. Moreover, Preamble (25) of the Regulation clarifies that the consent should be given explicitly by any appropriate method enabling a freely given specific and informed indication of the data subject's wishes, either by a statement or by an affirmative action of the data subject, ensuring that he or she is aware that they accept the processing of their personal data. Therefore, silence or inactivity should not create the consent. Consent has to cover all processing activities carried out for the same purpose. This Preamble also contains that if the data subject's consent is to be given following an electronic request, the request must be clear, concise and not unnecessarily disruptive to the use of the service for which it is provided.

Article 9 contains the rules of processing of special categories of personal data, revealing race or ethnic origin, political opinions, religion or beliefs, trade-union membership, and the processing of genetic data or data concerning health or sex life or criminal convictions or related security measures.

Article 11 introduces the obligation on controllers to provide transparent, easily accessible and understandable information, inspired in particular by the Madrid Resolution on international standards on the protection of personal data and privacy (Madrid Resolution, 2009).

Article 12 of the Regulation states the obligation of the controller to provide procedures and mechanism for exercising the data subject's rights, including means for electronic requests, requiring response to the data subject's request within a defined deadline (at the latest within one month of receipt of the request), and the motivation of refusals.

Article 14 further specifies the controller's information obligations towards the data subject, building on Articles 10 and 11 of DPD, providing additional information to the data subject, for example the contact details of the controller or the period for which the personal data will be stored. Article 15 contains the conditions of the right of access for the data subject. In this case, the data subject could request a confirmation from the controller at any time, whether or not personal data relating to the data subject are being processed.

Article 16 sets out the data subject's right to rectification, so he or she could request the completion of incomplete personal data, which provision is based on Article 12(b) of DPD.

Article 17 of the GDPR provides the data subject's right to be forgotten and to erasure. It further elaborates and specifies the right of erasure provided for in Article 12(b) of DPD and provides the conditions of the right to be forgotten, which are the following:

- The data are no longer necessary in relation to the purposes for which they were collected or otherwise processed;
- The data subject withdraws consent on which the processing is based, or when the storage period consented to has expired, and where there is no other legal ground for the processing of the data;
- The data subject objects to the processing of personal data pursuant to Article 19;
- The processing of the data does not comply with the Regulation for other reasons.

This means the obligation of the controller which has made the personal data public to inform third parties to erase any links to, or copy or replication of that personal data. The Preamble (54) of the Regulation contains that the controller should take all reasonable steps, including technical measures, in relation to data for the publication of which the controller is responsible, to ensure this above mentioned information. In relation to a third party publication of personal data, the controller should be considered responsible for the publication, where the controller has authorised the publication by the third party.

The controller shall carry out the erasure without delay, except to the extent that the retention of the personal data is necessary in the following cases:

- For exercising the right of freedom of expression;
- For reasons of public interest in the area of public health;
- For historical, statistical and scientific research purposes;
- For compliance with a legal obligation to retain the personal data by Union or Member State law to which the controller is subject;
- If the controller shall restrict processing of personal data.

Instead of erasure, the controller shall restrict processing of personal data where:

- Their accuracy is contested by the data subject, for a period enabling the controller to verify the accuracy of the data;
- The controller no longer needs the personal data for the accomplishment of its task but they have to be maintained for purposes of proof;
- The processing is unlawful and the data subject opposes their erasure and requests the restriction of their use instead;
- The data subject requests to transmit the personal data into another automated processing system.

Where the erasure is carried out, the controller shall not otherwise process such personal data. This right is particularly relevant, when the data subject has given their consent as a child, when not being fully aware of the risks involved by the processing, and later wants to remove such personal data especially on the Internet.

Article 18 introduces the data subject's right to data portability, i.e. to transfer data from one electronic processing system to, such as a social network, into another, without being prevented from doing so by the controller. As a precondition and in order to further improve access of individuals to their personal data, it provides the right to obtain from the controller those data in a structured and commonly used electronic format. The Preamble (55) of the Regulation clarifies that this option could apply where the data subject provided the data to the automated processing system, based on their consent or in the performance of a contract.

Article 19 provides for the data subject's rights to object at any time to the processing of personal data with some exceptions. Article 20 concerns the data subject's right not to be subject to a measure based on profiling solely on automated processing intended to evaluate certain personal aspects relating to this natural person or to analyze or predict in particular the natural person's performance at work, economic situation, location, health, personal preferences, reliability or behavior. In light of the Preamble (21) of the Regulation in order to determine whether a processing activity can be considered to "monitor the behavior" of data subjects, it should be ascertained whether individuals are tracked on the internet with data processing techniques which consist of applying a "profile" to an individual, particularly in order to take decisions concerning her or him or for analyzing or predicting her or his personal preferences, behaviors and attitudes. The Preamble (24) of the Regulation states that individuals may be associated with online identifiers provided by their devices, applications, tools and protocols, such as Internet Protocol addresses or cookie identifiers, when they use the online services. This may leave traces which, combined with unique identifiers and other information received by the servers, may be used to create profiles of the individuals and identify them. But the identification numbers, location data, online identifiers or other specific factors as such not necessarily be considered as personal data in all circumstances.

Article 21 contains the opportunity for the EU or Member States to maintain or introduce restrictions of principles laid down in Article 5 and of the data subject's rights. This provision is based on Article 13 of DPD and on the requirements stemming from the Charter of Fundamental Rights and the European Convention for the Protection of Human Rights and Fundamental Freedoms, as interpreted by the Court of Justice of the EU and the European Court of Human Rights.

In the following the new provisions for the general obligations of the controller and processor are summarized.

Article 22 takes account of the debate on a "principle of accountability" and describes in detail the obligation of responsibility of the controller to comply with the Regulation and to demonstrate this compliance, including by way of adoption of internal policies and measures for ensuring such compliance. The measures shall in particular include:

- Keeping the documentation;
- Implementing the data security requirements;
- Performing a data protection impact assessment;
- Complying with the requirements for prior authorization or prior consultation of the supervisory authority;
- Designating a data protection officer.

Moreover, mechanisms should be implemented to ensure the verification of the effectiveness of the measures by the controller. If proportionate, this verification shall be carried out by independent internal or external auditors.

Article 23 sets out the obligations of the controller arising from the principles of data protection by design and by default. Having regard to the state of the art and the cost of implementation, the controller shall, both at the time of the determination of the means for processing and at the time of the processing itself, implement appropriate technical and organizational measures and procedures in such a way that the processing will meet the requirements of the Regulation and ensure the protection of the rights of the data subject.

Articles 24 and 25 address some of the issues arise from Cloud Computing, more specifically from Cloud Federations. While these provisions do not indicate whether outsourcers are joint data controllers, they acknowledge the fact that there may be more than one data controller.

Article 24 clarifies the responsibilities of joint controllers as regards their internal relationship and towards the data subject. Where a controller determines the purposes, conditions and means of the processing of personal data jointly with others, the joint controllers shall determine their respective responsibilities for compliance with the obligations under the Regulation, by means of an arrangement between them.

Article 25 of the Regulation obliges under certain conditions those controllers, who are not established in the Union, to designate a representative in the Union, where the Regulation applies to their processing activities. The exception are when the controller is established in a third country ensuring an adequate level of protection, or the controller is a small or medium sized enterprise or a public authority or where the controller is only occasionally offering goods or services to such data subjects. The representative should act on behalf of the controller and may be addressed by any supervisory authority.

The main establishment of a controller in the EU should be determined according to objective criteria and should imply the effective and real exercise of management activities determining the main decisions as to the purposes, conditions and means of processing through stable arrangements. Only the presence and use of technical means and technologies for processing personal data do not constitute such main establishment themselves and are therefore no determining criteria for a main establishment. The main establishment of a controller or a processor should be the place of its central administration in the EU and implies the effective and real exercise of activity through stable arrangements according to the Preamble (27) of the Regulation.

Otherwise, regardless of whether the processing itself takes place within the EU or not, any processing of personal data in the context of the activities of an establishment of a controller or a processor in the EU should be carried out in accordance with the Regulation (Preamble (19)).

The Regulation also applicable for those processing of personal data by a controller not established in the Union, where the processing activities are related to the offering of goods or services to data subjects residing in the EU, or to the monitoring of the behavior of such data subjects (Preamble (20)).

Article 26 of the proposed Regulation clarifies the position and obligation of processors, partly based on Article 17(2) of DPD, and adding new elements, including that a processor who processes data beyond the controller's instructions is to be considered as a joint controller. The carrying out of processing by a processor shall be governed by a contract or other legal act binding the processor to the controller and stipulating in particular that the processor shall:

- Act only on instructions from the controller, in particular, where the transfer of the personal data used is prohibited;
- Employ only staff who have committed themselves to confidentiality or are under a statutory obligation of confidentiality;
- Take all required measures;
- Enlist another processor only with the prior permission of the controller;
- Insofar as this is possible given the nature of the processing, create in agreement with the controller the necessary technical and organizational requirements for the fulfillment of the controller's obligation;
- Assist the controller in ensuring compliance with the obligations;
- Hand over all results to the controller after the end of the processing and not process the personal data otherwise;
- Make available to the controller and the supervisory authority all information necessary to control compliance with the obligations laid down in this Article.

The controller and the processor shall document in writing the controller's instructions and the processor's obligations. The processor shall be considered to be a controller in respect of that processing and shall be subject to the rules on joint controllers, if a processor processes personal data other than as instructed by the controller.

Article 27 on the processing under the authority of the controller and processor is based on Article 16 of DPD.

Article 28 introduces the obligation for controllers and processors to maintain documentation of the processing operations under their responsibility, instead of a general notification to the supervisory authority required by Articles 18(1) and 19 of DPD. Article 29 clarifies the obligations of the controller and the processor for the co-operation with the supervisory authority.

The following provisions are designed for the data security. Article 30 obliges the controller and the processor to implement appropriate measures for the security of processing, based on Article 17(1) of DPD, but extending that obligation to processors. This means that they shall take the steps to protect personal data against accidental or unlawful destruction or accidental loss and to prevent any unlawful forms of processing, in particular any unauthorized disclosure, dissemination or access, or alteration of personal data. Articles 31 and 32 introduce an obligation to notify personal data breaches, building on the personal data breach notification in Article 4(3) of the e-privacy Directive 2002/58/EC.

Moreover, DPD provided for a general obligation to notify processing of personal data to the supervisory authorities, which notification could create administrative and financial burdens. According to the Commission, this general obligation should be replaced by effective procedures. Therefore Article 33 introduces a new element, namely the obligation of controllers and processors to carry out a data protection impact assessment prior to risky processing operations, which could present specific risks to the rights and freedoms of data subjects by virtue of their nature, their scope or their purposes. According to the new Regulation the following processing operations in particular present specific risks:

- "A systematic and extensive evaluation of personal aspects relating to a natural person or for analyzing or predicting in particular the natural person's economic situation, location, health, personal preferences, reliability or behavior, which is based on automated processing and on which measures are based that produce legal effects concerning the individual or significantly affect the individual;

- Information on sex life, health, race and ethnic origin or for the provision of health care, epidemiological researches, or surveys of mental or infectious diseases, where the data are processed for taking measures or decisions regarding specific individuals on a large scale;
- Monitoring publicly accessible areas, especially when using optic-electronic devices (video surveillance) on a large scale;
- Personal data in large scale filing systems on children, genetic data or biometric data;
- Other processing operations for which the consultation of the supervisory authority is required (..)."

According to this Article of the Regulation, general description of the envisaged processing operations, an assessment of the risks to the rights and freedoms of data subjects, the measures envisaged to address the risks, safeguards, security measures and mechanisms to ensure the protection of personal data and to demonstrate compliance with this Regulation should be included in particular in the assessment.

This provision should in particular apply to newly established large-scale filing systems, which aim at processing a considerable amount of personal data at regional, national or supranational level and which could affect a large number of data subjects – Preamble (71) of the Regulation.

Article 34 concerns the cases where authorization by, and consultation of, the supervisory authority is mandatory prior to the processing, building on the concept of prior checking in Article 20 of DPD.

The new Regulation, based on Article 18(2) of DPD, introduces the function of a mandatory data protection officer, who should be designated when the processing carried out for the public sector or for large enterprises, which employing 250 persons or more, or where the core activities of the controller or processor consist of processing operations which require regular and systematic monitoring. The data protection officer may be employed by the controller or processor, or fulfill his or her tasks on the basis of a service contract. Article 36 sets out the position, while Article 37 provides the core tasks of the data protection officer.

Article 38 concerns codes of conduct, building on the concept of Article 27(1) of DPD, clarifying the content of the codes and the procedures and providing for the empowerment of the Commission to decide on the general validity of codes of conduct. Article 39 introduces the possibility to establish certification mechanisms and data protection seals and marks. The Member States and the Commission shall encourage, in particular at European level, the establishment of data protection certification mechanisms and of data protection seals and marks, allowing data subjects to quickly assess the level of data protection provided by controllers and processors.

The Chapter V of the Regulation contains the rules for transfers of personal data to third countries or international organizations. In light of the new provisions, transfer could be carried out only when the third country, or a territory or a processing sector within that third country, or the international organization in question ensures an adequate level of protection. The novelty of the new provision is that it now confirms explicitly the possibility for the Commission to assess the level of protection afforded by a territory or a processing sector within a third country. The criteria which shall be taken into account for the Commission's assessment of an adequate or not adequate level of protection include expressly the rule of law, judicial redress and independent supervision.

Where the Commission decides that an adequate level of protection not ensured, any transfer of personal data to the third country, or a territory or a processing sector within that third country, or the international organization in question shall be prohibited. In this case, the Commission shall enter into consultations with this third country or international organization to remedying the situation resulting from this "inadequacy" decision. A list of those third countries, territories and processing sectors within a third country and international organizations, where it has decided that an adequate level of protection is or is not ensured, should be published by the Commission in the Official Journal of the European Union. When no adequacy decision has been adopted by the Commission, the Regulation requires for transfers to third countries, to adduce appropriate safeguards, in particular standard data protection clauses, binding corporate rules and contractual clauses. The possibility of making use of Commission standard data protection clauses is based on Article 26(4) of DPD. As a new component, such standard data protection clauses may now also be adopted by a supervisory authority and be declared generally valid by the Commission. The option of contractual clauses gives certain flexibility to the controller or processor, but is subject to prior authorization by supervisory authorities. Article 43 describes in further detail the conditions for transfers by way of binding corporate rules, based on the current practices and requirements of supervisory authorities.

Article 44 spells out and clarifies the derogations for a data transfer, based on the Article 26 of DPD. This applies in particular to data transfers required and necessary for the protection of important grounds of public interest, for example in cases of international data transfers between competition authorities, tax or customs administrations, or between services competent for social security matters or for fisheries management. In addition, a data transfer may, under limited circumstances, be justified on a legitimate interest of the controller or processor, but only after having assessed and documented the circumstances of that transfer operation.

The Regulation explicitly provides for international co-operation mechanisms for the protection of personal data between the Commission and the supervisory authorities of third countries, in particular those considered offering an adequate level of protection (Article 45).

Chapter VI of the Regulation contains the provisions for the independent supervisory authorities based on the rules of the DPD, but implementing the relevant case law by the Court of Justice of the European Union (CURIA judgment, 2010).

The one or more public, independent supervisory authorities should be provided by each Member State in order to monitor the consistent application of the Regulation throughout the EU and to protect the natural persons in relation to the processing of their personal data and to facilitate the free flow of personal data within the EU. These supervisory authorities shall co-operate with each other and the Commission. Chapter VII is on co-operation (mutual assistance and joint operations including a right of supervisory authorities to participate in such operations) and consistency.

The Regulation establishes the European Data Protection Board (EDPB), which replaces the Article 29 Data Protection Working Party set up by DPD (Working Party on the Protection of Individuals with regard to the Processing of Personal Data set up under Article 29 of Directive 95/46/EC.) This Board consists of the heads of the supervisory authority of each Member State and of the European Data Protection Supervisor, led by a chair and a secretariat. It is clarified that the Commission is not a member of the European Data Protection Board, but has the right to participate in the activities and to be represented. The tasks of the independent European Data Protection Board are based on Article 30(1) of DPD, but provides for additional elements, e. g. to advise the Commission on any issue related to the protection of personal data in the Union or to examine any question covering the application of the Regulation. In order to be able to react in urgent situations, it provides the Commission with the possibility to ask for an opinion within a specific time-limit. The EDPB shall prepare report annually on its activities, building on Article 30(6) of DPD.

The Regulation contains provisions for remedies, liability and sanctions. Article 75 concerns the right to a judicial remedy against a controller or processor, building on Article 22 of DPD, and providing a choice to go to court in the Member State where the defendant is established or where the data subject is residing.

Moreover some special data processing situations also clarified by the Regulation, namely the following: processing personal data in the employment context, processing personal data for processing for journalistic, health, historical, statistical or scientific research purposes. The Regulation obliges the Member States to adopt specific laws, exemptions and derogations from specific provisions of the Regulation where necessary to reconcile the right to the protection of personal data and ensure specific safeguards for processing. Article 85 allows in the light of Article 17 of the Treaty on the Functioning of the European Union for the continuous application of existing comprehensive data protection rules of churches if brought in line with the Regulation.

The Regulation creates the task of the Commission to evaluate the application and function of the Regulation itself after entry into force. The Commission's reports on the above mentioned evaluation shall be submitted to the European Parliament and the Council every four years.

Concerning the initial goal of the author's investigation, this proposal for a new regulation mostly clarifies, restates and strengthens the referred rules of the DPD and among other above mentioned things the so-called "right to be forgotten" introduces also a new responsibility for Cloud service providers. Some providers claim in the service usage terms and conditions to have the right to retain data, which may be affected by this new regulation. Even though it would definitely be a positive sign for the users and would encourage service utilization, but it would also place further development costs for providers, since the removal of all data replicas may also raise some technical problems.

As a summary, due to the legal nature of a regulation under EU law, the proposed data protection Regulation will establish a single rule that applies directly and uniformly. EU regulations are the most direct form of EU law. A regulation is directly binding upon the Member States and is directly applicable within the Member States. As soon as a regulation entered into force, it automatically becomes the part of the national legal system of each Member State and it is not allowed to create a new legislative text by each Member State. Contrarily, EU directives are flexible tools of the EU legislation; they are used to harmonize the different national laws in-line with each other. Directives prescribe only an end result that must be achieved by every Member State; the form and methods of implementing the principles included in a directive are a matter for each Member State to decide for itself. Each Member State must implement the directive into its legal system, but can do so in its own words. A directive only takes effect through national legislation that implements the measures.

In case of the Cloud federations: according to the Article 4 of the current DPD, the location of the data controller's establishment determines the national law applicable, which can be variable as we have seen in the use cases mentioned in the author's previous work (Kertesz et al. 2014).

However, the proposed Regulation with its unified rules after enter into force must be applied in every Member State in the same way, so there would be and could be not discrepancy among them. Moreover where the national law of a Member State applies by virtue of public international law, this Regulation should also apply to a controller not established in the EU, such as in a Member State's diplomatic mission or consular post. (Preamble (22) of GDPR).

CONCLUSION

Data protection legislation is fundamental to Cloud Computing as the consumer loses a degree of control over personal artifacts when they are submitted to the provider for storage and possible processing. To protect the consumer against the provider misusing their data, data processing legislation has been developed to ensure that the fundamental right to privacy is maintained. Since Cloud services are available from anywhere in the world, it makes is difficult to analyze every country's data protection laws for common Cloud usage evaluation criteria. Therefore it is important to know how the corresponding legislation affects the behavior of Cloud providers.

In this chapter the revised European legislation resulting in the General Data Protection Regulation was investigated, which will be used to set up the new European Data Protection Framework. The author gathered and summarized the most relevant changes this regulation brings to the field of Clouds, and draw relations to the previous legislation called the Data Protection Directive currently in force.

The future work of the author will address the extension of the set of use cases previously identified, representing the general scenarios of Cloud ecosystems. It will also determine how to place these cases in the future European data protection framework currently being formed by the General Data Protection Regulation.

REFERENCES

A Digital Agenda for Europe COM (2010) 0245 final. (2010). Commission to the European Parliament, the Council, the European Economic and Social Committee and the Committee of the Regions.

Birnhack, M. D. (2008). The EU Data Protection Directive: An Engine of a Global Regime (Paper no. 95). Tel Aviv University Law School: Tel Aviv University Law Faculty Papers.

Buyya, R., Yeo, C. S., Venugopal, S., Broberg, J., & Brandic, I. (2009). Cloud computing and emerging it platforms: Vision, hype, and reality for delivering computing as the 5th utility. *Future Generation Computer Systems*, 25(6), 599–616. doi:10.1016/j.future.2008.12.001

Bygrave, L. A. (2000). European Data Protection, Determining Applicable Law Pursuant To European Data Protection Legislation. *Computer Law & Security Report*, 16(4), 252–257. doi:10.1016/S0267-3649(00)89134-7

(COM(2012)0011 – C7-0025/2012 – 2012/0011(COD)). Draft opinion of the Committee on the Internal Market and Consumer Protection (IMCO) for the Committee on Civil Liberties, Justice and Home Affairs on the proposal for a regulation of the European Parliament and of the Council on the protection of individuals with regard to the processing of personal data and on the free movement of such data (General Data Protection Regulation). 25 September, 2012.

Commission / Germany, CaseC-518/07, ECR 2010 p. I-1885 (Judgement). (2010, March 9). Court of Justice of the EU.

(2000, August). Commission Decision no. 2000/520/EC of 26 July 2000 pursuant to Directive 95/46/ EC of the European Parliament and of the Council on the adequacy of the protection provided by the safe harbor privacy principles and related frequently asked questions issued by the US Department of Commerce. *Official Journal, 215*, 7–47.

Cs, A. Marosi, G. Kecskemeti, A. Kertesz & P. Kacsuk (2011). FCM: an Architecture for Integrating IaaS Cloud Systems. *Proceedings of the Second International Conference on Cloud Computing, GRIDs, and Virtualization (Cloud Computing 2011)*, Rome, Italy (pp. 7-12). IARIA.

Data Protection package: Report on progress achieved under the Cyprus Presidency, 16525/1/12 REV 1. (2012, March 12). Council of the European Union.

Opinion 1/2010 on the concepts of "controller" and "processor" (Ref. WP 169). (2010, February). *Data Protection Working Party*. Retrieved from http://ec.europa.eu/justice/policies/privacy/docs/wp-docs/2010/ wp169_en.pdf

Opinion 8/2010 on applicable law (Ref. WP 179). (2010, December). *Data Protection Working Party*. Retrieved from http://ec.europa.eu/justice/policies/privacy/docs/wp-docs/2010/wp179_en.pdf

Decision of the EEA Joint Committee, No. 83/1999 of 25 June 1999 amending Protocol 37 and Annex XI (Telecommunication services) to the EEA Agreement. (2000, November). Official Journal L 296, 41.

Directive 95/46/EC of the European Parliament and of the Council of 24 October 1995 on the protection of individuals with regard to the processing of personal data and on the free movement of such data. (1995, November). Official Journal L 281, 31-50.

EC Press release: Commission proposes a comprehensive reform of data protection rules to increase users' control of their data and to cut costs for businesses. (2012, January 25). European Commission. Retrieved from europa.eu/rapid/pressReleasesAction.do?reference=IP/12/46

Information Society and Media Directorate-General, Converged Networks and Services, Software & Service Architectures and Infrastructures, Cloud Computing: *Public Consultation Report*, European Commission. Brussels. (2011, 5th December). Retrieved from http://ec.europa.eu/information_society/ activities/cloudcomputing/docs/ccconsultationfinalreport.pdf

European Cloud Computing Strategy (CCS). (2012). *European Commission*. Retrieved from http:// ec.europa.eu/information_society/activities/cloudcomputing/cloud_strategy/index_en.htm

Impact Assessment SEC(2012) 72 final (Staff Working Paper). (2012, January 25). European Commission, Brussels.

Ferrer, A. J., Hernandez, F., Tordsson, J., Elmroth, E., Ali-Eldin, A., Zsigri, C., & Sheridan, C. et al. (2012). OPTIMIS: A Holistic Approach to Cloud Service Provisioning. *Future Generation Computer Systems, 28*(1), 66–77. doi:10.1016/j.future.2011.05.022

Gellman, R. (2009, February). Privacy in the Clouds: Risks to Privacy and Confidentiality from Cloud Computing. *World Privacy Forum*.

Greenleaf, G. (2012). Global Data Privacy Laws: 89 Countries, and Accelerating. *Privacy Laws & Business International Report*, Issue 115 (Special Supplement).

A. Kertesz & Sz. Varadi (2008): Legal Aspects of Data Protection in Cloud Federations. In S. Nepal & M. Pathan (Ed.), *Security, Privacy and Trust in Cloud Systems* (pp 433-455) Berlin, Heidelberg: Springer-Verlag.

Kroes, N. (2012, January). *Setting up the European Cloud Partnership.* Davos, Switzerland, World Economic Forum.

OPTIMIS FP7 project deliverable no. D7.2.1.1, Cloud Legal Guidelines. (n. d.). Retrieved from http://www.optimis-project.eu/sites/default/files/D7.2.1.1~OPTIMIS~Cloud~Legal~Guidelines.pdf

Privacy in a Connected World A European Data Protection Framework for the 21st Century, COM (2012) 09 final. (2012, January 25). (2012). Communication from the Commission to the European Parliament, the Council, the European Economic and Social Committee and the Committee of the Regions Safeguarding.

Proposal for a Directive of the European Parliament and of the Council on the protection of individuals with regard to the processing of personal data by competent authorities for the purposes of prevention, investigation, detection or prosecution of criminal offences or the execution of criminal penalties, and the free movement of such data COM (2012) 10 final. (2012, January 25). Brussels.

Proposal for a Regulation of the European Parliament and of the Council on the protection of individuals with regard to the processing of personal data and on the free movement of such data (General Data Protection Regulation) COM (2012) 11 final. (2012, January 25). Brussels.

Public Consultation on Cloud Computing by the European Commission. (n. d.). Retrieved from http://ec.europa.eu/your-voice/ipm/forms/dispatch?form=cloudcomputing&lang=en

Safe Harbor website of export.gov. Retrieved from https://safeharbor.export.gov

Svantesson, D., & Clarke, R. (2010). Privacy and consumer risks in cloud computing. *Computer Law & Security Report, 26*(4), 391–397. doi:10.1016/j.clsr.2010.05.005

The Madrid Resolution: International Standards on the Protection of Personal Data and Privacy, Adopted by the International Conference of Data Protection and Privacy Commissioners. (2009, November 5). *U.S. Department of Justice.* Retrieved from http://www.justice.gov/opcl/privacyactoverview2012/1974intro.htm

Unleashing the Potential of Cloud Computing in Europe. COM(2012) 529 final. (2012, September 27). Brussels: Communication from the Commission to the European Parliament, the Council, the European Economic and Social Committee and the Committee of the Regions.

What is EU Data Protection Directive 95/46/EC? (n. d.). *Whatis.com.* Retrieved from http://searchsecurity.techtarget.co.uk/definition/EU-Data-Protection-Directive

Whittaker, Z. (2011). *Safe Harbor: Why EU data needs "protecting" from US law.* Retrieved from http://www.zdnet.com/blog/igeneration/safe-harbor-why-eu-data-needs-protecting-from-us-law/8801

Wong, R. (2011). Data protection: The future of privacy. *Computer Law & Security Report, 27*(1), 53–57. doi:10.1016/j.clsr.2010.11.004

Chapter 3
Identity and Access Management in the Cloud Computing Environments

Manoj V. Thomas
National Institute of Technology Karnataka, India

K. Chandrasekaran
National Institute of Technology Karnataka, India

ABSTRACT

Nowadays, the issue of identity and access management (IAM) has become an important research topic in cloud computing. In the distributed computing environments like cloud computing, effective authentication and authorization are essential to make sure that unauthorized users do not access the resources, thereby ensuring the confidentiality, integrity, and availability of information hosted in the cloud environment. In this chapter, the authors discuss the issue of identity and access management in cloud computing, analyzing the work carried out by others in the area. Also, various issues in the current IAM scenario in cloud computing, such as authentication, authorization, access control models, identity life cycle management, cloud identity-as-a-service, federated identity management and also, the identity and access management in the inter-cloud environment are discussed. The authors conclude this chapter discussing a few research issues in the area of identity and access management in the cloud and inter-cloud environments.

INTRODUCTION

Even though cloud computing has become one of the most promising paradigms in the IT domain, many organizations and the enterprises are still reluctant to adopt the cloud for critical workloads or services because of the concern about the security of their personal data (King & Raja, 2012). Hence, managing user identities and their access in the cloud system is a critical problem to be solved effectively so that the cloud computing is safe and secure. Digital identity of a user represents who he is, and it is used to decide his access rights or privileges when he interacts with other users or accesses resources or services

DOI: 10.4018/978-1-5225-0153-4.ch003

online. The identity of a cloud user authorizes him to access data or resources from the cloud environment. When the users make requests to access the cloud resources and services, it is highly important that the identity and the access rights of the users are verified before granting the requested services.

An effective Identity and Access Management (IAM) mechanism is required to make the cloud computing platform trusted, secure, reliable and scalable. Normally, on-premise applications can rely on various on-premise identity infrastructure services such as Active Directory (Microsoft, 2009) and Lightweight Directory Access Protocol (Wahl et al., 1997) for verifying the user identity information. Similarly, an effective identity service in the cloud should solve this issue in the cloud environment. Identity and Access Management deals with the process of identifying entities in a computing system, and also managing access to the available resources in the system based on access rules or policies. In the cloud computing domain, the private data of the cloud customers are stored in the servers or the data centers of the CSPs; rather than keeping it on-premise on the user's computer. Hence, the CSPs need to address the privacy concerns of the cloud users through proper IAM mechanisms so that the trust level of the cloud users in the Cloud Computing domain is increased. Proper identity management is the first step to be enforced in the cloud environment, in order to avoid unauthorized access of cloud resources.

In this chapter, the authors discuss the issue of identity and access management in the cloud and inter-cloud environments. The analysis of the work done by the researchers in this area shows the merits and demerits of various approaches. The various issues in the identity and access management in cloud computing, such as authentication, authorization, access control models, identity life cycle management are discussed. The authors explain the emerging concepts in identity management, such as the federated identity management, Single Sign-On (SSO) and cloud identity-as-a-service. Also, the various issues in the identity and access management in the inter-cloud (cloud federation) environment are discussed in this chapter. Finally, the authors conclude the chapter discussing a few research issues in the area of identity and access management in the cloud and inter-cloud environments.

BACKGROUND

In the Cloud Computing domain, an efficient IAM is essential for maintaining the confidentiality, integrity and availability of the data stored in the cloud. Generally, in the cloud environment, access control mechanism is required at each of the following layers (Alliance, 2011):

1. **Network Layer:** An access control mechanism at the network layer should not allow a user to see any system or a specified portion of a network (Ping, Route commands) in the cloud unless the access policies allow him to do so.
2. **System Layer:** A user should not be allowed to access any particular host or system in the cloud unless the access policies allow him to do so.
3. **Application Layer:** Access to the cloud applications or any functionality of the applications should be governed by the access control rules, and the access should be permitted after verifying the identities and attributes of a cloud user.
4. **Process Layer:** Access control policies and rules should be effectively used to define the processes or functions that a user is allowed to run within an application.

5.   **Data Layer:** In the cloud domain, access policies or rules could be used to control the user's access to the data area and file system. Also, the individual files and the various fields (as in a database system) should be controlled from illegal access.

When an organization adopts cloud services, its trust boundary is more dynamic since the resources used by the organization extends into the domain of the CSP. Hence, there should be a proper IAM mechanism implemented in the cloud computing domain for its widespread adoption among the service consumers.

Literature Review

This section throws light on the research activities in the area of IAM in the cloud and inter-cloud environments, analyzing the works carried out by the researchers. The work carried out in (Wei et al., 2010) presents an attribute and role based access control (ARBAC) model. Before invoking services, requestors of various services provide their attribute information to the service providers. When the service providers receive the requests, they determine whether to permit or deny these requests according to their access control policies. In this work, access negotiation mechanism is not added into the ARBAC model. How to enforce access control, on the numerous users who are not defined in the system in the distributed computing environment is discussed in the work carried out in (Lang et al., 2007). The access control method based on trust makes decisions based on the trust evaluation of the requestor. In (Wang et al., 2007), the proposed scheme cryptographically provides role-based access control and delegation, based on Hierarchical Identity-Based Signature (IBS).

In (Feng et al., 2008), a Trust and Context based Access Control (TCAC) model, extending the RBAC model is proposed for open and distributed systems. A trust evaluation mechanism based on the local and global reputation, to compute the trust value of users in a distributed system is provided. When the trust value of the requester is not less than the trust threshold defined by the system policies, the user will be assigned to some roles. In (Gunjan et al., 2012), the authors discuss the issue of identity management in the cloud computing scenario. They also show the privacy issues associated with cloud computing. The paper gives a review of the existing approaches in identity management in cloud computing. In this work, loss of control, lack of trust and multitenancy issues are identified as major problems in the present cloud computing model.

The research in the field of IAM in the Inter-Cloud environment is still in its nascent stage, and some of the relevant approaches proposed by the researchers in that area follow. In (Stihler et al., 2012), the authors propose the architecture for Federated Identity Management in a scenario similar to the Inter-Cloud environment. The main objective of the proposed architecture is to provide a platform for the sharing of various resources and services among the Inter-cloud consumers. The work focuses on sharing of information or resources across all the three cloud service models such as SaaS, PaaS and IaaS. The works carried out in (Celesti et al., 2010a; Tusa et al., 2011) present a heterogeneous horizontal cloud federation model, for CLoud-Enabled Virtual EnviRonment (CLEVER). These works use the concept of a middleware component called the Cross-Cloud Federation Manager (CCFM) that could be integrated into the Cloud Manager component of the CSP. This helps the participating clouds to be a part of the cloud federation. The CCFM consists of three sub-components, called the Discovery Agent, Match-Making Agent and Authentication Agent, and they are responsible for performing the required functions for the cloud federation.

The work in (Bernstein & Vij, 2010a) discusses the inter-cloud security considerations. In (Bernstein & Vij, 2010b), the authors propose an authentication mechanism for inter-cloud environments using SAML profile over XMPP. The architecture discussed in this work is based on the internet scale. The work shown in (Yan et al., 2009) discusses a Federated Identity Management approach using Hierarchical Identity-Based Cryptography. This mechanism makes collaboration possible within a Hybrid Cloud, which is a combination of private and public clouds. The work focuses on the Private Key Generator (PKG) hierarchical model. This model assumes a root PKG for managing the entire Hybrid Cloud. Before applying this model to the inter-cloud scenario, issues regarding the control of the root PKG should be solved.

Many works related to the identity management and the Single Sign-On in the cloud computing domain have been published, and the relevant papers are discussed in this section. (Fugkeaw et al., 2007) have presented an SSO model based on Multi-Agent System (MAS) and strong authentication based on PKI. User authorization is not considered as part of this work. (Wang et al., 2013) present a security analysis of various Single Sign-On mechanisms in the distributed networks. They have identified various flaws such as impersonation of a user, impersonation of a service provider etc. during the authentication process. They have also proposed a secure scheme by using RSA-based signatures.

(Celesti et al., 2010b) have implemented a three-phase mechanism for cross-cloud Single Sign-On authentication. The three phases discussed in this paper are Discovery, Match-Making and Authentication. They have focused mainly on authentication in their work and tried to solve the issue by defining their own Security Assertions Markup Language (SAML) profile. They also extended their work in (Celesti et al., 2011) by developing a CLoud Enabled Virtual EnviRonment (CLEVER). Also, in this work, they have only focused on a single Identity Provider rather than having multiple Identity Providers. (Kumar & Cohen, 2000) have proposed the MAS based network security for authentication and authorization. They have implemented an Adaptive Agent Architecture based on MAS. (Chan & Cheng, 2000) present various security flaws in the authentication scheme using smart cards such as the off-line password guessing attacks, impersonation attacks, the intruder-in-the-middle attacks and the denial-of-service attacks.

In order to overcome the problems of guessing attacks in the authentication schemes, (Lee et al., 2002) have proposed an authentication scheme which uses one-way hash functions. (Ren & Wu, 2012) also proposed a dynamic approach for PAS. It uses One-Time Passwords (OTP) unlike traditional static passwords. This OTP is used for authentication along with the user's private identity information and also considering the current authenticating time. Major benefits of this work are its resistance to various real time attacks in the network such as the MITM, replay attacks etc. At the same time, the method is still vulnerable to types of phishing attacks.

Selected Case Studies

1. **Amazon Web Services (AWS) - IAM:** AWS Identity Management (AWS-IAM, 2015) provides the following security options for the cloud customers to secure their AWS account and control the access to it. AWS-IAM helps the cloud customers create multiple users and deal with the access permissions for each of these users within the AWS account. The customer AWS account considers a user as an identity having unique security attributes or credentials that could be used for accessing the AWS services. Using AWS-IAM, the customers can implement security features such as 'principle of least privilege' by providing unique identity credentials to each cloud user

within their AWS account, and thereby allowing a user to access the AWS services and resources that are required for the users to perform the designated job. AWS-IAM is considered secure by default, since new users are not allowed to access the AWS services until access permissions are granted explicitly.

2. **AWS-Multi-Factor Authentication (AWS-MFA):** AWS-MFA (AWS-MFA, 2015) offers additional control over AWS account settings, and also helps in the management of AWS services and resources. In order to use this security feature, the AWS users have to provide a six-digit single-use code, in addition to their standard username and password credentials while accessing their AWS account settings, services or resources. The AWS customers get this single-use code from the authentication device they keep with them. Since this authentication mechanism requires two factors, it is called two-factor authentication and it is considered to be more secure than the single factor authentication which normally requires user names and passwords.

3. **Eucalyptus - Identity and Access Management:** Eucalyptus is an open source cloud software for building private or hybrid clouds that are compatible with Amazon Web Service (AWS) APIs (Kumar et al., 2014). Identity and Access Management (IAM) in the Eucalyptus private cloud offers authentication, authorization, and accounting features along with the management of user identities and the enforcement of access controls over cloud resources. Access control policies and the user identities are stored in the local Cloud Controller (CLC) database of the Eucalyptus. Identity data of the cloud users can also be accessed from LDAP or Active Directory. Eucalyptus IAM offers various services such as secure credential management and also policy based resource access management.

4. **OpenStack Identity Service - Keystone:** OpenStack is an open source cloud computing software (Kumar et al., 2014). The default identity management service for OpenStack is the OpenStack Identity Service, Keystone. Keystone integrates the OpenStack functions for authentication, policy management, and catalog services (Rhoton, 2013). The implementation of Keystone uses a centralized architecture wherein all users are to be enrolled in its database before accessing any of the cloud services in the OpenStack. The enrolling of user identity details can be done either manually by the OpenStack administrator using the command line interface, or by using the bulk loading from an external corporate database such as LDAP.

5. **OpenNebula - Users and Group Management:** OpenNebula is an open source cloud computing platform used for the management of heterogeneous cloud infrastructures (Kumar et al., 2014). For the Identity and Access Management, OpenNebula provides a comprehensive user and group management system. In OpenNebula, the cloud resources are accessed by the users, and a permissions system similar to UNIX system is used to manage the access requests made by the users. By default, various resources such as VM images can be used and managed by the owner of the resources. Even though OpenNebula provides an internal username/password authentication system; an external authentication system may also be integrated if required. OpenNebula also supports three customizable authentication configurations such as Command Line Interface, Sunstone and Servers Authentication Mechanisms.

6. **Google IAM:** Google Cloud Identity and Access Management (IAM) mechanism helps the cloud users to manage access permissions for Google Cloud resources (Google Cloud IAM, 2015). This IAM mechanism unifies access control for the various Cloud Platform products into a single system and provides a consistent set of operations to the users. The IAM provides a simple and consistent

access control interface for all Cloud Platform products. Also, it provides resource-level access control such that cloud users can be assigned with suitable roles to access resources at a finer granularity level. It also helps to assign flexible roles to the cloud users. The Google Cloud IAM provides Google Cloud Console UI and REST-based IAM APIs that can be used by the cloud users to create and manage the IAM policies in the cloud environment. Using the Google Cloud IAM, access to different types of identities can be managed. A Google account used by a developer, an administrator, or any other person who interacts with Cloud Platform can be managed using the email address associated with the corresponding Google account. It can also be used to manage the service account that belongs to a cloud application other than the individual end user. Service account can be used to run the code that is hosted on Cloud Platform. Also, Google Group that is a named collection of Google accounts and service accounts can be managed using the unique email address associated with the group. In Groups, access is granted to a group, instead of granting access to individual users or service accounts. Also, a Google Apps domain that represents a virtual group of all the members in an organization can be managed. After the identity of the user making the access request is authenticated, IAM takes an authorization decision as to whether that identity is allowed to perform the requested operation in the system. IAM policies are used for deciding the access rights of a cloud user.

7. **Microsoft IAM:** Microsoft's Identity and Access Management (IAM) system (Microsoft Identity Manager, 2015) provides the identity management services to the cloud and on-premises environments. This system provides various services such as federation, identity management, user provisioning, application access control, and data protection. It offers the IAM services by combining Windows Server Active Directory, Microsoft Identity Manager, and Microsoft Azure Active Directory that can be used by various organizations to secure their hybrid cloud infrastructure. Microsoft Identity Manager combines Microsoft's IAM solutions together (Microsoft Identity Manager, 2015). It combines the various on-premises authentication stores such as Active Directory, LDAP and Oracle Azure Active Directory. Microsoft Identity Manager supports hybrid infrastructure by offering the features such as cloud-ready identities, powerful user self-service, and enhanced security.

Azure Active Directory (Microsoft Azure, 2015) can be used to provide Single Sign-On to various cloud (SaaS) apps and other on-premise web apps. It offers security features such as Multi-Factor Authentication (MFA), access control based on user location, and identity and holistic security reports, audits, and alerts. It can be used to connect Active Directory and other on-premises directories to Azure Active Directory easily. It employs unique machine learning-based mechanisms to identify potential security threats. It can be used to access the on-premises web applications of cloud users from everywhere.

FUNCTIONAL REQUIREMENTS AND CHALLENGES OF THE IAM

In this section, the functional requirements and the implementation challenges of the IAM mechanism in the cloud environment are discussed.

Functional Requirements

An efficient IAM should be implemented in the cloud environment in order to enforce mutual authentication, authorization and auditing in the cloud computing environment. Based on the digital identity of the user, the cloud recognizes who this user is and what he is allowed to do. The overview of the access control module of a CSP is shown in the Figure 1. Whenever an access request is received by a CSP, the IAM module deals with the authentication and authorization processes of the cloud customers. In order to avoid unauthorized or illegal access of the cloud resources, the implementation of the authentication and the authorization processes should be efficient. As shown in the figure, the major components in the access control module are:

1. **Policy Enforcement Point (PEP):** This component is a part of the authorization process in the cloud environment. PEP interacts with the Policy Decision Point (PDP) for validating the access requests of clients, and implements the authorization decisions taken by the PDP. Policy Enforcement Point is the access management layer that enforces the PDP's decisions.
2. **Policy Decision Point (PDP):** This component of the authorization process takes the authorization decision when an access request is received by a CSP. PDP interacts with policy storage database stored locally with the CSP. In cloud systems, PDP is the authorization layer where the access control policies are evaluated and authorization decisions are taken.

Thus, the major functional requirements of IAM in the cloud environment are Dynamic Provisioning and De-provisioning (Identification), Authentication, Authorization, Accounting and Auditing, Support for compliance, identity life cycle management (Hovav & Berger, 2009). Identity life cycle management manages the entire life cycle of user identities. These components are explained in later sections in this chapter.

Figure 1. Overview of the access control module

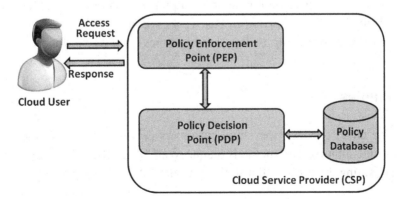

Identity Management Challenges in the Cloud

The present day business requirements of the organizations using cloud services are diverse. In order to have an effective access control system, the identity management in the cloud should consider the following issues or challenges.

1. It has to effectively deal with the authentication and authorization of various heterogeneous users who are accessing the cloud services from any place, any time and through any supported devices.
2. Due to various business reasons, the roles and responsibilities of users in an organization who use cloud services might change. How to rapidly and dynamically provision users in such cases is another issue.
3. How to manage the staff turnover as far as the identities of the users are concerned.
4. How to handle the user identities when there are merger or de-merger between companies or service providers is another issue which requires proper solutions. And also, the identity management in the cloud should take enough care to avoid duplication of identities, attributes or credentials of users in the system.
5. The IAM techniques also need to be user-friendly for its easier adoption among the business users.

Responsibilities of CSPs and CSCs

The CSPs and the Cloud Service Consumers (CSCs) have to understand their roles and responsibilities in the identity management, in order to have a secure access control in the cloud environment.

CSP Responsibilities

1. The CSPs should support the authentication of the cloud users through identity federation and SSO. Since the users will be accessing the cloud services from anywhere, any time round the clock, and also using any device, the authentication and authorization mechanisms adopted by the CSPs should support them.
2. CSPs need to communicate to the CSCs regarding any changes being made in the account management policies of the CSP.
3. The CSPs should have the required support for identity management when various services are integrated in scenarios such as hybrid clouds.
4. Also, the CSPs should support the regulatory and policy requirements of the cloud users such as Separation of Duty (SoD), least-privilege-based access control etc.
5. Provisioning and de-provisioning to the cloud instances should be done in time, as and when required.

CSC Responsibilities

1. When using the cloud services, the cloud customers need to understand the user provisioning, authentication and authorization methods unique to a CSP, as the CSPs may vary in terms of the lag time for activating the users, and also the attributes of the users supported.

2. Customers have to evaluate and utilize the support extended by the CSPs in identity federation features such as Single Sign-On (SSO).
3. Customers have to verify that whether the log files maintained by the CSPs would be made available to the user for security auditing purposes, if needed.
4. The cloud customers should also monitor the CSP's compliance with government regulations from time to time.

AUTHENTICATION

The cloud users have serious concerns about the confidentiality, integrity and availability of their data stored in the cloud (Sood, 2012). The users worry about the leakage of their sensitive data or their loss of privacy while using cloud services. All these points stress on the need for an effective authentication mechanism in the cloud environment. Authentication in the cloud is the process by which the identity of a user or an entity requesting some resources or service is verified by the CSP. The entity could be a person, process, program or software agent requesting access to cloud resources.

Authentication Requirements of the Cloud Environment

In open service-oriented systems such as the cloud computing systems, in many cases, the service providers and the service consumers are strangers. Since they do not have a pre-established trust value between them, the service provider must be able to authenticate the unfamiliar users and then determine whether the requestors have enough privileges to access the requested services. In the cloud, both the cloud users and the cloud service providers want the information to be secure and well protected in the cloud, irrespective of the service delivery models and the deployment models in the cloud computing paradigm.

Authentication Challenges

The cloud service consumers may use any type of device to connect to the cloud services, and also they may use the cloud service from any location, any time. Hence, a continuously available authentication mechanism is required in the cloud to verify that unauthorized users do not access the cloud resources.

Multi-Factor Authentication

The authentication mechanism in the cloud environment could be based on the four main approaches (Suhendra, 2011). 1. Authentication by something the user knows such as the username or password or PIN (Personal Identification Number) 2. Authentication by something the user has, such as the smart card. 3. Authentication by something the user is such as the bio-metric features of the user, such as fingerprint, retina or iris details. 4. Multi-factor authentication that could use a combination of any two or more of the above mentioned authentication approaches. In a cloud computing environment, the process of authentication needs to be implemented in such a way that the unauthorized users do not access the networks, hosts or the applications to use the data or resources in the cloud.

Authentication Solutions and Recommendations

Strong authentication mechanisms such as multi-factor authentication are required to protect the private information of cloud users. The enterprises can establish VPN tunneling (Padhy et al., 2012) from the CSP to the enterprise network and authenticate the cloud users using the enterprise user directory such as AD or LDAP. Risk-based authentication approaches considering various parameters such as device identifier, geo-location, heuristic information etc. could be employed in the cloud. In the cloud environment, high-risk transactions should be allowed only after strong authentication procedures.

The CSPs should have the capability to consume authentication tokens from authoritative sources using protocols such as SAML. It should be ensured that the authentication service is OAuth-compliant so that the organizations can avoid getting locked into one vendor's authentication credentials. The Cloud Security Alliance (CSA) (Kumaraswamy et al., 2010) suggests the use of user-centric authentication approaches such as OpenID so that the same user identity credentials could be used for availing services from multiple CSPs.

AUTHORIZATION

Authorization in cloud environment is the process by which the access rights or privileges of a user or entity are verified by the cloud system against predefined security policies. In order to avoid unauthorized access my malicious users, the authorization process should verify the access rights of a user who is requesting some service from a CSP.

Authorization Requirements of the Cloud Environment

The CSPs need to ensure that the user requesting some service has the necessary privileges to perform the requested operation in the system. Normally, the authorization process follows the authentication step. In the cloud computing, the business requirements and security requirements of the CSP are turned into access control policies or rules which are used to evaluate the access requests of cloud users. In the cloud environment, XML-based access control policy language, XACML (eXtensible Access Control Markup Language) could be used for managing the access control policies.

Access Control Models

Access control models come in between access control policies and access control mechanisms and, they bridge the gap between an access control policy and the corresponding mechanism. Security models describe what security properties are associated with an access control system. Security models help to formally present the security policy applicable to a computing system, and also to discuss and analyze any theoretical limitations of a particular system in ensuring the proper access control. An access control mechanism is designed according to the properties of the corresponding access control model. From a user's point of view, an access control model represents a clear and precise expression of the security requirements. From the vendor's point of view, access control models act as security design and implementation requirements.

Types of Access Control Models

An access control model should make sure that there is no leakage of access permissions to an unauthorized principal. In another way, the access control system should be 'safe'. Some of the access control models used in cloud computing paradigm are given as follows.

1. **Role-Based Access Control (RBAC):** This model is suitable for organizations where static hierarchy is maintained, and the members have defined roles such as Manager, Accountant or Clerk, and specific access rights are associated with each role. Here, the access rights of users are decided by the roles which they are members of (Ferraiolo et al., 2001). Users are mapped to roles and roles are mapped to privileges. The basic RBAC model is shown in the Figure 2. Apart from the basic or core RBAC model, there are extended models of RBAC (Hu et al., 2006) such as hierarchical RBAC, which supports the role hierarchy and inheritance of privileges; statically constrained RBAC, which supports static constraints; and dynamically constrained RBAC, which supports time-variant constraints.

2. **Attribute-Based Access Control:** In this model, access to the resources are allowed or rejected depending on the attributes of the subject, context, resource and action (Wei et al., 2010). Subject attributes include user id, group membership etc. Context attributes include time and location of access request made. Resource attributes include the resource id, and the action represents the type of operation requested by the user such as read or write. As shown in the Figure 3, whenever an access request is initiated, the attributes pertaining to the access request are compared with the stored access control policies, and then the Policy Evaluation module either accepts or rejects the access request.

3. **Risk-Based Access Control:** In a highly dynamic environment like the cloud, the prediction of resources to be accessed by users is not always possible, and risk-based access control models could be used in such environments (health care or military domain). If strict access control is enforced over the usage of resources in such environments, it might result in poor response during an emergency or crisis, and subsequent losses or damages. In the risk-based model, real time decisions are taken to allow or reject a user request, by calculating the risk involved in allowing the access. Figure 4 shows the Risk-Based Access Control model in which the access requests are given to the Policy Enforcement Point (PEP). The PEP contacts the Policy Decision Point (PDP) for the access decision and the PDP takes the access decision by calculating the risk involved in the access request made. In this case, the calculation of the risk considers various parameters such as the attributes of the user, his trustworthiness, context information of the access request such as

Figure 2. Role-based access control

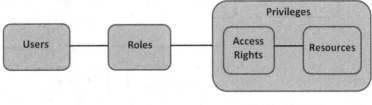

Figure 3. Attribute-based access control

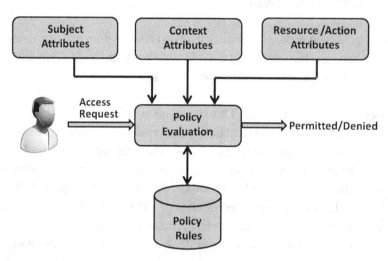

time, location and also, the sensitivity level of the resource requested and the previous access history. Risk threshold levels are specified by the security policy from time to time, and the decision to grant or deny the request is taken based on that threshold value.

Logging and Auditing in Identity Management

The logging process collects the identification details of a user, such as the time of access, resource accessed, etc. and they are entered in a log file which could be stored for future security auditing purposes (Wang et al., 2010). The log files should be updated to record all the events in the system. The process of auditing in the cloud environment involves monitoring the recorded actions performed by users in the cloud system which could later be used for security purposes. This process involves analyzing the log files to collect information about user behavior, resource usage, access requests for a particular resource etc. Hence, the process of logging and auditing involves the verification of the authentication and authorization records to ensure the compliance of the IAM procedures with security policies and procedures so that any violation of the security policies is detected. Auditing thus helps to improve the security of the cloud system by recommending the required changes in the IAM implementation strat-

Figure 4. Risk-based access control

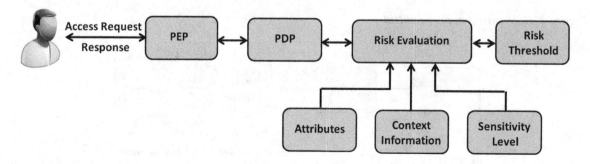

egy adopted in the organization. Hence, auditing requires proper and effective identity management for verifying the entities in the log file.

Recommended Practices

1. In the cloud computing domain, the CSPs should use access control languages such as XACML that provides a standardized method of access control and policy enforcement across various applications.
2. Open standards such as SAML could be used for authenticating the cloud users.
3. Wherever required, risk-based authorization to the cloud applications should be implemented in the cloud.
4. Temporal attributes of cloud users, such as the geo-location should undergo real-time attribute checking throughout the transaction, in order to provide effective authorization functions.
5. Logging of authorization decisions or access granted should be performed in a common format for later security analysis. The cloud service providers are requested to keep the log of the details of users' access to various resources in the cloud, and they should produce it for auditing, whenever required.

IDENTITY PROVISIONING AND DE-PROVISIONING

The process of identity provisioning associates digital identities to various users, and the process of identity de-provisioning removes the identities from a user so that the specified identity is no longer valid with that user.

Identity Provisioning and De-provisioning in the Cloud

In the case of Identity Provisioning in the cloud, it associates the user's identity to the applications or the systems, and provides the users with the required access rights to the data or resources maintained in the system. After the identity provisioning, various users can access the resources or services stored in the cloud using the unique user identity. That is, provisioning means in-time or on-demand provisioning of users to the cloud services so that the users can access the required services. In the case of Identity De-provisioning, it deletes or deactivates the identity of a user, or the access rights or privileges assigned to the user identity. Hence, de-provisioning is the real-time de-activation of the user accounts for the cloud services so that the users are no longer able to access them.

Requirements and Challenges in the Cloud

Nowadays, the cloud applications used by clients could be a mashup (Marston et al., 2011) of multiple cloud applications hosted on the same or different CSPs. In this case, how can the users be authenticated for accessing all these cloud applications seamlessly, and also, how can the user's attributes such as group association, access rights, roles are shared across these cloud applications are issues to be solved in the identity and access management in the cloud. Open standards such as SAML, OAuth, XACML could be used by the organizations for this purpose. There should be timely revocation of the user accounts or access rights in the cloud, when the user leaves or moves to another role in an organization with different access rights. The provisioning of user entities in a cloud system requires the understanding of the complete life cycle management of the user account, including its creation, management and the deletion. In cloud computing, user accesses various services from different cloud service providers, and the consumers are really sensitive to the delay involved in service provisioning. Hence dynamic provisioning and de-provisioning of user identities is required. The CSPs should use SPML for user provisioning. CSPs should follow the 'principle of least privilege' when provisioning an account.

Identity Life Cycle Management

Identity Life Cycle Management shows the various stages through which a user identity goes (Mather et al., 2009). That is, it shows how the identity is managed when it is created, used or terminated. The cloud Identity Life Cycle Management is shown in the Figure 5. As shown in the figure, the five stages in the Identity Life Cycle Management include Identity Provisioning, Authentication, Authorization, Self-Service, Password Management, Compliance and Audit, and the identity de-provisioning. The Identity Provisioning and de-provisioning, Authentication and Authorization have been explained in the previous sections.

Self-service

This phase shows how the user can maintain, update or reset his identity credentials. Ensuring self-service in the IAM in the cloud environment helps the users reset their account passwords, maintain and update the user information, and thereby accessing the services without the service provider's interaction.

Credentials Management

This phase of the identity life cycle shows how the user password is stored in the cloud servers. This focuses on various factors such as how the passwords of various cloud users are stored in the cloud database, which is the encryption algorithms used by the CSPs (such as MD5 or SHA1). It also supports the features to facilitate SSO to access the cloud services.

Compliance and Audit

In this phase, users' access to cloud resources will be monitored to ensure that the security requirements of the cloud system are not violated. Periodic auditing and the analysis of the log files maintained by the CSPs will help enforce the required access control policies from time to time.

FEDERATED IDENTITY MANAGEMENT IN THE CLOUD

Federation is an association between multiple entities or organizations that have predefined goals, and standards for operation (Ghazizadeh et al., 2012). Nowadays, a user or an organization may subscribe to services from multiple CSPs. The organization can also integrate the individual services from various cloud service providers and provide the final combined service to its customers. This scenario shows that

Figure 5. Identity life cycle management

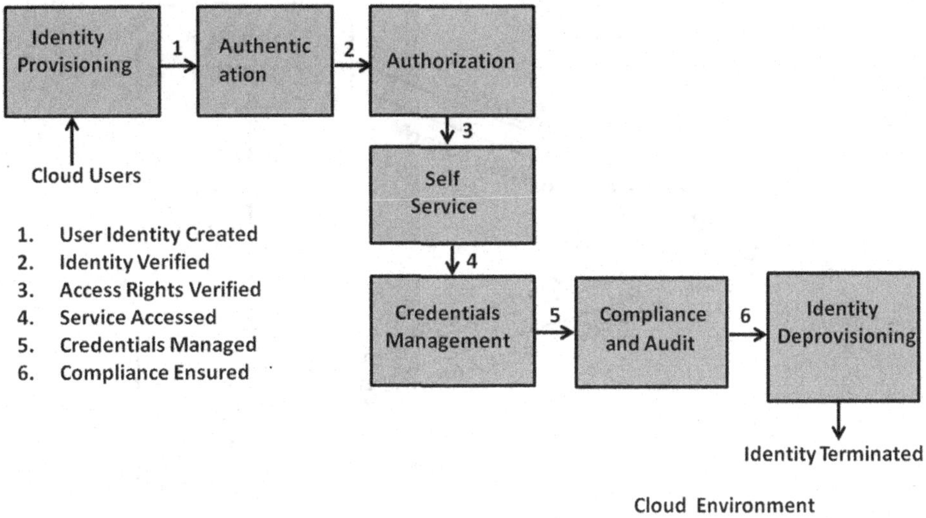

effective identity management is essential in the cloud computing domain. The current cloud computing paradigm can make use of federated identity management approaches such as Single Sign-On, for authentication of the cloud users. That is, in the cloud, user-centric identity management is preferred over the application-centric approach. The overview of the Identity Federation is shown in the Figure 6.

In the application-centric identity management, each application keeps track of the users using its own specific identity. In this case, if a user uses multiple services offered by more than one service provider, or by the same service provider itself, he has to create multiple accounts to use each application or service with the CSP. In the user-centric identity management (El Maliki & Seigneur, 2007), a user is uniquely identified by the user identifier which could be recognized by more than one CSP. Hence, in the federated identity management, identity of a cloud user is provided by the Identity Provider (IdP), and the same identity could be utilized by the CSPs who trust that IdP. CSP-specific identity credentials are eliminated in this case.

Single Sign-On (SSO)

Single Sign-On (SSO) is a mechanism used for authentication in which a service consumer is required to be authenticated only once while accessing various services from multiple service providers, or when accessing multiple services from the same service provider (Almulla & Yeun, 2010). The process of SSO involves the association between the following entities: Cloud Service Consumer (CSC), Relying Party or Cloud Service Provider (CSP) and the Identity Provider (IdP). The CSP and the IdP have mutual trust established between them. That is, IdP offers Identity Management functions to the CSP. Before accessing the services from the CSP, a Cloud Service Consumer has to get authenticated as a valid user from the IdP. Since the CSP and IdP are part of the association, and they have mutual trust with each other, the user is allowed to access the services from the CSP after successful authentication. Hence, in SSO, the users are able to access multiple services from the same or different CSPs using the identity token issued by the Identity Provider. Because of this association, the service providers can concentrate more on their core services, since the identity management operations are taken care of by the Identity Providers.

Figure 6. Overview of identity federation

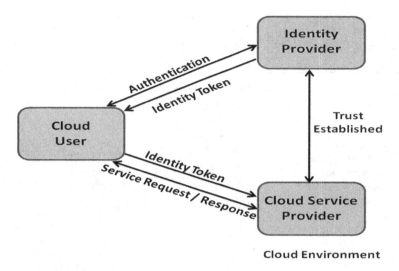

Identity Providers (IdPs)

The Identity Providers are trusted entities in the cloud computing environment that provide the identity tokens to the cloud users (Smith, 2008). These tokens could be used by cloud users for availing services from the CSPs. Examples of IdP are Ping Identity, Symplified etc. In the Cloud Computing domain, the IdP accepts the cloud user's credentials such as user ID, password, certificate etc. and returns a signed security token identifying the user. The CSP that has trust established with the IdP uses the identity token in order to allow services or resources to the user. In this case, the service provider has no direct information of the cloud user, but relies on the IdP. Thus, IdPs allow the CSPs to offload the task of identity management to the third parties and help the CSPs concentrate more on their core services.

Identity providers such as Symplified (Symplified, 2015) offers SSO systems which can synchronize and communicate with the Active Directory (AD) maintained in an organization to verify the identity credentials of users who want to log into a cloud application. The cloud customers are to be authenticated by the SSO provider, and it is synchronized with the AD maintained in the organization. This gives the organization the required flexibility to decide which of their accounts are used to access the cloud applications. When the user accounts in the AD are deactivated, no users will be able to utilize that account to access the cloud application. Federated Identity Management thus reduces the complexity of the authentication process for the cloud users by employing SSO. Similarly, Sun Microsystems' Open SSO (Oracle, 2015) externalizes the authentication and the authorization components from the applications. Various CSPs such as Salesforce.com, Google, Microsoft etc. support standards such as SAML that facilitates SSO using identity federation.

Types of Identity Federation

There are two types of identity federation possible for an organization in a cloud environment, depending on the implementation of the IdP in the domain (Radha & Reddy, 2012).

1. **Enterprise IdP within the Security Perimeter of the Organization:** In this case, the IdP is maintained in the organization that subscribes to the cloud services. The various CSPs establish trust relationships with this IdP in delivering services to the cloud consumers. In this case, more control in the authentication, authorization and the policy management is achieved as it is managed internally to the organization.
2. **Trusted Cloud-Based Identity Management Services:** In this case, for identity management purposes, cloud-based identity service providers are used. They are also known as Cloud Identity-as-a-service (IDaaS) providers. This concept is explained in the next section.

The Impact of Trust in the Federated Identity Management

Trust of an entity shows the level of confidence or reliance such that the entity would behave exactly as promised (Khan & Malluhi, 2010). In a multi-domain environment like cloud computing, the trust needs to be established between the cloud service provider and service consumers, and also between the providers of various services and the identity providers. Trust in the cloud computing domain is dynamic, and the trust value of the entities such as cloud users, CSPs or Identity Providers need to be calculated by considering various parameters such as the past behavior of the entities and also recommendations from other Trusted Third Parties (TTPs) in the system. Effective trust management in the cloud environment is still an issue which requires further research.

Identity Management Standards and Protocols

There are several standards and protocols which can be used for the identity management in the cloud environments. The various identity management protocols differ in their features such as the data format supported, protocols to exchange credentials between the entities involved etc. Some of the well-known identity management protocols which help in establishing a federation among the individual partners are given below. An organization can use the following IAM standards or specifications to implement efficient IAM mechanisms in the cloud environment. Since the different identity management protocols have non-similar features, the selection of a particular protocol depends on the requirements of the applications and also their architectural features.

1. **Security Assertion Markup Language (SAML):** The SAML (Cantor et al., 2005) includes a set of specifications for exchanging the authentication, authorization and attribute assertions across the federation. SAML uses XML-based data format and this protocol is managed under the Organization for the Advancement of Structured Information Standards (OASIS). The various use cases of SAML include SSO in the federation, identity/account linkage, session management and secure web services. Three releases of SAML namely SAML 1.0, SAML 1.1 and SAML 2.0 are available.
2. **Service Provisioning Markup Language (SPML):** This is an XML-based security framework developed by OASIS, and it could be used to exchange information related to the users, resources and service provisioning within a group of cooperating organizations (Standard, 2003). This helps in automating the provisioning and de-provisioning of user accounts with the CSP.
3. **eXtensible Access Control Markup Language (XACML):** In order to implement an access control mechanism, this XML-based access control language developed by OASIS could be used

(Godik et al., 2002). This language provides the XML-schema which could be used to protect the resources by making access decisions over these resources.

4. **Shibboleth:** Shibboleth (Cantor & SCAVO, 2005) is an open source Identity Management project and is based upon SAML. This protocol helps to establish SSO solutions in the federation. Shibboleth uses the SAML specifications to achieve the authentication and authorization in the federated environment. Shibboleth provides federated identity management, and it involves the two main components such as the Service Provider (SP) and the IdP. In line with their privacy policies, IdP can decide the SPs that are allowed to access the users' authentication data.

5. **OpenID:** OpenID (Recordon & Reed, 2006) provides a user-centric identity framework for the authentication purposes. OpenID 2.0 supports the identification of users through URL or XRI addresses. OpenID uses the concept of Relying Party (RP) and OpenID providers. Users' authentication data are stored by the OpenID provider, and the user has the flexibility to decide who have access to his authentication data maintained by the OpenID provider. In the OpenID mechanism, a user is associated with one primary user-id which could be used to authenticate the user against various CSPs.

6. **OAuth:** OAuth (Hardt, 2012) is an open source Identity Management protocol that could be used to provide the authorization of users across different applications without disclosing the user's identity credentials. Identity tokens, issued by the identity provider, are used by the third party applications to gain access to the user's protected data.

7. **OpenID Connect:** OpenID Connect (Sakimura et al., 2011) is an open source Identity Management protocol, which could be used to provide standardized authentication and authorization functions across federated applications. OpenID Connect combines the authentication and authorization processes of OpenID and OAuth. OpenID Connect protocol uses OpenID 2.0 and OAuth 2.0, and provides APIs to be used by the third party applications.

8. **WS-Federation:** WS-Federation (Goodner & Nadalin, 2009) is a part of the web services security specifications, and is meant for the federation of applications or web services. WS-Federation specifications are extensions to WS-Trust protocol. This protocol can be used to share the identity information of various users across multiple security domains and organizations. WS-* suite of protocols are developed in a collaborative effort by Microsoft, IBM, VeriSign, RSA Security and Ping Identity. It includes WS-Trust, WS-Security, WS-Federation and WS-Policy, and used for authentication, authorization and policy management in multiple security domains. In order to manage and exchange the security or identity tokens across various applications, WS-Federation uses the Security Token Service (STS), as used by the WS-Trust protocol specifications.

Recommended Practices

1. In the cloud computing paradigm, the implementers of the federation are required to understand the trust relationship between the various entities such as CSPs, Cloud users and Identity Providers involved in the federation, as bidirectional trust relationship is needed in the cloud federation for its successful implementation.

2. The cloud customers have the responsibility to check and verify the support extended by a CSP for IAM features such as SSO using identity federation. The cloud customers should select those CSPs who incorporate the latest security mechanisms, for availing the required services.

3. In the cloud computing domain, the customers should understand the federation protocols supported by the CSPs and the integration requirements for using multiple cloud services.

4. The CSPs should offer standard APIs such as OAuth for the management of authentication and authorization to various applications deployed on the cloud platform.

5. Organizations can rely on the identity federation products such as Sun's Open SSO, Oracle's Federation Manager (Oracle, 2015) and CA's federation Manager (CA, 2015) which could integrate with the directory services maintained in the organization such as LDAP or AD to enable the SSO feature for using various cloud services.

6. The CSPs implementing federation should use open standards such as SAML and OAuth.

7. The identity standards and the protocols used by a CSP and an IdP should be compatible in such a way that the CSP is interoperable with the third party IdP.

8. The usage of SAML and XACML protocols are recommended by the NIST (National Institute of Standards and Technology) (Linstrom & Mallard, 2003) for authentication and authorization purposes between any two cooperating environments such as cloud domains.

CLOUD IDENTITY-AS-A-SERVICE

Cloud Identity-as-a-Service (IDaaS) is an emerging cloud service delivery model where the management of user identities is performed outside the applications of the cloud service providers (Kumaraswamy et al., 2010; Mather et al., 2009). This is another type of service offered by the cloud domain wherein various identity and access management functions such as identity life cycle management and single sign-on etc. are provided by the specialized CSPs. Also, this SaaS model for identity management offers services such as user account provisioning and de-provisioning, account auditing, password management and user self services. By using this service model, an organization can automate the user account provisioning and auditing by offloading the activities to the third party CSP. The SaaS IdP stores the user identities in a trusted identity store, and acts as a proxy for the user's access to the cloud services. Various CSPs will find it attractive to use the services offered by the IDaaS provider, as it would help the CSPs offer quality services without being worried about the identity management functionalities.

The overview of the Cloud IDaaS model is shown in the Figure 7. As shown in the figure, in this service delivery model, the identity management functions offered by the Cloud Identity Service providers (IDaaS) are used by various clients such as cloud users and organizations. When these clients interact with heterogeneous CSPs, the IDaaS provider acts as a Multi-Protocol Federation Gateway offering the interoperability between various CSPs. In the case of IDaaS, an organization can also follow the hybrid approach where the user identities are managed internally within the organization, and other functionalities such as authentication are implemented using a Service Oriented Architecture (SOA) offered by the IDaaS service provider. Thus, using this model, an organization can outsource the identity management requirements of various cloud users to a third-party service provider, such as Ping Identity, TriCipher (TriCipher, 2015), or Symplified. IDaaS offers easier management of user identities with a wide range of integration options. (Rimal et al., 2009; Subashini & Kavitha, 2011). Even though this service model offers various advantages to the cloud users, this identity and access management model has several challenges also associated with its implementation. Outsourcing any part of identity management functions to third-party IDaaS provider introduces several security and privacy challenges related to the user's Personally Identifiable Information (PII).

Advantages of IDaaS

In case an organization does not have strong IAM practices, or if it doesn't have a federated architecture, it can make use of Identity management-as-a-service (IDaaS) for cooperating with different partners and cloud service federation schemes. In this case, the CSPs can delegate the authentication of the cloud users to an IDaaS provider. Hence, the CSPs can concentrate more on their core services rather than identity management functions, thereby improving the efficiency and productivity of the CSPs. It also supports federation gateways for the integration of multiple IAM protocols. That means, this model helps an organization to use the services from different CSPs supporting different identity federation standards, by utilizing the federation gateways offered by the cloud identity providers. Thus, a federation gateway reduces the complexity of integrating with multiple CSPs supporting different federation standards. If an organization outsources the identity management functionalities to a third party CSP, it would help the organization in using multiple services from different CSPs, each using different protocols such as SAML, OAuth for the identity management. Another benefit of using this service model is that the architectural changes required for an organization to use this model are comparatively less, as the users can sign on to the cloud services using their corporate identities, after the identity synchronization between the organization directory and the identity service directory in the cloud.

Federation Gateways

Federation Gateways (Kumaraswamy et al., 2010) are used in the federated identity management scenario to translate the identity tokens of cloud users from one format to another. Using this approach, organizations using different cloud services can achieve the required identity translation while accessing services from different cloud providers. If an organization has to interfere with more than one CSP each supporting different federation standards and procedures, it can benefit from the multi-protocol federation gateways. Organizations can set up the federation gateway either in their internal network, or it can be the part of various cloud identity-as-a-service providers. There are different IAM standards with different maturity levels, and their adoption rates by the CSPs in the cloud computing domain are also different. Assume that an organization accesses service-1 from CSP-1 and service-2 from CSP-2. Also, assume that CSP-1 supports, say SAML 1.1 for identity management functions, and CSP-2 supports, say

Figure 7. Cloud identity-as-a-service (IDaaS)

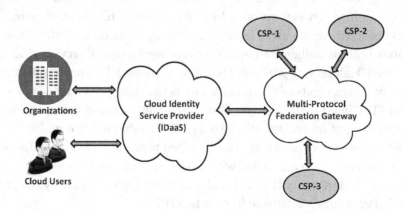

SAML 2.0 for identity management functions. In this case, the organization can use the multi-protocol federation gateways hosted by the identity providers such as Symplified or TriCipher. Multi-protocol federation gateways support both the standards, and hide the integration complexity from a cloud user adopting multiple services. Thus, these gateways provide federation among various cloud services supporting different IAM standards or protocols.

Challenges for Deployment

In this model, since an organization depends on a third party cloud service for identity management functionalities, it has little knowledge in the implementation and architecture details adopted by the identity service provider. Hence the organization has to rely on the SLA agreed by the identity service provider as far as the identity management functionalities of the users are considered. Hence, the performance and availability aspects of the IDaaS provider depend on the SLA, and also on the trust level shared between the CSP and the IdP. Thus, trust between the IdP and the cloud users and also between the IdP and the CSP is an important factor for the successful deployment of this service.

INTER-CLOUD IDENTITY MANAGEMENT

Inter-cloud is the federation of Cloud Providers (Celesti et al., 2010a). In the standard Cloud Computing model, a client gets the required service from a single Cloud Service Provider or data centre, and this approach introduces several challenges. Due to some reasons, if the CSP cannot handle the service requests initiated from the cloud customers, it can leave thousands of customers who depend solely on that Service Provider, without access to the required resources. Also, this approach of depending on a single cloud data centre makes it difficult to ensure adequate responsiveness and Quality of Service (QoS) to the clients. Thus, the motivating factors for the adoption of Inter-Cloud computing paradigm are the enhanced collaboration between the various Cloud Service Providers and the improved QoS delivered to the cloud consumers. Practically, the resources of a CSP are finite, and hence a CSP form the federation or inter-cloud environment with other CSPs where they cooperate with each other in delivering better QoS and achieve economy of scale. Inter-cloud is formed with the purpose of enlarging the computing and storage capacities of individual CSPs. Identity and Access Management of cloud users is an important activity in the inter-cloud environment.

Need for IAM in the Inter-Cloud

In the inter-cloud model, a CSP in the federation can use resources from another CSP in the federation. This collaboration ensures the support in terms of information and resource sharing among the partners in the inter-cloud environment ensuring better QoS. The QoS includes factors such as availability, reliability and response time of the services delivered by various cloud service providers. In the inter-cloud environment, the identity management systems should uniquely identify the inter-cloud users, and also various resources associated with different partner clouds of the cloud federation should be uniquely named and identified. In the cloud computing, the cloud deployments are dynamic with servers launched or terminated run-time. Hence, in the cloud domain, whenever a service or a machine is decommissioned, the information regarding this should be communicated to the IAM module so that future access to it are revoked or managed properly. Another issue in the cloud federation is how the authentication of cloud users could be performed among the heterogeneous inter-cloud partners in the cloud federation. Generally, the authentication and the identity management mechanisms adopted by each CSP may be different from that of the other clouds. Hence, the identity management technology and protocols should be interoperable in the inter-cloud environment. The inter-cloud environment is required to have proper Identity and Access Management mechanism to deal with the access requests of various cloud customers.

Federated Identity Management in the Inter-Cloud

One of the significant reasons for the widespread adoption and popularity of Cloud Computing paradigm is its ability to provide rapid elasticity and on-demand provisioning of computing, storage and network resources. Even though the cloud computing paradigm promises to offer infinite resources, in reality, the resources with each and every Cloud Service Provider are finite. When a CSP runs out of resources, it can get the required services from partners in the cloud federation or the inter-cloud. This scenario indicates that proper identity and access management is essential in the cloud federation. The current inter-cloud computing domain can make use of federated identity management approaches such as Single Sign-On, for authentication of the cloud users in the federation. The overall view of the SSO in Cloud Federation is shown in the Figure 8. The users in a cloud federation don't need to use separate credentials for each cloud service provider or service they subscribe to; instead, they can have the identity issued by the Identity Provider (Ping Identity, Symplified etc.). They can submit the security tokens (normally SAML assertions) issued by the identity provider, to the Service Providers in the cloud federation. This approach is both efficient and secure, and relieves the users of the multiple credentials problem when accessing services from multiple cloud service providers in the federation.

Thus, in the SSO mechanism in Cloud Federation, a user needs to verify his credentials and get authenticated himself only once during an active session of accessing the cloud services. The cloud users are benefitted in such a way that they will be able to access all the related services that are offered by a single CSP or multiple CSPs in the federation seamlessly, without the need to provide the identity credentials again and again for accessing different services. It also helps in increasing the productivity of the users as well as the developers by reducing the number of times a user must login, also reducing the number of credentials one has to remember.

Workflow Model of the Single Sign-On Approach

The sequence of steps involved in the workflow of the implementation of SSO in the Cloud Federation is shown in the Figure 9.

In this figure, the authors have shown only two CSPs in the Cloud Federation. As shown in the figure, the various steps involved are:

Step 1: The Cloud User wants to access the service hosted by the CSP-1, and submits the identity credentials to the CSP-1.

Step 2: The CSP-1 contacts the associated Identity Provider (IdP) for the authentication of the user.

Step 3: The CSP-1 gets the result of user verification from the IdP.

Step 4: The user submits the service request for accessing the resources from the CSP-1.

Step 5: User authorization is performed by the CSP-1 to decide whether to accept or reject the request.

Figure 8. Single Sign-On (SSO) in cloud federation

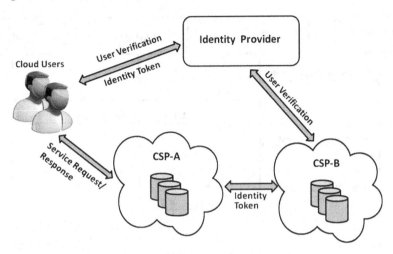

Step 6: The local resources (if available at the CSP-1) are allocated to the user.

Step 7: The CSP-1 contacts the other CSP(s) in the federation (CSP-2), if the local resources are not sufficient to satisfy the user's request.

Challenges for the Identity Management in the Inter-Cloud

The challenges for developing an effective Identity and Access Management mechanism in the inter-cloud environment can be broadly categorized as follows (Núñez et al., 2011; Dreo et al., 2013)

1. **Naming and Identification of the Inter-Cloud Resources:** All the resources (servers, storage systems, processors, virtual machines, applications) present in the inter-cloud environment could be considered as potential resources. Hence, the identity of each of these resources should be properly established in the inter-cloud so that the resources could be distinguished one from the other in a particular context.

2. **Interoperability of Identity Information in the Inter-Cloud:** The standards, protocols, formats and attributes used by the inter-cloud partners in the identity management should be such that they are interoperable with each other. Also, the identity management system used in the inter-cloud should be interoperable with the identity management systems in the organization or the individual CSP, in order to enable the CSP to join the inter-cloud or cloud federation, and deliver the services effectively.

3. **Identity Life Cycle Management in the Inter-Cloud:** In the life cycle of the identity of a cloud user, some changes could happen in its attribute values, authorization decisions or access rights from time to time depending on the policy of the CSP. Hence, whenever there is a change in the identity information of a cloud user, there should be proper synchronization among the inter-cloud partners so that the inter-cloud resources are protected from malicious access. The synchronization should be done in-time as any delay would cause security vulnerabilities.

4. **Single Sign-On for interactions in the Inter-Cloud:** The federated identity management in the inter-cloud should support SSO in such a way that the users are allowed to access the resources and

Figure 9. Workflow model of the Single Sign-On approach

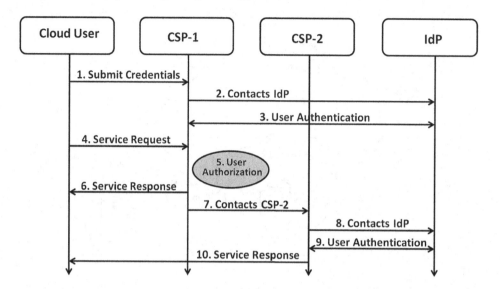

services offered by the inter-cloud partners, after the verification of their identities by the IdPs in the inter-cloud. That means, users are not required to be authenticated at individual CSPs if they are authenticated by a CSP where they make the initial access request.

5. **Exchange of Identity Information:** In the Inter-Cloud environments, multiple Identity Providers and Service Providers can be present. Hence, the extent of information about users, apps/devices etc. that need to be exchanged among the different service domain, is an issue to be solved as far as protecting the privacy of the cloud users is concerned. Also, the development of an interoperable data format and the protocols used for exchanging the information is another concern in the inter-cloud environment.

6. **Dynamic Extensibility:** In the Inter-Cloud environment, new Cloud services may be added from time to time. How can the existing IAM systems be dynamically extended with the new cloud services is an issue to be solved. Also, how the trustworthiness of such services will be verified by the existing users is also a concern to be addressed.

An efficient IAM system in the Inter-Cloud environments should support the various identity standards such as X.509 certificates, SAML, and WS-Federation (Bernstein & Vij, 2010b). Inter-Cloud environment should support XACML-compliant access management mechanisms (Bernstein & Vij, 2010b) as it offers a standardized language for access control and policy enforcement. Scalability is another issue to be considered for Identity management in the inter-cloud environments.

FUTURE RESEARCH DIRECTIONS

Based on the discussion carried out, it is seen that IAM is an important issue and surely there are many aspects which require further research and proper solution. Effective trust management in the cloud environment is still an issue which requires further research. It is necessary to have further research in the establishment of a dynamic trust relationship between user domains and cloud domains, and between various cloud domains and the identity providers to have a proper solution for the identity management. Single Sign-On mechanism implemented in the cloud environment should address the security issues such as impersonation of a user, impersonation of a Service Provider etc. during the authentication process. Also, it should be resistant against various attacks such as Man-in-the-Middle attacks, replay attacks, phishing attacks etc. The identity federation mechanism adopted in the cloud environment should support multiple identity providers, and hence the interoperability between various entities in the identity federation is an issue which requires effective solutions. In the case of cloud mashups, how can the users be authenticated for accessing all the cloud applications integrated in the mashups seamlessly, and also, how can the user's attributes such as group association, access rights, roles are shared effectively across these cloud applications are issues to be solved in the identity and access management in the cloud.

In the inter-cloud environment, the identity management systems should uniquely identify the inter-cloud users, and also various resources associated with different partner clouds of the cloud federation should be uniquely named and identified. Another issue in the cloud federation is how the authentication of cloud users could be performed among the heterogeneous inter-cloud partners in the cloud federation. Generally, the authentication and the identity management mechanisms adopted by each CSP could be different from that of the other clouds. Hence, the identity management technology and protocols adopted by the partner clouds should be interoperable in the inter-cloud environment. Hence, it is clear that the issue of identity and access management in the cloud computing domain has enormous potential for further active research, in order to make the cloud computing paradigm secure, reliable and scalable.

CONCLUSION

In this chapter, the authors have discussed the issue of Identity and Access Management (IAM) in the cloud and inter-cloud environments. The analysis of the work done by the researchers in this area is carried out. The important features and functionalities of IAM are discussed. The various issues in the identity and access management in cloud computing, such as access control models, identity life cycle management, federated identity management, Single Sign-On (SSO) and cloud identity-as-a-service are discussed. The emerging area of inter-cloud domain is discussed and the importance of an effective identity management in that domain is highlighted. Also, some of the future research directions in IAM in the cloud and inter-cloud domains are also highlighted.

REFERENCES

Almulla, S. A., & Yeun, C. Y. (2010, March). Cloud computing security management. *Proceedings of the 2010 Second International Conference on Engineering Systems Management and Its Applications (ICESMA)* (pp. 1-7). IEEE.

Amazon Web Services-Identity and Access Management. (2015). Retrieved from http://aws.amazon.com/iam

Amazon Web Services-Multi Factor Authentication. (2015). Retrieved from http://aws.amazon.com/mfa

Microsoft Azure. (2015). Retrieved from http://azure.microsoft.com/en- in/documentation/infographics/cloud-identity-and-access/

Bernstein, D., & Vij, D. (2010a, July). Intercloud directory and exchange protocol detail using XMPP and RDF. *Proceedings of the 2010 6th World Congress on Services (SERVICES-1)* (pp. 431-438). IEEE.

Bernstein, D., & Vij, D. (2010b, November). Intercloud security considerations. *Proceedings of the 2010 IEEE Second International Conference onCloud Computing Technology and Science (CloudCom)* (pp. 537-544). IEEE. doi:10.1109/CloudCom.2010.82

CA's Federation Manager. (2015). Retrieved from http://www.ca.com/in/securecenter/ca-federation.aspx

Cantor, S., & SCAVO, T. (2005). Shibboleth architecture. *Protocols and Profiles*, 10.

Cantor, S., Kemp, I. J., Philpott, N. R., & Maler, E. (2005, March). Assertions and protocols for the oasis security assertion markup language. *OASIS Standard*.

Celesti, A., Tusa, F., Villari, M., & Puliafito, A. (2010a, July). How to enhance cloud architectures to enable cross-federation. *Proceedings of the 2010 IEEE 3rd International Conference on Cloud Computing (CLOUD)* (pp. 337-345). IEEE. doi:10.1109/CLOUD.2010.46

Celesti, A., Tusa, F., Villari, M., & Puliafito, A. (2010b, July). Three-phase cross-cloud federation model: The cloud sso authentication. *Proceedings of the 2010 Second International Conference on Advances in Future Internet (AFIN)* (pp. 94-101). IEEE.

Celesti, A., Tusa, F., Villari, M., & Puliafito, A. (2011). Federation establishment between clever clouds through a saml sso authentication profile. *International Journal on Advances in Internet Technology*, 4(1 & 2), 14-27.

Chan, C. K., & Cheng, L. M. (2000). Cryptanalysis of a remote user authentication scheme using smart cards. *IEEE Transactions on* Consumer Electronics, 46(4), 992–993.

Dreo, G., Golling, M., Hommel, W., & Tietze, F. (2013, May). ICEMAN: An architecture for secure federated inter-cloud identity management. *Proceedings of the 2013 IFIP/IEEE International Symposium onIntegrated Network Management (IM 2013)* (pp. 1207-1210). IEEE.

El Maliki, T., & Seigneur, J. M. (2007, October). A survey of user-centric identity management technologies. *Proceedings of the International Conference on Emerging Security Information, Systems, and Technologies SecureWare '07* (pp. 12-17). IEEE. doi:10.1109/SECUREWARE.2007.4385303

Feng, F., Lin, C., Peng, D., & Li, J. (2008, September). A trust and context based access control model for distributed systems. *Proceedings of the 10th IEEE International Conference on High Performance Computing and Communications HPCC '08* (pp. 629-634). IEEE. doi:10.1109/HPCC.2008.37

Ferraiolo, D. F., Sandhu, R., Gavrila, S., Kuhn, D. R., & Chandramouli, R. (2001). Proposed NIST standard for role-based access control. *ACM Transactions on Information and System Security*, 4(3), 224–274. doi:10.1145/501978.501980

Fugkeaw, S., Manpanpanich, P., & Juntapremjitt, S. (2007, April). A robust single sign-on model based on multi-agent system and PKI. *Proceedings of the Sixth International Conference on Networking ICN '07.* (pp. 101-101). IEEE. doi:10.1109/ICN.2007.10

Ghazizadeh, E., & Zamani, M. Jamalul-lail Ab Manan, & Pashang, A. (2012, December). A survey on security issues of federated identity in the cloud computing. In CloudCom (pp. 532-565).

Godik, S., Anderson, A., Parducci, B., Humenn, P., & Vajjhala, S. (2002). *OASIS eXtensible access control 2 markup language (XACML) 3. Tech. rep.* OASIS.

Goodner, M., & Nadalin, T. (2009). Web Services Federation Language (WS-Federation) Version 1.2. OASIS Web Services Federation (WSFED) TC.

I am Google Cloud. (2015). Retrieved from https://cloud.google.com/iam/

Gunjan, K., Sahoo, G., & Tiwari, R. K. (2012, June). Identity management in cloud computing–a review. International Journal of Engineering Research and Technology, 1(4).

Hardt, D. (2012). *The OAuth 2.0 Authorization Framework.*

Hovav, A., & Berger, R. (2009). Tutorial: Identity management systems and secured access control. *Communications of the Association for Information Systems, 25*(1), 42.

Hu, V. C., Ferraiolo, D., & Kuhn, D. R. (2006). *Assessment of access control systems.* US Department of Commerce, National Institute of Standards and Technology.

Khan, K. M., & Malluhi, Q. (2010). Establishing trust in cloud computing. *IT Professional, 12*(5), 20–27. doi:10.1109/MITP.2010.128

King, N. J., & Raja, V. T. (2012). Protecting the privacy and security of sensitive customer data in the cloud. *Computer Law & Security Report, 28*(3), 308–319. doi:10.1016/j.clsr.2012.03.003

Kumar, R., Gupta, N., Charu, S., Jain, K., & Jangir, S. K. (2014). Open Source Solution for Cloud Computing Platform Using OpenStack. *International Journal of Computer Science and Mobile Computing, 3*(5), 89–98.

Kumar, S., & Cohen, P. R. (2000, June). Towards a fault-tolerant multi-agent system architecture. *Proceedings of the fourth international conference on Autonomous agents* (pp. 459-466). ACM. doi:10.1145/336595.337570

Kumaraswamy, S., Lakshminarayanan, S., Stein, M. R. J., & Wilson, Y. (2010). Domain 12: Guidance for identity & access management v2. 1. Cloud Security Alliance. Retrieved from http://www.cloudsecurityalliance.org/guidance/csaguide-dom12-v2,10

Lang, B., Wang, Z., & Wang, Q. (2007, July). Trust representation and reasoning for access control in large scale distributed systems. *Proceedings of the 2nd International Conference on Pervasive Computing and Applications ICPCA '07* (pp. 436-441). IEEE. doi:10.1109/ICPCA.2007.4365483

Lee, C. C., Li, L. H., & Hwang, M. S. (2002). A remote user authentication scheme using hash functions. *Operating Systems Review, 36*(4), 23–29. doi:10.1145/583800.583803

Linstrom, P. J., & Mallard, W. G. (2003, March). National Institute of Standards and Technology: Gaithersburg. MD, USA.

Marston, S., Li, Z., Bandyopadhyay, S., Zhang, J., & Ghalsasi, A. (2011). Cloud computing—The business perspective. *Decision Support Systems, 51*(1), 176–189. doi:10.1016/j.dss.2010.12.006

Mather, T., Kumaraswamy, S., & Latif, S. (2009). *Cloud security and privacy: an enterprise perspective on risks and compliance.* O'Reilly.

Microsoft Active Directory. (2009). Retrieved from http://www.microsoft.com/windowsserver2003/technologies/directory/activedirectory/default.mspx

Microsoft Identity Manager. (2015). Retrieved from http://www.microsoft.com/en-in/server-cloud/products/microsoft-identity-manager/

Núñez, D., Agudo, I., Drogkaris, P., & Gritzalis, S. (2011). Identity management challenges for inter-cloud applications. In Secure and Trust Computing, Data Management, and Applications (pp. 198-204). Springer Berlin Heidelberg.

Oracle: SunOpenSSO Enterprise 8.0 TechnicalOverview. (2015). Retrieved from http://docs.sun.com/doc/820-3740

Oracle's Federation Manager. (2015). Retrieved from http://www.oracle.com/identity

Padhy, R. P., Patra, M. R., & Satapathy, S. C. (2012). Design and implementation of a cloud based rural healthcare information system model. [VPN tunneling]. *Univers J Appl Comput Sci Technol, 2*(1), 149–157.

Radha, V., & Reddy, D. H. (2012). A Survey on single sign-on techniques. *Procedia Technology, 4*, 134–139. doi:10.1016/j.protcy.2012.05.019

Recordon, D., & Reed, D. (2006, November). OpenID 2.0: a platform for user-centric identity management. *Proceedings of the second ACM workshop on Digital identity management* (pp. 11-16). ACM.

Ren, X., & Wu, X. W. (2012, October). A novel dynamic user authentication scheme. *Proceedings of the 2012 International Symposium on Communications and Information Technologies (ISCIT)* (pp. 713-717). IEEE.

Rhoton, J. Discover OpenStack: the identity component keystone. Retrieved from http://www.ibm.com/developerworks/cloud/library/cl-openstack-keystone/

Rimal, B. P., Choi, E., & Lumb, I. (2009, August). A taxonomy and survey of cloud computing systems. Proceedings of the Fifth International Joint Conference on INC, IMS and IDC, NCM '09 (pp. 44-51). IEEE. (2013). doi:10.1109/NCM.2009.218

Sakimura, D. N., Bradley, J., Jones, M., de Medeiros, B., & Jay, E. (2011). OpenID Connect Standard 1.0-draft 20.

Security guidance for critical areas of focus in cloud computing v3. 0. (2011). Cloud Security Alliance.

Smith, D. (2008). The challenge of federated identity management. *Network Security, 2008*(4), 7–9. doi:10.1016/S1353-4858(08)70051-5

Sood, S. K. (2012). A combined approach to ensure data security in cloud computing. *Journal of Network and Computer Applications, 35*(6), 1831–1838. doi:10.1016/j.jnca.2012.07.007

OASIS Standard. (2003). Service Provisioning Markup Language (SPML) Version 1

Stihler, M., Santin, A. O., Marcon, A. L., & Fraga, J. S. (2012, May). Integral federated identity management for cloud computing. *Proceedings of the 2012 5th International Conference on New Technologies, Mobility and Security (NTMS)* (pp. 1-5). IEEE. doi:10.1109/NTMS.2012.6208751

Subashini, S., & Kavitha, V. (2011). A survey on security issues in service delivery models of cloud computing. *Journal of Network and Computer Applications, 34*(1), 1–11. doi:10.1016/j.jnca.2010.07.006

Suhendra, V. (2011). A survey on access control deployment. In *Security Technology* (pp. 11–20). Springer Berlin Heidelberg. doi:10.1007/978-3-642-27189-2_2

Symplified. (2015). Retrieved from http://www.symplified.com-Symplified

TriCipher. (2015). Retrieved from http://www.tricipher.com

Tusa, F., Celesti, A., Paone, M., Villari, M., & Puliafito, A. (2011, June). How clever-based clouds conceive horizontal and vertical federations. *Proceedings of the 2011 IEEE Symposium on Computers and Communications (ISCC)* (pp. 167-172). IEEE. doi:10.1109/ISCC.2011.5984011

Wahl, M., Howes, T., & Kille, S. (1997). Lightweight directory access protocol (v3).

Wang, C., Wang, Q., Ren, K., & Lou, W. (2010, March). Privacy-preserving public auditing for data storage security in cloud computing. Proceedings of the '10 INFOCOM '10 (pp. 1-9). IEEE. doi:10.1109/INFCOM.2010.5462173

Wang, G., Yu, J., & Xie, Q. (2013). Security analysis of a single sign-on mechanism for distributed computer networks. . *IEEE Transactions on* Industrial Informatics, *9*(1), 294–302.

Wang, J., Li, D., Li, Q., & Xi, B. (2007, September). Constructing Role-Based Access Control and Delegation Based on Hierarchical IBS. *Proceedings of the NPC Workshops IFIP International Conference on Network and Parallel Computing Workshops.* (pp. 112-118). IEEE. doi:10.1109/NPC.2007.106

Wei, Y., Shi, C., & Shao, W. (2010, May). An attribute and role based access control model for service-oriented environment. *Proceedings of the 2010 Chinese Control and Decision Conference* (CCDC) (pp. 4451-4455). IEEE.

Yan, L., Rong, C., & Zhao, G. (2009). Strengthen cloud computing security with federal identity management using hierarchical identity-based cryptography. In *Cloud Computing* (pp. 167–177). Springer Berlin Heidelberg. doi:10.1007/978-3-642-10665-1_15

KEY TERMS AND DEFINITIONS

Access Control Model: Access control models describe what security properties are associated with an access control system. They bridge the gap between an access control policy and the corresponding mechanism, and help to discuss and analyze any theoretical limitations of a particular system in ensuring the required access control.

Authentication: Authentication is the process of verifying the identity of an entity in a system. It verifies that the entity is really who it claims to be.

Authorization: Authorization is the process by which the access rights or privileges of an entity are verified by the system against predefined security policies. Normally, authorization process follows the authentication step and it is required to avoid unauthorized access of resources by malicious users.

Federation Gateway: Federation Gateways are used in the federated identity management scenario to translate the identity tokens of cloud users from one format to another. Using this approach, organizations using different cloud services can achieve the required identity translation while accessing services from different cloud providers.

Identity Federation: In the Identity Federation scenario, there is an association between CSPs and IdPs in such a way that the identity tokes issued by the IdP are used by the CSPs to deliver the requested services to the cloud users.

Identity Life Cycle Management: Identity Life Cycle Management shows the various stages through which a user identity goes through. That is, it shows how the identity is managed when it is created, used or terminated.

Identity Provider: The Identity Providers (IdPs) are trusted entities in the cloud computing environment that provides the identity tokens to the cloud users. These tokens could be used by the CSPs for delivering the requested services to cloud users.

Single Sign-On: Single Sign-On (SSO) is a mechanism used for authentication in which a service consumer is required to be authenticated only once while accessing various services from multiple service providers, or when accessing multiple services from the same service provider. The process of SSO involves Identity Federation, and it helps the users to access multiple services from the same or different CSPs using the identity tokens issued by the Identity Provider.

Chapter 4
Characterizing PaaS Solutions Enabling Cloud Federations

Tamas Pflanzner
University of Szeged, Hungary

Ákos Zoltán Gorácz
University of Szeged, Hungary

Roland Tornyai
University of Szeged, Hungary

Attila Kertesz
University of Szeged, Hungary

ABSTRACT

Cloud Computing has opened new ways of flexible resource provisions for businesses migrating IT applications and data to the cloud to respond to new demands from customers. Recently, many businesses plan to take advantage of the flexible resource provision. Cloud Federations envisage a distributed, heterogeneous environment consisting of various cloud infrastructures by aggregating different IaaS provider capabilities coming from both the commercial and academic area. Recent solutions hide the diversity of multiple clouds and form a unified federation on top of them. Many approaches follow recent trends in cloud application development, and offer federation capabilities at the platform level, thus creating Platform-as-a-Service solutions. In this chapter the authors investigate capabilities of PaaS solutions and present a classification of these tools: what levels of developer experience they offer, what types of APIs, developer tools they support and what web GUIs they provide. Developer experience is measured by creating and executing sample applications with these PaaS tools.

INTRODUCTION

Cloud computing providers offer services according to several models which can be categorized as follows: (i) Infrastructure as a Service (IaaS) – this is the most basic cloud-service model, where infrastructure providers manage and offer computers (physical or virtual) and other resources, such as a hypervisor that runs virtual machines. IaaS clouds often contain additional resources such as a virtual machine disk-image marketplace with pre-installed images, raw block storage and other file or object storage, load balancing, IP addresses and VLANs. Providers supply these resources on-demand from their large pools of computers installed in their datacenters; (ii) Platform as a Service (PaaS) – these providers deliver a computing platform, including an operating system, programming language execution

DOI: 10.4018/978-1-5225-0153-4.ch004

environment, database and web server. Developers can develop and run their software applications on the cloud platform without the cost and/or complexity of buying and managing their own server farms to match application demand. (iii) Software as a Service (SaaS) –such providers install and operate application software in the cloud and cloud users access the software from cloud clients. Cloud users do not manage the infrastructure nor the platform on which their application runs. Load balancers distribute the workload over the set of allocated virtual machines. The load balancing is transparent to the end user, who only sees one entry point to the application. This model has the potential to reduce IT operational costs by outsourcing maintenance of hardware and software to a provider, enabling the reallocation of IT operation costs to other goals.

According to a recent study, the Dzone Guide to cloud development (Dzone, 2015), over half of the companies use cloud computing in their development (53%), testing and quality assurance (44%), production and deployment work (52%), and these percentages are going up around 10% in surveys from the past years. Lot of the survey respondents replied that they are "planning to perform" testing, development and deployment in the cloud. This shows that cloud is growing ever more important in our world. From the over 600 IT professionals who responded to the survey, 50% see hybrid cloud as their ideal platform, and private cloud is second with 29%. When asked about hosting types, respondents preferred third party (56%) over on premise (41%) hosting. A good representation of the market could be seen by the data gathered in the survey. Respondents of the survey are most likely to deploy web applications (73%) and enterprise applications (54%) in the cloud. They are most likely to use Paas and IaaS types of service. It is interesting to note that Storage-as-a-Service and Database-as-a-Service have risen, and this relates to the impact of Big Data technologies in cloud environments.

Cloud computing is already a part of our everyday life, and there is so much data produced by humans and their machines. As the technology evolves, new kind of innovative use cases can be invented. These new capabilities are the motivation for developing even better cloud infrastructures (Rajkumar Buyyaa, 2009), (Michael Armbrust, 2009).

There are some concepts which create an additional abstraction layer above infrastructure cloud providers, such as (David Cunha, PaaS Manager: A Platform-as-a-Service Aggregation, 2014). Some of these offer standard APIs (David Cunha, A Platform-as-a-Service API Aggregator, 2013), while others try to avoid vendor lock in situations (Kolb S., 2014; Sellami M., 2013). These approaches are important in creating a standard for cloud platforms, but it is hard to integrate innovative ideas and their implementations.

Some of the most critical parts in cloud computing in general are security issues. The cloud technology is relativly new, and it has to gain the trust of its users (Yanpei Chen, 2010).The nature of it makes it hard, as in many cases the users does not know where or how their data is stored. The cloud is used by many users at the same time and it is the responsibility of the provider to make sure that the applications can not affect each other without permission (Luis Rodero-Merinoa, 2012).

The aim of this chapter is to present an overview of the state-of-the-art Platform-as-a-Service solutions that are used to develop applications over cloud federations. The authors investigated and provided an overview of the capabilities of the most advanced tools, both PaaS software stacks and PaaS providers: what levels of developer experience they offer, how they follow recent trends in cloud application development, what types of APIs they provide, what kind of developer tools they support and what web GUIs they provide. Primary sources for this investigation were public documentation of the relevant tools, research publications and trial or demo versions where applicable. Developer experience has been measured by creating and executing sample applications with some of these PaaS tools.

There are many PaaS solutions nowadays, therefore the authors tried to select the most popular ones that are used by many developers and have stood the test of time. The authors included some relatively new providers because of their innovative or specialized features. Some solutions were left out because of the instability and unacceptable quality.

The main challenge the authors identified during their research is that it is difficult to objectively compare providers belonging to the same category, as they all provide a slightly different set of services. Providers can advertise such qualities that may not be available or measurable compared to other providers.Therefore the authors followed the idea that there may be a difference between the feature that the user or developer experiences, and the features the providers advertise. Comparison data may be subjective and biased because of this, but they tried to remain as objective as possible.Similar research efforts have been performed in previous years by other research groups (Hoefer & Karagiannis, 2010; Rimal, Choi, & Lumb, 2009; Pivotal, 2014).

The structure of the chapter is as follows: Section 2 contains an overview of general PaaS providers and presents a classification of their main properties both in theory and in practice. Section 3 introduces and compares providers specialized in mobile support.Section 4 summarizes the findings with a discussion, and Section 5 concludes the chapter.

CHARACTERISING GENERAL PAAS PROVIDERS

Overview of the Investigated Providers

One of the first cloud platforms, Heroku (Heroku, 2015) has been in development since 2007, starting with support for Ruby, and adding support for many languages through the years, such as Java, Node.js, Scala, Clojure, Python, PHP and Perl. Heroku was acquired by Salesforce.com in 2010, as a subsidiary. Heroku's services run on the Amazon cloud systems. From the Developer Experience point-of-view, Heroku's interface is well-polished, intuitive and easy to use. Many times Heroku has been seen as an example by other PaaS providers, for their ease of use, features and reliability. One such example is Deis, which uses a Heroku inspired buildpack system in their deployments. The basic units of computing power in the Heroku ecosystem are the Dynos. A Dyno is a lightweight, isolated container that runs an instance of the application.

CloudFoundry (CloudFoundry, 2015) is an open source PaaS service, originally developed by VMware, later owned by Pivotal Software, primarily written in Ruby and Go. CloudFoundry is available in three flavors, Cloud Foundry OSS, an open source project available to everybody, which uses the developers own infrastructure and the BOSH shell to interact with it, Pivotal Cloud Foundry, a commercial product from Pivotal, which includes extra tools for installation and administration, and Pivotal Web services, which is an instance of Pivotal Cloud Foundry hosted on Amazon Web Services. Applications deployed to CloudFoundry access external resources via Services. All external dependencies such as databases, messaging systems, file system, etc. are Services. When releasing an application, the developer must specify the Services it should use. Many pre-defined services are available via an administration console, such as MySQL, PostgreSQL, MongoDB, etc. as database services, RabbitMQ as a messaging service, Jenkins for continuous integration, and API Gateway, Data Sync, Push Notifications for mobile development.

Apcera (Apcera Platform, 2015) is a startup company, launched in 2012, and was founded by some of the architects behind CloudFoundry. Apcera Platform lets companies create, run, manage applications in ways that conform to specific security and governance policies. Apcera works with a cloud based or on-premise servers and hybrid environments as well. It aims to provide a way to build and deploy applications with IT policies factored in from the start and to apply policies and governance to existing applications as well. Apcera blends the models of IaaS, PaaS, SaaS but overlays them all with technology that handles policy.

Google App Engine (Google App Engine, 2015) is a cloud computing platform for developing and hosting web applications. Applications that are run in the system are sandboxed, and run across multiple Google-managed servers. App Engine offers automatic scaling for web applications, automatically allocates more resources for the application to handle additional demand. App Engine supports a wide variety of programming languages such as: Python, Java (and by extension Groovy, JRuby, Scala, Clojure), Go, PHP, and many web frameworks. App Engine provides infrastructure to make it easy to write scalable applications, but can only run a limited range of applications designed for their infrastructure. App Engine requires developers to use only its supported languages, APIs and frameworks. By default data is stored in a BigTable non-relational database, and applications that require a relational database will not run on App Engine without modifications such as Google Cloud SQL. Some developers expressed worries that their applications will not be portable from App Engine and fear being locked into the technology. To address these concerns, a number of open-source projects have appeared to create backends for the various proprietary APIs of App Engine, such as AppScale.

Azure (Microsoft Azure, 2015) is a Cloud computing platform, which allows developers to publish web applications running on different frameworks, written in different programming languages such as any .NET language, node.js, php, Python and Java. Azure Web Sites supports a website creation wizard that can be used to create a blank site or use one of the several pre-configured sites. Developers can add or modify content of the website via multiple deployment methods: TFS, FTP, CodePlex, GitHub, Dropbox, Bitbucket, Mercurial or git. Developers can select the place where their website will be hosted from several Microsoft data centers around the globe. Azure Traffic Manager routes traffic manually or automatically between websites in different regions. Web sites are hosted on IIS 8.0, running on a custom version of Windows Server 2012.

Amazon Web Services (Amazon Web Services, 2015) is a collection of services that make up a cloud computing platform, which are based on 11 geographical regions across the world. The most central and well-known services are Amazon EC2 (Elastic Compute Cloud) and Amazon S3 (Simple Storage Service). The products are offered to large and small companies as a service to provide large computing capacity faster and cheaper than the client company building and maintaining an actual physical server farm. AWS automatically handles the details such as resource provisioning, load balancing, scaling and monitoring. One can create applications in PHP, Java, Python, Ruby, node.js, .NET, Go or in a Docker container that runs on an application server with a database. An environment using the default settings will run a single Amazon EC2 micro instance and an Elastic Load Balancer. Additional instances will be added if needed, to handle any peaks in workload or traffic. Each Amazon EC2 instance is built from an Amazon Machine Image which can be an Amazon Linux AMI or an Amazon Windows Server 2008 R2 AMI by default.

Mendix (Mendix, 2015) is a Netherlands based enterprise application company, which has developed a PaaS product called the Mendix App Platform. The platform allows the users and developers to build, integrate and deploy web and mobile applications. The Mendix App Platform uses a visual, model-driven software development approach. Mendix is also a member of the Cloud Foundry Foundation.

The company plans to evolve the open source standard as well as integrate the PaaS framework of Cloud Foundry with its own rapid app platform as a service. The rapid app platform as a service methodology prioritizes speed and agility and utilizes a "no code" principle. Using visual models simplifies app creation and migration and allows business users more insight and more direct participation in the development process. This method reduces the time to market of the app significantly.

Services and applications in the Mendix App Platform are oriented towards collaboration. Mendix offers a Community Edition of the app platform, which brings application development tools to a wider audience ranging from individual developers to large teams and companies. Recently Mendix made major enhancements to the Mendix App Platform, such as reducing time, cost and effort for app development and mobile application development. Mobile features include pre-defined layouts for smartphone, tablet and desktop user interfaces.

CloudControl (CloudControl, 2015) is a programming language agnostic PaaS service based in Germany. It's officially supported development languages are Java, PHP, Python and Ruby, and the services use the open buildpack API developed originally by Heroku. Pricing is based on usage. Computing containers are billed in Boxes per hour, where one Box is similar in power to a Dyno with Heroku, with the notable difference that it can answer two requests simultaneously. CloudControl features deployments that enable separate versions of the same application (e.g. development, staging, testing, live). A role based permission system is provided to authenticate multiple developers to work on the same application.

AppScale (AppScale, 2015) began as a research project at the University of California. It is an open source computing platform that deploys and scales unmodified Google App Engine applications over public and private cloud systems and on-premise clusters or a hybrid of these systems. The service is modeled on the App Engine APIs and supports Python, Go, PHP and Java languages. They are in close partnership with Google. One of the goals of AppScale is to make the applications of the developers truly mobile, to provide a way to migrate or fail over apps to another cloud or the developer's own servers if needed. It reduces the problem of vendor lock-in. They aim to provide developers with a rapid API-driven development platform that can run applications on every cloud infrastructure. AppScale uses many open source components and APIs such as Cassandra for data and blob storage, memcached, RabbitMQ for queueing, ejabberd for messaging, etc. AppScale can be run on the Google App Engine and in the Amazon Web Services cloud.

Deis (Deis, 2015) is a lightweight application platform that deploys and scales Twelve-Factor apps as Docker containers across a cluster of CoreOS machines. The Twelve-Factor app is a methodology for building modern applications that can be scaled across a distributed system. It provides a lightweight PaaS with a Heroku-inspired workflow (Twelve-Factor app, 2015). Deis creates the applications as Docker images, which are distributed across the cluster as Docker containers. It uses CoreOS, a minimal linux distribution that can be run and hosted everywhere, public or private, bare metal or virtualized. It uses Git as the main version control system, the developers can deploy new content with a simple "git push". It is free and open source.

IBM's latest cloud software is the Bluemix platform (Bluemix, 2015), which is using the Cloud-Foundry open source PaaS project. It is an implementation of the IBM's Open Cloud Architecture. Bluemix delivers enterprise-level services that can easily integrate with your cloud applications without you needing to know how to install or configure them. For developers, Bluemix further optimizes the time you spend creating cloud application. For organizations, it provides a cloud platform that requires very little in-house technical know-how as well as cost savings.

PaaS Comparison Categories

The authors compared the PaaS providers based on the following categories:

- **Cost:** The cost of the service can be a big factor in choosing a provider. Different tiers of service may be available for different fees. There are many different billing schemes, which differ on what kind of resource consumption they track.
    - Most providers offer free tiers with limited processing power, database size and connections, network bandwidth, and data storage.
    - Pricing is done in a pay-as-you-go system with most providers, by billing them based on the resources used monthly.
    - Higher tier services may increase monthly cost. These include a separate database instance instead of a shared one, High Availability, data rollback, encryption, different (higher) SLAs.
- **Workload:** With this category the authors tried to define what kind of workload and what type of data works well with each provider. The basic types of workloads that they were interested in are:
    - **Analytics:** This type of workload is about crunching the numbers, analyzing and processing data. This may be done in a distributed way, like Hadoop Clusters.
    - **Transactions:** With this kind of workload, stress is on the database actions, transactions, and data retrieval.
    - **Media:** Working with media, delivering large static files and other content.
    - **Mobile:** Do they offer any mobile apps and a backend?
    - **IoT:** Internet of Things support
- **Tooling / Developer Experience:** This category is about how easy it is for a developer to use the service and develop his own application on a day-to-day basis.
    - **IDE Support:** More and more providers supply developers with plugins and extensions to the major IDEs, (e.g. Eclipse, Visual Studio, NetBeans, IntelliJ, etc.)
    - **Targets:** Some providers offer the ability to run different instances of the applications simultaneously. One instance might be the live application with actual customer or user data, a second instance can be available for developers to test their new code of the application, maybe a third for testers to run their tests against, etc.
    - **APIs:** Providers may offer some public API endpoints for the developer to interface their own application with. Different interfaces can be used for parts of the service.
    - **Command Line Interface:** Most of the providers offer a Command Line Interface for managing the service. These can vary wildly in quality and usability.
    - **Git:** Nowadays Git is the most used distributed version control system. This category shows how well git is used within the service, how to deploy or push newer versions of the application.
- **Deployment:** Items in this category are about the deployment of the service and the containers used / promoted by the provider.
    - **Backend Type:** The big providers (Google, Microsoft, Amazon) have their own server farms that run the PaaS applications. In contrast, smaller providers host their services on Amazon servers, by using their own PaaS solution on top of the IaaS provided by Amazon.
    - **Container Solution:** Containers are the building blocks of PaaS services. In the age of virtualization, some different container types have appeared. One of the main container tech-

nologies is Docker, which many of the providers support. Other providers may use a different kind of method, or have a system based on Docker.

- ○ **Supported Containers:** This category shows if the provider supports more types of containers that might be beneficial for developers, because they might not need to rewrite their application for a new container solution.
- **Integration:** Some providers may offer solutions for managing the users of the application, e.g. a registry form, login pages, errors, and user management interfaces for administrators.
  - ○ **User Registry:** Adding, registering, managing, removing users in the application, and managing the details of the users.
  - ○ **Authentication / Authorization:** Methods, granularity of managing the access of users to content/data.
  - ○ **Security:** Security of users and user data.
- **SLAs:** Providers agree on some levels of service that is definitely provided by them. This could be imposed on uptime, scaling, performance, some kind of support for paying tiers of service, etc.
  - ○ **Availability / HA:** The type and amount of availability guaranteed by the provider. High Availability may be available for redundancy, switching over to other servers when one node goes down in the system.
  - ○ **Reliability:** This category shows how many and what size of outages happened in the last few years of service.
  - ○ **Horizontal Scalability:** The process of allocating more instances to serve a growing number of requests on the application.
  - ○ **Vertical Scalability:** The process of adding more resources (more processing power, more memory, more disk) to a node.
  - ○ Horizontal and vertical scalability may also depend on the application itself.
- **Datastores:** If the provider offers any kind of data storage methods that are mentioned here.
  - ○ **Relational (SQL), NoSQL, Key-value, Documents, etc.:** The provider may offer different types of data storage, with different backends and APIs.
- **Programming Models:** The more different languages and frameworks a provider supports, the more potential customers it might attract.
  - ○ **Programming Languages:** Amount and type of supported programming languages available for developers to use for writing their applications.
  - ○ **Frameworks:** Providers might support web frameworks, which may be pre-installed or easily installed from some kind of marketplace of the provider.
- **Management:** Managing the events and availability of the service can be done on many levels, they are aggregated in this category.
  - ○ **Logging:** Different levels and methods exist for logging different types of events or activities. Logs can be accessed in many different ways, there are some standard methods and frameworks (e.g. LogStash, etc.), which provide easy access and different search parameters and functions to find the relevant data.
  - ○ **Monitoring:** Monitoring the quality of the service and the application is an important aspect of the user and developer experience. Alerts can be sent out if different service-based failure criteria are met, developers and administrators can be notified. Monitoring is usually available as self service monitoring for the free and lower tier users, and enterprise grade monitoring might be available for higher tier customers.

- **Misc.:** Any other criteria that could not be fitted in their own group is mentioned here.
  - ○ **Open Source:** It might be important for a developer to know if the source of any parts of the provider solution is available.
  - ○ **Marketplace:** More and more providers offer an in-house marketplace of selected, pre-assembled containers or software images, made by the PaaS provider or even other developers.

Features in categories (where applicable) were measured, aggregated and ranked the following way: In the comparison table (shown in Table 1) the authors used numbers for four different levels. 0 means the provider has not implemented the feature, or there is no data available on it. 1 means the feature quality is basic, beta state, it can have major bugs. 2 indicates a stable quality, while 3 means the feature is excellent or innovative.

PaaS Workflow of Developer Roles

In order to understand what steps develppers should undergo during cteating a PaaS application, the authors present a workflow of developer roles. These basic roles and their connections in PaaS application development is depicted in Figure 1. In general, after the Authentication the user can Edit, Run or Monitor applications.In the authentication part the user can register or login and then use the features of the given PaaS system depending on the user's role and permissions.

Figure 1. Basic developer roles

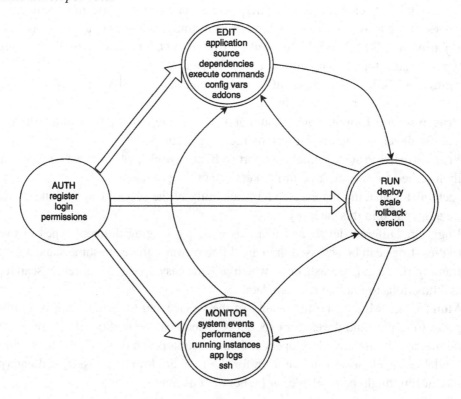

Table 1. Comparison of PaaS providers

		Apcera Platform	Heroku	CloudFoundry	Google App Engine	Microsoft Azure	Amazon Web Services	Mendix	CloudControl	AppScale	Deis	Bluemix
Cost	Billing schemes	n/a	free, scaling	free	free quota, priced above	free, pay-as-you-use	pay-as-you-go	free, 3 tiers	free, pay-as-you-go	N/A	free	free quota, priced above
Workload	Media, larger files	na	2	2	1	3	3	2	1	1	1	2
	Mobile	na	2	2	1	2	1	2	1	1	0	3
	IoT	0	2	2	3	3	2	0	0	0	0	2
Tools	IDE support	na	2	1	1	2	1	1	2	2	2	1
	Targets	na	3	3	1	3	2	2	3	1	2	3
	APIs	2	3	3	1	1	3	2	2	3	1	3
	Git usage	na	2	3	2	1	2	2	3	2	3	3
	CLI	2	3	3	2	1	3	1	3	2	3	3
Deployment	Backend	private	Amazon	Amazon	Google	Microsoft	Amazon	public, private	Amazon	Google, Amazon	Amazon, own	SoftLayer
	Own container	3	3	2	1	1	2	0	0	2	na	2
	Supported containers	Docker	na	na	na	na	na	na	buildpack	GAE	buildpack, docker	Docker
Integration	User registry	2	1	2	2	3	2	2	2	2	1	2
	Authentication / Authorization	2	2	2	2	2	3	2	2	2	1	2
SLAs	Security	3	2	2	2	2	2	1	1	2	1	2
	Availability - HA	na	2	1	3	3	3	1	1	1	2	2
	Reliability	1	2	3	3	3	3	2	2	2	2	2
	Vertical scalability	na	3	3	1	3	3	2	3	3	3	3
	Horizontal scalability	na	3	3	3	3	3	2	3	3	3	3
Datastores		SQL, K/V	• SQL, • Doc, • Graph, • K/V	• SQL • K/V • Doc	• Column-based, • K/V	• SQL • K/V • Doc • Graph	• SQL • ... • Column • K/V	na	na	3	1	SQL K/V

continued on following page

Table 1. Continued

		Apcera Platform	Heroku	CloudFoundry	Google App Engine	Microsoft Azure	Amazon Web Services	Mendix	CloudControl	AppScale	Deis	Bluemix
Programming models	Languages	3	3	3	3	3	3	1	2	3	2	3
	Frameworks	2	3	3	1	1	2	1	2	2	1	3
Management	Logging	2	3	3	1	2	2	1	1	2	2	3
	Monitoring	2	3	2	2	2	3	2	2	2	2	2
Misc	Open Source	yes, except core	no	yes	no	no	no	has Community Editon	no	yes	yes	based on open source
	Marketplace	yes	yes	yes	yes	yes	yes	yes	yes	no	no	yes

After the authentication in the Editpart, the user can create a new applicationin the system or use an existing one. Generally the sourcecode can be modified in this phase, and the runtime is automatically recognised by the system. The dependenciescan be modified by language specific ways, usually Java has maven *pom* files, Ruby use a *Gemfile*, in Python there is a *requirements text file*, while in Node.js a *package.json*, and so on. The executabletypes and commands can be added to the application, but some defaults are recognised by the system automatically. For example in Ruby on Rails, this is typically a rails server, in Django it is a python <app>/manage.py runserver, and in Node.js it is the main field in package.json. Some configuration variables can be added, these are good for having different settings for separate instances running the same code, for example use different credentials. The addons can provide extra functionality and services like logging, performance monitoring, data storage, etc.

The other option available for the authenticated user is to run the application. The first step is to deploy the application, this is usually made with a VCS or with direct upload, the PaaS system recognises the runtime and the dependencies and builds the application. With the recognised or given execute commands the user can select and run the application on the cloud. When starting more instances the application can be scaled, for example by starting more web frontend instances the application can handle more visitors with the help of a load balancer. To handle a bigger workload some worker instances can be started. To provide high availability is achievedin a similar way. If there is an issue with the latest release of the application, the user can use the rollback feature to restore a previous version. It is useful to have more versions of the application, for example a stable release for production, an unstable beta version with new features to demonstrate, and some developer versions for testing.

The monitoring part is interesting for managers and testers as well, not just for developers. The system events and application logs can be analysed for debugging purposes. The application's performance can be measured, and with the list of the running instance types and number of instances the application's scalability issues can be diagnosed. SSHand other type of connections with a running instance are useful for debugging or running one-time bugfix scripts.Every PaaS provider has their own tools and methods to provide these general features to the users.

The transitions between the main states (Edit, Run, Monitor) are shown with arrows in Figure 1. These state changes should be considered as an iterational application development workflow. As an example, consider the state after implementing a feature when the developer deploys the application. If the application fails, based on the logs the developer can go back to the Edit state, otherwise the Monitor state can be used to analyse the application behaviour, considering scalability. After drawing the conclusions based on the performance, they can return to the Edit state to fix some problems that have risen, or change the number of the running instances for further investigation and testing.

The authors took these identified roles into account for their practical investigation of the most widespread PaaS providers by developing and running a sample application for all of them. The authors introduce their experiences in the next subsection.

Experiences of PaaS Application Development with the Main Providers

In order to study PaaS provider's developer experience from the practical side, the authors decided to create a simple web application and deploy this application to different platforms to see what the biggest providers offer by the time of writing. The authors selected the following providers: Azure (Microsoft Azure, 2015), Heroku (Heroku, 2015), OpenShift (OpenShift, 2015) and Apcera (Apcera Platform, 2015). The researchers also spent considerable time with Cloud Foundry (CloudFoundry, 2015), but the service was very unstable and proved unusable for their purposes. They decided to use BlueMix (Bluemix, 2015) which is strongly based on Cloud Foundry. There were some hindering issues at the beginning, but with each modification that had to be done in order to get an application working at a certain provider, the application became better, more resilient and, in many cases, more convoluted.

The authors created their application in Python (Python, 2015) and Node.js (Node.js, 2015), therefore two versions of the same album manager application were made. While it was not exactly meant for production use, it aims to make use of various PaaS functionalities. During their tests some of the provider's services have changed, e.g. Azure requiring a credit card number even for the free services, and Heroku imposing an obligatory 6 hour waitperiod on free accounts.

The test application is a fairly basic image hosting service. Its components are:

- **Website:** For managing image uploads, comments and albums. The Node.js version also utilises websockets.
- **Worker:** For resizing images and uploading them to storage.

Their aim was to separate the website and the worker instances as much as possible, making them independently scalable and still connected, either through sharing the same code and services. The application has the following requirements:

- A Relational database for storing image, user and album data. While MongoDB (MongoDB, 2015) is more popular, Node.js users were still opted for RDBMS's in order to share the database between both Python and Node.js versions. ORM's have been used in both implementations, for both comfort and practical reasons.
- A Redis server for acting as a basic message queue, a session store and sharing the image processing status through basic keys and/or pubsub.
- A MongoDB server was needed when using the Celery version of the Python worker because it consumed most Redis providers' connection quota.
- Some kind of blobstore to store the images themselves. Current supported backends are Azure, Cloudinary (Cloudinary, 2015) (both with their own SDKs) and local file system, the latter can be used for NFS, too.

In both implementations the workers use the ImageMagick (ImageMagick, 2015) library in one way or another, which gave some complications. When faced with issues with either of these aforementioned services given by the PaaS providers themselves, some third party hosts were used, which offer services even outside of PaaS providers' reach, like:

- **MongoLab** for MongoDb,
- **Redis4You** (Redis4You, 2015) for Redis,
- **ClearDB** (ClearDB, 2015) for MySQL, and
- **Cloudinary** for blob storage (which is an odd one out since it features its own API).

This approach was most necessary on Azure, when all MSSQL libraries on both platforms were unusable and registering a Redis serveror any other service required a credit card. When everything else failed and the application felt very slow, local hosting was used for local testing or in an Azure based Linux VM.

Concerning general deployment issues, every popular web based PaaS provider offers git support. The way they are handling it is more or less uniform, such as following the deployment messages during the push, being able to revert previous versions through the web interface and such. The biggest difference between them is the way of authentication. Azure requires authentication through git itself, while OpenShift and Heroku have their own tools. A minor issue the authors had was that most of their git repos were not empty when creating new apps, but contained a sample application. Whenever they started a new app a local empty repository had to be created, the address given by the provider added as a remote, delete everything, add the remote to the project's local repo, pull it again and finally push it to deploy it. Azure can give an empty repo, so one can skip these initial steps. Sharing the same repository was feasible, the differences of the different platforms were that they only had to be taken into account during the credential setup stage.

As mentioned before, in some cases third party services were used. A lot of PaaS providers have marketplaces, where users can bind services to their applications with different pricing packages that are included in the user's subscription. Most of the time the services work as expected, without any major restrictions or special connection parameters. There are of course some exceptions. A lot of Redis providers require to have the "ready check" parameter disabled. A lot of them require passwords, which cannot be passed through connections strings with some bindings, such as Node's node-redis (node-redis, 2015). Azure's Microsoft hosted Redis service requires SSL by default, which can be disabled. A lot of these functions can only be accessed from the PaaS providers' network, but not from the developer's system. While this is perfectly understandable, for some operations using the REPL from the applications shell was not always feasible. This issue rose while trying to clear some identical MySQL tables, but being denied because of the presence of foreign keys. A SET foreign_key_checks=0; (MySQL table deletion workaround, 2015) instruction can be used in similar situations. Azure solves this issue by providing single IP exceptions to its database firewall and OpenShift by supplying a phpMyAdmin (phpMyAdmin, 2015) interface. Adding command line clients to the app shell could be also a nice solution.

Regarding language-specific requirements, the Python 3 version had a lot of useful libraries not ported yet, such as the majority of the Memcache (Memcache, 2015) ones for caching, gevent (gevent, 2015) for setting up a lightweight server to get around health checks, protobuf (Protocol Buffer, 2015) for precise data formating or supervisord (Supervisord, 2015) for process management. Therefore the requiements were modified as follows:

- **RDBMS:** Handled through the SqlAlchemy ORM, due to most service providers shipping with different database services by default (Apcera and Heroku with PostgreSQL (PostgreSQL, 2015), Azure with MSSQL, 3rd party free MySQL hosts) and it also has an amazing migration framework.
- A **Redis** server for communication between the worker and the website. It can also double as the message queue when the connection count constraints allow it.
- A **MongoDB** indirectly through PyMongo (PyMongo, 2015), because only Celery is using it.
- A **storage backend** to store images, since most service providers don't have any support for permanent file storage. It currently supports
  - **Local Storage:** As basic file operations
  - **Azure Blobstore:** Microsoft's own SDK worked fine
  - **Cloudinary:** Their own SDK(Cloudinary SDK for Python, 2015) worked fine.

For image processing the application originally used the Pillow (Pillow, 2015) library, as used by many Python developers, however installing it was not really user friendly, so a switch was made to Wand (Wand, 2015), an ImageMagick based solution. In the end the authors called convert (convert, 2015) directly on Apcera.

Concerning the Node.js version, creating the application was easier than the Python one. The basic idea of communicating through environment variables of these modern PaaS services remained similar, aside fromsome variable names. The application structure stayed the same, the following libraries were used:

- **Website:** The authors choseExpress 4 (Express, 2015) as every other Node developer. Its session store makes use of Redis as a backend. It notifies the client of the image processing status in real-time through websockets using the Socket.io (Socket.io, 2015) library.
- **Worker:** The same BLPOP queue applies here as well. Invoked as an external process from the website through forever. It also starts its own HTTP server through the default http (Node.js, 2015) module to fool the health check.

Requirements:

- **Database:** Uses Sequelize as the ORM for the same reasons, as it was already behind a Sqlite, MySQL and PostgreSQL database.
- **Redis:** Had some issues with the authentication since most hosts require passwords and by default the localhost Redis instance used by the developers did not. Passing the password in callbacks is a very inelegant solution using the "redis" library. In addition, the Redis connection's ready check setting had to be disabled on external services.
- **Storage:** The authors used easyimage to resize the images, which is an ImageMagick backed solution. For uploading, Cloudinary's and Azure's API worked as expected.

The experiences of the selected providers are listed as follows.

Deploying the Node.js version of the application on OpenShift went easily. The Python version however had a major issue in the early stages of deployment, in which it refused to install packages from the suppliedrequirements.txt. This problem like a system bug, but since the issue hasn't been fixed on such a large system for a long time seems to indicate otherwise. The SSO links on the dashboard to the 3rd party services rarely ever worked. Fortunately, all information needed was in environment variables. Scalability is not very well streamlined, one has to choose whether he wants to scale its app or not when creating it, conversion between these two types isn't possible.

The application-scaling system in Heroku was quite similar to the initial design ideas of the application, especially separating the worker and the web application. Theyuse the same repository, they are independently scalable, and share the same 3rd party services.Initial start-up commands are taken from Foreman's Procfile (Foreman and Procfile, 2015), to save an extra step after deployment.Heroku recently also started its own Redis service (Heroku hosted Redis, 2015), which offers bigger storage that any other competitors for free of charge (20MB vs 10MB).

Since applications on the Azure platform run on Windows-based systems, some major modifications were necessary on the application. Unfortunately, the administration website of Azure was generally slow. It provides a web based Powershell interface.When trying to use the interface to download and extract data from the system the HTTP download command refused to run, referring to a connection setup in

Internet Explorer. They provide a Web Job (Azure Web Job, 2015) abstraction, which allows setting up recurring tasks as: single use, scheduled and continuously running tasks, which shared some point with the design of the worker in the test application. Getting the application to work in a Windows-based environment requies a lot of work, sharing libraries between the web application and the Web Job is difficult.

The service provides many self hosted and third party services. The researchers only used the blobstore through theprovided Azure SDK (Azure SDK for Python, 2015), (Azure SDK for Node, 2015), because the message queue had a really small message size limit, making it unfit for the application.The MSSQL server they providecould have been also a good candidate for testing, but none of the ORM's that wereused (Sequelize (Sequelize, 2015) and SQLAlchemy (SQLAlchemy, 2015)) were supporting MSSQL.With the previous three sharing services between different apps weren't necessary, resulting in multiple registrations on the same email address to the same service.

The way Apcera Platform can share and bind services between applications is really useful, while the distinction between services and providers is not really trivial for the developer at first.It is a matured and well documented system, but it has some interesting quirks.The handling of NFS volumes might be cumbersome. Occasionally mounted volumes disappear and even terminate running applications. By logging in to such controllers via SSH however shows the volume as mounted. Occasionally the application maynot be reachable again, even after unbinding and deleting the NFS services and providers. The way toget the application deployed again was to delete and recreate it. The logs did not contain any proper error messages and reading them yielded very little.The lack of text editors really take away from the SSH's usefulness, resulting in regular redeploys in the application's infant state, which is lengthenedas the staging component downloads every single dependency during each indivudual deployment.

Installing Cloud Foundry through the bosh-lite (Bosh-lite, 2015) based method failed most of the times with a different error every week. The errors ranged from missing deployment manifest files, malconfigured default nginx configurations to dying connections during blob downloads. The authors eventually gave up when VM snapshots could not be restored without the virtual network cards stopping.There were short periods when the service was usable, but after additional efforts to make it more stable, such as installing 3rd party service packs for MySQL and Redis, it refused to work anymore and even restoring snapshots did not recover the previous working state.

In IBM Bluemix persistence had to be handled with special care, because it does not provide any blobstore service so far. The app usesthe following two solutions:

- MongoDB's GridFS feature to store files alongside the database, and
- Cloudinary, a 3rd party service reachable through an API using a Node.js package that specializes in media storage

The only Bluemix (or rather Cloud Foundry) specific step in the install procedure was to read the application's host and port from an environment variable, after that the application was ready to start. Imagemagick was installed on the app's container by default, so that could be used easily. Websockets were also supported outside-the-box.

IBM offers a marketplace for self-hosted and 3rd party services on its marketplace, just like many other PaaS providers. There are ones hosted by IBM itself, including in beta services such as message queues. Since IBM has interest in a company called Compose.io, their services are also plugged into the catalog, including free ones. To access these, however, one must provide his credit card number.

For the original application a Redis server, an SQL server and optionally a MongoDB server were needed.Redis was selected since it could be replaced with MongoDB. Compose.io provided Redis servers required additional service registration, so MongoDB was used instead.

IBM provides an SQL database without any sorts of obligations: a DB2 service. Aside from the Compose.io services, there were also some popular third party ones: ClearDB for MySQL and ElephantSQL for Postgres. During the testing of the application ClearDB and MongoDB were used.

Docker containers created within Bluemix can also be bound as services, which are also visible through environment variables.

The deployment process was simple. The only prerequisite was CloudFoundry's cf command line tool. A developer can deploy either through this tool or through a git repository. The development via the command line tool required only a single command after authentication.

No real special preparations were needed for deployment aside from specifying the required Node version in the package.json file, which installed the newest version without a hitch. During this test the application was uploaded without the Node.js package folder. Those were also downloaded during installation and cached for further deployments.

The Dashboard provides essential functions for managing an application, such as editing the description, managing the instance numbers, allocating resources, binding services through the Catalog, managing routes, settings environment variables and browsing logs in real time.

A feature missed however was some kind of settings option in the start command. This has to be done either though the (optional) Cloud Foundy manifest file, through a Procfile (only the web field is taken into account), or by the application's running environment (e.g. in Node.js's case, the npm run command in package.json)

Bluemix's documentation clearly states that they do not support Heroku's dyno system, meaning that there cannot be two different processes running from the same codebase in different containers. Instead, they suggest uploading the same application into a duplicate app dedicated to the task.

Health checks are done frequently by checking if the application's accepting connections. This means that an app has to have a port open, even if it does not communicate directly.

By the time of evaluating Bluemix, strating an sshconnection into an app's container did not work from command line. On the other hand, they have a web based file browser on the dashboard, however this only supports viewing files.

Docker images can be deployed and bound to apps. To manage these oneneeds to install the appropriate cf plugin, which assumes that Docker is also installed on the developer's machine.

Developer Experience Comparisons

Table 2 shows a comparison of the PaaS providers the authors encountered based on the differences found between them based on the experiences on both platforms.

The following expressions are used in the table:

- **Shareable Service:** In some cases binding the same service to different applications can be useful. A method that doesn't involve sharing the connection string directly by hand can make deployment somewhat easier in special cases.
- **Websocket Support:** A lot of web applications rely on real-time communication through websockets.

Table 2. Comparison table of PaaS functionalities based on application development experiences

	Apcera Platform	Heroku	OpenShift	Azure	BlueMix	Comment
Shareable services	+	-	-	-	+	can be shared by sharing the connection string
Websocket Support	+	+	+	+	+	-
Cached packages	+	+	+	+	+	-
Multiple independent instances of the same app	+	+ (Foreman)	-	+ (Web Job)	-	-
ImageMagick by default	-	+	+	-	+	-
Text editor in shell	-	-	+	-	-	-
Text editor outside of Git	-	-	+ (nano through SSH)	+ (web)	- (read-only)	-
3rd party service marketplace	-	+	+	+	+	-
Tailable logs	+	+	+	+	+	-
Git revertable from web	-	+	-	+	+	-

- **Cached Packages:** Most packages stash already installed packages away when redeploying the application, making the process faster.
- **Multiple Independent Instances of the Same App:** For the lack of better wording. Giving some sort of abstraction to run the same code on different environments independently from each other can make the maintenance easier.
- **ImageMagick Support by Default:** Most Node image processing libs rely on ImageMagick.
- **Text Editor in Shell and Text Editor Outside of Git:** Useful when encountering errors during deployment.
- **3rd Party Service Marketplace:** API and backend for 3rd party support
- **Tailable Logs:** Watching the running instance's output real-time.
- **Git Revertable from Web:** Following the deployment status and reverting mistakes in cases when using Git isn't an option.

Characterising PaaS Providers with Mobile Support

MBaaS (MBaaS wikipedia, 2015)(Mobile Backend as a Service) or also known as BaaS (Backend as a Service) is an emerging cloud category. Pre-built cloud hosted components help the mobile application and web developers to easily have features like data storage, user management, push notifications and connection with social media networks. The applications and the backend can be linked with SDKs (Software Development Kits) and APIs (Application Programming Interface).

There are many MBaaS providers in the market with different type of MBaaSs. Two big categories are the open source solutions and non-open source backends. The targeted applications can be different as well. There are providers to help startups, simple application developers, game developers with fast and easy development and deployment and the capability to scale. There are solutions for enterprises where integration with other systems and securityare important.

The list of the examined solutions in this chapter is not complete, there were some projects with not acceptable quality that were left out. The authors considered the popularity of the provider in the selection process, but the list contains some new, but innovative solutions, too. In these cases the beta state is not a reason to sort out, the vision of the product is remarkable.

Overviewed MBaaS Providers

The Google MBaaS's (Google Mobile Cloud Platform, 2015) biggest advantage is that many cloud services can be used, the server or cloud side is really great. There are some specialized services, for example the image processing service, and some general propose ones like Compute Engine. The storage part is advanced as well, and the big data processing is not a problem. The responsible service for the cloud and client connection is the Google Endpoints (Google Endpoints, 2015), which is just an extension to generate client side SDKs. The SDK is usable, because it can handle custom cloud calls, but requires too much coding.

Parse (Parse, 2015) is really great in the SDKs section, it has many efficient SDKs.The Android SDK is not just a REST call wrapper, it helps the developers with extra features like push notification for devices without Google Cloud Messaging (Kindle) and there is a library for UI elements to help the login implementation. It has a feature to save the data the next possible time when there is connection. The SDK gives sync and async options for every method. It supports mobiles (iOS, Android, Windows Phone, Xamarin, Unity), desktop and web apps (OS X, Windows, JavaScript, PHP) and embedded devices (Arduino, embedded C). The documentation is examplary and the admin site is really simple and useful with many features. The weakness is the lack of integration with enterprise databases and applications, this is the reason why it's not a good choice for business application developers. The CLI deployment method is not user-friendly. All of the SDKs are opensource projects. Parse support the Internet of Things, meaning different sensors can send data to the cloud and can recive push notifications. Beside the general embedded C SDK there are some manufacturer specific SDKs integrated (like Intel).

Backendless (Backendless, 2015) has an advantage of letting the developer host the service on their own or hybrid cloud systems. The most special feature is the media streaming, but this is just for iOS platform. There are some scenarios for working with live or recorded media for example: live video/audio broadcast, recording video/audio content on the server, video/audio chat, video/audio playback for live and on-demand content. Versioning is another great feature, this way the developers can work on a development version next to a stable release.

Amazon (Amazon Mobile, 2015) is a PaaS provider, and they have many "blocks" to build applications with. This allows for more general usage, but not so many details, that could make the developer's job easier. With the three main components (Cognito (User management), Mobile Analytics and Simple Notification Service) the mobile solution is a good piece for the whole Amazon cloud offering. This is still not mature enough for enterprise usage, because the lack of integration and security.

Firebase (Firebase, 2015) offers a secure, real-time, cloud-hosted, NoSQL database with a login service. This solution is specialized for low latency. Many features are missing, some basics like push notification and integration, but surprisingly great applications can be written through the service, as the sample apps greatly demonstrate.

FeedHenry (FeedHenry, 2015) is a Mobile Application Platform for enterprises, with many features. Supports the agile development, integrates with git, has many connectors like Salesforce, SAP and Oracle. It concentrates on security. Helps the reusability, has many plugins, templates and a drag and drop application builder, where the mobile application can be developed without coding.

Appcelerator (Appcelerator, 2015) started as a mobile development tool, to create mobile applications for all platforms with common code written in JavaScript. This main feature has been extended with its own IDE, testing tools and MBaaS features. The MBaaS part is really good for enterprises, it has many connectors, can be deployed with hybrid or fully private clouds. It's a full mobile development platform.

BaaSBox (BaasBox, 2015) is in beta stage by the time of writing, but will probably have a stable release in the near future. It has many features, performance is a priority. It is an open source project with Apache 2 license.

DreamFactory (DreamFactory, 2015) has many install guides for IaaS providers (Docker, Amazon Web Services, Microsoft Azure, Google Cloud Platform, VMware Marketplace, Bitnami Cloud Hosting), for PaaS providers (Red Hat OpenShift, Pivotal Web Services, IBM Bluemix, Heroku) for Desktop Computer (LAMP or WAMP) (Linux, OS X, Windows) IBM SoftLayer, Rackspace Marketplace. For push notification it uses the Amazon SNS. The SDK is moderately good, too general, requires too much coding. On the free hosted version the login window pops up for almost every click.

Strongloop's top features are the modularity, enterprise connectivity, API Explorer, generators, client SDKs. It has some advanced features like geolocation search. StrongLoop Arc seems to be a great tool to visually edit, deploy, and monitor LoopBack (Loopback, 2015)apps.

Apache Usergrid (UserGrid, 2015) is currently undergoing Incubation at the Apache Software Foundation. It already has many basic and some more advanced MBaaS features, and it has a potential to be a great solution.

The Heroku MBaaS solution Helios (Helios, 2015) is in beta stage. The main disadvantage is that it only supports the iOS platform at the time of writing. But the the support of this only platform is great, it has some more advanced features like In-App Purchases, Passbook, Newsstand, Logging and Analytics, A/B testing.

The authors also compared the overviewed PaaS providers with MBaaS support. In the following comparison table, if a property is measured by a number, the number can have 3 different levels. 0 means the provider has not implemented this feature or doesn't work. 1 means the feature is usable and it's on the same level as the average. 2 means the provider implemented it in an outstanding way.

Comparison of MBaaS Providers

The authors compared the PaaS providers based on the following categories:

- **Price:** This category is not really detailed, it is only used to indicate that what kind of prices the product usage requires. It can be time or function limited free trial, pay/month or pay/use. But it is important, because it is a good offer for startups, but if the application has more and more users and the bandwidth is growing the bill can grow extremely big.
- **Open Source:** An open source tool many benefits like security, quality, customizability, etc. If it's open source, the license type is shown too.
- **Hosting:** Some backend can be hosted on optional clouds, even on private clouds, while others are strictly hosted by the provider, and some can have both options. The hosting has more categories,

like multi tenant or dedicated, and if a private cloud hosts the application, the deployment can be managed by the provider or it can be the developer's job.

- **Custom Business Logic:** Can a developer customise the server side code? The type of the customisability can be different, it can be limited to add triggers on data modification or highly customisable when the developers can add their own API methods too.
- **Server Side Language:** If the server side can be customised, it can be done in one or more languages. The support of more languages is preferred because the developers can use the language that is closer to their knowledge and fits more to the task. The reusability is an option here too.
- **Admin Site:** The admin sites main function to manage the applications. The main goal is to be simple and still usable with many features. The admin site helps the developer or the manager to browse the data, send push notifications, see the analytic results and many more.
- **SDKs:** The number of supported platforms is important, because usually an application wants to reach as many people as it's possible with minimal effort. The most common platforms are the Android, iOS and JavaScript, but some providers have many more. The quality is more important than the quantity, it's important to be efficient with a few lines of code and still have the ability to handle custom actions.
- **IoT:** The Internet of Things capability is a new trend, many primitive sensors can provide data, and the cloud can gather the information and analyse it and visualise it.
- **Documentation:** The documentations are evaluated by their understability, accuracy, currency. Usually the documentation is an online website with fresh informations about the platform.
- **Tutorials:** The tutorials evaluated by their coverage, quality and variety. To start using the platform, it's great to have clear step-by-step instructions, and visions for other possibilities.
- **Sample Apps:** The sample apps are evaluated by their connection with real life applications, quality and variety. It's a great help for developers to see a working example with no effort, to see the complexity and usability of the provider's solution.
- **Storage:** This is a basic functionality for MBaaS, but it can have advanced features like file storage and external DB usage capability. The offline capability is a big plus, the synchronization can be a hard task.
- **User Management:** The user management is a basic feature too, It is connected with social media networks, it's a plus if the user can use their account of other sites. Beside the social media networks, LDAP can be used or OpenID. The login and registration is a common task, so it's a good idea to support it with customisable components on the client side.
- **Social Media Networks:** With the support of social media networks the users do not have to deal with the registration process. The most common social media sites are Google, Facebook and Twitter. Deeper integration is an extra, to use other features like Facebook graph search API.
- **Push Notification:** The push notification support for iOS (Apple Push Notification Service) and Android (Google Cloud Messaging), the A/B testing, client to client push notification capability and other extra features are valued.
- **Analytics:** The capability to track built-in user events like installing data, application start time and even custom events.

Table 3 shows a comparison of these providers based on these categories.

Table 3. Comparison of PaaS providers with mobile support

		Google Mobile Backend	Parse	Backendless	Amazon	Firebase	Kumulus	Kinvey
Pricing		free trial; pay/use	limited free version; pay/month	limited free version; pay/ month	limited free version, pay/use	limited free version, pay/month	free developer version, pay/month	free developer version, pay/month
Host		by provider	by provider	by provider, hybrid, or custom	by provider	by provider	by provider	by provider or custom
Open source, license		no	no	no	no	no	no	no
Custom business logic		yes	yes	yes	yes	-	n/a	yes
Scheduled task		yes	yes	n/a	n/a	-	-	n/a
Server side language	**JavaScript**	-	yes	-	-	-	n/a	yes
	Java	yes	-	yes	yes	-	n/a	-
	other	python, php, go	-	-	-	-	n/a	-
Admin site		2	2	2	1	1	1	1
SDKs	**Android**	yes	yes	yes	yes	yes	yes	yes
	iOS	yes	yes	yes	yes	yes	yes	yes
	JS	yes	yes	yes	-	yes	yes	yes
	other	-	.NET, PHP, python, unity, C, etc	.NET, ActionScript	fireOS	-	PHP, Unity	-
SDK		1	2	1	1	1	1	1
IoT		2	2	0	1	1	0	1
Documentation		2	2	2	1	1	1	2
Tutorials		2	2	1	1	1	1	2
Sample apps		1	1	1	1	2	n/a	1
Storage		2	2	2	2	1	1	2
User management		1	2	1	1	1	0	1
Social media networks		yes, Google	yes, FB, Twitter, Google	yes, FB, Twitter	yes, Amazon, FB, Google	yes, Twitter, Google, FB	-	yes, FB, Google
Push notification		1	2	1	1	0	0	n/a
Analytics		1	2	1	2	0	1	0

Table 4. Comparison of PaaS providers with mobile support

		FeedHenry	Appcelerator	BaasBox	DreamFactory	StrongLoop	UserGrid	Helios
Pricing		limited free trial, pay/month	limited free version, pay/month	free	free	free	free	free
Host		custom	by provider, hybrid or custom	by provider or custom	by provider or custom	custom	custom	custom
Open source, license		no	no	yes, Apache 2	yes, Apache	yes, MIT license, or StrongLoop License	yes, Apache	yes, MIT
Custom business logic		yes	yes	yes	yes	yes	yes	n/a
Scheduled task		yes	yes	yes	n/a	n/a	n/a	
Server side language	JavaScript	yes	yes	yes	yes	yes	-	n/a
	Java	-	-	-	-	-	yes	n/a
	other	-	-	-	-	-	-	n/a
Admin site		2	2	1	1	1	1	1
SDKs	Android	yes	yes	yes	yes	yes	yes	-
	iOS	yes	yes	yes	yes	yes	yes	yes
	JS	yes	yes	yes	yes	yes	yes	-
	other	WP8, HTML5, Xamarin, Cordova, Appcelerator	Windows, Blackberry, HTML5	-	WP, Titanium	-	ruby, .NET, PHP	-
SDK		2	2	1	1	1	1	2
IoT		0	0	0	1	0	0	0
Documentation		2	2	1	1	1	1	0
Tutorials		2	1	1	1	1	0	1
Sample apps		1	1	1	1	n/a	0	0
Storage		2	2	2	1	1	1	1
User management		1	1	2	1	1	1	1
Social media networks		n/a	yes, FB, Twitter, LinkedIn	yes, FB, Twitter, Google	n/a	yes, FB, Google, Twitter	yes, FB	n/a
Push notification		1	1	1	1	1	n/a	1
Analytics		2	2	1	0	0	0	1

COMPARISON DISCUSSIONS

PaaS Summary

All of the overviewed providers support the major development languages used nowadays. Providers can be grouped in two categories based on their size. The bigger providers, like Google, Amazon, Microsoft, they have been in the PaaS market for some time, so they have their own solution, and host on their own servers, integrate their solutions into their bigger infrastructures.

The smaller PaaS providers (e.g. CloudControl, AppScale, Deis, Mendix) are trying to offer some interesting features on the market, and have interesting ideas that are not available with the big providers, such as hosting on multiple cloud backends, running the PaaS service on the premise of the customer, or a new way of creating apps thereby shortening the time-to-market of the application. These smaller providers usually have their backends at larger providers, mostly at Amazon. This presents a dependency and a connection of reliability for them. If there is an outage with an IaaS provider that they use, than their product will be offline as well. Some of the providers (Mendix, AppScale) aim to provide an abstraction layer between different PaaS providers, with some kind of middleware or API system. The goal of this is to remove the dependency on a particular PaaS provider (to prevent vendor lock-in), and to make the applications more portable between providers.

The authors' recomandation differ based on the goals, but in general the Heroku provider provides had really great overall experience. The Google App Engine should be considered as a good choice because of the other Google services which can be cooperated with each other, and this kind of Google ecosystem clearly has its own benefits. But every situation has different priorities.The open source feature can be a major requirement in many cases.

MBaaS Summary

Most of the overviewed MBaaS solutions have some common features. Most of them are the basic features, but they still represent big categories. There are some extra capabilities for every feature that makes the solution special, even leading in some area.

The storage is one of the basic features, it enables to store, modify, delete and load data to and from the cloud. It can have some special advanced capabilities, like connectors to external DBs and systems, real time data sharing, offline working, data synchronization. The user management is also a basic feature, it can have specialities like using other systems (LDAP, OpenID, OAtuh, FB, Google, Twitter) or the capability to "follow" other users. The social media network integration usually ends in the existing user account usage, but it can have full integration, for example the capability of using the Facebook SDK and the FB Graph API. The push notification can be used for chat messaging and A/B testing. Analytics have key functionality to track the users and analyze them, the visualised data, and generated reports can help to accomplish these tasks. The developers are interested in crash reports, but the management probably more curious about the user behaviour. The other important feature is the server side customizability capability, which can have multiple levels, starting from database like data modification triggers to custom business logics and scheduled jobs. The most supported client side platforms are the Android, iOS and JavaScript. The support means usually just a generated SDK, but some services provide more features, such as UI components, utility modules. The viewpoint can be different, sometimes the cloud is the main focus, and the client side is just for minimal interaction and visualisation, but sometimes the client platform has the focus and the cloud side is just a helper tool. The admin site is important as well, as it has many features and options, but it must stay simple and user friendly.

The solutions can be categorised by the targeted developers for example. Some of them are for start-ups and indie developers, their goal is to create simple, fancy mobile applications as fast and efficiently as possible and still with little investments (at the beginning). Others are for big enterprise companies where the security, integration, analytics and monitoring are the key features. The other possible way to distinguish the overviewed solutions is based on their open source nature. At this point the open source projects are mostly in beta versions and only capable of basic features, but they have the advantages of the freedom of the deployment and the community support. Commercial providers usually provide SLAs.

Surprisingly, many companies have MBaaS solutions. There is a big chance that the ones with very special skill sets can satisfy special needs and survive in the long run. But the universal, general solutions can have a bright future too, but their MBaaS features are just one of the many other features to support the whole development, deployment and testing of the mobile and web development. These are can be called as Mobile Development Platforms. Most of the providers use Amazon's cloud as hosting, and Amazon has its own MBaaS solution. There is space for many MBaaS solutions because of the specializations (targeted developers, real time capability, streaming, game features, etc.)

There are many PaaS providers, and much more different requirements for every project, so it is not an easy task to decide which one is the best, but the authors conclude that Parse is a good choice in most of the cases. It has a strong background (by Facebook support), evolves fast and it's really userfriendly. The Parse SDKs are all open source projects, and they are not afraid of innovation. Further looking the Google MBaaS solution is a great option considering the opportunities offered by Google. As with the PaaS projects, every situation is different: if it is a small and simple project FireBase can be ideal in some cases, or BaaSBox has an adventage because of its open-sourceness.

The biggest challenges the authors identified are security problems, integration problems, the offline working capability and the automatic data synchronization features.

SUMMARY

In this chapter the authors gave an overview of the state-of-the-art Platform-as-a-Service solutions that are used to develop applications over clouds, therefore can be used to manage applications in cloud federations. Basic capabilities wereinvestigated of the most advanced providers: what levels of developer experience they offer, how they follow recent trends in cloud application development. Primary sources for this investigation were public documentation of the relevant tools, research publications and trial or demo versions where applicable. Developer experience was measured by creating and executing sample applications with some of these PaaS tools. Most of the examined providers proved to be usable, and some of them have special strengths. Comparison tables and classifications have been created for highlighting the generally supported and lacking functionalities.

ACKNOWLEDGMENT

The research leading to these results has received funding from Ericsson Hungary Ltd.

REFERENCES

Amazon Mobile. (2015, May). *Amazon*. Retrieved from http://aws.amazon.com/mobile/

Amazon Web Services. (2015, May). *Amazon*. Retrieved from http://aws.amazon.com/

Apcera Platform. (2015, May). Retrieved from https://www.apcera.com/continuum/

Appcelerator. (2015, May). Retrieved from http://www.appcelerator.com

AppScale. (2015, May). Retrieved from http://www.appscale.com/

Azure SDK for Node. (2015, May). *Github*. Retrieved from https://github.com/Azure/azure-sdk-for-node

Azure SDK for Python. (2015, May). *Github*. Retrieved from https://github.com/Azure/azure-sdk-for-python

Azure Web Job. (2015, May). *Microsoft*. Retrieved from https://azure.microsoft.com/en-us/documentation/articles/web-sites-create-web-jobs/

BaasBox. (2015, May). Retrieved from www.baasbox.com

Backendless. (2015, May). Retrieved from www.backendless.com

Bluemix. (2015, November). Retrieved from https://console.ng.bluemix.net/

Bosh-lite. (2015, May). Retrieved from https://github.com/cloudfoundry/bosh-lite

Clear, D. *B*. (2015, May). Retrieved from https://www.cleardb.com/

CloudControl. (2015, May). Retrieved from https://www.cloudcontrol.com/

CloudFoundry. (2015, May). Retrieved from http://cloudfoundry.org/

Cloudinary. (2015, May). Retrieved from http://cloudinary.com/

Cloudinary SDK for Python. (2015, May). *Github*. Retrieved from https://github.com/cloudinary/pycloudinary

convert. (2015, May). Retrieved from http://www.imagemagick.org/script/convert.php

David Cunha, P. N. (2013). A Platform-as-a-Service API Aggregator. In Advances in Information Systems and Technologies (pp. 807-818).

David Cunha, P. N. (2014). PaaS Manager: A Platform-as-a-Service Aggregation. *Computer Science and Information Systems*, *11*(4), 1209–1228. doi:10.2298/CSIS130828028C

Deis. (2015, May). Retrieved from http://deis.io/

DreamFactory. (2015, May). Retrieved from http://www.dreamfactory.com/

Dzone. (2015, May). *Guide to Cloud Development*. Retrieved from http://dzone.com/research/2015-guide-to-cloud-development

Express. (2015, May). Retrieved from http://expressjs.com/

FeedHenry. (2015, May). Retrieved from http://www.feedhenry.com/

Firebase. (2015, May). Retrieved from www.firebase.com

Foreman and Procfile. (2015, May). Retrieved from http://ddollar.github.io/foreman/

gevent. (2015, May). Retrieved from http://www.gevent.org/

Google App Engine. (2015, May). *Google*. Retrieved from https://cloud.google.com/appengine/

Google Endpoints. (2015, May). Retrieved from https://cloud.google.com/mobile/endpoints/

Google Mobile Cloud Platform. (2015, May). *Google*. Retrieved from https://cloud.google.com/solutions/mobile/

Helios. (2015, May). Retrieved from http://helios.io/

Heroku. (2015, May). Retrieved from https://www.heroku.com/

Heroku hosted Redis. (2015, May). *Heroku*. Retrieved from https://addons.heroku.com/heroku-redis

Hoefer, C., & Karagiannis, G. (2010). Taxonomy of cloud computing services. Proceedings of the 2010 IEEE GLOBECOM Workshops (GC Wkshps), Miami, FL, USA (pp. 1345 - 1350).

ImageMagick. (2015, May). Retrieved from http://www.imagemagick.org/script/index.php

Kolb, S. W. G. (2014). Towards Application Portability in Platform as a Service. *Proceedings of the 2014 IEEE 8th International Symposium on Service Oriented System Engineering (SOSE)* (pp. 218 - 229).

Loopback. (2015, May). Retrieved from http://loopback.io/

Luis Rodero-Merinoa, L. M. (2012). *Building safe PaaS clouds: A survey on security in multitenant software platforms* (pp. 96–108). Computers & Security.

MBaaS. (2015, May 8). *Wikipedia*. Retrieved from http://en.wikipedia.org/wiki/Mobile_Backend_as_a_service

Memcache. (2015, May). Retrieved from http://memcached.org/

Mendix. (2015, May). Retrieved from https://www.mendix.com/

Michael Armbrust, A. F. (2009). *Above the Clouds: A Berkeley View of Cloud.*

Microsoft Azure. (2015, May). *Microsoft*. Retrieved from http://azure.microsoft.com/

Mongo, D. B. (2015, May). Retrieved from https://www.mongodb.org/

MySQL table deletion workaround. (2015, May). Retrieved from http://stackoverflow.com/questions/2300396/force-drop-mysql-bypassing-foreign-key-constraint

node-redis. (2015, May). *Github*. Retrieved from https://github.com/mranney/node_redis

Node.js. (2015, May). Retrieved from https://nodejs.org/

Node.js HTTP module. (2015, May). Node.js. Retrieved from https://nodejs.org/api/http.html

OpenShift. (2015, May). Retrieved from https://www.openshift.com/

Parse. (2015, May). Retrieved from www.parse.com

phpMyAdmin. (2015, May). Retrieved from http://www.phpmyadmin.net/home_page/index.php

Pillow. (2015, May). Retrieved from https://python-pillow.github.io/

Pivotal. (2014, August). PaaS comparison. Retrieved from http://www.slideshare.net/Pivotal/paa-s-comparison2014v08

Postgre, S. Q. L. (2015, May). Retrieved from http://www.postgresql.org/

Protocol Buffer. (2015, May). Retrieved from https://github.com/google/protobuf/

PyMongo. (2015, May). Retrieved from http://api.mongodb.org/python/current/

Python. (2015, May). Retrieved from https://www.python.org/

Rajkumar Buyyaa, C. S. (2009). Cloud computing and emerging IT platforms: Vision, hype, and reality for delivering computing as the 5th utility. In Future Generation Computer Systems (pp. 599–616).

Redis4You. (2015, May). Retrieved from http://redis4you.com/

Rimal, B., Choi, E., & Lumb, I. (2009). A Taxonomy and Survey of Cloud Computing Systems. *Proceedings of the Fifth International Joint Conference on INC, IMS and IDC, NCM '09*, Seoul (pp. 44 - 51).

Sellami, M., Yangui, S., Mohamed, M., & Tata, S. (2013). PaaS-Independent Provisioning and Management of Applications in the Cloud. *Proceedings of the 2013 IEEE Sixth International Conference on Cloud Computing (CLOUD)*, Santa Clara, CA, USA (pp. 693 - 700).

Sellami, M. Y. S. (2013). PaaS-Independent Provisioning and Management of Applications in the Cloud. *Proceedings of the 2013 IEEE Sixth International Conference on Cloud Computing (CLOUD)*, Santa Clara, CA, USA (pp. 693 - 700).

Sequelize. (2015, May). Retrieved from http://docs.sequelizejs.com/en/latest/

Socket.io. (2015, May). Retrieved from http://socket.io/

SQLAlchemy. (2015, May). Retrieved from http://www.sqlalchemy.org/

Supervisord. (2015, May). Retrieved from http://supervisord.org/

Twelve-Factor app. (2015, May). Retrieved from http://12factor.net/

UserGrid. (2015, May). Retrieved from http://usergrid.incubator.apache.org/

Wand. (2015, May). Retrieved from http://docs.wand-py.org/en/0.4.0/

Yanpei Chen, V. P. (2010). *What's New About Cloud Computing Security? EECS Department,* University of California, Berkeley, CA, USA.

Section 2
Practice and Experience

Chapter 5
Highly Available Fault–Tolerant Cloud Database Services

Chetan Jaiswal
University of Missouri Kansas City, USA

Vijay Kumar
University of Missouri Kansas City, USA

ABSTRACT

Legacy database systems manage transactions under a concurrency control and a recovery protocol. The underlying operating system creates transaction execution platform and the database executes transactions concurrently. When the database system fails then the recovery manager applies "Undo" and/or "Redo" operations (depending upon the recovery protocol) to achieve the consistent state of the database. The recovery manager performs these set of operations as required by transaction execution platform. The availability of "Virtual" machines on cloud has given us an architecture that makes it possible to eliminate the effect of system or transaction failure by always taking the database to the next consistent state. We present a novel scheme of eliminating the effect of such failure by applying transaction "roll-forward" which resumes its execution from the point of failure. We refer to our system as AAP (Always Ahead Processing). Our work enables cloud providers to offer transactional HA-DBMS as an option that too with multiple data sources not necessarily relational.

We are what our thoughts have made us; so take care about what you think. Words are secondary. Thoughts live; they travel far. - Swami Vivekananda

1. INTRODUCTION

Cloud computing provides a global data management platform that is capable of satisfying data processing needs of all types of customers (individuals, organizations, etc.) It has changed the way data are managed (processing and data storage). The cloud exploits the power of virtualization in managing all its activities including transaction management. It has made the conventional way of dealing with

DOI: 10.4018/978-1-5225-0153-4.ch005

information nearly obsolete by offering a more user-friendly and need-matching computing platform to its users. Although users can have their desired computing platform, many issues still need innovative solutions to make the platform universally acceptable. One such issue is to provide high availability (HA) of a processing entity to provide database Fault Tolerance (FT) management services. These properties still remain complex and expensive to achieve. HA makes sure that irrespective of failures, the system is available whenever a user needs it. If the system is available 90% of the time then it is called as "One Nine" availability, if it is available 95% of the time then it is called as "Two Nines" and if it is available 99.999% of the times then it is called "Five Nines". FT systems are those systems that continue to work, possibly at a reduced level, rather than entirely failing (High Availability, n.d.) (Fault Tolerance, n.d.).

HA with FT can be achieved through hardware (replicated processors) or through software (advanced database architecture and commodity server and storage technology). Our goals are to make transaction management (processing and recovery) on the cloud cost-effective and to achieve HA of "Five Nines" or more. We achieve this by eliminating the effect of transaction and system failures on transaction processing. A natural inclination to do so is to alter or to extend the conventional data processing approaches for the cloud. This, however, would not work satisfactorily because of the following reasons.

A. It is not likely to utilize cloud resources efficiently and datacenters may become a bottleneck because they are geographically dispersed. A conventional approach assumes that databases are in the vicinity of the processing units.

B. Cloud virtualization can be exploited to achieve HA in a much better way than it is done in (Minhas, et al., 2013).

C. A conventional DBMS calls for a relational system at the core. The current trends is to use an RDF (Resource Description Framework), KV (Key-Value) or some other data format for information processing, but it creates a major challenge for the deployment of TM-DM (Transaction Manager-Data Manager) with ACID semantics on the cloud. We refer to a TM-DM model as a conventional RDBMS solution where components such as data management, concurrency control, and recovery management are bundled together. For further information refer to (Bernstein, Hadzilacos, & Goodman, 1987).

D. FT and HA are very expensive on conventional TM-DM systems because they need two completely replicated physical machines running in a lockstep fashion.

2. OUR IDEA

In conventional database systems, some serialization technique is used to execute transactions and "undo" or "redo" (or a combination of them is used to recover from) transaction or system failures. A checkpointing operation is used to reduce the cost of recovery (Bernstein, Hadzilacos, & Goodman, 1987). Undo and redo operations are expensive and do not help much in achieving our measure of HA and FT. Our idea is to eliminate the effect of failure from database processing. We introduce the idea of "roll-forward" to achieve our objective. A roll-forward of a transaction always takes its execution forward and eventually commits. Note that a roll-forward operation is different from a redo. In this chapter we refer to our system as Always Ahead Processing (AAP).

Undo and redo are executed by the database system in order to reach a consistent state. An undo operation is required in a situation when an uncommitted transaction is allowed to write on the database (update the database). Should this transaction fail (due to system failure or user initiated abort), the database contains the effect of a failed transaction making it inconsistent. These uncommitted updates must be removed from the database. Since a database system always follows a write ahead logging (WAL) protocol, the before image (BFIM) and after image (AFIM) of the updates are available in the transaction log. A recovery system installs the BFIMs of the failed transaction onto the database (by running another transaction), and thus undoing its effects that push the database to its last consistent state (Figure 1). A redo operation is required in a situation when a transaction is allowed to commit before the updates it made are written on the database. System failure at this point (after restart) will not be consistent since it contains partial updates of a committed transaction. In order to push the database to the next consistent state, the recovery system installs all AFIMs of this transaction onto the database (recall that every operation made by transaction is logged). In general, during recovery, the recovery manager applies undo to some transactions and redo to some transactions.

In our roll-forward, a transaction resumes forward execution from the point of interruption (resumption point). Unlike a conventional RDBMS' recovery system, which applies undo/redo operations, AAP takes a different approach on transaction failures. It identifies that if a transaction (or transactions) failure occurs because of a system or machine failure, then there is no need to abort and undo the transaction; instead, it takes the execution further from the point of interruption. We call this operation a roll-forward.

Figure 1. Undo

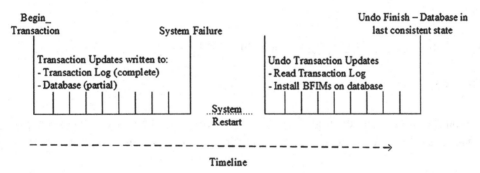

Figure 2. Redo

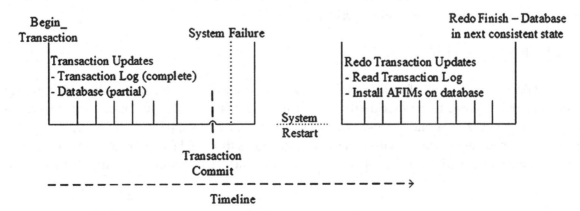

Figure 3. Failure and resumption

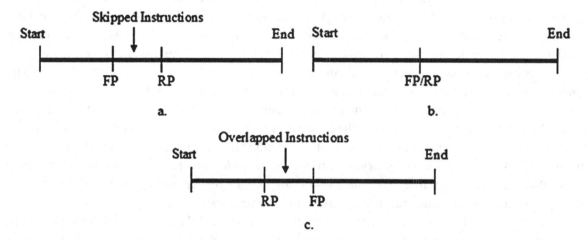

In order to work, a roll-forward requires state information and a back-up machine. Since this is the core of our approach, let us understand the roll-forward process with Figure 3. We assume

- **RP – Resumption Point (Interruption Point):** The point from where the transaction resumes forward execution.
- **FP – Failure Point:** The point where the execution of a transaction is interrupted because of some failure.

We envision three cases: Case 1, Case 2, and Case 3 (Figure 3).

Case 1: FP < RP

Resumption starts at a point that is greater than the failure point. This case will never happen, because its roll-forward will skip a few instructions resulting in an incorrect transaction execution. (Figure 3a)

Case 2: FP = RP

This is an ideal case. Here, the failed transaction begins forward execution exactly from the instruction of the transaction where the failure occurred. (Figure 3b)

Case 3: FP > RP

The failed transaction rolls-forward (forward execution) prior to the failure point. Although, this may re-execute some of the instructions of the transaction, this does not affect the data consistency. (Figure 3c)

We consider case-3, because case-2 is a special case of case-3. We define a threshold $T_{Overlap}$ that limits a worst case upper bound on the number of instructions that will be re-executed in a roll-forward (case-3). Our approach tries to reduce the $T_{Overlap}$ to a minimum (can be zero, case-2). In other words, we try to reduce the distance between the FP and RP on the execution line. $T_{Overlap}$ represents the distance between the FP and RP and thus, "$T_{Overlap} = FP - RP$" as shown in Figure 3.

The introduction of roll-forward helps us to achieve HA and FT for a DBMS for the cloud. We have discussed how this works in detail in section 4. In the current scenario, if a customer requires FT and HA just for the database service he rents, he has to pay for HA/FT for the whole VM (Virtual Machine) instance on which the service is provided. Also, the service provider has to create a new back-up VM on a different physical host and has to run two VMs in a lock-step fashion. This is still quite expensive for the customer and also for the service provider. Under our system, the customer can rent the HA/FT database services at a much lower cost.

We observe that the progress on achieving HA and FT for the cloud have been relatively slow because of several reasons. First, an RDBMS is a highly successful tool in Internet Client-Server technology for banking and finance sectors and even for web services. The cloud, in comparison, is still in its infant stage and lack desirable features, especially in security and system reliability. Second, most works have been focused mainly on deployment models and networking solutions. Third, over the last few years several NoSQL systems have implemented scalability, elasticity, and performance guarantees targeting OLTP and Web workloads that traditionally relied on a standard relational database. As authors of (Kyriazis, 2013) have mentioned, with the evolution of the cloud, a concept that hasn't yet completely evolved is the RDBMS. This is our effort to add to the evolution of relational systems. The SQL-like RDBMS, as offered by Amazon's RDS or Microsoft's SQL Azure, are not any different than their desktop versions. The only difference is reliability (because of replication) as we have covered in our literature review. Few works have been done in the past to extend the concept of an RDBMS to the federated cloud as a partitioned distributed database system with each partition independent or autonomous. This step (known as the Fault Tolerant Option, FTO) to some extent makes the system FT right down to each partition. This is not a new concept in the database world, many works have gone in this direction.

In an RDBMS, many different components such as Recovery Manager (RM), Concurrency Control (CCM), TP-Monitor (Transaction Processing Monitor), etc., work in sync. This model is commonly known as the TM-DM model (Bernstein, Hadzilacos, & Goodman, 1987) that binds the database, the underlying operating system, and communications among them in one package in which the user submits the request and receives a result. It also does load balancing, performance monitoring, fault monitoring, etc. A TP-Monitor may be built upon an ULT (user level thread) providing a child thread to each newly created transaction, or it can also use server classes (for further details please refer (Philip & Eric, 2009). In a conventional DBMS, the recovery manager applies a transaction roll-back followed by an (optional) transaction restart and redo. A conventional DBMS is inherently FT because the restart procedure takes the system to a consistent state, but it comes at a higher cost. Another way to achieve FT and HA in such systems is to run another physical machine (as a secondary replica) in parallel to the primary database machine that will imitate the state of the primary. This is likely to work but would be prohibitively expensive. We observe that there is actually no cost-effective way to achieve HA and FT in conventional systems.

In today's database systems more than 90% of transactions commit. If a failure (machine or system or hardware) happens then most of the transactions are redone. For example, an IMS Fast Path, (IMS Fast Path Solutions Guide, 1997) which is equipped with large RAM recovers from failure mainly by redoing transactions. This does improve recovery performance, but other issues (logging, database updates, etc.) affect the performance and cannot be eliminated from the underlying platform. AAP on the other hand continues the execution of incomplete active transactions (rolls forward) irrespective of a host failure. It has the following advantages:

- Reduces the cost of achieving HA/FT
- Provides flexibility and robustness
- Increases availability
- Improves throughput and response time
- Efficient resource utilization

3. LITERATURE REVIEW

We review relevant earlier works and illustrate the innovation of our scheme. The work presented in (Lomet, Fekete, Weikum, & Zwilling, 2009) deals with the de-coupling of conventional transaction management that can be implemented in a non-persistent cloud deployment model. In other words, the authors have proposed an architecture that unbundles the transaction component (TC) of the database with the data component (DC). This is an interesting and practical approach towards cloud deployments because cloud may have multiple heterogeneous databases. As noted in (Lomet, Fekete, Weikum, & Zwilling, 2009), unbundling a TC with a DC provides a better scalable and flexible model for data processing. However, this work lacks the HA/FT feature.

The works presented in (Minhas, et al., 2013) which is based on (Cully, et al., 2008) deal with the HA of a conventional DBMS on a VM instead of a physical host. Their architecture needs complete replication of the database at 2 physical hosts; one running the primary VM and the other, the secondary or backup VM. It is relatively harder to deploy this architecture on the cloud because the platform lacks scalability and flexibility. In other words, its requirements significantly affect the efficiency of the scheme, which is likely to get worse in real world scenario, because here a service provider could have tens of physical servers and hundreds of data storage elements running thousands of transactions.

Amazon's RDS (AWS | Amazon Relational Database Service (RDS), n.d.) is a deployment model provisioned and managed by Amazon. It provides multiple database (DB) instances each of which could be MySQL, Oracle, Microsoft SQL Server or PostgreSQL. It also provides HA by creating a standby instance along with primary and then synchronously replicating the primary to a standby database instance. They create the standby instance in a different availability zone (AZ); that is, in a different physical cluster. This replication provides HA for the database in case of infrastructure failure (for instance, hardware failure, storage failure, or network disruption). This idea is pretty similar to (Minhas, et al., 2013) which ran a primary machine and secondary replica in a lock-step fashion.

The authors of *ElasTras* (Das, Agrawal, & El Abbadi, 2013) proposed a solution that deals with the issue of scalability and elasticity of the data stored in the cloud. It extends elasticity while providing scalable transactional data access. It contains an HTM (High level transaction manager) that decides whether it can execute the transaction locally or has to route it to a suitable OTM (Owning Transaction Manager) that has exclusive rights to the data accessed by the transaction. It also has an MM (Metadata Manager) that contains all the critical state information of the system. There is another layer where the data are actually stored and they call it the distributed storage layer. Essentially, because of the partitioning of the database, it cannot provide global ACID guarantees, and that is why it only offers it to the transactions limited to a partition. The issue with such a prototype is that though it uses a partial decoupled architecture, it doesn't support a heterogeneous data configuration. Furthermore, the authors mention the replication of the system state or MM but how it would provide the HA for transactions is not clear and they haven't provided any metrics for the same. AAP, on the other hand, takes a set of heterogeneous databases (federated, multi-tenant, or multi-cloud) to begin with, decouples the execution and storage protocols of these databases, and on that provides ACID guarantees, Scalability, HA and FT for execution semantics, i.e., transactions and data storage. Based on this, we observe that AAP is more flexible, scalable, and cost-effective than (Das, Agrawal, & El Abbadi, 2013).

AAP compares well with (Elmore, Das, Agrawal, & El Abbadi, 2011) that is a live migration solution in shared nothing databases in a coupled database architecture. Note that there is a big difference between Live Migration and High Availability. Live migration is a one time job but HA is a continuing monitoring task to detect failure and it remains active until the service is requested. If failure is detected, the HA solutions tend to do a transparent failover so that the user doesn't notice the change in the service point. Although they look similar and might use similar techniques, HA is more complex because it deals with a transparent failover along with failure detection. Live migration, on the other hand, might not even be aware of a failure.

Spanner (Corbett, et al., 2013), a product of Google, is a distributed database that distributes data on a global scale and supports distributed transactions. Its primary focus is to manage cross-datacenter replication and partitioning. The idea of global scale data partitioning and replication improves availability, locality, and disaster recovery. It uses a commit timestamp in order to provide *linearizability* (Corbett, et al., 2013). In order to mark a consistent and synchronous timestamp, it uses a TrueTime API. Since Bigtable (Chang, et al., 2008) can be difficult to use by applications that consist of complex and changing schema, engineers from Google came up with another solution referred to as the Megastore (Baker, et al., 2011). It combines the scalability of NoSQL with the strong consistency of an RDBMS. It also provides ACID semantics over partitioned data processing. It is a good model that deals with schemas, partitioning, and synchronous replication and achieves HA to some extent. Because of its semi-relational data model and support for synchronous replication, it offers a relatively poor write throughput. In both, Spanner and Megastore, the transactions are strongly bound to the location where the data are stored using a homogenous data model.

We claim that our scheme offers HA by unbundling the transactional services from data storage and by simplifying the services for a global cloud deployment. It also has the ability to provision ACID transactional services over multi-type data stores (RDBMS/KV store/RDF etc.).

4. ALWAYS AHEAD PROCESSING

In this section, we focus on the recovery service of AAP for the cloud database. To achieve this, we use the unbundled (Lomet, Fekete, Weikum, & Zwilling, 2009) approach of transaction processing.

AAP replaces transaction redo by transaction roll-forwards for achieving failure-free transaction execution. Thus, in the presence of a system/hardware failure, it continues the forward processing of transactions as if no failure occurred. If there is a pause or an obstruction during the execution of transactions, AAP continues roll forward from the point of the pause. Note that in some situations a transaction roll-back cannot be avoided. For example, in a deadlock resolution, one of the transactions has to be rolled back. AAP takes care of such situations efficiently.

The cloud provides an ideal structure for developing AAP. It achieves two things: first it decouples data processing with data storage and makes the DBMS suitable for the cloud, and second, it revisits FT/HA specific to the cloud DBMS. It enables a service provider to provide flexibility to a customer in terms of an SLA (Service Level Agreement). AAP, unlike (Minhas, et al., 2013), creates intelligent snapshots of different sections of the transaction execution instead of doing a blind copy of the whole primary VM to the secondary VM. We do not have to log disks (.vmdk or .xvd) except for the virtual memory that belongs to the TP Monitor. This optimizes the whole process since it generates the least amount of traffic and data to be replicated or stored on the secondary VM. The service provider, using AAP, can now customize the FT/HA process and thus can provide service using the least amount of resources and network usage. In the following sub-sections, we present the architecture and workings of AAP. We begin with a conventional transaction processing scenario for continuity.

4.1. Current Transaction Processing Scenario

A TP monitor is a database software module responsible for creating, binding, executing and managing transactions. A transaction comes as input and is bound to an appropriate Transaction Server (TS). The TS is an application program that executes a transaction. The TP-Monitor does the following:

A. Accepts input from clients in a predefined message semantics
B. Examines the input requests to ascertain the type of request
C. Initiates and starts an appropriate transaction class (depending upon the type)
D. Commits/aborts the transaction
E. Acknowledges the client about the outcome of the transaction

A TP monitor acts like an API for the user's transactions and provides a layer of abstraction. It binds the database, the underlying operating system, and the communications as one package in which the user submits the request and receives a result (commit or abort). It also does load balancing, performance monitoring, fault monitoring, etc. (Philip & Eric, 2009). TS is invoked by a TP Monitor when a transaction request is received. We call this event "binding" (TS is bound to a transaction request and the state of this request).

There are a number of ways of mapping the TP Monitor and TS to operating system processes or threads (Philip & Eric, 2009). The most significant are

- **Use of ULT (User Level Thread Library):** A ULT library provides a clean approach to implement multithreading with a very small overhead. A ULT system has a different code and different execution for each thread and uses a single shared memory, as shown in Figure 4.

For example, a TP Monitor can implement multithreading and run a TS (bind to a transaction) in each thread. These worker threads can easily communicate with each other since they all share the process and memory. The operating system is unaware of this setup and it executes a TM process as any other process. However, this setup has a problem. Let us consider that one thread is blocked (due to I/O), then the operating system will assume that the process is blocked and therefore, it will suspend the process. In reality, there can be several threads that are in ready state. This issue can be remedied if the TP Monitor can trap any such thread's operation. By doing this, it can actually send an asynchronous message to the

Figure 4. ULT

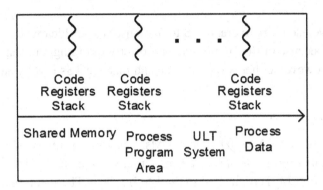

I/O controller and request to make a software interruption when the operation is complete. In this way, the TP Monitor can schedule other threads that are in a ready state, leaving the thread that requires I/O to wait. The advantage of using this approach is that it gives a clean execution structure in the form of an ULT, but the disadvantage is that each I/O has to go through the TP Monitor.

- **Use of Server Classes:** Server classes emulate ULT systems since they have a number of benefits. As shown in Figure 5, a single threaded TP Monitor can bind incoming transaction requests to the available TS Processes (single threaded). Any TS process can communicate to other TS processes using the inter-process communication service provided by their operating system. However, the TP Monitor still monitors the workings and state of each TS process.

   A pool of processes (single threaded) emulates a multithreading model of an ULT system. If a TS is implemented in this way, then each TS can run a transaction inside an operating system level process. This approach has advantages in the sense that a TP Monitor doesn't have to trap the I/O of each TS, thus, each TS can be blocked individually without affecting the whole system. This also avoids any conflict since in this model, the operating system is in charge of scheduling.

   A request from a client can result in the creation of one or more TSs (in the ULT or Server Classes), each under the control of a TP Monitor. This is a required control since creation, management, commit, abort, etc., are performed by the TP Monitor. Apparently, the TP Monitor has the privilege to monitor

Figure 5. Server Classes

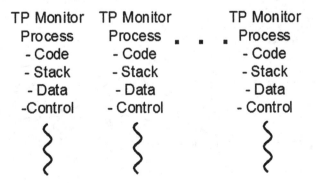

each TS's execution state. We also refer to the TP-Monitor as an HA-Monitor (High Availability Monitor) in this chapter.

In our validations, we used *fork* to create TS to demonstrate our idea while TP Monitor runs as the parent process. This is because of the simplicity, ease of programming and implementation associated with *fork* system call. However, either ways to create and manage TSs is fully adaptable in our scheme.

4.2. Architecture

Figure 6 shows the architecture of AAP. It uses two VMs; VM_p as the primary VM and VM_x as the backup VM. To record the execution progress, it uses a Log Server (LS) maintained at a separate location. The state of the TP-Monitor of VM_p is replicated to the LS for VM_x. There can be many transactions running on VM_p, all under the control of the HA-Monitor. In order to attain HA, instead of checkpointing the whole VM, AAP takes application level checkpointing that reduces the amount of memory to be checkpointed and in turn, reduces the communication costs. We have also designed a Replication Agent Stub (RAS) that is responsible for performing checkpointing and communicating with peer RASs at the LS (refer to section 4.3). Since concurrency control and recovery are both necessary for satisfying the ACID guarantee, we also use an LS for storing the transaction log (section 4.4) and Lock Manager (LM) for providing transaction isolation (section 4.5). AAP also provides a transparent failover by configuring the VM_x with the same IP address as that of VM_p. The HA-Monitor (hence, the transactions) is rolled forward from the point of failure with the same ports and state. We observe that this is quite the standard way to achieve a transparent failover (Minhas, et al., 2013).

Figure 6. Architecture

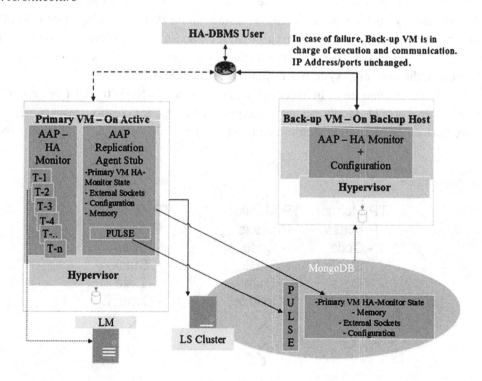

4.3. State Replication

In order to roll forward a transaction from the failure point, it is necessary to save the execution state up to the failure (interruption) point. Products like vSphere (vSphere, n.d.), hyperV (Hyper-V, n.d.) and research prototypes like Remus (Cully, et al., 2008), RemusDB (Minhas, et al., 2013) make a blind replication of the whole VM state at a predefined time interval. To complete the replication, the current VM execution is paused until the replication is complete. The execution of all active transactions is blocked, the state is saved, and then the execution of the blocked transactions is resumed. The approach is quite expensive because it involves full state and non-customized replications.

We observe that to roll forward any activity (transaction, thread, etc.), a full VM state replication is not necessary. What we need is the address of the next instruction of the application, the execution history of the completed operations stored in the log, and the necessary pointers for resuming execution. Thus, AAP instead of taking full state replications, creates an application (database) checkpoint image that is much smaller in size than the whole VM (we use snapshot and checkpoint interchangeably in this chapter). In addition, it applies *Event Based Replication (EBR)*. EBR creates a snapshot or checkpoint of the running transactions that enable us to restore or resume the execution from the last checkpoint.

Once the checkpoint is taken, it is replicated to a location (Log Server) other than the current host. If we store the image on the current host, then in the event of a failure, we need to wait until the host comes online. This jeopardizes the transparent failover and availability. The backup virtual machine is provided with the most recent checkpoint to resume the execution. We identify three events: (a) standard replication timeout (SRT), (b) a transaction creation and, (c) an end transaction.

The first event, SRT, refers to the frequency with which the replication is done (for example, after every 30 seconds). As soon as the timer expires, the SRT enables the checkpointer to take a checkpoint of the running transactions.

The transaction creation is the second event that occurs when a transaction is submitted to the TP Monitor. The event binds the transaction to a process (child).

As shown in Figure 7, checkpointing can be done at Instance-1, at Instance-2, or at Instance-3. However, checkpointing at Instance-1 or at Instance-2 will be inadequate because the snapshot will have no information about how many TSes (Transaction Server (Philip & Eric, 2009) got bound to T1 (i.e., the incomplete transaction execution structure). This is the reason we define Instance-3 as the "initial state event". We consider VM_p as the primary VM and VM_x as the backup VM. The state of the TP-Monitor of VM_p is replicated to the LS for VM_x at every "initial state event" for every transaction T_i. If T_i starts executing before transaction T_j, the intermediate state of T_i will be replicated while performing the "initial state" replication for T_j. This does not affect the logic and working of EBR. Thus, AAP avoids unnecessary replication by replicating only at the specific events (EBR) where it is affirmative that the transaction will be executed. The idea of fuzzy checkpointing would not work here, that is why TP Monitor has to be suspended to complete the replication. The event of transaction creation also resets the timer (SRT).

The third event refers to the situation where a transaction submits an ET (End Transaction). We consider it as an event to perform checkpointing. However, for us, an ET is no different than a conventional commit. Performing a replication at this point helps us to achieve a consistent lock table state (section 4.5) and also the need for *Commit Protection* (Minhas, et al., 2013) becomes obsolete (Section 6). Furthermore, in order to increase the overall efficiency and reduce the costs compressing the checkpoints is beneficial because the data contains redundancy. We found that this applies to database workloads because the memory writes often change only a small part of the pages on which they occur. This pres-

Figure 7. Transaction instances

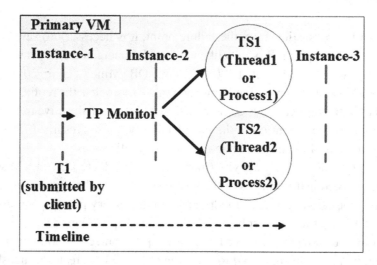

ents an opportunity to achieve a significant reduction in the replication traffic by only sending the actual changes to dirty pages. To achieve this, we use a bitmap scheme, which after every checkpoint, finds out the pages that are dirty in comparison to the previous checkpoint. Only these pages are sent to the LS and also only after XORing them with the pages of the previous checkpoint. After the XOR operation, the dirty pages mostly contain zeroes that are then picked up by the compression schemes we have used quite efficiently. We discuss the effects of different compression techniques in the behavior analysis section.

4.4. Pulse and Failover

To keep the failover transparent and fast, AAP uses pulse (a configurable parameter) messages. There is an LM running a CCM (Concurrency Control Mechanism) and LS which is managed by an RM (Recovery Manager). AAP has a RAS running at the LS (Figure 6) that identifies if any of the primary VMs (VM_ps) are down. To do so, it exchanges a pulse every 100ms (depend on the configuration) and if the RAS misses three consecutive pulses from VM_p then it assumes that it is down and enables VM_x with the latest state information. "λ" (pulse timeout = missing 3 consecutive pulses) is the total wait time observed by the RAS to initiate a failover. If both hosts fail, which is unlikely, the system would be left in a consistent state since all the information necessary to roll forward transactions is saved at the LS. In a host failover, which is transparent to a user, the data packets intended for VM_p (offline now) will now be routed to VM_x. Hypervisor makes sure that this happens. Since the old VM_x is now VM_p, the RAS makes the selection of a new VM_x for this VM_p in case it fails as well.

There are many hosts, and each one is running multiple VM's. There are multiple data centers and each has a database running on them. The transaction processing and recovery management is decoupled from the database. So the databases in this case are the *Data Components* (DCs) (Lomet, Fekete, Weikum, & Zwilling, 2009) that may have their own cache, own recovery schemes, and stable data storage (different from the transaction cache, log and crash recovery). As soon as a transaction is initiated on VM_p, the initial state (checkpoint image) of the TP-Monitor (which includes transactions) gets recorded at the LS. The transaction execution starts at VM_p where it makes entries to the cache, lock table (LM and local) and log as the transaction code gets executed. This instance of a DBMS running at VM_p is marked as an HA-DBMS; however, there can be other instances running in other VM's without HA. Since our idea is to offer an HA-DBMS as a service, this comes with an option.

Based on EBR the TP-Monitor running at the VM_p is checkpointed. There are three different types of communication between the LS and TP-Monitor: the log update, the checkpoint update, and the pulse. We propose a new communication protocol (Figure 8a) between the RASs to increase the efficiency of AAP and to standardize the communication.

The very first checkpoint update of the HA-Monitor at VM_p is stored at the LS as soon as it is generated based on the EBR. For all future updates, we do incremental checkpointing. This saves us a lot of communication costs and increases efficiency. At the LS, as soon as a checkpoint update is received, the AAP replication agent overwrites the old snapshot with the latest one (consolidating new and old snapshots). To summarize the steps of AAP towards high availability, we present an algorithm:

Begin

1. AAP identifies back-up VM set $VM_X = \{VM_{X1}, VM_{X2} \dots VM_{Xn}\}$ based on closest host using IGOD. Initializes LS, LM, RAS and DCs

2. User at VM_p submits one or more transaction(s). LM calls going as needed by the transaction, monitored by TP-Monitor. RAS identifies, configures, initializes and binds a back-up VM_{Xi} for this user but keeps it in suspended state.

3. Create checkpoint(s) based on EBR, ship them to LS.

4. <Transaction(s) execution>, updates sent first to LS (WAL) and then DC(s)

5. If system fails, VM_p, identify failure by missed pulses.

6. RAS Re-enables VM_{Xi} and provide it with latest checkpoint image.

7. VM_{Xi} starts executing transaction(s) from the point of failure and becomes VP_p. RAS identifies, configures, initializes and binds a back-up VM_{Xi} for this user but keeps it in suspended state. If system fails again, go to Step 5.

8. Transactions execution finish, user log-off, terminate the binding between VM_p and VM_{Xi}, VM_{Xi} returns to VM_X set.

End

Figure 8.

VM-ID	T-ID	Timestamp	T-Status
Sequence-Number	Payload Type	<Reserved>	
Payload			

a. Checkpointing Protocol

DC-ID	LSN	TransactionID (TID)	BFIM	AFIM

b. New Log Structure

4.5. Transaction Log

The transaction log is the most crucial data-structure of database recovery since it contains the BFIM (before image) for undoing an aborted transaction and AFIM (after image) for redoing a completed transaction. In our data model (Lomet, Fekete, Weikum, & Zwilling, 2009) we can have multiple DCs getting read/write from hundreds of transactions and since it also follows WAL protocol (Write Ahead Logging), we realize that conventional log storage would soon become a performance bottleneck. In a traditional SQL database hosting thousands of users, using a synchronously replicated log would risk interruptions that will have a widespread impact. In AAP, we do not rollback transactions. Situations like user initiated transaction abort, deadlock resolution, etc., or DC failure will require an undo or redo or both. To address these issues, AAP maintains the LS which is managed by a MongoDB cluster (Chodorow, 2010) for log management. This simplifies the log storage and also enhances the performance since we configure the cluster with write-optimization. We also shard (partition) the log that optimizes the writing log records for each DC. This improves the availability and throughput. We believe that most user generated queries would be directed towards a single DC, however a query could encompass more than one database and could go beyond the boundaries of one DC. Thus, a single query could result in data retrieval/manipulation from multiple types of DCs. Either way, since we shard the log on the basis of each DC, a transaction might result in entries towards more than one shard, which is easily handled by MongoDB doing parallel writes. Since we choose a partition key (compound shard key) as the DC-ID (unique *Data Component* id) and the T-ID (unique transaction id), this, in effect, results in multiple logs, each for its own DC. For MongoDB, our transaction log is a Document oriented database. We create the *AAP-TRANSACTION-LOG* database, the LOG *collection,* and configure the number of shards to be equal to the number of DCs.

The LOG is partitioned on the basis of the DC-ID. Each shard would have multiple chunks of the data. Chunk is a contiguous range of data from a particular collection. *Documents* of a collection are sorted lexicographically while managing chunks of a shard. In the above discussed scenario, chunks are first created on the basis of the DC-ID and then if that chunk grows to its maximum size, it is split in two on the basis of the T-ID. In other words, any chunk of a shard would at least belong to one transaction. This partitioning and organization of log records makes the recovery fast in case of a redo and/or undo.

There are three different types of servers in MongoDB: *mongod-config, mongod-data,* and *mongos* (as shown in Figure 9). Any client, in our scheme the HA-Monitors/RAS, interacts with only the mongos' processes. The mongos process is a front-end client interface and a routing agent. We create one mongos' process for each DC in the system; this improves the utilization and efficiency through servicing requests in parallel. AAP creates two databases in the LS cluster. One is *AAP-TRANSACTION-LOG* and the other is *VM-SNAPSHOT.* We have already discussed the organization of the former; the latter is required to store the latest checkpoint of the HA-Monitor running at a VM (refer section 4.3). We partition the database *VM-SNAPSHOT* using the compound shard key as the *VM-ID* and *USER-ID.* Since at any given time, only one user will own a VM and once that user gets logged off, the respective snapshot is deleted by the RAS. In our approach, the conventional log structure is not adequate for recovery because of the decoupling of transactional services with the data. Thus, we add a new piece of information that is DC-ID. Figure 8b illustrates this structure in a simplistic form with some of the fields including DC-ID.

AAP supports three recovery operations: redo, undo, and roll-forward. We have discussed roll-forward in detail and redo-undo in brief in previous sections. We present the scenarios in which undo-redo would be applied.

Figure 9. Log servers cluster

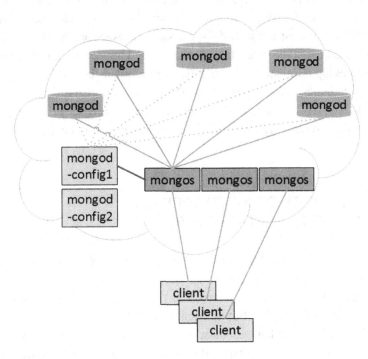

Undo and Redo: A transaction may be aborted by a user or in a deadlock resolution. Each DC is an independent data store that can fail independently. If a DC fails during a transaction execution, a straight forward choice could be to abort the transaction. However, we take the optimistic approach and keep executing the transaction only if the transaction does not make a read request for a new data item from the failed DC. Thus, in absence of a read request, a transaction will execute and eventually commit. All the updates will be logged in the LS. When the DC comes up, it sends its low water mark (LWM) (Lomet, Fekete, Weikum, & Zwilling, 2009) (LWM is the LSN of the last updated DC installed on the database) to the LS. The LS, after receiving the LWM, finds that there are still more updates to be written to the DB (by searching for log records having LSN > LWM for the same DC, identified by the DC-ID). Hence, the LS ships those updates to the DC (redo), the DC installs the updates and changes the value of the LWM to the LSN of the last installed update and communicates this LWM value to the LS. This is similar to the situation when a transaction is committed, but the DC failed before installing the updates. Since WAL is followed in our approach, the ET/commit record is present in the LS. The DC follows the same approach (redo) when it comes up to attain a consistent state. On the other hand, if a transaction makes a read request for a new data item from the failed DC, then we have no other choice but to abort the transaction when the DC comes up.

4.6. Concurrency Control

In order to guarantee consistency and isolation, we use an LM. We use two types of lock tables that are always kept in a consistent state. They are an *LM-* table and a *local lock* table. If a transaction wants to access (read or write) a data item, it has to first acquire a lock on that data item. The LM-table maintains this information. The local lock table stores this information for future references of the same transaction; however, this information is only valid until the transaction unlocks the data item after which it is removed from the local lock table. By keeping a consistent local copy with the HA-Monitor, we avoid many round trips for a lock request to the LM for the same transaction. As soon as a transaction commits, the locks are released for other requesting transactions. The locking mechanism that AAP uses is a version of 2-Phase Locking (Bernstein, Hadzilacos, & Goodman, 1987).

The LM has the metadata/catalog of the all the DCs. We support multi granularity locking. Since this chapter is towards HA, the concurrency management details are out of its scope. That being said, our model is well suited for scalability towards adding more DCs and is capable of managing scalable configurations.

5. AAP: ALONG THE LINES OF INTEROPERABLE AND FEDERATED CLOUD ARCHITECTURE

As cloud computing is evolving as a "ready-to-use-service", users and providers are both looking for ways to fit the cloud in personal or organizational needs. With this comes the private cloud, public cloud, hybrid cloud, and federated cloud (Navarro, n. d.). A private cloud is a type of cloud architecture that provides scalability and self-service, but through a dedicated hardware and architecture. This is, in principle, contrary to the public cloud, which offers services to multiple organizations; a private cloud is dedicated to a single organization. To safeguard data security and customer privacy, organizations tend to use a private cloud for sensitive information like customer information (including SSNs) and EHRs (electronic health records) and use a public cloud for non-sensitive data and analysis. Such features are offered by a hybrid cloud that bundles the best of both worlds. So it contains a private cloud as well as a public cloud, and an organization can fit its data storage and processing accordingly. Another type of cloud architecture is a federated cloud that is the latest addition in this series. It is essentially a multi-cloud architecture that contains multiple providers, each offering slightly different services, hardware, and focus. They also tend to have datacenters at different locations. A federated cloud is a result of interoperability between different cloud providers. The barriers between them have dropped because of open APIs and increasing compatibility. This has given a great opportunity to the customers since they can now actually use cloud environments that meet their needs more than any single provider could. It is now possible to move data easily across different platforms. To some people, it might seem that hybrid and federated clouds are similar (and they look quite similar) however, they are different in principle and purpose. It is also possible and not very uncommon that a federated cloud can be a hybrid cloud.

The key feature of AAP is that it is independent of the underlying cloud architecture. We have developed our scheme with virtualization and portability in mind. Though it can be part of a single cloud, it finds its application in a hybrid or federated cloud. AAP is actually compatible and can easily run in a VM's user space with VM_p and VM_x both in totally different cloud settings. It is pretty straight forward to create two identical VMs, each in a different cloud. The two VMs need to be physically close to each other, so that the failover is transparent and fast. The Datacenter's (DC) geographic location would be a key concern in identifying the VMs. This can be easily achieved by algorithms like IGOD (Jaiswal, Nath, & Kumar, A Location-Based Security Framework for Cloud Perimeter, 2014) (Jaiswal & Kumar, IGOD - Identifying Geolocation of Cloud Datacenter Hosting Mobile User's Data`, 2015) (Jaiswal & Kumar, IGOD: Identification of Geolocation of Cloud Datacenters, 2015) as it would find the closest datacenter, irrespective of the provider. The distance between the two VMs affects the failover time and thus, finding a host in the closest datacenter is a must. Now, since we can go across a provider's space (cloud datacenter) the communications between the two hypervisors might seem a little difficult if there is no open API available. However, this issue can be readily handled by creating a supervisor that can act as a transparent failover agent. Since AAP is independent of the underlying architecture, it can easily be deployed as a third party service over any cloud architecture. For third party providers, a federated cloud is the best choice for economic reasons, performance reasons, and ease of use. In essence, AAP offers high availability over parallel deployment of SQL/No-SQL data stores spread across one or more datacenters. It can be offered especially as a third party service, which is well suited for a federated cloud. We claim that none of the works are done in this direction and AAP is one of a kind that addresses this problem.

6. BEHAVIOR ANALYSIS

In this section, we present the merits of AAP with our preliminary experimental results. In these experiments, we focused on the distinct features of AAP: 1. Application Checkpointing, 2. Checkpoint Image Compression, and 3. Incremental Checkpointing. Before we hop into our evaluation, we would like to point out a semantic flaw in (Minhas, et al., 2013) and how AAP deals with it. Authors of RemusDB (Minhas, et al., 2013) proposed the idea of *Commit Protection*. We claim that commit protection is an overhead in transaction execution. It prohibits the release of commit acknowledgement until the backup VM is checkpointed. This means that if a transaction t1 commits, the commit message is released only after checkpointing is done after checkpoint timeout. This violates commit semantics. Consider the scenario in Figure 10. A failure occurred after the transaction executed an ET, but before it executed a commit.

In other words, according to *Commit Protection,* if a transaction fails after committing, but before checkpointing, then the transaction has to be rolled-back. This is an unnecessary overhead because the system (in case of failure) will end up re-executing already committed transactions. In AAP, there can be tens of VMs running hundreds of transactions and communicating with data components (Lomet, Fekete, Weikum, & Zwilling, 2009) along with the LS and LM. In this scenario, failure of one VM (or one instance of DBMS running on a VM) should not affect other transactions (i.e., should not initiate a restart procedure), but if we follow the *restart* procedure of (Lomet, Fekete, Weikum, & Zwilling, 2009) (Bernstein, Hadzilacos, & Goodman, 1987) then this cannot be achieved. Thus, instead of waiting for the checkpoint timeout, AAP takes the checkpoint as soon as a transaction reaches the ET and it then resets the timer (SRT). A general checkpoint and transaction execution timeline is shown in Figure 11. It can be noticed that checkpoints *i* to *i+2* were taken because of the SRT; however, *Checkpoint (i+3)* was taken due to a transaction commit even before the SRT expired. Later, the system failed, but the execution resumed on VM_x from the last consistent checkpoint, i.e., *Checkpoint (i+3)*.

Figure 10. Failure scenario

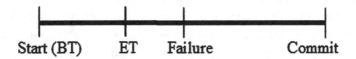

Figure 11. Transaction "Execution + Checkpointing" timeline

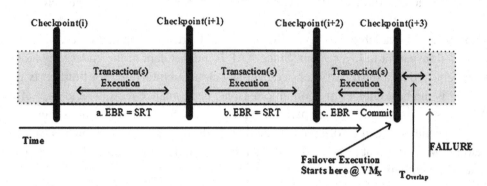

We conducted emulated experiments to demonstrate the cost-effectiveness and superior performance of AAP. Our preliminary results show that AAP is much more cost effective than any database HA scheme today, especially (Minhas, et al., 2013). For these experiments we used a university cluster with 2 servers (Microsoft Windows Server 2012 and vSphere) both with 16gb of memory, an Intel Xeon X3430 2.40-2.39 GHz processor, and a Ubuntu 14.04.1 guest operating system. Each guest OS had 4 GB of virtual memory and 4 virtual CPUs. For the LS, we used a MongoDB cluster with 3 shards each on a different desktop Windows 7 machine (each with an Intel i5-2400 3.10GHz processor and 4 GB of memory). We deployed two databases, one with MySQL and the other with a simple MongoDB KV (key, value) database. As mentioned earlier, we also deployed an LM on the Windows server running as a separate multi-threaded process. Since we used an LM, our queries did not use built in locks on these databases. In addition, we implemented range based locks and also, for simplicity, we made each as a *key* based query (*Primary* for MySQL and *_id* for MongoDB). The above setup imitates a *hybrid | federated | multi* cloud with different servers, configurations, and even databases, but it allows for the creation of identical VMs. In addition, the university cluster was running on a *1gbps* network.

We discussed in Section 4.3, the merit of compression schemes and their effectiveness when the amount of data to be replicated is large and contains redundancy. We evaluated three different compression schemes, namely, GZ (GZip), BZ (BZip2), and XZ (LZMA/LZMA2) with AAP's EBR checkpoints. We linearly generated transactions that were then picked up by a TP-Monitor and assigned a TS (see Section 4.1) for execution. Since transaction execution must be suspended during checkpointing and the duration of suspension affects throughput and response time, we measured this duration for different compression schemes. The "read:write" ratio for the transactions were "80:20", respectively. We collected data when the execution state reached a steady state. Figure 12 illustrates the TP-Monitor suspension time with respect to the number of transactions. We observed that with the number of transactions, the amount of memory and state information to be checkpointed increased. However, the difference was not too large; for example, with 10 transactions running in the system, the TP-Monitor was suspended for 30 ms (mean) for a checkpoint, whereas with 50 transactions in the system, it was suspended for 70 ms (mean).

Different compression schemes have different sets of advantages. For example, in our case of checkpoint images for more than 50 concurrent transactions, XZ compression (tar + xz) was very economical with a compression rate of more than 99%, but it took 45 times more time than archiving (tar). On the other hand, for the same image GZ compression (tar + gz) offers around a 90% compression rate and it takes around 5 times more time than tar. Such comparisons are illustrated in Figures 13a and 13b. Another

Figure 12. TP-Monitor (User transactions) Suspension delay with linear increase in # of transactions

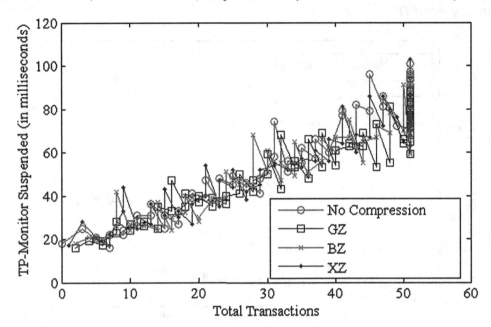

aspect which is dependent on the size of compressed checkpoint image and network bandwidth was the network delay to upload (replicate) this image to the LS, as shown in Figure 14. The random spikes in this figure are because of our university shared network. Figure 15 demonstrates the combined effect of Figure 13a and Figure 14. It also shows the percentage of time spent by the RAS in compression and replication. In these graphs, we turned off the incremental checkpointing feature so as to visualize the real compression values. It can be clearly observed that the XZ compression, although it has a very high compression ratio, is very slow. Thus, it is not a good choice for AAP. With careful observation, we decided to use GZ compression since its performance is acceptable in time, space, and network complexity.

These figures demonstrate important properties of AAP right from taking checkpoint on VM_p to replicating it on the LS. It is also equally important to verify how AAP performs during the transparent failover. Figure 16a illustrates the average delay observed in the transparent failover from VM_p to VM_x for $\lambda = 50$ ms. Recall "λ" (pulse timeout), which is the total time the RAS waits to initiate the failover. The total time to complete a transparent failover would require "λ + *checkpoint image transfer* + *resume execution*" ms. We observed that λ as 50 ms is a very small wait time if the RAS wants to detect that VM_p has failed, thus we considered several different values as illustrated in Figure 16b. Based on this figure, we deduced that the total transparent failover time was directly proportional to "λ". We also compared AAP's failover performance with RemusDB's (Minhas, et al., 2013) failover performance. It can be seen in the figure, that AAP performed much better and in addition, its flexibility can be configured based on the workload. If the transactions tend to be longer (of the order of few minutes) the administrator can increase the value of "λ" and vice versa. Furthermore, because of AAP's optimizations (compression and incremental checkpointing), the failover was partially independent of the number of transactions, rather "λ" was the key element. Since, "λ" is a parameter that can be tuned external as well, AAP's internal performance was consistent irrespective of the system load.

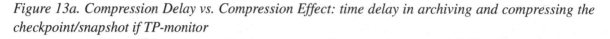

Figure 13a. Compression Delay vs. Compression Effect: time delay in archiving and compressing the checkpoint/snapshot if TP-monitor

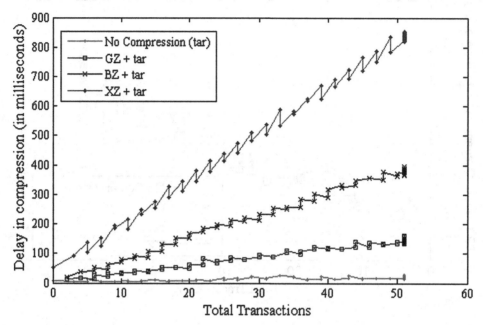

Figure 13b. Compression Delay vs. Compression Effect: effects of different compression schemes on checkpoint/snapshot of TP-monitor

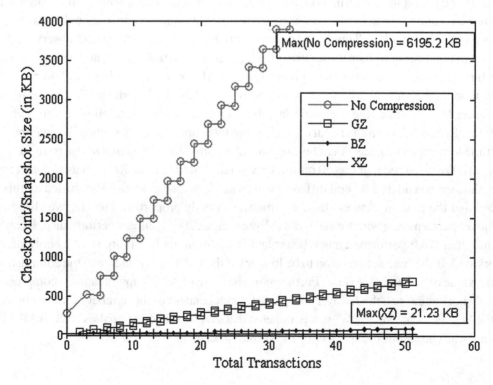

Figure 14. Checkpoint Image Transfer Delay (Primary VM to LS)

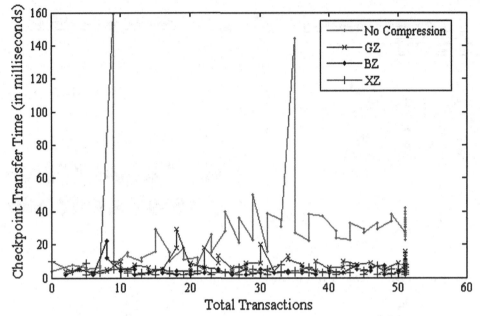

Figure 15. Checkpointing Archiving vs. Network Delay

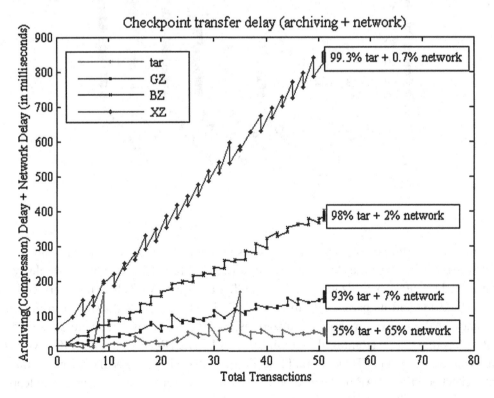

Figure 16. a. Failover Delay for λ=50 ms b. AAP Mean Failover Delay for λ = {100, 500, 1000} ms Vs. RemusDB Failover Delay

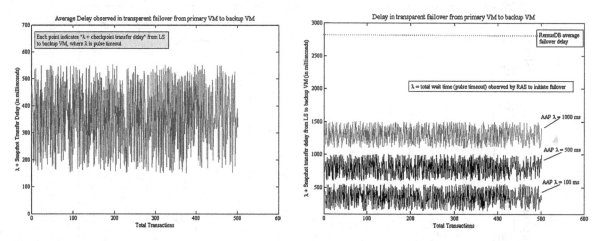

Figure 17. Replication Data Sent: AAP vs. {Remus, RemusDB}

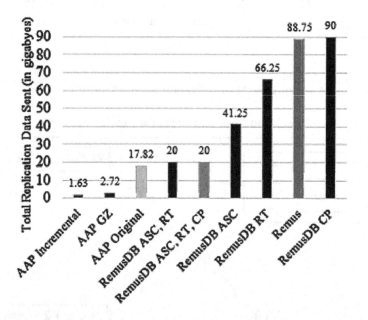

A very important feature of any replication based solution is the amount of data it sends for the sole purpose of providing HA because it is directly proportional to the efficiency of the whole system and the costs involved for network utilization and storage. In this aspect AAP also outperformed RemusDB (Minhas, et al., 2013) and its parent system Remus (Cully, et al., 2008). As shown in Figure 17, the amount of data AAP sent, even without optimizations, (AAP original) was much less than what earlier works sent with optimizations (RemusDB optimizations: RT – Disk Read Tracking, ASC – Asynchronous Checkpoint Compression, and CP – Commit Protection). With optimizations like compression (GZ) and incremental checkpointing, AAP performed 90% better than earlier works. This is a huge leap towards low cost HA when we talk about overall system efficiency.

7. CONCLUSION

In this chapter we presented a novel way to achieve HA and recovery in cloud database management systems running on virtual machines. We also proposed a scheme for fast recovery of unbundled transactions using log partitioning. To maintain consistency, we used MongoDB cluster as the LS and LM. Our scheme enabled the cloud community to offer transactional HA-DBMS as a service. Our preliminary experiments show that AAP is cost effective and faster than earlier works. AAP covers much bigger ground because it can be deployed in any cloud setting (federated, public, private, or hybrid) since it is independent of the underlying architecture. Furthermore, AAP incorporates multi type databases that are not necessarily relational and provides ACID guarantees along with HA that we believe is a unique solution.

8. REFERENCES

AWS | Amazon Relational Database Service (RDS). (n. d.). Amazon. Retrieved from http://aws.amazon.com/rds/

Baker, J., Bond, C., Corbett, J. C., Furman, J. J., Khorlin, A., Larson, J., . . . Yushprakh, V. (2011). Megastore: Providing Scalable, Highly Available Storage for Interactive Services. *Proceedings of the ACM Conf. Innovative Data Systems Research.*

Bernstein, P. A., Hadzilacos, V., & Goodman, N. (1987). Concurrency Control and Recovery in Database Systems - Microsoft Research. Boston: Addison-Wesley Publishing Company. Retrieved from http://research.microsoft.com/http://research.microsoft.com/en-us/people/philbe/ccontrol.aspx

Chang, F., Dean, J., Ghemawat, S., Hsieh, W. C., Wallach, D. A., Burrows, M., & Gruber, R. E. (2008). *Bigtable: A distributed storage system for structured data. CM Transactions on Computer Systems.* TOCS.

Chodorow, K. (2010). MongoDB: The Definitive Guide. Sebastopol: O'Reilly.

Corbett, J. C., Dean, J., Epstein, M., Fikes, A., Frost, C., & Furman, J. J. (2013). Spanner: Google's globally distributed database. *ACM Transactions on Computer Systems, 31*(3), 1–22. doi:10.1145/2518037.2491245

Cully, B., Lefebvre, G., Meyer, D., Feeley, M., Hutchinson, N., & Warfield, A. (2008). Remus: High availability via asynchronous virtual machine replication. *Proceedings of the 5th USENIX Symposium on Networked Systems Design and Implementation* (pp. 161-174).

Das, S., Agrawal, D., & El Abbadi, A. (2013). *ElasTraS: An elastic, scalable, and self-managing transactional database for the cloud. ACM Transactions on Database Systems.* TODS.

Elmore, A. J., Das, S., Agrawal, D., & El Abbadi, A. (2011). Zephyr: live migration in shared nothing databases for elastic cloud platforms. *Proceedings of the ACM SIGMOD International Conference on Management of data* (pp. 301-312). doi:10.1145/1989323.1989356

Fault Tolerance. (n. d.). *Wikipedia*. Retrieved from http://en.wikipedia.org/wiki/Fault_tolerance

High Availability. (n. d.). *Wikipedia*. Retrieved from http://en.wikipedia.org/wiki/High_availability

Hyper-V. (n. d.). Microsoft. Retrieved from https://technet.microsoft.com/en-us/magazine/hh127064.aspx

IMS Fast Path Solutions Guide. (1997). *IBM*. Retrieved from http://www.redbooks.ibm.com/: http://www.redbooks.ibm.com/redbooks/pdfs/sg244301.pdf

Jaiswal, C., & Kumar, V. (2015). IGOD - Identifying Geolocation of Cloud Datacenter Hosting Mobile User's Data. *Proceedings of the 16th IEEE International Conference on Mobile Data Management (MDM)* (pp. 34-37). Pittsburgh, USA: IEEE. doi:10.1109/MDM.2015.20

Jaiswal, C., & Kumar, V. (2015). IGOD: Identification of Geolocation Of Cloud Datacenters. *Proceedings of the 40th IEEE Conference on Local Computer Networks (LCN)*, Clearwater Beach, Florida, USA. IEEE.

Jaiswal, C., & Kumar, V. (2015, May). *Two-sce-doctoral-students-win-best-papermultimedia-presentation-awards*. Retrieved from sce.umkc.edu

Jaiswal, C., Nath, M., & Kumar, V. (2014). A Location-Based Security Framework for Cloud Perimeter. *IEEE Cloud Computing* (pp. 56-64).

Kyriazis, D. e. (2013). *Data Intensive Storage Services for Cloud Environments*. Hershey: IGI Global. doi:10.4018/978-1-4666-3934-8

Lomet, D., Fekete, A., Weikum, G., & Zwilling, M. (2009). Unbundling transaction services in the cloud. *Proceedings of the 4th Biennial Conference on Innovative Data Systems Research (CIDR)*, Asilomar, California, USA.

Minhas, U. F., Rajagopalan, S., Cully, B., Aboulnaga, A., Salem, K., & Warfield, A. (2013). Remusdb: Transparent high availability for database systems. *The VLDB Journal, 22*(1), 29–45. doi:10.1007/s00778-012-0294-6

Navarro, T. (n. d.). What Is The Relationship Between Hybrid Clouds And Federated Clouds? *Computenext.com*. Retrieved from https://www.computenext.com/blog/what-is-the-relationship-between-hybrid-clouds-and-federated-clouds/

Philip, B., & Eric, N. (2009). *Principles of transaction processing* (2nd ed.). Burlington: Morgan Kaufmann.

vSphere. (n. d.). *VMware journal*. Retrieved from http://www.vmware.com/products/vsphere/features/availability

Chapter 6
Distributed Multi–Cloud Based Building Data Analytics

Ioan Petri
Cardiff University, UK

Thomas H Beach
Cardiff School of Engineering, UK

Javier Diaz-Montes
Rutgers University, USA

Omer F. Rana
Cardiff University, UK

Mengsong Zou
Rutgers University, USA

Manish Parashar
Rutgers University, USA

Ali Reza Zamani
Rutgers University, USA

Yacine Rezgui
Cardiff University, UK

ABSTRACT

Cloud computing has emerged as attractive platform for computing data intensive applications. However, efficient computation of this kind of workloads requires understanding how to store, process, and analyse large volumes of data in a timely manner. Many "smart cities" applications, for instance, identify how data from building sensors can be combined together to support applications such as emergency response, energy management, etc. Enabling sensor data to be transmitted to a cloud environment for processing provides a number of benefits, such as scalability and on-demand provisioning of computational resources. In this chapter, we propose the use of a multi-layer cloud infrastructure that distributes processing over sensing nodes, multiple intermediate/gateways nodes, and large data centres. Our solution aims at utilising the pervasive computational capabilities located at the edge of the infrastructure and along the data path to reduce data movement to large data centres located "deep" into the infrastructure and perform a more efficient use of computing and network resources.

1. INTRODUCTION

Cloud computing has generally involved the use of specialist data centres to support computation and data storage at a central site (or a limited number of sites). The motivation for this has come from the need to provide economies of scale (and subsequent reduction in cost) for supporting large scale computation for multiple user applications over (generally) a shared, multi-tenancy infrastructure. The use of

DOI: 10.4018/978-1-5225-0153-4.ch006

such infrastructures requires moving data to a central location, undertaking processing on the data, and subsequently enabling users to download results of analysis. However, when applications need data to be captured and processed/analysed in real time, migrating all the data to a central site prior to analysis can create significant overhead. Examples include sensor network-based applications, such as smart buildings and smart grids, where sensors interface with real world artefacts and must respond to physical phenomenon that cannot be predicted apriori. The amount of data likely to be generated by a sensor and processing requirements in such applications cannot be pre-determined - they are often dependent on the rate of change of the physical phenomenon being measured and potential occurrence of "trigger events" which are non-deterministic.

Recently, there has been significant interest in creating "multi-clouds" or Cloud-of-Clouds federation to aggregate capabilities and capacities offered by a variety of cloud providers. Some of the efforts are focused on cloud interoperability. For example, the Open Cloud Computing Interface (OCCI) effort (OCCI), which defines a common interface for cloud providers; and the European FP7 "UNIFY" project (UNIFY EU FP7 project), which develops a Cloud Operating System (CloudOS) to connect distributed clouds and make use of in-network capabilities to process data (GENICloud project (GENICloud project)). Similarly, on-line sites such as CloudHarmony (CloudHarmony) report over 100+ cloud providers that offer capability ranging from storage and computation to complete application containers that can be acquired at a price, primarily using service-based access models. From the user's perspective these environments bring a variety of benefits: (i) reduced reliance on a single vendor's infrastructure; (ii) improved fault tolerance, as failure in one cloud system does not render the entire infrastructure inoperable; (iii) improved security – similar argument to fault tolerance, i.e. a breach in one cloud system does not impact the entire infrastructure; and (iv) the ability to utilise capability (and data) that may only be available in one cloud system and may not be transferable due to volume or legal constraints.

Resource elasticity and scalability offered through cloud computing enables researchers to explore complex problems in energy optimisation that are otherwise impractical or impossible to address (Perez-Lombard, Ortiz, & Pout, 2010; Thain, Tannenbaum, & Livny, 2008). In this chapter we describe how a distributed cloud system can be used to perform a number of different data analysis operations (in-situ vs. in-transit) based on pre-defined application requirements. We describe and evaluate the establishment of such a sensor-based application using a CometCloud (Diaz-Montes, AbdelBaky, Zou, & Parashar, 2015; Diaz-Montes, Zou, Singh, Tao, & Parashar, 2014) implementation with data collection from real building pilots and determine how processing can be distributed across multiple data centre locations to achieve QoS and cost targets. Building sensor data is analysed using EnergyPlus. EnergyPlus is as time-step based energy simulation package that can be used to model heating, cooling, lighting, ventilation and other energy flows within a building. Our solution enables resources to be utilised across geographically distributed cloud environments connected over the Internet. In this paper we propose a cost based multi-cloud framework for supporting real application deployment over three federated sites Cardiff University in Cardiff (UK), Rutgers University in New Jersey (USA), and Indiana University in Indiana (USA) – all hosting EnergyPlus; and a performance analysis of the application scenarios to determine how task submission could be supported across these three sites, subject to particular revenue targets. The reminder of this chapter is organised as follows: Section 2, outlines the development and use of distributed clouds, providing a key motivation for our research and analysing several related approaches. Section 3 presents our approach for cloud analytics. Section 4 presents our application scenario, followed by detailed information about building characteristics in Section 5. The evaluation of our implemented system is presented in Section 6. Section 7 introduces a multi-layer decision function and some preliminary results. We conclude and identify future work in section 8.

2. BACKGROUND AND RELATED WORK

2.1. Smart Buildings

Building controls and sensors have the potential to enable their users to become more "active" consumers of energy (through smart metering, for instance). Centralised building controls are often used to enable interactions between the different sensors, actuators, and controllers to perform appropriate control actions. "Intelligent" buildings have embedded monitoring and control equipment and the potential to reduce energy use along with operations and maintenance expenses, while improving comfort levels. For achieving an equilibrium in terms of consumption and comfort, these systems typically necessitate the deployment of a wide range of sensors (e.g., temperature, CO_2, zone airflow, daylight levels, occupancy levels, etc.), which are, in turn, integrated through an Energy Management Control System (EMCS) and an array of electronic actuators, terminal unit controllers to process sensor outputs, and control set-points. In particular, sensor systems can enable building energy simulations – enabling users to optimise various associated aspects of building use over time (Petri, Li, Rezgui, Chunfeng, Yuce, & Jayan, 2014). Energy optimisation demonstrates a real time use of sensor data, where a number of parameters need to be optimised based on a particular building representation. Based on such real-time readings from sensors it has become possible for building facility managers to take decisions in order to reduce energy consumption. As sensors can provide readings within an interval of 15-30 minutes, it is necessary for any simulation/ optimisation to also be carried out over a similar interval. Thus, the efficiency of the optimisation process depends on the capacity of the computing infrastructure available.

There has also been a significant recent focus on the integration of sensor networks with decentralised distributed systems based on the emergence of various network and IP-based technologies. Cuzzocrea et al. (Cuzzocrea, Fortino, & Rana, Managing Data and Processes in Cloud-Enabled Large-Scale Sensor Networks: State-of-the-Art and Future Research Directions, 2013) provide a survey of various sensor-based applications that make use of Cloud infrastructure to carry out data analytics and decision support. Such "Sensor Clouds" enable users to collect, access, process, visualise, archive, share and search large amounts of sensor data from different applications. Sensor clouds also facilitate the sharing of sensor resources by different users and applications under flexible usage scenarios, for instance, a single multi-purpose sensor (i.e. one able to measure multiple parameters around its vicinity) may be re-used by multiple applications at different time period. Sensor clouds also provide users with a mechanism to handle sensor devices as part of a general purpose resource management system, thereby allowing scheduling and allocation systems to treat these as resources that can be allocated to users based on a variety of different scheduling strategies (Petri, et al., 2014). Such sensor clouds can help to provision service instances automatically, to monitor sensors assets/resources and to control sensors via the use of a Web-based interface (Cohen, Dolan, Dunlap, Hellerstein, & Welton, 2009; Yuriyama & Kushida, 2010).

2.2. Sensor Clouds

In previous work, the STACEE system (Neumann, Bodenstein, Rana, & Krishnaswamy, 2011) was developed for dynamically creating storage distributed Clouds using edge devices, such as routers, routing switches, multiplexers, mobile phones, PCs/media centres, set-top boxes and modems. The functional architecture within STACEE makes use of edge device capacity in a Cloud using Peer-to-Peer (P2P) technology, thereby reducing energy consumption at a single site and maximising user engagement with the system. Recently researchers have investigated the integration of WSNs (Wireless Sensor Networks) with large-scale distributed computing infrastructures to support data analysis and decision support. Examples include an integration architecture of Cloud computing and WSNs (Kurschl & Beer, 2009), Sensor-Web (Chu & Buyya, 2009), SensorGrid (Cuzzocrea, Furfaro, Mazzeo, & and Sacca, 2004; Cuzzocrea, Furfaro, Greco, Masciari, Mazzeo, & and Sacca, 2005; Cuzzocrea & Sacca, 2013), the Sensor-Cloud infrastructure (Yuriyama & Kushida, 2010), the BodyCloud architecture (Distefano, Merlino, & and Puliafito, 2012), etc.

In (Kurschl & Beer, 2009), a SaaS architecture for sensor network analytical services is proposed. It is implemented atop a PaaS layer (e.g. Google App Engine, Microsoft Azure) and is organized into three layers: (i) sensor data management, focusing on the collection of sensor data streams from a SN gateway; (ii) filtering and analysis operations which involve the execution of processing workflows according to the pipe- and-filter paradigms; (iii) filter management, visualization and notification processes, which respectively allow for the definition and management of the processing filter chain, the visualization of the analysed data and generation of notification events to a user or a subsequent process.

SensorGrid is a Grid framework for providing approximate answers to aggregate queries on summarized sensor network data based on data compression and approximation paradigms. Aggregate queries are the basis for achieving Online Analytical Processing (OLAP) over sensor network readings in Data Grid environments. OLAP has a number of interesting applications for eScience, covering aspects such as visualization of scientific data, multi- dimensional analysis of data streams, privacy of multi-dimensional data (Cuzzocrea, Furfaro, Mazzeo, & and Sacca, 2004; Cuzzocrea, Furfaro, Greco, Masciari, Mazzeo, & and Sacca, 2005; Cuzzocrea & Sacca, 2013), etc.

In-transit data analysis refers to the manipulation and transformation of data using resources in the data path between source and destination, and can be extremely advantageous for data intensive applications. Various reactive management strategies for in-transit data manipulation have been undertaken (Klasky, Ludaescher, & Parashar, 2006; Bhat, Parashar, & Klasky, 2007; Bennett, et al., 2012). Studies have investigated the possibility of coupling these strategies with various application levels to create a cooperative management framework and in-transit data manipulation for data-intensive scientific and engineering workflows.

A method for optimising in-transit data analysis is to use Software Defined Networks (SDNs), where network control plane is decoupled and is directly programmable. This migration of control, formerly tightly bound in individual network devices, into accessible computing devices enables the underlying infrastructure to be abstracted for applications and network services, which can treat the network as a logical or virtual entity (Klasky, Ludaescher, & Parashar, 2006). An alternative to in-transit processing is in-situ data analysis, where the latter is based on the idea of performing analysis as the workflow is running, storing only the results and mitigating the effects of limited computing capacity. The major difference of these approaches is how and where the computation is performed. In-situ analysis typically shares the primary simulation compute resources whereas for in-transit analysis, processing is undertaken as data is transferred to different processors. An example use case that can benefit from in-transit and in-situ is the case of energy optimisation with EnergyPlus, where results are generated based on sensor readings recorded at different time intervals. Not all data may need to be moved to a central site to undertake the required analysis.

Our focus is on understanding how a distributed cloud could be constructed for a particular application use case. We focus on EnergyPlus and make use of an actual deployment to describe how data is captured, processed and analysed using an elastic (and distributed infrastructure).

2.3. Hybrid Federated Cloud

Dynamically federated "cloud-of-clouds" infrastructures are being explored as a way of aggregating distributed resources in support of heterogeneous and highly dynamic applications requirements. Typically a federated infrastructure can be composed by a variety of resources ranging from high performance computing (HPC) clusters and computational Grids to pure virtualized clouds. The key idea of a hybrid cloud federation is to offer all these resources as a single pool using cloud abstractions (i.e. elastic provisioning, scale up/down).

Current cloud platforms can provide effective platforms for certain classes of applications, for example high-throughput computing (HTC) applications. There have been several early projects that have reported successful deployments of applications on existing clouds (Fox & Gannon, 2012) (Deelman, Singh, Livny, Berriman, & Good, 2008) (Keahey & Freeman, 2008) (Vecchiola, Pandey, & Buyya, 2009). Additionally, there are efforts exploring other usage modes (Parashar, AbdelBaky, Rodero, & Devarakonda, 2013) and to combine clouds, such as AmazonEC2 (Amazon EC2), with integrated computing infrastructures (e.g. HPC clusters). Villegas et al. (Villegas, et al., 2012) proposed a composition of cloud providers as an integrated (or federated) cloud environment in a layered service model. Assuncao et al. (Assuncao, Costanzo, & Buyya, 2009) described an approach of extending a local cluster to cloud resources using different scheduling strategies. Along the same lines, Ostermann et al. (Ostermann, Prodan, & Fahringer, 2009) extended a grid workflow application development and computing infrastructure to include cloud resources, and experimented with AustrianGrid and an academic cloud installation of Eucalyptus using a scientific workflow application. Similarly, Vazquez et al. (Vazquez, Huedo, Montero, & Llorente, 2009)proposed architecture for an elastic grid infrastructure using the GridWay meta-scheduler, and extended grid resources to Globus Nimbus; Vockler et al. (Vockler, Juve, Deelman, & Rynge, 2011) used Pegasus and Condor to execute an astronomy workflow on virtual machine resources drawn from multiple cloud infrastructures based on FutureGrid, NERSC's Magellan cloud and Amazon EC2; Gorton et al. (Gorton, Liu, & Yin, 2010) designed a workflow infrastructure for Systems Biology Knowledgebase (Kbase) and built a prototype using Amazon EC2 and NERSC's Magellan cloud; and Bittencourt et al. (Bittencourt, Senna, & Madeira, 2010) proposed an infrastructure to manage the execution of service workflows in the hybrid system, composed of the union of a grid and a cloud. Riteau et al. (Riteau, Tsugawa, Matsunaga, Fortes, & Keahey, 2010) proposed a computing model where resources from multiple cloud providers are leveraged to create large-scale distributed virtual clusters. They used resources from two experimental testbeds, FutureGrid in the United States and Grid'5000 in France. In (Celesti, Tusa, Villari, & Puliafito, 2010), Celesti et al. proposed a cross-federation model based on using a customized cloud manager component placeable inside the cloud architectures. Other example is the Resevoir (Rochwerger, Breitgand, Levy, Galis, & others, 2009) that aims at contributing to best practices with a cloud and federation architecture. Others have explored the creation of federated marketplaces to facilitate resource sharing. Mashayekhy et al. (Mashayekhy, Nejad, & Grosu, 2015) proposed to use game theory to enable cloud federation by considering the cooperation of the cloud providers in offering cloud IaaS services. In (Hadji & Zeghlache, 2015), authors propose a mathematical model to decide when to outsource tasks to identify the most appropriate strategies and decisions (servingusers directly, outsourcing and insourcing decisions) for providers involved in cloud federations according. In (Petri, Diaz-Montes, Rana, Punceva, Rodero, & Parashar, 2015) explore the formation of federation using social networking mechanisms.

3. CLOUD DATA ANALYTIC APPROACH

We propose a layered cloud approach aimed at taking advantage of the pervasive capabilities distributed across the infrastructure to enable efficient data analytics. The architecture of this approach is presented in Figure 1. This architecture consists of three main layers: (i) L3: data capture point; (ii) L2: gateway nodes (in practice, multiple levels may exist); and (iii) L1: data centre/computing cluster. At L1 various data capture devices, such as sensors, mobile phones (with human input) record values based on an observed phenomena. These devices capture data with a pre-defined frequency (often dictated by the rate of change of the phenomenon being observed), depending on the capacity of the device to record/collect data and also based on specific system requirements that need to be satisfied. A variety of standards have recently been proposed at L3, such as the Constrained Application Protocol (CoAP) (Shelby, Hartke, & Bormann), which is supported through Erbium REST interface and Contiki (Kovatsch). L2 involves the use of multiple gateways, which may be realised in practice using building manager control resources, or software defined network (SDN) switches and routers (e.g., using OpenFlow). SDN decouples data and control planes, which facilitates performing operations over the data. Additionally, these gateways may also be computational devices that aggregate data from a variety of L3 sensors. Finally, L1 contains more complex computing clusters and data centre capability, where greater computational and storage capability is made available to application users, enabling more complex, generally long running, simulations to be carried out on the data.

Figure 1. System architecture

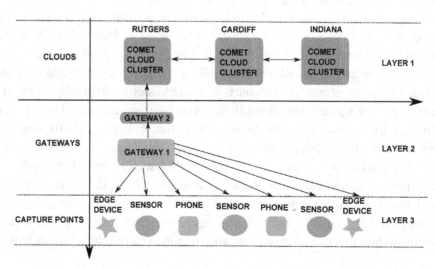

Devices at L2 can carry out various operations on the raw data collected at L3 – such as performing stream operations (average, min, max, filtering, etc.) on a time/sample window of data, carrying out encryption of an incoming data stream or a variety of other data encoding/transcoding operations before forwarding this data for subsequent analysis to L1. Hence, devices at L2 retrieve data but can also perform some preliminary analysis. We envision a distributed cloud to be composed of devices at all of these levels, and with a need to coordinate work across these levels to achieve particular data analysis and performance targets. Each level also has its own objective function which influences the types of operations carried out. For instance, L3 generally consists of resource-constrained devices (i.e., limited battery power, network range, etc.) which must carry out operations in the context of these constraints. Similarly, L2 consists of various network elements or computing nodes that need to be shared across multiple concurrent data flows, requiring any analysis to be constrained by the number of flows and time constraints in carry out the filtering/pre-analysis. Operations at L1 are based on Quality of Service (QoS) targets that have been pre-agreed between a client and a data centre provider, such as throughput, response time, cost, etc. Understanding how an application hosted on a Cloud at L1 can interact and coordinate with L3 and L2 we believe is an essential research challenge in such systems, particular for real time, streaming applications.

Distributing analysis of data across these different levels can improve the overall system performance and reduce the load on L1 infrastructure. We also observe that raw data collected at L3 may not necessarily be needed (in its entirety) at L1 – and aggregate operations on the data (e.g., average, summation, etc.) may be enough for the type of analysis required at L1. It is therefore not necessary to transfer all the collected data to the data centre (as often undertaken currently – even with the availability of recent systems such as Amazon Kinesis (Amazon Kinesis) or Google BigQuery for streaming data), wasting network bandwidth and buffer/ storage space at levels L2 and L1. We identify the following classes of data analysis:

- **In-Situ Analysis:** is carried out at L1, on a pre-agreed number of computing resource. This is the current mode of operation with many cloud systems – whereby data is aggregated at a central site prior to analysis. Typically, streaming systems chuck data prior to its transfer to remote cloud resources. This approach can have major disadvantages in terms of load and response time, as collection at a central server can be time consuming (and sometimes not necessary) – thereby limiting QoS targets that can be met in practice.

- **Data-Drop Analysis:** After data values are collected by edge devices, and sent over the network, the actual data analysis process starts when the data sets are dropped into a specific folder. Data-drop analysis is the ability to trigger on-demand analysis making use of elastic computing resources available at L1 (at the data centre). A key challenge in this type of analysis is to predict the number of computing resources needed (as data is dynamically made available) based on heuristics or prior execution history. This type of analysis can suffer from the same QoS limitations at In-situ analysis, as it still requires data to be shipped over the network from L3 to L1 infrastructure.

- **In-Transit Data Analysis:** Identifies the type of distributed analysis carried out at L3 and (more generally) L2. In-transit analysis makes use of capability available in resources along the path of the data, such as software defined network devices, to undertake partial analysis while the data is in transit from source (L3) to the data processing engine (generally L1). This approach can significantly improve overall analysis time (and limit use of resources at L1), as pre-analysis can help identify what needs to be carried out at L1. In-transit analysis therefore makes more effective use of computing capability available at L2.

3.1. CometCloud

Our multi-layer cloud analytics approach, depicted in Figure 1, has been implemented on top of Comet-Cloud to leverage CometCloud's orchestration mechanisms and federation model, which are described next. CometCloud is an autonomic framework for enabling real-world applications on software-defined federated cyberinfrastructure, including hybrid infrastructures integrating public & private Clouds, data-centres and Grids (Diaz-Montes, AbdelBaky, Zou, & Parashar, 2015). The overarching goal of CometCloud is to realize a software-defined federation with cloud abstractions that offer resources in an elastic and on-demand way and supporting the batch execution model. It also provides abstractions and mechanisms to support a range of programming paradigms and applications requirements on top of the federation. CometCloud is composed of a programming layer, autonomic management layer, and infrastructure/federation layer.

- **Infrastructure Layer:** it manages the dynamic resource federation and provides essential services. Two main components compose this layer. First, an information lookup system built on a content-based distributed hash-table (DHT) based on a structured peer-to-peer overlay (Parashar & Zhen, 2007). This information service maintains content locality and guarantees that content-based information queries, specified using keywords and wild cards, are satisfied with bound cost. The second is a scalable, decentralized shared coordination space built on top of the DHT, named CometSpace, which can be associatively accessed by all resources in the federation. CometSpace provides tuple-space like abstraction for coordination and messaging, and enables coordination in the federation model illustrated in Figure 2. Specifically, we define two types of coordination spaces. First, a single management space spans across all resource sites creating and orchestrating the federation. Second, multiple shared execution spaces are created on-demand during application workflow executions to satisfy computational or data needs. Execution spaces can be created within a single resource site, or can burst to others, such as public clouds or external HPC systems.

The CometCloud federation is created dynamically and collaboratively, where resources/sites can join or leave at any point, identify themselves (using security mechanisms such as public/private keys), negotiate terms of federation, discover available resources, and advertise their own resources and capabilities (Diaz-Montes, Xie, Rodero, Zola, Ganapathysubramanian, & Parashar, 2014).

- **Autonomic Management Layer:** it enables users and/or applications to define objectives and policies that drive resource provisioning and execution of application workflows while satisfying user constraints (e.g., budget, deadline) and application requirements (e.g., type of resources). The autonomic mechanisms in place not only provision the right resources when needed, but also monitor the progress of the execution and adapt the execution to prevent violations of established agreements (Diaz-Montes, Zou, Singh, Tao, & Parashar, 2014).
- **Programming/Interface Layer:** it provides interfaces to independently describe application workflows and resources. Application workflows are currently described using XML documents, as a set of stages defining input and output data, dependencies to other stages, scheduling policies, and possibly annotated with specific objectives and policies.

Figure 2. CloudCloud federation architecture

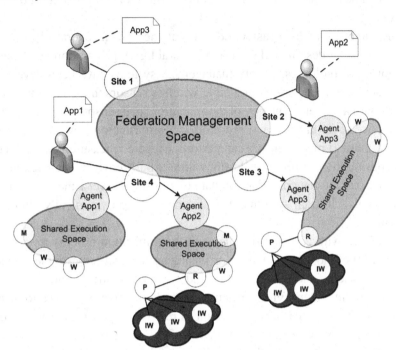

3.2. EnergyPlus Application

EnergyPlus has been validated as an efficacious tool for running energy simulations (Fumo, Mago, & Luck, 2010). EnergyPlus is an energy analysis and thermal load simulation tool for allowing building performance simulations such as lighting/daylighting, HVAC, service water heating, and on-site energy generations. Based on a user description of a building, EnergyPlus can calculate the heating and cooling loads necessary to maintain thermal control setpoints, conditions throughout a secondary HVAC system and coil loads, and the energy consumption of primary plant equipment. In EnergyPlus, inputs and outputs are accomplished by means of ASCII (text) files. On the input side, there are three files:

- The Input Data Dictionary (IDD) that describes the types (classes) of input objects and the data associated with each object;
- The Input Data File (IDF) that contains all the data for a particular simulation.
- The Weather Data File (EPW) that contains all the data for exterior climate of a building.

In addition, EnergyPlus can be used as an energy simulation engine employing a simultaneous load/ system/plant simulation methodology. In load calculation, different methods are used to calculate heat conduction through envelopes and then a heat balance method for zone load (Crawley, et al., 2001). Moreover, EnergyPlus makes use of a modular, loop-based method to simulate HVAC systems which helps accelerate the model construction process (Strand, 2001). Through the object of "Setpoint Manager" in EnergyPlus, many different kinds of variables such as supply air temperature and chilled water supply temperature can be controlled and this function facilitates the construction of modern advanced supervisory control.

Energy efficiency practices include passive design strategies which generally focus on building shape and orientation, passive solar design, and the use of natural lighting. To improve efficiency and enable more active monitoring of buildings, energy management systems have been developed that provide advanced controls such as motion sensors and other wireless sensors that allow more detailed monitoring to be carried out with a higher frequency of data capture. Such sensors also enable an automatic and instant distribution of receiver-tailored and pre-processed information (raw data, consumption trends, deviation alarms, etc.). Smart meter sensors can perform triggered measurement and record of electricity, water, or gas consumption at different levels within a built environment/ facility (sub-metering) and allow for remote access to the consumption data (e.g., using Power Line, GSM, or standard wired communication protocols). In such systems, it is also possibly to dynamically alter the rate at which data capture takes place.

As the time associated with carrying out the energy optimisation process represents a key aspect, both facility managers (i.e. those responsible for managing the built environment) and infrastructure providers (i.e. those providing the data analytics and networks platform) aim to minimise time and generate optimised set-points (identifying particular control objectives that need to be met by the facility managers). The time parameter is also important in real-time optimisation where delays can bring additional costs for the facility managers especially when build related parameters (such as temperature, occupancy, etc.) are frequently changing. The complexity of this process increases depending on the size of the facility involved – such as sports facility considered in this paper. In the context of this work, users are represented by building facility managers interested to minimise a number of objectives related to energy. Such users are interested in running the optimisation process and to obtain the required results in a limited time period. In practice, such an optimisation process will require multiple executions of an optimisation package, such as EnergyPlus, with different sensor data and parameter ranges, see Figure 3. In Figure 3, the simulation phase corresponds with our proposed cloud data analytic approach. We consider two key parameters here: (i) *Complexity of the building model* has a direct impact on the overall simulation time; and (ii) *Simulation period*, i.e. the time interval over which the energy optimisation is carried out – can range from 1 week to 1 year, for instance.

Similarly, the cloud system must comply with two parameters:

- **Time-to-Complete:** An optimisation plan needs to be completed by a particular time deadline. Assuming that sensors can deliver readings every 15 minutes, the optimisation process also needs to be carried out over an equivalent period. Each new execution uses as input the last configuration of the building and set points (for various control outputs) associated with the building.
- **Results Quality:** An optimisation process, as identified in this study, consists of a number of EnergyPlus simulations. Depending on the complexity of the building and the period to simulate, a time interval is associated with each optimisation process. If suitable computational resources are not available, it may become necessary to sacrifice the quality of results and complete only a part of the required rounds of simulation in order to comply with the time deadline. Returning a partial optimisation result may have a twofold impact: (i) reduces the number of resources needed to carry out the simulation/ optimisation; and (ii) influences the accuracy of the energy optimisation plan undertaken by facility managers.

Figure 3. Sensor based deployment

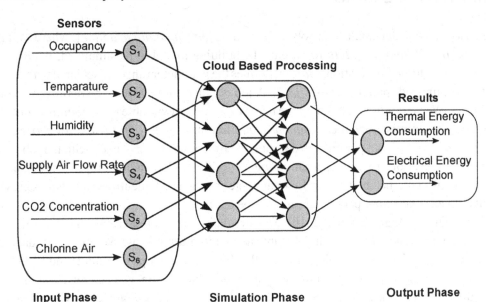

For instance, if a computing resource provider decides to stop the optimisation process after a certain number of simulations – lower quality results will need to be returned to the user. From a computational perspective, depending on the size of the building, the number and range of parameters being considered, EnergyPlus requires significant computational resources to execute. For relatively smaller building models (with a small number of surfaces, zones, and systems), which do not require large amount of computer memory, processor speed is generally more significant than I/O. For large models, main memory and internal cache have a greater influence on reducing run time. If an energy model run will produce lots of hourly or time step data, I/O access speed and latency also become important in reducing run time.

EnergyPlus has been demonstrated to provide an efficacious tool for running energy simulations (Fumo, Mago, & Luck, 2010). This energy analysis software package enables thermal load simulations, enabling an architect, engineer or facilities manager to carry out building performance simulations. Such simulations can include a pre-defined "run period" and involve the integrated coupling of building envelope (generally considered as the physical separator between the interior and exterior environments of a building), lighting/daylighting, Heating, Ventilation Air Conditioning (HVAC), service water heating and on-site energy generation (through solar panels and other sources). In EnergyPlus, inputs and outputs are specified by means of ASCII (text) files. On the input side, there are three files:

- Input Data Dictionary (IDD) that describes the types (classes) of input objects and the data associated with each object
- Input Data File (IDF) that contains all the data for a particular simulation
- Weather Data File (EPW) that contains all the data for exterior climate of a building

Based on a user description of a building, EnergyPlus can calculate the heating and cooling loads necessary to maintain thermal control setpoints, conditions throughout a secondary HVAC system and coil loads, and the energy consumption of primary plant equipment.

4. APPLICATION SCENARIO

In our scenario we consider that a user job is defined as *job*:[*input,obj,deadline*], where *input* data is represented as [*IDF,W,[param]*], *IDF* represents the building model to be simulated, *W* represents the weather file required for the simulation, [*param*] defines the parameter ranges associated with the *IDF* file that need to be optimized [param]=[$r_i \rightarrow (x_m,x_n)$]. A job *obj* therefore encodes the optimisation objective *objective*:[*outVarName,min/max*], defining the name of the output variable to be optimised *outVarName* and the target of the optimisation process *min/max*, *min*:minimising the *outVarName* or *max*:maximising the *outVarName*. *Deadline* is a parameters defining the time interval associated with the job submitted.

A job contains a set of tasks mapped into tuples within the CometCloud tuple-space. Each task is characterised by two parameters with the first parameter being a task identifier and *data* represents one set of results (given a particular parameter range). The application scenario used in this chapter is based on EnergyPlus (Fumo, Mago, & Luck, 2010). The simulation output represents an optimum setpoint to be implemented within the building using suitable actuation mechanisms. We use sensor data from the *SportE²* project (SportE2 EU FP7 project) pilot called FIDIA (FIDIA project pilot) and EMTE (EMTE project pilot), public sports buildings in Rome, Italy and Bilbao, Spain, respectively. The *SportE²* project, funded under the European FP7 ICT programme, focuses on developing energy efficient products and services dedicated to the needs and unique characteristics of sporting facilities. Figure 4 shows our application scenario which involves several buildings and cloud infrastructures.

4.1. Sensors Level

Each sensor in our pilot can communicate via a gateway or can be directly linked (using wired infrastructure) with the pilot automation server (identified as I/O to Automation Server (AS) in the table). Sensors are usually battery powered meters with a typical autonomy. Sensors can measure: (i) indoor temperature and air temperature inlet – usually battery powered with a Modbus IP protocol connected to the AS gateway; (ii) Water Temperature using a regular I/O operation to the AS gateway; (iii) Indoor

Figure 4. Application scenario

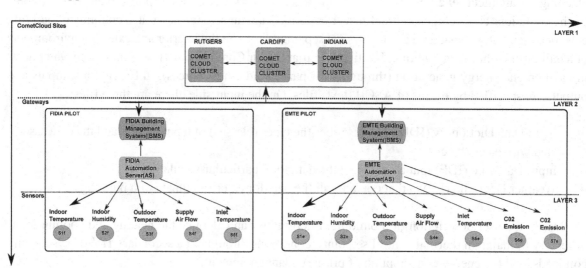

Humidity – battery powered, and communicating to the AS gateway; and (iv) Supplied Air Flow Rate measured with a velocity sensor and using I/O operations to the AS gateway.

4.2. Gateways Level - BMS and AS

There are two distinct gateways:Building Management System (BMS) and Automation Server (AS). The BMS gateway is a server machine that controls the activities and spaces within the building. BMSs are most commonly implemented in large projects with extensive mechanical, electrical, and plumbing systems and are a critical component to manage energy demand. In addition to controlling the building's internal environment, BMS systems are sometimes linked to access control (turnstiles and access doors controlling who is allowed access to the building) or other security systems such as closed-circuit television (CCTV) and motion detectors.

The AS gateway is a hardware-based server that is factory programmed with StruxureWare Building Operation software (for instance). In a small installation, the embedded AS acts as a stand-alone server, mounted with its I/O modules with a small footprint. In medium and large installations, functionality is distributed over multiple Automation Servers (ASs) that communicate over TCP/IP. Capable of co-ordinating traffic from above and below its location, the AS can deliver data directly to you or to other servers throughout the site. The AS can run multiple control programs, manage local I/O, alarms, and users, handle scheduling and logging, and communicate using a variety of protocols. Consequently, most parts of the system function autonomously and will continue to run as a whole even if communication fails or individual servers or devices go offline.

4.3. CometCloud Sites Level

At this level, we have a CometCloud-based federation of resources [31, 33], where each site has access to a set of heterogeneous and dynamic resources, such as public/private clouds, supercomputers, etc. These resources are uniformly exposed using cloud-like abstractions and mechanisms that facilitate the execution of applications across the resources. Each site decides on the type computation it runs, as well as the prices based on various decision functions that include factors such as availability of resources, computational cost, etc. This federation is dynamically created at runtime where sites can join or leave at any given time. Notably, this requires a minimal configuration at each site that amounts to specifying the available resources, a queuing system or a type of cloud, and credentials. We consider three sites in this scenario – one based at Cardiff, at Rutgers, and at Indiana. A federation site therefore refers to a deployment which is connected over a network and not co-located with a master node. Our sites are: Cardiff site: has a virtualized cluster-based infrastructure with 12 dedicated physical machines. Each machine has 12 CPU cores at 3.2 GHz. Each VM uses one core with 1GB of memory. The networking infrastructure is 1Gbps Ethernet with a measured latency of 0.706 ms on average. Rutgers site: has a cluster-based infrastructure with 32 nodes. Each node has 8 CPU cores at 2.6 GHz, 24 GB memory, and 1Gbps Ethernet connection. The measured latency on the network is 0.227 ms on average. FutureGrid site: make use of an OpenStack cloud deployment at Indiana University. We have used instances of type medium, where each instance has 2 cores and 4 GB of memory. The measured latency of the cloud virtual network is 0.706 ms on average.

5. THE TESTING PILOTS

We use sensor data from two project pilots called FIDIA and EMTE public sports building facilities. is a research project co-financed by the European Commission FP7 programme under the domain of Information Communication Technologies and Energy Efficient Buildings. This project focuses on developing energy efficient products and services dedicated to needs and unique characteristics of sporting facilities.

5.1. Building Properties

The sports facilities are equipped with sensors and actuators for monitoring, control and optimisation of the facility. The building has metering capability to determine consumption of electricity, gas, biomass, water and thermal energy. This data can be accessed through a specialist interface and recorded for analysis. The sub-metering of thermal and electrical consumption within grouped zones (gym/fitness and swimming pool is also provided along with "comfort" monitoring by functional area: gym, fitness room and swimming pool). In these areas the Predicted Mean Vote (PMV) index (which measures the average response of a group of people to a thermal sensation scale – such as hot, warm to cool and cold) – it is one of the most widely recognised thermal comfort models, and is measured as a function of the activity performed within a particular part of the building. The occupancy is also monitored in the gym, fitness room and around the swimming pool area. The structure of the facility does not allow the direct measurement of the total value of occupancy for the pilot, so the occupancy of the whole facility is provided as sum of number of people who have entered/exited the building over a particular time interval.

5.2. Optimisation Description

In our optimisation scenario, the objective is to reduce energy consumption while maintaining indoor thermal comfort. HVAC energy consumption consists of two components: thermal energy and electricity consumption, therefore energy consumption function can be described as follows: E = +, where, and represent thermal energy consumption and electricity consumption respectively. *E* represents total energy consumed by the building facility.

ConstraintsPMV is used as one constraint for the optimisation model. As mentioned previously, the acceptable comfort zone is defined as $-1 < PMV < +1$ in this scenario. Figure 5 shows data generated by sensors and the set points obtained after data optimization.

6. EVALUATION

In our experiments we use two different configurations – (a) Cloud level analysis where the tasks are executed exclusively at the cloud level with two configurations: (i) single cloud context where all the tasks have to be processed locally (within the local site) and (ii) federation cloud context where the sites have the option of outsourcing tasks to remote sites; and (b) Distributed Cloud analysis where the tasks are executed on a multi-cloud infrastructure.

Figure 5. Sensor application

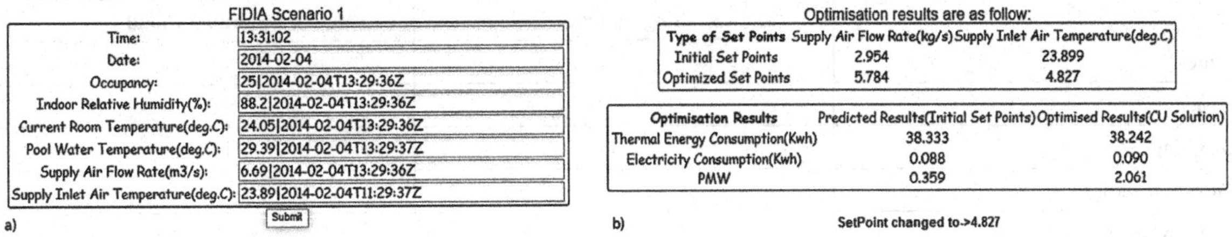

6.1. Clouds Level Analysis

In these experiments, we evaluate how the system works when only the cloud level is used for executing EnergyPlus simulations. In this part, we ignore other levels and the entire load of the system is exclusively on the clouds. We use as inputs for our calculation (i) CPU time of remote site as the amount of time spent by each worker to computer the tasks, and (ii) storage time on remote site as the amount of time needed to store data remotely.

Experiment 1: Job Completed

In this experiment we consider jobs submitted by the user based on parameter ranges identified in Table 1. In this instance, the master has two different options: (i) running the tasks on the local infrastructure (single cloud case) or (ii) outsourcing (using a distributed infrastructure) part of the task to a remote site (federation cloud case).

In Table 2we present the results obtained after running the tasks using the two setups. As tasks generated based on the job parameter ranges have a corresponding deadline of 1 hour, only 34 out of 38 managed can be completed on the local cloud system. As these tasks represent EnergyPlus simulations, part of an optimisation process with a given building model, running only a set of the simulations can impact the quality of results provided to a user. A higher quality of results would imply running all the 38 tasks generated from the job input. In the second part of this experiment we have tested the federation scenario where some tasks are outsourced to a federation site. From Table 2we observe that the total number of nodes used to compute the tasks within a federation context is 6 workers which has a direct impact on the total time consumed with job completion. In the federation context all the tasks are successfully completed in 55 minutes by outsourcing a number of 15 task requests (represented as tuples in the CometCloud system) to the remote site. From experiment 1 we can conclude that it is beneficial to process as many tasks as possible on the local resources. This is only possible when the parameters ranges are small and consequently the number of tasks derived can be deployed exclusively on the local infrastructure. However, in the local site only 34 out of 38 tasks are completed. When the

Table 1. Input parameters: experiment 1

P1	P2	P3	P4	Deadline
{16,18,20,22,24}	{0,1}	{0,1}	{0,1}	1 Hour

Table 2. Results: experiment 1

	Single Cloud	Federated Cloud
Nodes	3	6
Tasks	38	38
Deadline	1 hour	1 hour
Tuples exchanged	-	15
CPU on remote site	-	5626.45 Sec
Storage on remote site	-	1877.10 Sec
Completed tasks	34/38	38/38 in 55min 40s

parameters ranges are large resulting in a larger number of tasks, the federation option can reduce cost and increase the quality of results. When outsourcing to remote sites more tasks can be completed as illustrated inTable 2.

Experiment 2: Job uncompleted

In experiment 1 we explored the case when a significant percentage of the tasks can be completed on the local infrastructure according to the given deadline. In this experiment we stretch further the capabilities of the infrastructure by increasing the ranges associated with each of the parameters being considered and consequently the number of tasks that need to be processed. As illustrated in Table 3the parameters ranges are increased but we keep the same deadline of 1 hour.

Results are collected in Table 4. We observe that a deadline of 1 hour is too short for completing a higher number of tasks then in experiment 1. From Table 4it can be observed that in the context of a single cloud system (3 workers) only 37 out of 72 tasks are completed within the deadline of 1 hour. On the other hand, when using a federation cloud setup with 6 workers, we observe that a number of 58 tasks are completed in the 1 hour deadline. This takes place by exchanging 15 tuples between the two federation sites, thereby increasing the overall cost associated with using remote resources. Contrary to experiment 1 where most of the tasks are successfully completed within the single federation cloud, in this experiment we observe that only 58 out of 72 tasks are completed. We can conclude that in some cases, according to the inputs of the users, neither single cloud nor federated cloud is enough for completed all the tasks. However there is a significant improvement in terms of number of tasks completed that can be achieved when using cloud federation – in the context of experiment 2, 19 more tasks are completed by using federation. It must be noted, that the percentage of tasks completed has a direct impact on the quality of results. To enable a greater number of task completions, we need to increase the deadline or dynamically federate-in new resources from a public cloud, for instance.

Table 3. Input parameter: experiment 2

P1	P2	P3	P4	Deadline
{16,17,18,19,20,21,22,23,24}	{0,1}	{0,1}	{0,1}	1 Hour

Experiment 3: On-demand job execution

In this experiment we study how the system reacts to the availability of real-time data from building sensors. The objective is to better understand the overhead required to execute an EnergyPlus simulation dynamically, based on the availability of new data from sensors. In this experiment we run two different configurations: (i) multiple EnergyPlus instances are deployed locally within a single cloud environment (i.e. Cardiff site); and (ii) multiple EnergyPlus instances are executed remotely (i.e. Rutgers site) via outsourcing. Both of these configurations involve allocating new instances (i.e. reserve instance and start a worker) when new data becomes available.

Table 4. Results: experiment 2

	Single Cloud	**Federated Cloud**
Nodes	3	6
Tasks	72	72
Deadline	1 hour	1 hour
Tuples exchanged	-	15
CPU on remote site	-	5637.27 Sec
Storage on remote site	-	1869.41 Sec
Completed tasks	37/72	58/72

Figure 6. Summary of experimental results: cost, tasks completed, total tasks, time to complete

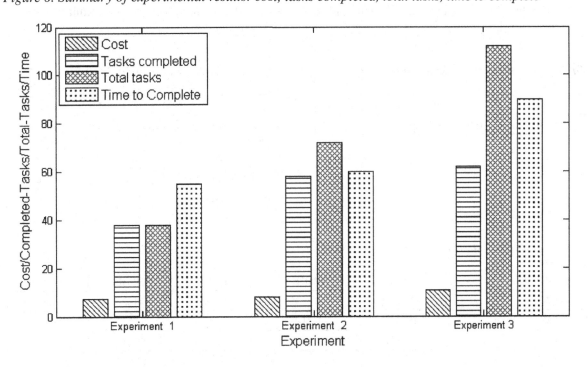

The input parameters of this experiment (provided in Table 5) are similar to those from Experiment 1. We use a predefined availability interval of 5 minutes to specify the frequency over which new sensor data becomes available – thereby leading to the submission of a new job (involving an EnergyPlus execution). From Table 6 it can be observed that on-demand job execution adds an additional overhead to job completion. We calculate an overhead per job as the difference between the expected time-to-complete and the actual time-to-complete. A local on-demand execution has an overhead of 33.15ms, whereas a remote on-demand execution has an overhead of 40.97ms per job. These are tolerable delays compared to the overall execution time of the job of 1-1.5 hours. In addition, in Table 7 we present the overhead recorded when launching EnergyPlus instances with different parameters ranges (R1(16-24)-R2(16-28)-R3(16-32)). We use a time-to-complete related to the number of EnergyPlus instances deployed (i.e. T1(18E+) is the time-to-complete for 18 EnergyPlus instances). It can be observed that the larger gets the parameter range, the higher is the time-to-complete associated with the job.

6.2. Distributed clouds analytics

In the second use case, information collected by sensors is processed in-transit in the Gateway layer to filter out various sensor information (e.g., values out of range or certain combination of parameters that cannot lead to reasonable results) and then create jobs to be sent to federations sites level. In this case, one job might require less computation capability due to in-transit filtering. We explore the benefit of in-transit data analysis by comparing differences between these two scenarios in terms of the total cost for each site to compute all jobs, the overall time spent and number of jobs completed successfully. The infrastructure used in these experiments is described on Section 4.3.

We consider sensors in two geographically distributed buildings that are collecting information about the status of the building and sending this information to gateways. In order to better explore the behaviour of in-transit data analysis and task distribution, we emulate the execution of the tasks and use a Poisson distribution to periodically generate sensor collected information every 100 minutes. A job is

Table 5. Input parameters: experiment 3

	P1	P2	P3	P4	Deadline
	{16,18,20,22,24}	{0,1}	{0,1}	{0,1}	–

Table 6. Results: experiment 3

	Single Cloud	Federated Cloud
Nodes	3	6
Tasks per job	38	38
Availability interval	5 min	5 min
Average Overhead	33.15 milisec	40.97 milisec

Table 7. Results: experiment 3- multiple instances

Ranges/Time	T1(18E+)	T2(32E+)	T3(48E+)	T4(64E+)	T5(72E+)
R1(16-24)	1301.293	2100,495	3363,904	4182,82	4619,82
R2(16-28)	1522,07	3384,452	4924,17	6482,12	7929,21
R3(16-32)	1823,37	4523,14	5832,432	7111,34	9332,12

Table 8. Parameters Range

Parameters	P1	P2	P3	P4	Deadline
Before filter	16,18	0,1	0,1	0,1	30 Min/task
After filter	16	0,1	0,1	0,1	30 Min/task

generated after the gateway has received data from sensors. One job will produce multiple EnergyPlus computation sub-tasks. All the three sites, Rutgers, FutureGrid and Cardiff, bid for computing those jobs based on their available resources and how many sub-tasks they can finish before the deadline. No single winner will get all the sub-tasks. Instead, these sub-tasks will be distributed to all bidder sites based on their estimation of job completion deadline. Each site will get *bidNum/allSitesTotalBidNum* sub-tasks to compute. We allocate two local and two external workers to each site. Once a site consumes a list of sub-tasks, these tasks will be sent to workers to finish computation.

- **No Filtering:** From Table 8 we can see that the original parameters we get from sensors includes four types of parameters which then gives a combination of 16 EnergyPlus sub-tasks per job. Each EnergyPlus sub-task takes 30 minutes to compute on all three sites. In Figure 7c, we can notice that due to resource limitation, some jobs are rejected because these sub-tasks cannot be completed before the deadline by these three sites. Among those accepted jobs, *Not 100% Completed* Jobs are those whose sub-tasks were completed within the given deadline. This is caused by various reasons such as network speed, scheduling constraints, placing multiple bids without knowing results of previous auctions, etc. Those *100% completed* jobs have all sub-tasks completed on time.
- **With Filtering:** After analysis of sensor data, we can filter out some of those unnecessary parameters. In Table 8, we can find that the number of sub-tasks for each job is reduced to eight. In order to better compare with this use case with the previous one, in this experiment we assume that jobs are generated following the same time series as the previous experiment. This means the total number of jobs is the same, only the sub-task number per job is smaller. Figure 7c shows that the number of rejected jobs is reduced significantly after filtering. The percentage of Not 100% Completed Jobs in accepted jobs is also decreased. From Figure 7a, we can see that the total execution time for completing all jobs is decreased. The total execution cost also shows rapid decrease in Figure 7b. This is mainly because the number of sub-tasks per job is reduced from 16 to eight after filtering part of the parameters. Therefore, we can prove the necessity of performing in-transit data analysis at different layers.

7. LAYER BASED DECISION FUNCTION

In the previous section we have considered that the system has a single decision function according to which the processing of the tasks is scheduled. Here, we evaluate individual layers by considering that each layer has its own decision function, whereby each layer decision function is dependent on the other layers. We also consider that each layer has a set of constraints based on which the decision function is built.

Figure 7. Summary of experimental results for use cases with filter and without filter. 7a collects the total execution time in each case; 7b collects the total cost spent on computing all jobs; 7c shows the number of rejected jobs, 100% Completed and Not 100% Completed jobs

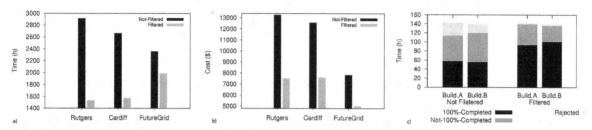

We consider the following set of constraints:

$$QoS_T = \min_{DC}(\text{cost}) \, \& \, \min_{G/W}(storage) \, \& \, \min_S(battery) \tag{1}$$

1. Sensors Level: *L3:Min(battery)* – For sensors we aim to reduce the battery consumption and the amount of data to record.
2. Gateway Level: *L2:Min(storage)*– At the gateway level we aim to reduce the amount of storage used with data.
3. Clouds Level: *L1:Min(cost)*– At this level we aim to reduce the cost associated with task processing.

We consider a quality of service metric composed by three individual layer metrics:

$$QoS_T = QoS_T^{DC} + QoS_T^{G/W} + QoS_T^{S} \tag{2}$$

where QoS_T represents the total quality of service that the system needs to comply, QoS_T^{DC} represents the quality of service for the clouds layer, $QoS_T^{G/W}$ is the quality of service at the gateway layer and QoS_T^{S}, the quality of service at the sensors layer, respectively.

In Algorithm 1 we present the protocol for processing the tasks with several parameters such as battery, storage and cost. The |*data*| parameter refers to the amount of data that is recorded for undertaking the required simulations. In accordance with the |*data*| parameter we calculate:(i) The cost at cloud layer required for running the simulations based on the amount of |*data*| collected; (ii) The storage at gateway layer required for storing the |*data*| collected; and (iii) The battery required at sensor layer for collecting the amount of |*data*|.

7.1. Real Deployment Validation

In this section we validate the presented approach by testing its efficiency in a real world scenario. For undertaking these experiments and providing a comparison base, we use the SportE2 (SportE2 EU FP7 project) pilots to deploy the cloud optimisation. In this section we evaluate the impact of our distributed cloud optimisation solution from two perspectives:

Algorithm 1. Protocol for distributed processing

```
1: if |data| > storage and |data| > battery and |data| < cost then
2: process (clouds);
3: else if |data| > storage and |data| > cost and |data| < battery then
4: process (sensor);
5: else if |data| > battery and |data| > cost and |data| < storage then
6: process (gateway);
7: else if |data| > battery and |data| > cost and |data| > storage then
8: process (clouds);
9: else
10: process (sensor);
11: end if
```

- Amount of energy that the pilots can save by running the optimisation process on a distributed cloud environment
- Amount of money that the pilots can save by using a cloud environment to run optimisation

We have recorded the "real energy consumption" as identified in the pilots over a period of one day and compared with the results obtained when running the optimisation within our cloud methodology. It must be noted that the cloud optimisation process was conducted based on real input data recorded from the pilots to whom we have applied an EnergyPlus optimisation process deployed on a cloud infrastructure.

In our evaluation cases we compare the distributed cloud optimisation, as identified in this chapter, with traditional optimisation techniques as existing in the pilot. A traditional optimisation technique refers to a number of operations that pilot personnel are adopting for reducing energy. All these operations are manually applied (e.g., switching off the boiler, the air fans, the lighting system, etc.) and have no automated implementation or consistent decision making process. A distributed cloud based optimisation, on the other hand, is based on a number of simulations undertaken with EnergyPlus. This is related to a set of input parameters and generates optimised values according to which set points within a building are automatically adjusted.

Case 1: Energy Consumption: Cloud Optimisation vs. Traditional Optimisation Method

Figure 8 illustrates how energy consumption evolves in the pilots over a monitored period of 1 day (24hours). It can be observed that the energy consumption, as recorded in the pilot and undertaken with traditional optimisation methods, fluctuates between 0 and 100Kwh with a peak value of 300Kwh. For the cloud based optimisation the energy consumption fluctuates over the interval of [0-38] Kwh. We can immediately conclude that cloud optimisation imposes uniformity over the energy consumption.

From Figure 8, it can also be identified two consumption schedules: (i) day schedule ([0-20] recording stages and [50-100] stages) and (ii) night schedules ([20-50] recording stages). During the day schedule the energy consumption is high, whereas over night the consumption is minimum. However, as traditional optimisation technique has no intelligent decision making process for some night schedule intervals energy consumption is still high. Cloud-based optimisation assumes a continuous adaptation based on the values read from sensors. This process of continuous adaptation associated with an intelligent optimisation mechanism facilitates significant energy savings. For a monitor period of 1 day(24

Figure 8. Energy Consumption: Cloud based Optimisation vs. Traditional optimisation method

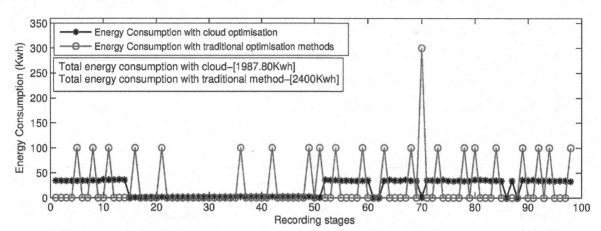

Figure 9. Price with Energy Consumption: Cloud based Optimisation vs. Traditional optimisation method

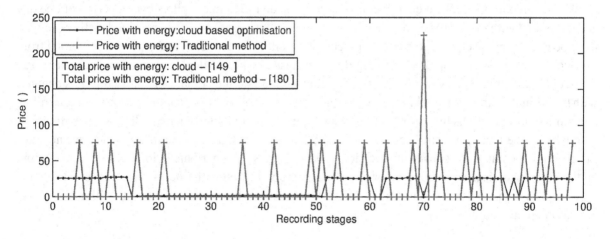

hours), the saving obtained by using cloud based optimisation is of 412.20KWh equivalent with a saving percentage of approximately 39%.

Case 2:   Price with energy consumption: Cloud optimisation vs. Traditional optimisation method

For undertaking this validation case, we have used the electricity prices for European stock markets, taking into account the average selling prices of electricity. In this case we want to reflect the money equivalent saved when using a cloud based optimisation.

As presented in Figure 9, the costs with energy are significantly reduced when using cloud optimisation. This reduction is identified not only during night schedule but also during day schedule by balancing between the comfort and the energy consumption in a cost effective way. Over a period of 24 hours we have identified a cost reduction with energy of 30.1 euros.

8. CONCLUSION

Distributed clouds have the capability of optimising the system workload in accordance to a number of computing requirements and timing constraints. In data-intensive applications executing tasks in a distributed way can lead to significant benefit – reducing the need to capture all the data at a single site (e.g., at a data centre). Energy efficiency practises include passive design strategies regarding building shape and orientation, passive solar design, and the use of natural lighting. Modern independent and wireless sensor technologies are allowing deeper monitoring with increased frequency and to enable an automatic and instant distribution of receiver tailored and pre-processed information (raw data, consumption trends, deviation alarms, etc.).

In this chapter, we have presented the design and implementation of a multi-cloud approach for in-transit analytics. We have experimentally evaluated a number of scenarios for distributed cloud optimisation. The experimental results have shown a number of benefits that our system provides with regards to task completion. As robust energy management needs to employ a set of computing mechanisms for addressing the end use and global energy consumptions, we use as inputs values from a pilot facility as recorded through the smart meters and a set of sensors, and carry out further processes for achieving a set of predefined set-points. We show how our federated cloud model facilitates EnergyPlus simulations to be deployed with data recorded from building sensors and how various analyses can be applied at intermediate architectural layers to ease the energy optimisation of buildings. The experimental results have shown a number of benefits that our system provides with regards to task completion and costs.

By using a cost perspective, an application user may therefore infer on how many concurrent simulations (jobs) to execute to achieve a discount from a cloud provider – which may subsequently influence the scheduling decisions made by a job manager. We present a real a federation framework that facilitates the orchestration of geographically distributed resources and creates a multicloud environment where user requests are handled based on a decision function (influenced by resource availability, cost, performance and other user-defined constraints such as access privileges)

ACKNOWLEDGMENT

The research presented in this work is supported by EU FP7 project, ICT for Energy Efficiency in European Sport Facilities. The research presented in this work is supported in part by National Science Foundation (NSF) via grants numbers ACI 1339036, ACI 1310283, CNS 1305375, and DMS 1228203, and by IBM Faculty awards. This project used resources from FutureGrid supported in part by NSF OCI-0910812. The research at Rutgers was conducted as part of the Rutgers Discovery Informatics Institute (RDI2).

REFERENCES

Amazon EC2. (n. d.). *Amazon*. Retrieved from http://aws.amazon.com/ec2/

Amazon Kinesis. (n. d.). *Amazon*. Retrieved from http://aws.amazon.com/kinesis/

Assuncao, M. D., Costanzo, A. d., & Buyya, R. (2009). *Evaluating the cost-benefit of using Cloud computing to extend the capacity of clusters*. ACM HPDC. doi:10.1145/1551609.1551635

Bennett, J. C., Abbasi, H., Bremer, P.-T., Grout, R., Gyulassy, A., Jin, T., ... (2012). Combining in-situ and in-transit processing to enable extreme-scale scientific analysis. *Proc. of the Int. Conf. on High Perf. Computing, Networking, Storage and Analysis (SC '12).*

Bhat, V., Parashar, M., & Klasky, S. (2007). Experiments with in-transit processing for data intensive grid workflows. *Proceedings of the 8th IEEE/ACM Inter. Conf. Grid Computing* (pp. 193-200). doi:10.1109/GRID.2007.4354133

Bittencourt, L. F., Senna, C. R., & Madeira, E. R. (2010). Enabling execution of service workflows in grid/cloud hybrid systems. Proceedings of the Network Operations and Management Symp. Workshop. doi:10.1109/NOMSW.2010.5486553

Celesti, A., Tusa, F., Villari, M., & Puliafito, A. (2010). *How to enhance cloud architectures to enable cross-federation.* IEEE CLOUD. doi:10.1109/CLOUD.2010.46

Chu, X., & Buyya, R. (2009). Service-Oriented Sensor Web. In *Sensor Networks and Configuration.* Springer.

CloudHarmony. (n. d.). Retrieved from http://cloudharmony.com

Cohen, J., Dolan, B., Dunlap, M., Hellerstein, J., & Welton, C. (2009). MAD Skills: New Analysis Practices for Big Data. *Proceedings of the VLDB Endowment.* doi:10.14778/1687553.1687576

Crawley, D. B., Lawrie, L. K., Winkelmann, F. C., Buhl, W., Huang, Y., & Pedersen, C. O. et al.. (2001). *Energyplus: creating a new-generation building energy simulation program.* Energy and Buildings.

Cuzzocrea, A., Fortino, G., & Rana, O. (2013). Managing Data and Processes in Cloud-Enabled Large-Scale Sensor Networks: State-of-the-Art and Future Research Directions. Proceedings of the DPMSS workshop alongside CCGrid (pp. 583-588).

Cuzzocrea, A., Furfaro, F., Greco, S., Masciari, E., Mazzeo, G., & Sacca, D. (2005). A Distributed System for Answering Range Queries on Sensor Network Data. In Proc. of PerComW'05.

Cuzzocrea, A., Furfaro, F., Mazzeo, G., & Sacca, D. (2004). A Grid Framework for Approximate Aggregate Query Answering on Summarized Sensor Network Readings. *Proc. of OTMW '04.* doi:10.1007/978-3-540-30470-8_32

Cuzzocrea, A., & Sacca, D. (2013). Exploiting Compression and Approximation Paradigms for Effective and Efficient OLAP over Sensor Network Readings in Data Grid Environments. *Concurrency and Computation.* doi:10.1002/cpe.2982

Cuzzocrea, A., & Sacca, D. (2013). Exploiting Compression and Approximation Paradigms for Effective and Efficient OLAP over Sensor Network Readings in Data Grid Environments. *Concurrency and Computation.* doi:10.1002/cpe.2982

Deelman, E., Singh, G., Livny, M., Berriman, B., & Good, J. (2008). The cost of doing science on the cloud: the Montage example. *Proceedings of the 2008 ACM/IEEE conference on Supercomputing.*

Diaz-Montes, J., AbdelBaky, M., Zou, M., & Parashar, M. (2015). CometCloud: Enabling Software-Defined Federations for End-to-End Application Workflows. *IEEE Internet Computing*, *19*(1), 69–73. doi:10.1109/MIC.2015.4

Diaz-Montes, J., Xie, Y., Rodero, I., Zola, J., Ganapathysubramanian, B., & Parashar, M. (2014). Federated computing for the masses - aggregating resources to tackle large-scale engineering problems. *CiSE Magazine*, 2014, 62-72.

Diaz-Montes, J., Zou, M., Singh, R., Tao, S., & Parashar, M. (2014). *Data-driven workflows in multi-cloud marketplaces*. IEEE Cloud.

Distefano, S., Merlino, G., & Puliafito, A. (2012). *SAaaS: a Framework for Volunteer-Based Sensing Clouds*. Parallel and Cloud Computing.

EMTE project pilot. (n. d.). *EMTESport*. Retrieved from http://www.emtesport.com/

FIDIA project pilot. (n. d.). *ASFIDIA*. Retrieved from http://www.asfidia.it

Fox, G., & Gannon, D. (2012). *Cloud Programming Paradigms for Technical Computing Applications*. Indiana University.

Fumo, N., Mago, P., & Luck, R. (2010). Methodology to Estimate Building Energy Consumption Using EnergyPlus Benchmark Models. In *Energy and Buildings* (pp. 2331-2337).

Garg, V., Chandrasen, K., Tetali, S., & Mathur, J. (2010). Energyplus Simulation Speedup Using Data Parallelization Concept. *Proceedings of the ASME Energy Sustainability Conference, New York: American Society of Mechanical Engineers* (pp. 1041-1048). doi:10.1115/ES2010-90509

GENICloud project. (n. d.). Retrieved from http://groups.geni.net/geni/wiki/GENICloud

Gorton, I., Liu, Y., & Yin, J. (2010). Exploring architecture options for a federated, cloud-based system biology knowledgebase. Proceedings of the IEEE Intl. Conf. on Cloud Computing Technology and Science. doi:10.1109/CloudCom.2010.79

Hadji, M., & Zeghlache, D. (2015). Mathematical Programming Approach for Revenue Maximization in Cloud Federations. Proceedings of the IEEE Transactions on Cloud Computing.

Keahey, K., & Freeman, T. (2008). Science Clouds: Early Experiences in Cloud Computing for Scientific Applications. *Cloud Computing and Its Applications (CCA-08)*.

Klasky, S., Ludaescher, B., & Parashar, M. (2006). The Center for Plasma Edge Simulation Workflow Requirements. *Proceedings of the 22nd Int. Conf. on Data Engineering Workshops (ICDEW'06)*. doi:10.1109/ICDEW.2006.143

Kovatsch, M. (n. d.). *Erbium REST Engine and CoAP implementation of Contiki*. Retrieved from http://people.inf.ethz.ch/mkovatsc/erbium.php

Kurschl, W., & Beer, W. (2009). Combining Cloud Computing and Wireless Sensor Networks. In Proc. of iiWAS'09.

Mashayekhy, L., Nejad, M., & Grosu, D. (2015). *Cloud federations in the sky: formation game and mechanism*. IEEE Transactions on Cloud Computing.

Neumann, D., Bodenstein, C., Rana, O. F., & Krishnaswamy, R. (2011). STACEE: Enhancing Storage Clouds using Edge Devices. *Proceedings of the ACM/IEEE workshop on Autonomic Computing in Economics (ACE)*. doi:10.1145/1998561.1998567

OCCI. (n. d.). Retrieved from http://occi-wg.org/

Ostermann, S., Prodan, R., & Fahringer, T. (2009). Extending grids with Cloud resource management for scientific computing. *IEEE/ACM Grid*.

Parashar, M., AbdelBaky, M., Rodero, I., & Devarakonda, A. (2013). Cloud Paradigms and Practices for Computational and Data-Enabled Science and Engineering. *Computing in Science & Engineering*, *15*(4), 10–18. doi:10.1109/MCSE.2013.49

Parashar, M., & Zhen, L. (2007). *A computational infrastructure for grid-based asynchronous parallel applications* (pp. 229–230). HPDC.

Perez-Lombard, L., Ortiz, J., & Pout, C. (2010). A review on buildings energy consumption information. In *Energy and Buildings* (pp. 394-398).

Petri, I., Diaz-Montes, J., Rana, O., Punceva, M., Rodero, I., & Parashar, M. (2015). *Modelling and Implementing Social Community Clouds*. IEEE Transactions on Services Computing.

Petri, I., Li, H., Rezgui, Y., Chunfeng, Y., Yuce, B., & Jayan, B. (2014). A modular optimisation model for reducing energy consumption in large scale building facilities, Renewable and Sustainable Energy Reviews. *Renewable & Sustainable Energy Reviews*, *38*, 990–1002. doi:10.1016/j.rser.2014.07.044

Petri, I., Rana, O., Rezgui, Y., Li, H., Beach, T., Zou, M., ... (2014). Cloud Supported Building Data Analytics. *Proceedings of the 14th IEEE/ACM International Symposium on Cluster, Cloud and Grid Computing (CCGrid)*, (pp. 641-650).

Riteau, P., Tsugawa, M., Matsunaga, A., Fortes, J., & Keahey, K. (2010). *Large-Scale Cloud Computing Research: Sky Computing on FutureGrid and Grid'5000*. ERCIM News.

Rochwerger, B., Breitgand, D., Levy, E., Galis, A., & others. (2009). The Reservoir model and architecture for open federated cloud computing.

Shelby, Z., Hartke, K., & Bormann, C. (n. d.). Constrained Application Protocol (CoAP). Retrieved from https://datatracker.ietf.org/doc/draft-ietf-core-coap/

SportE2 EU FP7 project. (n. d.). Retrieved from http://www.sporte2.eu/

Strand, R. K. (2001). Modularization and simulation techniques for heat balance based energy and load calculation programs: the experience of the ASHRAE Loads Toolkits and EnergyPlus. Proceedings of Building Simulation, (pp. 747-753).

Thain, D., Tannenbaum, T., & Livny, M. (2008). Distributed Computing in Practice: The Condor Experience. *Concurrency and Computation*, 2008, 323–356.

UNIFY EU FP7 project. (n. d.). Retrieved from http://www.fp7-unify.eu/

Vazquez, C., Huedo, E., Montero, R., & Llorente, I. (2009). Dynamic provision of computing resources from grid infrastructures and Cloud providers. *Proceedings of the Grid and Pervasive Computing Conf.*

Vecchiola, C., Pandey, S., & Buyya, R. (2009). High-Performance Cloud Computing: A View of Scientific Applications. *Proceedings of the 10th Intl. Symposium on Pervasive Systems, Algorithms, and Networks*, (pp. 4--16). doi:10.1109/I-SPAN.2009.150

Villegas, D., Bobroff, N., Rodero, I., Delgado, J., Liu, Y., Devarakonda, A., & Parashar, M. et al. (2012). Cloud federation in a layered service model. *Journal of Computer and System Sciences*, *78*(5), 1330–1344. doi:10.1016/j.jcss.2011.12.017

Vockler, J.-S., Juve, G., Deelman, E., & Rynge, M. (2011). Experiences using cloud computing for a scientific workflow application. *Proceedings of the 2nd Workshop on Scientific Cloud Computing in conjunction with ACM HPDC*. doi:10.1145/1996109.1996114

Yuriyama, M., & Kushida, T. (2010). Sensor-Cloud Infrastructure-Physical Sensor Management with Virtualized Sensors on Cloud Computing. *Proc. of NBiS'10*. doi:10.1109/NBiS.2010.32

Chapter 7

Decentralised Repositories for Transparent and Efficient Virtual Machine Operations:
Architecture of the ENTICE Project

Simon Ostermann
University of Innsbruck, Austria

Radu Prodan
University of Innsbruck, Austria

Gabor Kecskemeti
MTA-SZTAKI, Hungary

Thomas Fahringer
University of Innsbruck, Austria

Salman Taherizadah
University of Ljubljana, Slovenia

Vlado Stankovski
University of Ljubljana, Slovenia

ABSTRACT

ENTICE is an H2020 European project aiming to research and create a novel Virtual Machine (VM) repository and operational environment for federated Cloud infrastructures to: (i) simplify the creation of lightweight and highly optimised VM images tuned for functional descriptions of applications; (ii) automatically decompose and distribute VM images based on multi-objective optimisation (performance, economic costs, storage size, and QoS needs) and a knowledge base and reasoning infrastructure to meet application runtime requirements; and (iii) elastically auto-scale applications on Cloud resources based on their fluctuating load with optimised VM interoperability across Cloud infrastructures and without provider lock-in, in order to finally fulfil the promises that virtualization technology has failed to deliver so far. In this chapter, we give an inside view into the ENTICE project architecture. Based on stakeholders that interact with ENTICE, we describe the different functionalities of the different components and services and how they interact with each other.

INTRODUCTION

Virtualisation is a key technology in Cloud computing that allows users run multiple *virtual machines (VM)* with their own application environment on top of physical hardware. Virtualization enables scaling

DOI: 10.4018/978-1-5225-0153-4.ch007

up and down of applications by elastic on-demand provisioning of VMs in response to their variable load to achieve increased utilization efficiency at a lower operational cost, while guaranteeing the desired level of *Quality of Service (QoS)*, such as response time to the end-users. Typically, VMs are created using provider specific templates, so-called *VM images* (VMI) stored in proprietary repositories, leading to provider lock-in and hampering portability or simultaneous usage of multiple federated Clouds.

In this context, optimization at the level of the VMIs is needed both by the applications and by the underlying Cloud providers for improved resource usage, operational costs, elasticity, storage use, and other desired QoS-related features. The project team identified in this projective critical barriers that prevent many users from industry, business and academia to effectively use Cloud resources and virtualized environments for their computing and data processing needs:

- Manual, error-prone and time consuming VM image creation;
- Monolithic VM images with large deployment and migration overheads;
- Proprietary un-optimized VM repositories;
- Inelastic resource provisioning;
- Lack of information to support effective VM image optimization.

The goal of this chapter is to present a comprehensive overview of the common requirements, a high-level architecture, and initial use cases for the three main technological components of *ENTICE: dEcentralised repositories for traNsparent and efficienT vIrtual maChine opErations*, an H2020 EU project:

1. The distribution of Virtual Machine images, Container Images, or any other complete application representation (in short VMIs) that can be applied in the scope of the ENTICE project.
2. The VMI analysis and synthesis;
3. The VMI images portal and its associated knowledge base, acting as glue for the distributed, highly optimised repository.

In this chapter, the project partners made every effort to analyse and present the high-level architecture that gives a preview of the ENTICE functionality to be expected towards the end of the project. The ENTICE environment will let Cloud federations benefit by delivering VMIs in a faster way and in the right format for different hypervisors that are in use within a Cloud federation.

STATE OF THE ART

The following sections describe the state-of-the-art of the key technologies to be developed in the ENTICE project: lightweight creation of VMIs and storage. This is the key technology that Cloud federations will be able to utilize to provide faster and more portable VMIs that can be exchanged fast from one individual Cloud host to another.

Image Format and Interoperability

Tang et al. (Tang 2011) present Fast Virtual Disk (FVD) as a new virtual machine VMI format and the corresponding block device driver developed for QEMU, an emulator for multiple hypervisors, including

KVM, Xen-HVM, and VirtualBox. Its feature set includes flexible configurability, storage thin provisioning without a host file system, compact image, internal snapshot, encryption, copy-on-write, copy-on-read, and adaptive prefetching. As a principle, functions are intentionally orthogonal so that each feature can be configured independently yielding flexibility. The work is centred around VM mobility in a Cloud focusing on subtle details of copy-on-read, and adaptive prefetching enabling instant VM creation and instant VM migration, even if the VM image is stored on direct-attached storage. Experiments show that the throughput of FVD is 249% higher than that of QCOW2 for file creation. The proposed FVD, however, needs heavy adoption by the IaaS providers to provide useful benefits for the other players in the Cloud landscape.

The separation of application and the (virtual) infrastructure appears again in paper by Nguyen et al. (Nguyen 2013). The work introduces an elastic instrument (called high-level Cloud Abstraction Layer – CAL) allowing easy development and deployment of services on resources of multiple infrastructure-as-a-service (IaaS) Clouds simultaneously. Technically, the CAL provides an approach with emphasis on abstraction, inheritance and code reuse. Its advantage is that Cloud-based services can be easily developed by extending available classes provided by the CAL or other developers. Interoperability between different Clouds is solved by the basic abstraction classes of the CAL and all services are inherited and benefited from the advantage. Since this approach builds a higher level, object-oriented (OO) layer on top of IaaS, and applications can be controlled by defined interfaces, it largely resembles an OO PaaS construction.

Image Transfer, Distribution, and Placement

Schmidt et al. (Schmidt 2010) analysed the distribution of VM images in a multi-Cloud computing environment. They survey and analyse Network File System (NFS), unicast distribution, binary tree distribution, Fibonacci-tree distribution, peer-to-peer distribution (BitTorrent), multicast, cross-Cloud and layered copy-on-write (UnionFS) distribution methods. Furthermore, they take into consideration the security of VM image distribution such as encryption. Their performance is compared experimentally and conclusions claim multicast as the one with best performance while a layered copy-on-write approach can save significant (up to 90%) data traffic in cross-Cloud scenario. Their layering approach is more relevant for the runtime of the VMs as the layers are established once there are several executed VMs based on the same original VMI.

Zhou et al. (Zhou 2013) investigate VM image migration techniques in case of a heterogeneous (both regarding type and performance) storage system focusing on multiple criteria, i.e. user experience, device wearing and manageability. Based on a migration cost metric three new storage migration strategies are put forward towards (i) least amount of redundant writes (ii) highest IO performance and (iii) balance between IO performance and write redundancy. The multi-criteria optimisation of transferring VM images is also an objective of ENTICE. However, the consideration of device heterogeneity and consequently, the differentiation between criteria accordingly, is a novel and outstanding dimension. The prototyped system outperforms existing live storage migration by a significant margin that can be further improved by adaptive combination of the proposed schemes.

Xu et al. (Xu 2014) address the management of huge amount of VM images. Earlier approaches to optimize images usually focused on either improving performance or decreasing image size, which cannot satisfy the requirements of high IO performance, low storage consumption, and low management cost simultaneously. Typically, high IO performance requires images storing close to VMs, but this increases redundant data and consumes extra storage, and closer image means more data stored in local disks rather than a normal shared storage, which increases management cost as well. They propose a zone-based model to balance the requirements by partitioning computing nodes into many zones, and construct a shared storage in each zone to cache data. They also managed to improve the normal Copy-on-Write and cache mechanisms, providing new image types and cache functions to enhance the eventual effectiveness. Their performed evaluations show that this solution improves IO performance by more than 100% in general and even 10 times while adopting a friendly VM placement strategy. Though they improve IO performance and storage utilization with the propose solution, it also introduces some management overhead. To use this model, the whole image of a VM should be separated to a base image, a work image, and caches, which increase redundant data.

Bazarbayev et al. (Bazarbayev 2013) present a content-based scheduling algorithm for the placement of VMs in data centres. Their approach tries to find identical disk blocks in different VM disk images with similar operating systems, and schedule VMs with high content similarity to a previously deployed image on the same hosts. In this way they can reduce the amount of data transferred when deploying a VM on a destination host. Their analysis showed that content similarity between VMs with the same operating system and close version numbers can be as high as 60%. It is also found that there is close to zero content similarity between VMs with different operating systems. They also designed a content-based scheduling algorithm that lowers the network traffic associated with transfer of VM disk images by skipping similar contents. Their experimental results show that the amount of data transfer associated with deployment of VMs and transfer of virtual disk images can be lowered by more than 70%. The approach is limited to simulation results with no information how it performs in a real data centre.

Reich et al. (Reich 2012) propose a P2P streaming technique for storing VM images in a tool called vmTorrent. It is able to cope with read-intensive processes unlike network storage solutions. It uses a novel combination of block prioritization, profile-based execution prefetch, on-demand fetch and decoupling of VM image presentation from underlying data-stream. They also performed an experimental evaluation of vmTorrent, and found that it achieves comparable execution time to that achieved using local disks. This solution is also able to maintain this performance while scaling to 100 instances, providing 11x speedup over current state-of-the-art and 30x over traditional network storage. In order to use this approach, a custom file system server needs to be deployed that effectively virtualizes the VM images.

The work by Razavi et al. (Razavi 2013) is aimed at solving a common scenario when many VM images are to be transferred to many compute nodes simultaneously resulting slow VM start-up times, negatively impacting both dynamic scaling of web applications and the startup of high-performance computing applications consisting of many VM nodes. The work is based on the observation that only a tiny part of the VM image is needed for the VM to be able to start up hence, small caches for VM images are able to overcome the VM start-up bottlenecks. VM image caches are implemented as an extension to QCOW2, QEMU's implementation of copy-on-write. Once caches are warm, a large amount of network traffic can be avoided. While cold caches can cause significant performance degradation in certain environments, the current implementation is strongly tied to the structure of QEMU/QCOW2.

Duplication, De-Duplication, Chunks and Image Similarity

The core of the work by Peng et al. (Peng 2012) is an analysis of VM instance traces collected at six production data centres during four months with the aim of finding certain behavioural patterns that may enhance VM distribution. Results indicate that the number of instances created from the same VM image is relatively small at a given time and consequently conventional file based p2p sharing approaches may not be effective. Based on the understanding that different VM image files often have many common chunks of data, a chunk-level (as opposed to file-level) VMI Distribution Network (VDN) is proposed. Furthermore, the distribution scheme takes advantage of the hierarchical network topology of data centres to reduce the VM instance provisioning time and to minimize the overhead of maintaining chunk location information. Evaluation shows that VDN achieves as much as 30–80x speed up for large VM images under heavy traffic. The aims of this work are in strong relation to some objectives of ENTICE, the chunk based image distribution corresponding to the notion of small reusable parts of ENTICE where also the concept of image decomposition and reconstruction are put forward. Although they use a hierarchical metadata server, it still represents a bottleneck.

The paper by Keren et al. (Keren 2009) shows that with simple block level de-duplication techniques, one can identify nearly 70% of identical parts in frequently used VMIs. The paper shows several chunk identification techniques, but these chunks never reach over the level of file systems. In order to support online VM image assembly, the project has a chance to investigate chunking over file systems as well (allowing the use of more metadata and easier identification of likely de-duplicable content in the images). Finally, the paper addresses the issue of the package management systems and their effect on the efficiency of de-duplication. The different behaviour and dependencies in the widely available package management systems lead to some variance in data chunks on the VMIs. This variance is expected to be unavoidable even if one processes the metadata offered by file systems. They have shown that with even simple chunk-level de-duplication methods the size of a single image file can be reduced up to 80%. On the negative side, the block level handling of the images hides several important inter-relationships between the image parts.

Liquid is introduced as a lightweight distributed file system heavily building on ideas from the fields of de-duplication and peer-to-peer computing (Zhao 2014). The new file system is especially targeted on storing VMIs. The authors consider de-duplicating both running and offline VM images, and they allow rapid cloning mechanisms with the help of copy on read. As Liquid is implemented as a file system it can be rather transparent for the IaaS system, on the other hand the authors require the IaaS systems to completely adopt Liquid in order to achieve the best performance. Liquid provides good IO performance while doing deduplication in the background by caching frequently used data blocks and organizing them into chunks to reduce disk operations. P2P technique provides good scalability. On the other hand, an own file system should be used to track VM lifecycle with a metadata server.

Over several hundred VM images were analysed by Jayaram et al. (Jayaram 2011). The analysis consisted of checking how efficiently 5 de-duplication techniques could work on the images, and also the authors introduced several similarity metrics. The used metrics and techniques were both checked in inter and intra VM image contexts. Unfortunately, this paper does not go further than point out the chance of optimizing image storage or delivery with the help of de-duplication. The authors showed in a real world scenario that choosing the right chunk-size for de-duplication is crucial, as the chunk size increases so the de-duplication factor decreases. The analysed techniques were not checked for their capabilities of VM image size optimization.

The paper by Ng et al. (Ng 2011) goes further than the regular de-duplication techniques applied in past research. First of all, it analyses if the de-duplication actually reduces the performance of VM operations. Next, they consider how a changing ecosystem of VM images could be followed with a more dynamic de-duplication technique (which does not assume immutable VM image contents). Finally, the paper aims at improving the performance of running VM images by changing how de-duplication is applied to the constantly updating images. The authors propose the LiveDFS file system to answer the previously discussed 3 challenges. The authors even show the applicability of their file system in an OpenStack based Cloud environment where a single LiveDFS instance is shared amongst the physical machines in the Cloud and their storage systems. Unfortunately, the levels of intrusion they introduce make their file system hard to apply in the context of ENTICE. On the other hand the combination of such de-duplicating file system and the ENTICE VMMT concept might introduce a transparent technique for VM image delivery in Clouds that did not incorporate de-duplication over ENTICE managed VM images.

Lei et al. (Lei 2014) present their method for de-duplicating data in existing image files for virtual machines. Their work is based on two methods: first the entire image is checked whether it exists in a repository, if not the image is chunked into fix sized blocks and the blocks are checked individually (block level de-duplication or fixed-size partition [FSP] method). The authors used different OS images and images that are based on these images to test their method. They used 4, 8, 16 and 32KB blocks. They found that as the block size increases the de-duplication decreases, since there is a higher possibility of changed data within a block. Their proposed technique can significantly reduce the transmission time of image files that have already existed in storage. The calculation of fingerprints of blocks, on the other hand, is compute intensive that could be improved. Lowering the computational cost would allow to use smaller block sizes.

Xu et al. (Xu 2014, July) propose a VM image de-duplication method to speed up the Cloud operation. Since different images have a large amount of same data segments, these duplicated data can lead to serious waste of storage resource. Although previous solutions could achieve a good result in removing duplicate copies, they are not very suitable for VMI de-duplication in a Cloud environment, since it could lead to serious performance interference to the hosting virtual machines. The paper proposes a local de-duplication method which can speed up the operation progress of VMI de-duplication and reduce the operation time. The proposed method is based on an improved k-means clustering algorithm, which could classify the metadata of backup image to reduce the search space of lookups for the de-duplication. The experiments show that this approach can significantly reduce the performance interference to the hosting virtual machine with an acceptable increase in disk space usage. While re-duplication is still done during runtime – hence the interference – in ENTICE we will aim at reducing the interference caused by our techniques by exploiting periods of underutilisation.

Deshpenade et al. (Deshpande 2013) introduce the so called gang migration for the simultaneous live migration of multiple Virtual Machines from one set of physical machines to another. This process generates a large volume of network traffic and can overload the core network links and switches in a datacentre. To reduce this network overhead, gang migration uses global de-duplication (GMGD), which identifies and eliminates the retransmission of duplicate memory pages among VMs running on multiple physical machines in the cluster. They designed a GMGD prototype using QEMU/KVM VMs. The performed evaluations on a 30-node Gigabit Ethernet cluster having 10 GigE core links show that GMGD can reduce the network traffic on core links by up to 65% and the total migration time of VMs by up to 42%, when compared to the default migration technique in QEMU/KVM. The disadvantage of this method are its overheads, especially in worst-case scenarios.

Kochut et al. (Kochut 2012) leverage similarity in VMIs to reduce the data volume transferred from the storage server to the hypervisor on which the virtual machine is being instantiated. Really, the virtual machine instances are created using copy-on-write technology and based on read-only images. Therefor read-only images, originally obtained from the storage server, can be used to create other images. They presented an analytical model of such a provisioning process using image similarity, and validated it using a discrete event simulator. They found that the proposed provisioning scheme can achieve significant (up to 80%) reduction in data transfer between storage server and hypervisors. However, they use image redundancy information to supplement capacity based placement, which is only effective when overlaps across images present on direct attached storage for reconstituting a virtual image.

The work by Nicolae et al. (Nicolae 2015) focuses again on a common pattern, collective on-demand read, accessing the same image or dataset from a large number of VM instances concurrently. The work is based on the collaboration of unrelated VM instances belonging to different groups to and exchanging common data in order to reduce the I/O pressure on the storage system. A mirror is a local view of the virtual disk image stored remotely on the VM repository to the hypervisor. From the perspective of the hypervisor, the local mirror appears to have already fetched and created a copy of all necessary content, however, the mirror gets populated with content only as needed during runtime. Mirrors advertise chunks to each other in a peer-to-peer collaborative scheme and prefetch any missing chunk soon as an advertisement about it has been received, in anticipation of future read requests. Nevertheless, the exact details (selection of peers, prefetching vs. conserving bandwidth) is said to be out of scope in this work. Detection of content similarity is realized by a low-overhead fingerprint based approach (a strong hash function) and duplicated content can be detected and exchanged on-the-fly. The authors observed a speedup of completion time up to 11x compared to a naïve solution and a speed-up of 1.88-2x compared with collaborative schemes. Even with a single group, the authors have measured a 4% overhead compared with an approach that is specifically aimed at a single group. The proposed mirroring technique is mostly efficient only when the mirrors are placed close to the VMs' hosting locations.

Virtual Machines Analysis

Jebessa et al. (Jebessa 2013) discuss a case study of analysing the dependency network of a virtual machine hosting a few software and it discusses that security threats can be minimized in optimized systems by just eliminating unnecessary kernel functionalities. In this respect, the work identifies some even bigger challenges than ENTICE faces (namely open source systems can be tightly optimized by analysing their entire source code). In addition, the paper discusses some aspects of describing the purpose of a virtual machine. The proposed solution is a pre-requisite for any VM analysis and transformation procedures. In order to use this approach, VMs should be declaratively described in a domain-specific language by providing descriptions such as used set of packages, kernel features and system configurations for software, and so on.

Razavi et al. (Razavi 2014) investigate the effects of VM image size and contents on VM start-up time in Amazon EC2. They developed an approach (analysing the dependency graph, creating a pruned dependency graph of the needed components and moving these components into a blank image) for consolidating size and contents of VMIs within the ConPaaS project. Their proposed approach applied to the VMIs resulted in four times reduction of the disk size, three times speedup for the VM start-up time, and three times reduction of storage costs, compared to an unmodified VMI. The authors do not take into account that VM start-up times are not constant (especially on Amazon).

Menzel et al. (Menzel 2013) provide an analysis of one of the regions of Amazon's Cloud. Through this analysis, they show that only a few users dare to publish VMIs (because of the technical issues faced while constructing one). And they highlight that even just focusing on a single region one can find over 10 thousand images stored which are often based on similar software thus these images would be ideal for identifying their smaller building blocks. The paper also provides insight on how to identify configuration setups of VMIs. The approach relies on starting up each and every tracked VMI. And the authors require the deployment of custom configuration management software (if not already installed there) on the virtual machine created from the image, before they can extract configuration information. In work package 3 of the project, we expect to not just analyse the configuration of the images but also other similarities amongst the VMIs. The paper shows that one can achieve significant performance improvements even in commercial Clouds by just adhering some image content requirements. The disadvantage of this method is that it requires specific components to be pre-installed on every VM.

Luo et al. (Luo 2013) introduce S-CAVE, an extension to contemporary virtual machine monitors (VMM) so they can efficiently manage caching and access to the increasingly widespread SSD drives that represent the ephemeral storage for VMs. Although this paper shows significant improvements for VMs in environments with multi tenancy, the VMs must be running and they also expect the Cloud provider to upgrade their VMMs so they also support the S-CAVE extension. As the objectives of EN-TICE are mainly targeted on pre-utilization behaviour of the VMs and their images, S-CAVE cannot have significant effects on the VM instantiation process. On the other hand, the VMMT concept could exploit S-CAVE extensions if multiple ENTICE created VM images are instantiated on a single host. Thus, ENTICE should investigate when it is possible to detect both being on a single host and having a host that supports S-CAVE. If one can detect these circumstances, then the VMMTs running on the single host should synchronize their installation and configuration activities allowing the VMs to exploit S-CAVE based caching

Malhotra et al. (Malhotra 2013) propose VMCloner to reduce time needed for cloning VMIs by using multi-threaded cloning. The designed framework improves the behaviour of Virtual Box by reducing the time taken by clonevdi API to create multiple copies of the virtual disk. The clonevdi function simply reads a bunch of blocks from the source drive and writes them to the destination drive. By sequential block-by-block copying, the cloning time increases with the increase in virtual disk size and can be optimized in the range of 32 KB to 16 MB as buffer sizes. VMCloner implements multi-threaded VM cloning with an optimum buffer size to decrease cloning time. They observed that the time taken to clone a virtual machine decreases with the increase in cluster size. For small sized virtual disk, no significant time decrease is seen because the context switching is high as compared to the size of the disk. The multi-threaded cloning mechanism developed by the authors is efficient for larger sized virtual disk cloning. The proposed technique is restricted to single hosts as well as to the proprietary VMI format of Virtual Box.

Image Reconstruction

The solution proposed by Zhang et al. (Zhang 2013) is focusing on providing software on demand, i.e. deploying VMs without software installation and adding the necessary program components on the fly. The solution is based on a "double isolation" mechanism, introducing user level virtualization of the on-demand software and a central distribution system in order to decouple application software from VM to improve the deployment flexibility. The user-level virtualization isolates applications from the OS (and then the lower-level VM); so that a user can choose which software will be used after setting the virtual machines' configuration. Moreover, the chosen software is not pre-installed (or pre-stored) in the VM image; instead, it can be streamed from the application depository on demand when the user launches it in a running VM to save the storage overhead. During the whole process, no software installation is needed. Further, the enormous existing desktop software can be converted into such on-demand versions without any modification of source code. The current concept is based on centralized storage servers that hinder scalability and deployment is realized for applications but not for VM images.

STAKEHOLDERS

There are various individuals and organizations that may be considered as stakeholders in the Cloud computing domain (Foster et al. 2008), and may be highly interested in a technology (expected to be provided through the implementation of the ENTICE architecture discussed in the paper) that is capable of automatically organizing VMIs both regarding their contents and their storage locations. In the following, we list the most relevant stakeholders for the architecture discussed below and we not only define them but also show how such stakeholder is represented by some of ENTICE consortium members:

1. End-Customers are expected to utilize various services/applications provided by our second stakeholder. The users of the satellite image service of DEIMOS (a member of ENTICE) can serve as an example for these customers.
2. Cloud Application Providers and/or Software as a Service provider, offer preconfigured and customised applications deployed in cloud infrastructures to serve many customers dynamic needs (e.g., including availability). In the context of ENTICE this stakeholder is represented by the company, Wellness Telecom (WT).
3. Application Developers design and develop highly efficient, scalable cloud ready applications specialized for particular customer needs. In the context of ENTICE, the company DEIMOS is in such role, who operates several satellites and develops an Earth observation application for its customers (see above). We expect (just like in the case of DEIMOS) that some application developers who intend to keep their developments in house will directly act as cloud application providers and/or cloud providers (below) as well.
4. Cloud Operators are offering solutions for managing and operating cloud systems and applications on top of multiple cloud systems. In the context of ENTICE, the well-known company Flexiant (FLEX) fills the role who pioneered its solutions for the management of Cloud applications across multiple Clouds.
5. Cloud Providers are the maintainers of actual computing infrastructures. Typical public commercial Cloud Providers are Amazon EC2, Microsoft Azure, or Google AppEngine, while private Clouds of interest include EGI Federated Cloud and Grid5000 infrastructures. In the context of ENTICE, University of Innsbruck (UIBK), MTA SZTAKI, and University of Ljubljana (UL) are acting as private academic Cloud providers in the project for test bed and internal evaluation purposes.

The project present in the following a complete list of the stakeholders representative for the ENTICE environment in detail, depicted in Figure 1.

End-Customer

End-Customers of Cloud applications, e.g. Software-as-a-Service (SaaS) applications, will most likely not be aware of ENTICE as this should transparently operate in the background as a supporting service for Cloud Application Providers, Cloud Operators, and Cloud Providers. Therefore, the End-Customers

Figure 1. ENTICE stakeholders

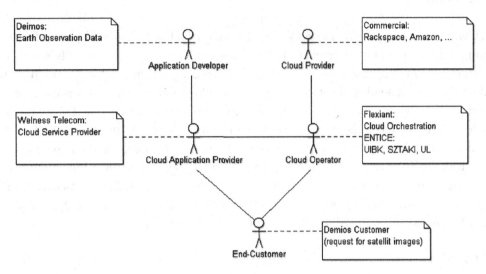

will indirectly benefit from the ENTICE technology, as their Cloud applications will be able to utilize this highly efficient system for VMI delivery during runtime which will improve the Quality of Service (QoS) (Vaquero 2008) in the runtime of their used applications. By using the ENTICE repository technology, Cloud applications will be able to efficiently and elastically scale up and down upon fluctuating load, which will transparently maintain or improve their responses to the End-Customers' requests.

Cloud Application Provider

Cloud Application Providers (or SaaS providers) are a special category of companies engaged in business with the End-Customers. The Cloud Application Provider usually does not own a large-scale data centre to host its Cloud applications, but it rather relies on the services of other existing public (or private) Cloud Providers. Cloud Application Providers are in great need to provide scalable and dynamic applications that dynamically instantiate VMs in background with the benefit of a high elasticity. ENTICE addresses the needs of Cloud Application Providers by providing RESTful application programming interfaces that may be used for dynamic provisioning of highly-optimized VMIs during the Cloud application runtime.

Application Developer

The Application Developer, is a company (may also be an individual) that develops an application that serves a specific purpose and achieves a certain functionality. ENTICE does not put any constraint on the application that may be a legacy one and makes use of any kind of software technology. In particular, the application may be aware of the underlying Cloud infrastructure or not. Through the provisioned GUI provided by ENTICE (also called VMI image portal), the Cloud Application Developers may be given the opportunity to search for VMIs across the distributed repository according to various, sometimes even conflicting criteria, e.g., cost, performance, security, storage, or a trade-off mixture of them.

Cloud Operator

A Cloud Operator, is a company that provides an operating panel and high-quality tools for monitoring (Rosenblum et al. 2005) and management of Cloud installations. As such, it usually serves the needs of both individuals who are developing Cloud applications, as well as companies (such as WT) that are providing SaaS (i.e. Cloud applications) to a large number of customers. As it is the case of FLEX, Cloud Operators usually provide a VMI storage capacity to their customers. Cloud Operators give their users the flexibility to choose the parameters of the needed VMIs, and the VMI chunk distribution. Cloud Operators usually support a wide range of Clouds for VMI storage and chunks for instant and flexible provisioning of VMIs. Unfortunately, in their current operation, many of the provisioned VMIs lack appropriate optimization and therefore perform with a lower expected performance. ENTICE will seamlessly operate alongside the repositories of such Cloud Operators by distributing highly optimized VMIs and VMI chunks, thus providing added value for the Cloud Operators.

Cloud Provider

A traditional Cloud Provider (public or private) provides an Infrastructure-as-a-Service (IaaS) (Prodan et al. 2009) environment for running VMIs coming from a Cloud Operator. The VMIs obtained by using an ENTICE repository may be higher-priced goods, as they will be highly optimized compared to VMIs obtainable from traditional VMI storages (Reimer et al. 2008). Optionally, a Cloud Provider may wish to provide additional storage capacities for VMIs directly at its data center by deploying ENTICE architectural components. Additionally, federated Clouds can directly benefit from the optimizations resulting from the architecture because of its support for multiple hypervisors image size and delivery optimization techniques allow extending the federation towards more diverse cloud infrastructures.

REQUIREMENTS ENGINEERING AND ANALYSIS

Based on an extensive review within the project, generalized requirements were collected for the three pilot use cases, systematically presented in this section. The use cases are presented on the ENTICE homepage (http://www.entice-project.eu) and their requirements can be found in a public deliverable called "Requirements specification for the ENTICE environment". These requirements will represent the basis for the design of the overall architecture of the ENTICE repository, which is the main scope of this chapter.

Application Data-Related Requirements

REQUIRMENT-1: Files or Directories Containing Files to be Delivered Alongside the VMIs

Motivation: Some applications need the delivery of various content alongside the VMI. For example, in the case of the Earth Observation Data (EOD) processing and distribution pilot case, ENTICE need to deliver satellite images together with the image containing a function that processes them using the ENTICE environment as a content delivery mechanism at geographic locations. This may require using scalable storage by the Cloud application at designated geographic locations.

The components of the ENTICE architecture addressing this need are the following:
- ○ The *functional descriptions* should contain the references to these files/folders and evaluate their presence in terms of files, folders, sizes, distribution, and so on;
- ○ *Virtual Machine* Management *Templates (VMMT)* are a mechanism to inject these files during runtime. In case the files/folders to be injected are large (e.g. several GBs in size), the VMMT should employ scalable transfer techniques to allow prompt delivery, i.e. by providing VMI with Graft servers / network file system / Bit-torrent or similar solutions optimised for fast transfer of large files.

The files and directories here refer to such data items needed for the normal prolonged operation of an image (and thus not data processed once and then thrown away).

REQUIRMENT-2: Hierarchical Data (not VMIs) for Fast Medium, and Low-Speed Access

Motivation: Since our pilots are big data applications, some of the data must be frequently accessed and some not, as there are different demands for it. Therefore, a mechanism is needed to allow for moving data from one hierarchy level to another, supported by adequate technology for fast, medium and low-speed content delivery.

The components of the ENTICE architecture addressing this need are the following:
- ○ In the *functional descriptions*, application developers should be able to specify how their application accesses the various hierarchical levels;
- ○ The employed *image optimisation technique* should utilize these requirements to validate if the access to the various storage levels is guaranteed, whenever needed.

Security-Related Requirements

REQUIRMENT-3: Support for Encryption Methods for VMI and Data Delivery

The contents of some VMIs and data could be business-critical and not available under any circumstance to intruders. For this purpose, the repository must support content delivery through encrypted channels. Moreover, the analysis methods for VMIs of the ENTICE environment should not compromise the privacy and security of the Cloud application owners.

The components of the ENTICE architecture addressing this need are the following:

- The *functional descriptions* should not breach details about the contents of obfuscated images;
- The *knowledge base* should not expose business-critical functional descriptions that could introduce unauthorised insights into application logic;
- *Image optimisation* should not ease the identification of business-critical functionalities and should not make it easier to understand the internal functionality and behaviour of the application;
- The *distributed image delivery* techniques should ensure encrypted image transfer and storage, if prescribed by the Pareto SLA (P-SLA), and exclusive owner access to the distributed images/fragments (i.e. the Cloud Operators, Cloud Providers, Application Developers).

VMI and Fragment Management-Related

REQUIREMENT-4: VMI and/or Fragment Delivery at Hierarchical Levels: Fast, Medium, and Low-Speed

Motivation: Since the repository of VMIs has to provide fast delivery, and the "fast storage" may be expensive, it is necessary to provide mechanisms for storing images at three hierarchical levels. Moreover, it is necessary to move these images from one hierarchical level to another, supported by adequate technology. VMI fragments might also be stored on different levels of storage depending on the optimized distribution process.

The components of the ENTICE architecture addressing this need are the following:

- ◦ The *distributed image delivery* optimisation should organize the images and fragments according to the needs for them. The optimisation should not only consider bandwidth and geographical availability of the images, but also storage prices;
- ◦ The *VMMTs* of ENTICE should be always stored in rapid access storage.

REQUIREMENT-5: Access to VMIs at Geographic Locations

Motivation: Firstly, distributed storage system storage for VMIs is a prerequisite for our work. Since Cloud operators may wish to deploy the applications at distant locations, it should be possible to deploy storage capacity at distant locations where the Cloud Providers reside. Secondly, an application is composed of a pipeline that should scale based on its demands at different geographic locations. In such cases, an automatic delivery mechanism of VMIs is needed at these locations, preferably to the repositories of the closest Cloud Providers.

The components of the ENTICE architecture addressing this need are the following:

- ◦ The *image* delivery *techniques* researched by ENTICE should consider *SLA* requirements for geographical availability and/or geographical access speeds/times.

REQUIREMENT-6: Different Operating Systems and VMI Types

The ENTICE environment should support various VMI types including Debian, CentOS, Ubuntu, and Windows.

The components of the ENTICE architecture addressing this need are the following:

- • The *image optimisation* techniques should be agnostic to the applied operating systems by the Cloud Application Providers and must support the operating systems necessary to run all pilot cases as a minimum.

REQUIREMENT-7: Recorded use History of Specific VMI Functionalities

Motivation: This functionality is necessary to allow faster delivery of VMIs at geographic locations, by quickly reconstructing it nearby based on fragments available at the location and perhaps few fragments from remote locations of the repository (this is the expected main functionality of VM-MTs). This will significantly improve the delivery time for VMIs.

The components of the ENTICE architecture addressing this need are the following:

- Distributed image store should be able to determine where is it possible to keep both image fragments as well as complete VMIs;
- If necessary, the distributed image store could use on site non-VMI-related storage for storing image fragments, for example by S3 alongside OpenNebula Image store;
- VMMTs should be able to extract image fragments both from VMI-related and from non-VMI-related storage of the various providers in the ENTICE environment;
- If a Cloud Provider does not support non-VMI-related storage (e.g. Flexiant's FCO-based Providers), the distributed image store should be capable of creating a VM in the Cloud that will act as a fragment store. This functionality is required only for storing fragmented VM images on site of such providers.

REQUIRMENT-8: Docker and CoreOS/Rocket Container Management

Motivation: Some applications require use containers for their execution. Similarly, to VMIs and image fragments, the ENTICE environment should be designed to also support the management of containers, such as those of CoreOS/Rocket and Docker.

The components of the ENTICE architecture addressing this need are the following:

- The image analysis and synthesis tools should not restrict their use to hardware virtualisation, but should support operating system level virtualization too if there is a clear image format for such virtualised containers;
- Conversion of images should be possible within the same kind of virtualisation techniques (e.g. Docker to Rocket or KVM to VMWare). A conversion between different kinds of virtualisation solutions should first resynthesize the images for the new virtualisation type needed. For example, a Docker to KVM conversion should be implemented directly in KVM by reusing the Docker's optimised image functional description.

REQUIRMENT-9: 40% Faster Delivery of VMIs

Motivation: A mechanism is necessary for VMI delivery at distant locations, as the current mechanism is inefficient across geographic locations. The distributed repository will help it store images (and/or their fragments) at distant locations, which in turn will improve significantly their delivery time.

The components of the ENTICE architecture addressing this need are the following:

- The ENTICE *knowledge base* should provide means for monitoring for the QoS metrics (Armstrong et al. 2009) related to the delivery time for particular VMIs (e.g. by using time stamps). It should further provide a mechanism to move VMIs and/or fragments across repository locations to change the distribution based on the systems QoS metrics.

REQUIRMENT-10: Latest Optimized VMI for the Needed Functionality

Motivation: During the Cloud application lifecycle, VMIs may be upgraded (e.g. operating system or software component changes) several times. As the existing Cloud application may be long running, an upgrade to a new VMI must happen during its execution. The ENTICE environment must provide the latest needed VMI at all the geographic locations where the Cloud application is currently running.

The components of the ENTICE architecture addressing this need are the following:

- ○ The image synthesis should allow rapid optimisation of VMIs based on past optimisation results and the differences between the current and past un-optimised VMIs;
- ○ Distributed image storage should invalidate not up-to-date VMIs, ensuring that after a new un-optimised upload to the image portal, the old VMIs are no longer served anywhere. It should also redistribute the newly optimised images to the appropriate locations.

REQUIRMENT-11: SLA Provisioning to Service based on Optimized VMI Delivery

Motivation: To design the Pareto Service Level Agreement (P-SLA) towards the Cloud Application Providers explaining the deployment location, the performance, and other QoS requirements using knowledge of the Cloud Providers are needed. The internal optimization of the repository and its operation could employ Pareto multi-objective methods.

The components of the ENTICE architecture addressing this need are the following:

- ○ The *P-SLA* should be able to express policies on VMI operation including delivery time, fragmentation options, storage costs, performance and QoS requirements, and so on. The P-SLA design should also be able to capture the trade-off of possible optimised solutions.

REQUIRMENT-12: Standardized Interfaces with Proprietary Repositories

Motivation: Synchronizing VMIs from the ENTICE repository with proprietary repositories (e.g. VMI repositories of Cloud Operators or Cloud Providers) may be necessary to speed up the deployment process. ENTICE should be able to upload and download VMIs (if download might not be possible, the ENTICE repository needs to keep a copy) from such Cloud operators or Cloud Providers automatically using standard interfaces that allow for access to Cloud operators or Cloud Providers.

The components of the ENTICE architecture addressing this need are the following:

- ○ The primary storage for VMIs should be at the Cloud Provider side and ENTICE should perform the *distributed storage* of VMIs over these primary storage entities;
- ○ For those Cloud Providers that do not offer image extraction options, the *multi-objective image delivery technique* of ENTICE should keep a downloadable image at either in another primary storage, or on its own secondary storage if this is not possible;
- ○ The *knowledge base* should be able to tell the upload/download capabilities (both for VMIs and for fragments) of every ENTICE-managed image store.

REQUIRMENT-13: API for Automatic VMI Type Conversion

Various Cloud Providers could have restrictions on the supported VMI types (e.g. KVM Debian-based). For this purpose, it may be necessary to design a conversion mechanism that provides the necessary functionality to the Cloud Provider while transforming the image to the specific supported VMI type (e.g. to Xin Ubuntu-based). ENTICE should support advance orders for specific VMI types, too.

The components of the ENTICE architecture addressing this need are the following:

- ENTICE stores images in *interoperable forms* whenever the performance requirements allow a transformation before delivery;
- For some VMIs the image should also hold certain runtime requirements, such as the number of processors, memory, and so on. This has been taken care in the initial conceptual model of the knowledge base. During the conversion, this information should be collected either directly from the Cloud Application Provider (through the *image portal* or its *APIs*) who will operate the VMIs or from the *P-SLAs*.

Information and Metadata Management-Related Requirements

REQUIRMENT-14: Indexed Application Data Files or Folders

Motivation: The ENTICE environment must support in some cases the delivery of data in the form of files or folders containing satellite images. In such cases, ENTICE must provide appropriate storage and data delivery mechanism together with the VMIs. ENTICE will have to index the data properly, so that it can search and efficiently deliver to certain geographic locations.

The components of the ENTICE architecture addressing this need are the following:

- *Knowledge base and reasoning* should keep track of the files associated with certain VM images and make sure that they are moved together;
- *Image portal* should provide means to specify the association between files (folders) and applications (images).

REQUIRMENT-15: Proper VMIs Functional Description

Motivation: The stakeholders of the ENTICE environment need to search for various VMIs according to their needed functionality. For this reason, properly connecting VMIs and image fragments in an index is needed. The semantic model will contain information about the actual VMIs and their functionality, the geographic location, the URI, and other details for the search facility. The P-SLA multi-objective optimization algorithms may require this feature too.

The components of the ENTICE architecture addressing this need are the following:

- *Functional description* should provide means of capturing and describing the functionality of VM images;
- *Knowledge base and reasoning* should maintain descriptions of VM images and allow transformations of the functional descriptions. For example, if images are split, merged or synthesised, the corresponding descriptions must be kept consistent, in a preferably automated way;
- *Image synthesis* should be able to follow the functional descriptions and fabricate VM images accordingly.

REQUIRMENT-16: Free Selection of Source and Destination for VMIs and/or Fragment Movements

Motivation: ENTICE will design and maintain an internal the network topology to be able to calculate the "best" delivery of VMIs. ENTICE will consider this capability for the Pareto multi-objective optimization techniques.

The components of the ENTICE architecture addressing this need are the following:

- *VM image distribution* should provide means (elementary operations) for moving images and fragments.

REQUIRMENT-17: Recorded use History of Specific VMI Functionalities

Motivation: During a long running Cloud application, the Application Developer may decide to change certain deployment characteristics. For example, a particular VMI may receive an upgrade by changing of the operating system, the storage size, and so on. In such cases, ENTICE should deliver the newest VMI to the Cloud application for future uses.

The components of the ENTICE architecture addressing this need are the following:

- *Knowledge base and reasoning* should record each event when a specific functionality is delivered at a specific geographic location, to a specific Cloud Provider for a specific Cloud application. The ENTICE ontology in its initial version allows for the recording the VMI use history. The Cloud application could then rely on this mechanism so that it can always use the newest VMI corresponding to a needed functionality.

REQUIRMENT-18: VMI Repository Statistics

Motivation: ENTICE needs to collect information about the usage of the VMI repository and store it in the knowledge base for later statistics.

The components of the ENTICE architecture addressing this need are the following:

- *Knowledge base and reasoning* should collect statistics of the use of repository.

REQUIRMENT-19: Metadata for VMI Conversions

Motivation: ENTICE environment should store information about the Cloud Providers on which the Cloud application will execute, including the underlying resource architecture. ENTICE will use this information to decide about the conversions to apply, for example when moving from an Open Nebula installation to an Open Stack installation. Many-to-many transformations of images types (e.g. from KVM Debian to Xen Ubuntu) may be needed depending on the specific policies and requirements of various Cloud Providers.

The components of the ENTICE architecture addressing this need are the following:

- *Knowledge base and reasoning* should collect and provide information regarding the use of repository, such as information on Cloud Providers, computing architecture for optimised conversion, and many others.

QoS Metrics-Related

REQUIRMENT-20: Monitoring of QoS Metrics

Monitoring of QoS metrics is necessary to be able to observe the time needed to move VMIs and/or fragments among repository locations and to deploy a VMI needed by a particular Cloud application. A further requirement is to monitor the infrastructure on which the ENTICE repository is deployed to ensure that the scaling and speed of operation is adequate. It may be necessary to monitor how the ENTICE repository scales – e.g. based on increasing number of requests for VMIs (usage peaks).

The components of the ENTICE architecture addressing this need are the following:

- The *knowledge base* should collect QoS metrics to support decisions related to P-SLA driven operations;
- The *multi-objective optimisation and image delivery* technique should consider the QoS metrics of its various first and second level of storage options, and optimize VMI storage amongst these so that the expected P-SLA is fulfilled;
- The multi-objective image delivery technique should monitor changes in the QoS of the currently utilised storage for a particular P-SLA. If a certain QoS metric increases the chances of P-SLA violation, image storage needs to be pre-emptively reorganised.

REQUIRMENT-21: Elasticity of Cloud Applications

Motivation: Cloud applications which are designed by Cloud applications developers should be able to implement elasticity mechanisms which will be supported by the ENTICE environment. For example, if an application needs to vertically scale (i.e. having multiple instances of the application running supporting more application throughput) or horizontally (i.e. running bigger problems in the application needing more VM for execution), the ENTICE environment should be able to supported this by providing optimized VMIs.

External Interface-Related

REQUIRMENT-22: VMI Search based on Functional Descriptions

Motivation: The user interface will allow for semantic search of various images based on functionality, such as for example, Redmine (project management software) for chart drawing purposes.

The components of the ENTICE architecture addressing this need are the following:
- Functional descriptions should have a simple searchable textual equivalent (maybe mapped with an ontology) in the knowledge base;
- Some functional descriptions should only be visible to authorised parties, allowing the invisibility of the obfuscated VMIs.

REQUIRMENT-23: Requesting and Running VMIs.

Motivation: The user interface should allow the stakeholders express their multi-objective QoS needs as part of P-SLAs.

The components of the ENTICE architecture addressing this need are the following:

- ◦ The *image portal* and APIs of the ENTICE components should allow the specification of the P-SLAs in relation to functional descriptions to enable the distributed VMI delivery optimisation framework store the Cloud application provider's images to best meet their performance requirements;
- ◦ The *image portal* should offer a GUI to formulate an initial P-SLA document and to point to currently existing images and fragments (stored in one or more primary Cloud storages) that support its fulfilment.

REQUIRMENT-24: Application Data Download

Motivation: The external Interface shall allow for data download needed by the application through an API, which allows the delivery of a pointer (i.e. URI) so that the Cloud application can access and use the data (files or folders) while running at the Cloud Provider.

The components of the ENTICE architecture addressing this need are the following:

- ◦ The *VMMTs* should be able to programmatically query the *knowledge base* about the "best" (e.g. most rapid, least expensive) location of a particular VMI fragment.

REQUIRMENT-25: VMIs Upload and Download Mechanism

Motivation: When the Cloud application developer prepares an un-optimized VMI, he might need to use the repository to optimize it by uploading it to the ENTICE repository along with its functional descriptions and the necessary functionality testing process.

The components of the ENTICE architecture addressing this need are the following:

- ◦ The *image portal* should allow the upload of an un-optimised VMI, first stored in the ENTICE storage;
- ◦ After the size optimisation of the VMI, the *image portal* should allow downloading the new VMI for third party use or for further validity analysis of the image contents. The result of this process should be a URL to a secondary or a primary *VMI storage* that holds the optimised VMI.

REQUIRMENT-26: VMI Functionality Testing Descriptor

Motivation: A Cloud Application Developer may use the ENTICE repository to optimized an own prepared and un-optimized VMI. For this purpose, he needs to upload the VMI along with its functional description and all the necessary functionality testing mechanism to the repository. The functionality testing mechanism should then assure that the optimized VMI preserves the original functionality.

The components of the ENTICE architecture addressing this need are the following:

- ◦ In the VMI *functional description*, the application developers describe the required functionality (typically a single path of execution) with a validation technique, which can range from traditional unit and integration testing, to uploading a specialised VMI hosting the validation environment, or even some manual validity checks.

The Application Developer considers that the validator functions in the functional descriptions could execute up to thousands of times.

REQUIRMENT-27: Collection of Location Information

Motivation: The user interface should support the selection of information about the Cloud Provider and the computing architecture (hardware) where the image will execute.

The components of the ENTICE architecture addressing this need are the following:

- ○ The multi-objective repository optimisation should consider the expected execution locations (e.g. specific Cloud Providers or geolocations) of the VMIs and ensure that they can be instantiated according to the P-SLAs at these locations.

REQUIRMENT-28: user comments

Motivation: The ENTICE repository should be able to support user comments.

The components of the ENTICE architecture addressing this need are the following:

The *knowledge base* should offer interfaces where P-SLA violations can be automatically reported allowing the multi-objective optimizer to re-evaluate the repository layout and request changes in the image distribution. It can be implemented similar to a ticketing system within the GUI, if needed.

ENTICE ARCHITECTURAL DESIGN

In the ENTICE project, a multidisciplinary team of computer scientists (UIBK, SZTAKI, and UL), Application Developers (DEIMOS), Cloud Application Providers (WT), Cloud Operators, and Cloud Providers (FLEX) will research a ubiquitous repository-based technology for VM management called *ENTICE environment*. The environment depicted in Figure 2 aims to prove a universal backbone for IaaS VM management operations, which accommodate the needs for different use cases with dynamic resource (e.g. requiring resources for minutes or just for a few seconds) and other QoS requirements. The ENTICE technology is completely decoupled from the applications and their specific runtime environments, but continuously supports them through optimized VM image creation, assembly, migration and storage.

The ENTICE environment is designed to receive unmodified and functionally complete VM images from users, and transparently tailor and optimize them for specific Cloud infrastructures with respect to their size, configuration, and geographical distribution, such that they are loaded, delivered (across Cloud boundaries), and executed faster and with improved QoS compared to their current behaviour. ENTICE will gradually store information about the VMI and fragments in a knowledge base that will be used for interoperability, integration, reasoning and optimization purposes (e.g. repositories should decide at which other repositories one needs replicas of a heavily requested image and at which time such an image is replicated).

VM images management will be supported by ENTICE on an abstract level, independent of the middleware technology supported by the underlying Cloud computing infrastructure. To further shield the users from the complexity of underlying Cloud technologies and simplify the development and the execution of complex use cases, ENTICE will research a repository, which will provide the flexibility for tailoring the VM images to specific Cloud infrastructures. This allows easier integration and support for federated Cloud infrastructures that might consist of different hypervisors and Cloud middleware

Figure 2. ENTICE overall architecture

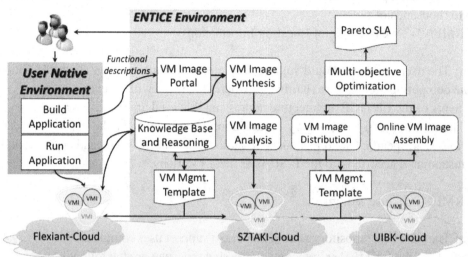

combined to a single sign on system. Current used approaches to form Cloud federation can there for be simplified when using ENTICE as image repository for the environment.

The ENTICE repository will include, among other features, techniques to optimize the size of VM images while maintaining their functionality, automatically share images (or parts of the images) among repositories (even in multiple administrative domains or Cloud infrastructures), and optimally deploy them in response to application and data centre requirements.

Interoperable and Decentralized VM Image Synthesis, Analysis, and Storage

The project's *VMI synthesis* tool will allow the creation of new VMIs with several approaches. First, it will allow the use of generic user provided images or (software) recipes to act as the foundation of specialization. Next, the synthesis tool will collaborate with the image portal to identify the functional requirements a newly created image must meet. Then project's synthesis technique will alter the user provided images either directly or indirectly (through recipes). These alterations will target partial content removal from the original images allowing them offering only their single purpose, namely the functions identified in the image portal. Once the initial optimized image is ready, the VMI Synthesis will offer image maintenance operations (like managing software updates on the image).

Next to synthesis, ENTICE will introduce *VMI analysis* functionality to allow discovery of identical portions in apparently unrelated VM images coming from even different stakeholders and communities, regardless of the Cloud Provider where they are physically stored. This information will be automatically stored in the ENTICE knowledge base for later use. The environment will also allow splitting of VM images into *fragments* for storing the frequently shared image components only once (e.g. a particular flavour of Linux used by two different images), this operation allows the *VM image distribution* component (Peng et al. 2012) to optimize the overall storage space throughout the distributed repository.

As VM images are now fragmented, the ENTICE will distribute VMMT to the various repositories in the ENTICE environment. The VMMTs will allow VMs be assembled at runtime from the previously identified fragments. The templates will be stand-alone VM images containing the necessary components to access the distributed repository. After a VM is instantiated from a VMMT, it will customize the contents of the instantiated VM with the VM fragments required to match the user's functional requirements (even allowing new files/directories be placed in particular VMs to meet the demands of the various stakeholders). This will also be supported thorough user-defined functional and non-functional descriptions about the application in the ENTICE knowledge base and the implemented reasoning mechanisms that will feed in necessary information for the decision making process.

Federated Multi-Objective VM Image Repository Optimization

To deal with the rather large heterogeneity of existing VM monitors (e.g. Xen, VMware, KVM) and IaaS Cloud systems (e.g. Flexiant, OpenStack, OpenNebula, Amazon EC2) currently available, an interoperable VM image format will be supplied supported by a unified user interface for storing VM images. The purpose of this solution is to hide the IaaS Cloud Provider-specific functionality and enable users to interact with their Cloud application deployments from a pure functional perspective. The ENTICE repository interfaces will therefore eliminate the provider lock-in barriers experienced in IaaS Clouds, and allow efficient and straightforward migration of workloads across Cloud boundaries. With the use of VMMTs, ENTICE will also foster Cloud Provider-independent VM migration techniques across federated Clouds that only transfer the VM fragments (such as memory or disk) changed by the VM on the sender side to significantly reduce the data transfer overhead. This technology also promises nearly instantaneous creation of a VM at the receiving side to meet the stringent auto-scaling and QoS requirements of Cloud applications.

To allow the VM image distribution and placement to run as efficiently as possible, investigating the use of software-defined network (SDN) capabilities to create a complete virtual network overlay on top of the federated public/private Cloud infrastructure with secure connectivity between individual repositories will be done. ENTICE needs to configure the SDN-defined network overlays automatically based on current VM image locations and transfer frequencies in the distributed repository in order to optimize image delivery across Cloud boundaries. On the other hand, placing VM images for fast deployment and instantiation in Clouds is a multi-objective optimization problem that needs to consider a number of simultaneous and equally important objectives such as VM transfer and deployment latency, expected execution time of a VM, data locality, storage size, operational costs, resource utilization, or availability. For this purpose, ENTICE will research a generic *multi-objective optimization* framework targeting a number of important objectives such as performance-related (e.g. time, CPU utilization, data locality, functional QoS parameters), operational cost (e.g. price per hour of resource use) and storage size. The framework will be applied on two particular problems: *VM image distribution* in the repository and *online image discovery and assembly* (using the VMMTs).

First, based on the performance requirements (e.g. processing speed, number of cores, memory size), use patterns (e.g. originating Cloud Provider, download frequency), and structure (i.e. fragments) of images or location of input data, ENTICE (assisted by its knowledge base and monitoring system) will automatically optimize in the background the distribution and placement of VM images. The main purpose is to significantly lower their provisioning time for complex resource requests (which can be in the orders of hours using today's provider lock-in technologies) and for executing the Cloud applications (thus focusing on their functional use scenarios). The optimization will consider the requirements of applications built as a composition of VMs and arrange for simultaneous delivery of multiple VM images to selected Clouds, optionally enhanced with application input data. The users will be able to describe these requirements both within the ENTICE environment and with IaaS Cloud Provider provided tools such as Flexiant Bento Boxes (http://www.flexiant.com/2012/12/03/application-provisioning/). The VM image delivery will occur both offline, as well as online during application execution by proactively moving the most demanded VM image fragments close to the resources the application is currently running on. In case of online image delivery, ENTICE will automatically discover user demand patterns by analysing the metadata (e.g. sequence and number of downloads of particular images or fragments) published by the Cloud Provider-operated repositories (e.g. similar to Glance from OpenStack) and replicate the highly demanded images or fragments according to user demands. For example, if some VM images are always instantiated at a high frequency, ENTICE will place them at other Cloud Providers where the users might need them. ENTICE's offline image distribution techniques will also aim for a global storage size and cost minimization while ensuring that on-site repositories are prepared so they can meet the requirements of subsequent application executions.

As many of these objectives may conflict with each other (e.g. resource speed versus operational cost, storage size versus number of replicated VM image fragments), the result of this complex problem is usually a set of trade-off solutions called *Pareto front*. A Pareto front is an essential tool for decision support and preference discovery, whose shape can provide new insights and allow Cloud Providers and users explore the space of non-dominated solutions with certain properties, possibly revealing regions of interest that are impossible to see otherwise. Concretely, a Pareto front can answer questions such as "are my optimization goals conflicting?", "can I always simultaneously improve the VM deployment latency, execution time and computation cost?" and "how big is the trade-off between my optimization criteria?", or it can ease the selection process for the best fitting solution to the user's particular requirements. For example, it may happen that by conceding up to 1% in performance, the computing cost halves by using slower and cheaper resources. On the other hand, it can occur that by increasing the overall storage by 10%, the performance improves by over 70% due to better VM image replication and data locality. Those solutions are points on the Pareto front, presented to the user or selected automatically based on requirements. Moreover, a Pareto front can expose alternative solutions if the importance of objectives changes, for example by giving costs priority over execution time.

ENTICE will publish the multi-objective optimization results as part of a novel *Pareto SLA (P-SLA)* by researching a corresponding template capable of modelling the complete front of trade-off solutions. A *decision making* tool will support the optimisation by allowing to selection of the "best" Pareto point from the P-SLA that fulfils the user-specified deployment characteristics (e.g. deployment time, QoS metrics, data locality, operational costs) and the Cloud Provider's operational requirements (e.g. resource utilization, number of VM accesses). ENTICE will use the lightweight VM creation, management, and optimization researched in this project to improve the elasticity of three carefully chosen pilot use case applications.

VMI Portal and Knowledge-based Modelling and Reasoning

The users of the ENTICE environment are not expected to create ready-to-use VM images, but only to prepare their applications in their own environments, as they are normally used to. While preparing their applications, the users has to provide *functional descriptions* of their applications (e.g. an Apache web server for static web pages). By using the Virtual Machine Images and Container Images (VMI) (He et al. 2012) portal and the associated knowledge base the users will receive adequate support to search, discover and select appropriate software components. By using an implemented reasoning mechanism, the ENTICE environment will obtain information necessary to extract and *synthesize* highly optimized VM images (e.g. even preconfigured for user needs) that are focused on the specific functionality described by the users. This will be complemented by automatic detection and removal of unnecessary VMI contents, sensitive data (e.g. private key files, external-party login details, non-anonymized documents), like log files belonging to some old past executions, unused libraries (or even entertainment software) that are usually present in user-prepared VMIs. The knowledge base will be also designed to support the ENTICE runtime by providing latest statistics and logistics information to the VMI distribution.

RDF Schema (RDFS) provides a data-modelling vocabulary for RDF data (Klyne et al. 2006). Actually, RDFS is an extension of the basic RDF vocabulary. On top of RDF, the simple schema language RDFS has been defined to offer a distinguished vocabulary to model class and property hierarchies and other basic schema primitives that can be referred to from RDF models. Both RDF and RDFS constitute a newly emerging standard for metadata that is about to turn all kinds of information (structured, semi-structured and even unstructured data) into a machine-understandable knowledge base. RDFS is an XML application that allows for the denotation of facts and schemata in a machine-readable format, building on an elaborate object model for describing concepts and relations. In other words, RDFS exploits the means of XML to allow for disjoint namespaces, linking and referring between namespaces and, hence, is a general methodology for sharing machine-readable knowledge in a distributed setting. To phrase the role of RDFS in knowledge engineering terminology, it defines a simple ontology for checking particular RDF documents against to determine consistency.

Moreover, the Web Ontology Language (OWL) (McGuinness et al. 2004) targets applications that need to process the content of information instead of just presenting information to humans. OWL facilitates greater machine interpretability of content than that supported via XML by providing additional vocabulary along with a formal semantics.

Reasoning with the languages such as RDFS and OWL, which allow for adding rich semantics to the data, can help the system derive facts and obtain complete answers for queries over linked data. That is reasoning capabilities enabled by the three following necessary tools: (1) first of all by defining RDF as a universal data format; (2) secondly by defining SPARQL, a standard query language for RDF; and (3) lastly by providing schema languages such as RDFS and OWL. Therefore, all these components together might turn up as a natural choice for a widely useable ontology modelling and reasoning.

Interoperable and Decentralised VM Image Synthesis, Analysis and Storage

The image synthesis and image analysis play a central role in the ENTICE architecture (see Figure 2). Section 4.1 describes the overall purpose of image synthesis and analysis, and the aim of this section is to define their internal functionalities, their interplay, and their relations to stakeholders.

Figure 3 presents a use case diagram for image synthesis and analysis. The nodes (use cases) in this diagram were distilled from overall requirements (both pilot cases and architectural ones) and overall principles of the project objectives. In other words, these use cases must cover the requirements and the project objectives where applicable, with the focus strictly set to image synthesis and analysis aspects.

As it can be seen, image analysis (initiate image analysis) is a central part of the diagram (and hence a central notion of the conceptual architecture) and it is accessed by the most stakeholders. On the other hand, the Application Developer is the central actor that interacts with most of the use cases and can initiate

Figure 3. Use case diagram for image synthesis and analysis

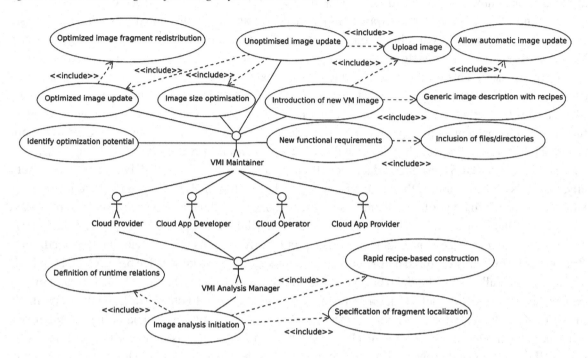

most of the activities. In the following, a list of the descriptions of these use cases by paying particular attention to their requirements (or some of their specific aspects), and how to achieve them is given.

Optimized Image Fragment Redistribution

Stakeholders: Cloud Operator, Cloud Provider, Cloud Application Developer, Cloud Application Provider

In case an updated VMI was previously fragmented by the ENTICE environment, the repositories of the previous fragments must be updated so they reflect the changes in the updated VMI then to ensure its new usability. This step might avoid the need for immediately rerunning the image analysis and the repeated planning of the distribution of the various fragments. As a result, the use case reduces initial redistribution costs in alignment with the requirement of ensuring geographically diverse and rapid access to image fragments previously designated as fast access fragments by the VM image distribution component of the architecture.

This use case addresses requirements: REQUIRMENT-10 and REQUIRMENT-16.

Definition of Runtime Relations

Stakeholders: Cloud Operator, Cloud Provider, Cloud Application Developer, Cloud Application Provider

If a stakeholder often observes a specific pattern of VMs (e.g. a sequence, or parallel occurrence of VMs) on particular Cloud infrastructure, the image analysis tool could receive information about the VMIs used to instantiate such a constellation. With the knowledge about this constellation, the analysis tool could identify shared image fragments in the constituent VMIs. As a result, the analysis tool may prepare fragments that allow for better distribution optimization supporting the movement of such constellations altogether to other Clouds.

This use case addresses requirements: REQUIRMENT-17

Image Size Optimization

Stakeholders: Cloud Operator, Cloud Provider, Cloud Application Developer, Cloud Application Provider

If there are several functional requirements paired within a VMI, ENTICE should allow the optimization of the VMI so that it provides mostly (or only) the functionality described and nothing more. In ENTICE, the VMIs will undergo over several treatments that reduce their size to reduce their delivery time and storage needs for a particular functional requirement set. The Application Developer will primarily run the optimization before the VMI is becoming widely used. After the optimization phase, the Application Developer expects to approve the optimized VMI in two ways: (1) automatic when it completely trusts the previously defined functional requirements of the image, or (2) manual if the functionality defined might not completely cover the VMI's expected behaviour. The Application Developer could decide on an optimization termination condition, which might limit the possible size reduction. In some cases, the image distribution facility of ENTICE might recognize that further optimization of the image might bring significant gains in application performance for the Cloud Application Providers. In these cases, the image distribution facility will initiate the optimization based on the P-SLA requirements of the Cloud Application Provider. Finally, the Application Developer will receive the newly optimized image for approval again.

This use case addresses requirements: REQUIRMENT-2, REQUIRMENT-3

Generic Image Description with Recipes

Stakeholders: Cloud Operator, Cloud Provider, Cloud Application Developer, Cloud Application Provider

When the Application Developer aims to avoid uploading of a large VMI, it can describe the raw VMI's contents with the preferred configuration management tool. Instead of the complete VMI, the Application Developer now will have a chance to upload the custom contents of the image and the configuration description. This approach could significantly reduce the time to reach the Cloud with new VMIs, and introduces a generic approach to create a non-optimized VMI, which on can be exploited later during the image optimization. In some cases, the user-provided configuration description might be updated based on the previous experience with the generic approach.

This use case addresses requirements REQUIRMENT-8 (re-synthesis aspects), REQUIRMENT-19

Inclusion of Files/Directories

Stakeholders: Cloud Operator, Cloud Provider, Cloud Application Developer, Cloud Application Provider

As the presence of data files are a primary concern of some of the pilot cases, their specification should not need to be in the form of generic functional requirements. ENTICE will allow to specify custom stop filters for files and directories in VMIs, so that they will never be touched by the image optimization and analysis tools. The optimization tool will not try to decrease the size of the image by eliminating them, while the analysis tool will not place them on separate fragments, as their delivery will be bundled with specific functionalities. As an advanced option, some Application Developers or Cloud Application Providers might plan to customize their VMIs with data files added later on. This customization operation will happen after such new functional requirements are specified. This case will directly lead the Application Developers and Cloud Providers to the update of an optimized image.

This use case addresses requirements: REQUIRMENT-1 and REQUIRMENT-14.

Specification of Fragment Localization

Stakeholders: Cloud Operator, Cloud Provider, Cloud Application Developer, Cloud Application Provider

The role of this case is to find and specify the exact location of image fragments for image analysis, usually initiated by a Cloud Operator or Cloud Provider or the image distributor component. It is important to analyse the location of the already stored fragments, and use this information for optimally storing additional ones. This process is directly related to the VM image analysis part of the ENTICE overall architecture. Concerning the requirements of ENTICE architecture design, it is important to store and retrieve the image fragments according to the predefined hierarchical levels: fast, medium and low-speed. This use case should take into account the geographic location of the fragments too.

This use case addresses requirements: REQUIRMENT-4, REQUIRMENT-

Un-Optimized Image Update

Stakeholders: Cloud Operator, Cloud Provider, Cloud Application Developer, Cloud Application Provider

The Application Developer may decide to release a new version of the application. If the image containing the application is a new image or an updated version of a previously submitted un-optimized image, it needs to be uploaded to the ENTICE repository and treated as an un-optimized one. Later on, it should undergo an optimization process as defined in the "Optimize image size" use case. This use case may reuse the steps executed for optimizing the previous version of this VMI. Concerning the requirements of ENTICE architecture design, this process is related to the "Information and metadata management requirements". Therefore, it is important to update the meta-data information after the update.

This use case addresses requirements: REQUIRMENT-10.

Introduction of New VM Image

Stakeholders: Cloud Operator, Cloud Provider, Cloud Application Developer, Cloud Application Provider

Both the Application Developer and the Cloud Application Provider can introduce a new image to the ENTICE environment. For example, the application developer may release a new application independent of the previously uploaded VMIs. After this process the new image should be uploaded and undergo an optimization process. This process is directly related to the VM image synthesis and the image portal of the ENTICE overall architecture. Concerning the requirements of ENTICE architecture design, this process is related to the Information and metadata management requirements, because it is important to add meta-data information for the newly created image.

New Functional Requirements

Stakeholders: Cloud Operator, Cloud Provider, Cloud Application Developer, Cloud Application Provider

The Application Developer can add generic functional requirements at any time to new or existing VMIs. It can add special requirements to a subcase by including files or directories in the image. This information can help the optimization processes of ENTICE, as it is directly related to the VM image synthesis part of the ENTICE overall architecture. Concerning the requirements of ENTICE architecture design, this process is related to the "Information and metadata management" requirements.

This use case addresses requirements REQUIRMENT-15, REQUIRMENT-26.

Rapid Recipe-based Construction

Stakeholders: Cloud Operator, Cloud Provider, Cloud Application Developer, Cloud Application Provider

A set of pilots, such as natural disaster scenarios, require the deployment of VMs in a time critical manner. This may involve applying overlays to a base VMI as well as calculating the difference between two VMIs. Hence, rapid recipe based construction requires precise information about the content and structure of an image provided by image analysis. More precisely, this can support configuration management tools by providing the necessary and appropriately optimized images and fragments to be added to the construction.

Image Analysis Initiation

Stakeholders: Cloud Operator, Cloud Provider, Cloud Application Developer, Cloud Application Provider

Image analysis has a central role in manipulating the VMIs once uploaded to the repository and passed to the optimization stage. Virtually all activities related to VMI construction (either synthesis or joining existing fragments), dissection and transformation require information about the content and structure of the image. Image analysis can be initiated by a Cloud Provider to eliminate duplicates at different sites, by a Cloud Application Provider to introduce new services and ease the distribution of fragments and by a Cloud Operator to optimize image size and the method of distribution. Image analysis may involve detecting runtime relations, such as temporal or spatial coexistence, specifying fragment locations for better fragment distribution, and providing analysis for rapid recipe based construction.

This use case addresses requirement: REQUIRMENT-11.

Optimized Image Update

Stakeholders: Cloud Operator, Cloud Provider, Cloud Application Developer, Cloud Application Provider

The Application Developer may request the update of an optimized VMI. Subsequently, updating an optimized image may be part of updating an un-optimized image, as the changes introduced to an un-optimized image need to be propagated to the optimized image too. Updating an optimized image involves deciding the inclusion of an update by a Cloud Application Provider, for example if the update may take place or not (e.g. if a certain service is no longer used, its update is not necessary) and if so, redistributing the optimized image fragments.

This use case addresses requirements: REQUIRMENT-10.

Upload Image

Stakeholders: Cloud Operator, Cloud Provider, Cloud Application Developer, Cloud Application Provider

Uploading an image means introducing previously non-existing (with respect to structure and/or content) images into the repository and adding some structurally and/or semantically new content. Uploading an image is not an individual use case, but can be part of introducing a new VMI (adding an entirely new image) or part of updating an un-optimized image (modifying some existing images and uploading the new image). Thus, both Cloud Application Provider and Application Developer may indirectly initiate uploading an image.

This use case addresses requirements: REQUIRMENT-25.

Automatic Image Update

Stakeholders: Cloud Operator, Cloud Provider, Cloud Application Developer, Cloud Application Provider

If an image is described by means of recipes, the application (execution) of recipes may yield different images due to updates, different versions, and so on. Hence, despite functionally equivalent, these images need potentially completely different optimizations than before. Thus, automatic update of these images may have adversary effects and therefore, the Application Developer may allow or disallow automatic updates of the image at this stage.

Identification of Optimization Potential

Stakeholders: Cloud Operator, Cloud Provider, Cloud Application Developer, Cloud Application Provider

Estimating the optimization potential of a VMI is essential to make a trade-off between the time and resource devoted for the optimization and its benefits. If the anticipated benefits in terms of storage space and transfer times are too small, the optimization is not initiated. The Cloud Operator and the Application Developer are responsible for initiating such requests for analysis. Upon the results of the analysis, they may initiate the image size optimization.

Figure 4. Use case diagram for multi-objective VMI repository optimisation

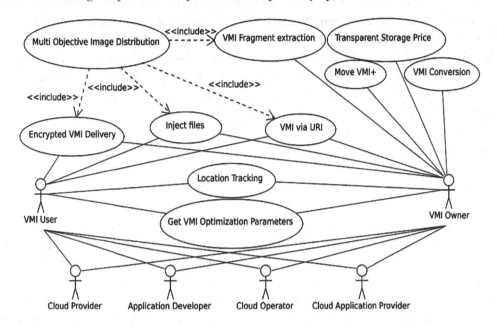

FEDERATED MULTI-OBJECTIVE VM IMAGE REPOSITORY OPTIMISATION

For the use cases regarding the distributed VMI storage, the stakeholders are classified in two major categories with different roles:

- **VMI Owner:** The Owner of a VMI is responsible for selecting its optimisation parameters, resulting storage location, storage cost, and for maintaining or updating the image to latest versions. After uploading a VMI to the ENTICE repository, the owner can choose to optimise the image by providing functional descriptions and setting the parameters for the optimised distribution of the VMI or its fragments. A Cloud Provider or Cloud Operator can move their own images to the ENTICE repository and thus become VMI owners. An Application developer and a Cloud Provider will need to be able to upload a VMI to the ENTICE repository if they are not already provided by the Cloud Provider (which is the typical case for our applications from DEIMOS and WT).
- **VMI User:** The stakeholders allowed to use a VMI are the second important category. Every VMI Owner has the VMI User rights included. The user is missing the functionalities, which can result in changes to the VMI, its optimisation or cost. For example, moving a VMI to a different location might change the resulting cost for the VMI Owner, and is therefore prohibited for the VMI User. Again, a Cloud Provider and a Cloud Operator might need to test and/or use VMI for which they received user rights for (i.e. debugging tasks or support for users). A Cloud Application Provider might only get VMI User rights on applications developed by an Application Developer. Finally, an Application Developer might use VMI from other entities within their application structure and therefore, can have the VMI User role.

For ENTICE it does not make a difference if the Cloud used is private, public or a federation of Clouds as multiple image formats will be supported and the conversation to the requested format needed for a special platform. This is especial useful to avoid vendor locking or within federated Clouds, where different sub providers might use different technologies for their Cloud implementation. This helps building federated Clouds by closing the gap between image formats by supporting smooth transformation from one format in the other or by providing different images that fulfil the user requirements best matching the target Cloud platform.

Multi-Objective Image Delivery

Stakeholders: VMI Owner and VMI User

The ENTICE environment will be able to specify one or multiple objectives to optimize the VMI and fragments distribution and the resulting delivery. The objectives are from three types of conflicting metrics: QoS-related, operational cost, and storage. The ENTICE environment will enable the opportunity to specify what objectives to optimize for, or select a trade-off point from a Pareto front. Each image will be delivered to the VMI User based on the optimized distribution. The VMI Owner and user are not direct stakeholders of this use case. The VMI Owner, VM user or both will use the different child-sub use cases affiliated to this functionality. A good example is the VMI fragment extraction and encrypted VMI delivery (sub-use cases of the multi-objective image delivery). The VMI Owner can use the functionality of VMI Fragment extraction, while the VMI Owner and user use encrypted VMI delivery.

This use case addresses requirements: REQUIRMENT-11, REQUIRMENT-20.

VMI Fragment Extraction

Stakeholders: VMI Owner

The VMI Owner will have the permission to extract fragments from VMI or complete VMI stored in the storage systems to which they have access. These fragments should be lightweight, suitable to fit within the storage system, which may be a conventional or a specialized VMI storage system. The VMI fragments are also available internally for dynamic VMI creation. The VM Owner can access the VMIs as a whole based on their fragments. The importance lies in the fact to discourage redundancy of common chunks to optimize the VM repository. At the same time, it is important to enhance and synchronize the communication to enable the access of common fragments, specifically in the case of fluctuating load, resulting to the sudden change in number of nodes. A typical example in the ENTICE Environment is the Unified Communications pilot, where the number of nodes in the VoIP and/or video cluster can vary based on the number of users using the infrastructure.

This use case addresses requirements: REQUIRMENT-4.

VMI Movement

Stakeholders: VMI Owner

The VMI Owner can request the move of a VMI, fragments or associated files, such as satellites imagery. The ingesting of such files onto a memory location could be triggered either due to the re-evaluation of optimized VMI parameters as a consequence of changes in QoS requirements and in user image specifications, or in case the target storage location is receiving the file for the first time. Another cause could be the movement of associated data files as a part of content delivery. If the concerned data file has a co-relation to any of the VMI or the fragments, its location can be changed to enhance the proximity with the latter. The concern with these transfers is to avoid the queues and to maintain the elasticity of the system. Another significant issue is to handle the storage, by archiving the recent transferred images or files with respect to some lease or validation period. However, ENTICE should be finally archive or store all the data onto a disk as a backup.

This use case addresses requirements: REQUIRMENT-1.

Retrieval of VMI Optimization Parameters

Stakeholders: VMI Owner and VMI User

The parameters associated to each VMI are stored into the ENTICE distributed repository to enable the VMI Owner and user read the values related to the VMI. This could be significant in identifying whether the concerned VMI corresponds to the End-Customer specifications. The local storage of VMI and its acting parameters also facilitates the portability of VMI, independent of the used infrastructure. Thus, the ENTICE environment guarantees remote access to VMs for testing, validation, and demonstration of the performance with respect to image transfer and storage. A typical example is Flexiant Cloud Orchestrator, where the download of a VMI to local storage will facilitate portability independent of the infrastructure, and will enable unitary tests. The VM user can access the image portal to see information about VMI, including the associated parameters in read mode. This functionality enables the VM user to match its own specifications the stored ones, specifically in the case of any updates or optimizations.

This use case addresses requirements: REQUIRMENT-24.

VMI Access via URI

Stakeholders: VMI Owner and VMI User

The VMI Owner can access the images via a unified resource identifier (URI), if it has rights to obtain the specified VMI. The importance of this functionality lies in the lightweight VMI, to provide an easy access via URI and a decreased deployment time. This functionality also enables the ENTICE environment to deliver the optimized VMI over varying operating systems. A typical example is FLEX Cloud Orchestrator, where ENTICE shall allow reservation of VMs in Debian, CentOS, Ubuntu and Windows.

A VMI via URI is also accessible by authorized VM users. Using this functionality, the ENTICE environment provides the flexibility of faster download of optimized images due to its lightweight deployment on a number of operating systems. Hence, ENTICE provides an easy integration into various external Cloud platforms. The VM users also benefit from the facility of creating VM with varying sizes and configurations.

This use case addresses requirement REQUIRMENT-25.

VMI Update

Stakeholders: VMI Owner and VMI User

The VM Owner has access to the VMI and its corresponding parameters. Every time after an optimization of an image, it results in the invalidation of its predecessor image state. Hence, all the previous versions of the concerned optimized image stored within the distributed data store at all memory locations will be certified invalid and thus removed. The provisioning of the latest optimized image remains the only existent VMI delivered for the deployment. The VM user is enabled by the ENTICE environment to read the optimized VMI and its relative optimization parameters. Further, the VM user can download the latest updated version of the VMI from the repository.

This use case addresses requirement: REQUIRMENT-10.

Location Tracking

Stakeholders: VMI Owner and VMI User

The location of a VMI and its corresponding fragments are stored onto the ENTICE repository, which can be further tracked by the VM Owner. The access the information regarding distribution of VMI and its fragments can facilitate the migration of VMI, providing portability across various platforms, irrespective of the infrastructure. It also enables the VM Owner to keep track over the redundant chunks and remove them, and at the same time replicating the VMI at various locations within the distributed repository. This functional capability has also internal use, while invalidating older versions in case of any recent updates or optimizations. The VM user can use this functionality to keep track of the corresponding uploaded VMI, and download the latest optimized state from the ENTICE repository.

This use case addresses requirements: REQUIRMENT-16.

P-SLA Parameters

Stakeholders: VMI Owner and VMI User

The ENTICE environment will facilitate VM Owners to support the VM users in selecting a Pareto Service Level Agreement (P-SLA) for the corresponding VMI or additional files stored. This functionality helps in providing portability of the system, with the deployment capability across distributed nodes at different locations. For example, a VM Owner may receive the request to deliver a processed satellite image at a particular location with respect to the satellite, achieved by supporting deployment between various clusters stationed at different geographical locations. The ENTICE users are able to select a P-SLA for the VMI stored in the distributed storage system. Hence, their requests are served as per chosen P-SLA parameters. For example, a VM user can request for a processed satellite imagery corresponding to satellite at a particular geographical location.

This use case addresses requirement: REQUIRMENT-5.

File Injection

Stakeholders: VMI Owner and VMI User

The additional files such as collection of satellite imagery might also be included with VMI. This functionality provisions automatic cataloguing of such files in the form of metadata to describe it. The storage of these files happens in hierarchical levels such as the short-term backup used to archive recently or frequently used files. However, the final backup completes by storing every files onto the backup disk for future reference. This helps VM Owner in achieving an information infrastructure for strategic and dynamic reasoning. The association of these files to certain VMI can trigger the transfer of these files to bring them to closer to the location where corresponding VMI is stored in order to improve the response time. The transfer of additional files should avoid queuing the requests to maintain the elasticity of the system. A VM user might request a VMI with additional files included. These files, which are either associated with the VMI or stored within the ENTICE storage system or their location provided via a URI, can be requested and downloaded by the VM user from the distributed repository, provided the user has an access to such files. The ENTICE environment allows faster response to attain high performance.

This use case addresses requirements: REQUIRMENT-1.

Encrypted VMI Delivery

Stakeholders: VMI Owner and VMI User

The delivery of VMI can be done in an encrypted fashion to increase security and allow VMI to contain confidential information or software. Using this functionality, the ENTICE environment secures confidentiality to prevent disclosure of any information to unauthorized individuals or systems. For example, in case of Earth Observational Data, the concern is that while some resources are to be shared between users, there are resources subjected to only one user, to guarantee specific levels of performance. Hence, the VM Owner would facilitate the secure authentication by making sure that data transactions and communications are genuine. Every request for a VMI from a VMI User or deployment tool can indicate if the delivery shall be encrypted, resulting in an overhead for encryption, or faster unencrypted delivery is allowed.

This use case addresses requirements: REQUIRMENT-3

Transparent Storage Price

Stakeholders: VMI Owner and VMI User

Storage price needed for VMI will be transparent. Each location of the distributed image repository will have its own machine-readable prices for storage and the resulting price for the VMI Owner will become available. Every VMI Owner will be able to collect the cost for each VMI hosted within the ENTICE environment at the granularity provided by the underlying storage systems prices. In order to address the cost of storage, the VM Owner can optimize the distributed repositories to store redundant chunks or lightweight images. ENTICE can increase or decrease the storage nodes depending upon the load of the system. This will help in optimizing the storage price in case of systems with high fluctuating load. A good example is the Unified Communications pilot, for which the ENTICE environment should increase the number of nodes in each functional block based on the system load (i.e. number of users using the infrastructure).

This use case addresses requirements: REQUIRMENT-4

VMI Conversion

Stakeholders: VMI Owner and VMI User

Converting VMI for different software stacks within their environment aim to support different hypervisors or Cloud Providers. The VM Owner will provide an API to integrate third party conversation tools and a selected range needed for the use case applications will be included into this part of the distributed image repository. VM users will have the option to specify the environment where they want their image delivered. The Converted VMIs are stored in the storage system to avoid the repetition of the expensive and time-consuming conversion processes. This allows easier Cloud federation integration and might help building even bigger federations then currently available by helping to allow interoperability between different technologies in a transparent way.

This use case addresses requirements: REQUIRMENT-8.

VMI IMAGES PORTAL AND KNOWLEDGE-BASED MODELLING AND REASONING

A distributed repository like ENTICE needs to store a large amount of metadata and information about items present in the system (e.g. VMIs, repositories and users). All this data will be stored in a knowledge base, representing the primary source of information needed for the repository operations. The knowledge base will expose functionality via both a GUI and APIs. Both external and internal services of analysis and synthesis and distribution parts can use the API. This task implements client libraries and a reasoning infrastructure to facilitate the management of information in the knowledge base both by the administrators and by the ENTICE supporting services. The early stage of the project fundamentally models the information and knowledge needed by ENTICE for the optimization and management of VMs through a semantic model for both VMs and the federated ENTICE environment and through interlink concepts for reasoning at both strategic (design time) and dynamic (runtime) levels. The GUI interface will use the same API to retrieve and store the data presented through a Web-based dashboard. In what follows, an elaboration of the initial use cases for the VMI portal, GUI and the functionality of knowledge base and its modelling and reasoning is presented.

Building exploration interfaces for a complex environment like ENTICE is a major research and technology development task, bearing in mind that the knowledge bases must support many decisions. From the beginning of the project, it was necessary to rationalize the significance and relevance of the users' requirements. Figure 5 presents the initially identified use cases. In the following use case diagram, two actors refer to several stakeholders depending on the particular use case. Application Developers and Cloud Application Providers are primary users of the external GUI interfaces while Cloud Providers and Cloud Operators usually interact with ENTICE via internal APIs.

Figure 5. Use cases of the external and internal interfaces of the ENTICE environment

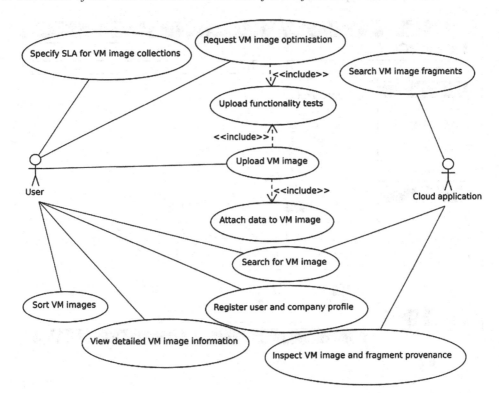

VMI Images Portal

During the early stages of the project, UL performed detailed analysis of the requirements related to the GUI, based on which several preliminary designs of the user interface were developed. These designs were presented to the potential users of ENTICE (DEIMOS, WT and FLEX) for comments and suggestions. This chapter presents an initial version of the design for the VMI images portal that will continuously be improved in the forthcoming period.

Figure 6 shows a design of the first page of the VMI images portal. The user will have the possibility to see a very flexible page organized similarly to familiar services in the Web. The idea of this design is to allow for both simple and more complex browsing capabilities of the distributed collection of VMIs. The user may be interested to search the collection according to the needed functionality or maybe according to other criteria (e.g. operating system). Once the user decides that an image satisfies all the selection criteria, he/she can download the image or manipulate it in some other way (e.g. optimize the given VMI for own purposes). Moreover, it allows the user to instruct ENTICE for distributing the selected image in ENTICE distributed repositories for the own Clouds. The same functionality will be offered also to automated services accessing the ENTICE repository via an API.

Some ENTICE users (Application Developers or Cloud Operators) developing or operating applications that are more complex may need to manage a larger amount of VMIs. In such case, they can decide to sign up in the system. Signing up in the system (see Figure 13) will allow them to include their personal profile as well as the details about the company that is operating the Cloud application

Figure 6. Initial design of the first page of the VMI images portal

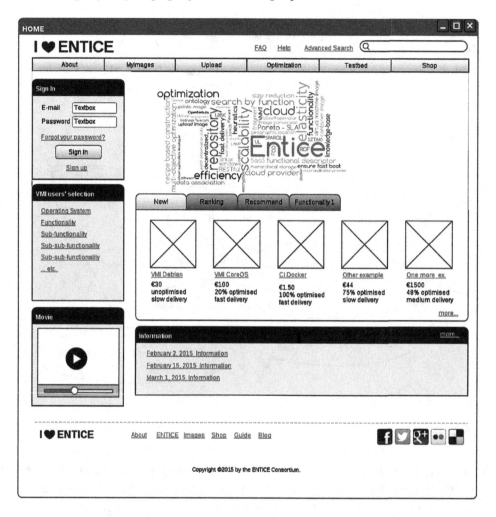

(or more Cloud applications) and is actual owner of the provided images and data. Obfuscation is more an "internal" requirement for DEIMOS use case. All binaries with proprietary components (gs4EO product) deployed on the machines are generated with an obfuscation mechanism to conceal its purpose (security through obscurity) and its logic, in order to prevent tampering and deter reverse engineering from potential competitors. This does not include external linked libraries with open source or even third-party proprietary code.

An important feature of the ENTICE repository is the management of Priority Levels for the delivery of VMIs. By logging in the system, the users can specify the availability of individual VM images (i.e. countries, regions and/or repositories, where the VMIs should reside or not due to legislation reasons) and the priority level of delivery speed levels (i.e. 1: fast, 2: medium and 3: slow). ENTICE will reduce the delivery time of the images, nowadays still in the range of minutes, to three delivery speed levels. The first level is around 10 seconds for most cases, the second level is around 2 minutes in average, and the third level is regularly around 15 minutes. The users will also be able to associate data (usually big data files) with the same Priority Levels together with the images (at same Priority Level). Additionally,

Figure 7. Search for VM images

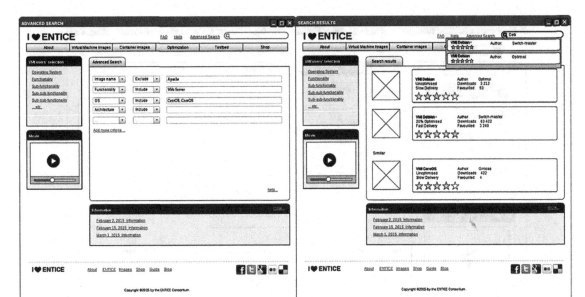

users of ENTICE (Application Developer, Cloud Operator, and Cloud Provider) will be able to inspect QoS parameters for each particular VMI, and to inspect and edit the P-SLA with the ENTICE distributed repository. All this information can be provided during image upload (Figure 8) or image update (Figure 9). In what follows, the VMI portal is described as a set of individual provisioned functionalities.

Image Search

Stakeholders: Cloud Operator

One of the basic functionalities provided by the GUI is the VMI search (see Figure 7). The user of the ENTICE repository will first come across an intuitive GUI that provides VMI search functionality based on different criteria such as name or some textual or semantic description. To provide this functionality, each VMI will be equipped with functional descriptors, which describe all the information known about the VMI. The search will allow users to simply use text search functionality and more detailed functionality according to the various purposes of the VMIs. Some functional descriptors will be searchable only by authorized parties, allowing the invisibility of the obfuscated VMIs (see requirement REQUIRMENT-3). Auto-complete and sorted image results will further enhance the functionality and thus upgrade similar solutions seen on the market. Functional and non-functional descriptions of the software components will be stored, including information on their computational, memory, storage, and communication complexity, and all the necessary dependencies, libraries and environmental variables for deployment on a VM in the ENTICE knowledge base. The purpose is to support the overall lifecycle of applications deployed as VMIs and to facilitate automatic optimization, setup and management in the ENTICE environment.

This use case addresses requirements: REQUIRMENT-22.

Figure 8. Uploading a new VM image

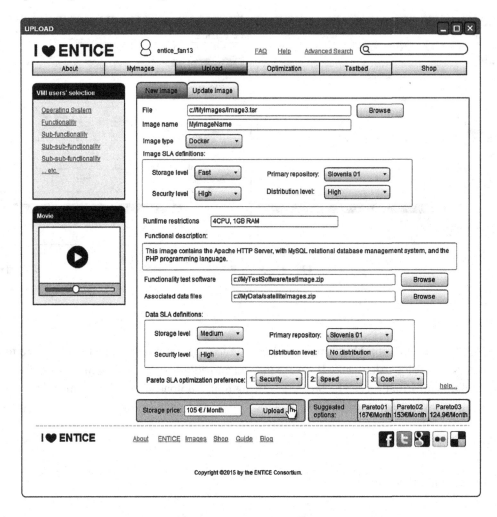

Image Upload and Image Update

Stakeholders: Application Developer, Cloud Operator, Cloud Provider

Uploading a VMI image means introducing previously non-existing (with respect to structure and/or content) image into the repository. Uploading a VMI image is not an individual use case, but it can be either part of introducing an entirely new image to the repository, or part of updating an existing image (i.e. replacing already existing image with a new version or possibly only updating the P-SLA conditions of the image).

A Cloud Provider, a Cloud Operator, or an Application Developer may initiate uploading a VMI image referred in the following as the user. During the upload process, the user should have the means for providing metadata related to the uploaded image. As presented in Figure 8, this metadata consists of specifying the image name and type, initial P-SLA requirements (e.g. storage level, security level, distribution level, primary repository) of the image, any possible runtime restrictions, functional de-

Figure 9. Updating an existing image

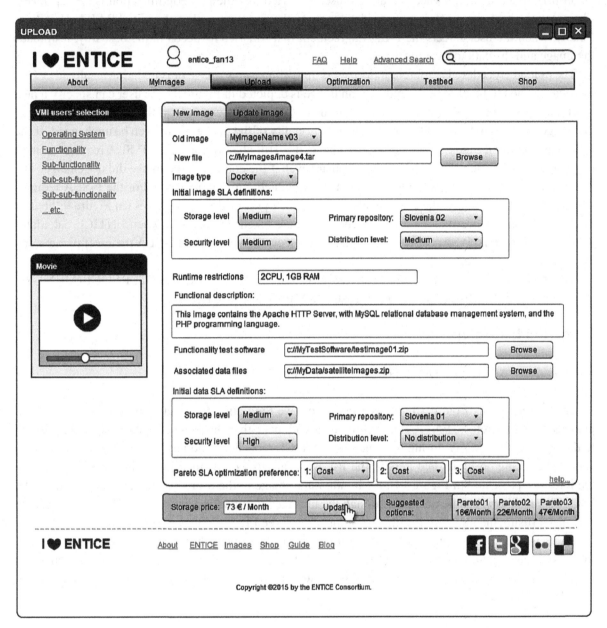

scriptions of the image, and the software for automatic functionality testing. Additionally, the user can specify any associated data files to upload together with the image. The initial P-SLA requirements for these data files can also be specified. Based on the initial image and data P-SLA definitions, the ENTICE repository calculates the storage price and presents it to the user. Additionally, the user can also specify the preferences for the P-SLA optimization. For example, the user might select that the most important P-SLA parameter is security, followed by speed and the cost (see Figure 8). The P-SLA optimizer might then propose to the user several additional options (with different settings than the initial P-SLA), optimized based on its preferences. Figure 8 shows that the proposed optional P-SLA definitions have larger price than the initial one, because the user specified that the price optimization is not a priority. The user can check these offers and see if they satisfy the needs more than the initial P-SLA definition. Finally, when the user selects the P-SLA agreement that satisfies its needs in the best way, it uploads the image and the data to the repository.

The upload procedure is different if the user is uploading a new image or is updating an already existing image. The GUI interface for updating an image is depicted in Figure 9. The user can specify a new version of the image (file) as a replacement of the old image. For example, if the user slightly changed the image, perhaps only a small part of it, the functionality of the image might even be unchanged. If the user does not specify the new version of the image, it is still able to change the P-SLA requirements of the image, which is also consider as image update, even if the content of the image did not change. The user can also specify the new version of the data associated with the image and/or the P-SLA requirements for the data. Finally, the user can also specify the optimization preferences (in Figure 9 the user is obviously only concerned about the price), which are taken into account when ENTICE calculates the proposed optional P-SLA offers. When the user selects the appropriate P-SLA trade-off parameters, it can update the image.

This use case addresses requirements: REQUIRMENT-1, REQUIRMENT-3, REQUIRMENT-10, REQUIRMENT-14, REQUIRMENT-15, REQUIRMENT-24, REQUIRMENT-25.

Image Set Management

Stakeholders: Application Developer, Cloud Operator, Cloud Provider

As can be seen in the Figure 10, the user needs to have the option to manage the images he/she is in possession of. Therefore, ENTICE must provide a Web page that shows a list of the images that belong to the user (i.e. the user is storing this image in ENTICE repository and pays a monthly fee for its storage). By clicking on individual item in the list, user can inspect detailed image information (through the interface presented in Figure 14). Each individual image in the user's list can be removed from the ENTICE repository, can be updated (through the interface for updating image – see Figure 9) or can be optimized (using the interface for image optimization – see Figure 11).

There is no explicit requirement for the image set management; however, this functionality to allow easy image manipulation needs to be provided. We try to avoid showing the type of the image as ENTICEs integrated conversions of image types will support multiple hyper visors currently used in Clouds and federations.

Image Optimization Request

Stakeholders: Application Developer, Cloud Operator, Cloud Provider

The primary user of the image optimization portal is the Application Developer, referenced in the following as user for brevity reasons. A request for image optimization is accessible from the GUI when the user is logged in. The user interface exposes several options for the selected image. The first option allows updating existing functional descriptions and tags of the target, since functional tests provided later in the process might not cover some existing functionality and will be eventually eliminated in the optimization process. A potential use case addressing such a scenario is the user uploading a single

Figure 10. Personal image management

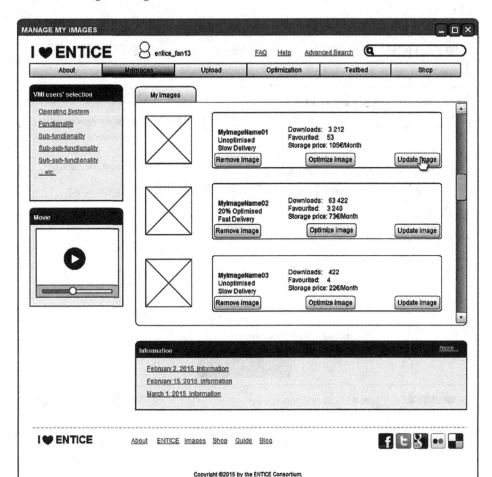

un-optimized image with a very general functionality consisting of several services and/or applications. The functional description for this general-purpose image is expected to be broad. Based on this general image, the user may later decide to create several optimized instances, each covering very specific functionality, controlled by appropriate functional tests. Accordingly, the textual functional description needs to be updated as well, while the functional description of the un-optimized image is left intact.

Due to the way optimization algorithm operates, the user needs to specify functional tests, preferably packed in a single uploaded file. The optimization algorithm should provide some completion constraints too. Therefore, the user interface includes several options to address these requirements:

- Maximum allowed iterations of the optimisation algorithm;
- Maximum wall-clock execution time;
- Lower bound of the target size;
- Achieved ratio of size reduction;
- Absolute size reduction.

Figure 11. VMI optimisation request

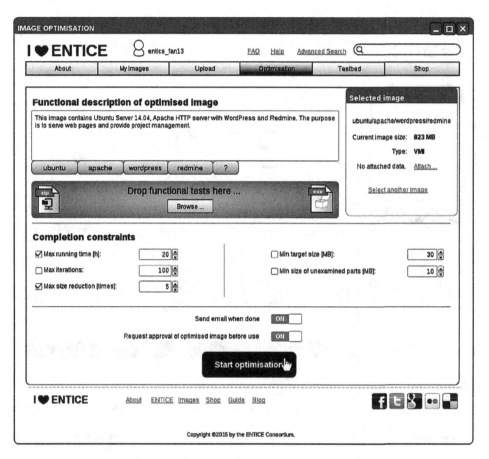

Figure 12. VM image sort

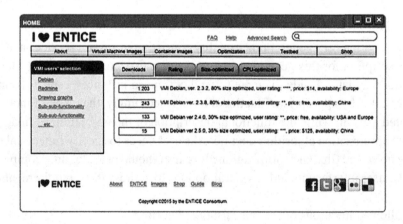

Figure 13. Register user and company profile

Functional tests could be unit or integration tests that are able to validate the functionality of the application in the image, but are restricted to be executable in the context of the target image. However, the user interface has no means to check for proper files format and validity of tests against un-optimized images, as this cannot be determined prior to the first run of the optimization algorithm. Eventually, the optimization algorithm delivers feedback and, if anything goes wrong on the first run, notifies the user and gives the chance to revise and update the functional tests. As the optimization might not start instantly but later, communication channels like email trigger the notification.

The optimization process will require several hours or even days to complete. Because this task is not only depending on VM instantiation time but also on the way the functional descriptions are given (e.g. if there is a long integration test included then the optimization process might take days). Thus, it might be reasonable to notify the user upon completion, preferably via email, with an additional on/off switch.

Users can express the confidence about the functional tests provided. In case of a complete trust, an optimized image is immediately ready for use after optimization facility completes, while in the case of incomplete trust the user has to approve validity of functionality of the optimized image before the image is ready to use. Figure 11 presents the proposed GUI for VMI optimization request. Stakeholders such as Application Developer or VMMTs and other ENTICE components (such as image distribution and analysis) may initiate the image size optimization. The latter interacts with ENTICE via APIs and initiates optimization based on the P-SLA requirements of the Cloud Application Provider.

Regardless of stakeholder, the role of the knowledge base is always the same. Size optimization facility requires non-fragmented image, while un-optimized image in the repository may be fragmented. The knowledge base knows where these parts are stored. Moreover, the result of the optimization is new optimized image related to the un-optimized one, which needs to be properly handled in the knowledge base as well.

This use case addresses requirements: REQUIRMENT-25 and REQUIRMENT-26.

Figure 14. Detailed image information

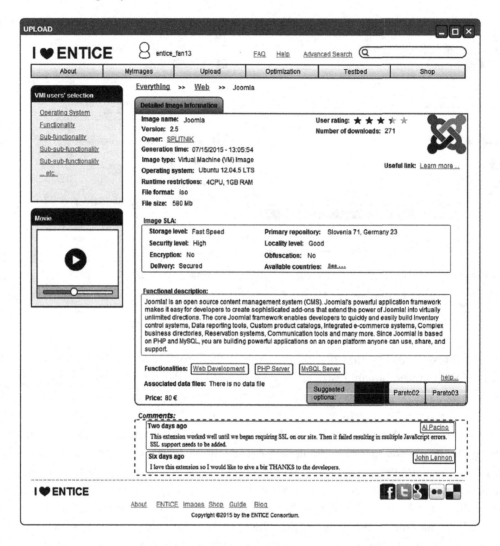

Image Sort

Stakeholders: Cloud Operator

A basic feature offered by many services in the Web, such as booking.com or youtube.com, is the possibility to sort the search results according to a given criterion. The goal of this exercise is to identify key properties according to which the users of the ENTICE repository would be interested to sort the results. These include technology for fast, medium and low-speed content delivery, runtime restrictions (e.g. amount of memory and processing units), number of VMI downloads, users' rating of VMIs (e.g. from 0 to 5 points, as is common in many Websites), upload date, geographic location where the image is available, level of optimization according to a selected functionality, and so on. In the following an initial design of this part of the user interface sketched is shown in Figure 12.

User and Company Profile Registration

Stakeholders: End-Customer, Application Developer, Cloud Application Provider, Cloud Operator, Cloud Provider

The Web-based image portal should provide means for registering the users and creating their profile information, as presented in Figure 13, achieved through a standard three-step sequence: sign-up, confirm and profile update. The Web interface will provide different options for each stakeholder involved in the ENTICE project based on the information they provide during the signup process.

There is no explicit requirement for such use case; however, virtually any existing Cloud operator provides this functionality.

Some related requirements are: REQUIRMENT-28 (regarding user comments) and REQUIRMENT-3 (addressing security issues).

Image Fragment Search

Entities that Use the Feature: VMMTs and other ENTICE components (like image distribution and analysis).

The ENTICE knowledge base reasoning mechanisms will also support the search for particular images fragments via VMMTs and other ENTICE components (like image distribution and analysis) needed for the images synthesis part. However, most likely the GUI for fragments will not be needed at this stage of the project development, as it is too early to characterize the various fragments fully. Fragments are often not easily adaptable for different operating systems. Looking for fragments is useful if someone wants to find locations where VMMT based instantiations is rather rapid.

Inspect Image or Fragment Provenance

Entities that Use this Feature: VMMTs and other ENTICE components (like image distribution and analysis).

The provenance of VMIs and images fragments is an important detail for smarter decisions at both strategic (i.e. software, VM, QoS, SLA design time) and dynamic (i.e. runtime VM) levels of the ENTICE environment. Similar to the image fragment search, implementing this functionality in the RESTFul APIs of the knowledge base too is required. It is, however, too early to be able to define exact reasoning criteria for this part. The early version of the ontology takes care about basic provenance tracing methods.

Data File Attachment to Disk Image

Stakeholders: Application Developer, Cloud Operator, Cloud Provider

Regarding DEIMOS use case, some of the ENTICE pilot applications require the option to deliver data together with the VMI (e.g. satellite images together with the image containing a function that processes them using the ENTICE environment as a content delivery mechanism at geographic locations). This means that these kinds of data must be semantically pre-linked (pre-attached) to the VMI for further use. The methods for doing this could be delivery of data in a separate file, or injection of data inside the VMI. Both options are possible; however, it is not clear at this early stage of the project which method to use. For this purpose, the conceptual modelling of this part is kept rather basic and extend in the future versions of the GUI and of the ontology as part of the upcoming project progress. However, in this early stage it is clear that data attachment during runtime is not the ENTICE's task. What ENTICE could do in this concept is to prepare pre-attached data files for the images, or to prepare the data files on the expected future runtime locations so that they can be easily attached.

This use case addresses requirements: REQUIRMENT-1.

Detailed Image Information

Stakeholders: Cloud Operator

One of the basic functionalities of the GUI is to show detailed information about a selected disk image. This use case is very basic and it addresses most of the requirements for the usability of the VMI images portal. As can be seen in the example Figure 14, the user goes to the "Web" category and clicks to see all detailed information related to a particular VMI named "Joomla".

CONCLUSION

We summarised in this chapter the ENTICE architecture by first identifying the stakeholders and the requirements for the different parts of the main software components developed of the project. We systematically analysed the requirements of the ENTICE stakeholders which to a list of 37 functional and non-functional requirements used to develop the use-cases for the different components of the ENTICE architecture. Based on the requirements, we presented an overview of the envisaged architecture of the ENTICE environment. We concluded the paper with a description of the summary of the functionality to be developed in the three main project workpackages: interoperable and decentralised VM synthesis, analysis and storage, federated multi-objective VMI repository optimisation, and VMI portal and knowledge-based modelling and reasoning.

REFERENCES

Abecker, A., & Tellmann, R. (2003). Analysis of Interaction between Semantic Web Languages, P2P architectures, and Agents. *EU-IST Project SWWS–Semantic Web Enabled Web Services project IST-2002-37134.*

Armstrong, D., & Djemame, K. (2009, July). Towards quality of service in the Cloud. *Proc. of the 25th UK Performance Engineering Workshop.*

Bazarbayev, S., Hiltunen, M., Joshi, K., Sanders, W. H., & Schlichting, R. (2013, July). Content-based scheduling of virtual machines (VMs) in the Cloud. *Proceedings of the 2013 IEEE 33rd International Conference on Distributed Computing Systems (ICDCS)* (pp. 93-101). IEEE.

Deshpande, U., Schlinker, B., Adler, E., & Gopalan, K. (2013, May). Gang migration of virtual machines using cluster-wide deduplication. *Proceedings of the 2013 13th IEEE/ACM International Symposium on Cluster, Cloud and Grid Computing (CCGrid)* (pp. 394-401). IEEE. doi:10.1109/CCGrid.2013.39

Foster, I., Zhao, Y., Raicu, I., & Lu, S. (2008, November). Cloud computing and grid computing 360-degree compared. *Proceedings of the Grid Computing Environments Workshop GCE '08* (pp. 1-10). IEEE.

He, S., Guo, L., Guo, Y., Wu, C., Ghanem, M., & Han, R. (2012, March). Elastic application container: A lightweight approach for Cloud resource provisioning. *Proceedings of the 2012 IEEE 26th international conference on Advanced information networking and applications (AINA)* (pp. 15-22). IEEE. doi:10.1109/AINA.2012.74

Jayaram, K. R., Peng, C., Zhang, Z., Kim, M., Chen, H., & Lei, H. (2011, December). An empirical analysis of similarity in virtual machine images. *Proceedings of the Middleware 2011 Industry Track Workshop* (p. 6). ACM. doi:10.1145/2090181.2090187

Jebessa, N. D., van't Noordende, G., & de Laat, C. (2013, February). Towards Purpose-Driven Virtual Machines. *Proceedings of the ESSoS Doctoral Symposium.*

Jin, K., & Miller, E. L. (2009, May). The effectiveness of deduplication on virtual machine disk images. *Proceedings of SYSTOR 2009: The Israeli Experimental Systems Conference* (p. 7). ACM. doi:10.1145/1534530.1534540

Klyne, G., & Carroll, J.J. (2006). Resource description framework (RDF): Concepts and abstract syntax.

Kochut, A., & Karve, A. (2012, April). Leveraging local image redundancy for efficient virtual machine provisioning. *Proceedings of the Network Operations and Management Symposium (NOMS)* (pp. 179-187). IEEE. doi:10.1109/NOMS.2012.6211897

Lei, Z., Li, Z., Lei, Y., Bi, Y., Hu, L., & Shen, W. (2014, September). An Improved Image File Storage Method Using Data Deduplication. *Proceedings of the 2014 IEEE 13th International Conference on Trust, Security and Privacy in Computing and Communications (TrustCom)* (pp. 638-643). IEEE. doi:10.1109/TrustCom.2014.82

Luo, T., Ma, S., Lee, R., Zhang, X., Liu, D., & Zhou, L. (2013, October). S-cave: Effective ssd caching to improve virtual machine storage performance. *Proceedings of the 22nd international conference on Parallel architectures and compilation techniques* (pp. 103-112). IEEE Press.

Malhotra, A., & Somani, G. (2013, September). VMCloner: A Fast and Flexible Virtual Machine Cloner. *Proceedings of the 2013 Third International Conference on Cloud and Green Computing (CGC)* (pp. 181-187). IEEE. doi:10.1109/CGC.2013.34

McGuinness, D. L., & Van Harmelen, F. (2004). OWL web ontology language overview. *W3C recommendation*, 10(10), 2004.

Menzel, M., Klems, M., Le, H. A., & Tai, S. (2013, March). A configuration crawler for virtual appliances in compute Clouds. *Proceedings of the 2013 IEEE International Conference on Cloud Engineering (IC2E)* (pp. 201-209). IEEE. doi:10.1109/IC2E.2013.12

Ng, C. H., Ma, M., Wong, T. Y., Lee, P. P., & Lui, J. (2011, December). Live deduplication storage of virtual machine images in an open-source Cloud. *Proceedings of the 12th International Middleware Conference* (pp. 80-99). International Federation for Information Processing. doi:10.1007/978-3-642-25821-3_5

Nguyen, M. B., Tran, V., & Hluchy, L. (2013). A generic development and deployment framework for Cloud computing and distributed applications. *Computing and Informatics*, *32*(3), 461–485.

Nicolae, B., Kochut, A., & Karve, A. Discovering and Leveraging Content Similarity to Optimize Collective On-Demand Data Access to IaaS Cloud Storage. *Proceedings of the CCGrid'15: 15th IEEE/ACM International Symposium on Cluster, Cloud and Grid Computing.* doi:10.1109/CCGrid.2015.156

Peng, C., Kim, M., Zhang, Z., & Lei, H. (2012, March). VDN: Virtual machine image distribution network for Cloud data centers. Proceedings of INFOCOM '12 (pp. 181-189). IEEE.

Prodan, R., & Ostermann, S. (2009, October). A survey and taxonomy of infrastructure as a service and web hosting Cloud providers. *Proceedings of the 2009 10th IEEE/ACM International Conference on Grid Computing* (pp. 17-25). IEEE. doi:10.1109/GRID.2009.5353074

Razavi, K., & Kielmann, T. (2013, November). Scalable virtual machine deployment using VM image caches. *Proceedings of the International Conference on High Performance Computing, Networking, Storage and Analysis* (p. 65). ACM. doi:10.1145/2503210.2503274

Razavi, K., Razorea, L. M., & Kielmann, T. (2014, January). Reducing VM Startup Time and Storage Costs by VM Image Content Consolidation. In Euro-Par 2013: Parallel Processing Workshops (pp. 75-84). Springer Berlin Heidelberg. doi:10.1007/978-3-642-54420-0_8

Reich, J., Laadan, O., Brosh, E., Sherman, A., Misra, V., Nieh, J., & Rubenstein, D. (2012, December). VMTorrent: scalable P2P virtual machine streaming. In CoNEXT (pp. 289-300).

Reimer, D., Thomas, A., Ammons, G., Mummert, T., Alpern, B., & Bala, V. (2008, March). Opening black boxes: using semantic information to combat virtual machine image sprawl. *Proceedings of the fourth ACM SIGPLAN/SIGOPS international conference on Virtual execution environments* (pp. 111-120). ACM. doi:10.1145/1346256.1346272

Rosenblum, M., & Garfinkel, T. (2005). Virtual machine monitors: Current technology and future trends. *Computer*, *38*(5), 39–47. doi:10.1109/MC.2005.176

Schmidt, M., Fallenbeck, N., Smith, M., & Freisleben, B. (2010, February). Efficient distribution of virtual machines for Cloud computing. *Proceedings of the 2010 18th Euromicro International Conference on Parallel, Distributed and Network-Based Processing (PDP)* (pp. 567-574). IEEE. doi:10.1109/PDP.2010.39

Tang, C. (2011, June). FVD: A High-Performance Virtual Machine Image Format for Cloud. *Proceedings of the USENIX Annual Technical Conference.*

Vaquero, L. M., Rodero-Merino, L., Caceres, J., & Lindner, M. (2008). A break in the Clouds: Towards a Cloud definition. *Computer Communication Review*, *39*(1), 50–55. doi:10.1145/1496091.1496100

Xu, J., Zhang, W., Ye, S., Wei, J., & Huang, T. (2014, July). A lightweight virtual machine image deduplication backup approach in Cloud environment. *Proceedings of the 2014 IEEE 38th Annual Computer Software and Applications Conference (COMPSAC)* (pp. 503-508). IEEE. doi:10.1109/COMPSAC.2014.73

Xu, X., Jin, H., Wu, S., & Wang, Y. (2014). Rethink the storage of virtual machine images in Clouds. *Future Generation Computer Systems.*

Zhang, Y., Li, Y., & Zheng, W. (2013). Automatic software deployment using user-level virtualization for Cloud-computing. *Future Generation Computer Systems, 29*(1), 323–329. doi:10.1016/j.future.2011.08.012

Zhao, X., Zhang, Y., Wu, Y., Chen, K., Jiang, J., & Li, K. (2014). Liquid: A scalable deduplication file system for virtual machine images. . *IEEE Transactions on* Parallel and Distributed Systems, *25*(5), 1257–1266.

Zhou, R., Liu, F., Li, C., & Li, T. (2013, March). Optimizing virtual machine live storage migration in heterogeneous storage environment. In ACM SIGPLAN Notices, 48(7), 73-84. ACM. doi:10.1145/2451512.2451529

Chapter 8

EUBrazilCC Federated Cloud:
A Transatlantic Multi-Cloud Infrastructure

José Luis Vivas
Federal University of Campina Grande, Brazil

Francisco Brasileiro
Federal University of Campina Grande, Brazil

Abmar Barros
Federal University of Campina Grande, Brazil

Giovanni Farias da Silva
Federal University of Campina Grande, Brazil

Marcos Nóbrega Jr
Federal University of Campina Grande, Brazil

Francisco Germano de Araújo Neto
Federal University of Campina Grande, Brazil

Ignacio Blanquer
Polytechnic University of Valencia, Spain

Erik Torres
Polytechnic University of Valencia, Spain

Giovanni Aloisio
Euro-Mediterranean Centre on Climate Change, Brazil

Sandro Fiore
Euro-Mediterranean Centre on Climate Change, Italy

Rosa M. Badia
Barcelona Supercomputing Center, Spain

Daniele Lezzi
Barcelona Supercomputing Center, Spain

Antonio Tadeu A. Gomes
National Laboratory for Scientific Computing, Brazil

Jacek CaÅa
Newcastle University, UK

Maria Julia de Lima
Pontifical Catholic University of Rio de Janeiro, Brazil

Cristina Ururahy
Pontifical Catholic University of Rio de Janeiro, Brazil

ABSTRACT

Many e-science initiatives are currently investigating the use of cloud computing to support all kinds of scientific activities. The objective of this chapter is to describe the architecture and the deployment of the EUBrazilCC federated e-infrastructure, a Research & Development project that aims at providing a user-centric test bench enabling European and Brazilian research communities to test the deployment and execution of scientific applications on a federated intercontinental e-infrastructure. This e-infrastructure exploits existing resources that consist of virtualized data centers, supercomputers, and even opportunistically exploited desktops spread over a transatlantic geographic area. These heterogeneous resources are federated with the aid of appropriate middleware that provide the necessary features to achieve the established challenging goals. In order to elicit the requirements and validate the resulting infrastructure, three complex scientific applications have been implemented, which are also presented here.

DOI: 10.4018/978-1-5225-0153-4.ch008

INTRODUCTION

It is largely recognized today that many recent scientific advances have only been possible because of the increasing ability of researchers to draw upon information technologies (IT) in a comprehensive and efficient way. The use of these technologies allows them to process massive amounts of data and execute increasingly sophisticated simulation models, generating thereby new knowledge on an unprecedented scale. The intensive use of IT to generate new scientific knowledge is called *e-Science* (Hey, 2009).

Cloud computing technologies provide greater efficiency, agility and innovativeness in the delivery of IT services by facilitating economies of scale, sharing of irregularly used resources, and adoption of advanced approaches towards resource management (Armbrust et al., 2010). It is therefore not surprising that many e-science initiatives are currently considering the use of cloud computing to support many kinds of scientific activities (Yang et al., 2014).

The *EU-Brazil Cloud infrastructure Connecting Federated Resources for Scientific Advancement* (EUBrazilCC) is a R&D project that aims to provide a user-centric test bench enabling European and Brazilian research communities to test the deployment and execution of scientific applications on a federated intercontinental e-infrastructure. The resulting e-infrastructure exploits existing resources that include virtualized data centers, supercomputers, and even opportunistically exploited desktops spread out over a transatlantic geographic area. These heterogeneous resources are federated by means of a middleware that provides the necessary features to achieve the challenging established goals.

The objective of this chapter is to describe the architecture, implementation and deployment of the EUBrazilCC federated e-infrastructure, which has been developed according to the requirements of the following three complex applications involving three different scientific areas:

- **Leishmaniasis Virtual Laboratory:** An application integrating and processing genomic and clinical data from Leishmania and its vectors.
- **Cardiovascular Simulation Service**: An application integrating a cloud-based simulator of the human arterial vascular system with an HPC-based heart simulator.
- **Climate Change and Biodiversity Scientific Gateway**: A platform for the integration and processing of big data in order to study the interaction between biodiversity and climate change.

Although the design decisions were driven by the particular needs of these three applications, the resulting solutions are intended to be general enough to be useful also for many other similar types of scientific applications, and the tools used to build the federated e-infrastructure – some of them developed within the project – should be useful also to other distinct e-Science initiatives.

With the end of meeting the requirements of these three applications, each one demanding the integration of expertise, data and computing resources distributed in some cases over the two continents, we decided to adopt a user-centric approach in the development of a federation of private clouds and other computing resources belonging to different partners involved in the project. In order to support the federation of private clouds, a new middleware called fogbow[1] was developed within the EUBrazillCC project.

However, since not all applications can be executed efficiently in the cloud, the EUBrazilCC e-infrastructure also incorporates HPC clusters. These resources are different from those typically obtained from cloud providers, not only with regard to the processing and communication capabilities they provide but, most importantly, in the way that they may be accessed. When interacting with cloud providers, users and applications commonly have access to virtual machines over which they have full control. In contrast, HPC clusters are accessed via specific job submission services that may vary from one HPC provider to another. In the EUBrazilCC federated e-infrastructure, uniform access to HPC resources is enforced by a standard API provided by the CSGrid middleware (de Lima et al., 2006). Both this API and fogbow will be presented in detail below.

The rest of this chapter is structured as follows. We start with a presentation of the architecture designed to address the requirements of the three applications. Thereafter we give an overview of the design and implementation of fogbow; in particular, we present the security model designed to allow a seamless, flexible and simple authentication and authorization procedure for both users and applications across the whole federation. We follow by discussing how CSGrid was tailored in order to comply with the EUBrazilCC security model and be able to interact with fogbow, allowing thereby the execution of jobs with resources that are dynamically instantiated by cloud providers. This feature is particularly useful when applications are required to run partially on HPC clusters and partially on virtual machines.

We complete the description of the EUBrazilCC e-infrastructure by presenting details about a number of services deployed on top of the federation middleware to facilitate the contextualization of the execution environments that have been customized for the applications. We show also a set of higher-level services needed for the three applications such as management of highly parallel applications, elastic enactment of scientific workflows, and advanced parallel data analysis services. After the presentation of the EUBrazilCC e-infrastructure, we describe how it is being used within the project to deploy and execute the three use case applications.

Finally, we conclude the chapter with a presentation of the lessons learnt during the development of the federated EUBrazilCC e-infrastructure supporting efficient transatlantic scientific cooperation.

ARCHITECTURAL VIEW

The EUBrazilCC federated e-infrastructure aims at giving support to complex scientific applications characterized by heterogeneity in terms of requirements and programming models. Some of these applications need only simple batch processing facilities, while others may require parallel processing capabilities, workflow execution engines, and advanced data analytics functionalities. This is further compounded by the fact that some applications may need specific types of resources or to be executed at determined locations, while others would benefit from holding a wholly agnostic view of the underlying resources allowing for a seamless execution on any type of resources available in the federated e-infrastructure.

The three applications targeted by the EUBrazilCC project provide good examples of such heterogeneity of requirements. The Leishmaniasis Virtual laboratory requires the dynamic instantiation of complex workflows that, depending on the input parameters, might impose quite different computational demands on the underlying execution infrastructure and require workflow enactment services capable of dynamically increasing or decreasing the amount of compute resources allocated to run the application. On its turn, the data privacy concerns of the Cardiovascular Simulation Service might forestall the transmission of these data outside the countries in which they are initially stored. Likewise, the complexity of the Ayla-Red simulation runs in some of the scenarios of interest might require their execution in high-end HPC clusters such as the MareNostrum supercomputer hosted by the Barcelona Supercomputing Center. These requirements call for appropriate orchestration of the remote execution of two complex pieces of software over a Wide Area Network (WAN) connection. Finally, the massive amounts of data that need to be processed and correlated in the Biodiversity and Climate Change Scientific Gateway require high throughput data analysis services that scale well in a federated e-infrastructure.

In order to meet the different requirements of the target applications, the EUBrazilCC e-infrastructure is structured as a collection of independent layers, as shown in Figure 1.

At the bottom of the figure we have the Federation Layer, which provides a unified interface for accessing the federated e-infrastructure. Figure 2 gives a graphical view of the structure of the Federation Layer, which will be described in more detail in the next section.

Immediately above the Federation Layer, the Contextualization Layer provides functionalities that facilitate the customization of execution environments. Above it, the Scientific Platform Layer integrates a set of programming frameworks and data services. The architecture does not prescribe the adoption of a specific programming model, providing developers instead with a toolbox for code optimization and enhancement of the functionalities of the applications, possibly by combining the functionalities of different tools. Finally, above all these layers we have the Application Layer.

As mentioned above, EUBrazilCC federated e-infrastructure consists of a set of widely heterogeneous resources, including both private clouds and HPC clusters. The private clouds belonging to the federation

Figure 1. EUBrazil General Architecture

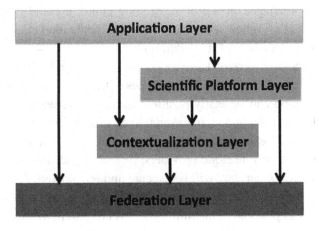

Figure 2. The Federation Layer

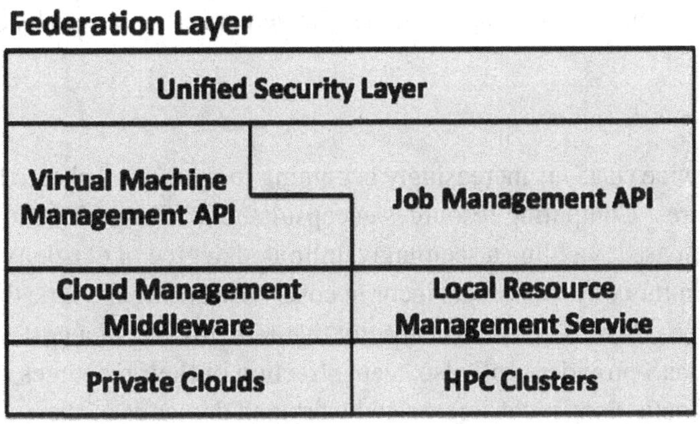

Federation Layer

Unified Security Layer	
Virtual Machine Management API	Job Management API
Cloud Management Middleware	Local Resource Management Service
Private Clouds	HPC Clusters

may run different cloud management middleware, such as OpenStack[2], OpenNebula[3], and CloudStack[4], while the HPC clusters may also use different local resource management services. In addition, these two types of resources are accessed through quite different APIs. The EUBrazilCC architecture provides support for APIs based on well-accepted standards. VM management is provided through an extended OCCI API, while job-based interaction is provided through an API that follows the DRMAA standard. In order to provide a unified view of such a heterogeneous e-infrastructure, we have adopted a single security model that is supported by both these APIs.

FEDERATING PRIVATE CLOUDS

Fogbow is a middleware for sharing underused resources, evolved from the OurGrid[5] and JiT Cloud[6] projects. Its goal is to provide computing power catering to *highly elastic* and *ephemeral* workloads (workloads that are operational only for short periods of time) according to a non-monetary delayed exchange business model, i.e. an exchange of resources between two parties that is not immediate and thus may give rise to a debt or obligation to return, in consequence involving aspects of trust and fairness among the members of the federation. To this end, we developed a model of delayed exchange called the Network of Favors (NoF), explained in detail in a separate section below.

By installing a fogbow-manager on top of an existing cloud, a cloud administrator can make its administrative domain part of a fogbow federation, allowing local cloud clients to make use of surplus resources belonging to other members of the federation.

Applications that produce such workloads are very common in several scientific domains. For instance, bag-of-tasks applications, one of the most important types of this class of applications, are characterized by the fact that their execution can be easily parallelized. A simple work queue scheduler that keeps dispatching pending tasks for execution at any available processing resource, until all tasks have been executed, can control the parallel execution of the application. If the resources provided are homogenous, which is commonly the case in private cloud providers, then obviously the more resources are available to run these applications, the sooner they will be execute and terminated. As a result, clients that need to run this type of applications could fully explore the elasticity property of clouds by requesting as many computing resources as possible to maximize the level of parallelization in the execution of their applications. This would allow these clients to run their applications in the shortest possible time when compared to other scheduling options. Hence, the optimal execution of these applications in resources obtained from private clouds requires the requisition of very large numbers of resources in relatively short periods of time, yielding in this way highly elastic and ephemeral workloads.

Challenges

Infrastructure-as-a-Service (IaaS) is increasingly becoming the preferred choice for the provisioning of computing infrastructures. Computing resources encapsulated in Virtual Machines (VMs) can be rapidly provisioned and released, yielding a seemingly unlimited degree of elasticity in the provisioning of computing resources. In this way, customers incur in costs only during the time that the VMs are in use.

During off-peak times there is an excess capacity that remains idle at a cost for the provider. Moreover, most of the time IaaS providers will also keep a fraction of their resources in an idle state in order to deal with eventual fluctuations in the aggregated workload demands of their clients or with transient failures in the infrastructure, which also implies a cost. By establishing a federation of IaaS clouds, the aggregated excess capacity of all of its members can be used as a shared pool of resources that may serve applications with highly elastic and ephemeral workloads. The federated members might in this way make their idle resources available to other IaaS providers in the federation that may have momentarily exhausted their own local resources. Local clients need not suffer here since resource providers may give them priority in the use of resources by keeping the right to claim them back whenever more resources are requested by those clients.

In this way, as long as the resources provided to the federation during times of low local demand are paid back during times of excess local demand, and also that the costs derived from participating in the federation are negligible, it will always be advantageous to make idle resources available to the federation. In large federations, this will make it possible to fall back on a large pool of resources available on demand and catering to highly elastic and ephemeral workloads without significantly increasing the costs of provision and without detriment to the quality of service provided to local clients.

The success of such a federation of private clouds depends on the costs incurred by each member in joining and participating in the federation. Since no extra physical resources are required, the cost of federating depends exclusively on the operation of the service. Executing remote workloads with local resources increases power expenditure, even when idle resources are not as a rule switched off. In consequence, these extra costs will be acceptable only if approximately the same amount of computing power incurred by running external workloads is saved by having internal workloads executed remotely by other members of the federation. The next section will explain how this balance can be achieved.

Issues related to security and interoperability must also be solved without introducing significant costs. In this case, the key is to provide solutions that are transparent and impose minimal changes, if any, to local policies and configurations. Members should keep their autonomy to define their own security policies and how their resources are provided to the federation. These requirements should be met independently of the middleware used by each member to manage the local private cloud, respecting local features such as user authentication methods, image types, VM flavors, and computing power.

The fact that the federation is geographically spread out also brings about new challenges. It should be possible to locate other members of the federation with little or no assumptions concerning real IP addresses, firewall or NAT (Network Address Translation) configurations. The same rationale applies for accessing VMs that have been instantiated in remote private clouds, which are commonly not accessible from outside the perimeter of the local area network of the provider. Hence, a solution for the federation of private clouds must provide a means to bypass these obstacles.

Summing up, the ultimate challenge is to implement a business model that: (i) guarantees that providers are duly compensated for allocating their resources to external workloads without substantially increasing the cost of provision; (ii) enhances interoperability; and (iii) ensures that security goals are met without imposing excessive costs.

The Network of Favors

An important challenge for building stable federations concerns the promotion of cooperation between rational selfish individuals in a context without any centralized trusted authorities. In this kind of peer-to-peer oriented system, participants (peers) are usually left to themselves with only limited information to estimate the trustworthiness of other peers within the federation, who may not be reliable and willing to reciprocate later a received favor. Each peer must therefore rely solely on its own experience, acquired solely through direct interaction with other peers, in order to estimate the trustworthiness of each one of them.

Initially, participants will have an incentive to become free riders, consuming but not providing resources. Moreover, collaborative peers may defect from the federation if not satisfied with the results of participation. Some form of individual incentive must therefore exist in order to promote cooperation and sustained voluntary participation. The challenge is to find a scheme that ensures that collaborative peers will not defect and free riders will be marginalized. In fogbow, this is done by a refinement of an early proposal called the Network of Favors (NoF) (Cirne et al., 2006).

The goal of the NoF is to provide mechanisms that allow peers to make correct decisions about whom to collaborate with, giving priority to honest participants that are more likely to reciprocate received favors in the future. In order to assess the effectiveness of these mechanisms for our business model, we have defined two metrics: satisfaction and fairness. *The satisfaction* of a federated member at any point in time is defined as the ratio between the total amount of resources it has received so far from the federation and the total amount of resources it has requested so far to the federation. *Fairness*, on the other hand, is defined as the ratio at any point in time between the total amount of resources received so far from the federation, and the total amount of resources provided so far to the federation. The challenge is to find a scheme that guarantees that, on the long run, the value of fairness approaches unity for all collaborative members, and that at the same time their satisfaction values are also sufficiently high. Moreover, the cost of running a scheme that guarantees these goals should also be negligible. In particular, one should avoid relying on centralized services provided either by a particular member of the federation or by any specialized external agent.

The NoF is basically a mechanism that aids participants in deciding to whom they should provide idle resources. To perform this task, the member of the NoF keeps a local record of the total value of all resources provided to and received from each other member of the federation with which it has interacted in the past. Whenever a peer provides or obtains a certain amount of resources, the total value of the resources exchanged with the collaborating peer is updated. Based on these values, each peer calculates a balance value associated with each collaborating peer. For a peer A, the balance value of peer B is given by the total amount of resources provided by peer B to A, minus the total amount of resources provided to B by A. In case of resource contention, a peer will always prioritize those peers against which it has a higher balance, thus encouraging collaboration.

The NoF was initially proposed as an incentive mechanism for resource sharing within P2P opportunistic desktop grids. We call here this notion of the NoF the Satisfaction-Driven NoF (SD-NoF). In the SD-NoF a collaborator always supply all of its idle resources to the federation, with the expectation of accumulating credits with other peers that may result in future received favors. This strategy ensures the best possible levels of satisfaction for collaborators, independently of the level of resource contention. The scheme is suitable for opportunistic desktop grids, since in this case the cost of providing resources that are intended primarily for in-house consumption is assumed to be so low that collaborators may disregard fairness and focus instead only on maximizing satisfaction. However, in the case of private and P2P federated clouds, resources are dedicated, and the associated overhead costs (management staff, energy, space etc.) may not be negligible. Fairness can thus become an important goal that may be met by limiting the amount of supplied resources, thereby isolating free riders more efficiently, especially in scenarios with low resource contention. In contrast to the SD-NoF, we call this scheme the Fairness-Driven NoF (FD-NoF). Fogbow supports both these models.

Conceptual Architecture

The architecture of a fogbow federation of private clouds consists of two basic components: the *membership manager* and the *allocation manager*. Any private cloud that wants to join the federation must deploy both these components (see Figure 3).

The role of the membership manager is to keep track of which members of the federation are currently active. The several membership managers implement a gossip-style communication protocol to spread information about the addresses and the estimated capacity of their associated allocation managers. To this end, the membership managers periodically exchange with each other information on their current state. The allocation managers provide their currently available idle capacity to the associated membership managers, and manage information about the currently active allocation managers, together with an estimation of the resources that each of them can provide to the federation.

A client interacts with the federation by sending requests to one of the allocation managers. Upon reception of the request, the allocation manager will interact with the local cloud and try to fulfill the request using at first hand internal idle resources. If these are not enough, it will try to reclaim the local resources, if any, that are being used to fulfill previous remote requests received from other allocation managers in the federation, using in this case a local prioritization policy in such a way as to promote fairness. If these resources are still not enough, the allocation manager will finally try to obtain the needed resources from other members of the federation.

Although resources will be exchanged over the Internet, local security policies should nevertheless be enforced. Hence, the deployment of the federation components should be as little intrusive as possible with regard to e.g. user authentication methods, firewall rules, NAT isolation, and demand for public IPs. Service endpoints (compute, storage, network, identity, etc.) should no be exposed. To this end, the allocation manager should provide a new layer of abstraction that will forward remote instance

Figure 3. Fogbow basic components

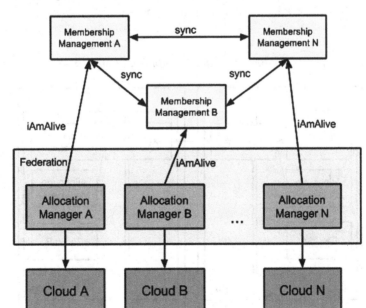

requests to the underlying cloud management middleware, keeping these endpoints behind the firewall. In addition, allocation managers must communicate with each other regardless of the public IPs or ports exposed through the firewall.

In order to address both these issues, we adopted an architecture based on components that communicate through a messaging service that assigns a logical and DNS-resolvable address and multiplexes all message packets through a single common port located at a so-called DeMilitarized Zone (DMZ). Both the allocation manager and the membership manager should be implemented in this way, as shown in Figure 4.

With regard to authentication and authorization, the existing user base and local policies concerning quotas and permissions constrain the resources that may be made available by the allocation manager. In order to allow federation users to obtain resources from other members, the allocation manager provides a three-layer authentication and authorization schema (Figure 5). The first layer authenticates and authorizes users to create requests at the allocation manager; the second layer interacts with the underlying private cloud and associates the requesting user to a local quota, if there is one; finally, the third layer is responsible for managing authentication and authorization between allocation managers, deciding whether an allocation manager will receive or supply resources to other allocation managers. The proposed schema assumes the existence of a mapping function that associates with each authenticated and authorized federation user a credential that can be used to access a subset of the resources offered by the local cloud. Cloud administrators are free to define this mapping at their will, ultimately deciding by themselves which resources in their clouds will be made available to each other user of the federation. The simplest implementation of this mapping is by using the credential associated with a single special user at each private cloud created with the sole purpose of acting as proxy to remote requests, which means that all requests coming from remote members will share a single quota at the underlying cloud.

Federation members could be isolated by NATs and firewalls, resulting in poor connectivity to external resources. This issue is addressed by means of a reverse tunneling component, a service responsible for exposing connectivity endpoints to resources beyond the DMZ of the domain, as shown in Figure 6.

The distributed and complex nature of the federation and the heterogeneity of the many cloud management middleware products available today turn interoperability into a big challenge. The proposed

Figure 4. Internet-friendly intra-member and inter-member communication

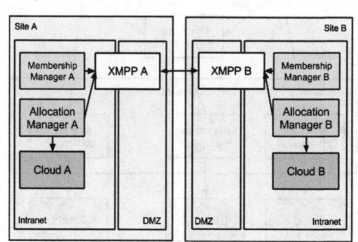

Figure 5. Three-Layer Authentication and Authorization Schema

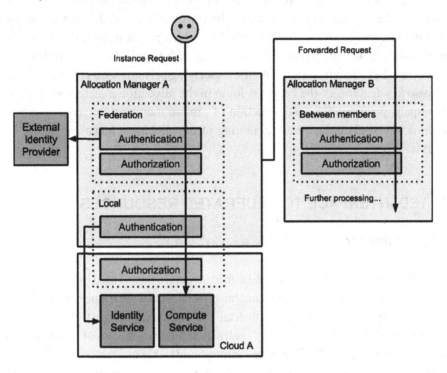

Figure 6. Reverse tunneling

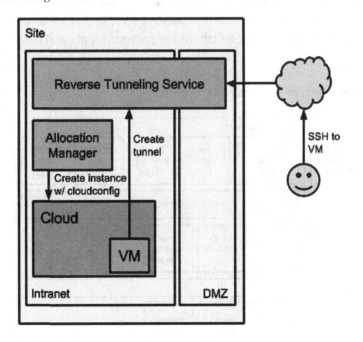

architecture for the allocation manager broadens the range of compatible IaaS technologies by concealing communication with the various services provided by the private cloud through the implementation of a set of well-defined *interoperability plugin* interfaces, which play a major role in the architecture and design of the allocation manager, enhancing in this way the extensibility capabilities of the federation middleware. Not only the communication with the underlying private cloud is defined in terms of plugin interfaces, but also key features of the business logic in the allocation manager such as authentication, authorization, request prioritization, and selection of remote members for request outsourcing. These *behavioral plugins* ultimately define the functioning of the allocation manager. Figure 7 shows all the specified plugin interfaces.

JOB-ORIENTED INTERFACE TO FEDERATED RESOURCES

Conceptual Architecture

The job-based API in the EUBrazilCC federated e-infrastructure is provided by the CSGrid[7] middleware. CSGrid is a freely distributed open source system based on the CSBase framework (de Lima et al., 2006) and has been used for both academic and industrial purposes over the past 10 years. CSGrid offers a collaborative and extensible environment as an abstraction layer for the use of distributed computational and storage resources—e.g. High Performance Computing (HPC) clusters—, providing functionalities that can be used either directly by end users or by the applications themselves with the aid of programming interfaces (e.g. the mc[2] toolset, described below.)

CSGrid is a client-server system that supports a working model based on a project-centric approach. Users cooperate with each other by checking and comparing results for different input data sets. In fact, users typically work only on a limited set of programs that are available for running on resources managed by the system. Each project represents a data storage area, organized as a hierarchical structure. Users create their own projects by defining collaboration contexts for pre and post processing programs.

Figure 7. The allocation manager's architecture

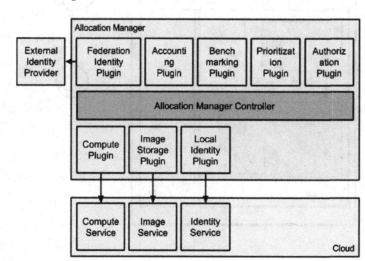

This project-centric approach aims at supporting data-intensive operations in which data is moved as little as possible.

Different executions of a single program can be associated with a common project, allowing simulations to run in parallel in the same project input files and the different results to be organized in a single area.

The system runs by batch submissions of non-interactive programs previously uploaded and shared by the users in the CSGrid server. These programs — called algorithms in CSGrid — are composed of executables and configuration files. CSGrid typically creates the associated command to execute an algorithm dynamically, using parameters provided by the user. Executable programs, like project data, are stored in server repositories and are under permission-related access restrictions.

The main components of the CSGrid system are illustrated in Figure 8 and described below.

The *Authentication and Service Discovery Layer* lies on top of OpenBus[8], a CORBA-based middleware used for integrating multi-platform and multi-language systems in a service-oriented architecture. OpenBus provides a service directory, access control mechanisms, and peer-to-peer communication.

Figure 8. CSGrid Architecture

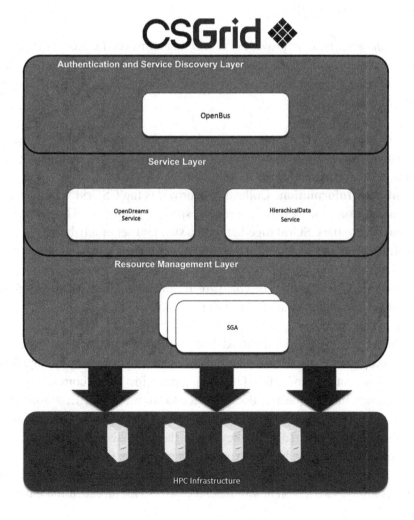

The *Service Layer* publishes its services as OpenBus components, allowing clients to be written in a number of programming languages and operating systems. The OpenBus components offered by the CSGrid server are the following:

- *OpenDreams* (OpenBus Distributed Resource and Algorithms Management Service): provides a set of operations for the submission, monitoring and control of jobs on remote execution resources, and for monitoring the execution resources themselves. The OpenDreams interface is based on OGF's DRMAA 1.0 specification (Global Grid Forum, 2008).
- *Hierarchical Data Service*: provides a set of operations for accessing and manipulating files in the user's project area. Each project is organized as a hierarchical structure that stores related files. All data files needed as input to an algorithm submission should be previously available in a user project area. Submitted algorithms also write output files to the associated project area.
- *Algorithm Service*: provides a set of operations for obtaining algorithm descriptions. As stated above, each algorithm is composed of executables and configuration files. One of these files (config.xml) describes the input and output arguments of the algorithm. It is similar in purpose to the JSDL files of the UNICORE middleware and the CTD files of the OpenMS library (Sturm et al., 2008). Nevertheless, it allows providing more details about how the arguments of the algorithm can be rendered in a user interface.

The *Resource Management Layer* provides the API that abstracts the access to a number of different execution resources, possibly encompassing clusters as well as individual machines with specific hardware capabilities. This API, called SGA (a Portuguese acronym for Algorithm Management System) provides the following functionalities:

- **Resource Configuration Information:** Provides mechanisms for querying the configuration of available computational resources for the execution of algorithms, identifying the attributes and requirements of the platform.
- **Specific Platforms Information:** Collects and provides the CSGrid with information about the computational environment, which depends on specific platforms. This information is consolidated and provided to the CSGrid together with a standard set of attributes.
- **Job Control:** Provides mechanisms for the execution, monitoring and control of jobs that depend on specific platforms.
- **Sandbox to Algorithms:** Provides mechanisms for the configuration of an optional sandbox area used for the input and output data of algorithm executions.

The SGA API hides the complexities involved in using the computational environment. This makes it possible to manage a complex and heterogeneous resource farm in a user friendly way. When an execution takes place, the user does not have to bother if it is taking place in a single computer or in an HPC cluster with hundreds of nodes. Similarly, the user does not need to know if a specific algorithm is implemented in C, Java or Fortran, or if it runs on a 64-bit Linux or 32-bit Windows system: the implementation of the SGA API in the specific resource will take care of these details. This facilitates collaboration by allowing computational resources to be transparently shared by the CSGrid users.

Moreover, the SGA API is flexible and can be instantiated in different scenarios. An SGA implementation can be deployed as a daemon in host machines to provide an execution interface to these hosts individually, or it can be set as a gateway to third party Resource Management Systems (RMSes). In the former case, each host machine becomes a resource for the execution of algorithms. In the latter case, a module within the SGA implementing the integration with a specific system is used, whereas the SGA intermediates execution requests from the CSGrid to the other systems and manages the executions. Currently, there are SGA gateway implementations for the following RMSes: SGE, TORQUE/PBS, and SLURM.

So far, there are bindings for the SGA API in Java and Lua[9] programming languages. The use of Lua makes it easy to provide a single interface irrespective of the implementation being a script with command-line tools or relying on other libraries for job submission. When a SGA is implemented with the Lua binding it runs as a daemon, and the communication with CSGrid is performed through a CORBA interface. When a SGA is implemented with the Java binding, it may be provided as a local plug-in to the CSGrid server, which is particularly useful when it is not possible to run a daemon or open the necessary TCP ports for CORBA communication within the resource. When the SGA is provided as a local Java plug-in to the CSGrid server, it can employ conventional resource access protocols (e.g. SSH) to manage the resources.

Integration with Fogbow

In EUBrazilCC, a new implementation of the SGA API—called *SGA fogbow*—has been developed to allow the execution of jobs on resources dynamically instantiated by fogbow on cloud providers. This SGA implementation brings together the job-oriented and VM-oriented APIs shown in Figure 2 by overseeing the job lifecycle and staging the files needed to execute each job in the resources of the cloud.

Figure 9. gives an overall picture of the CSGrid integration with private clouds and HPC resources in the context of the EUBrazilCC federation. An allocation manager is deployed on each private cloud participating in the EUBrazilCC federation. The SGA-fogbow interacts with one allocation manager, dynamically allocating resources in its local cloud as well as in any other cloud that is a member of the federation.

Figure 9. Integration with fogbow

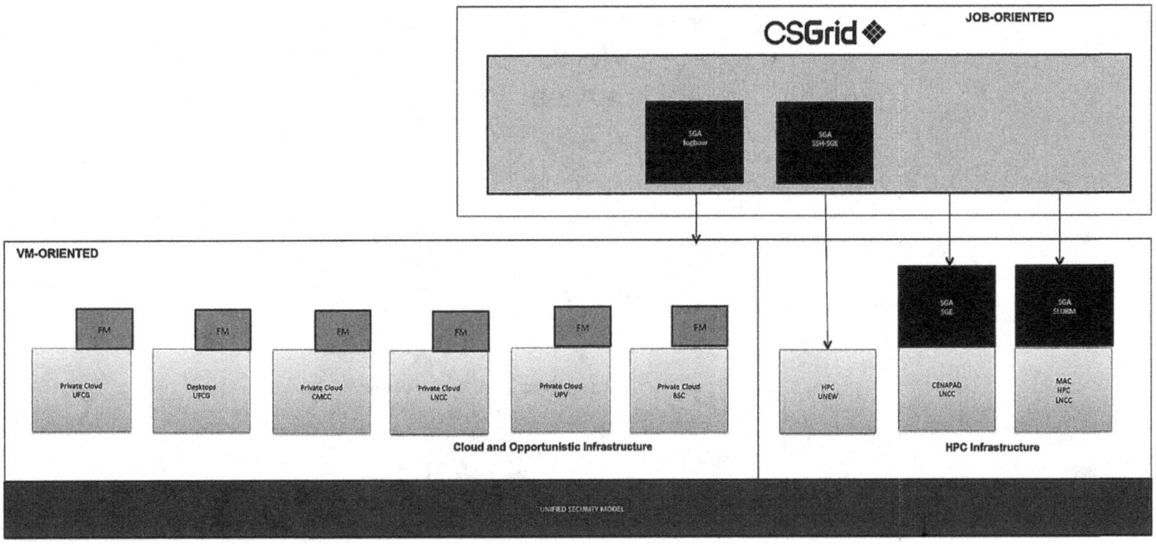

CONTEXTUALIZATION SERVICES

Managing VMIs in a Federated Environment

The management of Virtual Machine Images (VMIs) in a cloud environment poses important challenges to the use of cloud-based infrastructures. A VMI encapsulates both software configurations and virtual hardware specifications. The software and hardware requirements of some applications may lead to a massive creation of VMIs that must be properly indexed in order to leverage both reuse and sharing (Tordsson, Montero, Moreno-Vozmediano, & Llorente, 2012). Identifying the proper VMI may be a complex and burdensome task. As an example, there are currently almost 41.000 public images in the North Virginia region of Amazon AWS. This database is queried for very basic information, such as the key words in the VMI description. Moreover, minimum requirements on the software for running the VMIs are not clearly exposed in the associated metadata. Therefore, selecting a compatible instance type is not a straightforward task. Another important feature that VMI catalogues should have is the ability to store a high volume of data, since the size of a VMI is commonly in the order of a few gigabytes.

In order to meet these challenges, Carrión et al. (2010) propose a catalogue and repository of VMIs that enables users and cloud administrators to index and store the VMIs together with the appropriate metadata describing their hardware and software features. The Virtual Machine Resource Catalogue (VMRC) system can be deployed within a private cloud to store the different VMIs required to provision the services (see Figure 10), and can also index VMIs stored within other cloud providers.

A single VMRC entity can provide the VMIs to different clouds in a federation. The catalogue itself is hypervisor-agnostic and uses the open virtual format (OVF) specification. In this way, VMIs are in-

Figure 10. VMRC Architecture Schema

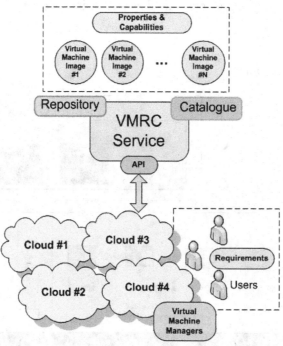

cluded in the catalogue, and the different Cloud Management Platforms (CMPs) may use the catalogue to retrieve the appropriate VMIs. The VMRC can be used only to index the location of the VMIs that can be accessed by the different CMPs via shared directories. The URIs of the VMIs stored by the cloud providers are included in each one of the entries in the metadata, so the query can be restricted to the set of providers in which a user can have credentials. Finally, the repository service enables the implementation of synchronization mechanisms between files in different repositories. As replication and distribution are key to fault tolerance, this approach paves the way to having multiple repository services in order to better cope with failures and prevent the loss of data stored in the repository.

The catalogue is extended with a repository of Ansible-based recipes (Hochstein, 2014), which allows setting up not only the proper basic VMI but also the software to be configured in the virtual appliance. In this way, software configurations are described as a set of modules to be included in the final set-up. Details about automated configuration and contextualization are provided in the next section.

Configuration and Contextualization

VMIs contain the disk and virtual hardware specification needed to instantiate a Virtual Machine (VM). In the process of deployment of a VM, several actions have to be performed in order to configure it properly (Quinton, Haderer, Rouvoy, & Duchien, 2013; Armstrong, Espling, Tordsson, Djemame, & Elmroth, 2015). Literature (Caballer, Segrelles, Molto, & Blanquer, 2014) and software tools that address the deployment of virtual infrastructures are currently available. Amazon Web Services (AWS) provides CloudFormation[10] to facilitate the creation and management of AWS resources. The Nimbus project has developed a set of tools to deploy virtual infrastructures: the Context Broker (Keahey & Freeman, 2008), the Recontextualization Broker (Marshall, Tufo, Keahey, LaBissoniere, & Woitaszek, 2012; Marshall, Keahey, & Freeman, 2010; Armstrong, Espling, Tordsson, Djemame, & Elmroth, 2012), and cloudinit.d (Bresnahan, Freeman, LaBissoniere, & Keahey, 2011). In particular, cloudinit.d automates the VM creation process, the contextualization, and the coordination of service deployment, supporting multiple clouds and the synchronization of different "run levels". In spite of the fact that cloudinit.d provides a system to monitor the services that check for service errors, re-launching failed services or launching new VMs, the contextualization is described by simple scripts, which is insufficient in complex scenarios with multiple VMs and different operating systems.

Apache Whirr[11] supports the deployment of clusters both on EC2 and Rackspace. The user specifies in the beginning the number of instances, the roles, and the VMIs. It does not support elasticity, so after the deployment of the infrastructure the configuration will remain static. Wrangler (Juve & Deelman, 2011) uses XML files and scripts to specify requirements and configuration. SixSq SlipStream enables defining the list of packages to install and a script file that can be executed by each VM. Again, SlipStream defines a static configuration that cannot be automatically reused to recontextualize the infrastructure if nodes are added or removed. Fine-grain level orchestration and recontextualization is performed by SALSA (Le, Truong, Copil, Nastic, & Dustdar, 2014), enabling the definition of configuration plans that best fit the changes on a configuration.

One common limitation in these systems is the employment of manually selected base images to launch the VMs. This is an important limitation because it implies that users must create and maintain their own images. This limitation affects the reutilization of the previously created VMIs, forcing the user to dedicate time and effort for customizing the existing images or creating new ones. Another important limitation is the usage of simple scripts in the contextualization, instead of DevOps tools (except for Nimbus) such as Puppet (Puppet, 2015), Chef (Opscode, 2015), or Ansible (DeHaan, 2013), which create system-independent configurations.

Therefore, a cloud deployment service should consider the following points:

- It should separate the management of the VMIs, the infrastructure descriptions, the software dependencies installation and the VMI deployment on a cloud to facilitate integration and interoperability.
- The platform should not focus exclusively on a specific cloud management platform or even a specific type of infrastructure (PC clusters, grid test beds, parallel environments, etc.), in order to be able to deal with any kind of complex infrastructure. The same complex infrastructure can be deployed both in on-premise and public clouds, thus enabling the outsourcing of computation to public clouds when there is a shortage of computational resources on-premise.
- The usage of pre-packaged VMIs is an important limitation because users are constrained to use the preselected software of the VMIs or manually install the desired software after the virtual infrastructure has been provisioned. The service, on the other hand, should support the automated installation at runtime of the software and the configuration of the complex data dependencies in the virtual infrastructure as well as in the physical infrastructure. This facilitates keeping the infrastructure updated, since new version of packages can be installed at each new deployment.
- There should be the possibility to reuse both the infrastructure descriptions, with the aid of a repository of high-level infrastructure descriptions, and the VMIs, by means a catalogue with their corresponding metadata).

The Infrastructure Manager (IM) is a tool that facilitates the access of IaaS clouds by automating the selection of the rightmost Virtual Machine Image, as well as the deployment, configuration, software installation, monitoring and updating of virtual appliances. Its architecture is shown in Figure 11.

The IM provides an abstraction layer to make it interoperable with different IaaS cloud back-ends. This layer has been designed using a plug-in scheme that currently supports libvirt, Docker containers, OCCI, OpenStack, OpenNebula, Amazon EC2, Google Cloud and Windows Azure. This set of plug-ins enables the access to a large number of cloud deployments and virtualization platforms. This approach prevents vendor lock-in and facilitates the seamlessly migration from a simple virtualization system to a large-scale cloud deployment. It integrates Ansible as the contextualization system to enable the installation and configuration of any software dependency. Ansible has shown better scalability and robustness against failures of the provisioning system, which is highly desirable in federated environments. Although multiple cloud providers offer services for the deployment of software configurations (e.g. HEAT from OpenStack or the Software Management and Catalogue service of OpenNebula), IM recipes are compatible to all the platforms supported via plug-ins.

To describe both the hardware characteristics and the software configuration of an infrastructure, the IM uses formal descriptive documents. These documents are expressed using the Resource Application Description Language (RADL) (Caballer, Blanquer, Molto, & de Alfonso, 2015; de Alfonso, Caballer, Alvarruiz, Molto, & Hernández, 2011), which is a simple high level and declarative Domain Specific Language (DSL) to describe the hardware and software features of a virtual infrastructure. A RADL

Figure 11. The IM Architecture

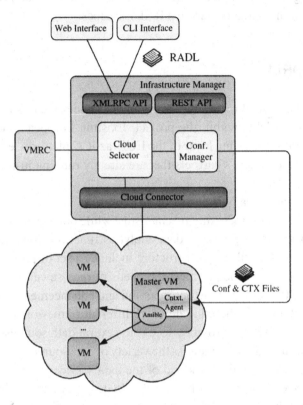

document specifies the requirements of each type of VM needed in the infrastructure and the number of instances of each type to be deployed on top of the IaaS cloud. A RADL document comprises four points:

- The description of the virtual hardware.
- The deployment of the node.
- The common configuration recipes.
- The instantiation of variables specific to this node.

The configuration in run-time of the VA introduces an overhead, which however is negligible due to the time scale of the experiments. On-the-fly configuration hides the platform specificities and mitigates the degradation that continuous operation may have on the workers. In case that the configuration time impacts the quality of service perceived by the user, the VMs can be preserved through snapshots and registered in a catalogue for longer-term hibernation. An interesting alternative, which is also supported by the IM, is the use of docker containers enabling a binary-compatibility level with cloud providers (including public clouds like the container service of Amazon). The IM can instantiate those containers, which can be registered in a catalogue for reuse.

Finally, automatic contextualization opens the door to dynamic recontextualization of running virtual appliance by means of the addition or removal of new or existing VMs. Caballer et al. (2013) introduce the concept of elastic virtual clusters using the IM as a contextualization and recontextualization mechanism. Adding or removing VMs through the IM's API leads to an automatic recontextualization of the virtual appliance, based on the initial declarative RADL recipes.

SCIENTIFIC PLATFORM

The programming frameworks enable the implementation of the use cases and their execution on the federated cloud resources available within the project. Existing European and Brazilian technologies build the foundation of the programming layer of the EUBrazilCC platform, extending and adapting the environments provided by the project's partners that are already running in several e- Infrastructures in Europe, such as the EGI.

Scientific applications vary greatly in terms of requirements and programming models. Many applications need only simple batch-processing mechanisms, while others may require parallel processing capabilities, workflow execution engines, or data analytics functionalities. In order to support those different requirements, the EUBrazilCC infrastructure includes a set of programming frameworks that provide complementary features needed to meet the needs of the use cases. The aim is to provide application developers with a toolbox for code optimization and enhancement of the functionalities of the applications, possibly combining the functionalities of different frameworks.

The EUBrazilCC architecture also provides access to several data sources offered by multiple data providers and needed by the use cases. To address the variety of data sources, an adaptation layer (specific components/libraries) is included in the back-end of the data services provided in the architecture. To address efficiency requirements, scalable solutions able to deal with large volumes of data are needed. The EUBrazilCC platform relies on parallelization techniques to efficiently manage large datasets (from GBs to TBs) on multiple nodes, and exploits the cloud paradigm for scalability purposes.

In the next sections we provide a description of the two programming frameworks available in the infrastructure, COMPSs and eScience Central, of the PDAS data analytics service, which provides a framework for parallel I/O and data analysis, and of the mc^2 toolset (Gomes, Bastos, Medeiros, & Moreira, 2015), which allows the rapid prototyping of application-specific science gateways over the EUBrazilCC federated e-infrastructure.

COMPSs

COMPSs is a programming framework consisting of a programming model and an execution runtime that supports it. Its main objective is to ease the development of applications for distributed environments. The COMPSs programming model aims at keeping programmers unaware of the execution environment and parallelization details. The users are only required to create a sequential application and specify which methods of the application code will be executed remotely. This selection is done by the provision of an annotated interface in which these methods are declared with metadata about them and their parameters. COMPSs has also the capability of orchestrating workflows composed of services mixed with regular methods (pieces of code not intended to be services). Both services and methods can be COMPSs tasks and part of a COMPSs application workflow. The programming model provides bindings for Java, C/C++ and Python applications, and a graphical interface is available to help programmers port their code to COMPSs and deploy the application on the infrastructure.

The COMPSs runtime is in charge of optimizing the performance of the application by exploiting its inherent concurrency. The runtime intercepts any call to a selected method creating a representative task and finding the data dependencies with other tasks that must be considered along the application run. The task is added to a task dependency graph as a new node and the dependencies are represented by edges on the graph. Tasks with no dependencies enter the scheduling step and are assigned to available resources. This decision is made according to a scheduling algorithm that takes into account data locality, task constraints, and the workload of each node. According to this decision, the input data to the scheduled task are transferred to the selected host and the task is remotely submitted. Once a task finishes, the task dependency graph is updated, possibly yielding new dependency-free tasks to schedule. Through the monitoring of the application workload, the runtime determines the excess or lack of resources and turns to cloud providers enforcing a dynamic management of the resource pool. In order to make COMPSs interoperable with different types of providers, a common interface is used that implements the specific cloud provider API. In the EUBrazilCC platform the OCCI interface is used to deploy VMs through fogbow (see Figure 12).

The Programming Model Enactment Service (PMES) is a web service that allows the execution of applications programmed with the COMPSs programming model. A client is used to contact an OGF BES compliant endpoint in order to submit the execution of the application. This request is expressed through a JSDL document containing the application name, the input parameters and data references. When a request is received, a virtual machine is requested to the Cloud Provider in order to deploy the application by downloading its package from a storage location. Once the runtime machine is deployed, the COMPSs application is remotely started. On its turn, the COMPSs runtime will schedule the tasks on a set of machines created on demand. This phase includes the staging of input files from remote loca-

Figure 12. COMPSs deployment in EUBrazilCC

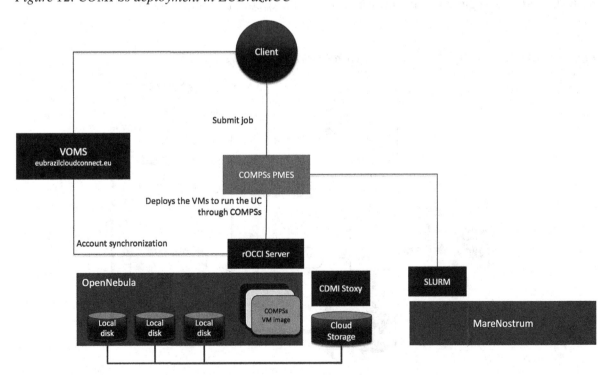

tions as specified in the execution request. The COMPSs-PMES service can be also configured to boot a predefined number of VMs on the provider where the service is deployed; this solution allows serving requests that involve the execution of smaller operations in a reasonable amount of time, avoiding the overhead of VM creation; if the requests requires more resources than currently available, the service is still able to dynamically deploy new instances in order to cope with the load burst.

eScience Central

e-Science Central (e-SC) is a cloud-based workflow management system that provides capabilities to store, analyze and share data among scientists (Hiden, Woodman, Watson, & Cala, 2013). It provides both SaaS and PaaS for scientists who want to carry out own analyses, manage data, and collaborate with each other. The key feature of e-SC is to allow users to process and manipulate data by means of specified workflows. Using the in-browser workflow editor, they can build workflows by dragging blocks and connecting them together to form a direct acyclic graph. Edges in the graph define the flow of data, whereas the vertices denote data processing blocks. The workflows can thereafter be executed and the results displayed in the web application and stored in the system for later use. The system collects also provenance information; in this way, for any data produced in the system the users are able to access complete logs on how the data was generated, including input data, workflows, and the blocks involved.

Currently, e-SC provides the palette of about 250 data processing blocks such as CSV file import, data column selection, and neural model builder. Users can add custom blocks with their own algorithms, which can be implemented in Java, R, Octave and JavaScript.

The architecture of e-Science Central follows the common master-worker pattern (see Figure 13). The central server provides core services such as data and workflow repository, versioning, security, and web user interface. It also manages the invocation queue into which all workflow invocations are pushed. Workflow engines pull the invocations from the queue and process them.

Figure 13. Architecture of the e-Science Central Workflow Management System

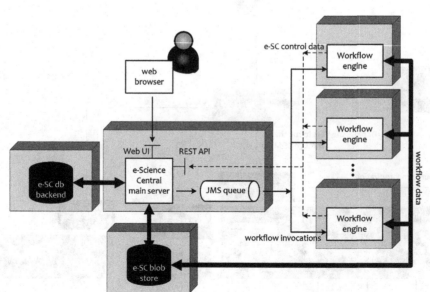

The system is portable across a wide range of devices ranging from laptops to clusters and clouds. In the cloud, it can take advantage of the processing and storage facilities provided by an underlying IaaS. For example, the workflow engine can transfer data directly to or from a cloud storage such as Amazon S3 and Azure Blob Store, which greatly improves performance in large scale workflow applications.

Most importantly, e-SC implements also basic deployment procedures in which each processing node only requires the installation of a relatively small workflow engine service. Later, any block and library pieces of code required by the workflows are downloaded and installed on demand, while the workloads continue executing. The benefit of this approach is at least three-fold. First, it avoids the need to configure in advance all data processing nodes with the required software and tools. Second, it improves reusability of VM images in the cloud because the same workflow engine image can be used in different system deployments. Finally, it facilitates application updates. The task of updating workflow blocks and libraries is executed directly by the engine, so whenever a new version of a component has been registered in the system, the engines that are going to use it will first download and install the updated version. Also, updating the engine service is a straightforward operation supported by the Ansible automation facility[12].

Data Analytics and PDAS

The EUBrazilCC project deals also with big data analytics challenges. More specifically, in the context of the use case on climate change and biodiversity, multiple, large and heterogeneous scientific data sources need to accessed, analyzed and visualized. To address these requirements, the project exploits and extends a software framework developed at CMCC and called Parallel Data Analysis Service (PDAS) (Fiore et al., 2015).

The PDAS provides a big data analytics framework for knowledge discovery on large scientific datasets (Fiore, Palazzo, D'Anca, Foster, Williams, & Aloisio, 2013; Fiore, D'Anca, Palazzo, Foster, Williams, & Aloisio, 2013). It supports data-intensive analysis and I/O by exploiting parallel computing techniques and smart data distribution methods. It provides a framework for parallel I/O and data analysis, an array-based storage model, and a hierarchical storage organization for partitioning and distributing multi-dimensional scientific datasets. By design, the storage model is both format and dimension independent. This means that the PDAS can be exploited within different scientific domains with very heterogeneous sets of data. The internal storage model is based on a key-value pair approach to store multi-dimensional data (called *datacubes*). From a physical point of view, a datacube is horizontally partitioned into several blocks (called fragments or chunks) that are distributed across multiple I/O nodes. Each I/O node hosts a set of I/O servers optimized to manage n-dimensional arrays. The I/O servers manage a set of databases consisting of one or more datacube fragments.

The PDAS comes with an extensive set of primitives to operate on n-dimensional arrays (i.e. on the arrays contained in the datacube fragments). To address flexibility and extensibility requirements, all the primitives are implemented as dynamic libraries, so that they can be added to the framework at runtime without re-building the I/O servers. A large set of array-based primitives (e.g. data sub-setting, data aggregation, array concatenation, algebraic expressions, predicate evaluation, and compression) is already available as a core module. It is worth mentioning that the implementation of numerical and statistical primitives relies on well-known GNU Scientific Library (GSL) routines. Besides the array-based primitives, the PDAS provides also many operators addressing data (e.g. datacube sub-setting, datacube aggregation, array-based primitives at the datacube level, datacube duplication, intercomparison, and file import and export) and metadata (e.g. datacube schema, size, provenance).

In the context of the EUBrazilCC project, the PDAS has been enhanced in a variety of ways to meet the requirements of the application on climate change and biodiversity. More specifically, the following extensions have been provided:

1. A set of three VMIs (PDAS server, compute node, and I/O node/datastore), jointly with RADL and Ansible scripts to transparently instantiate a PDAS cluster in a private cloud;
2. New data analytics operators and primitives to manage climate and satellite datasets;
3. Extended support for scientific data formats (e.g. GeoTIFF, NetCDF);
4. A new GSI/VOMS server interface to address interoperability with grid-based environments (e.g. EGI-FedCloud); and
5. An extended and user-friendly version of the PDAS terminal.

The mc² Toolset

The EUBrazilCC federated e-infrastructure provides a toolset called *mc²* (Gomes et al., 2015) specifically built for the rapid prototyping of application-specific science gateways over the CSGrid system. The mc² toolset has been developed and used for the past 5 years by the Brazilian national HPC network (SINAPAD)[13], which employs CSGrid to integrate its geographically distributed and highly heterogeneous computational and data resources. While focused on rapid prototyping of science gateways, the mc² toolset does not provide only basic gateway features such as management of user jobs and data — which are dealt with in the CSGrid system by the OpenDreams and the Hierarchical Data Services, resp. — but also advanced features not commonly found in similar solutions (e.g. Gridsphere, GENIUS Grid Portal, Vine Toolkit, and EnginFrame), such as: (i) file sharing between gateway users and file publishing through "tiny URLs"; (ii) provenance tracking of an experiment's data inputs and outputs; and (iii) support for restricted anonymous access to gateway services. The mc² toolset also allows simple configuration and deployment — an mc²-based gateway can be deployed in any ordinary Java-based Web application container and, when first started, allows configuring all features of a gateway and the communication of the gateway with the CSGrid system. Most of this simplicity derives from the use of the CSGrid Algorithm Service, which allows the dynamic assembling of Web interfaces in the gateway.

SCIENTIFIC USE CASES

Three scientific use cases were selected for implementation in the EUBrazilCC federated cloud. They all share the common objective of investigating new ways of enabling collaborative environments to support interdisciplinary research, specifically in areas where the emergence of massive data sources, combined with the availability of large-scale computing capabilities based on dynamic resources, is changing the way that knowledge is generated and used.

Moreover, the implementation of the use cases provides also evidence of the successful collaboration between Brazil and Europe in providing computing and data resources as well as joint expertise to address scientific problems in a way that would not be feasible without extensive cross-border collaboration. In this way, EUBrazilCC is bringing together related scientific communities from across Europe and Brazil, helping them to learn how to work with each other.

The potential users of the use cases include researchers, international organizations, governmental agencies (both research and education), and commercial companies. Non-scientific users come from the field of forestry, earth science, biology, and environmental conservation, among others.

In the three use cases, the advantages of the federation are threefold:

- The availability of a simple mechanism for accessing an increasing amount of resources in an elastic scenario through cloud-bursting, since it is the federation service that provides resources to the workflow engines and programming models.
- The availability of a homogeneous mechanism to deploy and configure virtual appliances by means of the synchronization of VMI catalogues and the use of platform-independent configuration recipes and a cloud-agnostic deployment service.
- The use of a single authentication and authorization mechanism and standard APIs to access the individual resources.

The use cases have addressed different requirements regarding the integration of geographically distributed data and computing resources. Intensive computing pipelines benefit from the availability of a federated set of resources transcending the resource capacity of a single provider, whereas recipe-based automation enables the customization of environments, including reference data, regardless of the particular features of each provider (OpenNebula and OpenStack in the case of EUBrazilCC).

Use Case on Climate Change and Biodiversity

The use case on climate change and biodiversity is data-driven, aiming at a better understanding of the interaction between biodiversity and the climate system through the temporal analysis of a selected set of indicators in conjunction with Ecological Niche Modeling (ENM) techniques. A novel approach is to regard the Land Use Land Cover (LULC) system as a proxy for changes in the biodiversity system. Interactions can be studied at various scales, ranging from the microscopic to the macroscopic, and also at the genomic, taxonomic and ecosystem scales of individual plant and animal species. Dataflows have to be produced to combine the analysis of data acquired through technologies such as LiDAR, hyperspectral imagery, satellite images, ground level sensors, and meteorological and biodiversity data, in order to study the impact of climate change in regions where there is a high interest in biodiversity conservation, such as the Amazon and the semi-arid Caatinga regions in Brazil. The co-operation between Brazilian and European centers constitutes an added value, as it brings together complementary expertise in biodiversity modeling and climate change data analysis.

To address the scientific challenges, this use case draws together into single federated environment different components such as heterogeneous data sources, on-premises cloud infrastructures, data access and analysis services, and a scientific gateway. The Scientific Gateway (see Figure 14) constitutes a unique web-based platform for end users able to address climate change and biodiversity research, providing an integrated and interactive support for data exploration, analysis and visualization. More specifically, with the aid of the Scientific Gateway the user can:

- Create a new experiment by choosing a set of target climate and biodiversity indicators;
- Define the spatial and temporal domains of the experiment (for climate indicators, future scenarios are also available);
- Submit the experiment to the federated cloud infrastructure and monitor its status through the available real-time dashboard, each experiment consisting of a set of sub-tasks, each one associated to a data analytics workflow running on PDAS clusters;
- Display the experiment results, perform visual comparison of different indicators, download the output, and (optionally) store the results in a clearinghouse system to for data re-use.

A key point in the implementation of this use case is the dynamic use of the federated cloud infrastructure. In particular, the entire set of experiments submitted by end users is managed by a smart agent, called *elastic-job engine*, running in the back-end of the Scientific Gateway. Its goal is to provide both dynamic job scheduling and elastic deploy/undeploy of PDAS cluster instances in the federated cloud infrastructure, based on the experiment's workload.

The cloud scenario involves IaaS components like IM and the fogbow middleware for the federation of private cloud infrastructures. In this context, specific VMIs for the PDAS have been created and made available on the VMRC repository. COMPSs is responsible for providing advanced workflow-

Figure 14. Scientific Gateway Environment

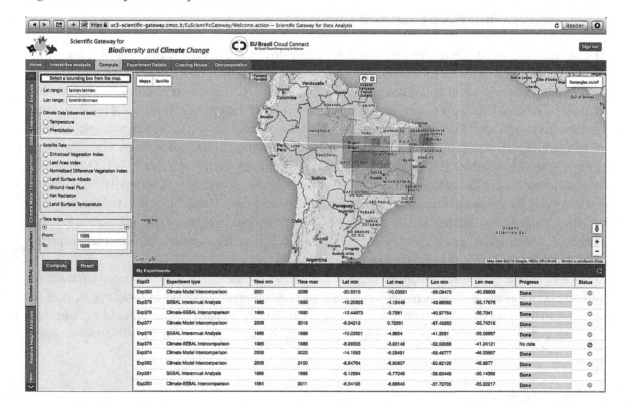

based capabilities. Besides the Scientific Gateway, the use case implements another user interface, called "Analysis Term", targeting more expert users by providing a bash-like terminal environment for interactive data analysis.

Leishmaniasis Virtual Laboratory (LVL)

Leishmaniasis is one of the world's most neglected diseases. It is caused by protozoan parasites of the *Leishmania* genus, which are transmitted by an insect vector: the sandflies. The disease is currently spreading because control efforts are crimped by three escalating risk factors: (i) human-made and environmental changes; (ii) immune status (essentially because of *Leishmania*/HIV co-infection); and (iii) treatment failure and drug resistance. Today, 350 million people are considered to be at the risk of contracting Leishmaniasis, and 1.5 to 2.0 million new cases appear every year.

The Leishmaniasis Virtual Laboratory (LVL) has created a database of molecular markers of Leishmania and sandflies, integrating biological, geographical, clinical and other relevant data from external sources (CLIOC[14], COLFLEB[15], the collection of *Leishmania* of the ISCIII-WHO-CCL[16], speciesLink[17], GenBank[18] and PubMed[19]). This database provides the data required for the correct identification of the etiological agent, which can be crucial for the prognostics of the disease since different species or strains may have different clinical outcomes. Moreover, the genetic structure of vector populations is important for control management strategies.

The LVL leverages on the EUBrazilCC federated cloud to execute molecular pipelines based on molecular methods, such as Multilocus Sequence Analysis (MLSA) and Multilocus Microsatellite Typing (MLMT), for enabling the identification of the *Leishmania* species and strains and thereby being able to assess its population structure. Moreover, the LVL relies on computing resources provided by EUBrazilCC for generating an atlas of parasite/vector, thereby increasing the knowledge about their species and genetic population distribution.

Given its multi-user nature and the complexity of its processing pipelines, the LVL might require an unpredictable and potentially unlimited amount of resources. Therefore, it must be able to rely on an elastic provisioning of resources. If run on a public production cloud, the LVL resource requirements could transcend the maximum amount of resources available to the user. In the case of on-premise cloud facilities, it is might also be bounded by the availability of resources. The IaaS federation enables treating cloud bursting in the same way as in the case of a single infrastructure, since individual jobs from multiple users do not communicate at all. In this case, the workflow management system requests individual resources to the federation and dispatches the jobs accordingly. The federation also synchronizes the VMIs among the providers, thus reducing deployment time.

The LVL is available as an online[20] open-access portal and also as preconfigured virtual appliances[21] compatible with the EGI federated cloud, and can be used locally to study unreleased datasets. Furthermore, the source code[22] of the LVL is provided under an open-source license.

Cardiovascular Simulation Services

Simulating a heartbeat is a complex multi-scale problem. This means that many scales covering different orders of magnitude are involved, from the descriptions of electrical propagation and cells arrangement into a spatial description (generally known as myofibre orientation), to the geometry of the cardiac chambers.

EUBrazilCC leverages the integration of heterogeneous supercomputing and virtualized infrastructures with the orchestration of the components of two simulation codes, one from Brazil and other from Spain, integrated in the platform and addressing two complementary problems in cardiovascular modeling: the Alya Red System[23], a Cardiac Computational Model at organ level simulating fluid-electro-mechanical coupling; and the Anatomically-Detailed Arterial Network (ADAN)[24] model which, starting from anatomical data and physiological concepts, performs cutting-edge cardiovascular research supported by the modeling of physical phenomena and simulation-based techniques.

The EUBrazilCC integrated environment leverages on the existing codes of Alya Red System and ADAN to create and submit experiments for execution within High-Performance Computing (HPC) systems and cloud environments (for details, see Figure 15). In a typical experiment, a 3D model of a computational heart and a 1D model of the arterial network will run closely connected to each other (the AlyaADAN application). Two different scenarios are foreseen: direct solution and parameters estimation. In the first one, large-scale cases are solved. In the second one, a large number of problems are simulated on a coarse level to explore the space of certain parameters using optimization software. Parametric runs, used for tuning the models, are orchestrated by the COMPSs runtime in cloud environments. Full runs use HPC resources managed by the CSGrid middleware, coupled through a connector in the cloud that regulates the flow of temporary files between the two models over the network and across organizational boundaries. A COMPSs application orchestrates the complete workflow that includes execution of parametric runs with low definition data, post processing to evaluate the best configuration of the parameters, and execution with full resolution data. Independently of the type of execution of AlyaADAN and of the computational backend, a web service interface performs the executions by providing the basic methods to transfer input and output data, and to configure the execution.

The federation provides a unique authentication and authorization mechanism for both types of infrastructure resources as well as a communication channel set-up during the execution of the tasks. This communication channel is used to cross-feedback and communicates both sets of jobs (HPC and cloud-based).

Figure 15. Cardiovascular Simulation architecture

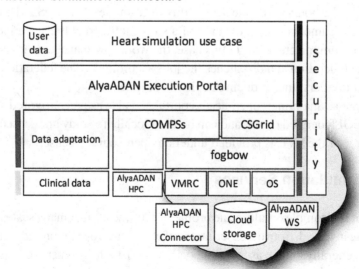

Other Use Cases

Along with these three use cases, the EUBrazilCC federation platform can be applied to other cases addressing elasticity, cooperation and interoperability. From the application's point of view, the federation provides a mechanism to facilitate the migration from one infrastructure to another, thanks to the use of customizable VMIs, standard interfaces, and high-level services. For instance, the same virtual appliance can be instantiated in OpenNebula, OpenStack, or in a combination of both. This reduces maintenance costs also at the level of the VMI management.

From the infrastructure provider's point of view, the federation model can facilitate meeting QoS requirements without subscribing computing resources on public infrastructures. Federation models based on delayed exchange, such as fogbow, defines an in-kind payment of resource provision. This model has been successfully applied to other utility markets.

CONCLUSION

The EUBrazilCC is an R&D project whose main objective is to provide a user-centric test bench enabling European and Brazilian research communities to test the deployment and execution of scientific applications on a federated intercontinental e-infrastructure. In this work, the architecture and deployment of the EUBrazilCC federated e-infrastructure has been presented. The EUBrazilCC project is a first step towards providing a user-centric, cross-Atlantic test bench for European and Brazilian research communities.

The requirements have been elicited with the aid of three real world scientific use cases, and the development has been carried out in close collaboration between European and Brazilian excellence centers. Since its inception, the EUBrazilCC has been successfully exploiting and coordinating existing heterogeneous e-Infrastructures (virtualized datacenters, supercomputers, and resources exploited opportunistically) with more than 5500 CPU and 17000 GPU cores. EUBrazilCC has studied three multidisciplinary and highly complementary scenarios, covering Epidemiology, Health, Biodiversity, and Natural Resources & Climate Change, all presented here. The scientific scenarios involve complex workflows and access to huge datasets. EUBrazilCC draws upon experience and knowledge coming from both Brazil and Europe concerning federation of resource providers (JiT Cloud, OurGrid, CSGrid and InterCloud), programming environments, scientific gateways (mc^2, COMPSs, eScienceCentral), and distributed scientific data access (parallel data analysis). For the use cases, EUBrazilCC is involving leading institutions such as the Brazilian FIOCRUZ, world leader in Leishmaniasis, the Spanish Barcelona Supercomputing Center, developer of the heart simulator Alya, which received an HPC Innovation Excellence Award; and the Italian CMCC, a key node in the Earth System Grid Federation. EUBrazilCC has been building a strong dissemination network to promote the resulting infrastructure among other communities, leveraging on the networks of SINAPAD, the Brazilian National Institutes of Science and Technology, LifeWatch-ESFRI, and the European Network for Earth System Modelling.

An all-round account of the EUBrazilCC federated e-infrastructure, built as a collection of independent layers, was provided. A security model giving a unified view of the heterogeneous e-infrastructure was outlined. An overview was given of fogbow, a middleware for sharing underused resources according to a non-monetary delayed exchange business model and catering to highly elastic and ephemeral workloads. A conceptual architecture was provided. CSGrid was introduced, a middleware that provides the job-based API to the EUBrazilCC federated e-infrastructure. Its integration with fogbow was also presented.

For the management of VMIs, the Virtual Machine Resource Catalogue (VMRC) was presented, used to store the different VMIs required to provision the services. The Infrastructure Manager (IM), a tool facilitating access to IaaS clouds, was also presented, together with the Resource Application Description Language (RADL), a high level declarative Domain Specific Language (DSL), used by the IM, for describing the hardware and software features of a virtual infrastructure. A description was provided of the two programming frameworks available in the infrastructure, COMPSs and eScience Central. An overview was given of the PDAS data analytics service, which provides a framework for parallel I/O and data analysis, and of the mc² toolset, which enables the rapid prototyping of application-specific science gateways over the EUBrazilCC federated e-infrastructure. Finally, a detailed account was given of the three scientific use cases selected for implementation in the EUBrazilCC federated cloud, including areas as diverse as climate change and biodiversity, the Leishmaniasis disease, and cardiovascular simulation.

The development of the project has so far been successful and has met widespread interest in the workshops and events in which it has been presented, in spite of the difficulties involved in integrating and federating systems with such a degree of heterogeneity and decentralization in the absence of any central coordinating agents. The challenge is compounded by the fact that the developed infrastructure includes resources from two distinct continents, and by the inherent complexity of thee the use case applications, involving widely different scientific fields and disciplines. In addition, more possibilities of increased international cooperation than initially predicted have been detected, which forebodes well for the prospects of the project legacy, which impact may go well beyond the established duration of the project.

ACKNOWLEDGMENT

The results of this work have been partially funded by EUBrazil Cloud Connect (614048), a Small or medium-scale focused research project (STREP) funded by the European Commission under the Co-operation Programme, Framework Programme Seven (FP7), and CNPq/Brazil (grant 490115/2013-6).

REFERENCES

Armbrust, M., Fox, A., Griffith, R., Joseph, A. D., Katz, R., Konwinski, A., & Zaharia, M. et al. (2010). A View of Cloud Computing. *Communications of the ACM, 53*(4), 50–58. doi:10.1145/1721654.1721672

Armstrong, D., Espling, D., Tordsson, J., Djemame, K., & Elmroth, E. (2012). Lecture Notes in Computer Science: Vol. 7640. *Runtime Virtual Machine Recontextualization for Clouds. Euro-Par 2012: Parallel Processing Workshops* (pp. 567–576). Springer. doi:10.1007/978-3-642-36949-0_66

Armstrong, D., Espling, D., Tordsson, J., Djemame, K., & Elmroth, E. (2015). Contextualization: Dynamic configuration of virtual machines. *Journal of Cloud Computing, 4*(1), 1–15.

Bresnahan, J., Freeman, T., LaBissoniere, D., & Keahey, K. (2011). Managing appliance launches in infrastructure clouds. Proceedings of the TeraGrid Conference: Extreme Digital Discovery (TG '11) (pp. 12:1-12:7). New York: ACM.

Caballer, M., Blanquer, I., Molto, G., & de Alfonso, C. (2015). Dynamic management of virtual infrastructures. *Journal of Grid Computing, 13*(1), 53–70. doi:10.1007/s10723-014-9296-5

Caballer, M., de Alfonso, C., Alvarruiz, F., & Moltó, G. (2013). EC3: Elastic Cloud Computing Cluster. *Journal of Computer and System Sciences, 79*(8), 1341–1351. doi:10.1016/j.jcss.2013.06.005

Caballer, M., Segrelles, D., Molto, G., & Blanquer, I. (2014). A Platform to Deploy Customized Scientific Virtual Infrastructures on the Cloud. *Proceedings of the 6th International Workshop on Science Gateways (IWSG),* Dublin (pp. 42-47). IEEE. doi:10.1109/IWSG.2014.14

Carrión, J. V., Moltó, G., de Alfonso, C., Caballer, M., & Hernández, V. (2010). A Generic Catalog and Repository Service for Virtual Machine Images. *Proceedings of the 2nd International ICST Conference on Cloud Computing (CloudComp '10)* (pp. 1-15).

Cirne, W., Brasileiro, F. V., Andrade, N., Costa, L., Andrade, A., Novaes, R., & Mowbray, M. (2006). Labs of the World, Unite!!! *Journal of Grid Computing, 4*(3), 225–246. doi:10.1007/s10723-006-9040-x

de Alfonso, C., Caballer, M., Alvarruiz, F., Molto, G., & Hernández, V. (2011). Infrastructure Deployment over the Cloud. *Proceedings of the IEEE Third International Conference on Cloud Computing Technology and Science* (pp. 517–521). IEEE. doi:10.1109/CloudCom.2011.77

de Lima, M., Ururahy, C., de Moura, A., Melcop, T., Cassino, C., & dos Santos, M. … Cerqueira, R. (2006). CSBase: A framework for building customized Grid environments. Proceedings of the 15th IEEE International Workshops on Enabling Technologies: Infrastructure for Collaborative Enterprises (pp. 187–194). IEEE.

DeHaan, M. (2013). *Ansible*. From www.ansible.com

Fiore, S., D'Anca, A., Palazzo, C., Foster, I., Williams, D. N., & Aloisio, G. (2013). *Ophidia: Toward Big Data Analytics for eScience. ICCS 2013. 18* (pp. 2376–2385). Barcelona: Elsevier.

Fiore, S., Mancini, M., Elia, D., Nassisi, F., Brasileiro, F. V., & Blanquer, I., … Aloisio, G. (2015). Big data analytics for climate change and biodiversity in the EUBrazilCC federated cloud infrastructure. *Proceedings of the Workshop on Analytics Platforms for the Cloud, ACM International Conference on Computing Frontiers '15*, Ischia. doi:10.1145/2742854.2747282

Fiore, S., Palazzo, C., D'Anca, A., Foster, I. T., Williams, D. N., & Aloisio, G. (2013). A big data analytics framework for scientific data management. Proceedings of the *IEEE Big Data Conference, 2013*, 1–8.

Global Grid Forum. (2008, June). Distributed resource management application API specification 1.0.

Gomes, A. T., Bastos, B. F., Medeiros, V., & Moreira, V. M. (2015). Experiences of the Brazilian national high-performance computing network on the rapid prototyping of science gateways. *Concurrency and Computation, 27*(2), 271–289. doi:10.1002/cpe.3258

Hey, T. (2009). *The Fourth Paradigm: Data-Intensive Scientific Discovery*. Microsoft Research.

Hiden, H., Woodman, S., Watson, P., & Cala, J. (2013). Developing cloud applications using the e-Science Central platform. *Philosophical Transactions of the Royal Society A: Mathematical, Physical and Engineering Sciences, 371* (1983).

Hochstein, L. (2014). *Ansible: Up and Running*. O'Reilly Media.

Juve, G., & Deelman, E. (2011). Automating Application Deployment in Infrastructure Clouds. In I. C. Society (Ed.), *Proceedings of the IEEE Third International Conference on Cloud Computing Technology and Science (CLOUDCOM '11)* (pp. 658–665). Washington, DC: IEEE Computer Society. doi:10.1109/CloudCom.2011.102

Keahey, K., & Freeman, T. (2008). Contextualization: Providing One-Click Virtual Clusters. *Proceedings of the Fourth IEEE International Conference on eScience* (pp. 301–308).

Le, D.-H., Truong, H.-L., Copil, G., Nastic, S., & Dustdar, S. (2014). SALSA: A Framework for Dynamic Configuration of Cloud Services. *Proceedings of the 6th International Conference on Cloud Computing Technology and Science (CloudCom)* (pp. 146-153). Singapore: IEEE. doi:10.1109/CloudCom.2014.99

Marshall, P., Keahey, K., & Freeman, T. (2010). Elastic Site: Using Clouds to Elastically Extend Site Resources. *Proceedings of the 10th IEEE/ACM International Conference on Cluster, Cloud and Grid Computing (CCGrid)* (pp. 43 - 52). Melbourne: IEEE. doi:10.1109/CCGRID.2010.80

Marshall, P., Tufo, H., Keahey, K., LaBissoniere, D., & Woitaszek, M. (2012). Architecting a Large-Scale Elastic Environment: Recontextualization and Adaptive Cloud Services for Scientific Computing. *Proceedings of the 7th International Conference on Software Paradigm Trends (ICSOFT)* (pp. 409–418). Rome.

Opscode. (2015). *Chef*. From http://ww.opscode.com

Puppet Labs: IT Automation Software for System Administrators. (2015). Retrieved from http://puppetlabs.com/

Quinton, C., Haderer, N., Rouvoy, R., & Duchien, L. (2013). Towards multi-cloud configurations using feature models and ontologies. *Proceedings of the 1st International Workshop on Multi-Cloud Applications and Federated Clouds,* Prague (pp. 21-26). ACM. doi:10.1145/2462326.2462332

Sturm, M., Bertsch, A., Gröpl, C., Hildebrandt, A., Hussong, R., Lange, E., & Kohlbacher, O. et al. (2008). OpenMS - an open-source software framework for mass spectrometry. *BMC Bioinformatics*, *9*(163). PMID:18366760

Tordsson, J., Montero, R. S., Moreno-Vozmediano, R., & Llorente, I. M. (2012). Cloud brokering mechanisms for optimized placement of virtual machines across multiple providers. *Future Generation Computer Systems*, *28*(2), 358–367. doi:10.1016/j.future.2011.07.003

Yang, X., Wallom, D., Waddington, S., Wang, J., Shaon, A., Matthews, B., & Kershaw, P. et al. (2014). Cloud Computing in e-Science: Research Challenges and Opportunities. *The Journal of Supercomputing*, *70*(1), 408–464. doi:10.1007/s11227-014-1251-5 PMID:25309040

KEY TERMS AND DEFINITIONS

Big Data: Large volume of complex structured and/or unstructured data sets that are difficult to process by traditional database techniques.

E-Science: Computationally intensive science using very large data sets requiring some form of distributed processing like grid or cloud computing.

Infrastructure-as-a-Service: A form of cloud computing in which virtualized computing resources are provided over the Internet.

Landsat: A series of satellites built by the Landsat program enterprise for acquisition of satellite imagery of the Earth.

Leishmaniasis: A disease caused by an intracellular protozoan parasite of the genus *Leishmania* and transmitted by the bite of certain types of sandflies.

LiDAR: A remote sensing method for measuring variable distances to the Earth by illuminating a target with a pulsed laser and analyzing the reflected light.

Virtual Laboratory: A virtual workbench where researchers can easily access data and tools related to specific domains, and that also provides computer-mediated cooperation environments.

Virtual Machine: A software emulation of a physical machine.

ENDNOTES

[1]   http://www.fogbowcloud.org/

[2]   http://www.openstack.org/

[3]   http://opennebula.org/

[4]   http://cloudstack.apache.org/

[5]   http://www.ourgrid.org/

[6]   http://jitclouds.lsd.ufcg.edu.br/site/index.php/en/

[7]   http://www.tecgraf.puc-rio.br/csgrid/

[8]   http://www.tecgraf.puc-rio.br/openbus/

[9]   http://www.lua.org/

[10]   AWS CloudFormation: http://aws.amazon.com/es/cloudformation/

[11]   Whirr. From Apache Whirr™: http://whirr.apache.org/

[12]   http://www.ansible.com/

[13]   http://www.lncc.br/sinapad/

[14]   Coleção de Leishmania do Instituto Oswaldo Cruz (CLIOC): http://clioc.fiocruz.br/

[15]   Coleção de Flebotomíneos do Instituto Oswaldo Cruz (COLFLEB): http://colfleb.fiocruz.br/

[16]   Collection of Leishmania of the WHO-Collaborating Centre for Leishmaniasis ISCIII: http://www.isciii.es/

[17]   speciesLink: http://splink.cria.org.br/

[18]   GenBank: http://www.ncbi.nlm.nih.gov/genbank/

[19]   PubMed: http://www.ncbi.nlm.nih.gov/pubmed/

[20]   Leishmaniasis Virtual Laboratory (LVL): http://lvl.i3m.upv.es/

[21]   LVL at EGI AppDB: https://appdb.egi.eu/store/vappliance/leishmaniasis.virtual.lab.lvl/

[22]   LVL project: https://github.com/eubrazilcc/leishmaniasis-virtual-lab/

[23]   The Alya System: https://www.bsc.es/computer-applications/alya-system/

[24]   ADAN-WEB: http://hemolab.lncc.br/adan-web/

Chapter 9
Federated IaaS Resource Brokerage

Bruno Veloso
Instituto Superior de Engenharia do Porto,
Portugal

Benedita Malheiro
Instituto Superior de Engenharia do Porto,
Portugal

Fernando Meireles
Instituto Superior de Engenharia do Porto,
Portugal

Juan Carlos Burguillo
Universidade de Vigo, Spain

ABSTRACT

This paper presents the CloudAnchor brokerage platform for the transaction of single provider as well as federated Infrastructure as a Service (IaaS) resources. The platform, which is a layered Multi-Agent System (MAS), provides multiple services, including (consumer or provider) business registration and deregistration, provider coalition creation and termination, provider lookup and invitation and negotiation services regarding brokerage, coalitions and resources. Providers, consumers and virtual providers, representing provider coalitions, are modelled by dedicated agents within the platform. The main goal of the platform is to negotiate and establish Service Level Agreements (SLA). In particular, the platform contemplates the establishment of brokerage SLA – bSLA – between the platform and each provider or consumer, coalition SLA – cSLA – between the members of a coalition of providers and resource SLA – rSLA – between a consumer and a provider. Federated resources are detained and negotiated by virtual providers on behalf of the corresponding coalitions of providers.

INTRODUCTION

The emergence of Cloud Computing as a new trend computing paradigm is attractive to business owners as it eliminates the requirement to plan ahead for provisioning and gives enterprises the flexibility to manage the contracted resources according to the current workload. The market for the cloud services, specifically the IaaS cloud computing market, is still maturing and brokers are emerging as the preferential middleware to match demand and offer between stakeholders. In particular, Small and Medium sized Enterprises (SME), which are typically in the early stages of adopting the cloud paradigm or provid-

DOI: 10.4018/978-1-5225-0153-4.ch009

ing cloud services, require support services and platforms to increase their competitiveness. For SME providers, brokers offer additional business opportunities and simplify the management and integration of disparate cloud services – potentially across different providers – fostering the creation of provider coalitions; for SME consumers, brokers provide seamless provider lookup and invitation as well as SLA negotiation services, increasing the chances of meeting their resource requirements at the best price and in time. The ultimate goal of this research is to support the adoption and provision of IaaS by SME both as consumers and as providers.

This paper addresses the design and development of the CloudAnchor business-to-business (B2B) brokerage platform with provider discovery and invitation as well as negotiation, establishment and management of resource service level agreements regarding single provider and federated resources. This problem is by nature distributed, decentralised, dynamic and involves multiple stakeholders (consumer and provider businesses) continuously entering and leaving the system (open system). The stakeholders are, not only, loosely coupled, but, depending on the situation, can either compete (consumers and providers compete for getting and leasing resources) or cooperate (coalitions of providers). Furthermore, these businesses wish to retain autonomy, privacy and the control of their strategic knowledge, leading to the adoption of the agent-based paradigm.

The CloudAnchor brokerage platform implements an open event-driven multi-layered agent-based architecture. Businesses are represented by dedicated autonomous agents and are, thus, able to specify their self-models, by uploading their strategic knowledge (lookup, invitation, acceptance and negotiation strategies), resource offers (providers) or resource requests (consumers), as well as build peer models of their business partners based on the outcomes of their previous interactions (individual peer trust). The layered approach allows the distribution and delegation of the interface, agreement, enterprise (knowledge and processes) and negotiation related tasks to corresponding dedicated agents, representing each business by a set of task specialized agents rather than by a single agent to increase the overall responsiveness.

The platform provides multiple services, including (consumer or provider) business registration/deregistration, provider lookup and invitation, provider coalition creation/termination and agreement negotiation/termination. To support these functionalities, the platform contemplates the negotiation, establishment and termination of brokerage, coalition and resource agreements: (*i*) a brokerage SLA (bSLA) is a contract between the platform and a business (provider or consumer); (*ii*) a coalition SLA (cSLA) is a contract between a coalition of providers and the resulting virtual provider; and (*iii*) a resource SLA (rSLA) is a contract between a consumer and a provider (single or a virtual provider) regarding a given resource.

In terms of external events, there are business registration/deregistration, resource request/offer and SLA fulfilled/violated events. These events drive the execution of the business registration service, business deregistration service, resource provider lookup and invitation service, provider resource availability publication service and SLA termination service. In particular, whenever a consumer requests a new resource via its interface agent (resource request event), it triggers the resource finding process. The consumer enterprise agent automatically looks up and invites providers for negotiation. If the invited provider enterprise agents accept the invitation, dedicated delegate market agents are created by both consumer and provider enterprise agents to negotiate and establish the rSLA. If the providers were not able to provide single-handedly the resource, the platform attempts to create a virtual provider. Virtual providers are temporary coalitions of single providers established on the fly to provide federated resources, *i.e.*, resources which were not offered by any single provider. When an rSLA terminates, the parties involved (consumer and provider) receive an agreement fulfilled or agreement violation event.

Each consumer and provider enterprise agent creates and maintains local trust models of their peers based on the outcomes of their direct interactions: partner invitation (accepted or rejected), negotiation (success or failure to establish a SLA) and SLA enforcement feedback (fulfilled or violated). These models support all future peer interaction, namely, provider invitation, consumer and coalition invitation acceptance and negotiation of SLA instances. From a platform's perspective, the local peer trust models constitute a decentralised trust system.

In terms of contributions, the proposed brokerage platform provides: (*i*) federated resources through the creation of virtual providers, representing provider coalitions; (*ii*) the negotiation and establishment of brokerage, coalition and resource SLA instances; (*iii*) a decentralised trust model regarding providers, consumers and the platform for the negotiation and renegotiation of SLA.

This paper is organized in five sections. Section 1 presents the context of the project, identifies the problems addressed and describes the approach adopted. Section 2 presents and compares the most relevant features of related agent-based cloud resource brokerage platforms, including our proposal, and discusses the issues associated with federated cloud resources. Section 3 describes our approach, including platform design, architecture and services, and details the different SLA types contemplated and their negotiation. Section 4 describes the future developments. Finally, Section 5 draws the main conclusions.

AGENT-BASED CLOUD RESOURCE BROKERAGE

Brokerage platforms frequently adopt the agent-based paradigm since resource, service or partner brokerage is an inherently distributed, decentralised complex problem involving autonomous entities. In this context, consumers compete for provider resources, providers compete or cooperate to fulfil consumer requests and, finally, consumers and providers play opposite roles (buyer and seller). Businesses are then represented within the brokerage platform as autonomous intelligent agents, regardless of their competitive or cooperative nature, maintaining autonomy and privacy. In this section we explore the state of the art regarding agent-based trust and reputation systems, agent-based SLA negotiation frameworks and cloud brokerage systems.

Trust and Reputation

Trust and reputation are central to effective interactions in open multi-agent systems (MAS) in which agents, owned by a variety of stakeholders, continuously enter and leave the system (Huynh, Jennings & Shadbolt, 2006). Trust can arise from individual and societal perspectives. While the individual perspective results from the direct interactions with peers, the societal perspective – usually referred as reputation – is based on the observations by a collection of agents. Trust is a one to one subjective perception between truster and trustee, which depends on their mutual interaction experiences. A trustee is considered to be trustworthy if it has, according to the truster, a high probability of performing a particular service, *i.e.*, has fulfilled its obligations (Teacy, Patel, Jennings & Luck, 2006).

The reputation of a Web service provider can be, according to He, Kowalczyk, Jin and Yang (2007), established using the past performance of the provider service and, then, applied by the consumers to assess and select service providers. Cascella, Blasi, Jegou, Coppola and Morin (2013) evaluate the reputation of cloud providers based on the number of SLA violations observed and the set of explicit user preferences and use it to filter provider offers. To select the best available provider, Alhamad, Dillon and Chang (2010) propose a trust model built from three different sources: (*i*) the local experience with cloud providers; (*ii*) opinions of external cloud services; and (*iii*) the reports provided by the SLA management agent.

In CloudAnchor we build a decentralised peer trust model from the past direct interactions between stakeholders (consumers, providers and platform) and apply this model when consumers invite potential providers, providers assess invitations to negotiate and when consumers choose the best provider proposal during a negotiation. The model is built from the outcomes of three stages: the partner invitation/acceptance, SLA negotiation and SLA enforcement. In the future, we plan to reuse the model for the renegotiation of bSLA and cSLA.

SLA Negotiation

SLA negotiation is essential to cloud brokerage since it is the stage where provider and consumer negotiate the terms of the service provision with the intent to establish a binding contract. From the large number of agent-based SLA negotiation frameworks available in the literature, we selected the following illustrative and relevant subset:

1. The Web Services SLA negotiation framework presented by Al Falasi, Serhani and Elnaffar (2011) is an agent-based system composed of provider and consumer agents. WS SLA adopts the Foundation for Intelligent Physical Agents (FIPA) Iterated Contract Net Interaction Protocol (FICNIP) to negotiate SLA instances. The proposed framework follows the W3C Web Service Policy Specification (WS-Policy) to describe the negotiation policies and adopts a utility-based negotiation strategy.

2. The Framework for Automated Service Negotiation in Cloud Computing proposed by Pan (2011) is a multi-agent system for the negotiation of cloud computing resources. It is composed of autonomous provider and consumer agents and includes a marketplace where resource offers and requests are registered and matched. The negotiation between consumer and provider agents implements a bilateral multi-step monotonic concession negotiation protocol.

3. Cloudle is an agent-based search engine for cloud service discovery. It is composed of a service discovery agent, a cloud ontology, a database of cloud services and multiple cloud crawlers. It relies on a utility-oriented strategy for coordinating concurrent negotiations and establishing multiple SLA instances (Sim, 2012).

4. The Policy-based Web Services SLA Negotiation System by Zulkernine, Martin, Craddock and Wilson (2009) encompasses provider and consumer agents. The negotiation protocol is the FICNIP. The system provides a flexible framework for SLA negotiation by incorporating multiple strategy models based on high level policies.

5. The Framework for Negotiation and SLA Management described by He *et al.* (2007) is an agent-based platform that negotiates, interacts and cooperates to facilitate autonomous and flexible SLA management. It is composed of SLA initiator and responder agents and includes a store where resource offers and requests are registered and matched. The system relies on a Universal Description Discovery and Integration (UDDI) service registry to publish the resource announcements. The framework supports SLA formation, SLA recovery and, finally, SLA profiling. The negotiation between initiator and responder agents implements the OGF WS-Agreement negotiation specification.

6. CloudAnchor contemplates the negotiation, establishment and termination of brokerage, coalition and resource agreements regarding single and federated resources. In particular, the platform: (*i*)

handles three types of SLA (brokerage, resource and coalition SLA); (*ii*) implements two SLA specifications (WS-Agreement and WS-Agreement Negotiation); (*iii*) adopts two standard negotiation protocols (one shot and FICNIP); (*iv*) uses Business Process Modelling Notation (BPMN) to define the SME behaviour within the platform, including the SLA negotiation strategies; (*v*) maintains and uses a decentralised trust model of business counterparts to negotiate SLA instances; and (*vi*) negotiates and establishes coalitions between providers (virtual providers) to provide federated resources.

Table 1 summarises the most relevant features of these agent-based cloud resource brokerage platforms. Each platform is analysed in terms of service level agreement approach, negotiated resources, service interface and implemented peer model. In terms of specifications, Al Falasi *et al.* (2011) implement the WS-Policy specification to describe negotiation policies and CloudAnchor implements the WS-Agreement specification. In terms of negotiation protocols, there is a wider diversity, ranging from the implementation of specifications, adoption of standard negotiation protocols to custom-made approaches. Al Falasi *et al.* (2011), Zulkernine *et al.* (2009) and CloudAnchor use FICNIP; Cloudle by Sim (2012) uses a variant of FCNIP; and CloudAnchor adopt the one shot negotiation protocol included in the WS-Agreement. Al Falasi *et al.* (2011) adopt a utility-based negotiation strategy; He *et al.* (2007) adopt the one shot protocol; and Pan (2011) implements a bilateral multi-step monotonic concession negotiation protocol. Regarding the service interfaces, the most recent platforms, including CloudAnchor, expose Representational State transfer (REST) Web Service (WS) interfaces, while the others adopt Simple Object Access Protocol (SOAP) Remote Procedure Call (RPC) WS interfaces. Peer modelling is implemented only by He *et al.* (2007) and CloudAnchor.

CloudAnchor not only implements several specifications and adopts several standards, *e.g.*, the WS-Agreement and WS-Agreement negotiation specifications, the FICNIP one-to-many standard negotiation protocol and RESTful WS endpoints, but is the only platform that negotiates agreements regarding brokerage, coalition and single and federated resources with the support of a decentralised trust-based peer model.

Table 1. Comparison of agent-based SLA negotiation frameworks

Platform	SLA Specification	SLA Negotiation Protocol	Service Interface	Resources	Peer Model
Al Falasi *et al.*, 2011	WS-Policy	FICNIP	SOAP RPC	Single	
Pan, 2011		Bilateral multi-step monotonic concession	REST	Single	
Sim, 2012		FCNIP based	REST	Single	
Zulkernine *et al.*, 2009		FICNIP	SOAP RPC	Single	
He *et al.*, 2007	WS-Agreement	One shot	SOAP RPC	Single	Reputation
CloudAnchor	WS-Agreement WS-Agreement Negotiation	One shot FICNIP	REST	Single & Federated	Trust

Brokerage Platforms

Brokerage platforms manage the use, performance and delivery of cloud services and negotiate relationships between cloud providers and cloud consumers, including the aggregation, customisation and integration of services (Fowley, Pahl & Zhang, 2014). In particular, cloud brokerage platforms can be enriched with marketplaces to bring providers and customers together, supporting partner discovery, service negotiation, agreement establishment and enforcement. The following platforms provide a representative overview of the state of the art regarding brokerage platforms:

1. Stantchev and Schröpfer (2009) describe an approach to map business processes requirements to grid and cloud infrastructures, including SLA negotiation and corresponding quality of service (QoS) enforcement. The authors formalize a structure to describe the service level requirements of the business processes and the technical services of the providers. This approach uses on-demand service level objective (SLO) structures, specifying response time, throughput and transaction rate and contemplates only single resources. The proposed scheme supports the specification of trust relations.

2. The S-Cube project described by Mahbub and Spanoudakis (2010) proposes a proactive SLA Negotiation for Service Based Systems composed of monitor, service listener, negotiation broker and runtime service discovery tool. The services are described using the Organization for the Advancement of Structured Information Standards (OASIS) Business Process Execution Language (BPEL). This system is event-driven, *i.e.*, reacts to events created by providers or consumers. The broker module uses system-defined negotiation rules regarding both single and composite provider resources.

3. The Cross-cloud Federation Model (CCFM), proposed by Celesti, Tusa, Villari and Puliafito (2010), contemplates four distinct stages: discovery, *i.e.*, the search for available resources, matchmaking, *i.e.*, the selection of the resource which best fits the requirements; and authentication, *i.e.*, the establishment of a trusted context with the selected cloud. The overall system is structured in virtual machine manager layer, virtual infrastructure layer and cloud manager layer. The CCFM is implemented in the cloud manager layer by three different agents, corresponding to the three main stages, and provides single and federated resources.

4. The Cloud Agency architecture described by Venticinque, Aversa, Di Martino, Rak and Petcu (2011) includes service discovery, SLA negotiation and enforcement as well as peer trust models. It generates and monitors SLA as well as negotiates single and federated cloud resources. SLA violation is checked by monitoring the QoS and, thereafter, applying penalties to the failing providers. The development of Cloud Agency was supported by a multi-agent toolset which provides different protocols together with authentication, agent migration, workload balance and dynamic resource allocation services.

5. The OPTIMIS toolkit, described by Ferrer *et al.* (2012), offers a set of components to enable the use of multiple cloud architectures. This toolkit supports four types of implementation scenarios: federated architecture, multi-cloud architecture, aggregation of resources by a third party broker and hybrid cloud architecture. OPTIMIS provides monitoring and automated management of services and infrastructures as well as compares different configurations to enhance business efficiency. The toolkit, which includes components for resource discovery, SLA negotiation and enforcement, supports the provision of federated resources and implements trust-based peer models.

6. The STRATOS cloud broker service described by Pawluk, Simmons, Smit, Litoiu and Mankovski (2012) has three main constituents: cloud manager, broker and monitoring modules. The broker requires information about the desired configuration and the set of objectives to submit to a multi-criteria optimization process. In order to minimise costs and avoid provider lock-in, the broker uses two specific objective functions. To support different cloud providers, the authors chose the Apache Deltacloud abstraction layer. STRATOS provides resource discovery and provides federated resources.

7. The cloud brokering architecture described by Tordsson, Montero, Moreno-Vozmediano & Llorente (2012) implements federated resource discovery. It has two main components: the cloud scheduler and the virtual infrastructure manager. The cloud scheduler adopts templates to store the provider VM configurations which will be used by the cloud scheduling algorithms. The virtual infrastructure manager, which is based on the OpenNebula virtual infrastructure manager, provides a generic user interface to deploy, monitor and control the VM instances.

8. The mOSAIC project proposed by Amato, Di Martino and Venticinque (2012) includes a multi-agent system composed of Broker, Vendor, Meeter, Tier, Mediator and Archiver agents to discover and negotiate cloud infrastructure single provider resources. The SLA negotiation protocol is FICNIP. The brokering policy sets constraints and objectives on multiple parameters. The broker analyses a number of SLA proposals and chooses the SLA proposal that satisfies the applicable constraints and objective rules, including provider reputation.

9. The Cloud@Home project reported by Cuomo *et al.* (2013) adopts an SLA-based broker for the discovery cloud infrastructure resources, including federated resources. It has a modular architecture composed of resource management, SLA management and resource abstraction modules. The SLA management module supports one shot negotiations and implements the Open Grid Forum (OGF) Web Service Agreement (WS-Agreement) specification. The negotiation policies are setup only by the administrator.

10. The Contrail project described by Cascella *et al.* (2013) is a MAS dedicated to the discovery and negotiation of single and federated cloud computing resources. The SLA instances are described by the SLA@SOI template as well as the Open Virtualization Format (OVF) descriptors and the SLAs include the reputations of each cloud provider calculated by the Contrail federation. The negotiation between agents adopts the Contrail protocol.

11. The Sky model proposed by Al Falasi *et al.* (2013) allows the creation of a marketplace where cloud providers can exchange services and infrastructure resources using the premise of social networking. This marketplace supports federated service lookup, substitution, recommendation and supervision as well as provider collaboration and provider competition. In terms of architecture, Sky is structured in a socialization modules and a federation module. This model follows the concept of community with several relationships, reputations, penalties and rewards.

12. The Cloud broker described by Pawar, Rajarajan, Dimitrakos and Zisman (2014) works as a mediation layer and integrates a trust and reputation model for the cloud environment. This broker supports multi-cloud and federated cloud deployments. The trust model is based on the SLA monitoring and user feedback ratings. The cloud broker has four different components: the cloud service recommendation (discovery), the cloud service intermediation, the cloud service aggregation and the cloud service arbitrage modules.

13. The SLA-based service virtualization architecture described by Kertész, Kecskemeti and Brandic (2014) includes a meta-negotiator, a meta-broker, a broker and an automatic service deployment

module. The users use high level meta-negotiation constructs to describe the resource requirements and the meta-broker selects a broker capable of deploying the required service. The meta-negotiation documents are published in a searchable registry service. The service provides individual resources.

14. The CompatibleOne project proposes a cloud broker, based on open standards like Cloud Data Management Interface (CDMI) and Open Cloud Computing Interface (OCCI), for the discovery and transaction of single resources. This broker uses a model called CompatibleOne Resource Description System (CORDS) to describe applications, services and cloud resources. There is an external module named service level agreement manager which oversees all negotiated SLA, The SLA instances are described according to the WS Agreement standard (Yangui, Marshall, Laisne & Tata, 2014).

15. The Multi-Cloud Provisioning and Load Distribution for Three-Tier Applications approach described by Grozev and Buyya (2014) is intended for adaptive, dynamic and reactive resource provisioning. It provides load distribution algorithms to optimize cost and response delays without violating legislative and regulatory requirements. On top of the standard three-tier architectural pattern, *i.e.*, Data, Domain and Data Centre layers, it includes two additional layers – Entry Point Layer and Data Centre Control Layer – that enable legislation-compliant user routing to eligible clouds as well as manage the incoming workload and the dynamic provision of resources, without relying on advances in SLA specifications, *i.e.*, novel SLA formalisms. It takes into account the application regulatory requirements when selecting a data centre site and considers the cost as well as the degree of utilization of the employed resources within the data centre.

16. CloudAnchor offers trust-based discovery, negotiation and coalition establishment services regarding single and federated resources. It implements a business model where brokerage (bSLA), coalition (cSLA) and resource (rSLA) agreements and their dependencies are contemplated and builds trust based peer models to support provider invitation/acceptance, coalition establishment and resource negotiation. The adopted multi-agent paradigm allows businesses to enter/leave freely the platform, retain their autonomy and privacy as well as cooperate or compete to get/place resources.

Table 2 displays the comparison of the selected brokerage platforms in terms of services offered, namely service discovery, SLA negotiation and enforcement, type of resources transacted and adopted peer modelling approach. All platforms include service discovery, 94 % provide SLA negotiation and enforcement services regarding single and federated resources and 50% build and use peer models.

CloudAnchor, when compared with other platforms, implements two distinctive features: (*i*) a business model contemplating the negotiation, establishment and termination of brokerage, coalition and resource agreements; and (*ii*) a decentralised trust model of the peers, taking into account all past interactions, including provider invitation, resource negotiation and resource provision, and not just those regarding resource provision. The latter corresponds to the feedback from SLA monitoring and enforcement, which in our case is implemented by an external module. This novel approach allows consumers to invite providers based on the outcomes from past provider invitations and resource provisions as well as helps providers to decide whether or not to accept a consumer's invitation for negotiation based on the outcome of their common resource negotiation and resource provision history.

Table 2. Comparison of cloud brokerage platforms

Platform	Service Discovery	Service Negotiation	Service Enforcement	Peer Model	Resources
Stantchev *et al.*, 2009	Yes	Yes	Yes	Trust	Single
Mahbub *et al.*, 2010	Yes	Yes	No		Single & Federated
Celesti *et al.*, 2010	Yes	No	Yes		Single & Federated
Venticinque *et al.*, 2011	Yes	Yes	No	Trust	Single & Federated
Ferrer *et al.*, 2012	Yes	Yes	Yes	Trust	Single & Federated
Pawluk *et al.*, 2012	Yes	Yes	No		Single & Federated
Tordsson *et al.*, 2012	Yes	No	Yes		Single & Federated
Amato *et al.*, 2012	Yes	Yes	Yes	Reputation	Single
Cuomo *et al.*, 2013	Yes	Yes	Yes		Single & Federated
Cascella *et al.*, 2013	Yes	Yes	Yes	Reputation	Single & Federated
Al Falasi *et al.*, 2013	No	Yes	Yes	Trust	Single & Federated
Pawar *et al.*, 2014	Yes	Yes	No	Trust	Single & Federated
Kertész *et al.*, 2014	Yes	Yes	No		Single
Yangui *et al.*, 2014	Yes	Yes	Yes		Single
Grozev *et al.*, 2014	Yes	Yes	Yes		Single & Federated
CloudAnchor	Yes	Yes	No	Trust	Single & Federated

Federated Cloud Resources

Federated resources, in the context of this work, are sets of decomposable resources, *i.e.*, which can be broken into a collection of standard packages, serviced by multiple providers. The provision of such services suffers from the lack of interoperability and standardised interfaces between provider solutions and requires a versatile middleware capable of addressing the dynamic, distributed, decentralised nature of the resource brokerage problem. The adoption of a common abstraction layer minimises the lack of interoperability and standardisation in the application domain at the cost of customisation. On the one hand, abstraction layers offer a unique Application Programming Interface (API) and return single resource endpoints and, on the other hand, do not support the level of customisation offered by standalone provider solutions. In terms of the middleware and given the nature of the cloud resource brokerage problem at hand, the adoption of a multi-agent brokerage platform is the most appropriate solution.

Cloud service brokers play an essential role in this context, since they facilitate partner lookup, resource discovery and abstract the management and integration of disparate cloud services – potentially across different providers – allowing SME to migrate seamlessly to the cloud while meeting their unique requirements. However, at the cloud broker level, there are also several issues to be tackled: (*i*) the adoption of specifications and standards to represent SLA instances, *e.g.*, WS-Agreement (OGF) or WSLA (IBM); (*ii*) the definition of a standard model to represent cloud resources; (*iii*) the definition of a security mechanism to protect the negotiation strategies of each cloud provider as well as business information; and (*iv*) the provision of the federated resources. In the latter case, while existing approaches undertake one-to-one negotiations and merge the results into a single resource package in the end, our approach creates coalitions of providers – virtual cloud providers – which negotiate directly with the consumers.

CLOUDANCHOR

CloudAnchor was a 24 month research, development and innovation (RD&I) project funded by the Portuguese Agency for Innovation. The main focus of the project was the development of a modular platform for connecting and managing federations of IaaS cloud service providers. It integrates, among other components, a brokerage platform, including an automated partner lookup and resource negotiation mechanism on behalf of the stakeholders, and an abstraction framework, interfacing with different IaaS platforms. The CloudAnchor architecture presented in Figure 1 is composed of the broker layer (the CloudAnchor brokerage platform), the abstraction layer (Deltacloud framework) and the different IaaS provider platforms.

This approach offers a single API for the broker to manage and interact with the different underlying cloud computing and storage resource platforms' interfaces, acting as an abstraction layer. The IaaS resources are virtualized computing elements with standardised packages, *e.g.*, a standard Virtual Machine (VM) comprising four virtual Central Processing Units (CPU), 16 GiB of Random Access Memory (RAM) and an Operating System (OS) image.

Abstraction Layer

The goal of the abstraction layer, which is composed by the Deltacloud framework, is to overcome the lack of interoperability, vendor lock-in, terminology issues and distinct authentication methods, while exposing a common API to manage resources across different IaaS clouds. There are other cloud abstrac-

Figure 1. CloudAnchor approach

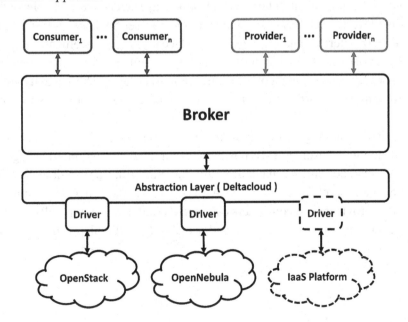

tion solutions *e.g.*, jClouds and Libcloud that are standard programming libraries and, unlike Deltacloud, do not integrate additional development tools. Thus, Deltacloud exposes broadly used interface libraries, Cloud Infrastructure Management Interface (CIMI) API and AWS EC2 API, making the overall development project more complete and also provide documentation for the development of new drivers to integrate unsupported IaaS platforms. Meireles and Malheiro (2014) provide further details on the selection, adoption and integration of several IaaS platforms in the Deltacloud framework.

Deltacloud is composed of three main layers: (*i*) Driver's Layer; (*ii*) Core Layer; and (*iii*) User Interface Layer. The Driver's Layer contains the individual drivers to interact with the specific back-end IaaS platforms and process the HTTP requests/responses. It uses external cloud clients to interact with the corresponding IaaS platform API and libraries with methods to perform API calls that comply with the IaaS API. The Core Layer is composed of modules and classes that support the remaining two layers. It defines the group of operations (also called collections) and the features that each API currently exposes and that each driver supports, and maps them to the syntax that is exposed by the User Interface Layer. The User Interface Layer is responsible for the exposure of the Deltacloud Web services. Deltacloud integrates a REST API and a graphical user interface Web dashboard as well as a Distributed Management Task Force (DMTF) open standard CIMI REST API and the Amazon Web Services (AWS) EC2 API. By default, Deltacloud provides drivers for multiple IaaS cloud providers and platforms including the open-source OpenNebula and OpenStack. The list of supported cloud platforms is available at the official project page (Apache DeltaCloud, 2013).

Broker Layer

The brokerage platform architecture is presented in Figure 2. It is organized in interface, agreement, enterprise and market layers and comprises of five types of specialised dedicated agents: (*i*) interface agents to interact with consumer and provider SME businesses; (*ii*) agreement agents to manage SLA instances; (*iii*) enterprise agents to model consumer and provider SME businesses; (*iv*) market delegate agents to negotiate specific resources on behalf of consumer and provider SME businesses; and (*v*) layer manager agents (interface, agreement, enterprise and market layer agents) responsible for the management of the corresponding layers. Each business (consumer or provider SME) is represented in the platform by the corresponding: (*i*) interface agent located in interface layer; (*ii*) agreement agent located in agreement layer; (*iii*) enterprise agent in the enterprise layer; and (*iv*) an undetermined number of delegate agents involved in specific resource negotiations in the market layer. These agents are identified by a trading code, preventing third parties from intruding in undergoing negotiations (Veloso, Malheiro & Burguillo, 2015).

In terms of standard technologies, the platform adopts: (*i*) standard REST WS interfaces for the interaction with provider and consumer SME businesses (via the dedicated interface agents); (*ii*) BPMN to define the provider and consumer behaviour within the platform; (*iii*) standard specifications for the representation of Service Level Agreements (SLA); and (*iv*) standard SLA negotiation protocols. The platform is open (*i.e.*, providers and consumers can register and deregister at will), modular, (*i.e.*, functionalities can be added and removed at will), and scalable (*i.e.*, the platform can be distributed over multiple computing nodes).

Figure 2. CloudAnchor approach

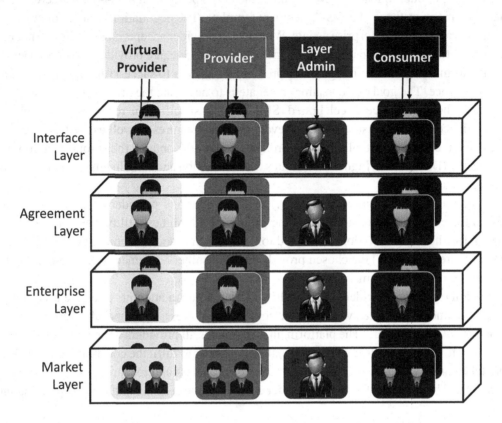

Brokerage Platform Workflow

The brokerage workflow encompasses six stages; (*i*) business registration, negotiation and establishment of the bSLA; (*ii*) consumer resource request; (*iii*) provider lookup and invitation; (*iv*) negotiation and establishment of the rSLA and provision of the resource endpoint to the consumer; (*v*) reputation update based on the SLA enforcement feedback data; and (*vi*) creation of virtual providers to supply federated resources.

In order to join the platform, a consumer or provider SME first needs to register with the interface administrator agent. Once registered, the interface layer administrator creates a dedicated interface agent to interact with the business and the agreement administrator creates a dedicated agreement agent to maintain the business SLA templates and instances. The first task of the agreement agent is to establish a bSLA with the platform on behalf of the business using the provided negotiation strategy according to the WS-Agreement one shot protocol. In the case of a consumer, the bSLA specifies that the consumer must invite all providers for negotiation with resources matching their future needs. In the case of a provider, the bSLA states that it must accept all resource negotiation invitations issued by potential partner consumers. The business agreement agent launches the two-step bSLA negotiation process: (*i*) obtains the SLA template; and (*ii*) negotiates the platform services fruition conditions, using the single proposal WS-Agreement Negotiation protocol. Upon success, the business completes its registration in the platform and is ready to take advantage of the platform brokerage services.

Every time a provider uploads a new resource, the corresponding agreement agent creates an rSLA template, which is an instance of a WS-Agreement template. The negotiation strategy of any resource is stored in the corresponding enterprise agents. Whenever a provider accepts an invitation to negotiate one of its resources, the provider and consumer launch ephemeral delegate provider and consumer agents to negotiate the terms of the rSLA. The goal of a provider delegate is to successfully negotiate the resource for the highest price. The goal of a consumer delegate is to negotiate the provision of a resource matching its needs at the lowest price. A celebrated rSLA not only specifies the resource provision terms, but implies that the consumers must share the relevant resource features as well as feedback data with the provider. Once the rSLA is established, the brokerage platform obtains the resource endpoint via the abstraction layer (Deltacloud). Figure 3 illustrates the negotiation and establishment of an rSLA between a consumer and a provider.

This process is conducted in three steps; (*i*) the consumer and provider delegates negotiate using FICNIP and the consumer delegate chooses the proposal with highest utility (represented by A and B in Figure 3); (*ii*) the outcome is communicated to the enterprise and agreement agents (represented by C and D in Figure 3); and (*iii*) the chosen provider and consumer agreement agents establish the rSLA according to the negotiated terms.

The creation of virtual providers is event-driven. The platform attempts to create a virtual provider based on a consumer request, *i.e.*, whenever the consumer requires a decomposable resource that cannot be provided by single providers. The platform, in turn, invites all providers with compatible, but insufficient resources to establish a virtual provider coalition in order to fulfil the consumer request. All invited providers take part in a negotiation to define the set of providers and resources to be committed to the virtual provider. The creation of a virtual provider consists of the creation of the corresponding interface,

Figure 3. rSLA negotiation

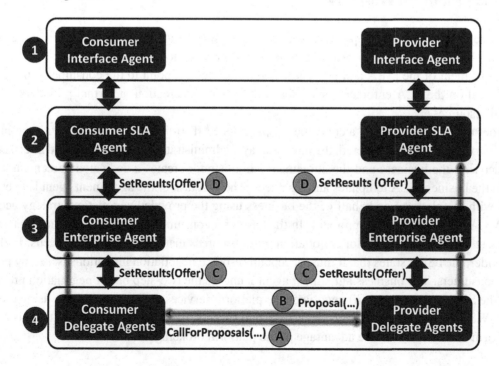

agreement and enterprise agents. Although the operation of a virtual provider coalition is identical to a single provider, once a federated resource is successfully negotiated, the brokerage platform obtains the corresponding collection of resource endpoints via the abstraction layer (Deltacloud).

The SLA enforcement feedback data feeds the distributed reputation system. Each provider and consumer builds a local reputation model of its business counterparts. This reputation model will condition any future negotiations with these counterparts.

Service Level Agreements

The platform implements two OGF specifications: (*i*) the WS-Agreement, used to represent all SLA templates used and to support the one shot bSLA negotiation; and (*ii*) WS-Agreement Negotiation, used to support the multi-round rSLA negotiation. These specifications are, in our case, implemented on top of the FIPA Agent Communication Language (ACL) in order to minimise the communication latency between parties. Additionally, to include a multi-round negotiation mechanism within the WS-Agreement Negotiation Protocol, we added FICNIP. Since the structure of a WS-Agreement template is highly extensible, bSLA, cSLA and rSLA are instances of WS-Agreement templates as displayed in Figure 4.

The SLA template presented in Figure 5 refers to an rSLA and includes context (validity, parties, etc.), terms (service terms and guarantee terms) and constraint fields. The service terms specify the service functionalities and the guarantee terms stipulate the service obligations and penalties. The constraints define the acceptable parameter negotiation range. All SLA instances are negotiated according to the negotiation strategy defined by the corresponding business.

The lifespan (validity) of a bSLA is typically longer than that of an rSLA. Figure 6 illustrates these different SLA lifecycles. In fact, multiple rSLA, involving a given business, can be celebrated, applied and terminated within the scope of the same bSLA. The arrows between the rSLA and the bSLA life cycles represent the feedback provided by the rSLA instances to the consumer and provider bSLA monitoring modules. When an rSLA expires, the provider pays the platform for the brokerage service, and the distributor reimburses the platform and the producer for the brokerage and the resource provisioning services, respectively. The lifecycle of a cSLA – which corresponds to the lifespan of a virtual provider – is identical to the corresponding bSLA. The main difference between the lifespan of a virtual and an individual provider is that the former tends to have a shorter life than the latter.

Figure 4. SLA template hierachy

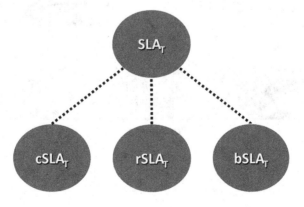

Figure 5. rSLA template

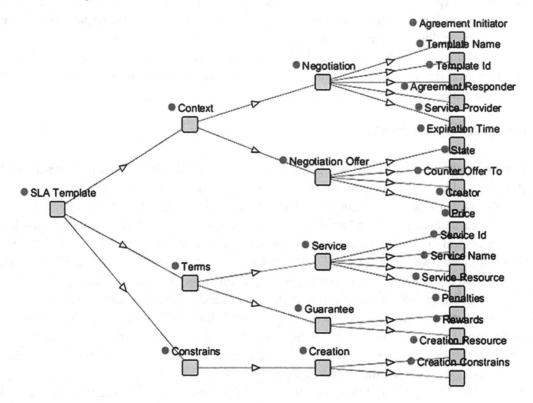

Figure 6. SLA lifecycle

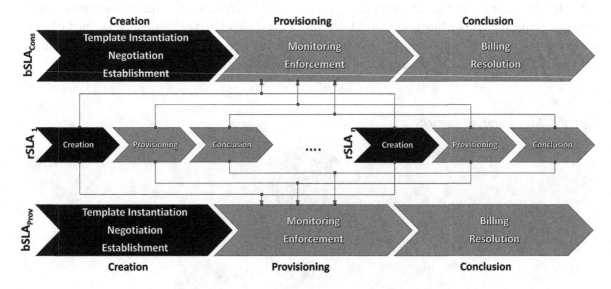

At the business level, the platform adopts a pay-per-use model together with the hierarchical SLA model illustrated in Figure 7.

Under this hierarchical model, bSLA instances define the brokerage service provisioning terms under which all cSLA and rSLA are established. The cSLA instances specify the federated resource provisioning terms under which the individual federated resources (rSLA) are provided. The rSLA regarding a provider resource inherits the terms of the bSLA established between the platform and the provider, and the rSLA of a federated resource inherits the terms of the bSLA established between the platform and the federated providers as well as the terms of the cSLA celebrated between the federated providers. The celebrated rSLA remain latent until the resources are actually provisioned, *i.e.*, when consumers use the service/resources. Only then, the corresponding rSLA instances are activated. Figure 8 illustrates the provision of Resource_01 by Provider_01 to Consumer_01, which implies fulfilling the terms of two bSLA and one rSLA.

Figure 7. SLA instance hierarchy

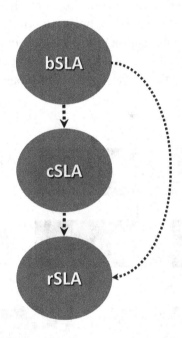

Figure 8. Single provider rSLA

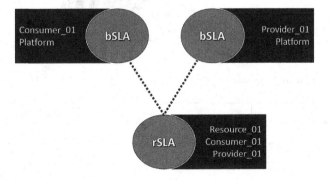

Figure 9. represents, in terms of SLA instances, the provision of Resource_01 by Virtual_Provider_01 to Consumer_01. On the one hand, it involves fulfilling the terms of one bSLA and one cSLA and, on the other hand, since the cSLA is composed by three rSLA from three providers, it, additionally, has to fulfil the terms of the corresponding bSLA.

The provision of a resource results in several payments: (*i*) the consumer pays the provider the established resource provisioning fee; (*ii*) the provider pays to the platform of the accorded brokerage fee; and (*iii*) the consumer pays the platform of the negotiated brokerage fee. In the case of a federated resource, there is an additional brokerage fee that the federated providers pay the platform. These fees are typically distinct. Table 3 and Table 4 illustrate the payment fees involved in the case of a single and a virtual resource provider, respectively.

SLA Negotiation

The platform negotiates the establishment of brokerage, resource and coalition SLA. A business wishing to join and benefit from the platform services needs first to establish a bSLA with the platform. The bSLA negotiation strategy is stored in the corresponding business agreement agent and the negotiation with the platform adopts the WS-Agreement one shot protocol. In the case of a consumer, the bSLA implies that it must invite all trusted providers for negotiation with resources matching its needs (IaaS resource profiles). The provider bSLA implies that it must accept all resource negotiation invitations issued by

Figure 9. Virtual provider rSLA

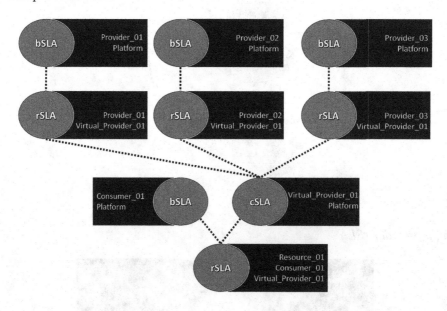

Table 3. Single provider resource service fees

		Platform
	Provider	bSLA Fee
Consumer	rSLA Fee	bSLA Fee

Table 4. Virtual provider resource service fees

					Platform
				Provider$_k$	bSLA Fee
			Provider$_j$		bSLA Fee
		Provider$_i$			bSLA Fee
	Virtual Provider	rSLA Fee	rSLA Fee	rSLA Fee	bSLA Fee
Consumer	rSLA Fee				bSLA Fee

trusted consumers. For the platform, the bSLA stipulates the level of the brokerage service. A provider may reject an invitation and a consumer may not invite a provider for negotiation if they are untrusted. For a given consumer or provider business, a peer is untrustworthy when its local trustworthiness is below the average local trust of the set of peers under consideration.

During registration, the business agreement agent launches the two-step bSLA negotiation process: (*i*) obtains the SLA template; and (*ii*) negotiates the conditions of the fruition of the platform services, using the single proposal WS-Agreement Negotiation protocol. Upon success, the business completes its registration in the platform and is ready to take advantage of the platform brokerage services. Figure 10 illustrates the negotiation of a bSLA, using the one shot negotiation protocol, where the business agent represents a consumer or a provider and the endpoint reference (EPR) corresponds to the business endpoint in the platform, *i.e.*, the corresponding business interface agent. This negotiation involves the business agreement agent, acting as the initiator and representative of the business, and the agreement layer agent, playing the role of respondent and representative of the platform. The business agreement agent sends gets a negotiation template, fills it with its proposal and sends the negotiation proposal to the platform agreement agent. The platform agent accepts the proposal, establishing the bSLA and registering the business in the platform, or sends a counter-offer. If the business agent rejects the counter-offer, the negotiation of the bSLA fails and the business registration aborts.

Figure 10. bSLA one-shot negotiation

On the one hand, every time a provider business generates a new resource offer event, the corresponding agreement agent creates an rSLA template instance. On the other hand, when a consumer business uploads a new resource request, it triggers the provider lookup and invitation, resulting in the invitation of the set of providers with compatible resources. In the case of the trust-based invitation, the consumer invites the sub-set of providers with trustworthiness higher or equal to the mean trustworthiness of the set of providers with compatible resources. A provider, by default, accepts all invitations as long as it has resources. In the case of trust-based acceptance, the provider accepts invitations from consumers with trustworthiness higher or equal to the mean trustworthiness of the set of known consumers. Alternatively, the provider business can define a threshold. Whenever the provider accepts a consumer invitation and selects this resource for negotiation, the provider and consumer launch ephemeral delegate provider and consumer agents to negotiate the terms of the provision of the resource (rSLA). The goal of a provider delegate is to negotiate the resource successfully. The goal of a consumer delegate is to negotiate the terms of usage and ensure that the resource under negotiation matches the profile of the required IaaS resource. The provisioning of the resource implies the payment off the fees described in the previous section. Virtual providers, which are coalitions of single providers, offer federated resources. The negotiation of a federated resource is identical to the negotiation of a single provider resource. Renegotiation of long lasting bSLA and cSLA can be performed periodically or on request from one of the parties involved.

Each consumer or provider may participate in multiple trading rooms by launching multiple delegate agents, *i.e.*, a provider business can negotiate multiple resources simultaneously. Each delegate agent is identified by a universally unique identifier (UUID) code generated when the provider is invited to negotiate. The negotiation protocol is the FICNIP, where the consumer delegate and provider delegates play the roles of the initiator and participant agents, respectively. At the end of each iterative multi-round, the consumer delegate assesses the set of received provider delegate proposals, accepts the one with highest utility and rejects the remaining others or rejects all proposals. When the consumer accepts a provider's proposal, it corresponds to the establishment of the corresponding rSLA, which additionally implies that the consumer must share feedback data with the provider and that the provider must make the resource available for use in the accorded terms. The consumer delegate agent assesses provider proposals through the resource utility function presented in Equation 1:

$$Utility\left(c,p,r\right) = Trust_{ENF}\left(c,p\right)\left(\alpha_c\left(1-price\left(p,r\right)\right)+\left(1-\alpha_c\right)time\left(p,r\right)\right) \tag{1}$$

where *Utility(c,p,r)* represents the utility that the consumer c attributes to the resource r proposed by provider p, $Trust_{ENF}\left(c,p\right)$ is the trustworthiness that consumer c attributes to provider p based on the ratio of fulfilled SLA, *price(p,r)* is the normalise resource price proposed by provider p, *time(p,r)* is the proposed resource uptime and, finally, α_c is the weight attributed to the price by consumer c.

Whenever a consumer c requires a decomposable resource which cannot be supplied single-handedly by any provider, it requests to the platform the creation of a virtual provider (*vp*). The platform attempts to create a virtual provider on behalf of the consumer capable of providing the requested resource. First, it creates a potential virtual provider agent, which looks up and invites trustworthy provider agents holding resources of the requested type to negotiate a cSLA, *i.e.*, the terms of a joint commitment to provide federated resources. The cSLA negotiation, which occurs in the market layer between delegate agents of the virtual provider and of the invited providers, follows the FICNIP protocol. During the negotiation, the providers offer to commit a given number of standard resource packages to the coalition under the specified terms. In the end, the virtual provider agent assesses the utility of the different provider offers through Equation 1. $Trust_{ENF}(vp, p)$, which is the SLA-based trustworthiness the virtual provider vp attributes to provider p, corresponds to $Trust_{ENF}(c, p)$, *i.e.*, the SLA-based trustworthiness that consumer c attributes to provider p. The negotiation succeeds if the resulting federated resource package fulfils the initial consumer request and fails otherwise.

Finally, the brokerage platform interacts with the abstraction layer to provide the negotiated IaaS resources. The interaction with the brokerage platform is conducted via the Deltacloud API. The brokerage platform is limited to the IaaS platforms supported by Deltacloud.

Decentralised Trust Model

The platform creates and maintains a distributed decentralised trust model of all business counterparts (platform, providers and consumers) based on their past behaviour, *i.e.*, the number of invitations, acceptances as well as the number of negotiated, established and fulfilled SLA. Each entity (platform, consumer, provider and virtual provider) builds and maintains a model of its counterparts. While consumers, providers and virtual providers hold a partial incomplete trust model of their counterparts, the platform is in a unique position as it keeps a global and complete trust model.

The trust model supports the invitation, acceptance and negotiation stages and is based on the past interaction data, including the number of invitations *versus* acceptances to negotiate, the number of SLA negotiated *versus* SLA established and the number of SLA established *versus* SLA fulfilled. In the future, it will also support bSLA and cSLA renegotiation stage. Whereas the number of invitations *versus* acceptances and negotiated *versus* established SLA is known by each partner, the SLA enforcement, which is based on the QoS and the payment of service (PoS), is communicated by an external SLA monitoring and enforcement module. This feedback is received when a bSLA, cSLA or rSLA terminates and is maintained by the involved entities. In the case of a bSLA, it is maintained by the platform and the consumer, the platform and the provider or the platform and the virtual provider; in the case of a cSLA, is kept by the virtual provider and the set of providers; and, in the case of an rSLA, by the consumer and the provider or the consumer, the virtual provider and the set of providers. Internally, the local trust model is kept by the corresponding agreement agents. Each entity determines the trustworthiness of a counterpart, *i.e.*, a business partner, based on this data. The trustworthiness varies between 0% (untrustworthy) and 100% (trustworthy) and, by default, a new business partner is 100% trusted. The trust model supports the invitation (*INV*), SLA negotiation (*NEG*) and SLA enforcement (*ENF*) stages. Equation 2 represents the dynamic trustworthiness attributed by a trustor a to a trustee b in stage S after concluding n interactions:

$$Trust_S(a,b)_n = \frac{n-1}{n} Trust_S(a,b)_{n-1} + \frac{1}{n} Out_{S,n} \qquad (2)$$

where $Out_{S,n}$ is the Boolean outcome of the last interaction within stage S: success (1) or failure (0).

The trustworthiness of the peers is updated every time new data is available and has three components: the ratio of accepted invitations between a consumer and a provider $\left(Trust_{INV}(c, p)_n\right)$, the ratio of established SLA between a provider and a consumer $\left(Trust_{NEG}\left(p,c\right)_n\right)$ and the ratio of fulfilled SLA $\left(Trust_{ENF}\left(c,p\right)_n\right)$ and $\left(Trust_{ENF}\left(p,c\right)_n\right)$.

In the invitation stage, a consumer invites providers to negotiate a resource based on their published resource availability and local trustworthinesses. The providers are filtered by the ratio of fulfilled SLA $\left(Trust_{ENF}\left(c,p\right)_n\right)$ and the ratio of accepted invitations $\left(Trust_{INV}\left(c,p\right)_n\right)$. Identically, a provider accepts a consumer invitation to negotiate a resource based on its resource availability and on the consumer's local trustworthiness. In this case, consumers are selected according to the ratio of fulfilled SLA $\left(Trust_{ENF}\left(p,c\right)_n\right)$ followed by the ratio of established SLA $\left(Trust_{NEG}\left(p,c\right)_n\right)$. A consumer chooses a provider based on its proposal and local trustworthiness by applying the resource utility function presented in Equation 1, which takes into account the ratio of fulfilled SLA $\left(Trust_{ENF}\left(c,p\right)_n\right)$.

TESTS AND RESULTS

We performed several tests to verify the correct operation of the platform in terms of: (*i*) single resource provision; (*ii*) federated resource provision; and (*iii*) mixed resource provision. In these experiments, according to the default SLA terms, if a business fails to fulfil an established SLA, it reimburses the partner. At start up consumers and providers are equally and fully trusted (100% trustworthiness). During these tests, consumers remain fully trusted, while providers experience changes in trustworthiness, *i.e.*, do not fulfil all established SLA. These experiments were performed with and without the application of the decentralised trust model, and using equal and diverse provider price adaptation strategies for the generation of negotiation proposals.

Providers can implement diverse price adaptation strategies. In the single price (SP) policy all providers adopt the same strategy. It corresponds to a linear descending price adaptation strategy with a maximum value of 47 € per standard VM, a reference value of 37 € per standard VM and a minimum value of 27 € per standard VM package. The providers start by issuing a proposal with the reference price and will, subsequently, lower the price of the next proposal if their previous proposal is rejected. In the multiple price (MP) policy scenario, providers adopt different price policies (linear, quadratic and exponential descending as well as random and static). The descending price strategies start at the reference price, the random strategy varies between the maximum and minimum prices and the static strategy.

In terms of hardware, the tests were executed on a platform with one quad-core i7-2600 3.40 GHz Central Processing Unit (CPU) with 2 threads per core, 15 GiB Random Access Memory (RAM) and a 1.8 TiB of storage capacity.

Table 5 displays the six configuration settings used in the single, federated and mixed resource provision experiments.

The focus will be on the multiple price scenarios rather than on the single price scenarios. The single price scenarios have been included for completeness and comparison.

Single Resources

The first set of tests involves one consumer and fifty providers holding twenty standard virtual machine packages (VM) each, *i.e.*, the offer meets demand. The consumer fulfils all rSLA and each provider

Table 5. Test configuration

Test	Price Strategy	Trust-based invitation	Trust-based negotiation
SP	Single	No	No
MP	Multiple	No	No
SP+TN	Single	No	Yes
MP+TN	Multiple	No	Yes
SP+TIN	Single	Yes	Yes
MP+TIN	Multiple	Yes	Yes

will fail to provide 5 out of the 20 VM with the negotiated QoS, ending with a trustworthiness of 75% and obtaining revenues which depend on the price adaption strategy adopted. The goal is to assess the impact of the provider trustworthiness in the invitation and negotiation stages. Each consumer request is provided by a single provider. Table 6 presents the results.

This first set of test involves one thousand resource negotiations. The multiple price results show that trust-based invitation and negotiation decreases the runtime by 51% and increases the average VM price by 1. The slight difference in the average resource price in the multiple price strategy (1%) results from the fact that providers are being selected according to their trustworthiness, and not to the price of their proposal. This first test is the base test for all future comparisons.

In the following set of tests, the only change is that the offer exceeds the demand. It involves one consumer and hundred providers holding twenty standard virtual machine packages (VM) each, *i.e.*, the offer doubles demand. Table 7 holds the results of this second test.

When compared with the first set of tests, the average VM price decreases by 12% in the SP case and by 6% in the MP_TIN as expected. The test involved a thousand negotiations, but now, in this oversupply scenario, the number of provider agents per negotiation is considerably higher than the number of the first test, and the runtime increases 215%. Moreover, the results indicate that, in this oversupply scenario, the trust-based negotiation runtime increases by 5% and, in the trust-based invitation and negotiation case (MP+TIN), decreases by 48%. This increase in runtime in the case of trust-based negotiation results from the fact that, in the trust-based negotiation, not only the consumer needs the provider trustworthi-

Table 6. Single resources: offer meets demand

Test	SP	MP	SP+TN	MP+TN	SP+TIN	MP+TIN
Consumers	1	1	1	1	1	1
Providers	50	50	50	50	50	50
Requests per consumer	1000	1000	1000	1000	1000	1000
Resources per consumer request (VM)	1	1	1	1	1	1
Resources available per provider (VM)	20	20	20	20	20	20
Provider rSLA violation (%)	25	25	25	25	25	25
Total Runtime (s)	268	206	209	208	105	106
Average VM price (€)	36.39	31.56	36.39	31.88	36.39	31.88

Table 7. Single resources: offer exceeds demand

Test	SP	MP	SP+TN	MP+TN	SP+TIN	MP+TIN
Consumers	1	1	1	1	1	1
Providers	100	100	100	100	100	100
Requests per consumer	1000	1000	1000	1000	1000	1000
Resources per consumer request (VM)	1	1	1	1	1	1
Resources available per provider (VM)	20	20	20	20	20	20
Provider rSLA violation (%)	25	25	25	25	25	25
Total runtime (s)	562	456	483	477	236	228
Average VM price (€)	36.39	27.71	36.39	30.51	36.39	30.02

ness to assess each provider proposal, but he is negotiating with all potential providers, including the ones with low trustworthiness.

Federated Resources

The following set of tests focusses on federated resource provision. The setup involves one consumer and fifty providers, holding 20 VM each. The consumer requests 40 packages of 25 VM sequentially. Since no single provider can provide this number of resources, it forces the establishment of provider coalitions. The goal is to assess the impact of the provider trustworthiness in the invitation, coalition establishment and negotiation stages. Each consumer request is provided by a coalition of providers. Table 8 holds the results.

This set of tests encompasses 40 cSLA negotiations, 40 virtual provider bSLA negotiations and 40 federated resource rSLA negotiations. For the multiple price strategies, the average VM price is identical in the three cases; in the case of trust-based negotiation (MP+TN test), runtime increases 14% when compared to the unfiltered invitation and negotiation (MP test) and, in the case of trust-based invitation and negotiation (MP+TIN test), runtime remains unchanged when compared to the unfiltered invitation and negotiation (MP test). This increase in runtime in the case of trust-based negotiation results from

Table 8. Federated resources: offer meets demand

Test	SP	MP	SP+TN	MP+TN	SP+TIN	MP+TIN
Consumers	1	1	1	1	1	1
Providers	50	50	50	50	50	50
Requests per consumer	40	40	40	40	40	40
Resources per consumer request (VM)	25	25	25	25	25	25
Resources available per provider (VM)	20	20	20	20	20	20
Provider rSLA violation (%)	25	25	25	25	25	25
Total runtime (s)	38	29	38	33	36	29
Average VM price (€)	37.93	36.87	37.93	36.89	37.93	36.85

the fact that, in the trust-based negotiation, not only the consumer needs the provider trustworthiness to assess each provider proposal, but he is negotiating with all potential providers, including the ones with low trustworthiness. When compared with the corresponding single resource results, runtime decreases 73% and the average VM price increases 16%. Runtime improves because, although the total number of negotiated resources is the same, the number of negotiations drops from 1000 to 120. The average price increases because federated resources are more expensive.

In the second set of tests with federated resources the offer doubles the demand. These tests involve the same number of 120 negotiations. Table 9 summarises the results. When compared with the previous set of tests, runtime increases 234% in the MP test, 200% in the MP-TN and 230% in the MP+TIN test. The average VM price is equal in all cases and identical to the previous test results. These federated resource results show that oversupply affects significantly runtime opposed to the average VM price, which remains unchanged. The runtime increases because the number of agents involved in the establishment of the virtual providers is considerably large in the oversupply scenario than in the offer meets demand scenario.

Single and Federated Resources

The mixed resource provision tests contemplate the negotiation of single and federated resources. One consumer requests 40 sets of 25 VM sequentially, while the other requests 1000 VM sequentially. Table 10 presents the results.

This set of tests involves a total of 560 negotiations: 20 coalition negotiations, 20 brokerage negotiations, 20 federated resource negotiations and 500 single resource negotiations. Comparing the results of the MP+TIN test and of the MP test, there is a 32% decrease of the runtime and a 1% increase of the average VM price. The runtime decrease is due to the fact that the number of invited providers is smaller in the MP+TIN test.

The second test is identical to the previous one, but has twice the number of providers, reproducing an oversupply scenario. Table 11 holds the results.

Each test involves a total of 560 negotiations: 20 coalition negotiations, 20 brokerage negotiations, 20 federated resource negotiations and 500 single resource negotiations. When compared with the previous set of tests, these results show a significant increase in runtime and a slight decrease in average

Table 9. Federated resources: offer exceeds demand

Test	SP	MP	SP+TN	MP+TN	SP+TIN	MP+TIN
Consumers	1	1	1	1	1	1
Providers	100	100	100	100	100	100
Requests per consumer	40	40	40	40	40	40
Resources per consumer request (VM)	25	25	25	25	25	25
Resources available per provider (VM)	20	20	20	20	20	20
Provider rSLA violation (%)	25	25	25	25	25	25
Total runtime (s)	73	68	75	66	71	67
Average VM price (€)	37.93	36.39	37.93	36.39	37.93	36.39

Table 10. Mixed resources: offer meets demand

Test	SP	MP	SP+TN	MP+TN	SP+TIN	MP+TIN
Consumers	1	1	1	1	1	1
Providers	50	50	50	50	50	50
Requests per consumer	20	20	20	20	20	20
	500	500	500	500	500	500
Resources per consumer request (VM)	25	25	25	25	25	25
	1	1	1	1	1	1
Resources available per provider (VM)	20	20	20	20	20	20
Provider rSLA violation (%)	25	25	25	25	25	25
Total runtime (s)	131	104	121	104	101	71
Average VM price (€)	37.16	34.87	37.16	35.40	37.16	35.23

Table 11. Mixed resources: offer exceeds demand

Test	SP	MP	SP+TN	MP+TN	SP+TIN	MP+TIN
Consumers	1	1	1	1	1	1
Providers	100	100	100	100	100	100
Requests per provider	20	20	20	20	20	20
	500	500	500	500	500	500
Resources per consumer request (VM)	25	25	25	25	25	25
	1	1	1	1	1	1
Resources available per provider (VM)	20	20	20	20	20	20
Provider rSLA violation (%)	25	25	25	25	25	25
Total runtime (s)	298	271	287	255	232	145
Average VM price (€)	37.16	32.04	37.16	34.20	37.16	34.09

VM price, *e.g.*, in the case of MP+TIN, a runtime increase of 204% and an average VM price decrease of 3%. From the comparison of the MP+TIN and the MP results in Table 10, runtime decreases 46% and the average VM price increases 6%. These results are compatible with the selection of providers by trustworthiness and not by the price of their resources.

FUTURE RESEARCH DIRECTIONS

At the broker level and in order to improve the overall quality of the services provided, we plan: (*i*) to implement the renegotiation of bSLA and cSLA based on the trust model and on the success of the business in the platform and in the coalition, respectively; (*ii*) to refine the trust model using a sliding window rather than using the complete SLA enforcement history; (*iii*) to enrich SLA templates with new parameters to meet increasing business demands, *e.g.*, the time of provision in the case of rSLA;

and (*iv*) create virtual providers not only at the request of consumers, but also at the request of providers, *i.e.*, providers may, in order to try to increase their profits, decide to join efforts and provide federated resources.

At the abstraction layer, it is important to define conventions for the network advertisement of the provisioned resources, in particular the usage of a single domain name for resources that are created in a federated context and shared by multiple cloud providers. Currently, for the federated resources, there are as many endpoints as cloud providers involved. The goal would be to have an agreement between the parties to name the resources on behalf of the created virtual provider and, then, to change the Domain Name System (DNS) entries accordingly, providing a single endpoint for the federated resources.

Concerning the validation of the platform, we are performing experiments to assess the impact of the distributed trust model from the perspective of the providers, *i.e.*, when consumers violate agreements and, thus, exhibit different levels of trustworthiness.

CONCLUSION

This paper presents the CloudAnchor brokerage platform which offers brokerage services for SME cloud infrastructure vendors and SME cloud infrastructure consumers. It handles the negotiation and provision of infrastructure resources from single or colligated vendors (virtual providers). The brokerage services include the discovery of resource providers, the selection of providers via the negotiation of the resource provision terms, the establishment of the binding SLA with the brokerage platform, and the establishment of the resource SLA between cloud infrastructure consumer and vendor. When there are no single vendors capable of fulfilling a consumer request, the coalition mechanism is triggered with the goal to find providers able to deliver the required resources. These resources, which must be decomposable in standard VM packages, are then offered as federated resources.

In terms of contractual relationships, we identified and modelled three types: (*i*) bSLA – which defines the platform service provision terms for each business; (*ii*) rSLA – that specifies the resource provisioning terms between businesses; and (*iii*) cSLA – that details the platform coalition service provision terms between all businesses that form the federation. Any rSLA is celebrated under the scope of the involved business bSLA or cSLA, *i.e.*, they must fulfil the agreed brokerage and coalition service provision terms.

To improve the performance of the platform we designed a decentralised trust model. This model takes into account all past interactions, including provider invitation, resource negotiation and resource provision. The typical approach focusses on the resource provision outcome, *i.e.*, the feedback from SLA monitoring and enforcement, and disregards the outcomes from other interactions. Our approach allows consumers to rely on the outcomes from past provider invitations and resource provisions to invite providers as well as helps providers to decide whether or not to accept a consumer's invitation for negotiation based on the outcome of their common resource negotiation and resource provision history. In terms of contract negotiation, while bSLA adopts and implements the WS Agreement single round negotiation, the rSLA and cSLA implement the WS Agreement multi-round negotiation (FICNIP). In the case of rSLA and cSLA negotiations, the proposals are according to their utility, taking into account the resource price, the uptime and the trustworthiness of the provider. The subsumption of the individual rSLA terms by the terms of the involved bSLA or cSLA together with the three types of SLA are, as far as we know, a novel and relevant approach.

ACKNOWLEDGMENT

This work was partially financed by: (*i*) the ERDF – European Regional Development Fund through the COMPETE Programme (operational programme for competitiveness) and by National Funds through the FCT – Fundação para a Ciência e a Tecnologia (Portuguese Foundation for Science and Technology) within project «23151 – CloudAnchor: Plataforma Modular de Interligação e Gestão de Federações de Fornecedores de Cloud Computing»; and (*ii*) the European Regional Development Fund (ERDF) and the Galician Regional Government under agreement for funding the Atlantic Research Center for Information and Communication Technologies (AtlantTIC).

REFERENCES

Al Falasi, A., Serhani, M. A., & Elnaffar, S. (2013). The sky: A social approach to clouds federation. *Procedia Computer Science*, *19*, 131–138. doi:10.1016/j.procs.2013.06.022

Alhamad, M., Dillon, T., & Chang, E. (2010). SLA-based trust model for cloud computing. *Proceedings of the 2010 13th International Conference on Network-Based Information Systems (NBiS)* (pp. 321-324). IEEE. doi:10.1109/NBiS.2010.67

Amato, A., Di Martino, B., & Venticinque, S. (2012). Evaluation and brokering of service level agreements for negotiation of cloud infrastructures. *Proceedings of the 2012 International Conference for Internet Technology and Secured Transactions* (pp. 144-149). IEEE.

Cascella, R. G., Blasi, L., Jegou, Y., Coppola, M., & Morin, C. (2013). Contrail: Distributed application deployment under SLA in federated heterogeneous clouds. In A. Galis & A. Gavras (Eds.), *The Future Internet (LNCS)* (Vol. 7858, pp. 91–103). Berlin, Germany: Springer. doi:10.1007/978-3-642-38082-2_8

Celesti, A., Tusa, F., Villari, M., & Puliafito, A. (2010). How to enhance cloud architectures to enable cross-federation. *Proceedings of the 2010 IEEE 3rd International Conference on Cloud Computing (CLOUD)* (pp. 337-345). IEEE. doi:10.1109/CLOUD.2010.46

Cuomo, A., Di Modica, G., Distefano, S., Puliafito, A., Rak, M., Tomarchio, O., & Villano, U. (2013). An SLA-based broker for cloud infrastructures. *Journal of Grid Computing*, *11*(1), 1–25. doi:10.1007/s10723-012-9241-4

Deltacloud Drivers. (2013, October). Apache Software Foundation. Retrieved from https://deltacloud.apache.org/drivers.html#drivers

Ferrer, A. J., Hernández, F., Tordsson, J., Elmroth, E., Ali-Eldin, A., Zsigri, C., & Sheridan, C. (2012). OPTIMIS: A holistic approach to cloud service provisioning. *Future Generation Computer Systems*, *28*(1), 66–77. doi:10.1016/j.future.2011.05.022

Fowley, F., Pahl, C., & Zhang, L. (2014). A comparison framework and review of service brokerage solutions for cloud architectures. In A. R. Lomuscio et al. (Eds), *Proceedings of the Service-Oriented Computing–ICSOC 2013 Workshops*, LNCS (Vol. 8377, pp. 137-149). Cham, Switzerland: Springer International Publishing. doi:10.1007/978-3-319-06859-6_13

Grozev, N., & Buyya, R. (2014) Multi-Cloud Provisioning and Load Distribution for Three-Tier Applications. ACM Transactions on Autonomous and Adaptive Systems, 9(3), 13:1-13:21. New York, USA: ACM.

He, Q., Yan, J., Kowalczyk, R., Jin, H., & Yang, Y. (2007). An agent-based framework for service level agreement management. *Proceedings of the 11th International Conference on Computer Supported Cooperative Work in Design CSCWD '07* (pp. 412-417). IEEE. doi:10.1109/CSCWD.2007.4281471

Huynh, T. D., Jennings, N. R., & Shadbolt, N. R. (2006). An integrated trust and reputation model for open multi-agent systems. *Autonomous Agents and Multi-Agent Systems, 13*(2), 119–154. doi:10.1007/s10458-005-6825-4

Kertész, A., Kecskemeti, G., & Brandic, I. (2014). An interoperable and self-adaptive approach for SLA-based service virtualization in heterogeneous Cloud environments. *Future Generation Computer Systems, 32*, 54–68. doi:10.1016/j.future.2012.05.016

Mahbub, K., & Spanoudakis, G. (2010). Proactive SLA negotiation for service based systems. *Proceedings of the 2010 6th World Congress on Services (SERVICES-1)* (pp. 519-526). IEEE. doi:10.1109/SERVICES.2010.15

Meireles, F., & Malheiro, B. (2014). Integrated Management of IaaS Resources. In L. Lopes et al. (Eds.), Proceedings of the Euro-Par 2014: Parallel Processing Workshops (pp. 73-84). Cham, Switzerland: Springer International Publishing. doi:10.1007/978-3-319-14313-2_7

Pan, L. (2011). Towards a framework for automated service negotiation in cloud computing. *Proceedings of the 2011 IEEE International Conference on Cloud Computing and Intelligence Systems (CCIS)* (pp. 364-367). IEEE.

Pawar, P. S., Rajarajan, M., Dimitrakos, T., & Zisman, A. (2014). Trust Assessment Using Cloud Broker. In J. Zhou et al. (Eds.), *Trust Management VIII* (pp. 237–244). Berlin, Germany: Springer.

Pawluk, P., Simmons, B., Smit, M., Litoiu, M., & Mankovski, S. (2012). Introducing STRATOS: A cloud broker service. *Proceedings of the 2012 IEEE Fifth International Conference on Cloud Computing* (pp. 891-898). IEEE. doi:10.1109/CLOUD.2012.24

Sim, K. M. (2012). Agent-based cloud computing. *IEEE Transactions on* Services Computing, 5(4), 564–577.

Stantchev, V., & Schröpfer, C. (2009). Negotiating and enforcing QoS and SLAs in grid and cloud computing. In N. Abdennadher & D. Petcu (Eds.), *Advances in grid and pervasive computing (LNCS)* (Vol. 5529, pp. 25–35). Berlin, Germany: Springer. doi:10.1007/978-3-642-01671-4_3

Teacy, W. L., Patel, J., Jennings, N. R., & Luck, M. (2006). Travos: Trust and reputation in the context of inaccurate information sources. *Autonomous Agents and Multi-Agent Systems, 12*(2), 183–198. doi:10.1007/s10458-006-5952-x

Tordsson, J., Montero, R. S., Moreno-Vozmediano, R., & Llorente, I. M. (2012). Cloud brokering mechanisms for optimized placement of virtual machines across multiple providers. *Future Generation Computer Systems, 28*(2), 358–367. doi:10.1016/j.future.2011.07.003

Veloso, B., Malheiro, B., & Burguillo, J. C. (2015). Media Brokerage: Agent-Based SLA Negotiation. In A. Rocha, A. M. Correia, S. Costanzo, & L. P. Reis (Eds.), *New Contributions in Information Systems and Technologies (Advances in Intelligent Systems and Computing)* (Vol. 353, pp. 575–584). Cham, Switzerland: Springer International Publishing.

Venticinque, S., Aversa, R., Di Martino, B., Rak, M., & Petcu, D. (2011). A cloud agency for SLA negotiation and management. In M. R, Guarracino et al. (Eds), Proceedings of the Euro-Par 2010 Parallel Processing Workshops, LNCS (Vol. 6585, pp. 587-594). Berlin, Germany: Springer. doi:10.1007/978-3-642-21878-1_72

Yangui, S., Marshall, I. J., Laisne, J. P., & Tata, S. (2014). CompatibleOne: The open source cloud broker. *Journal of Grid Computing*, *12*(1), 93–109. doi:10.1007/s10723-013-9285-0

Zulkernine, F., Martin, P., Craddock, C., & Wilson, K. (2009, July). A policy-based middleware for web services SLA negotiation. *Proceedings of the IEEE International Conference on Web Services ICWS '09*. (pp. 1043-1050). IEEE. doi:10.1109/ICWS.2009.157

Chapter 10
GPGPU as a Service:
Providing GPU-Acceleration Services to Federated Cloud Systems

Javier Prades
Technical University of Valencia, Spain

Carlos Reaño
Technical University of Valencia, Spain

Fernando Campos
Technical University of Valencia, Spain

Federico Silla
Technical University of Valencia, Spain

ABSTRACT

Current data centers leverage virtual machines (VMs) in order to efficiently use hardware resources. VMs allow reducing equipment acquisition costs as well as decreasing overall energy consumption. However, although VMs have noticeably evolved to make a smart use of the underlying hardware, the use of GPUs (Graphics Processing Units) for General Purpose computing (GPGPU) is still not efficiently supported. This concern might be addressed by remote GPU virtualization solutions, which may provide VMs with GPUs located in a remote node, detached from the host where the VMs are being executed. This chapter presents an in-depth analysis about how to provide GPU access to applications running inside VMs. This analysis is complemented with experimental results which show that the use of remote GPU virtualization is an effective mechanism to provide GPU access to applications with negligible overheads. Finally, the approach is presented in the context of cloud federations for providing GPGPU as a Service.

INTRODUCTION

Virtual machines (VMs) are a well-known and established technology commonly used in nowadays data centers due to their demonstrated ability to provide economic savings. These savings are originated in the fact that several VMs can be concurrently executed in the same host computer, allowing for what is commonly known as server consolidation. In this way, different VMs share the hardware resources of such computer, thus increasing their overall utilization, what allows faster amortizing the initial economic investment done for the acquisition of the data center equipment. Furthermore, initial acquisition costs can also be reduced given that a smaller amount of computers is required to address the same workload.

DOI: 10.4018/978-1-5225-0153-4.ch010

Moreover, the use of VMs also reduces the operation costs of data centers, given that the reduced size of the equipment requires a smaller amount of energy to be operated, what additionally translates into lower cooling requirements. The smaller electricity bill causes that the stage where economic benefits are provided is reached earlier, thus ensuring the viability of the company that runs the data center. All these features have caused that VMs become the building block in cloud systems, where VMs are dynamically created and destroyed under customers' demand, thus allocating the computing resources only during the utilization time. This allows the cloud platform provider to present VMs to their customers as dedicated resources while the needs of real resources are dramatically decreased.

Given the many benefits reported by the use of VM, several VMMs (Virtual Machine Monitors) can be currently found, such as VirtualBox (Oracle, 2015), VMware (VMware, 2015), KVM (KVM, 2015), and Xen (Xen, 2105). Actually, the advantages provided by these virtualization technologies have motivated the main processor manufacturers, such as Intel or AMD, to include virtualization support into their designs (Semnanian, 2011), so that VMs become an even more efficient way to achieve server consolidation. In this way, although VMs reduced application performance in the past with respect to executions in the native (or real) domain, current VMMs, in conjunction with modern hardware, are able to host VMs where the execution of applications is carried out without significant performance losses, as shown in (Felter, 2014). Furthermore, in addition to CPUs, other computer components have also been enhanced in order to efficiently support the use of VMs. This is the case, for example, of network adapters. In this regard, not only those at the highest performance end, as Mellanox Technologies with the InfiniBand network cards, but also other manufacturers of more basic technologies, such as Intel with its Ethernet NICs (Network Interface Controller), have incorporated hardware supported virtualization mechanisms into their designs. These mechanisms, known as Single Root I/O Virtualization, basically allow replicating, at the logical level, the network card (or, more accurately, creating virtual instances of the card, named virtual functions) so that each of the virtual functions is assigned to one of the virtual machines running in the host computer.

Nevertheless, although the VM technology has been widely enriched during the last years in order to provide more efficient virtualization, the use of GPUs (Graphics Processing Units) as accelerators is still not efficiently supported. In this way, current VMs do not efficiently support the increasing use of GPGPU (General Purpose computing on GPUs), which allows a significant reduction of the execution time of applications from many different areas, such as data analysis (Big Data) (Wu, 2014), chemical physics (Playne, 2009), computational algebra (Yamazaki, 2014), image analysis (Yuancheng, 2008), finance (Surkov, 2010), biology (Agarwal, 2013), and artificial intelligence (Luo, 2014), to name just a few. In this regard, several proposals have been made in order to leverage GPUs within VMs, like the NVIDIA GRID K1 and K2 boards (NVIDIA, 2013). These graphics cards, composed of 4 or 2 GPUs respectively, can be shared among up to eight VMs in order to achieve efficient desktop virtualization with increased graphics performance by allowing the graphics commands of each VM to be directly forwarded to one of these GPUs, without any translation by the hypervisor. Furthermore, although these GPUs feature a non-negligible amount of CUDA cores, this amount is noticeably smaller than that of the Tesla K40 GPU, for instance. Another example is the recent KVMGT technology by Intel (Song, 2014), which provides virtualization support for Intel GPUs within KVM VMs. Nevertheless, the fact that current VMMs are not able to provide efficient support for CUDA-compatible GPUs (CUDA, 2015) causes that accelerated applications being executed inside VMs cannot easily benefit from the GPUs available in the computer hosting the VMs.

The reason why current VMMs cannot easily take advantage of the acceleration characteristics of GPUs is mainly due to the fact that, in general, current accelerators do not feature virtualization capabilities, contrary to what happens with other computer components such as advanced network cards, for example. However, what the hardware is not providing may be supplied by making use of software mechanisms. In this regard, several software-based GPU sharing mechanisms have appeared, such as, for example DS-CUDA (Oikawa, 2102), rCUDA (Reaño, 2013), vCUDA (Shi, 2009), or GViM (Gupta, 2009). Briefly, these middleware proposals share a GPU by virtualizing it, so that these GPU virtualization solutions provide applications with the illusion of a real device, which can therefore be concurrently shared. Furthermore, from a logical perspective, these middleware solutions detach GPUs from cluster nodes, thereby making it possible that applications access virtualized GPUs regardless of the specific node the GPUs are attached to. As can be seen, these GPU virtualization solutions provide GPGPU services to the applications being executed inside VMs. In this regard, GPU virtualization frameworks offer to cloud environments the possibility of providing GPGPU as a service. Moreover, GPGPU services are provided in a transparent way, so that applications are not aware that their acceleration requests are in fact being serviced by a virtual device instead of a real one. Hence, the fact that GPU virtualization solutions detach GPUs from cluster nodes at the logical level may be used to overcome, in an easy and efficient way, the current limitations of VMs with respect to the use of these powerful accelerators.

In this book chapter we explore the use of the GPU virtualization mechanism in order to provide GPGPU services to federated clouds. The main motivation is that GPU virtualization solutions may be used in VM environments in order to address their current limitations with respect to GPGPU. In addition to motivate the use of GPU virtualization solutions to address current concerns of VMs regarding the use of GPUs as accelerators, in this book chapter it is also assessed the overhead that applications experience when demanding GPU services to accelerators located outside their VM by using the GPU virtualization mechanism. A thorough performance evaluation is presented in the context of Xen and KVM VMMs using the rCUDA GPU virtualization middleware, which is currently the most modern one. Two different scenarios are considered for a cloud provider offering High Performance Computing (HPC) services. In the first one, the VM accesses the GPU located in the same node of the HPC cluster that is acting as VM host, by using the internal virtual network provided by the VMM. In the second scenario, it is assumed that a high performance network fabric such as InfiniBand is already available in the HPC cluster and VMs access a GPU located in a different cluster node.

BACKGROUND

Basically, there are two basic ways of providing applications running inside VMs with access to CUDA accelerators: the hardware-based approach and the software-based one. The first category is based on the PCI passthrough technique (Walters, 2014). This approach makes use of the virtualization extensions currently available in HPC servers. These extensions allow assigning a PCI device to one of the VMs being executed in the host computer, although this assignment is made in an exclusive way, that is, only the VM that the PCI device was assigned to can access it. Hence, the device remains invisible for the other VMs running in the host and for the host itself. Regarding performance, the PCI passthrough mechanism does not reduce performance significantly with respect to that achieved when using the PCI device in the native domain. As it can be derived from the previous discussion, it is possible to assign the GPU installed in the host to one of the active VMs. However, as this technique assigns GPUs to a VM in an exclusive way, it is not possible to concurrently share the accelerator among the different VMs running in the host. Several proposals have been made to address this concern. For example, the one presented in (Jo, 2013) dynamically changes on demand the GPUs assigned to VMs. Unfortunately, these proposals do not provide an efficient solution given that they present a high time overhead for changing the GPU assignment. Actually, in the best case, at least two seconds are required to modify the assignments of GPUs to VMs.

Regarding the software-based approach for providing CUDA acceleration to VMs, it is possible to leverage recent middleware proposals which are able to share a GPU among several computers. In this way, solutions such as DS-CUDA, rCUDA, vCUDA, or GridCUDA, among others, share a GPU by virtualizing it, hence providing applications running inside a VM with virtual instances of the real device, which can be concurrently shared. Moreover, these GPU-sharing middleware solutions usually place the virtualization boundary at the GPU API level, which is CUDA in the case of NVIDIA GPUs. Hence, virtualization frameworks intended for NVIDIA GPUs usually offer the same API as the NVIDIA CUDA Runtime API (CUDA, 2015) does.

The architecture usually implemented in these GPU virtualization solutions, shown in Figure 1, follows a distributed client-server approach. The client side of the middleware is installed in the computing system (either native or virtual) where the application requesting GPU services is being executed. The server part of the middleware is usually executed as a daemon in the non-virtualized domain that owns the real GPU device. Notice that the non-virtualized domain owning the GPU may be either the native host computer or a remote server. The exact choice mainly depends on the features of each particular GPU virtualization middleware. On the other hand, communication between the client and server sides may use shared-memory mechanisms or the network fabric, depending on the exact characteristics of the GPU virtualizing middleware and the underlying system configuration.

The way these virtualization solutions provide access to GPUs is the following one: when the accelerated application executes a CUDA request, this request is intercepted by the client part of the middleware, which forwards it to the server middleware. In the server side, the request is received and executed in the real GPU, which performs the required computations and produces the associated results. Once the

Figure 1. Typical architecture used by GPU virtualization solutions

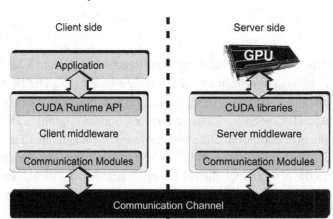

results are available, they are returned by the server middleware to the client side, which delivers them to the accelerated application that triggered the process. It is important to remark that the entire GPU virtualization process is carried out in a transparent way for applications, which are not aware that their GPU requests are actually being serviced by a virtual accelerator instead of by a real device.

CUDA-based GPU virtualization solutions can be divided into two broad types: those designed to be used in the context of VMs and those intended to be used as general purpose virtualization solutions, originally intended to be used in native domains although they can also be used within VMs. GPU virtualization solutions that fall in the first category usually make use of shared-memory mechanisms in order to exchange data between main memory of the VM and the GPU in the native domain. Shared-memory mechanisms can be used because both middleware sides are executed in the same computer. On the contrary, the general purpose GPU virtualization solutions from the second category leverage the network fabric available in the cluster in order to transfer data between main memory in the computer executing the client side and the GPU memory in the remote server. Given that solutions in this second category access GPUs installed in other cluster nodes, they are commonly referred to as remote GPU virtualization solutions.

Several implementations have been developed for each of the two categories mentioned above. In the first one, which comprises solutions to be used in the context of VMs, developments such as vCUDA (Shi, 2009), GViM (Gupta, 2009), gVirtuS (Giunta, 2010), and Shadowfax (Merrit, 2011) can be found:

- **vCUDA:** This technology, intended for Xen VMs, only supports an old CUDA version (v3.2) and implements an unspecified subset of the CUDA Runtime API. Moreover, its communication protocol presents a considerable overhead, because of the cost of the encoding and decoding stages, which causes a noticeable drop on overall performance.
- **GViM:** This framework targets Xen VMs and is based on the obsolete CUDA version 1.1 and, in principle, does not implement the entire CUDA Runtime API.
- **gVirtuS:** This virtualization solution is based on the old CUDA version 2.3 and implements only a small portion of its API. Despite being designed for VMs, it also provides TCP/IP communications for remote GPU virtualization, thus allowing applications in a non-virtualized environment to access GPUs located in other nodes.
- **Shadowfax:** This middleware allows Xen VMs to access the GPUs located at the same node, although it may also be used to access GPUs at other nodes of the cluster. It supports the obsolete CUDA version 1.1 and, additionally, neither the source code nor the binaries are available in order to evaluate its performance

Regarding the second type of GPU virtualization solutions, which are intended to provide general GPU virtualization, frameworks such as rCUDA (Peña, 2014) (Reaño, 2013), VGPU (ZILLIANS, 2015), GridCuda (Liang, 2011), DS-CUDA (Oikawa, 2012), or Shadowfax II (Keeneland, 2015) can be found:

- **rCUDA:** This middleware, further described in next section, features CUDA 6.5 and provides specific communication support for TCP/IP compatible networks as well as for InfiniBand fabrics.
- **VGPU:** This framework is a recent tool supporting CUDA 4.0. Unfortunately, the information provided by the V-GPU authors is fuzzy and there is no publicly available version that can be used for testing and comparison.

- **GridCUDA:** This technology also offers access to remote GPUs in a cluster, but supports an old CUDA version (2.3). Moreover, there is currently no publicly available version of GridCuda that can be used for testing.
- **DS-CUDA:** This solution integrates a more recent version of CUDA (4.1) and includes specific communication support for InfiniBand. However, DS-CUDA presents several strong limitations, such as not allowing data transfers with pinned memory or limiting the maximum size of data transfers to 32MB.
- **Shadowfax II:** This solution is still under development, not presenting a stable version yet and its public information is not updated to reflect the current code status.

Among the several GPU virtualization solutions described in our exploration about how to provide GPGPU services to VMs, we will select the rCUDA remote GPU virtualization solution because of two reasons. First, it supports the latest CUDA version whereas the rest of GPU virtualization solutions either support old CUDA versions or support versions that are completely obsolete nowadays. Second, among the several publicly available GPU virtualization solutions, rCUDA is the one that presents the best performance, as shown in Figure 2. This figure presents a comprehensive comparison among the three publicly available GPU virtualization solutions: DS-CUDA, rCUDA, and gVirtuS. The figure also shows the performance of CUDA as the baseline reference. Notice that the performance of DS-CUDA, rCUDA, and gVirtuS is normalized to that of CUDA. The well-known bandwidthTest benchmark from the NVIDIA CUDA Samples (NVIDIA, 2014) has been employed. The reason for using bandwidth for measuring performance is that, when transferring data between main memory and GPU memory, data copy sizes are, in general, large (in the order of MB). The throughput of these large data transfers is mostly influenced by achieved bandwidth, which thus turns out to be the most limiting factor regarding the performance of remote GPU virtualization solutions. Consequently, other metrics such as latency become less relevant in this context.

The experimental platform used in the performance experiments depicted in Figure 2 is the one presented in the later section devoted to describe the testbeds used in this work, although no virtual machine has been used in the experiments in Figure 2 in order to simplify the tests. In this way, the bandwidth test was run in a native domain whereas the server side of the several middleware systems considered was executed in a remote computer. The InfiniBand FDR network technology was used to connect both computers. Therefore, both the rCUDA and DS-CUDA frameworks made use of the InfiniBand Verbs API. In the case of gVirtuS, given that it is not able to take advantage of the InfiniBand Verbs API, TCP/IP over InfiniBand was used.

One additional consideration to be made regarding the experiments shown in Figure 2 is that the three GPU virtualization solutions analyzed support different versions of CUDA. In this regard, DS-CUDA is compatible with CUDA 4.1, gVirtuS supports the old CUDA 2.3 version and rCUDA supports CUDA 6.5. Thus, each of the considered solutions in this experiment has been analyzed with the respective version of CUDA supported. In this regard, it is important to remark that, in order to avoid introducing additional noise in this particular test, we have previously compared the bandwidth attained by the three versions of CUDA and results show that differences in performance for the bandwidth test are negligible from one CUDA version to another.

Several conclusions can be derived from the results presented in Figure 2. First, it can be seen that CUDA presents the highest performance when pinned memory is used in the client node, as shown in Figures 2a) and 2b) for the host to device and device to host directions, respectively. In both cases at-

Figure 2. Performance comparison among three different GPU virtualization solutions: gVirtuS, DS-CUDA, and rCUDA. The comparison is performed in terms of attained bandwidth. The performance of CUDA is also depicted. Tests have been carried out in native domains with the hardware and software settings described in the later section, devoted to introduce the testbeds. a) Shows the performance of data copies from host pinned memory to device memory. b) Depicts throughput for data transfers from device memory to host pinned memory. c) Presents the performance of transfers from host pageable memory to device memory. d) Shows the performance of data copies from device memory to host pageable memory. Bandwidth results for rCUDA, gVirtuS, and DS-CUDA are normalized to that of CUDA

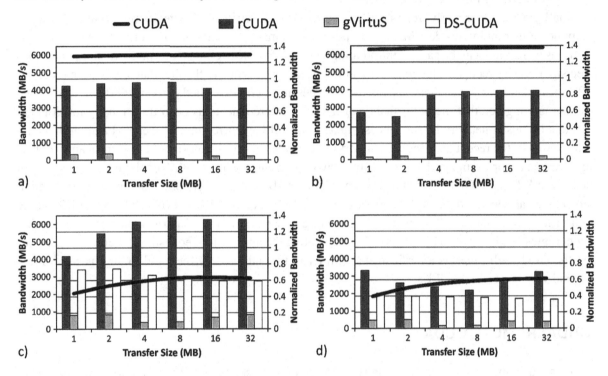

tained bandwidth is around 6000 MB/s. Notice that this bandwidth is reduced for copies using pageable memory in the client, as depicted in Figures 2c) and 2d). Second, Figure 2 shows that rCUDA presents better performance than the other two remote GPU virtualization solutions. Actually, for copies from host to device memory using pageable memory rCUDA also provides more performance than CUDA. This is a well-known effect thoroughly described in several works on rCUDA, such as (Peña, 2014). The reason for this improved performance is the use of an efficient pipelined communication based on the use of internal pre-allocated pinned memory buffers, which are known to provide more bandwidth than pageable memory, as shown in Figure 2c). On the other hand, notice that both rCUDA and DS-CUDA make use of the InfiniBand Verbs API. This API provides a noticeable high performance given that data transfers are directly managed by the InfiniBand network adapters. Thus, both rCUDA and DS-CUDA have access to all the bandwidth available in the InfiniBand interconnect. However, although rCUDA is able to struggle an important fraction of the available bandwidth, DS-CUDA presents much less performance. Therefore, it must be assumed that the difference in attained bandwidth is due to the different ways that both GPU virtualization solutions manage the InfiniBand interconnect. It should also be remarked that DS-CUDA supports neither memory copies larger than 32MB nor the use of pinned memory. On the other hand, notice that the performance of gVirtuS is extremely low, despite of using the InfiniBand fabric. One may think that this low performance is due to the fact that gVirtuS is using TCP/IP over InfiniBand instead of using the InfiniBand Verbs. It is well-known that using TCP/IP over InfiniBand clearly achieves lower performance than the use of the InfiniBand Verbs API. However, according to our measurements with the iperf3 tool (iperf3, 2015), InfiniBand FDR provides around 1190 MB/s, which is a noticeably larger bandwidth than the one attained by gVirtuS in our experiments. Hence, the low performance of this middleware is not due to the use of TCP/IP over InfiniBand but to the way it internally manages communications.

Finally, in order to properly understand the approach presented in this chapter for providing GPU access to applications running inside VMs, it is important to remark that although remote GPU virtualization solutions were known in the past for introducing a non-negligible overhead, this performance penalty has been significantly reduced. Notice that the initial overhead was due to the fact that applications access a GPU located in a remote cluster node instead of accessing a GPU attached to the local PCI Express link. In this regard, given that the performance of the PCIe interconnect has been traditionally much larger than that of cluster network fabrics, accessing a remote GPU incurred in a noticeable bandwidth reduction. However, the recent advances in networking technologies have contributed to significantly reduce this overhead. For example, the rCUDA framework currently achieves 98% of the total bandwidth of the NVIDIA Tesla K40 GPU when InfiniBand Connect-IB dual-port network adapters are used. Similar percentages are obtained when the previous technology generation is used (NVIDIA Tesla K20 along with InfiniBand ConnectX-3 adapters). As can be seen, with current high performance interconnection technologies, the bandwidth of the path communicating the application requesting acceleration services and the GPU itself presents a performance similar to that attained by the local PCIe link used in the original way of accessing GPUs.

rCUDA: REMOTE CUDA

As revisited in the previous section, the rCUDA technology stands out among the several GPU virtualization solutions. Furthermore, given that the other GPU virtualization frameworks support obsolete versions of CUDA, the rCUDA solution is the only one able to properly execute the applications used in this study. These circumstances have motivated its use in this work. In this section rCUDA is introduced in more detail.

The rCUDA middleware supports version 6.5 of CUDA. Additionally, it supports both the Runtime and Driver APIs of CUDA (except for graphics functions) and also provides support for the different CUDA libraries, like cuFFT, cuBLAS, cuSPARSE, etc. rCUDA is binary compatible with CUDA, what means that CUDA programs do not require to be modified in order to use the rCUDA middleware. Additionally, the rCUDA server has been devised to provide GPU-acceleration to several concurrent remote clients that simultaneously demand access to the GPU. This is accomplished by creating independent GPU contexts, which are assigned to different clients (Peña, 2014). Contrariwise, a single rCUDA client can make use of several rCUDA servers located at different nodes of the cluster in order to enjoy several GPUs.

Regarding communications between rCUDA clients and servers, this middleware provides specific support for several network fabrics (Peña, 2014). Support for several underlying interconnects is achieved by means of a set of runtime-loadable, network-specific communication modules. These modules have been carefully hand crafted in order to attain as much performance as possible from the underlying network. The current version of rCUDA includes two different communication modules: one intended for TCP/IP compatible networks and another one specifically implemented for the InfiniBand interconnect. Additionally, regardless of the exact interconnect used, data exchange between main memory in the client side and GPU memory in the remote server is pipeline in order to attain higher performance, as explained in (Peña, 2014). Furthermore, internal pipelined buffers within rCUDA make use of preallocated pinned memory because this kind of memory provides higher throughput.

With respect to the InfiniBand communication module, it makes use of the InfiniBand Verbs API. This API provides two different communication approaches: the channel semantics and the memory semantics. The first one comprises the regular send/received operations usually found in networking environments. On the other hand, the second approach makes use of RDMA operations where the communicating side initiating the RDMA operation specifies the source and destination memory regions of the data transfer and then the RDMA engines in both communicating ends collaborate in order to achieve zero-copy transfers with no involvement of the CPUs. The rCUDA middleware uses both communication approaches in order to improve performance, selecting one or the other depending on the exact communication task to be carried out (Peña, 2014).

TESTBEDS USED FOR THE Xen AND KVM VMMS

In this work we consider the use of the rCUDA remote GPU virtualization technology in the context of Xen and KVM VMMs. In this section we describe the Xen and KVM VMMs and also present the testbeds used for the experiments. Notice, however, that the Xen and KVM VMMs present different characteristics, what directly influences the test platforms used for each VMM.

The Xen and KVM VMMs

Figures 3 and 4 show, respectively, the configuration usually found in Xen and KVM environments where a computer hosts several VMs. The computer hardware is composed of several devices, such as a GPU and an Ethernet network adapter.

In the Xen configuration, depicted in Figure 3, the hypervisor can be found on top of the hardware. This hypervisor is a very thin software layer that provides the basic virtualization features to the upper VMs. These VMs are denoted in the figure as Dom0 and DomU$_i$. The Dom0 VM is a special VM preconfigured to use the Xen Linux kernel. This special VM provides system administrators with a configuration and management interface to the underlying hypervisor. On the other hand, the DomU$_i$ VMs are regular and unprivileged VMs that can be assigned to users. Regarding the devices shown in the figure, it can be seen that the network adapter is owned by the Dom0 VM. This VM makes use of a software bridge in order to provide connectivity among the real device and the DomU$_i$ VMs. Regarding the GPU, the figure shows how it is assigned in an exclusive way to one of the DomU$_i$ VMs by making use of the PCI passthrough mechanism.

The KVM configuration shown in Figure 4 is similar to the Xen configuration, the main difference being that the KVM VMM does not make use of a thin software layer on top of the hardware, but a regular Linux operating system is used instead. This Linux operating system is extended with the KVM virtualization extensions along with the qemu software in order to convert it into the KVM VMM or,

Figure 3. Typical configuration of a Xen-based system showing how the Ethernet adapter and the GPU available in the host are provided to VMs

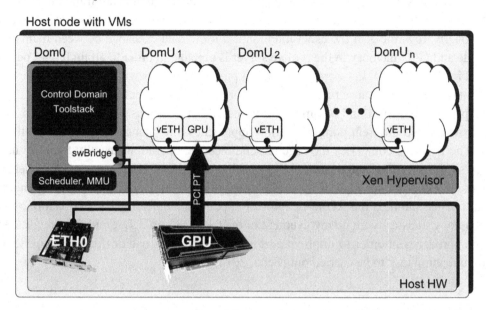

Figure 4. Typical configuration of a KVM-based system showing how the Ethernet adapter and the GPU available in the host are provided to VMs

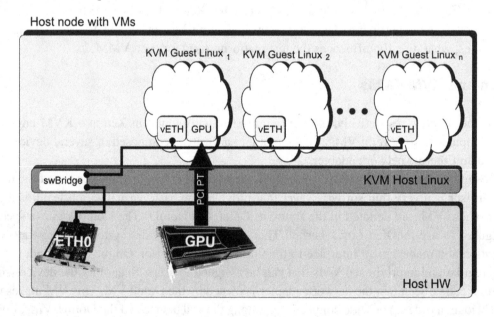

using the same terminology as for the Xen configuration, the KVM hypervisor. In this way, the KVM configuration does not need an especial VM to provide management and configuration interfaces.

Testbeds

After reviewing the basic configuration of Xen and KVM systems, we can proceed with the description of the testbeds used in our experiments. Two different testbeds have been used. In the first one, VMs on a single node access a GPU located in the computer hosting them by making use of the internal virtual network. In the second testbed, it is assumed that an InfiniBand fabric is already present in the cluster. This already existing network allows VMs to access a GPU owned by another node in the cluster. Next we describe both test platforms in more detail.

In the first testbed, depicted in Figure 5, the rCUDA middleware uses the virtual network provided by Xen or KVM VMMs to access the real GPU. The different approach between Xen and KVM VMMs requires a different configuration for this testbed. In the case of Xen (Figure 5a)), the GPU cannot be used at the hypervisor level and hence the rCUDA server must be executed inside a $DomU_i$ VM (Dom0 VM cannot be used because NVIDIA does not provide support for the Xen Linux kernel). The PCI passthrough mechanism will be used in order to assign the GPU, in an exclusive way, to one of the $DomU_i$ VMs. We will assume that the GPU is assigned to the $DomU_1$ VM. This VM will make use of the server part of the rCUDA middleware in order to provide the other $DomU_i$ VMs with GPU access. Accordingly, the other $DomU_i$ VMs will use the client side of the rCUDA solution in order to access the GPU. To that end, they will employ the virtual Xen network along with the TCP/IP based communications provided by rCUDA.

In the case for KVM (Figure 5b)), given that the KVM VMM is a complete Linux operating system providing full functionality, the rCUDA server can be directly executed within it. In this way, in order to provide GPU access to the different KVM VMs in execution in the host, the rCUDA server will be installed at the KVM VMM. Another important difference is that the PCI passthrough mechanism is

Figure 5. Single-node testbed, where VMs employ the virtual network to access the rCUDA server by means of the TCP/IP protocol stack. Figure 5a) depicts the single-node testbed when Xen VMs are considered and Figure 5b) shows the same testbed when KVM VMs are used

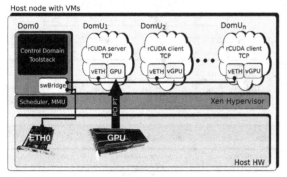
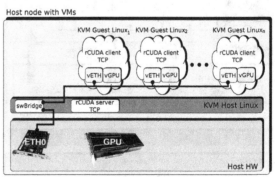

a)   b)

not necessary to provide the rCUDA server with GPU access. In this case the rCUDA server will use the GPU as any other regular process in the system could do.

With respect to the second platform test, which is depicted in Figure 6, an InfiniBand network already available in the cluster is used in order to access the GPU, which is located in a different node than that executing the VMs. In this case the original firmware in the InfiniBand network adapter has been replaced by a new version provided by the network manufacturer, according to the Mellanox User's Guide (Mellanox, 2015). This replacement allows the network card to provide several virtual instances of it. These virtual instances are usually referred to as virtual functions (VF). The real instance of the network device is still available. In this context, the real instance is known as physical function (PF). Notice that having several virtual copies of the InfiniBand card allows assigning each of them, in an exclusive way, to a different VM by making use of the PCI passthrough technique. Furthermore, in this second scenario, communications between rCUDA clients inside VMs and the remote rCUDA server can take advantage of the InfiniBand Verbs API instead of being based on the use of the TCP/IP protocol stack. The use of the InfiniBand Verbs API will further increase network performance, attaining almost all the effective bandwidth provided by network card. Moreover, notice that the rCUDA server is being executed in a native domain. That is, the remote computer has not been virtualized. Accordingly, the firmware of the InfiniBand network adapter of that computer has not been replaced by the new one in order to provide virtualization features, given that they are not required in this computer. Furthermore, notice that although the testbeds shown in Figures 5 and 6 consider the use of a single GPU, it could also be possible to share multiple GPUs among the VMs by using the rCUDA middleware. From the point of view of the rCUDA clients the exact location of the GPUs is not a concern. In this regard it could even be possible to share several GPUs, some of them located in a remote cluster node and some of them owned by a VM.

Figure 6. Testbed using a remote GPU. This testbed represents the case when an InfiniBand fabric is available, and thus VMs use such interconnect to access a remote rCUDA server. Figure 6a) depicts the testbed when Xen VMs are considered and Figure 6b) shows the same testbed when KVM VMs are used

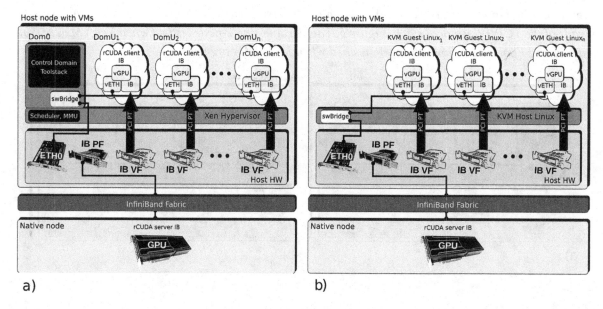

Regarding the hardware used in the experiments, it is based on the use of 1027GR-TRF Supermicro servers. Three nodes have been used. One of them will host the VMs. The other two nodes will not make use of VMs but will execute the tests in the native domain. One of these two nodes will host the rCUDA server shown in Figure 6 and the other one will be used for several comparison purposes. All the three servers leverage two Intel Xeon E5-2620 v2 processors (six cores with Ivy Bridge architecture) operating at 2.1 GHz and 32 GB of DDR3 SDRAM memory at 1600 MHz. They also include a Mellanox ConnectX-3 VPI single-port InfiniBand network adapter. The three nodes are interconnected by a Mellanox Switch SX6025 (InfiniBand FDR compatible), which provides a maximum data rate of 56 Gb/s. The nodes also include each of them an NVIDIA Tesla K20 GPU.

The software configuration used in these nodes is the following one. When Xen VMM is used, SUSE Linux Enterprise Server 11 SP3 (x86_64) was installed in the three nodes with the kernel version 3.0.76-0-11 and the Xen version 4.2.2. was used in the server hosting the VMs. Additionally, the Dom0 kernel was appropriately recompiled in order to activate the Xen options. In the case of KVM, the GNU/Linux CentOS 7.0 distribution has been used, along with kernel version 3.10.0-123.20.1.el7.x86-64. Notice that the KVM version is the same one, given that the KVM VMM is already integrated into the Linux version used. Therefore, the same Linux and kernel versions were used inside the KVM VMs. Regarding the network and GPU software, the Mellanox OFED 2.3-1.0.1 (InfiniBand drivers and administrative tools) was used, along with CUDA 6.5 and NVIDIA driver 340.29. rCUDA 5.0 was used, which supports CUDA 6.5. Finally, VMs were configured to make use of 4 cores and 12 GB of RAM memory.

NETWORK PERFORMANCE OBSERVED BY VMS

One of the key contributors to overall performance when making use of the remote GPU virtualization mechanism is the bandwidth of the underlying network connecting clients and servers. More accurately, the bandwidth attained by the path between the main memory in the client computer and the GPU memory in the remote server will mostly determine the performance of the remote GPU virtualization solution. In this section we analyze the performance of the network fabrics used in the later experiments. Remember that two different scenarios are considered. In the first one, the internal virtual network within the VMM is used. In the second scenario, the InfiniBand FDR network fabric is used to interconnect rCUDA clients and servers. We will explore both scenarios for each of the VMMs considered in this work. The results presented in this section will allow us to better understand the behavior of rCUDA within Xen and KVM VMs in later sections.

Performance Attained by the Internal VMM Network

As described in the previous section, when the applications demanding GPGPU services access the GPU located in the same host that is executing the VMs, the internal virtual network is used along with the TCP/IP protocol stack. Hence, the TCP/IP communications module of rCUDA should be selected for communicating rCUDA clients and server. Therefore, in order to assess the performance of the network connecting client and server sides, the performance of the TCP protocol over this virtual network should be analyzed.

To that end, the iperf3 tool (iperf3, 2015) has been used. Figure 7 depicts the performance reported by this tool as transfer size increases. The experiments carried out for gathering the bandwidth numbers in the figure consist of two different VMs located in the same host computer exchanging data with each other. In this regard, the client side of the iperf tool was run in one of the VMs whereas the sever side of the iperf tool was executed in the other VM. Notice that the Supermicro server used in the experiments presents two CPU sockets. Thus, the experiments should be carefully carried out in order to avoid that both VMs are placed in the same socket. This would introduce several side effects related to the use of the L3 cache of the socket, hence providing bandwidth numbers noticeably higher than usual. Therefore, for the experiments shown in Figure 7, one of the VMs was forced to be executed in one of the CPU sockets (NUMA node) whereas the other VM was located in the other socket, both belonging to the same machine. On the other hand, the performance of the 1Gigabit Ethernet network adapter included in the servers, when used from the inside of the VMs, is also included for comparison purposes. In this case, the virtualization features already included in the Xen and KVM VMMs have been used in order to provide the Ethernet adapter to VMs. It can be seen in the figure that the virtual network provides much higher bandwidth than the external 1Gbps Ethernet fabric, achieving even higher bandwidth than a 10 Gbps Ethernet network. In this regard, the internal virtual network within Xen provides a maximum bandwidth around 1600 MB/s, whereas the internal virtual network within KVM provides a maximum bandwidth of 1700 MB/s. Notice also that starting from transfer sizes equal to 32 KB, the performance of both virtual networks remain steady.

The higher performance of the internal virtual networks with respect to the external 1Gbps Ethernet fabric was actually expected, given that the internal switch used to interconnect VMs inside the same host is a software switch, which basically has to carry out memory copies inside the host computer without really transferring information across any wire (except those for accessing the RAM memory from the memory controller of the CPU).

Performance Attained by the External InfiniBand Network

Remember from Figures 6a) and 6b) that in the second scenario considered in this work it is assumed that an InfiniBand fabric is already present in the cluster. Thus, applications being executed inside VMs access a GPU located in another node of the cluster thanks to that InfiniBand interconnect. This

Figure 7. Bandwidth attained by the virtual network among VMs. The use of Xen and KVM environments is considered in the figure

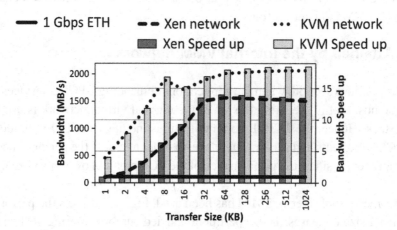

configuration is supposed to provide better performance than using the internal virtual network given that the bandwidth of the InfiniBand fabric is higher than that of the internal VMM network. On the other hand, notice that the performance study of the external InfiniBand interconnect requires a wider analysis than the one carried out for the internal virtual network. The reason is that InfiniBand cards provide several possibilities for this study, given that the InfiniBand Verbs API are used over the virtual instances of the InfiniBand cards in order to communicate rCUDA clients and servers. In this regard, the InfiniBand Verbs API allows the use of three different approaches for exchanging data between both communicating ends: regular send operations, RDMA reads and RDMA writes. Notice that the rCUDA middleware makes use of the three communication primitives. In this way, CUDA commands, including their parameters, forwarded from the client side to the rCUDA server, as well as CUDA responses sent in the opposite direction, make use of regular send operations. On the other hand, memory copies between the client main memory and the remote GPU memory in the server make use of the RDMA operations. More precisely, for transferring data from the client memory to the GPU memory, RDMA read operations are executed from the rCUDA server to the client side. On the contrary, for copying data from the GPU memory to the client main memory, RDMA write operations are used. Hence, the bandwidth attained by the three different methods for exchanging data must be explored. Therefore, in order to carry out the performance analysis, the ib_write_bw, ib_read_bw, and ib_send_bw tests from the perftest benchmarks, developed by the OpenFabrics Alliance and distributed within the Mellanox OFED software distribution, were employed. This way the use that the rCUDA framework makes of the InfiniBand fabric is mimicked. Notice that the ib_write_bw and ib_read_bw tests make use of the memory semantics (that is, RDMA write and RDMA read) whereas the ib_send_bw benchmark uses the channel semantics (that is, regular send and receive operations). Finally, in order to put their performance into the right perspective, the bandwidth of the virtualized InfiniBand card when using these three data transfer mechanisms should be compared against the performance of the non-virtualized network adapter. Firstly we present the bandwidth attained in the context of Xen VMs, and later the performance achieved when KVM VMs are used.

In the case of Xen VMs, Figure 8 shows the bandwidth achieved by the InfiniBand card for different transfer sizes in the scenario depicted in Figure 6a). The behavior of the memory semantics (RDMA) is shown in Figure 8a), where only results for the RDMA write case are presented, given that the RDMA read benchmark provided very similar performance. Figure 8b) shows the channel semantics bandwidth (non-RDMA) when using the ib_send_bw benchmark. For comparison purposes, in the experiments carried out with this scenario, we have also considered the performance attained when the tests are executed in the Dom0 VM using both the physical function of the InfiniBand adapter and also one of the virtual functions. The results labeled as "PF" and "VF" refer to the use of the physical and virtual functions, respectively, from the Dom0 VM. In a similar way, results labeled as "VM" refer to the use of the InfiniBand network from the inside of a regular DomU VM. Finally, results labeled as "Native" have been included for comparison purposes and refer to the use of a non-virtualized InfiniBand card from a native domain. Notice that, in Figure 8, the performance of the "Native" experiments are considered as the reference for the other three cases under study, which are depicted in the figure as a percentage of the difference with respect to the performance attained in the "Native" configuration. Presenting the results in this way allows better displaying the small differences among them.

As it can be seen in Figure 8, the performance of the InfiniBand card, when used in the four different configurations analyzed, is very similar. Actually, differences with respect to the baseline configuration

Figure 8. InfiniBand bandwidth tests using ConnectX-3 network cards executed in the different scenarios under study. Xen VMs are used in the experiments, which have been carried out in the scenario presented in Figure 6a). Figure 8a) presents results for the InfiniBand RDMA write bandwidth test whereas Figure 8b) depicts the performance attained by the InfiniBand send bandwidth test

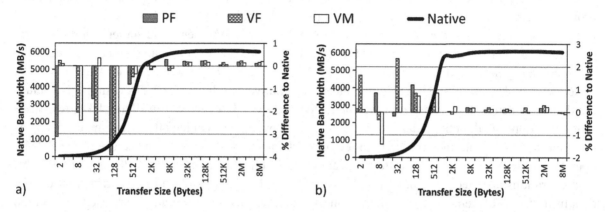

remain in the range from -4% up to 3%. Furthermore, as transfer size increases, differences become smaller. In this regard, for transfer sizes starting at 2KB, differences in performance are close to zero.

In the case of KVM VMs, similar results are obtained, as shown in Figure 9. It can be seen in this figure that differences in performance remain within a similar range as for the Xen VMs.

PERFORMANCE OF rCUDA WITHIN VMS

Once the bandwidth of the underlying interconnects has been characterized in both the Xen and KVM VM environments, in this section the performance of the rCUDA remote GPU virtualization middleware is explored. This exploration is focused on the context of the Xen and KVM VMs, although other contexts are also considered in order to perform a comprehensive analysis.

Figure 9. InfiniBand bandwidth tests using ConnectX-3 network cards executed in the different scenarios under study. KVM VMs are used in the experiments, which have been carried out in the scenario presented in Figure 6b). Figure 9a) presents results for the InfiniBand RDMA write bandwidth test whereas Figure 9b) depicts the performance attained by the InfiniBand send bandwidth test

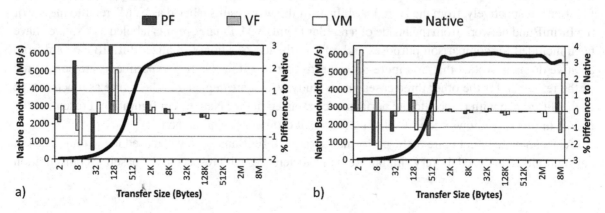

To that end, the performance of CUDA is used as the baseline reference, so that the performance attained by rCUDA is properly put into the right perspective. Notice that in this analysis CUDA is used as the reference because it is the purpose of any remote GPU virtualization solution to minimize its own overhead with respect to CUDA. Furthermore, it is important to remark that the analysis carried out in this section will be performed from the point of view of attained bandwidth, given that this metric is the most limiting factor regarding the performance of remote GPU virtualization solutions, as discussed in the background section. Hence, the bandwidthTest benchmark from the NVIDIA CUDA Samples will be used for copying data from main memory in the client VM to the memory of the Tesla K20 GPU, which could be located either in the same host or in other cluster node, depending on the exact scenario considered.

One more concern that should be addressed in this study is which is the exact hardware/software configuration that should be used for gathering bandwidth numbers for CUDA, so that they are the right reference. In this regard, the absolute reference would be the execution of an application in a native domain. From this starting point, the application might be moved to a VM and some performance might be expected to be lost. Thus, the performance of CUDA in a native domain accessing the GPU attached to that node should be considered as the right reference. However, notice that from a different point of view, one may consider that the right CUDA performance reference should be that achieved by an application when executed within a VM that has been assigned a GPU by making use of the PCI passthrough mechanism. The key point for this different perspective is that in this work we are providing GPU access to applications being executed within VMs and, hence, the original way to access a GPU from the inside of a VM is by assigning it the GPU by means of the PCI passthrough technique. Given that both points of view seem to be reasonable, in the performance analysis carried out in this section we will use both configurations, so that a complete analysis is carried out.

In order to use the proper hardware/software configuration for the baseline CUDA reference, on the one hand we made use of a configuration that makes use of the GPU attached to the node executing the bandwidthTest benchmark, in the traditional way and within a native domain (no Xen or KVM VM is used). These executions were carried out in the node that is used as remote rCUDA server in Figures 6a) and 6b). It is important to remark that the rCUDA software was disabled in order to avoid any kind of interference in the test. Results for this scenario will be referred to as "CUDA" in the figures. On the other hand, in order to satisfy the second point of view, when CUDA is used from the inside of a VM that owns the GPU by means of the PCI passthrough mechanism, the label "CUDA VM PT" will be used. The performance from these two scenarios will be used as the reference for the rCUDA experiments.

Regarding the rCUDA performance tests, when this middleware is used between native domains (no VM is involved) making use of the InfiniBand network, the label "rCUDA non-VM" will be used. Notice that this scenario is not strictly required for assessing the performance of rCUDA when used from the inside of VMs, but it is included for comparison purposes. Finally, when VMs are involved in the tests, the label "rCUDA VM IB" will be used to refer to the performance of rCUDA when a remote cluster node is used to execute the rCUDA server, according to scenarios depicted in Figures 6a) and 6b). On the contrary, when rCUDA is used by VMs in order to access the GPU installed in the host executing the VMs, according to Figures 5a) and 5b), the label "rCUDA VM Local" will be used. As in the previous section, we first present in Figure 10 the performance analysis carried out in the context of Xen VMs and later the study that analyzes the performance of rCUDA in the context of KVM VMs is presented in Figure 11.

Figure 10. Bandwidth tests for copies between host and device memory, using CUDA and the rCUDA middleware in the context of Xen VMs. Tests have been carried out in the different scenarios depicted in Figures 3, 5a), and 6a) as well as in native domains. Figure 10a) shows the performance of data copies from host pinned memory to device memory. Figure 10b) depicts throughput for data transfers from device memory to host pinned memory. Figure 10c) presents the performance of transfers from host pageable memory to device memory. Figure 10d) shows the performance of data copies from device memory to host pageable memory

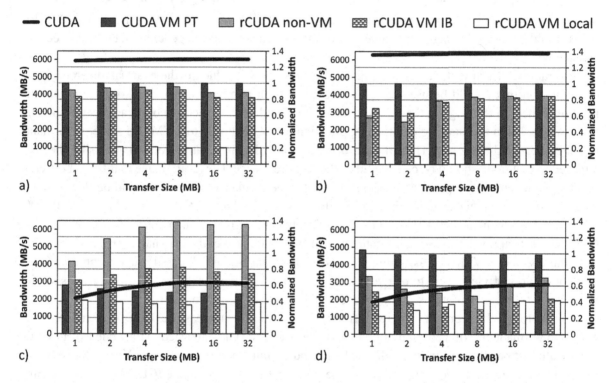

The bandwidth results for pinned memory, presented in Figures 10a) and 10b), show that the bandwidth attained for CUDA copies in the native domain and in the Xen VM using PCI passthrough present almost the same performance. In the case of rCUDA using InfiniBand to communicate with a remote GPU server, scenario shown in Figure 6a), a slightly smaller bandwidth is achieved when tests are executed from a Xen VM. Finally, when rCUDA is used employing the virtual network among VMs according to Figure 5a), maximum bandwidth for the CUDA memory copies is slightly lower than the one obtained when using the iperf tool, shown in Figure 7.

With respect to the use of pageable memory within Xen VMs, it can be seen in Figures 10c) and 10d) that in the case of copies from host memory to device memory, there is an important difference between the performance achieved by CUDA in the native domain and that obtained in the Xen VM using the PCI passthrough mechanism, since performance in the former doubles the bandwidth in the latter. Nevertheless, this effect does not appear in the opposite direction, where both scenarios present almost the same performance. Regarding the use of rCUDA when the InfiniBand network is leveraged, the ratio between the performance obtained in the native domain and that in the VM follows the same trend as for CUDA: the native domain attains twice the performance achieved in the VM. Notice, how-

Figure 11. Bandwidth tests for copies between host and device memory, using CUDA and the rCUDA middleware in the context of KVM VMs. Tests have been carried out in the different scenarios depicted in Figures 4, 5b), and 6b) as well as in native domains. a) Shows the performance of data copies from host pinned memory to device memory. b) Depicts throughput for data transfers from device memory to host pinned memory. c) Presents the performance of transfers from host pageable memory to device memory. d) Shows the performance of data copies from device memory to host pageable memory

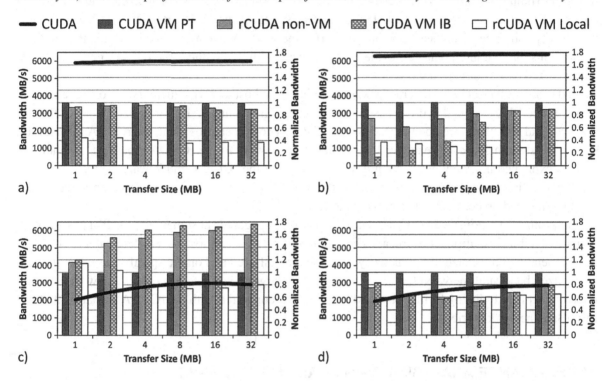

ever, that the beneficial effect commented in the Background Section and already analyzed in (Peña, 2014), does not appear when rCUDA is used within a Xen VM. Regarding the performance of rCUDA when the virtual network is used along with TCP/IP based communications, Figure 10c) shows that this scenario achieves the lowest bandwidth, as it was expected from the results shown in Figure 7. On the other hand, when the device-to-host direction is considered, results are quite different. First, the performance of the baseline CUDA and that of CUDA when used within a VM with PCI passthrough are very similar. Second, the performance of rCUDA in the native and virtualized domains follow the same trend as for the host-to-device direction, but now performance is noticeably reduced. Third, the bandwidth results of rCUDA when the virtual network is used are similar to the performance achieved in the opposite direction.

In summary, we can conclude that the bandwidth attained by PCI passthrough is almost identical to the one achieved by CUDA, except for copies from host pageable memory to device memory, where the bandwidth is reduced to the half. On the other hand, rCUDA over the Xen virtual network results in a very stable behavior in all the scenarios, the bandwidth being limited by the network performance (see Figure 7). Finally, the bandwidth obtained by rCUDA over an InifiniBand network is very close to that of CUDA when using pinned host memory, regardless whether accessing from a VM or not. In the case of pageable host memory, the bandwidth when accessing from a VM is reduced to the half of the one obtained by rCUDA without using VM. This reduction in the performance when involving the VM is more evident in the case of copies from device memory to host memory, where the bandwidth obtained by rCUDA using the VM is the same, regardless of using the Xen virtual network or the InfiniBand one.

In case KVM VMs are considered, Figure 11 presents the results for the same experiments carried out in Figure 10. In this case, we can observe that CUDA copies from pinned host memory to or from device memory to pinned host memory achieve a bandwidth over 6000 MB/s. The normalized bandwidth of the compared scenarios is very close to 1 showing a very small overhead. The rCUDA VM local scenario is the exception since we are using the internal virtual network. As we have already seen in the previous section, this internal interconnect provides a lower bandwidth that reduces the rCUDA performance to a normalized bandwidth around 0.4.

In the case of pageable host memory, when copying from host to device memory, we observe that the VM with the GPU assigned by PCI passthrough mechanism remains in the normalized bandwidth with a value equal to 1, therefore no overhead is appreciated. Those scenarios using the rCUDA middleware show a bandwidth speed up reaching 1.8 in some cases, owing to the rCUDA pipelined communication, as explained in a previous section devoted to present the rCUDA middleware. The exception to this bandwidth improvement is represented by the rCUDA VM local, which presents a limitation to the bandwidth speed up because of the internal network.

In the other direction, when copying data from device to pageable host memory, the PCI passthrough scenario exhibits insignificant overhead. The different rCUDA scenarios show different degree of overhead depending on the size of the memory area being transferred and on the specific case, leading to a normalized bandwidth between 0.5 and 0.8. In the two largest sizes, we can observe how the internal interconnect is introducing further bandwidth limitations compared with the rCUDA scenarios that use InfiniBand network fabric.

PERFORMANCE ANALYSIS USING REAL APPLICATIONS

In the previous sections it has been analyzed how the performance of the internal virtual VMM network and that of the InfiniBand ConnectX-3 network cards, when used from the inside of Xen and KVM VMs, influence the performance of the rCUDA remote GPU virtualization middleware. To that end, synthetic benchmarks were used. These benchmarks allow us to focus on specific characteristics of the remote GPU virtualization framework. However, remember that the real purpose of the study presented in this chapter is exploring the use of the remote GPU virtualization technology in order to provide CUDA acceleration to applications running inside VMs. Furthermore, this exploration should provide as an outcome the overhead experienced by applications when they access GPUs outside their VM by making use of a remote GPU virtualization middleware. Therefore, in this section it is analyzed how the performance attained by the interconnects analyzed in the previous sections, along with the use of Xen and KVM VMMs, influence the execution time of real applications. In order to carry out this exploration, four different applications are considered. These applications, which are listed in the NVIDIA GPU-Accelerated Applications Catalog (NVIDIA-app, 2014), are the following:

- **LAMMPS:** This application, further described in (Sandia, 2013) is a classic molecular dynamics simulator that can be used to model atoms or, more generically, as a parallel particle simulator at the atomic, mesoscopic, or continuum scale. For the tests shown in this section, it has been used the release from Dec. 9, 2014 of this application, along with the benchmarks in.eam and in.lj, which are automatically installed with the application. We run these benchmarks scaling them by a factor of 5 in all three dimensions (i.e., a problem size of 4 million atoms).

- **CUDA-MEME:** This application is a parallel formulation and implementation of the MEME motif discovery algorithm using the CUDA programming model. The complete description of this application can be found in (Liu, 2010). For the study in this section we have used its latest release, version 3.0.15, along with the test cases available in the application website (Liu, 2014).

- **CUDASW++:** This application, whose complete description can be found in (Liu, 2013), is a bioinformatics software for Smith-Waterman protein database searches that takes advantage of the massively parallel CUDA architecture of NVIDIA Tesla GPUs to perform sequence searches. In particular, we have used its latest release, version 3.1, for our study, along with the latest Swiss-Prot database and the example query sequences available in the application's website: http://cudasw.sourceforge.net.

- **GPU-BLAST:** This application, described in (Vouzis, 2010) has been designed to accelerate the gapped and ungapped protein sequence alignment algorithms of the NCBI-BLAST (http://www.ncbi.nlm.nih.gov) implementation using GPUs. It is integrated into the NCBI-BLAST code and produces identical results. We used release 1.1 in our experiments, where we have followed the installation instructions for sorting a database and creating a GPU database. To search the database, we then use the query sequences that come with the application package.

As in previous sections, we first analyze these applications in the context of Xen VMs and later we present a similar study conducted in the context of KVM VMs. Similar scenarios as in previous sections are explored. Thus, in the figures presented in this section, the label "CUDA" will refer to a scenario without VM, using regular CUDA in a native domain. The label "CUDA VM PT" will indicate that CUDA is used from the inside of a VM that owns the GPU by means of the PCI passthrough technique. The label "rCUDA non-VM" will refer to the performance of rCUDA when used between native domains (no VM is involved) making use of an InfiniBand network. Finally, when rCUDA is used and VMs are involved, the label "rCUDA VM IB" will refer to the performance of rCUDA when a remote cluster node is used to execute the rCUDA server over an InfiniBand network, whereas the label "rCUDA VM Local" will refer to a scenario where rCUDA is used by VMs in order to access the GPU installed in the host executing the VMs.

Figure 12 shows results regarding Xen VMs, whereas Figure 13 shows results concerning KVM VMs. As we can see, the results, in general, are the expected ones. In this manner, the best execution time is obtained when using regular CUDA from a native domain (labeled as "CUDA"), followed by CUDA used from inside a VM employing the PCI passthrough mechanism ("CUDA VM PT"). Next, rCUDA not involving VMs over an InfiniBand network ("rCUDA VM IB") achieves better performance and, finally, when rCUDA is used over the local network provided by the VM ("rCUDA VM Local") achieves the highest executions times.

For the sake of clarity, we present in Figure 14 the average overhead of the results shown in Figures 12 and 13. For so, we used as reference the results obtained when using regular CUDA not involving VMs (label "CUDA" in Figures 12 and 13). Regarding Xen-based systems, shown in Figure 14a), the overhead is, in general, below 6%. The two only exceptions are the LAMMPS and CUDA-MEME applications when using rCUDA from the inside of a Xen VM by means of the local network provided by Xen. This is due to the low performance provided by this network, as shown in Figure 7. With respect

Figure 12. Execution time of several applications when executed in different local and remote scenarios in the context of Xen VMs. Figure 12a) shows the results of LAMMPS application, Figure 12b) the results of CUDA-MEME, Figure 12c) the results of CUDASW++ and Figure 12d) the results of GPU-BLAST

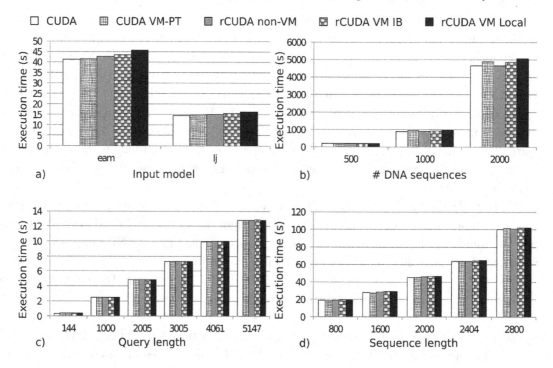

Figure 13. Execution time of several applications when executed in different local and remote scenarios in the context of KVM VMs. Figure 13a) shows the results of LAMMPS application, Figure 13b) the results of CUDA-MEME, Figure 13c) the results of CUDASW++ and Figure 13d) the results of GPU-BLAST

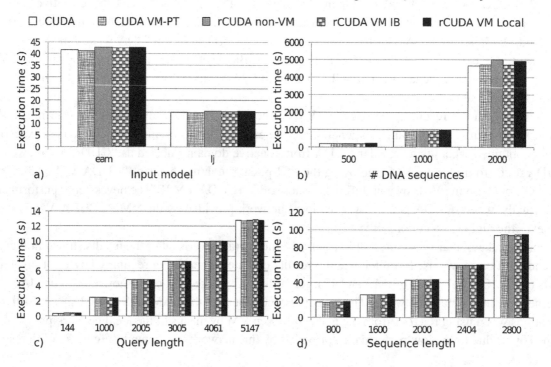

to the scenarios using KVM, shown in Figure 14b), the overhead is under 4% except for the case of CUDA-MEME when using rCUDA from the inside of a KVM VM over the virtual KVM network. As in the case of Xen VMs, this higher overhead is due to the low bandwidth attained by this network.

In summary, the results exposed in this section show that the use of remote GPU virtualization is an effective mechanism to provide GPU access to applications, featuring, in general, low overheads. With respect to the two different VMMs tested, the results when using KVM offered slightly better performance than the ones using Xen VM.

ADDING GPGPU SERVICES TO FEDERATED CLOUDS

Federated clouds can be seen as the merging of different kind of services, such as storage, database, computing, or web services. These services are offered by different cloud providers, which can be public or private. The result is a hybrid cloud computing environment. One possible scenario could be the one shown in Figure 15. As we can see, in this figure we introduce a new kind of service: GPGPU as a Service. It can be seen as a regular SaaS (Software as a Service), in which the users provide the input data, select the software, and the service consists in running the software with the input data, and returning the output data to the user. The main distinction from a regular SaaS is that the software provided by a GPGPU service can be accelerated by using GPUs.

In this section we exemplify one possible way of introducing GPGPU services to federated clouds using the approach exposed in previous sections. For the sake of clarity, we will consider a simple federated cloud composed by four cloud providers: a web service provider for handling user accounts and login to the federated cloud, a storage service provider to manage and support the storage layer, an HPC service provider to execute non-GPU-accelerated applications, and a GPGPU service provider offering GPU-accelerated software. With a view to connect this section with the rest of the chapter, the software services provided will be the same applications previously analyzed in this chapter (i.e., LAMMPS, CUDA-MEME, CUDASW++ and GPU-BLAST).

Figure 14. Average overhead with respect to executions with CUDA in a native domain for the four applications depicted in Figures 12 and 13. Figure 14a) shows the overhead when applications are executed in Xen-based systems whereas Figure 14b) depicts the overhead when a KVM VMM is used

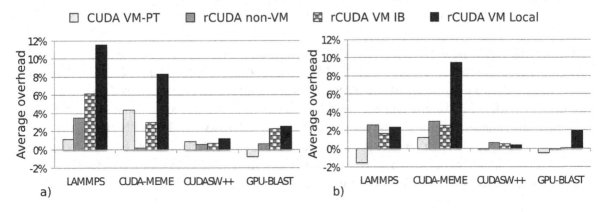

Figure 15. Federated cloud sample scenario

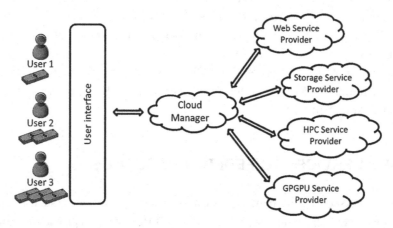

In first place, as shown in Figure 15, we could expect different kind of users. For instance, there will be users which do prefer to pay less money for a service and do not mind the time it takes to be completed (referred to as "User 1" in the figure). In contrast, there will be users willing to pay more money in order to have the best service quality (referred to as "User 3" in the figure). It is also possible that some users search for a good relation between quality of service and price (referred to as "User 2" in the figure).

In this context, Quality of Service (QoS) can be offered in several ways. For example, it is possible to have a centralized cloud federation broker to take decisions related to QoS. Another option will be having predefined agreements. After detailing how to install and configure rCUDA in next section, we then explain the second option, which is simpler than the first one, while the first option will be addressed in the section afterwards.

Installation and Configuration of rCUDA

In this section we detail how to install and configure rCUDA. The binaries of the rCUDA software are distributed within a tarball which has to be decompressed manually by the user. The steps to install rCUDA binaries are:

1. Decompressing the rCUDA package
2. Copying the rCUDA/lib folder to the client(s) node(s) (without GPU)
3. Copying the rCUDA folder to the server node (with GPU)

On the one hand, the rCUDA client is distributed in a set of files: "libcuda.so.$m.n$[1]", "libcudart. so.$x.y$[2]", "libcublas.so.$x.y$", "libcufft.so.$x.y$", "libcusparse.so.$x.y$", "libcurand.so.$x.y$" and "libcudnn. so.$x.y$". These shared libraries should be placed in those machines accessing remote GPGPU services. The LD_LIBRARY_PATH environment variable must be set according to the final location of these files (typically "/opt/rCUDA/lib", "/usr/local/rCUDA/lib", or "$HOME/rCUDA/lib", for instance). On the other hand, the rCUDA server is configured as a daemon (rCUDAd) that must be executed in those nodes offering GPGPU acceleration services. The rCUDA server listens in a TCP port for GPGPU requests. The LD_LIBRARY_PATH environment variable must also be set according to the location of the CUDA libraries (typically "/usr/local/cuda/lib64"). Notice that this is the path to the original CUDA libraries, not to the rCUDA ones.

In order to properly execute the applications using the rCUDA middleware, the following environment variables must be set at the client side:

- RCUDA_DEVICE_COUNT: indicates the number of GPUs granted to the application. The syntax for using this variable is: "RCUDA_DEVICE_COUNT=<number_of_GPUs>". For example, if the is assigned two remote GPUs: "RCUDA_DEVICE_COUNT=2"
- RCUDA_DEVICE_X: indicates where GPU X, for the client being configured, is located. The usage of this variable is: "RCUDA_DEVICE_X=<server[@<port>]>[:GPUnumber]". For instance, if GPUs 0 and 1 assigned to the current client are located at server "192.168.0.1" using the default rCUDA port (8308), then two variables should be set: "RCUDA_DEVICE_0=192.168.0.1:0; RCUDA_DEVICE_1=192.168.0.1:1"
- RCUDAPROTO: This environment variable must be set to "IB" in order to make use of the InfiniBand Verbs API. If this variable is not set, or if it is set to "TCP", then the TCP/IP sockets API will be used even if an InfiniBand network is available. For example: "RCUDAPROTO=IB" will use the InfiniBand Verbs API where "RCUDAPROTO=TCP" will use the TCP/IP sockets API over a TCP/IP compatible network (Ethernet, InfiniBand, etc.)

In the case of the rCUDA server, only the RCUDAPROTO environment variable must be set. The value of this variable must be the same at both the client and server side. Given that the rCUDA middleware is based on the use of these variables, it is very easy to comply with the elasticity requirement of virtual machine instances (Boob, 2014). In this manner, adding a new virtual GPU to a virtual machine simply consists in setting a new RCUDA_DEVICE_X environment variable and adjusting the RCUDA_DEVICE_COUNT variable. On the contrary, reducing the amount of GPUs that a given virtual machine can access can be achieved by reducing the value of the RCUDA_DEVICE_COUNT variable and adjusting the value of the RCUDA_DEVICE_X environment variables.

Managing the New GPGPU Service in Cloud Environments

In order to provide GPGPU in cloud environments, a new cloud service arises offering new endpoints in the form of GPUs able to execute CUDA code. As detailed in the previous section, the IP address of one GPU server and the GPU identifier number in that server are enough to access the new GPGPU service. Common mechanisms could be used to interact with this service, such as web-based management console and command line interface (CLI). Among other features, it is possible to allocate GPGPU services and manage them, as well as mapping GPGPU endpoints to instances. Regarding the instances configuration, it is required to install the rCUDA client in them and afterwards configure some environment variables prior to the execution of the accelerated applications. This configuration stage may either be performed in the virtual images that the instances will run, or by using one of the available mechanisms to execute commands at the instances start, such as basic shell script passed as user data (Amazon, 2015) or making use of more advanced options such as cloud-init (Canonical, 2015), both of them widely available in current cloud solutions. Furthermore, the GPGPU service could expose a RESTful API to allocate and manage resources. This API could also be used in order to allow instances to request GPGPU resources and to query the proper values they should use in the rCUDA related environment variables, bursting the possibilities of dynamically managing GPGPU resources from within the virtual instances.

Then, the required steps to deploy instances formations with access to CUDA computing capability are as follow:

1. Pre-allocate GPGPU resources to be used by the instances using the management console or the CLI offered by the cloud service provider
2. Deploy the instances formation to execute the GPU accelerated application
3. Installation of rCUDA client could be included in the instance's image. Otherwise, it should be installed when the instances boot, using a shell script as user data parameter or cloud-init commands
4. Each instance should receive the information about the GPGPU endpoints (i.e. number of remote GPUs, IP addresses, ports and GPU ids) and export it in the corresponding environment variables. This information could be passed using the shell script or cloud-init commands at boot time, or requested by the instance itself using the RESTful API of the GPGPU service
5. The instances are able to run applications with CUDA code being executed by the GPGPU service

Summarizing, all the necessary steps that allow an instance to access the GPGPU service are based on the installation of the rCUDA software and on setting the corresponding environment variables, showing this GPGPU service as a cloud-provider-agnostic solution. This would also avoid issues such as provider lock-in.

Once the GPGPU service layout is described, the number of different configurations enabled thanks to the flexibility offered by rCUDA is unveiled: some scenarios would take advantage of the availability of InfiniBand networks to allow flexible access to remote GPUs achieving high performance; other cases would make use of Gigabit Ethernet interconnects in order to offer a lower cost and performance solution; some cloud providers could warranty the execution of the instances in nodes owning GPUs, what would provide CUDA applications with access to the accelerator by leveraging the virtual network provided by the VMM, thus achieving a compromise between price and performance.

Federated Clouds with Predefined Agreements

In this section we assume that there are predefined agreements in order to decide which cloud provider attends each user. In this manner, following our example from Figure 15, there are two different cloud providers able to provide HPC services. These two providers are the "HPC Service Provider" on one hand and the "GPGPU Service Provider" on the other. The first one, which does not offer GPU acceleration, will be responsible for offering HPC services to users requiring a lower QoS level whereas the second one will service customers requiring a higher QoS level thanks to the GPU acceleration it provides. Furthermore, the "GPGPU Service Provider" will be composed, in turn, by two different cloud providers, as shown in Figure 16: one for users requiring a medium QoS level (referred to as "GPGPU Service Provider 1" in the figure), and another one for high QoS (referred to as "GPGPU Service Provider 2" in the figure). We will assume that, following the directions of the predefined agreements, services requested from "User 1" will be provided by "HPC Service Provider", the requests from "User 2" by "GPGPU Service Provider 1", and the ones from "User 3" by "GPGPU Service Provider 2".

Figure 17 presents the HPC and GPGPU Service Providers in more detail. Regarding the "HPC Service Provider", shown in Figure 17a), it can be seen as a high performance computing cluster composed

Figure 16. Detail of the GPGPU service provider shown in Figure 15

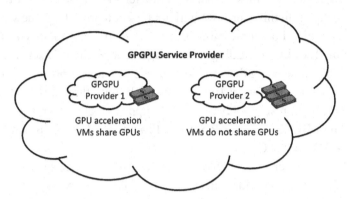

Figure 17. Detail of the different configurations of HPC and GPGPU service providers from Figure 16

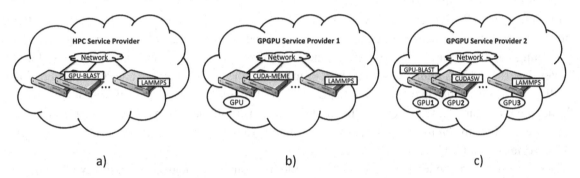

of several nodes similar to the ones used in previous experiments, but without featuring GPUs. This means that services offered by this provider will not have GPU acceleration and, therefore, the QoS will be lower. Notice that applications such as LAMMPS or GPU-BLAST can be executed without being accelerated by GPUs, although some performance would be obviously lost.

With respect to "GPGPU Service Provider 1", shown in Figure 17b), we can think about it as the same HPC cluster as in Figure 17a) but in this case some of the nodes have installed a GPU. In this way, one GPU will be shared among several nodes. This implies that the QoS will be better than when using the "HPC Service Provider". Nevertheless, given that GPUs are shared among several nodes, the performance will be lower than if GPUs were not shared.

Finally, "GPGPU Service Provider 2", shown in Figure 17c) would be an HPC cluster similar to the previous one but, in this case, each node has its own GPU and it is used exclusively by only one virtual instance at a time. Therefore, this will turn into the best QoS in our sample scenario.

Federated Clouds with Brokers

In the context of hybrid cloud computing environments, federated cloud brokers can be used to regulate the access to resources supplied by the different cloud providers, dynamically balancing and scheduling the load among them. For this purpose, different models can be used to perform such regulation, as, for instance, the ones presented in (Samaan, 2014), (Rochwerger, 2009), or (Goiri, 2012), to name only a few. In this section we explain how these models can benefit from the flexibility provided by the approach exposed in this chapter. In this sense, we will not focus on providing a new model or detailing the existing ones, but in explaining how these models can use the rCUDA GPU virtualization middleware to improve the degree of flexibility regarding the management of GPGPU services providers.

To this end, we will continue using the sample scenario previously presented in Figures 15, 16, and 17. As before, we have three kinds of users (types 1, 2 and 3), with three different types of QoS requirements (low, medium and high, respectively). We will suppose that: "User 1" is running two applications, LAMMPS and GPU-BLAST, in "HCP Service Provider"; "User 2" is running two applications, LAMMPS and CUDA-MEME, in "GPGPU Service Provider 1"; and "User 3" is running three applications, LAMMPS, GPU-BLAST and CUDASW++, in "GPGPU Service Provider 2".

In the event that "HPC Service Provider" decides to consolidate some of its nodes, there already exist a lot of solutions allowing VM migration, (Li, 2013), (Xu, 2011), (Wang, 2010). Therefore, the current active services (GPU-BLAST and/or LAMMPS) could be migrated to one single node, and the rest of the nodes could be switched off.

In contrast, if "GPGPU Service Provider 1" or "GPGPU Service Provider 2" will decide to consolidate some of its nodes, as far as we are concerned, there are no solutions capable of migrating VM which are running GPGPU applications. However, when virtualizing GPUs with the approach exposed in this chapter (i.e., the rCUDA middleware), the task of migrating the GPU context of a GPGPU application is simplified. The reason lies in the fact that rCUDA internally has all the necessary information to properly migrate the GPU part of the process, as this middleware tracks all the activity between applications and GPUs (i.e. CUDA invocations). Hence, now it is possible to transparently provide solutions for migrating VM offering GPGPU services.

The net result is that federated cloud brokers could have one more degree of flexibility when managing workloads, being able to accommodate more appropriately fluctuations on demand. Notice, however, that this flexibility is referred to intra cloud provider, and it cannot be extrapolated to inter cloud providers. Nevertheless, users would be able to concurrently use the services of several cloud providers with GPGPU service in order to manage their workload. In this regard, a given user may concurrently submit application execution requests to "GPGPU Service Provider 1" and "GPGPU Service Provider 2". The user would select, for each application, the use of "GPGPU Service Provider 1" or "GPGPU Service Provider 2" depending on the desired QoS level. At the end of the submission process, the user has requested "GPGPU Service Provider 1" to execute some applications with a lower QoS and some other applications have been submitted to "GPGPU Service Provider 2" so that they are executed with a higher QoS. However, it could happen that while these execution requests are serviced, "GPGPU Service Provider 2" modifies its GPGPU service details, such as modify prices, increase or decrease the amount or type of its resources (different GPU models, larger amount of available instances, etcetera). At this point, the user may decide to migrate the still pending requests to "GPGPU Service Provider 2". Notice that this is possible because applications do not need to be modified in order to use the rCUDA middleware, and the GPGPU service utilization only requires configuring a few environment variables. In a similar way, in the previous scenario, if after submitting the request for application execution to "GPGPU Service Provider 1" and "GPGPU Service Provider 2", it happens that "GPGPU Service Provider 1" decides to offer better GPGPU service (regarding price, GPU resources, higher performance interconnection network, etcetera), then the user may migrate the pending jobs to that provider.

CONCLUSION

In this chapter we have proposed an approach for providing GPGPU as a Service. For so, we have first analyzed the available technologies for using GPU accelerators from inside VMs. After this analysis, we have showed that the use of remote GPU virtualization is an effective mechanism to provide GPU access to applications running inside VMs, featuring, in general, low overhead. Finally, we have explained how the proposed approach can be introduced in cloud federations in order to provide GPGPU services.

In addition, this chapter has presented a practical way for offering GPGPU as a service, using a specific remote GPU virtualization technology, such as rCUDA, employing particular virtualization solutions, like Xen or KVM, and proposing one possible cloud federation scenario, integrating our proposed GPGPU service in the cloud providers with other typical services present in actual cloud computing environments.

In addition to introducing a new type of cloud service and a possible practical deployment, notice that the envision proposed in this chapter can be extended, not only by using different remote GPU virtualization technologies, distinct VM environments or other cloud federation scenarios, but also by providing different services. In this manner, different kind of hardware accelerators could be used apart from CUDA capable GPUs, resulting in new services which also can be interesting for the HPC community. In any case, many issues that need further research are still open. For instance, the efficient migration of accelerated applications that are in execution is a hot topic that can be simplified with the use of a remote GPU virtualization middleware. In this way, once an efficient migration mechanism for HPC applications is developed, the CUDA section of these applications is already able to be migrated using rCUDA middleware. The result is that live applications can be migrated among cloud providers depending on the evolution of their respective SLAs. Another issue that needs further research is how to efficiently share a GPU among several VMs. In this regard, these VMs may be using a GPU local to the computer hosting them or may be using a remote GPU located in another node of the cluster. In both cases it is required to define GPU sharing policies that maximize overall throughput (in terms of jobs per time unit) at the same time that power consumption is reduced. GPU accounting is one more example: given that remote GPU virtualization allows users to make a more flexible usage of GPU resources, which are additionally shared among several customers, the definition and implementation of new accounting methods is required in order to bill customers more accurately. This would move the billing granularity from the GPU grain to the resource grain, being resource possibly defined in several different ways.

REFERENCES

Agarwal, P. K., Hampton, S., Poznanovic, J., Ramanthan, A., Alam, S. R., & Crozier, P. S. (2013). Performance modeling of microsecond scale biological molecular dynamics simulations on heterogeneous architectures. *Concurrency and Computation*, *25*(10), 1356–1375. doi:10.1002/cpe.2943

Boob, S., González-Vélez, H., & Popescu, A. M. (2014). Automated Instantiation of Heterogeneous Fast Flow CPU/GPU Parallel Pattern Applications in Clouds. *Proceedings of the 22nd Euromicro International Conference on Parallel, Distributed and Network-Based Processing* (pp. 162-169)

Canonical. (2015). *Cloud-init*. Retrieved from http://cloud-init.org/

Felter, W., Ferreira, A., Rajamony, R., & Rubio, J. (2014). *An Updated Performance Comparison of Virtual Machines and Linux Containers*. Retrieved from http://domino.research.ibm.com/library/cyberdig.nsf/papers/0929052195DD819C85257D2300681E7B

Giunta, G., Montella, R., Agrillo, G., & Coviello, G. (2010). A GPGPU Transparent Virtualization Component for High Performance Computing Clouds. Proceedings of Euro-Par 2010 - Parallel Processing (pp. 379-391). Springer Berlin Heidelberg. doi:10.1007/978-3-642-15277-1_37

Goiri, I., Guitart, J., & Torres, J. (2012). Economic Model of a Cloud Provider Operating in a Federated Cloud. *Information Systems Frontiers*, *14*(4), 827–843. doi:10.1007/s10796-011-9325-x

Gupta, V., Gavrilovska, A., Schwan, K., Kharche, H., Tolia, N., Talwar, V., & Ranganathan, P. (2009). GViM: GPU-accelerated Virtual Machines. *Proceedings of the 3rd ACM Workshop on System-level Virtualization for High Performance Computing HPCVirt '09* (pp. 17-24). ACM. Retrieved from https://github.com/esnet/iperf

Jo, H., Jeong, J., Lee, M., & Choi, D. H. (2013). *Exploiting GPUs in Virtual Machine for BioCloud*. BioMed Research International.

KVM Home page. (2015). *KVM*. Retrieved from http://www.linux-kvm.org/page/Main_Page

Lammps molecular dynamics simulator. (2013). *Sandia National Laboratories*. Retrieved from http://lammps.sandia.gov/

Li, K., Zheng, H., & Wu, J. (2013). Migration-based virtual machine placement in cloud systems. *Proceedings of the IEEE 2nd International Conference on Cloud Networking (CloudNet)* (pp. 83-90). IEEE Computer Society. doi:10.1109/CloudNet.2013.6710561

Liang, T., & Chang, Y. (2011). GridCuda: A Grid-Enabled CUDA Programming Toolkit. *Proceedings of 2011 IEEE Workshops of International Conference on Advanced Information Networking and Applications* (pp. 141-146). IEEE Computer Society. doi:10.1109/WAINA.2011.82

Liu, Y. (2015). *Cuda-meme*. Retrieved from https://sites.google.com/site/yongchaosoftware/mcuda-meme

Liu, Y., Schmidt, B., Liu, W., & Maskell, D. L. (2010). CUDA–MEME: Accelerating motif discovery in biological sequences using CUDA-enabled graphics processing units. *Pattern Recognition Letters*, *31*(14), 2170–2177. doi:10.1016/j.patrec.2009.10.009

Liu, Y., Wirawan, A., & Schmidt, B. (2013). CUDASW++ 3.0: Accelerating smith-waterman protein database search by coupling CPU and GPU SIMD instructions. *BMC Bioinformatics*, *14*(1), 1–10. doi:10.1186/1471-2105-14-117 PMID:23557111

Luo, G., Huang, S., Chang, Y., & Yuan, S. (2014). A parallel Bees Algorithm implementation on GPU. *Journal of Systems Architecture*, *60*(3), 271–279. doi:10.1016/j.sysarc.2013.09.007

Mellanox OFED for Linux User Manual. (2015). *Mellanox* Retrieved from http://www.mellanox.com/related-docs/prod_software/Mellanox_OFED_Linux_User_Manual_v2.0-2.0.5.pdf

Merritt, A. M., Gupta, V., Verma, A., Gavrilovska, A., & Schwan, K. (2011). Shadowfax: Scaling in Heterogeneous Cluster Systems via GPGPU Assemblies. *Proceedings of the 5th International Workshop on Virtualization Technologies in Distributed Computing* (pp. 3-10). ACM. doi:10.1145/1996121.1996124

More Than A Programming Model. (2015). *NVidia*. Retrieved from https://developer.nvidia.com/about-cuda

NVIDIA GRID Technology. (2013). *NVIDIA*. Retrieved from http://www.nvidia.com/content/grid/pdf/GRID_K1_BD-06633-001_v02.pdf

The NVIDIA GPU Computing SDK Version 6.5. (2014). *NVIDIA*. Retrieved from https://developer.nvidia.com/cuda-toolkit

NVIDIA Popular GPU-Accelerated Applications Catalog. (2014). *NVIDIA-app*. Retrieved http://www.nvidia.es/content/tesla/pdf/gpu-accelerated-applications-for-hpc.pdf

Oikawa, M., Kawai, A., Nomura, K., Yasuoka, K., Yoshikawa, K., & Narumi, T. (2012). DS-CUDA: A Middleware to Use Many GPUs in the Cloud Environment. Proceedings of the 2012 SC Companion: High Performance Computing, Networking, Storage and Analysis (SCC) (pp. 1207-1214). IEEE Computer Society. doi:10.1109/SC.Companion.2012.146

Oracle VM VirtualBox User Manual. (2015). *Oracle*. Retrieved from http://download.virtualbox.org/virtualbox/UserManual.pdf

Peña, A. J., Reaño, C., Silla, F., Mayo, R., Quintana-Ortí, E. S., & Duato, J. (2014). A complete and efficient CUDA-sharing solution for HPC clusters. *Parallel Computing*, *40*(10), 574–588. doi:10.1016/j.parco.2014.09.011

Playne, D. P., & Hawick, K. A. (2009). Data Parallel Three-Dimensional Cahn-Hilliard Field Equation Simulation on GPUs with CUDA. *Proceedings of the International Conference on Parallel and Distributed Processing Techniques and Applications* (pp. 104-110). CSREA Press.

Reaño, C., Mayo, R., Quintana-Orti, E. S., Silla, F., Duato, J., & Peña, A. J. (2013). Influence of InfiniBand FDR on the performance of remote GPU virtualization. *Proceedings of the 2013 IEEE International Conference on Cluster Computing* (pp. 23-27). IEEE Computer Society. doi:10.1109/CLUSTER.2013.6702662

Rochwerger, B., Levy, E., Galis, A., Nagin, K., Llorente, I. M., Montero, R., & Galan, F. et al. (2009). The Reservoir Model and Architecture for Open Federated Cloud Computing. *IBM Journal of Research and Development*, *53*(4), 1–11. doi:10.1147/JRD.2009.5429058

Running Commands on Your Linux Instance at Launch. (2015). *Amazon*. Retrieved from http://docs.aws.amazon.com/AWSEC2/latest/UserGuide/user-data.html

Samaan, N. (2014). A Novel Economic Sharing Model in a Federation of Selfish Cloud Providers. *IEEE Transactions on Parallel and Distributed Systems*, *25*(1), 12–21. doi:10.1109/TPDS.2013.23

Semnanian, A. A., Pham, J., Englert, B., & Wu, X. (2011). Virtualization Technology and its Impact on Computer Hardware Architecture. *Proceedings of Eighth International Conference on Information Technology: New Generations (ITNG)* (pp. 719-724). IEEE. doi:10.1109/ITNG.2011.127

Shadowfax II - scalable implementation of GPGPU assemblies. (2015). Keeneland. Retrieved from http://keeneland.gatech.edu/software/keeneland/kidron

Shi, L., Chen, H., & Sun, J. (2009). vCUDA: GPU accelerated high performance computing in virtual machines. *Proceedings of IEEE International Symposium on Parallel & Distributed Processing* (pp. 23-29). IEEE Computer Society.

Song, J., Lv, Z., & Tian, K. (2015). *KVMGT: a Full GPU Virtualization Solution*. Retrieved from http://www.linux-kvm.org/images/f/f3/01x08b-KVMGT-a.pdf

Surkov, V. (2010). Parallel option pricing with Fourier space time-stepping method on graphics processing units. *Parallel Computing*, 36(7), 372–380. doi:10.1016/j.parco.2010.02.006

The Xen Project. (2015). *Xen*. Retrieved from http://www.xenproject.org/

vSphere 6.0 Datasheet. (2015). *VMware*. Retrieved from http://www.vmware.com/files/pdf/vsphere/VMW-vSPHR-Datasheet-6-0.pdf

Vouzis, P. D., & Sahinidis, N. V. (2010). GPU-BLAST: Using graphics processors to accelerate protein sequence alignment. *Bioinformatics (Oxford, England)*. PMID:21088027

Walters, J. P., Younge, A. J., Dong, I. K., Ke, T. Y., Mikyung, K., Crago, S. P., & Fox, G. C. (2014). GPU Passthrough Performance: A Comparison of KVM, Xen, VMWare ESXi, and LXC for CUDA and OpenCL Applications. *Proceedings of the IEEE 7th International Conference on Cloud Computing (CLOUD)* (pp 636-643). IEEE Computer Society. doi:10.1109/CLOUD.2014.90

Wang, W., Zhang, Y., Lin, B., Wu, X., & Miao, K. (2010). Secured and reliable VM migration in personal cloud. *Proceedings of the 2nd International Conference on Computing Engineering and Technology (ICCET)* (pp. 705-709). IEEE Computer Society. doi:10.1109/ICCET.2010.5485376

Wu, H., Diamos, G., Sheard, T., Aref, M., Baxter, S., Garland, M., & Yalamanchili, S. (2014). Red Fox: An Execution Environment for Relational Query Processing on GPUs. *Proceedings of Annual IEEE/ACM International Symposium on Code Generation and Optimization* (pp. 44-54). ACM. doi:10.1145/2581122.2544166

Xu, H., & Li, B. (2011). Egalitarian stable matching for VM migration in cloud computing. *Proceedings of the IEEE Conference on Computer Communications Workshops (INFOCOM WKSHPS)* (pp. 631-636). IEEE Computer Society. doi:10.1109/INFCOMW.2011.5928889

Yamazaki, I., Dong, T., Solcà, R., Tomov, S., Dongarra, J., & Schulthess, T. (2014). Tridiagonalization of a dense symmetric matrix on multiple GPUs and its application to symmetric eigenvalue problems. *Concurrency and Computation*, 26(16), 2652–2666. doi:10.1002/cpe.3152

Yuancheng, L., & Duraiswami, R. (2008). Canny edge detection on NVIDIA CUDA. *Proceedings of IEEE Computer Society Conference on Computer Vision and Pattern Recognition Workshops*. (pp. 1-8). IEEE.

Zillians GPU Virtualization Middleware (vGPU). (2015). *Zillians*. Retrieved from https://github.com/zillians/platform_manifest_vgpu

KEY TERMS AND DEFINITIONS

GPU Accelerator: Graphic Processing Unit (GPU) which is able to accelerate some parts of applications, mainly in scientific and engineering areas, but was initially designed for graphics processing

GPGPU: General Purpose computing on GPUs. Computing paradigm that uses GPU accelerators to perform other computations not related to graphics.

Remote GPU Virtualization: Software mechanism that transparently provides applications being executed in a node of a cluster with access to a remote GPU located in a different cluster node.

Middleware: Intermediate software, usually located among the application layer and the operating system or other API layer, whose function is supporting applications in communication and other interaction tasks, thus simplifying programmers' development.

InfiniBand: Interconnection network that provides high bandwidth and low latency, being commonly used in high performance computing (HPC).

InfiniBand Verbs: Programming API for InfiniBand networks that exposes read, write and send operations instead of the TCP/IP protocol stack

Network Adapter, Network Card, Physical Network Interface or NIC: Network Interface Controller. Computer hardware device present on every node for connecting computers in a computer network.

Network card Virtual Function: Virtual instance of a physical network interface that provides the illusion of a different independent device when actually uses the same hardware.

HPC Cluster: High performance computing system composed of several servers, also referred to as computing nodes, interconnected by a high performance network.

RDMA: Remote Direct Memory Access. Direct transmission of a memory region from one computer to another with no involvement of the operating system or the CPUs, based on hardware support in the network adapters.

ENDNOTES

[1] *m.n* are based on the exact version of the CUDA driver.

[2] *x.y* refer to the exact version of CUDA supported by the provided rCUDA package.

Chapter 11
Volunteer Clouds:
From Volunteer Computing to Interconnected Infrastructures

Attila Csaba Marosi
MTA SZTAKI, Hungary

Péter Kacsuk
MTA SZTAKI, Hungary

ABSTRACT

Cloud Computing (CC) offers simple and cost effective outsourcing in dynamic service environments and allows the construction of service-based applications extensible with the latest achievements of diverse research areas. CC is built using dedicated and reliable resources and provides uniform seemingly unlimited capacities. Volunteer Computing (VC) on the other hand uses volatile, heterogeneous and unreliable resources. This chapter per the authors makes an attempt starting from a definition for Cloud Computing to identify the required steps and formulate a definition for what can be considered as the next evolutionary stage for Volunteer Computing: Volunteer Clouds (VCl). There are many idiosyncrasies of VC to overcome (e.g., volatility, heterogeneity, reliability, responsiveness, scalability, etc.). Heterogeneity exists in VC at different levels. The vision of CC promises to provide a homogeneous environment. The goal of this chapter per the authors is to identify methods and propose solutions that tackle the heterogeneities and thus, make a step towards Volunteer Clouds.

INTRODUCTION

Compute capacity is either used or wasted. Unused capacity cannot be stored for later use. The term cycle scavenging refers to (distributed) systems that utilize these idle computing cycles of connected computers. Desktop Grids (DGs) cycle-scavenge institutional desktop computers to solve compute intensive problems. On the other hand Volunteer Computing utilizes the idle resources (i.e., CPU cycles and storage) of private donated computers. These are typically home desktop computers behind firewalls and routers that can be considered even more heterogeneous and volatile. Cloud Computing offers simple and cost

DOI: 10.4018/978-1-5225-0153-4.ch011

effective outsourcing in dynamic service environments and allows the construction of service-based applications extensible with the latest achievements of diverse research areas, such as Grid Computing, Service-oriented computing, business processes and virtualization. CC is built using dedicated and reliable resources and provides uniform seemingly unlimited capacities. Heterogeneity exists in VC at different levels. The vision of CC promises to provide a homogeneous environment. The goal of this chapter per the authors is to identify methods and propose solutions that tackle the heterogeneities and thus, make a step towards Volunteer Clouds.

This chapter is intended to systematize, extend and streamline the previous papers of the author regarding Volunteer Computing and Volunteer Clouds (Marosi, Kovács, & Kacsuk, 2012; Marosi, Balaton & Kacsuk, 2009; Marosi, Gombás, Balaton & Kacsuk, 2008; Marosi, Kacsuk, Fedak, & Lodygensky, 2010; Marosi, Gombás, Balaton & Kiss, 2008; Balaton et al. 2007). The chapter is divided into four main sections with related work discussed at each section. The first section defines scenarios and methods for interconnecting VC. The second section details a previously defined scenario: hierarchy of desktop grids in institutes and universities. The third section discusses Volunteer Clouds. Finally the last section concludes the chapter.

INTERCONNECTING VOLUNTEER COMPUTING

The term federation is used as a specific method for interconnecting distributed computing systems. For a generic interconnection the *Inter-** phrase can be used. For example for the generic interconnection of clouds the term *Inter-Cloud* was created and formulated by the Global Inter-Cloud Technology Forum (Global Inter-cloud Technology Forum, 2010). This definition can be adapted for the notion of interconnected volunteer computing systems:

Definition 1: Inter-Volunteer Computing is a volunteer computing model that, for purpose of guaranteeing service quality (e.g., performance), allows on-demand transfer of workload through the collaboration of volunteer computing systems based on the coordination of each users requirements for service quality and the use of standard interfaces.

Based on this definition Figure 1 shows the different possible interconnected architectures for volunteer computing adapted from cloud construct architectures defined in (Grozev & Buyya, 2012) separated into two groups: In multi-constructs the different volunteer computing systems are accessed in a centralized manner which can be either a multi-access service (see a. in Figure 1) where users can access multiple VCSs through a single service or a meta-middleware library (see b. in Figure 1) that users can use to develop their own brokers to access multiple infrastructures. In contrast federations allow the infrastructures to collaborate with each other. This can be achieved either by using a central component (see c. in Figure 1) to facilitate workload distribution or by directly in generally using some peer-to-peer manner (see d. in Figure 1). While multi-constructs can be established by third parties using APIs or tools provided by the different VCSs, federations are mainly volunteer formations that require the agreement between the two or more parties. Basically a federation is established when a set of providers interconnect their infrastructures to share resources among each other (Rochwerger et al., 2009):

Figure 1. Possible architecture types for interconnecting volunteer computing systems

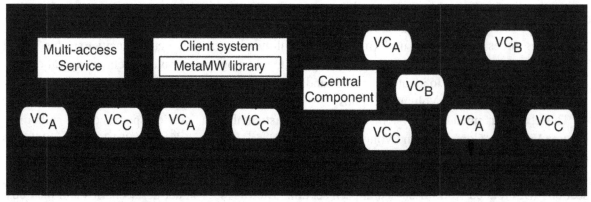

Definition 2: A federation of volunteer computing systems is formed through the direct interconnection of the systems based on the agreements of their providers for workload sharing.

Scenarios

For a deployment of a volunteer computing middleware the BOINC deployment term ``project'' will be used from now on. The authors identified three real world scenarios for federation that my method and model aims at solving. Figure 2 depicts these. There the directed edges denote the direction of the workflow transfer, thus the ``flow'' of jobs. Contrary to the federations' part of Figure 1 where the direction is not specified. The federated projects are ordered into levels based on their distance from the root of the graph (see L0, L1, etc. on Figure 2). The scenarios are as follows:

Figure 2. Proposed scenarios for desktop grid and volunteer computing federations

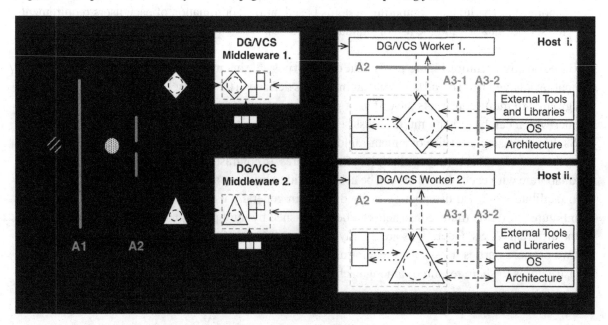

Scenario 1: Hierarchy of desktop grids in institutes and universities.

DGs do not collaborate with each other since they are usually deployed within different organizational units. There can be multiple DGs present within an institution, e.g., used by different departments or faculties. Institutes and companies have mostly a hierarchical organization structure (e.g., departments form a faculty and faculties form the university as whole). Combining the resources of the different organizational units in a hierarchical way similar to their administrative structure seems self-evident. For example in universities departments can be considered as the lowest element in the hierarchy (e.g., see DG_D and DG_E in Figure 2/a). Each department has its own computing resources, e.g., office machines or computers in laboratories. The unused resources of these can be utilized by a department-wide desktop grid. A faculty consists of multiple departments and the department-wide DGs can be joined together into a faculty wide one (e.g., see DG_B in Figure 2/a). This allows combining the resources of the different departments that would allow solving larger scientific challenges faster. Finally the different department-wide DGs can be joined into a university DG (e.g., see DG_A in Figure 2/a). The collaboration of deployments are solved in some extent by middleware specific methods (e.g., the flocking mechanism of HTCondor (Epema, Livny, van Dantzig, Evers & Pruyne, 1996)), but for example creating a collaboration that honors the hierarchical structure of the organization is troublesome. Such a hierarchical structure would allow that each organizational unit retains the control of their resources, but still the resources are pooled at a higher level and made available for larger compute intensive challenges.

Scenario 2: Company supporting a volunteer computing project.

Companies and institutes generally have many office computers that are not utilized to their full potential during the daily office hours and are turned off for the non-office hours, thus a lot of computing capacity is wasted. This capacity cloud be used to support a volunteer computing project. Usually most companies prohibit direct (or any) access to the internet for their computers thus, prohibit access to any VC project. This can be solved by opening access to the selected VC projects (either directly or via some proxy network solution) however, this is not desired since: (*i*) all hosts must have access to the VC project; (*ii*) for each new VC project network access must be granted to each host; (*iii*) each host must be individually connected to each new VC project and (*iv*) there is no easy (centralized) method for monitoring the flow and status of the jobs. For this scenario a ``proxy'' DG project within the institute that has no own application only transfers jobs from the selected VC projects is a possible solution. In this case all hosts can be connected to this proxy project and solving problems *i-iv*. The scenario is depicted in Figure 2/b.

Scenario 3: Volunteer computing projects collaborating.

BOINC is currently the most popular VC framework with more than 2.5 Million donors and 8.7 Million hosts in 80 distinct volunteer projects (BOINCstats/BAM!, n. d.). Each of these has its own grand scientific goal and does not collaborate with others. Some of these projects provide jobs for their donors 24/7 and would require more resources. On the other hand some projects provide jobs in batches (e.g., they run distinct experiments that do not overlap in time) and are not able to supply all their donors continuously with work. These are currently mitigated by the donors by signing up and contributing to multiple projects. Volunteer projects are either created specifically for solving a single scientific problem or nurturing multiple third party applications. In the latter case they are referred as umbrella projects. In either case they may not be able to provide jobs for their volunteers continuously as jobs usually arrive in batches. In such cases an "idling" project could transfer part of the workload to help out the other project. The scenario is depicted as Figure 2/c. Although the graph of this scenario contains one or possibly more cycles it is assumed that the workload transfer is unidirectional, thus it always flows in one direction at once. For example workload from VC_A is only transferred to VC_B only if VC_B is willing to accept it. In this case there is no reason to transfer back the same workload in parallel. Thus any cycle in the graph will not cause problems. It is assumed that the federation is used for workload transfer (e.g., in case it has free capacity one project accepts jobs from another) thus jobs won't traverse the graph in cycles (back and forth between parties) under normal circumstances.

HIERARCHY OF DESKTOP GRIDS IN INSTITUTES AND UNIVERSITIES

The hierarchical desktop grid allows a set of projects to be connected in a form of a directed acyclic graph. The projects are the vertices and work is distributed along the edges. The projects are ordered into levels based on their distance from the top level (see Figure 3).

In a hierarchy every project is in a parent-child relationship. A project may request work from a project above (*child*) or may provide work for a project below (*parent*). The hierarchical interaction is always between a parent and a child regardless of how many levels of hierarchy are above or below. For a child every job is originating from its parent regardless where it is originally from or where were the input data for the job fetched (although the data are not always from the parent). It is allowed for a project to have more children and parents. Figure 3 shows a three-level example.

A project in the hierarchy serves two roles (see Figure 4): a master side which puts retrieved jobs in the database of the project and retrieves the completed results, and a client side which downloads jobs

Figure 3. Roles in the hierarchy of DG/VC projects

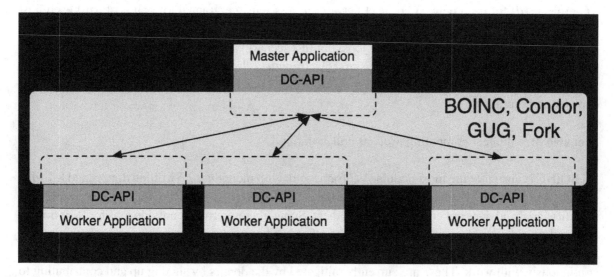

Figure 4. The split architecture of the Gateway: It acts both as a Host and as an UI

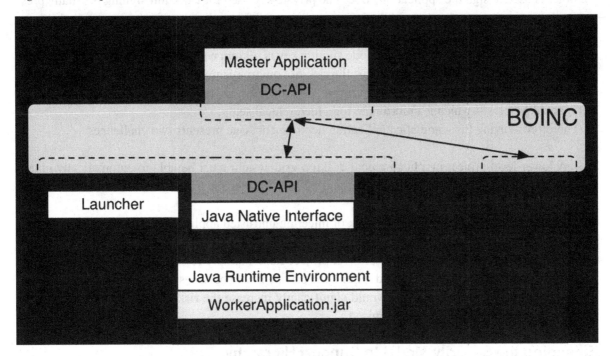

from the parent and uploads final results. Extending BOINC with this functionality allows providing basic hierarchical functionality without further (deeper) modifications, but it has drawbacks:

- The application of the job has to be deployed previously at each project. All implementations of the application.
- Application mapping between source and destination is required.
- Work distribution is based on the local scheduling method implemented by BOINC, which might not be ideal in a hierarchical setup as it was not designed for this task.

Extending BOINC for Use in Hierarchy

Although the hierarchy prototype presented is very simple and was easy to implement, it had a major drawback: applications must be installed manually at each child in order to be able to process jobs originating from the parent. Overcoming this limitation also requires replacing of the security model of BOINC. The most important factor in desktop grid computing is the trust between the clients and the project providing the application. Allowing foreign code to run on a computer always has a risk of either accidental or intended misbehavior. BOINC mitigates this risk by only allowing to run code that has been digitally signed by the project the client is connected to. Clients trust the operators of the BOINC project not to offer malicious code, and digitally signing the application provides technical means to ensure this trust relation. Of course it is not enough to only sign the application binary, the input data must be signed as well (think of the case when the application is some kind of interpreter and the input data can instruct it to do just about anything). Therefore BOINC uses two separate key pairs: one is used to sign the workunits (which in this context means the set of input files and a link to the application binary), the other is used to sign the application code. The private key used for workunit signing is usually present on the project's central server, while the private key used for application signing is usually kept at a separate location. The different handling of the private keys stems from their usage pattern: the workunit signing key is used very often while the code signing key is seldom needed therefore it can be protected better. This technique significantly reduces the risk of compromising the application signing key even if the machine hosting the project is compromised, but this also means that installing new applications is a manual process -- which is unfortunate for a hierarchical setup.

Therefore, solving the automatic application deployment issue presents two challenges:

- A lower-level project in a hierarchical desktop grid system must be able to automatically obtain an application's binary from its parent and be able to offer the application to its clients without manual intervention.
- This process must not increase the risk of injecting untrusted applications into the system.

These requirements mean that a lower-level project cannot simply re-sign the application it has obtained from the parent, since that would require the private key to be accessible on the machine hosting the lower-level project which in turn would significantly increase the risk of a key compromise if the machine hosting the project is compromised.

Extending the Security Model to Support Hierarchy

As discussed above the security model used by BOINC is not adequate in a hierarchical setup and a new model is needed. The model must provide enough information for the operator of the client machine (*Donor* from now on) to decide if a downloaded workunit should be trusted to run on the client machine or not, independent from where in the hierarchy the workunit is originated from. The model must provide enough information for the following decision scenarios:

1. The *Donor* wants to trust any workunits of applications installed locally on the BOINC project she is directly connected to (i.e., the *Donor* trusts the project itself). This is the original trust model of BOINC.
2. The *Donor* wants to trust any workunits from a given project, regardless of how many levels of hierarchy did the workunit travel through. This is in fact a generalization of the previous requirement.
3. The *Donor* wants to trust a specific application regardless of where in the hierarchy it is hosted and regardless of what other applications does the hosting project offer.

The $t(<subject>, <object>)$ trust relation for a workunit can be broken down to three parts:

1. Trusting the application code: $t(Donor, App)$.
2. Trusting the set of input files: $t(Donor, Input)$.
3. Trusting the link between the application, its inputs and the desired location of its outputs to prevent the application from processing data that was meant for another application: $t(Donor, <App, Input, Output>)$. Shorthand *WUDesc* for the $<App, Input, Output>$ triplet will be used from now on.

A workunit *WU* is trusted if all components are trusted:

$$t(Donor, App) \bigwedge t(Donor, Input) \bigwedge t(Donor, WUDesc) \rightarrow t(Donor, WU)$$

The trust relation is realized by digital signature verification. Therefore, each of the three classes of objects *App*, *Input* and *WUDesc* are accompanied by one or more digital signatures:

$$Sig_X: X \in \{ App, Input, WUDesc\}$$

It is assumed that *User* has a set of trusted identities marked TrustedID_{Donor}. Thus the trust relation becomes:

$$t(User, X) \Leftrightarrow \exists s \in Sig_X: verify\_sig(X, s) \bigwedge subject\_of(s) \in TrustedID_{Donor}$$

The *subject_of(s)* function provides the identity that created the signature *s*. Special elements (Any_X) which satisfy the relation are also allowed:

$$Any_X: X \in \{ App, Input, WUDesc\}$$

$$\forall s: verify\_sig(Any_X, s) = TRUE$$

The $Any_X \in TrustedID_X$ means that the user does not require a valid signature for that particular component.

REALIZATION

The authors decided to use the X.509 Public Key Infrastructure, since it is a widely accepted and used infrastructure that provides all the technical elements we need. Therefore, the $TrustedID_{Donor}$ set becomes a list of X.509 certificates. The authors define 3 entities responsible for signing various components of the system. The Application Developer (*AppDev* from now on) can sign application code. This kind of signature testifies that the application binary comes from a known source and does not contain malicious code. The *Project* is the administrative body of the BOINC project and it may also sign application code testifying that said application is in fact part of the project. The *Server* is the machine where the project is hosted, and it signs input files and workunit descriptors. Using the original BOINC terms the *AppDev* provides the code-signing key, while the *Server* provides the workunit-signing key.

The $TrustedID_{Donor}$ list of trusted certificates must be determined by the user, since the trust is ultimately a human relation. This may be simplified by the *Project* by providing a list of *Server* and optionally *AppDev* certificates it trusts -- this means the user can delegate the trust to the *Project*. This realizes the first scenario described in Section Scenarios. The second scenario is realized if the *Project* also provides the aggregated list of certificates from all levels above it in the hierarchy. The third scenario is realized if the user lists only the certificate of the appropriate *AppDev* and specifies that she does not care about the signature of *Input* or *WUDesc*. The authors described a model how a user can trust work received from a hierarchical desktop grid system. In a restricted environment however more is needed: it is not enough for the user to trust the workunit, but the project must also trust the user before it gives out possibly confidential information. Also it is not enough just to trust the receiving user, but the data also has to be protected from being disclosed to untrusted parties. This is a new requirement that is not present in public projects.

Protecting the confidentiality of the data can be easily achieved. BOINC by default uses plain HTTP protocol for communication, but it also supports the HTTPS protocol where the communication is encrypted. The *Server* certificate can be used with the HTTPS protocol to ensure that the *Donor* in fact talks to the server she thinks is talking to. Although BOINC uses a simple shared-secret based authentication scheme to identify users, this authentication applies only to interactions with the scheduler. Together with the use of HTTPS this may be adequate to prevent unauthorized users from uploading results, but it does not prevent unauthorized users to download application code and input data if they are able to guess the file name used on the server.

The protection of input data from unauthorized download can be achieved by giving every user a certificate. The *Project* can act as a Certificate Authority and can sign the certificates of all authorized users. Then, the web server that is used for downloading the input files can be configured to only allow downloading if the client authenticated itself with a properly signed certificate.

The workunits are always signed by the server running a specific project, so the projects need a way to make their known and accepted signing certificates available for their clients and other projects. This is solved by an extension to the web based interface of the BOINC project allowing to query for the certificates via the HTTP(S) protocol and depending on the trust model described in Section Extending the Security Model to support Hierarchy.

Application Deployment

BOINC allows the creation of a workunit that refers to external servers for the input files. This means that lower-level projects in a hierarchy do not need to install the input files locally, they may just refer to the original location of the files in the workunit description. However due to security considerations BOINC does not allow to refer to outside of the project for application binaries, they must always reside on the project's server. Thus, lower-level (child) projects must deploy all applications whose workunits they offer locally.

The automatic deployment of applications presents two problems. The first problem arises from the need to properly sign the binary and is solved by the introduction of the *AppDev* role as described in the previous section. If the users have configured their $TrustedID_{Donor}$ sets to contain the appropriate certificate of the *AppDev*, then the project does not need to sign the application binary, thus its secret key is not needed for application deployment.

The second problem arises from the fact that BOINC uses the <*AppName*, *Version*> tuple to identify applications and in a complex hierarchy it is possible that at different levels different applications are installed under the same name.

This problem can be solved by automatically renaming the application when a workunit is transferred from a parent to lower level child project. Using a Universally Unique Identifier (UUID) as the new application name ensures that there will be no name collisions.

For the following the authors assume that the application consists of just a single binary. The *Gateway* (see Section Interconnecting Volunteer Computing) keeps track of the name mapping of the application between parent projects and child project. Such a renaming is possible because on the sever side only the workunit-generating master application cares about the name of the application, and in this case this master application is the link between the members of the hierarchy and therefore has full control. The

UUID is generated by the hierarchy after downloading it from the parent project, before registering at the child project. Additionally, the following requirements have to be met for the application deployment:

- The registration method should be consistent with the original registration method, allowing already deployed projects to be added to a hierarchy without any modification and any project to leave the hierarchy anytime.
- Different versions of the same application should be allowed to run in parallel, since each parent may run different version of the same application.
- Since each application instance is tied to a platform, the application name should be the same for all platforms, allowing any child to query for the different platform instances of the application.
- Instances of the same application originating from different parents should be treated as different ones, to ensure that results are reported to the appropriate parent.

The flow of the deployment is the following:

1. The *Gateway* periodically queries higher level projects for new applications. When a new application is available it receives the *<App, AppName, Version, Signatures>* tuple identifying the application for a given *Platform*.
2. The *Signatures* are checked against the *TrustedID$_{Project}$* set of the child project containing all accepted *AppDev* and *Project* certificates.
3. The *<AppName, Version, Signatures>* triplet is checked against the list of applications already registered for a specific parent.
   a. If found, the application is already available at the child project.
   b. If not found, the *Gateway* creates a new mapping: *<AppName, Version, Signatures, Parent>*→ *<UUID, 1.0>*
4. The *Gateway* registers the application with BOINC using *UUID* as the application name and 1.0 as application version.

The above procedure ensure that applications can still be installed manually as in a regular BOINC project and that will not cause inconsistency between the configuration files of the project, the database of the project and the

Gateway: There is one significant difference though: an automatically deployed application is not signed using the code-signing key of BOINC, instead the signature retrieved by the *Gateway* is used. This requires that the Core Client requesting work (and receiving applications) is able to retrieve the certificates (depending on the trust scenario described in Section Extending the Security Model to Support Hierarchy) from the given project, and is able to validate the signature of the application (and the ones of the workunits belonging to it) using the certificates.

Workload Transfer

This section gives an overview of the application and work distribution in the Hierarchical Desktop Grid. In the example scenario the authors use the simplest setup, which consists of just two projects *Project$_A$* and *Project$_B$*, one application *App* and one *Donor*. The flow of the deployment and distribution process is the following (see also Figure 5):

Figure 5. Flow of the workload transfer in a block: Steps 1-6

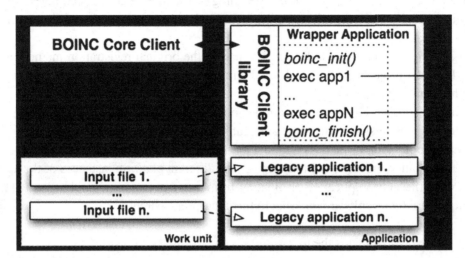

1. The application developer *AppDev* may initially sign the *App* using her secret key.
2. The certificate of the *AppDev* may be added, if not already done so, to the list of certificates belonging to *Project*$_A$ where the application is about to be installed by the administrator of the project. The list of certificates belonging to an entity (server, project, or client) holds all the certificates of the application developers, projects, servers and clients accepted by the entity.
3. The application is installed by the administrator manually. This initial procedure is the same as the normal application install process of BOINC.
4. The *Project* may also sign the application. This signature may either be appended to the signature of the *AppDev* or it may replace the original signature if the project does not wish to disclose the origin of the application. This step must be performed manually since the secret key of the *Project* should not be kept on the same machine where BOINC is running.
5. Workunits are created by the master application or submitted by a user and are passed to BOINC.
6. For each workunit the input data (*Input*) and workunit descriptions (*Desc*) are signed by the *Server*$_I$(*Sig-I, Sig-D*).

At this point the results are ready to be sent to any client attached to the project. Clients may be normal ones or other *Gateways*. The next steps are the following (see also Figure 6):

7. The *Gateway* connects. *Server*$_I$ has a list of the certificates of all accepted clients. If the certificate of the *Gateway* is among them, it can continue to attach to the desired project running on the server. The project has a list of certificates too, containing the certificates of the accepted clients.
8. The *Gateway* checks for new applications. Each application is tied to a BOINC platform (OS and architecture combination). The *Gateway* will query for applications tied to each predefined platform. The application binary and the belonging signatures are downloaded.
9. The signatures of the application binary are verified using the client's list of certificates. *User*s have a *TrustedID*$_{User}$ set defined, but the *Gateway* delegates the trust to the child project, in this case to *Project*$_B$. It will accept any application *Project*$_B$ is trusting.

Figure 6. Flow of the workload transfer in a block: Steps 7-12

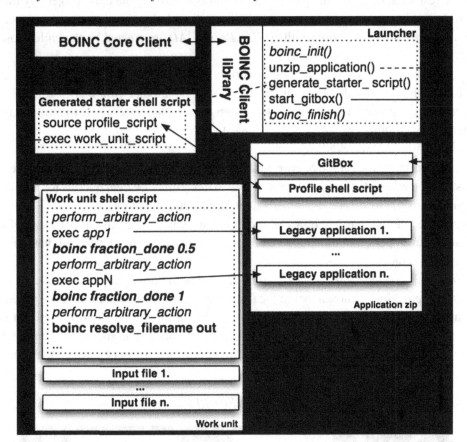

10. A unique name for the application is created, and the *Gateway* stores the name mapping as described in Section Application Deployment. The unique name guarantees that there will be no name collisions in the hierarchy, and the mapping allows the *Gateway* to update or remove applications at the child project. *Project$_B$* might add its signature to the application, certifying the path of origin for its children.

At this point the application is deployed at the child project with the unique name. *Gateway* will continue querying for new applications (checking all available platforms) and repeat this procedure (steps 7-10.) until there are no new ones available.

11. The *Gateway* will now query for work for the applications deployed at *Project$_B$*. The name mapping is used in this process, since for the same application a different name is set at the child and at the parent. A successful query will fetch a result, which consists of one or more input files, their signatures, and a workunit description (it is the same for each result created from the same workunit) and its signature.

The signatures of the input files and workunit descriptions *(Sig-I, Sig-D)* are checked against the *TrustedID$_{Project}$* set of the child project.

12. From the result fetched from the parent a workunit is created at the child project by the *Gateway*. *Server$_2$* may add its signature to the inputs and descriptions belonging to the newly created workunit. From the workunit one or more results (*WU1-Result1-AI*) are created by the child project.

At this point the application (*UUID*) and a workunit belonging to it is fully deployed at the child project, waiting to be downloaded by a client, which may be another *Gateway* or a regular host. If a *Gateway* connects, the procedure is the same from step 7. , if a *Donor* connects the following steps will be executed (see also Figure 7):

13. A *Donor* connects to the server. *Server$_2$* and *Project$_B$* has all the certificates of the accepted clients pre-installed, meaning they can authenticate her. Afterward her *Client* queries for new applications belonging to its platform, and downloads their binary and signatures.
14. The signature belonging to the downloaded application is verified that it is by one of the trusted application developers, and if there are additional signatures, they are verified that they are by one of the trusted projects.
15. The *Client* will now query for work (results) belonging to one of the applications available at the client (the application is chosen by the local scheduling implemented in the Core Client). On success one or more results (*WU1-Result1-AI*) consisting of input files (*Input*), workunit description (*Desc*) and their signatures (*Sig-I*, *Sig-D*) will be downloaded. The signature(s) of the description and the input files are verified to ensure they are signed by (one of) the trusted servers.

Figure 7. Flow of the workload transfer in a block: Steps 13-21

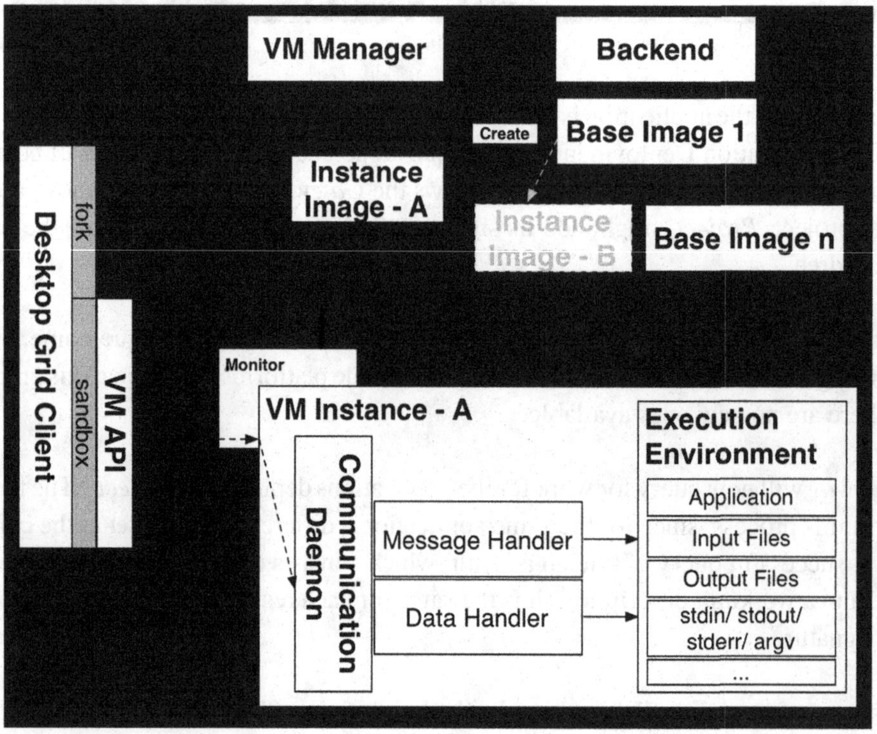

16. The result *WU1-Result1-AI* is ready to be processed by the application. Processing it, will produce one or more output files *Output*. The *Client* signs these files.

17. The output files and signatures *(Output, Sig-O)* are uploaded to *Project$_B$* by the *Client*, and the result is reported as finished.

18. The signatures of the uploaded files are checked if they are created by one of the trusted clients, using the list of certificates of *Project$_B$*.

19. The *Gateway* notices that a result belonging to a workunit that was created by it is complete. It fetches the output files from *Project$_B$*, so it is able to upload it to the parent when needed. It adds its signature to the output(s) of the result (*Sig-O-HC*). For the parent project the *Gateway* is the *Client* processing work, but in reality it is acting as a middle-man relaying work and binaries between the two projects.

20. The *Gateway* contacts *Server$_1$*, *Project$_A$*, and uploads the output files and their signatures belonging to the result.

21. The *Output* is verified using the signature and the list of certificates by *Project$_A$*.

At this point the completed result is available at *Project$_A$* for validation.

Workunit validation is performed only here at the originating project, the child projects use a trivial validator which is part of the *Gateway*, and it is accepting all incoming results. This may be adequate in a controlled environment, where only the selected clients allowed to return results, but this does not filter out syntactically incorrect results at the lower levels caused for example by some hardware defect.

Remarks

BOINC uses majority based voting (i.e., redundancy) for job. Redundancy aims at increasing the probability that every job will have a correct result by simply sending the same piece of work to multiple clients and comparing the results to filter out corrupt ones.

Figure 8 shows a three level layout with the redundancy of three on each level. In this case each parent on each level creates three copies of any workunit received. By the second level there will be nine redundant ones. This means that nine clients will compute the same workunit instead of the supposed three (which was the requested redundancy on the first level). If more levels are added to the hierarchy this number will exponentially grow. This problem can be solved by forcing redundancy to be disabled on all but the top level. This way exactly the requested number of redundant workunits will be distributed.

TOWARDS VOLUNTEER CLOUDS

Virtualization is the mechanism when a logical representation is created on top of the real, physical software or hardware component(s). Virtualization, for example, enables decoupling software services and their resources, i.e., separating the actual resources (CPU, storage, and network) from the physical hardware. Virtualization provides more flexibility for maintenance and improves the utilization rate of the physical resources. Cloud Computing builds on the achievements of diverse research areas, such as Grid Computing, Service-oriented computing, business processes and virtualization. There are several works (trying) to define cloud computing e.g., (Choi & Buyya, 2009), (Armbrust et al., 2009) or (Foster,

Figure 8. Growing number of redundant workunits in the hierarchy demonstrated with a simple three level layout

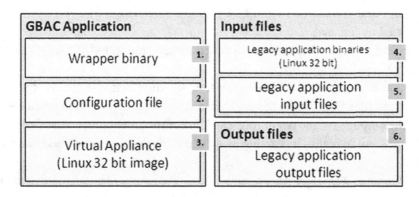

Zhao, Raicu, & Lu, (2008). The National Institute of Standards and Technology (NIST) provides the following definition for cloud computing (Mell & Grance, 2011) that became widely adopted:

Cloud computing is a model for enabling ubiquitous, convenient, on-demand network access to a shared pool of configurable computing resources (e.g., networks, servers, storage, applications, and services) that can be rapidly provisioned and released with minimal management effort or service provider interaction. This cloud model is composed of five essential characteristics, three service models, and four deployment models.

Essential characteristics: First (*i*) Any consumer should be able to provision the computing capabilities (e.g., storage or server time) she needs without human interaction with each provider (*on-demand self-service*); (*ii*) the capabilities are available over the network through standardized mechanisms (*broad network access*); (*iii*) provider's resources are pooled to serve multiple consumers in a multi-tenant model (*resource pooling*). (*iv*) Capabilities can be provisioned and freed in an elastically fashion to scale up or down as demand requires. To the consumer capabilities often appear as unlimited (*rapid elasticity*) and (*v*) resource usage can be controlled, monitored and reported providing transparency both for the consumer and provider (*measured service*).

Service models: Three service models are defined: (1) Infrastructure-as-a-Service (IaaS) provides the capability to the consumer to provision fundamental computing (processing, storage or network) resources where arbitrary applications and software can be deployed. (2) Platform-as-a-Service (PaaS) allows for the consumer to deploy applications on the cloud infrastructure that were created using programming tools (e.g., models, libraries, services) supported or provided by the provider. (3) Software-as-a-Service (SaaS) provides the capability to use a specific application running on a cloud infrastructure.

Deployment models: The (*a*) *private* deployment model provides an infrastructure to be used only by consumers from a single organization; (*b*) a *community* cloud is provisioned for the specific needs of a community of consumers (of different organizations) that have some shared concern; (*c*) a *public* cloud is provided for the open public and finally (*d*) a *hybrid* cloud is a composition of two or more distinct infrastructures (public, private or community). These remain separate entities, but are glued together by some technology that enables data and application portability.

Defining Volunteer Clouds

Volunteer Cloud (VCl) is the term used in this thesis for a cloud infrastructure based on volunteer resources. Considering the special characteristics of VC it is most likely that a definition will contain a subset of the service and deployment models described by the NIST definition (see Section Towards Volunteer Clouds), but should fulfill all essential characteristics. To achieve a definition first the relevant characteristics of VC must be considered. In a volatile and unreliable environment such as volunteer computing establishing a cloud(-like) infrastructure faces several challenges.

Service models: Based on these considerations the following scenarios are proposed for volunteer clouds for the different service models:

1. **IaaS:** Direct access (e.g., deploying VMs and accessing them) to donated resources is not feasible. Proposed scenario: Volunteer data archive. There are several works that investigate the storage/archiving potential of volunteer computing (Lázaro, Kondo & Marquès, 2012; Anderson, 2004; Anderson & Fedak, 2006)
2. **PaaS:** Proposed scenario: Scientific computation platform. Arbitrary applications conforming to the requirements set by the platform can be executed. Methods and mechanisms are required for deploying the application. Science gateways can provide the thin-client interface while methods presented in Section Application Deployment can be used for example in case of BOINC to deploy the application. Other possibility is to not to deploy the application rather execute them in containers.
3. **SaaS:** Proposed scenario: Scientific application execution service. By the provider deployed applications can be executed. These applications are made available through standardized interfaces and/or thin clients by the providers.

Deployment models: All four deployment models (see section Towards Volunteer Clouds) should be supported. The private deployment model (it does not mean here desktop grids a.k.a. private desktop grids) means that a single organization is able to run the scenarios defined above. The community deployment model denotes that a community can use the cloud while the public denotes that anyone could use the volunteer cloud. Hybrid model can utilize the federation approach described in Section Interconnecting Volunteer Computing.

ABSTRACTION FRAMEWORKS FOR VOLUNTEER COMPUTING

One of the major rules in VC is that the donor always retains full control of her computer while a VC worker is running. This in turn requires that the VC worker has fine-grained control over the application(s) it is executing. Additionally the donor needs detailed information about the state of the worker and application to make decisions whether to intervene. Complementing these the middleware tries to provide additional features that makes the VC 'experience' as seamless as possible for the donor, e.g., screensavers, check-pointing support or dynamic process priority during execution. These are usually achieved by requiring specific modifications to the source code of the application and/or linking with specific libraries that the middleware provides like in the case of BOINC. This true not just for VC, but for distributed computing in general as well (e.g., the standard universe of HTCondor). Additionally VC utilizes a diverse and heterogeneous set of donated (computing) resources consisting of different CPUs and architectures, operating systems, installed libraries and tools that the applications must be prepared to handle. However modifying source code and relinking applications are not always possible or feasible.

Such example is the *ISDEP* application (Velasco et al., 2012) with around 10,000 lines of C source code that is evolving constantly. Modifying it to meet the requirements of a single middleware requires effort, but to apply the modifications for each new version is not feasible. Also there are applications which have no source code available or rely on external libraries or using environments like R (The R Project for Statistical Computing, n.d.). These would require that all VC donors deploy R on their donated resources and that the VC middleware supports R, which is not feasible at all for a single scientific application. All the constraints detailed in this paragraph are going to be referred as *external dependencies* (EDs).

This section discusses the three abstraction frameworks (see Figure 10 for an overview and Table 1 for summary) that allow the rapid and simplified development of new, and adaptation (also referred as '*porting*') of existing scientific applications to VC environments. The authors going to show that ultimately all EDs can be resolved using these abstraction methods bringing the VC system closer to a PaaS scientific computing service detailed in the previous Section.

Related Work

There are efforts like the GAT (Allen et al., 2005), SAGA (Goodale et al., 2006) or DRMAA (Tröger, Rajic, Haas & Domagalski, 2007) for creating a unified API for applications on distributed systems. However, these are usually modeled after traditional grid middleware and batch schedulers but are not aimed at volunteer computing systems such as BOINC (Anderson, 2004). The above mentioned APIs are

Figure 9. Taxonomy of frameworks for application adaptation and development

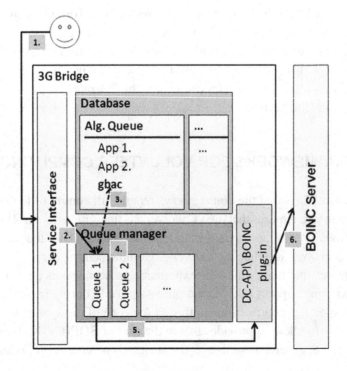

Table 1. Summary of frameworks and their supported abstractions

	A1	A2	A3-1	A3-2
1. BOINC API	-	-	-	-
2. BOINC Wrapper	-	+	-	-
3. DC-API	+	-	-	-
4. GenWrapper	+	+	+	-
5. GBAC	+	+	+	+

Figure 10. Abstraction frameworks for application porting

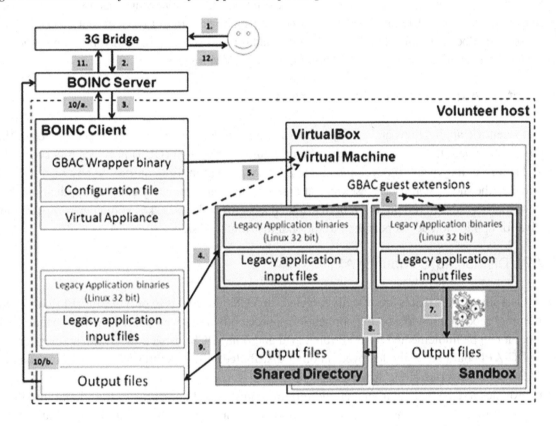

overly complex for such a restricted environment that BOINC provides and they also fail to cover areas like logical file name resolution, checkpoint control, redundant execution and result validation that are required in a BOINC environment. Also the volatility of desktop grid environments where clients may come and go at any time, there is no guarantee that a client that started a computation will indeed finish it, presents a problem for interface designs based on traditional job submission principles. Ferreira et al. (Ferreira, Araujo & Domingues, 2011) designed a common set of VM manipulation functions to hide the hypervisor specific details. Five methods have been defined by the API covering information query, VM startup, file copy, checkpoint and finally command execution inside the virtual machine. In this experience they have implemented the API for local execution, VMWare and VirtualBox. Finally, they have integrated this library as an application into the BOINC wrapper and performed tests to measure the overhead. Its most powerful feature is the easy switching between different virtualization environments however, this work is somehow a duplication of the virtualization.

API and its libraries provided by libVirt. The BOINC VBoxWrapper is a virtualized environment providing wrapper for BOINC created by the developers of BOINC. It interfaces between the BOINC client and VirtualBox. It is a BOINC specific wrapper as it relies on middleware specific functionalities (e.g., file transfer between the host and the shared directory, application execution) and does not aim at being a generic one. CernVM (Sanchez et al., 2011) is also based on the BOINC VBoxWrapper tool however, the main difference is in the virtual appliance and work distribution. Usually, in a BOINC environment the downloaded work unit (including the image as well) contains inputs and results are uploaded to the BOINC server when the job finished. The CernVM solution follows a new approach where the virtual appliance contains a complete job scheduler that performs job fetching from an external server by itself. So, this solution does not utilize BOINC work unit scheduling and the application validation framework rather uses the BOINC server only for distributing the CernVM images.

Abstraction A1: Cross-Middleware Transparency

Users of scientific applications are usually concerned only about the amount of computing power they can get and not about the details how a distributed computing system (DCS) provides this computing power. Therefore, they want to develop a single application that in turn can run on any infrastructure that provides the most appropriate resources at a given time. Unfortunately existing applications have to be modified in order to run on different distributed systems and this makes volunteer computing less attractive for application developers than traditional distributed systems.

DC-API: Distributed Computing API

DC-API is a simple API that is specifically targeted for VCSs. Its goal is to provide an API that requires only minimal modification to existing application source code. However, the DC-API is opaque in the sense that it can be implemented for traditional grid and other DCSs as well therefore, applications using the DC-API could be easily deployed on other distributed infrastructures as well, without the need to modify the source code of the application.

VC provides a restricted environment and programming model compared to traditional distributed computing systems. This means that some application categories like generic parallel applications cannot be supported. On the other hand due to this restricted programming model the DC-API can be small and simple. Although the original motivation for creating the DC-API was to help porting existing applications, DC-API also provides extra features on top of the functionality provided by BOINC. Among these features are the proper support of client applications that create multiple output files (the BOINC API only provides support for accessing the first output file), or the suspension of workunits by transferring a checkpoint file back to the master when it can be submitted and continued on another resource. DC-API also makes it easier to run multiple independent applications under the same BOINC project.

DC-API backends exist to use the Condor job manager, BOINC and XtremWeb (Cappello et al., 2005) as well. A simple fork-based implementation that runs all workunits on the local host is also available. The ability of running the workunits locally makes application debugging easier. Since switching the application from using such a local implementation to e.g., BOINC needs only a recompilation without any changes to the source code, the complete application can be tested on the developer's machine before deploying it to a complex grid infrastructure.

To accommodate the restrictions of different grid environments and to facilitate converting existing sequential code written by scientists not comfortable with parallel programming, the DC-API supports a limited parallel programming model only. This implies the following restrictions compared to general parallel programming:

- Master/ Worker concept: there is a designated master process running somewhere on the grid infrastructure. The master process can submit worker processes called workunits.
- Every workunit is a sequential application.
- There is support for limited messaging between the master and the running workunits. However, this it is not suitable for parallel programming, it is meant to be used for sending status and control messages only.
- No direct communication between workunits.

Following the Master/ Worker model, DC-API applications consist of two major components (see Figure 11): a master and one or more client applications. The master is responsible for dividing the global input data into smaller chunks and distributing them in the form of workunits. Interpreting the output generated by the workunits and combining them to a global output is also the job of the master. The master usually runs as a daemon, but it is also possible to write it so it runs periodically (e.g. from *cron*), processes the outstanding events, and exits. Client applications are simple sequential programs that take their input, perform some computation on it and produce some output.

A typical master application written using DC-API does the following steps:

1. Initialises the DC-API master library by calling the *DC_initMaster* function.

Figure 11. DC-API application components

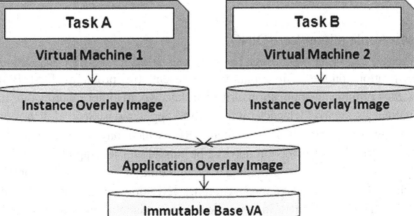

2.   Calls the *DC_setResultCB* function and optionally some of the *DC_setSubresultCB*, *DC_setMes-sageCB*, *DC_setSuspendCB* and *DC_setValidateCb* functions, depending on the advanced features (messaging, subresults, etc.) it wants to use.

3.   In its main loop, calls the *DC_createWU* function to create new workunits when needed and after specifying the necessary input and output files (*DC_addWUInput*, DC_addWUOutput) it can hand them over to the infrastructure for processing by calling the *DC_submitWU* function. If the total number of workunits is small (depending on the infrastructure), then the master may also create all the workunits inadvance. If the number of workunits is large, the master may use the *DC_getWUNumber* function to determine the current number of workunits processed by the grid infrastructure, and create new workunits only if it falls below a certain threshold.

4.   Also in its main loop the master calls the *DC_processMasterEvents* function that checks for outstanding events and invokes the appropriate callbacks. Alternatively, the master may use the *DC_waitMasterEvent* and *DC_waitWUEvent* functions instead of *DC_processMasterEvents* if it prefers to receive event structures instead of using callbacks.

A typical client application performs the following steps:

1.   Initializes the DC-API client library by calling the *DC_initClient* function.

2.   Identifies the location of its input/output files by calling the *DC_resolveFileName* function. Note that the client application may not assume that it can read/ create/ write any files other than the names returned by *DC_resolveFileName*.

3.   During the computation, the client should periodically call the *DC_checkClientEvent* function and process the received events.

4.   If possible, the client should call the *DC_fractionDone* function with the fraction of the work completed. On some infrastructures (e.g., BOINC) this will allow the client's supervisor processsto show the progress of the application to the user. Ideally the value passed to this function should be proportional to the time elapsed so far compared to the total time that will be needed to complete the computation.

5.   The client should call the *DC_finishClient* function at the end of the computation. As a result, all output files will be sent to the master and the master will be notified about the completion of the workunit.

Use Case: Java Applications for BOINC

Running Java applications on the BOINC platform represents two problems. First, BOINC API does not support Java, thus running an application written in Java would either require compiling it to native code or to use a wrapper designed for legacy (non-BOINC) applications. Second, Java requires a runtime environment on its own (Java Runtime Environment, JRE), which may not be already deployed on any client node or the already deployed version may not be suitable for the application. DC-API solves the lack of Java support in BOINC API by providing a Java binding of its API for Java applications via the Java Native Interface (JNI) (Java Native Interface, n.d.). JNI allows Java code to call and be called by native applications and libraries written in other programming languages, such as C or C++. The Java runtime deployment problem is solved either by bundling the JRE zipped with the application (license issues apply), or if the application is run in a Local Desktop Grid, then it can be assumed that the appropriate runtime is already deployed. Here the authors present the scenario when the Java runtime is assumed to be already deployed (see Figure 12).

In this case Client 1 receives the following files as part of the application bundle:

- DC-API Java bindings and libraries.
- A launcher application.
- Java application .jar file(s) (*WorkerApplication.jar*)

A typical execution does the following steps:

1. The launcher is executed, but it does not contact the client. From the point of view of the BOINC client it's an invisible application, it does not use any BOINC API or DC-API functions.
2. If the runtime is to be deployed with the application, then the launcher checks if it is already there (the application might be resuming from a checkpoint). If not found, then it has to be either installed, or uncompressed in the working directory.
3. The launcher starts the Java application using the Java runtime. After that the launcher will wait for its termination. This step is necessary because the BOINC client determines the outcome of the task based on the exit status of the application, in this case on the exit status of the launcher.
4. The Java application behaves like a normal DC-API client application, it has access to the full set of DC-API client functions via the interface provided with JNI. Typically the following steps are executed:
   a. The application initializes the DC-API client library via the *DCClient.init* method.
   b. Resolves the location of its input and output files by calling the *DCClient.resolveFileName* method.
   c. During computation it calls periodically the *DCClient.checkEvent* method and processes the received events. One of the events is *Event.isCheckpointRequest*, upon this event the application should checkpoint itself.
   d. Whenever possible, the application should call the *DCClient.fractionDone* method with the percentage of the work completed. This will report the BOINC client, thus the user, the completion ratio of the current task.

Figure 12. A DC-API Java application on BOINC

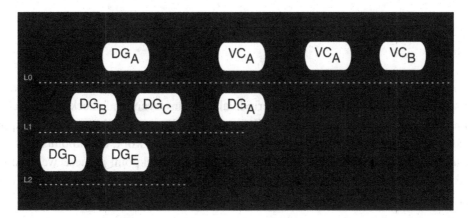

e.   The *DCClient.finish* method should be called at the end of the computation with zero value (or anytime if error occurs with non-zero value). This will finish the execution.

5.   After the application has finished, the launcher picks up its exit status and exits with the same value. The output files are sent back to the master, and it is also notified about the completion of the task.

Besides BOINC, the DC-API backend also supports Condor, and a simple fork-based implementation, thus the DC-API - Java interface is available on any of these platforms. Currently only DC-API client side functions are available via this Java interface, there is no support for using them on the master side yet. There is no restriction to use the same programming language both on client and master side, master applications should use the C/ C++ DC-API now.

Next I'll show a functional demonstration and overhead measurements via a simple application: It searches for the first given number of prime numbers. It is a deterministic and CPU intensive application, thus fits perfectly the needs. It is configured to search for the first 100000 prime numbers (from 2 to 1299709) since this has a moderate, but similar run-time as a normal BOINC work unit (around 1 hour) on a nowadays PC. Two versions of the application was evaluated, one which uses DC-API (and BOINC) and a standalone version stripped of any DC-API dependencies.

The following is a Structure of the DC-API enabled Java application

```
DCClient cli = new DCClient();
long x=2, c=0;
Event e;
cli.init();
readCheckpoint();
while (true) {
    if (c == count)
        break;
    c = isPrime(x);
    if (x % 1000 == 0) {
        e = cli.checkEvent();
        if (e == Event.isCheckpointRequest)
            doCheckpoint(x, c);
    }
    x++;
}
cli.finish(0);
```

The DC-API enabled one (see Box 1) initializes the DC-API library, reads the checkpoint file if any exists and continues the work. It checks periodically for any event and checkpoints itself on *Event. isCheckpointRequest*. When finished it calls *DCClient.finish(0)* which will terminate the application.

The standalone version reads the checkpoint file, does periodic work, checkpoints during the work and quits when finished. Since there is no event to signal the checkpoint request, we used the default interval of BOINC, which is 300 seconds, for checkpointing period. The invoked checkpoint function is only chekpoints when at least 300 seconds passed since the last invocation.

The measurements made do not consider the overhead of downloading it with the application and uncompressing it later at the start of each run. The authors chose not to directly measure the overhead of the JNI calls, since they just act as forwarders to the DC-API library, rather to compare the overhead of the whole infrastructure (JNI + DC-API + BOINC) against the standalone version.

Each application was executed 15 times (chosen arbitrarily), the standalone one was executed from shell, and the DC-API enabled one via BOINC. Measurements (see Table 2) were made using the Linux *time* command, the DC-API enabled application was wrapped in a shell script (acting as the launcher application) which invoked the *time* command with the application. The results show that the JNI + DC-API + BOINC infrastructure in this case has only a minimal (~0.8529%) overhead compared to the standalone run.

Abstraction A2: Middleware Detachment

Any application to be deployed on a BOINC infrastructure needs special preparations. However, there are many so called legacy applications, which have either no source code available to modify or simply would require too much effort to port. For these applications BOINC provides a wrapper which can be used to handle the communication with the Core Client, while executing the legacy application as a subprocess. This wrapper can handle the simple cases but it is not very flexible. It is configurable, but it can only be used to execute a list of legacy executables (tasks) one after the other. This is because the XML file it uses only allows describing the order of execution of the binaries. To make the wrapper more flexible this configuration file could be extended with new features to provide a required level of flexibility each time a shortcoming is discovered, but ultimately a general solution would require a generic scripting language for describing all possible configuration options.

Realizing this, GenWrapper aims to provide a generic solution for wrapping and executing an arbitrary set of legacy applications by utilizing a POSIX like shell scripting environment to describe how the application is to be run and how the work unit should be processed. This choice provides great flexibility and a powerful tool to adapt legacy applications to VC with very little effort.

Applications under BOINC

Donors can join a BOINC based VC project by installing and running the BOINC Core Client and attaching to the project. Besides handling communication with the project servers, the BOINC Core Client is responsible for: i) starting, stopping, suspending and resuming the application; ii) enforcing resource limits and resource shares between different projects set by the user; iii) instructing the application to checkpoint itself and iv) accepting various statistics reported by the application (its completion percentage, used CPU time).

Table 2. Run-time (real, in seconds) of the sample DC-API enabled and standalone application

Type	Slowest Run	Fasters Run	Mean Time
JNI + DC-API + BOINC	4409.86 sec	4407.99 sec	4408.82 sec
Standalone	4371.76 sec	4369.60 sec	4370.71 sec

To use the distributed resources gathered by BOINC, the application performing the computation also needs some preparation to be able run on the client machines under the control of the Core Client. Apart from having executables for all possible platforms that are member of the DG, the application also has to be prepared to be run by the BOINC Core Client which has two main aspects: i) it should be able to run in the directory structure used by the client, i.e. application executables are placed in the project directory while the working directory is a separate slot directory where input and output files are linked; ii) it should be able to interact with the Core Client, i.e. handle suspend, resume and quit requests and report used CPU time and checkpoints.

BOINC provides an API that applications should use to communicate with the Core Client and handle running in the DG environment. This API provides functions for resolving links to files that are accessed from the slot directory, communicate exit status to the Core Client so it can handle errors and report statistics as needed.

Legacy applications or applications which cannot be modified to use the API are not able to run under BOINC because without calling the right API functions they would find links instead of their input files, write their outputs to the wrong place and without properly reporting statistics to the Core Client the application would be restarted over and over and eventually it would be marked as failed. For these applications BOINC offers the BOINC Wrapper (see Figure 12) which acts as a main program managing communication with the Core Client calling the appropriate API functions and running the real application executable as a subprocess. An application using the BOINC Wrapper contains the wrapper executable besides the application files.

Applications with GenWrapper

A typical GenWrapper application consists of a zip file holding all the files belonging to legacy application(s), the two GenWrapper components: GitBox and Launcher executables and a *profile script* to perform platform specific preparations. A typical work unit for a GenWrapper wrapped application contains the input files and another shell script (the *work unit shell script*), which allows to control and execute the legacy applications in an arbitrary manner for each work unit. The work unit shell script should be platform independent as the work unit can be executed by any supported platform.

GenWrapper consists of an extended version of BusyBox (Perens, n.d.), a single binary providing essential UNIX commands (such as *sed, grep, unzip, tar, awk*, etc.) and a POSIX shell interpreter (based on *ash*). GenWrapper is ported to run on Windows, Linux and Mac OS X platforms and it is extended to make BOINC API functions accessible from the shell (e.g. *boinc resolve_filename* or *boinc fraction_done*). GitBox is a stripped-down Windows only port of BusyBox originally created for the Windows version of the git version control system which internally relies on running shell scripts. Although GIT on Windows later abandoned GitBox, this port was used as the basis for GenWrapper after extracting it from GIT and porting back to UNIX preserving functionality on Windows. Later the GenWrapper GitBox version was updated to match newer BusyBox releases, and thus diverged from the original GitBox significantly, although it is still referred to as GitBox in the GenWrapper distribution for historical reasons. Besides Windows the GenWrapper GitBox (which we will simply call GitBox now) is also supported on Linux and Mac OS X, some of the stripped down parts were put back and new BusyBox functionality (e.g. lzma compression) were added and it was extended with BOINC specific shell commands.

A GenWrapper wrapper legacy application is executed as follows (see Figure 13). The client downloads the Launcher executable (named like the application as BOINC expects), an application zip file and an optional profile script as the BOINC application and a work unit (input files and a work unit shell script). The Launcher is started by BOINC and acts as a BOINC application, handling all communication with the Core Client. After starting, the Launcher looks for a .zip file with the same name as itself and extracts all files from it to the slot directory. Storing application files in a .zip file is optional, if not found no extracting is performed and the work unit script should access it by resolving its logical name as any other input files. It is recommended to use application zip files, because the BOINC server stores all application files in one common location on the project web server and when files with the same name, but different content are required by different applications a conflict may happen which is prevented by storing application specific files in a zip archive. The most obvious scenario would be that different applications require different versions of the same DLL (Windows shared library) files. These files commonly have the same 8 character filename (plus the ".dll" extension) regardless of their version. Without packaging application files together in a zip, a later deployed application could overwrite the same named files belonging to a previously installed application. The application zip file may also contain a ``profile script'' which serves as a platform specific bootstrap script for the application (e.g. on Linux the library include path may need to be adjusted or local optimization options could be enabled depending on the presence of optional features, etc.). After unzipping the application archive, the Launcher generates a starter script which first sources the profile script if exists and then executes the work unit shell script. Then Launcher calls the built in POSIX shell interpreter (*ash*) of GitBox which starts to execute this generated script.

The Launcher remains running while GitBox executes the script and handles communication with the Core Client and performs similar tasks as the BOINC Wrapper. In fact Launcher was originally based on BOINC Wrapper, but it is heavily modified to fit the needs of GenWrapper. Modifications include: i) suspending and resuming GitBox and all the subprocesses started by it when the Core Client asks for this; ii) measuring and reporting the CPU time used by the running subprocesses and iii) killing the subprocesses if the requested or the client is stopped. The Launcher is spawning a new process for GitBox which is also spawning a new process for each legacy application it is executing. If the functionality of the original BOINC Wrapper were used here, only the GitBox process could be controlled and

Figure 13. Legacy application using BOINC wrapper

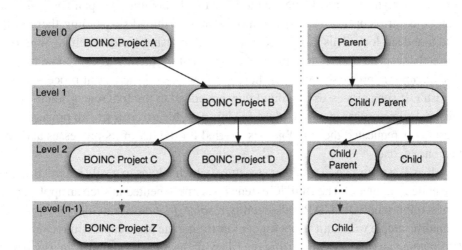

Figure 14. Legacy application using GenWrapper

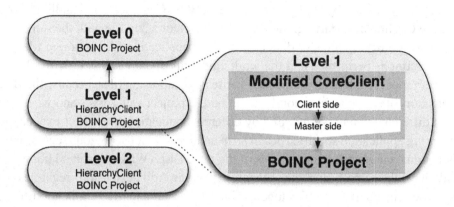

measured, while losing control over the legacy application processes (which do the actual work) and the Core Client having no information about them. These tasks are implemented differently on UNIX and Windows systems due to the lack of common API concepts and Windows' limited support of POSIX.

On Linux and Mac OS X there are process groups that the Launcher utilizes by simply putting the spawned GitBox process in a new process group and by default all its child processes will also belong to the same group. The limitation here is that no child process should break away from the process group, thus currently no subshells are supported (scripts should not create background processes or in practice & and parenthesizes should be avoided) and also the legacy applications should avoid create new process groups (although they can spawn subprocesses which are not breaking away from the process group).

On Windows, there are no process groups (a feature with the same name exists, but it is only vaguely similar to UNIX process groups and cannot be used the same way). The closest feature the WIN32 API provides is called JobObject. Each JobObject represents a collection of processes. But the problem with them is twofold: i) by default a process started by a process in a JobObject (child) should also belong to the same JobObject as its parent, but unfortunately it depends which system function was used to create the child process (*CreateProcess()* is fine, but *_spawn()* is not always), thus not every child process may end up in the JobObject; ii) there is no official, documented API function to suspend or resume a process, only threads can be controlled; if a process has more than one thread suspending them in the wrong order might lead to a dead-lock. This last problem is solved by using undocumented Windows NTAPI calls that can directly suspend and resume processes. The first problem was overcome by periodically checking the list of running processes whether there is a new one whose parent process belongs to the JobObject but it isn't. If such processes are found they are added to the JobObject. There is no function to suspend or resume all processes in a JobObject, but it is possible to terminate all processes of it. Thus, if suspend or resume is requested the JobObject is queried for the list of its processes and each one of those is handled one by one.

GitBox (as well as BusyBox) has a modular structure, which allows to easily extend it with arbitrary commands by so called ``applets''. The BOINC extension is implemented in such an applet and currently consists of the most important BOINC API calls such as, *resolve_filename, fraction_done, fraction_done_ percent*. A minimalist sample work unit script for demonstrating the basic capabilities can be seen in Box 2. This sample is reading an (integer) value from the file with the logical filename 'in' (by first resolving the link to the real file), performing a loop which: i) calculates how much of the total work is done; ii) print the fraction done in percent into the file with logical name 'out' and iii) sleep for a second in each iteration. There is no need to provide or call *boinc_init()* or *boinc_finish()* from the script itself, because it is called by the Launcher, which also takes care of forwarding the exit status to *boinc_finish* (thus the script can normally exit with a non-zero status to signal an error). The Launcher also measures used CPU time and reports to the Core Client automatically. The only BOINC API functionality required for this simple example is to resolve logical filenames and report the fraction done which is also the case for the majority of legacy applications.

The following is a Sample GenWrapper work unit shell script

```
IN=`boinc resolve_filename input `
OUT=`boinc resolve_filename output `
NUM=`cat ${IN}`
PERCENT_PER_ITER=`expr 10000 / $NUM`
for i in `seq $NUM`; do
                PERCENT_COMPLETE=` expr ${PERCENT_PER_ITER} \ $i / 100`
                boinc fraction_done_percent ${PERCENT_COMPLETE}
                echo -e "I am ${PERCENT_COMPLETE}% complete ." >> "${OUT}"
                sleep 1;
done
```

GenWrapper utilizes Abstraction A1 (relies on DC-API) and further extends it (Abstraction A2) by removing the need to modify application binaries. It also provides support for custom application environments (Abstraction A3-1). GenWrapper provides a robust and mature method to adapt existing scientific applications for volunteer computing.

Abstraction A3-1 and A3-2: Environment Detachment

Sandboxes provide an isolated execution environment for applications. Unix-like systems have traditionally supported this by techniques and tools like *chroot*} or BSD *jail*. The problem with these solutions is that they are only available for Linux/BSD, while VC is aimed at the general public thus; it is not enough to provide a solution for a single platform. With the emergence of hypervisors for the desktop computer (like VMware Player/ Fusion, VirtualBox, Bochs or QEMU) which are *cross-platform* this obstacle can be easily mitigated.

However it is not a solution to simply take and use any of these existing tools, since donors cannot be expected to be distributed computing or operating system administrators thus to have the knowledge (or be willing) to *deploy* (in Table 3) any ``complicated'' piece of software. For the long term if the donor notices any slowdown or the computer becomes less responsive while the sandbox is run the VC client will be removed (*"slowdown"* in Table 3). So in the first place a transparent sandbox should comply with the philosophy of VC and should not be noticeable for the donor *transparent for the donor*.

There are many already deployed VC projects. If applying a sandbox would require either to perform modifications to on the server deployed applications, for example they needed to be moved in a disk image no administrator can be expected to do this. Also there should be no restrictions for the application whether it is run in a sandbox or just simply executed by the client meaning the same capabilities

Table 3. Comparison of major "desktop" hypervisors and emulation software

	Bochs	QEMU	QEMU+KVM (or KQEMU)	VMware Player	VirtualBox
Method (Emulation/ Virtualization)	E	E	V	V	V
1. Transparency for the donor	+	+	-	-	-
a. deployment	+	+	- (KQEMU)	-	-
b. slowdown	-	+	+	+	+
2. Transparency for the middleware	-	+	+	-	+
a. Checkpoint and resume	+	+	+	+	+
b. Suspend and continue	+	+	+	+	+
c. Remote control (API)	-	+	+	+	+
d. Backdoor	-	+	- (KQEMU)	-	+
3. Isolation	+	+	+	+	+
4. Cross-platform	+	+	-	-	+
5. Performance	-	-	+	+	+
6. Instantiation	-	+	+	-	-
7. Background	-	+	+	-	+
8. Licensing	LGPL	GPL	GPL	Proprietary	Proprietary

should be available that are normally provided by the client, namely: checkpoint and resume, suspend and continue, start and stop and to report data about the running application (percent complete, resources used, etc.). These facilities should be available not just from a graphical interface, but also from an API-like one so the sandbox can be ``remote controlled''. So in the second place transparent sandbox should mean *transparent for the system.*

A sandbox should *isolate* the running application inside meaning should have no access to the resources of the host and should prohibit any outside connection. It should be also *"bulletproof",* thus no malicious application may render the sandbox unusable or requiring administrator intervention. This may be impossible to fulfill for any currently running task since an application might destroy it, but at least for the next task the sandbox should be once again available (and the current one should be stopped and marked as failed). The *transparency for the system* criteria requires that the there is no restriction for the client whether running applications normally or inside a sandbox, thus it needs a ``backdoor'' to copy applications and input data into the sandbox and later to extract results from it to be uploaded to the server. It is not enough for this backdoor to provide a simple file put/get interface it also should enable to start or stop and to get status information about the work unit running. This backdoor should be *one way*, meaning the client can put and extract data from the sandbox, but the sandbox cannot reach the host via this interface.

Multi-core processors are common for desktop computers thus more instances can be executed parallel. In this case independent ``copies'' of the sandbox should be started for each application (running on different cores) meaning that the sandbox should provide *instantiation*. Worst case this means that a copy is made every time of an immutable sandbox (``base'') and the copy is started for the application.

Best case no copy is need to be made, just a thin overlay which references the base and every modification to the instance should be stored there. This would also lower the used disk space and the time required for creating new instances. The immutable sandbox ensures the ``*bulletproof*'' criteria, since the instance can be thrown away whether the work unit finished successfully or not and a new instance can be created for the next one.

When using virtualization software *licensing* issues apply, meaning that the software should be preferably open source and freely redistributable at best, but worst case it must still allow the software to be deployed with the Desktop Grid client. Manual download and installation might be too much of a task for any user. It should be able to run in the background without any windows or pop-ups presented at the user (*"background"* in Table 3).

Any potentially to be used virtualization software must fulfill these requirements in order to be used as a transparent sandbox.

VIRTUAL MACHINES

Although all tools described in this section are referred as ``virtual machines'', two approaches must be distinguished. *Pure emulation* models the desired architecture/ platform from software. No code from the guest is ever run on the host CPU, everything is emulated. The biggest benefit is portability, since there is no dependency between the emulated platform and the hosting one, the trade-off is a significant performance loss, and a typical example is Bochs (Lawton, 1996). The second approach is usually referred as machine virtualization: it is used to implement a virtual machine environment so that it provides simulation of the underlying hardware. There are several levels of virtualization which can be accomplished. *Full virtualization* provides a complete abstraction of the underlying hardware enabling execution of all software that runs on the raw hardware to be run in the virtual machine, examples for full virtualization are VMware and VirtualBox (Watson, 2008). *Hardware-assisted virtualization* (or native virtualization) is a virtualization approach that enables efficient full virtualization using help from hardware capabilities like AMD-V (originally codenamed Pacifica and AMD Secure Virtual Machines) (Vincent, 2005) or Intel VT-x (Uhlig et al., 2005), primarily from the host processors. *Paravirtualization* presents a software interface to virtual machines that is similar but not identical to that of the underlying hardware. It may allow the virtual machines that run on it to achieve performance closer to non-virtualized hardware. However, operating systems must be explicitly ported. The best example for paravirtualization is XEN (Barham et al., 2003).

Bochs is an open source x86 *emulator* written in C++. It is running in user-space, and emulates the x86 processor with several I/O devices, and provides a custom BIOS. Bochs is highly portable, but rather slow since it emulates every instruction and I/O device. The primary author of Bochs reported 1.5 MIPS on a 400 MHz Pentium II, compared to the processor's original speed of ~1100 MIPS.

QEMU (Bellard, 2005) is an open source processor emulator and virtual machine, released under the Lesser GNU Public License and BSD License. It is available on every major platform and is able to host every major platform and can boot many guest operating systems. It runs as a single user process and is intended as a desktop product, but can be run as a background process presenting no windows or terminals at the user. Since it is emulating the guest architecture the performance is far from native, but on x86 Windows/Linux it has an accelerator named *KQEMU* or QEMU Accelerator, which speeds up x86 emulation to near native level. This is accomplished by running user mode code directly on the host computer's CPU, and using processor and peripheral emulation only for kernel mode and real mode code. However KQEMU was deprecated in the favor of KVM (Kivity, Kamay, Laor, Lublin & Liguori, 2007). QEMU implements overlay images, meaning it can keep a snapshot of the guest system, and write changes to a separate image file. If the guest system breaks, the original image or an earlier snapshot can be used to resume. It can save and restore the state of the running instance (checkpoint itself), also to an overlay image. QEMU does not need administrative rights to run. It Implements copy-on-write disk image formats, meaning that images only use that much disk space what they actually use and supports compressing images. Has a console for managing, running instances, and this console can be accessed either from a user interface or via a socket. It has support for virtual network card emulation, or can disable outside network at all, but still can forward a specific port to the host and bind it to a socket or port allowing one way communication with applications within the guest. It has a set of command line tools which provide full control over QEMU without having to run a separate graphical client.

VMware Player is a free, but not open source x86 virtualization product with the limitation of not being able to create, only able to start VM images. It provides the appearance of full virtualization by using binary translation. It requires Windows or Linux to run. It consists of several components: a user-level application (VMApp), a device driver (VMDriver) for the host system, and a virtual machine monitor (VMM). I/O initiated by a guest system is trapped the the VMM and forwarded to the VMApp, which executes in the host's context and performs the I/O using regular system calls, this way it achieves nearly native performance. VMware Player has a graphical interface and needs administrative rights to run on Windows.

VirtualBox is an x86 only virtualization software with optional support for hardware-assisted virtualization (through AMD-V and Intel VT). Its main components are open source released under the GNU Public License V2. Some additional components (e.g., USB support) is not open source, but still free for personal use and evaluation. VirtualBox originally relied on some QEMU components, it tries to run as much code as possible native, but if problems arise it falls back to a dynamic recompiler, which based on QEMU, to emulate the x86 processor. Actually VirtualBox makes use of QEMU in two ways: first, some of the virtual hardware devices have their origin in the QEMU project. Secondly it utilizes the recompiler of QEMU as a fallback mechanism for situations where it's Virtual Machine Manager (monitor) cannot correctly handle a certain situation. VirtualBox needs administrative privileges to run.

Containers like Linux Containers (LXC) are an operating system level virtualization environments on Linux based systems. The Linux kernel allows the prioritization and limitation of resources (e.g., memory, CPU, I/O, network, etc.) via its control groups (*cgroups*) feature. This allows the complete isolation of applications and their environments' (networking, process tree, user/ group IDs) without the need for virtual machines (VMs) making them lightweight, however with the drawback of they require explicit OS level support. The most popular software in relation with containers is Docker (Docker, n.d.). Docker automates the management and deployment of applications in containers.

By using some kind of virtualization, preferably VMs, as sandbox providing tool would provide several additional benefits:

- **Simplified Application Development:** Separate the host operating system from the guest, which allow running the same OS (preferably Linux) on the guest regardless of the host os. This would allow having a single version of the application, but it would still run on all resources connected.
- **System-Level Checkpointing:** VMs usually provide a method to save or serialize their current state to disk which can be later used to resume the VM, thus running applications do not need

to have the capability to checkpoint themselves. For example in the case of BOINC where each application implements its own checkpoint function (application-level checkpointing) this would mean that there is no need to write this non-trivial function. Combining system-level checkpointing with *instantiation* would allow easy migration of the task, if the same base image is used amongst clients, only the instance image needs to be migrated to a new client which would greatly reduce upload times and save bandwidth.

- **Legacy Applications:** By having a separate operating system available inside the VM, applications could be run whose source code is not available, so cannot be ported to any new platform, or those that have too many dependencies to be run on a volunteer's computer.
- **Enforce Resource Limits:** Any application running is guaranteed not to exceed the resource limits (e.g.: memory, disk or CPU) allocated for the VM.

Middleware Based Approach

The main goal was to design a generic architecture that can be later integrated with DGs (especially with SZTAKI DG and XtremWeb). The basic concept is to provide tools and APIs which allow creating and starting VM instances, uploading input files and executables into the instance, start tasks using the uploaded files, request status information and when finished retrieve the output files. The architecture is shown in Figure 15, the main components are the following:

- The *VM API* is to hide the under laying architecture and to provide a simple API for creating VM instances using the VM Manager and interacting with the created instances.
- The *Backend* stores metadata about the status of each created VM Instance. This allows the sandbox to be shut down and resumed any time.
- The *Base Image(s)* serve as immutable basis for the sandbox. Each instance is created from one of these base images. It contains a minimalist installation of an operating system (preferably Linux) and the Communication Daemon.
- The *Instance Image(s)* store the difference between the base image and the created instances. This way nothing is written back to the Base Image whether something is created, modified or removed. Also checkpoints should be stored here.
- The *Communication Daemon* handles the communication and data transfer between the VM Instance and the host. Communication is always initiated by the host, the daemon can only reply to requests, thus the host has to poll the daemon periodically for updates.
- The *Execution Environment* acts is where all application and task data is put and the task is run inside the VM Instance.

The client downloads a new task which consists of a binary executable, input files for the binary and several other files (libraries and other dependencies). Normally these are to be run by the client using a *fork* based execution method, but this approach provides a *sandbox* based one. A separate sandbox for each task is created with the capability to suspend, continue, checkpoint and resume if requested by the client. For managing sandboxes a C API is provided and a JAVA API is being developed, now we detail the C API to demonstrate how the sandbox works. Sandboxes consist of a VM instance and a library providing the VM API to manage the instance.

Figure 15. Architecture of the sandbox

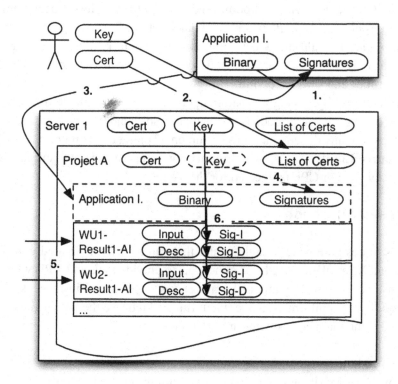

The VM API consists of two parts, first the *vm_sb_* * API functions are to control tasks inside an instance, the remaining *vm_* * API functions are to manage the instance(s). The functionality of this API is similar to the one provided by libvirt, but for this approach the authors did not need the complexity and most of the features of libvirt, and so the authors choose to go with their simpler one.

The *vm_init* and *vm_cleanup* API functions are called by the client on startup and before exit. All *vm_* * functions operate on a *VM_STATE* structure which represents the VM Instance. The state and metadata of the instance is always kept updated in the Backend, thus no need to serialize this structure manually. When needed any previous (not deleted) instance can be loaded using *vm_load*.

First the sandbox is created by calling the *vm_create* function, which creates a new VM instance using a selected Base Image as basis. *vm_start* starts the instance, the instance might not be available instantly, so the client waits and issues *vm_get_state* periodically. When the instance is running the files of the current task are copied in to the sandbox inside the instance using the *vm_sb_put* function. Any disk operation is written to the instance image not the base image, this way even if a malicious application destroys somehow the VM Instance, it cannot make any damage to the Base Image or to any other existing instances.

Inside the VM Instance the Communication Daemon handles the incoming messages and passes them either to the Message Handler which is responsible for controlling the application or to the Data Handler which is responsible for moving data in or out from the instance. *vm_sb_start* is used to start the execution of the application, any additional parameters (e.g., environment variables, command line, etc.) are passed by this function. Since the sandbox cannot initiate outward communication the client needs to periodically poll the status of the running application using *vm_sb_ping*. After the application finished (whether successfully or failed) the output files are copied back to the client using *vm_sb_get*, and the sandbox will report the client that the application exited and the results can be uploaded to the server. After finished the VM Instance is not needed anymore, so first it is shut down by issuing *vm_stop* and second it is deleted by calling *vm_destroy*.

The client may be instructed to suspend computation for example by local policies or user request. In this case the *vm_suspend* function suspends the VM Instance, but it still remains resident in memory waiting for *vm_continue* to continue operation. If the client is shutdown all running instances need to checkpoint, this is done via *vm_checkpoint*. Each checkpoint is assigned a unique id which can be used later to resume using *vm_resume*, or from the last checkpoint if the uuid is omitted.

There are messaging functions provided for sending custom messages from/to the instance, which can be used also to upload partial results to the host while the task is active. *msg_from_host* function is for sending custom messages to the task running in the VM Instance, while the *msg_to_host* is used to send a message from the task to the host. Since the VM Instance cannot initiate any communication outwards, the host needs to periodically call this function to check if there are any messages from the guest. A type is assigned for every task which identifies the DG the task is originating from. Currently BOINC and XTREMWEB types are supported (and UNKNOWN type is set as default). The Communication Daemon allows installing custom message/ data handlers for the different task types; this allows easily extending and customizing it according the needs of the selected DG.

GBAC: An Application Based Approach

In the previous section the authors (i) defined a criteria system for comparing different desktop virtualization solutions for desktop grids; (ii) evaluated the available tools (Bochs, QEMU, KQEMU, VMWare Player and VirtualBox); (iii) defined a generic architecture which allows building virtualized environments for task execution on desktop grid and volunteer resources; and (iv) did a reference implementation with focus on integration with BOINC and XtremWeb. The authors chose QEMU and KQEMU as the virtualization software for the implementation since at that time it was the solution best fitting to criteria system of the authors. The second best solution was VirtualBox. There are two considerations that need to be taken into account and thus, result in a different approach:

1. The original proposition was an integrated solution where the virtualization based execution service is integrated with the given (desktop) grid middleware client. Others chose this approach as well (Ferreira, Araujo & Domingues, 2011). The problem is that this would require extensive modifications in the client desktop grid software. In case of BOINC there are currently ~8.7 million hosts running the client software (BOINCstats/BAM!, n.d.) and only after an update would these hosts be able to run virtualization enabled tasks. This is not feasible and the authors think that a solution is required that is not tightly coupled with the client software and does not impose any modifications to the client. This can be achieved the easiest by including all virtualization related parts in a "traditional" application which would act as a wrapper.

2. QEMU dropped support for KQEMU and is left without acceleration support on Windows. QEMU itself (without KQEMU) is too slow, as the evaluation of the authors has shown (see Section Abstraction A3-1 and A3-2: Environment detachment), to be considered as a viable alternative.

Contrary, VirtualBox has progressed a lot in the recent years. It was improved in many ways and currently based on the authors criteria system (see Section Abstraction A3-1 and A3-2: Environment detachment) it is considered the best virtualization solution for desktop grids. Several other implementations aiming at utilizing virtualization for desktop grids have emerged and these also build upon VirtualBox. For example, CernVM (Sanchez et al., 2011) and VBoxWrapper (BOINC VirtualBox Applications, n.d.) are available for BOINC. The common in these solutions is that both are explicitly developed for BOINC and are not intended to become a generic framework.

Based on these two considerations the authors decided that instead of relying on QEMU in the future (without KQEMU support) they would switch to VirtualBox (see (1)); and instead of tight integration they have chosen a wrapper like approach (see (2)). The authors put the QEMU based implementation aside and chose VBoxWrapper as basis for a new implementation. The difference between their implementation and the basic VBoxWrapper one is that the authors intend to provide a generic framework and not a BOINC specific one. Currently the implementation supports BOINC, Condor and XtremWeb middleware beside standalone execution. The approach differs in the following: (a.) the authors are providing a generic framework that can be used with multiple middleware, although for demonstration purposes in this work we use BOINC; (b.) they want to support multiple virtualized environments through multiple layered virtual appliances (see Section Virtual Appliance Management); and (c.) the authors consider GBAC as one of the foundations for volunteer clouds rather than only a wrapper able to execute applications within a virtualized environment.

The Generic BOINC Application Client (GBAC) is a virtualization based wrapper. Contrary to its name it aims to be a generic framework providing virtualized environments for various distributed computing infrastructures (DCIs). GBAC is implemented using the DC-API Meta API and does not rely on any middleware specific functionalities, thus it is possible to use it on any DCIs that are supported by DC-API. In the following the BOINC version of GBAC is assumed for demonstrating its concepts and internals.

GBAC wrapper consists of the following components as shown in Figure 16: First, the wrapper binary (see 1. in Figure 16) itself is a BOINC enabled DC-API application that contains all BOINC related parts and handles communication with the BOINC client. Its task is to set up the client execution environment and manage the virtual machine on the client machine. Second, a supplied XML based configuration file (see 2. in Figure 16) is used to set the different parameters of the virtual machine: (i) the operating system type (e.g., Linux 64bit); (ii) the size of the allocated memory for the virtual machine; (iii) whether the machine should have network access; (iv) which virtual appliance to use; and (v) whether to enable a shared directory between the host and the guest (the virtual machine). The third component is a virtual appliance (see 3. in Figure 16) that contains the operating systems and libraries for the virtual machine. This image contains a 32bit Linux installation with some GBAC related components that will be detailed later in the next section "Architecture".

The wrapper sets up the client execution environment first by creating a shared directory for the virtual machine. It puts all input files in this directory. GBAC does not separate the binaries of the legacy application (typically a parameter sweep application as described in the introduction) and its input files (see 4. and 5. in Figure 16). This means that all legacy application binaries and their input files are normal input files for GBAC and are not part of the GBAC BOINC application. As a next step the virtual machine is started using VirtualBox. GBAC does not contain VirtualBox; it is a prerequisite that every host has VirtualBox preinstalled before GBAC can be used. Next, the legacy application is executed in

Figure 16. GBAC: application, inputs and outputs

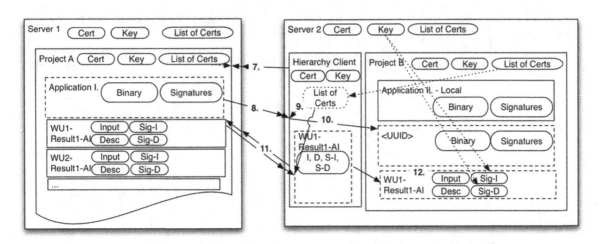

the virtual machine and the results are copied to the shared directory. Once the application finished the virtual machine shuts down and finally GBAC copies the results from the shared directory to the work directory of the BOINC client and terminates.

In the following subsections the functionality of GBAC is going to be detailed by describing a job submission generated from a parameter sweep application that is not registered at the BOINC server and hence without GBAC BOINC would not be able to handle it. In this description of BOINC it is assumed that the PS application is initiated either in a service grid VO (gLite, ARC or UNICORE) that is extended with a BOINC DG system. 3G Bridge (Farkas, Kacsuk, Balaton & Gombás, 2010) plays a crucial role connecting the SG systems with BOINC and enabling the job submission from WS-PGRADE to BOINC.

Architecture

The 3G Bridge provides a job handler service interface for accepting job submissions (see 1. in Figure 17). It assigns jobs to different job queues and stores them in its job database. Different DCI plug-ins can be used to submit (forward) jobs to different DCIs. 3G Bridge also provides extended services like a web service interface to add and query jobs.

3G Bridge keeps a list of the supported algorithms (applications in case of desktop grids) for each configured DCI. When a job is received (see 2. in Figure 17), 3G Bridge checks if the job fits to a registered algorithm (see 3. in Figure 17). If the algorithm is not registered it means that the application is not deployed so the job cannot be executed. When GBAC is registered in the algorithm Queue of 3g Bridge the job for the "unknown" PS application is redirected to it with one constraint, namely the task should contain not only the input files (which is normal for desktop grid job submission) but the application binaries as well or else the execution will fail. It is possible to include all application related files in a special named bundle (zip or tar.gz). This is only for user convenience and it eases job submission. Once the job is internally redirected to the GBAC queue, 3G Bridge submits it to the desktop grid via its configured DC-API plug-in (see 5. and 6. in Figure 17) that generates a GBAC work unit for the connected BOINC server (see 6. in Figure 17). After this BOINC will register the new work unit for the deployed

Figure 17. GBAC: server side related parts

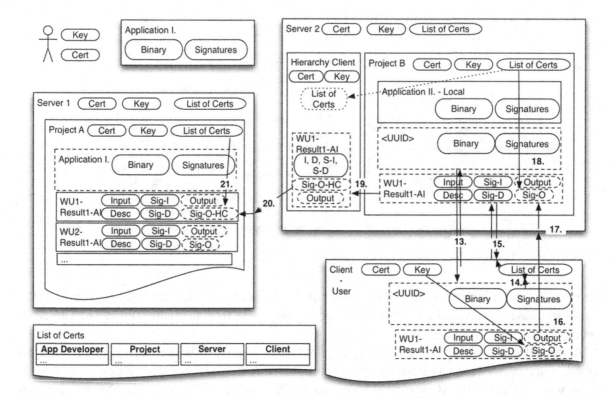

GBAC application and when a client with deployed VirtualBox asks for tasks BOINC will assign the work unit to the client. The current client side implementation of GBAC is based on VirtualBox and the BOINC client is able to detect and report to the BOINC server whether VirtualBox is installed on the client. The BOINC server will assign GBAC tasks only for those hosts that have VirtualBox preinstalled.

First a legacy application with its inputs is submitted via the 3G Bridge to BOINC (see 1. and 2. in Figure 18) and it is transformed into a GBAC application work unit containing the binaries and input files of the legacy application as inputs of the GBAC application. When a BOINC client connects, from a host where VirtualBox is installed, to the BOINC server and asks for tasks, it receives the work unit containing the GBAC application with its inputs. The BOINC client first downloads the GBAC binary, its configuration file and the virtual appliance along with the legacy application binaries and the input files (see 3. in Figure 18).

After the download finished the client starts the GBAC application. The first task of GBAC is to bootstrap the execution environment: it creates a directory that will be shared between the host and guest and all legacy application binaries and input files are copied here (see 4. in Figure 18). Also a special file is put into this directory that contains additional parameters of the application (e.g., command line parameters and environment variables). After this the virtual machine is started (see 5. in Figure 18) using the VirtualBox command line interface ("VBoxManage"). All parameters for the virtual machine are set in a configuration file for GBAC. This configuration file is currently part of the application and common for every GBAC application work unit, but it can also be supplied individually for each task

Figure 18. GBAC: execution of a sample task

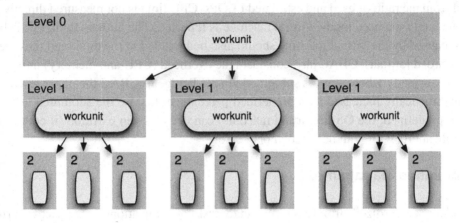

allowing more customization for the virtual machine. The configuration file also contains a reference to the virtual appliance to be used. Currently a single Linux appliance has been developed for GBAC but using more appliances is not prohibited by the GBAC concept. The appliance contains the GBAC guest extensions (see 6. in Figure 18) and these are started right after the boot process finished. First, a component checks if there are any application bundles found in the shared directory. If yes, it extracts the contents to a separate sandbox within the virtual machine. If not, then all files are simply copied to the sandbox. After this the legacy application is started in the sandbox (see 7. in Figure 18). Volunteer resources are highly volatile and any application running on these resources in the framework of a volunteer computing project should be prepared for interruption or shut down. This problem is usually solved by including an application specific (application-level) checkpointing mechanism in each application. The advantage of GBAC is clear here: application-level checkpointing is not needed since GBAC uses the system-level mechanism provided by the virtual machine monitor. GBAC can be suspended or stopped at any time regardless of what application it is executing and the suspended GBAC application can be resumed either on the current client or on a new client. While the virtual machine is running, GBAC continuously monitors its status through the virtual machine monitor.

After the execution of the legacy application has finished, all new and changed files are copied to the shared directory by the guest extensions (see 8. in Figure 18). Finally the virtual machine is instructed to shut itself down. Next GBAC notices that the virtual machine has terminated and it will copy all changed files from the shared directory to the working directory and terminate itself (see 9. in Figure 18). From here the BOINC client takes over, it will contact the BOINC server (see 10/a. in Figure 18), upload the output files (see 10/b. in Figure 18) and report the completion of the task. Next 3G Bridge fetches the results from BOINC (see 11. in Figure 18) and will return it to the submitter (see 12. in Figure 18).

BOINC employs reporting techniques which allow (i) the native applications to report their status (e.g., completion ratio) and (ii) measure the CPU time used for computation of the current task. These data are visualized in the BOINC client so that volunteers know what the status of the current task is and what to expect. Also for each task an upper limit for used resources (FLOPs, disk and memory) is set by the entity that created the task (in this case by 3G Bridge). In case of applications running in a virtualized environment (which acts basically like a sandbox) the reporting techniques do not work. The current implementation of GBAC does not allow reporting completion status (see (i)), instead the ratio is calculated from the ratio of used and estimated FLOPs. CPU time is not measured directly either (see (ii)) rather the total time used by the virtual machine is reported. The authors think this is better since the overhead caused by the virtual machine should also be included in the total (and thus the volunteer should be rewarded for that). GBAC also considers the overhead (CPU and memory) introduced by the virtualization. Currently when a task is submitted via 3G Bridge to GBAC the upper resource limit for the task is automatically increased by a predefined percentage. In case the submitted task takes more memory than predefined, the OS (in virtual machine) can use its swap partition (if configured) or the app will simply aborts with "run out of memory" error.

Virtual Appliance Management

GBAC provides a standardized virtual environment for tasks of applications and services. Currently there are base virtual appliances available that are based on Debian Linux and Scientific Linux. For each task a new virtual machine instance is started with the appliance by GBAC and shut down after the task is finished. There are two concerns with this: (i) although tasks are executed inside a sandbox within the virtual machine, if a task is somehow able to break out and do modifications to the file system of the virtual machine (e.g., the kernel is deleted) that might render it unusable permanently; (ii) after each execution a cleanup procedure is required to remove the remnants of the previous task.

To overcome these problems the authors chose to compose the virtual appliance for GBAC of multiple overlay images (appliances) as shown in Figure 19. First the base virtual appliance is immutable, meaning that no modifications can be done to it (see (i)). This is enforced not at the file system level, rather it is guaranteed by the hypervisor. It redirects all disk I/O to a separate overlay image which is specific to each running virtual machine instance. This also solves the problem of cleaning up the sandbox (see (ii)) after each execution, since the instance image can be simply thrown away. Second, the authors introduce optional application specific overlay images which can contain all application specific dependencies that are supplementary for the base image. In this case the immutable image is a composite of the base and the application image and all file system modifications initiated in the virtual machine are redirected to the instance image.

Figure 19. A virtual appliance for GBAC is composed of a base image, an optional application overlay image and an instance image

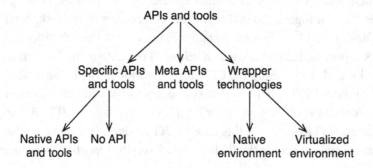

CONCLUSION

Volunteer Computing utilizes the idle resources (i.e., CPU cycles and storage) of private donated computers. CC is built using dedicated and reliable resources and provides uniform seemingly unlimited capacities. Heterogeneity exists in VC at different levels. The vision of CC promises to provide a homogeneous environment. This chapter per the authors identified methods and proposed solutions that tackle the heterogeneities and thus, make a step towards Volunteer Clouds.

REFERENCES

Allen, G., Davis, K., Goodale, T., Hutanu, A., Kaiser, H., Kielmann, T., & Ullmer, B. et al. (2005). The grid application toolkit: Toward generic and easy application programming interfaces for the grid. *Proceedings of the IEEE*, *93*(3), 534–550. doi:10.1109/JPROC.2004.842755

Anderson, D. P. (2004). BOINC: A System for Public-Resource Computing and Storage. In R. Buyya (Ed.), *Proceedings of the Fifth IEEE/ACM International Workshop on Grid Computing* (pp. 4–10). doi:10.1109/GRID.2004.14

Anderson, D. P., & Fedak, G. (2006). The Computational and Storage Potential of Volunteer Computing. *Proceedings of the Sixth IEEE International Symposium on Cluster Computing and the Grid (CC-GRID'06)* (pp. 73–80). IEEE. doi:10.1109/CCGRID.2006.101

Armbrust, M., Fox, A., Griffith, R., Joseph, A. D., Katz, R. H., Konwinski, A., & Zaharia, M. (2009). *Above the clouds: A Berkeley view of cloud computing (Technical Report No. UCB/EECS-2009-28)*. Retrieved from http://www.eecs.berkeley.edu/Pubs/TechRpts/2009/EECS-2009-28.html

Balaton, Z., Gombas, G., Kacsuk, P., Kornafeld, A., Kovacs, J., & Marosi, A. C., ... Kiss, T. (2007). SZTAKI Desktop Grid: a Modular and Scalable Way of Building Large Computing Grids. *Proceedings of the 2007 IEEE International Parallel and Distributed Processing Symposium* (pp. 1–8). IEEE. doi:10.1109/IPDPS.2007.370665

Barham, P., Dragovic, B., Fraser, K., Hand, S., Harris, T., Ho, A., & Warfield, A. (2003). Xen and the art of virtualization. *Operating Systems Review*, *37*(5), 164–177. doi:10.1145/1165389.945462

Bellard, F. (2005). QEMU, a Fast and Portable Dynamic Translator. *Proceedings of the USENIX Annual Technical Conference, FREENIX Track* (pp. 41–46).

BOINC VirtualBox Applications. (n. d.). Retrieved from http://boinc.berkeley.edu/trac/wiki/VboxApps

BOINCstats/BAM! (n. d.). Retrieved from http://boincstats.com

Cappello, F., Djilali, S., Fedak, G., Herault, T., Magniette, F., Neri, V., & Lodygensky, O. (2005). Computing on large-scale distributed systems: XtremWeb architecture, programming models, security, tests and convergence with grid. *Future Generation Computer Systems*, *21*(3), 417–437. doi:10.1016/j. future.2004.04.011

Choi, S., & Buyya, R. (2010). Group-based adaptive result certification mechanism in Desktop Grids. *Future Generation Computer Systems*, *26*(5), 776–786. doi:10.1016/j.future.2009.05.025

Docker – Official Site. (n. d.). Retrieved from http://www.docker.com/

Epema, D., Livny, M., van Dantzig, R., Evers, X., & Pruyne, J. (1996). A worldwide flock of Condors: Load sharing among workstation clusters. *Future Generation Computer Systems, 12*(1), 53–65. doi:10.1016/0167-739X(95)00035-Q

Farkas, Z., Kacsuk, P., Balaton, Z., & Gombás, G. (2010). Interoperability of BOINC and EGEE. *Future Generation Computer Systems, 26*(8), 1092–1103. doi:10.1016/j.future.2010.05.009

Ferreira, D., Araujo, F., & Domingues, P. (2011). libboincexec: A Generic Virtualization Approach for the BOINC Middleware. *Proceedings of the 2011 IEEE International Symposium on Parallel and Distributed Processing Workshops and Phd Forum (IPDPSW)* (pp. 1903–1908). doi:10.1109/IPDPS.2011.349

Foster, I., Zhao, Y., Raicu, I., & Lu, S. (2008). Cloud Computing and Grid Computing 360-Degree Compared. Proceedings of the 2008 Grid Computing Environments Workshop (pp. 1–10). IEEE. doi:10.1109/GCE.2008.4738445

Use Cases and Functional Requirements for Inter-Cloud Computing. (2010). *Global Inter-cloud Technology Forum*. Retrieved from http://www.gictf.jp/doc/GICTF_Whitepaper_20100809.pdf

Goodale, T., Jha, S., Kaiser, H., Kielmann, T., Kleijer, P., Von Laszewski, G., & Shalf, J. (2006). SAGA: A Simple API for Grid Applications. High-level application programming on the Grid. *Computational Methods in Science and Technology, 12*(1), 7–20. doi:10.12921/cmst.2006.12.01.07-20

Grozev, N., & Buyya, R. (2012). Inter-Cloud Architectures and Application Brokering: Taxonomy and Survey. doi:10.1002/spe

Java Native Interface. (n. d.). Retrieved from http://java.sun.com/javase/6/docs/technotes/guides/jni/index.html

Kivity, A., Kamay, Y., Laor, D., Lublin, U., & Liguori, A. (2007). KVM: the Linux virtual machine monitor. *Proceedings of the Linux Symposium* (Vol. 1, pp. 225–230).

Lawton, K. P. (1996). Bochs: A portable pc emulator for Unix. *Linux Journal, 1996*(29), 7.

Lázaro, D., Kondo, D., & Marquès, J. M. (2012). Long-term availability prediction for groups of volunteer resources. *Journal of Parallel and Distributed Computing, 72*(2), 281–296. doi:10.1016/j.jpdc.2011.10.007

Marosi, A., Balaton, Z., & Kacsuk, P. (2009). GenWrapper: A generic wrapper for running legacy applications on desktop grids. *Proceedings of the 2009 IEEE International Symposium on Parallel & Distributed Processing* (pp. 1–6). IEEE. doi:10.1109/IPDPS.2009.5161136

Marosi, A., Gombás, G., Balaton, Z., & Kacsuk, P. (2008). Enabling Java applications for BOINC with DC-API. In P. Kacsuk, R. Lovas, & Z. Németh (Eds.), *Distributed and Parallel Systems SE - 1* (pp. 3–12). Springer, US; doi:10.1007/978-0-387-79448-8_1

Marosi, A., Kovács, J., & Kacsuk, P. (2012). Towards a volunteer cloud system. *Future Generation Computer Systems*. doi:10.1016/j.future.2012.03.013

Marosi, A. C., Gombás, G., Balaton, Z., Kacsuk, P., & Kiss, T. (2008). SZTAKI Desktop Grid: Building a Scalable, Secure Platform for Desktop Grid Computing. In Making Grids Work (pp. 363–374). Springer.

Marosi, A. C., Kacsuk, P., Fedak, G., & Lodygensky, O. (2010). Sandboxing for Desktop Grids Using Virtualization. *Proceedings of the 2010 18th Euromicro Conference on Parallel, Distributed and Network-based Processing* (pp. 559–566). IEEE. doi:10.1109/PDP.2010.90

Mell, P., & Grance, T. (2011). *The NIST Definition of Cloud Computing*. Gaithersburg, MD. Retrieved from http://csrc.nist.gov/publications/nistpubs/800-145/SP800-145.pdf

Perens, B. (n. d.). BusyBox: The Swiss Army Knife of Embedded Linux. Retrieved from http://www.busybox.net

Rochwerger, B., Breitgand, D., Levy, E., Galis, A., Nagin, K., Llorente, I. M., Galan, F. (2009). The Reservoir model and architecture for open federated cloud computing. *IBM Journal of Research and Development, 53*(4), 4:1–4:11. doi:10.1147/JRD.2009.5429058

Sanchez, C. A., Blomer, J., Buncic, P., Chen, G., Ellis, J., Quintas, D. G., & Yadav, R. (2011). Volunteer Clouds and Citizen Cyberscience for LHC Physics. *Journal of Physics: Conference Series, 331*(6), 62022. http://stacks.iop.org/1742-6596/331/i=6/a=062022 doi:10.1088/1742-6596/331/6/062022

The R Project for Statistical Computing. (n. d.). Retrieved from http://www.r-project.org/

Tröger, P., Rajic, H., Haas, A., & Domagalski, P. (2007). Standardization of an API for distributed resource management systems. *Proceedings of the Seventh IEEE International Symposium on Cluster Computing and the Grid CCGRID '07* (pp. 619–626). doi:10.1109/CCGRID.2007.109

Uhlig, R., Neiger, G., Rodgers, D., Santoni, A. L., Martins, F. C. M., Anderson, A. V., & Smith, L. (2005). Intel virtualization technology. *Computer, 38*(5), 48–56. doi:10.1109/MC.2005.163

Velasco, J. L., Bustos, A., Castejón, F., Fernández, L. A., Martin-Mayor, V., & Tarancón, A. (2012). ISDEP: Integrator of stochastic differential equations for plasmas. *Computer Physics Communications, 183*(9), 1877–1883. doi:10.1016/j.cpc.2012.04.005

Vincent, A. (2005). AMD64 Virtualization Reference Manual. Retrieved from http://www.mimuw.edu.pl/~vincent/lecture6/sources/amd-pacifica-specification.pdf

Watson, J. (2008). VirtualBox: Bits and Bytes Masquerading As Machines. *Linux J., 2008*(166). Retrieved from http://dl.acm.org/citation.cfm?id=1344209.1344210

Compilation of References

(2000, August). Commission Decision no. 2000/520/EC of 26 July 2000 pursuant to Directive 95/46/EC of the European Parliament and of the Council on the adequacy of the protection provided by the safe harbor privacy principles and related frequently asked questions issued by the US Department of Commerce. *Official Journal, 215*, 7–47.

(COM(2012)0011 – C7-0025/2012 – 2012/0011(COD)). Draft opinion of the Committee on the Internal Market and Consumer Protection (IMCO) for the Committee on Civil Liberties, Justice and Home Affairs on the proposal for a regulation of the European Parliament and of the Council on the protection of individuals with regard to the processing of personal data and on the free movement of such data (General Data Protection Regulation). 25 September, 2012.

A Digital Agenda for Europe COM (2010) 0245 final. (2010). Commission to the European Parliament, the Council, the European Economic and Social Committee and the Committee of the Regions.

A. Kertesz & Sz. Varadi (2008): Legal Aspects of Data Protection in Cloud Federations. In S. Nepal & M. Pathan (Ed.), *Security, Privacy and Trust in Cloud Systems* (pp 433-455) Berlin, Heidelberg: Springer-Verlag.

Abecker, A., & Tellmann, R. (2003). Analysis of Interaction between Semantic Web Languages, P2P architectures, and Agents. *EU-IST Project SWWS–Semantic Web Enabled Web Services project IST-2002-37134*.

Agarwal, P. K., Hampton, S., Poznanovic, J., Ramanthan, A., Alam, S. R., & Crozier, P. S. (2013). Performance modeling of microsecond scale biological molecular dynamics simulations on heterogeneous architectures. *Concurrency and Computation, 25*(10), 1356–1375. doi:10.1002/cpe.2943

Al Falasi, A., Serhani, M. A., & Elnaffar, S. (2013). The sky: A social approach to clouds federation. *Procedia Computer Science, 19*, 131–138. doi:10.1016/j.procs.2013.06.022

Alhamad, M., Dillon, T., & Chang, E. (2010). SLA-based trust model for cloud computing. *Proceedings of the 2010 13th International Conference on Network-Based Information Systems (NBiS)* (pp. 321-324). IEEE. doi:10.1109/NBiS.2010.67

Al-Hazmi, Y., Campowsky, K., & Magedanz, T. (2012). A monitoring system for federated clouds. *Proceedings of 1st International Conference on Cloud Networking (CLOUDNET)*, Paris, France: IEEE.

Allen, G., Davis, K., Goodale, T., Hutanu, A., Kaiser, H., Kielmann, T., & Ullmer, B. et al. (2005). The grid application toolkit: Toward generic and easy application programming interfaces for the grid. *Proceedings of the IEEE, 93*(3), 534–550. doi:10.1109/JPROC.2004.842755

Almulla, S. A., & Yeun, C. Y. (2010, March). Cloud computing security management. *Proceedings of the 2010 Second International Conference on Engineering Systems Management and Its Applications (ICESMA)* (pp. 1-7). IEEE.

Amato, A., Di Martino, B., & Venticinque, S. (2012). Evaluation and brokering of service level agreements for negotiation of cloud infrastructures. *Proceedings of the 2012 International Conference for Internet Technology and Secured Transactions* (pp. 144-149). IEEE.

Amazon AWS Cloudfront. (2014). *Amazon*. Retrieved from http://aws.amazon.com/cloudfront/

Amazon EC2. (2015). Retrieved from http://aws.amazon.com/ec2/

Amazon EC2. (n. d.). *Amazon*. Retrieved from http://aws.amazon.com/ec2/

Amazon Kinesis. (n. d.). *Amazon*. Retrieved from http://aws.amazon.com/kinesis/

Amazon Mobile. (2015, May). *Amazon*. Retrieved from http://aws.amazon.com/mobile/

Amazon Web Services. (2015, May). *Amazon*. Retrieved from http://aws.amazon.com/

Amazon Web Services-Identity and Access Management. (2015). Retrieved from http://aws.amazon.com/iam

Amazon Web Services-Multi Factor Authentication. (2015). Retrieved from http://aws.amazon.com/mfa

An open, global, cloud interoperability project. (2015). Intercloud Testbed. Retrieved from http://www.intercloudtestbed.org

Anderson, D. P. (2004). BOINC: A System for Public-Resource Computing and Storage. In R. Buyya (Ed.), *Proceedings of the Fifth IEEE/ACM International Workshop on Grid Computing* (pp. 4–10). doi:10.1109/GRID.2004.14

Anderson, D. P., & Fedak, G. (2006). The Computational and Storage Potential of Volunteer Computing. *Proceedings of the Sixth IEEE International Symposium on Cluster Computing and the Grid (CCGRID'06)* (pp. 73–80). IEEE. doi:10.1109/CCGRID.2006.101

Andrieux, A., Czajkowski, K., Dan, A., Keahey, K., Ludwig, H., Nakata, T., . . . Xu, M. (2005). *Web services agreement specification (WS-Agreement)* (Tech. Rep.). Global Grid Forum, Grid Resource Allocation Agreement Protocol (GRAAP) WG.

Antonopoulos, N., & Gillam, L. (2010). *Cloud computing: principles, systems and applications*. London, UK: Springer Publishing Company, Incorporated. doi:10.1007/978-1-84996-241-4

Aoyama, T., & Sakai, H. (2011). Inter-cloud computing. *Business & Information Systems Engineering*, 3(3), 173–177. doi:10.1007/s12599-011-0158-4

Apache Qpid. (2015). *Qpid*. Retrieved from https://qpid.apache.org/

Apcera Platform. (2015, May). Retrieved from https://www.apcera.com/continuum/

Appcelerator. (2015, May). Retrieved from http://www.appcelerator.com

AppScale. (2015, May). Retrieved from http://www.appscale.com/

Ardagna, D., di Nitto, E., Mohagheghi, P., Mosser, S., Ballagny, C., D'Andria, F., & Sheridan, C. et al. (2012). Modaclouds: A model-driven approach for the design and execution of applications on multiple clouds. *Proceedings of Workshop on Modeling in Software Engineering (MiSE) in Internation Conference on Software Engineering (ICSE)*, Zurich, Switzerland (pp. 50-56). doi:10.1109/MISE.2012.6226014

Armbrust, M., Fox, A., Griffith, R., Joseph, A. D., Katz, R. H., Konwinski, A., & Zaharia, M. (2009). *Above the clouds: A Berkeley view of cloud computing (Technical Report No. UCB/EECS-2009-28)*. Retrieved from http://www.eecs.berkeley.edu/Pubs/TechRpts/2009/EECS-2009-28.html

Armbrust, M., Fox, A., Griffith, R., Joseph, A. D., Katz, R. H., Konwinski, A., ... Zaharia, M. (2009). *Above the clouds: A Berkeley view of cloud computing* (Tech. Rep. No. UCB/EECS-2009-28). EECS Department, University of California, Berkeley.

Armbrust, M., Fox, A., Griffith, R., Joseph, A. D., Katz, R., Konwinski, A., & Zaharia, M. et al. (2010). A View of Cloud Computing. *Communications of the ACM, 53*(4), 50–58. doi:10.1145/1721654.1721672

Armstrong, D., & Djemame, K. (2009, July). Towards quality of service in the Cloud.*Proc. of the 25th UK Performance Engineering Workshop.*

Armstrong, D., Espling, D., Tordsson, J., Djemame, K., & Elmroth, E. (2012). Lecture Notes in Computer Science: Vol. 7640. *Runtime Virtual Machine Recontextualization for Clouds. Euro-Par 2012: Parallel Processing Workshops* (pp. 567–576). Springer. doi:10.1007/978-3-642-36949-0_66

Armstrong, D., Espling, D., Tordsson, J., Djemame, K., & Elmroth, E. (2015). Contextualization: Dynamic configuration of virtual machines. *Journal of Cloud Computing, 4*(1), 1–15.

Assis, M. R. M., & Bittencourt, L. F. (2015). An Analysis of the Voluntary Aspect in Cloud Federations. *Proceedings of the4rd International Workshop on Clouds and (eScience) Applications Management (CLOUDAM 2015).* Limassol, Cyprus.

Assis, M. R. M., Bittencourt, L. F., & Tolosana-Calasanz, R. (2014). Cloud federation: Characterisation and conceptual model.*Proceedings of 3rd International Workshop on Clouds and (eScience) Applications Management (CLOUDAM 2014).*London, UK.

Assuncao, M. D., Costanzo, A. d., & Buyya, R. (2009). *Evaluating the cost-benefit of using Cloud computing to extend the capacity of clusters.* ACM HPDC. doi:10.1145/1551609.1551635

AWS | Amazon Relational Database Service (RDS). (n. d.). Amazon. Retrieved from http://aws.amazon.com/rds/

Azure SDK for Node. (2015, May). *Github.* Retrieved from https://github.com/Azure/azure-sdk-for-node

Azure SDK for Python. (2015, May). *Github.* Retrieved from https://github.com/Azure/azure-sdk-for-python

Azure Web Job. (2015, May). *Microsoft.* Retrieved from https://azure.microsoft.com/en-us/documentation/articles/web-sites-create-web-jobs/

BaasBox. (2015, May). Retrieved from www.baasbox.com

Backendless. (2015, May). Retrieved from www.backendless.com

Baker, J., Bond, C., Corbett, J. C., Furman, J. J., Khorlin, A., Larson, J., . . . Yushprakh, V. (2011). Megastore: Providing Scalable, Highly Available Storage for Interactive Services. *Proceedings of theACM Conf. Innovative Data Systems Research.*

Balaton, Z., Gombas, G., Kacsuk, P., Kornafeld, A., Kovacs, J., & Marosi, A. C., … Kiss, T. (2007). SZTAKI Desktop Grid: a Modular and Scalable Way of Building Large Computing Grids. *Proceedings of the2007 IEEE International Parallel and Distributed Processing Symposium* (pp. 1–8). IEEE. doi:10.1109/IPDPS.2007.370665

Banerjee, P., Friedrich, R., Bash, C., Goldsack, P., Huberman, B., Manley, J., & Veitch, A. et al. (2011). Everything as a service: Powering the new information economy. *Computer, 44*(3), 36–43. doi:10.1109/MC.2011.67

Barham, P., Dragovic, B., Fraser, K., Hand, S., Harris, T., Ho, A., & Warfield, A. (2003). Xen and the art of virtualization. *Operating Systems Review, 37*(5), 164–177. doi:10.1145/1165389.945462

Bazarbayev, S., Hiltunen, M., Joshi, K., Sanders, W. H., & Schlichting, R. (2013, July). Content-based scheduling of virtual machines (VMs) in the Cloud. *Proceedings of the 2013 IEEE 33rd International Conference on Distributed Computing Systems (ICDCS)* (pp. 93-101). IEEE.

Bellard, F. (2005). QEMU, a Fast and Portable Dynamic Translator. *Proceedings of theUSENIX Annual Technical Conference, FREENIX Track* (pp. 41–46).

Bennett, J. C., Abbasi, H., Bremer, P.-T., Grout, R., Gyulassy, A., Jin, T., ... (2012). Combining in-situ and in-transit processing to enable extreme-scale scientific analysis. *Proc. of the Int. Conf. on High Perf. Computing, Networking, Storage and Analysis (SC '12)*.

Bermbach, D., Kurze, T., & Tai, S. (2013). Cloud federation: Effects of federated compute resources on quality of service and cost.*Proceedings of the IEEE International Conference on Cloud Engineering (IC2E),*San Francisco, California, USA (pp. 31–37). IEEE Computer Society. doi:10.1109/IC2E.2013.24

Bernsmed, K., Jaatun, M. G., Meland, P. H., & Undheim, A. (2011). Security SLAs for federated cloud services.*Proceedings of IEEE International Conference on Availability, Reliability and Security (ARES),*Vienna: Austria (pp. 202-209). IEEE Computer Society.

Bernstein, D., & Vij, D. (2010a, July). Intercloud directory and exchange protocol detail using XMPP and RDF. *Proceedings of the 2010 6th World Congress on Services (SERVICES-1)* (pp. 431-438). IEEE.

Bernstein, D., & Vij, D. (2010b, November). Intercloud security considerations. *Proceedings of the 2010 IEEE Second International Conference onCloud Computing Technology and Science (CloudCom)* (pp. 537-544). IEEE. doi:10.1109/CloudCom.2010.82

Bernstein, D., & Vij, D. (2104) Intercloud federation using via semantic resource federation API and dynamic SDN Provisioning. *Proceedings ofInternational Conference and Workshop on the Network of the Future (NOF)*, Paris, France (pp.1–8). IEEE Computer Society.

Bernstein, P. A., Hadzilacos, V., & Goodman, N. (1987). Concurrency Control and Recovery in Database Systems - Microsoft Research. Boston: Addison-Wesley Publishing Company. Retrieved from http://research.microsoft.com/http://research.microsoft.com/en-us/people/philbe/ccontrol.aspx

Bernstein, D., Ludvigson, E., Sankar, K., Diamond, S., & Morrow, M. (2009). Blueprint for the intercloud - protocols and formats for cloud computing interoperability.*Proceedings of the Fourth International Conference on Internet and Web Applications and Services (ICIW)*, Washington, DC, USA. IEEE Computer Society. doi:10.1109/ICIW.2009.55

Bestavros, A., & Krieger, O. (2014). Toward an open cloud marketplace: Vision and first steps. *IEEE Internet Computing*, *18*(1), 72–77. doi:10.1109/MIC.2014.17

Bhardwaj, S., Jain, L., & Jain, S. (2010). Cloud computing: A study of infrastructure as a service (IaaS). *International Journal of Engineering and Information Technology*, *2*(1), 60–63.

Bhat, V., Parashar, M., & Klasky, S. (2007). Experiments with in-transit processing for data intensive grid workflows. *Proceedings of the8th IEEE/ACM Inter. Conf. Grid Computing* (pp. 193-200). doi:10.1109/GRID.2007.4354133

Birnhack, M. D. (2008). The EU Data Protection Directive: An Engine of a Global Regime (Paper no. 95). Tel Aviv University Law School: Tel Aviv University Law Faculty Papers.

Bittencourt, L. F., Senna, C. R., & Madeira, E. R. (2010). Enabling execution of service workflows in grid/cloud hybrid systems. Proceedings of theNetwork Operations and Management Symp. Workshop. doi:10.1109/NOMSW.2010.5486553

Bittencourt, L. F., & Madeira, E. R. M. (2011). HCOC: A cost optimization algorithm for workflow scheduling in hybrid clouds. *Journal of Internet Services and Applications*, *2*(3), 207–227. doi:10.1007/s13174-011-0032-0

Bluemix. (2015, November). Retrieved from https://console.ng.bluemix.net/

BOINC VirtualBox Applications. (n. d.). Retrieved from http://boinc.berkeley.edu/trac/wiki/VboxApps

BOINCstats/BAM! (n. d.). Retrieved from http://boincstats.com

Boob, S., González-Vélez, H., & Popescu, A. M. (2014). Automated Instantiation of Heterogeneous Fast Flow CPU/GPU Parallel Pattern Applications in Clouds. *Proceedings of the 22nd Euromicro International Conference on Parallel, Distributed and Network-Based Processing* (pp. 162-169)

Bosh-lite. (2015, May). Retrieved from https://github.com/cloudfoundry/bosh-lite

Bresnahan, J., Freeman, T., LaBissoniere, D., & Keahey, K. (2011). Managing appliance launches in infrastructure clouds. Proceedings of the TeraGrid Conference: Extreme Digital Discovery (TG '11) (pp. 12:1-12:7). New York: ACM.

Buyya, R., Ranjan, R., & Calheiros, R. N. (2010). Intercloud: Utility-oriented federation of cloud computing environments for scaling of application services. *Proceedings of the 10th International Conference on Algorithms and Architectures for Parallel Processing,* Busan, Korea (Vol. part I pp. 13–31). Springer-Verlag Berlin, Heidelberg. doi:10.1007/978-3-642-13119-6_2

Buyya, R., Broberg, J., & Goscinski, A. M. (2011). *Cloud computing principles and paradigms. Hoboken.* New Jersey, USA: John Wiley & Sons, Inc. doi:10.1002/9780470940105

Buyya, R., Pandey, S., & Vecchiola, C. (2012). Market-oriented cloud computing and the cloudbus toolkit. In S. Azad & H. Zomaya (Eds.), *Large Scale Network-Centric Distributed Systems.* Wiley-IEEE Press.

Buyya, R., Yeo, C. S., & Venugopal, S. (2009). Market-oriented cloud computing: Vision, hype, and reality of delivering computing as the 5th utility. *Proceedings of the 2009 9th IEEE/ACM International Symposium on Cluster Computing and the Grid (CCGRID),* Shanghai, China (p. 1). IEEE Computer Society. doi:10.1109/CCGRID.2009.97

Buyya, R., Yeo, C. S., Venugopal, S., Broberg, J., & Brandic, I. (2009). Cloud computing and emerging it platforms: Vision, hype, and reality for delivering computing as the 5th utility. *Future Generation Computer Systems, 25*(6), 599–616. doi:10.1016/j.future.2008.12.001

Bygrave, L. A. (2000). European Data Protection, Determining Applicable Law Pursuant To European Data Protection Legislation. *Computer Law & Security Report, 16*(4), 252–257. doi:10.1016/S0267-3649(00)89134-7

CA's Federation Manager. (2015). Retrieved from http://www.ca.com/in/securecenter/ca-federation.aspx

Caballer, M., Segrelles, D., Molto, G., & Blanquer, I. (2014). A Platform to Deploy Customized Scientific Virtual Infrastructures on the Cloud. *Proceedings of the 6th International Workshop on Science Gateways (IWSG),* Dublin (pp. 42-47). IEEE. doi:10.1109/IWSG.2014.14

Caballer, M., Blanquer, I., Molto, G., & de Alfonso, C. (2015). Dynamic management of virtual infrastructures. *Journal of Grid Computing, 13*(1), 53–70. doi:10.1007/s10723-014-9296-5

Caballer, M., de Alfonso, C., Alvarruiz, F., & Moltó, G. (2013). EC3: Elastic Cloud Computing Cluster. *Journal of Computer and System Sciences, 79*(8), 1341–1351. doi:10.1016/j.jcss.2013.06.005

Calheiros, R. N., Toosi, A. N., Vecchiola, C., & Buyya, R. (2012, October). A coordinator for scaling elastic applications across multiple clouds. *Future Generation Computer Systems, 28*(8), 1350–1362. doi:10.1016/j.future.2012.03.010

Campbell, R., Gupta, I., Heath, M., Ko, S. Y., Kozuch, M., Kunze, M., & Soh, Y. C. et al. (2009). Open CIRRUS™ cloud computing testbed: Federated data centers for open source systems and services research. *Proceedings of the 2009 Conference on Hot Topics in Cloud Computing (HotCloud),* San Diego, CA, USA. USENIX Association.

Canali, C., Cardellini, V., Colajanni, M., & Lancellotti, R. (2008). Content delivery and management. In R. Buyya, M. Pathan, & A. Vakali (Eds.), *Content Delivery Networks* (Vol. 9, pp. 105–126). Springer Berlin Heidelberg. doi:10.1007/978-3-540-77887-5_4

Canonical. (2015). *Cloud-init*. Retrieved from http://cloud-init.org/

Cantor, S., & SCAVO, T. (2005). Shibboleth architecture. *Protocols and Profiles*, 10.

Cantor, S., Kemp, I. J., Philpott, N. R., & Maler, E. (2005, March). Assertions and protocols for the oasis security assertion markup language. *OASIS Standard*.

Cappello, F., Djilali, S., Fedak, G., Herault, T., Magniette, F., Neri, V., & Lodygensky, O. (2005). Computing on large-scale distributed systems: XtremWeb architecture, programming models, security, tests and convergence with grid. *Future Generation Computer Systems*, *21*(3), 417–437. doi:10.1016/j.future.2004.04.011

Carrión, J. V., Moltó, G., de Alfonso, C., Caballer, M., & Hernández, V. (2010). A Generic Catalog and Repository Service for Virtual Machine Images. *Proceedings of the 2nd International ICST Conference on Cloud Computing (CloudComp '10)* (pp. 1-15).

Cascella, R. G., Blasi, L., Jegou, Y., Coppola, M., & Morin, C. (2013). Contrail: Distributed application deployment under SLA in federated heterogeneous clouds. In A. Galis & A. Gavras (Eds.), *The Future Internet (LNCS)* (Vol. 7858, pp. 91–103). Berlin, Germany: Springer. doi:10.1007/978-3-642-38082-2_8

Celesti, A., Tusa, F., Villari, M., & Puliafito, A. (2010a, July). How to enhance cloud architectures to enable cross-federation. *Proceedings of the 2010 IEEE 3rd International Conference on Cloud Computing (CLOUD)* (pp. 337-345). IEEE. doi:10.1109/CLOUD.2010.46

Celesti, A., Tusa, F., Villari, M., & Puliafito, A. (2010b, July). Three-phase cross-cloud federation model: The cloud sso authentication. *Proceedings of the 2010 Second International Conference on Advances in Future Internet (AFIN)* (pp. 94-101). IEEE.

Celesti, A., Tusa, F., Villari, M., & Puliafito, A. (2011). Evaluating a distributed identity provider trusted network with delegated authentications for cloud federation. *Proceedings of the 2th International Conference on Cloud Computing, Grids and Virtualization (CLOUD COMPUTING 2011)*, Rome, Italy (pp. 79–85). International Academy, Research, and Industry Association.

Celesti, A., Tusa, F., Villari, M., & Puliafito, A. (2011). Federation establishment between clever clouds through a saml sso authentication profile. *International Journal on Advances in Internet Technology*, *4*(1 & 2), 14-27.

Celesti, A., Tusa, F., Villari, M., & Puliafito, A. (2010). Security and cloud computing: Intercloud identity management infrastructure. In S. Reddy (Ed.), *Enabling Technologies: Infrastructures for Collaborative Enterprises (WETICE)* (pp. 263–265). IEEE Computer Society. doi:10.1109/WETICE.2010.49

Chadwick, D. K., Siu, K., Lee, C., Fouillat, Y., & Germonville, D. (2013). Adding Federated Identity Management to OpenStack. *Journal of Grid Computing*, *12*(1), 3–27. doi:10.1007/s10723-013-9283-2

Chan, C. K., & Cheng, L. M. (2000). Cryptanalysis of a remote user authentication scheme using smart cards. *IEEE Transactions on Consumer Electronics*, *46*(4), 992–993.

Chang, F., Dean, J., Ghemawat, S., Hsieh, W. C., Wallach, D. A., Burrows, M., & Gruber, R. E. (2008). *Bigtable: A distributed storage system for structured data. CM Transactions on Computer Systems*. TOCS.

Chaurasiya, V. K., Srinivasan, K., Thyagarajan, K., Govil, S. B., & Das, S. (2012). An approach to identify the optimal cloud in cloud federation. *International Journal of Cloud Computing and Services Science*, *1*(1), 35–44.

Chen, D., & Doumeingts, G. (2003). European initiatives to develop interoperability of enterprise applications - basic concepts, framework and roadmap. *Annual Reviews in Control, 27*(2), 153–162. doi:10.1016/j.arcontrol.2003.09.001

Chodorow, K. (2010). MongoDB: The Definitive Guide. Sebastopol: O'Reilly.

Choi, S., & Buyya, R. (2010). Group-based adaptive result certification mechanism in Desktop Grids. *Future Generation Computer Systems, 26*(5), 776–786. doi:10.1016/j.future.2009.05.025

Chu, X., & Buyya, R. (2009). Service-Oriented Sensor Web. In *Sensor Networks and Configuration.* Springer.

Cirne, W., Brasileiro, F. V., Andrade, N., Costa, L., Andrade, A., Novaes, R., & Mowbray, M. (2006). Labs of the World, Unite!!! *Journal of Grid Computing, 4*(3), 225–246. doi:10.1007/s10723-006-9040-x

Cisco Intercloud Fabric: Hybrid Cloud with Choice, Consistency, Control and Compliance. (2015). *Cisco.* Retrieved from http://www.cisco.com/c/en/us/td/docs/solutions/Hybrid_Cloud/Intercloud/Intercloud_Fabric.pdf

Clayman, S., Galis, A., Chapman, C., Toffetti, G., Rodero-Merino, L., Vaquero, L. M., & Rochwerger, B. (2010). Monitoring service clouds in the future internet. In G. Tselentis, A. Galis, A. Gavras, S. Krco, & T. Zahariadis et al. (Eds.), *Towards the Future Internet - Emerging Trends from European Research,* Amsterdam, Netherlands (pp. 115–126). IOS Press.

Clear, D. *B.* (2015, May). Retrieved from https://www.cleardb.com/

Cloud infrastructure management interface (CIMI) model and restful http based protocol an interface for managing cloud infrastructure (Standard No. DSP0263). (2012). Distributed Management Task Force.

CloudControl. (2015, May). Retrieved from https://www.cloudcontrol.com/

CloudFoundry. (2015, May). Retrieved from http://cloudfoundry.org/

CloudHarmony. (n. d.). Retrieved from http://cloudharmony.com

Cloudinary SDK for Python. (2015, May). *Github.* Retrieved from https://github.com/cloudinary/pycloudinary

Cloudinary. (2015, May). Retrieved from http://cloudinary.com/

Cohen, J., Dolan, B., Dunlap, M., Hellerstein, J., & Welton, C. (2009). MAD Skills: New Analysis Practices for Big Data.*Proceedings of the VLDB Endowment.* doi:10.14778/1687553.1687576

Commission / Germany, CaseC-518/07, ECR 2010 p. I-1885 (Judgement). (2010, March 9). Court of Justice of the EU.

Comuzzi, M., Kotsokalis, C., Spanoudakis, G., & Yahyapour, R. (2009). Establishing and monitoring SLAs in complex service based systems.*Proceedings of the IEEE International Conference of Web services (ICWS),*Miami, FL, USA (pp. 783–790). IEEE Computer Society. doi:10.1109/ICWS.2009.47

convert. (2015, May). Retrieved from http://www.imagemagick.org/script/convert.php

Corbett, J. C., Dean, J., Epstein, M., Fikes, A., Frost, C., & Furman, J. J. (2013). Spanner: Google's globally distributed database. *ACM Transactions on Computer Systems, 31*(3), 1–22. doi:10.1145/2518037.2491245

Crawley, D. B., Lawrie, L. K., Winkelmann, F. C., Buhl, W., Huang, Y., & Pedersen, C. O. et al.. (2001). *Energyplus: creating a new-generation building energy simulation program.* Energy and Buildings.

Cs, A. Marosi, G. Kecskemeti, A. Kertesz & P. Kacsuk (2011). FCM: an Architecture for Integrating IaaS Cloud Systems. *Proceedings of the Second International Conference on Cloud Computing, GRIDs, and Virtualization (Cloud Computing 2011),* Rome, Italy (pp. 7-12). IARIA.

Cully, B., Lefebvre, G., Meyer, D., Feeley, M., Hutchinson, N., & Warfield, A. (2008). Remus: High availability via asynchronous virtual machine replication. *Proceedings of the5th USENIX Symposium on Networked Systems Design and Implementation* (pp. 161-174).

Cuomo, A., Modica, G., Distefano, S., Puliafito, A., Rak, M., Tomarchio, O., & Villano, U. et al. (2013). An SLA-based broker for cloud infrastructures. *Journal of Grid Computing, 11*(1), 1–25. doi:10.1007/s10723-012-9241-4

Cuzzocrea, A., Fortino, G., & Rana, O. (2013). Managing Data and Processes in Cloud-Enabled Large-Scale Sensor Networks: State-of-the-Art and Future Research Directions. Proceedings of the DPMSS workshop alongside CCGrid (pp. 583-588).

Cuzzocrea, A., Furfaro, F., Greco, S., Masciari, E., Mazzeo, G., & Sacca, D. (2005). A Distributed System for Answering Range Queries on Sensor Network Data. In Proc. of PerComW'05.

Cuzzocrea, A., Furfaro, F., Mazzeo, G., & Sacca, D. (2004). A Grid Framework for Approximate Aggregate Query Answering on Summarized Sensor Network Readings.*Proc. of OTMW '04*. doi:10.1007/978-3-540-30470-8_32

Cuzzocrea, A., & Sacca, D. (2013). Exploiting Compression and Approximation Paradigms for Effective and Efficient OLAP over Sensor Network Readings in Data Grid Environments. *Concurrency and Computation*. doi:10.1002/cpe.2982

Das, S., Agrawal, D., & El Abbadi, A. (2013). *ElasTraS: An elastic, scalable, and self-managing transactional database for the cloud. ACM Transactions on Database Systems*. TODS.

Data Protection package: Report on progress achieved under the Cyprus Presidency, 16525/1/12 REV 1. (2012, March 12). Council of the European Union.

David Cunha, P. N. (2013). A Platform-as-a-Service API Aggregator. In Advances in Information Systems and Technologies (pp. 807-818).

David Cunha, P. N. (2014). PaaS Manager: A Platform-as-a-Service Aggregation. *Computer Science and Information Systems, 11*(4), 1209–1228. doi:10.2298/CSIS130828028C

de Alfonso, C., Caballer, M., Alvarruiz, F., Molto, G., & Hernández, V. (2011). Infrastructure Deployment over the Cloud. *Proceedings of theIEEE Third International Conference on Cloud Computing Technology and Science* (pp. 517–521). IEEE. doi:10.1109/CloudCom.2011.77

de Lima, M., Ururahy, C., de Moura, A., Melcop, T., Cassino, C., & dos Santos, M. … Cerqueira, R. (2006). CSBase: A framework for building customized Grid environments. Proceedings of the 15th IEEE International Workshops on Enabling Technologies: Infrastructure for Collaborative Enterprises (pp. 187–194). IEEE.

Decision of the EEA Joint Committee, No. 83/1999 of 25 June 1999 amending Protocol 37 and Annex XI (Telecommunication services) to the EEA Agreement. (2000, November). Official Journal L 296, 41.

Deelman, E., Singh, G., Livny, M., Berriman, B., & Good, J. (2008). The cost of doing science on the cloud: the Montage example. *Proceedings of the 2008 ACM/IEEE conference on Supercomputing*.

DeHaan, M. (2013). *Ansible*. From www.ansible.com

Deis. (2015, May). Retrieved from http://deis.io/

Deltacloud Drivers. (2013, October). Apache Software Foundation. Retrieved from https://deltacloud.apache.org/drivers.html#drivers

Deshpande, U., Schlinker, B., Adler, E., & Gopalan, K. (2013, May). Gang migration of virtual machines using cluster-wide deduplication. *Proceedings of the 2013 13th IEEE/ACM International Symposium on Cluster, Cloud and Grid Computing (CCGrid)* (pp. 394-401). IEEE. doi:10.1109/CCGrid.2013.39

Diaz-Montes, J., Xie, Y., Rodero, I., Zola, J., Ganapathysubramanian, B., & Parashar, M. (2014). Federated computing for the masses - aggregating resources to tackle large-scale engineering problems. *CiSE Magazine*, 2014, 62-72.

Diaz-Montes, J., AbdelBaky, M., Zou, M., & Parashar, M. (2015). CometCloud: Enabling Software-Defined Federations for End-to-End Application Workflows. *IEEE Internet Computing*, *19*(1), 69–73. doi:10.1109/MIC.2015.4

Diaz-Montes, J., Zou, M., Singh, R., Tao, S., & Parashar, M. (2014). *Data-driven workflows in multi-cloud marketplaces*. IEEE Cloud.

Directive 95/46/EC of the European Parliament and of the Council of 24 October 1995 on the protection of individuals with regard to the processing of personal data and on the free movement of such data. (1995, November). Official Journal L 281, 31-50.

Distefano, S., Merlino, G., & Puliafito, A. (2012). *SAaaS: a Framework for Volunteer-Based Sensing Clouds*. Parallel and Cloud Computing.

Distributed management task force. (2015). *DMTF*. Retrieved from http://www.dmtf.org/

Docker – Official Site. (n. d.). Retrieved from http://www.docker.com/

Docker: open platform for developers and sysadmins of distributed applications. (2015). *Docker*. Retrieved from http://www.docker.com/

DreamFactory. (2015, May). Retrieved from http://www.dreamfactory.com/

Dreo, G., Golling, M., Hommel, W., & Tietze, F. (2013, May). ICEMAN: An architecture for secure federated inter-cloud identity management. *Proceedings of the 2013 IFIP/IEEE International Symposium onIntegrated Network Management (IM 2013)* (pp. 1207-1210). IEEE.

Dreo, G., Golling, M., Hommel, W., & Tietze, F. (2013). ICEMAN: An architecture for secure federated inter-cloud identity management.*Proceedings of the IFIP/IEEE International Symposium on Integrated Network Management (IM),*Ghent, Belgium (p. 1207–1210).

Dzone. (2015, May). *Guide to Cloud Development*. Retrieved from http://dzone.com/research/2015-guide-to-cloud-development

EC Press release: Commission proposes a comprehensive reform of data protection rules to increase users' control of their data and to cut costs for businesses. (2012, January 25). European Commission. Retrieved from europa.eu/rapid/pressReleasesAction.do?reference=IP/12/46

El Maliki, T., & Seigneur, J. M. (2007, October). A survey of user-centric identity management technologies. *Proceedings of the International Conference on Emerging Security Information, Systems, and Technologies SecureWare '07* (pp. 12-17). IEEE. doi:10.1109/SECUREWARE.2007.4385303

Elmore, A. J., Das, S., Agrawal, D., & El Abbadi, A. (2011). Zephyr: live migration in shared nothing databases for elastic cloud platforms. *Proceedings of theACM SIGMOD International Conference on Management of data* (pp. 301-312). doi:10.1145/1989323.1989356

Emeakaroha, V. C., Netto, M. A., Calheiros, R. N., Brandic, I., Buyya, R., & De Rose, C. A. F. (2012). Towards autonomic detection of SLA violations in cloud infrastructures. *Future Generation Computer Systems*, *28*(7), 1017–1029. doi:10.1016/j.future.2011.08.018

EMTE project pilot. (n. d.). *EMTESport*. Retrieved from http://www.emtesport.com/

Epema, D., Livny, M., van Dantzig, R., Evers, X., & Pruyne, J. (1996). A worldwide flock of Condors: Load sharing among workstation clusters. *Future Generation Computer Systems*, *12*(1), 53–65. doi:10.1016/0167-739X(95)00035-Q

European Cloud Computing Strategy (CCS). (2012). *European Commission*. Retrieved from http://ec.europa.eu/information_society/activities/cloudcomputing/cloud_strategy/index_en.htm

European Commission. (2015). Retrieved from http://ec.europa.eu/index/

Express. (2015, May). Retrieved from http://expressjs.com/

Extensible markup language. XML. (2015). Retrieved from http://www.w3.org/standards/xml/

Farkas, Z., Kacsuk, P., Balaton, Z., & Gombás, G. (2010). Interoperability of BOINC and EGEE. *Future Generation Computer Systems*, *26*(8), 1092–1103. doi:10.1016/j.future.2010.05.009

Fault Tolerance. (n. d.). *Wikipedia*. Retrieved from http://en.wikipedia.org/wiki/Fault_tolerance

FeedHenry. (2015, May). Retrieved from http://www.feedhenry.com/

Felter, W., Ferreira, A., Rajamony, R., & Rubio, J. (2014). *An Updated Performance Comparison of Virtual Machines and Linux Containers*. Retrieved from http://domino.research.ibm.com/library/cyberdig.nsf/papers/0929052195DD819C85257D2300681E7B

Feng, F., Lin, C., Peng, D., & Li, J. (2008, September). A trust and context based access control model for distributed systems. *Proceedings of the 10th IEEE International Conference on High Performance Computing and Communications HPCC '08* (pp. 629-634). IEEE. doi:10.1109/HPCC.2008.37

Ferraiolo, D. F., Sandhu, R., Gavrila, S., Kuhn, D. R., & Chandramouli, R. (2001). Proposed NIST standard for role-based access control. *ACM Transactions on Information and System Security*, *4*(3), 224–274. doi:10.1145/501978.501980

Ferreira, D., Araujo, F., & Domingues, P. (2011). libboincexec: A Generic Virtualization Approach for the BOINC Middleware. *Proceedings of the 2011 IEEE International Symposium on Parallel and Distributed Processing Workshops and Phd Forum (IPDPSW)* (pp. 1903–1908). doi:10.1109/IPDPS.2011.349

Ferrer, A. J., Hernandez, F., Tordsson, J., Elmroth, E., Ali-Eldin, A., Zsigri, C., & Sheridan, C. et al. (2012). OPTIMIS: A Holistic Approach to Cloud Service Provisioning. *Future Generation Computer Systems*, *28*(1), 66–77. doi:10.1016/j.future.2011.05.022

FIDIA project pilot. (n. d.). *ASFIDIA*. Retrieved from http://www.asfidia.it

Fiore, S., Mancini, M., Elia, D., Nassisi, F., Brasileiro, F. V., & Blanquer, I., … Aloisio, G. (2015). Big data analytics for climate change and biodiversity in the EUBrazilCC federated cloud infrastructure. *Proceedings of the Workshop on Analytics Platforms for the Cloud, ACM International Conference on Computing Frontiers '15*, Ischia. doi:10.1145/2742854.2747282

Fiore, S., D'Anca, A., Palazzo, C., Foster, I., Williams, D. N., & Aloisio, G. (2013). *Ophidia: Toward Big Data Analytics for eScience. ICCS 2013. 18* (pp. 2376–2385). Barcelona: Elsevier.

Fiore, S., Palazzo, C., D'Anca, A., Foster, I. T., Williams, D. N., & Aloisio, G. (2013). A big data analytics framework for scientific data management. Proceedings of the *IEEE Big Data Conference*, *2013*, 1–8.

Firebase. (2015, May). Retrieved from www.firebase.com

Flake, S., Tacken, J., & Zoth, C. (2012). Real-time rating and charging in federated cloud environments. *Proceedings of the IEEE 17th Conference of Emerging Technologies Factory Automation (ETFA),* Krakón, Poland (pp. 1–6). IEEE Computer Society. doi:10.1109/ETFA.2012.6489791

Foreman and Procfile. (2015, May). Retrieved from http://ddollar.github.io/foreman/

Foster, I., Zhao, Y., Raicu, I., & Lu, S. (2008, November). Cloud computing and grid computing 360-degree compared. *Proceedings of the Grid Computing Environments Workshop GCE '08* (pp. 1-10). IEEE.

Foster, I., Zhao, Y., Raicu, I., & Lu, S. (2008). Cloud computing and grid computing 360-degree compared. *Proceedings of the Grid Computing Environments Workshop (GCE),* Austin, TX (pp. 1–10). USA: IEEE Computer Society. doi:10.1109/GCE.2008.4738445

Fowley, F., Pahl, C., & Zhang, L. (2014). A comparison framework and review of service brokerage solutions for cloud architectures. In A. R. Lomuscio et al. (Eds), *Proceedings of the Service-Oriented Computing–ICSOC 2013 Workshops,* LNCS (Vol. 8377, pp. 137-149). Cham, Switzerland: Springer International Publishing. doi:10.1007/978-3-319-06859-6_13

Fox, G., & Gannon, D. (2012). *Cloud Programming Paradigms for Technical Computing Applications.* Indiana University.

Fugkeaw, S., Manpanpanich, P., & Juntapremjitt, S. (2007, April). A robust single sign-on model based on multi-agent system and PKI. *Proceedings of the Sixth International Conference on Networking ICN '07.* (pp. 101-101). IEEE. doi:10.1109/ICN.2007.10

Fumo, N., Mago, P., & Luck, R. (2010). Methodology to Estimate Building Energy Consumption Using EnergyPlus Benchmark Models. In *Energy and Buildings* (pp. 2331-2337).

Gang, L., & Mingchuan, W. (2014). Everything-as-a-service platform for on-demand virtual enterprises. *Information Systems Frontiers, 16*(3), 435–452. doi:10.1007/s10796-012-9351-3

Ganglia monitoring system. (2015). *Ganglia.* Retrieved from http/ganglia.sourceforge.net/

Garcia, A. L. C., & Puel, M. (2013). Identity Federation with VOMS in Cloud Infrastructures. *Proceedings of the 5th IEEE International Conference on Cloud Computing Technology and Science (CLOUDCOM),* Bristol, UK (pp. 42–48). IEEE Computer Society. doi:10.1109/CloudCom.2013.13

Garg, V., Chandrasen, K., Tetali, S., & Mathur, J. (2010). Energyplus Simulation Speedup Using Data Parallelization Concept. *Proceedings of the ASME Energy Sustainability Conference, New York: American Society of Mechanical Engineers* (pp. 1041-1048). doi:10.1115/ES2010-90509

Geelan, J., Klems, M., Cohen, R., Kaplan, J., Gourlay, D., Gaw, P., . . . Berger, I. W. (2008). *Twenty-one experts define cloud computing.* Retrieved from http://virtualization.sys-con.com/node/612375

Gellman, R. (2009, February). Privacy in the Clouds: Risks to Privacy and Confidentiality from Cloud Computing. *World Privacy Forum.*

GENICloud project. (n. d.). Retrieved from http://groups.geni.net/geni/wiki/GENICloud

gevent. (2015, May). Retrieved from http://www.gevent.org/

Ghazizadeh, E., & Zamani, M. Jamalul-lail Ab Manan, & Pashang, A. (2012, December). A survey on security issues of federated identity in the cloud computing. In CloudCom (pp. 532-565).

Giunta, G., Montella, R., Agrillo, G., & Coviello, G. (2010). A GPGPU Transparent Virtualization Component for High Performance Computing Clouds. Proceedings of Euro-Par 2010 - Parallel Processing (pp. 379-391). Springer Berlin Heidelberg. doi:10.1007/978-3-642-15277-1_37

Global Grid Forum. (2008, June). Distributed resource management application API specification 1.0.

Godfrey, R., Ingham, D., & Schloming, R. (2012). *OASIS advanced message queuing protocol (AMQP) version 1.0.* Retrieved from http://docs.oasis-open.org/amqp/core/v1.0/os/amqp-core-complete-v1.0-os.pdf

Godik, S., Anderson, A., Parducci, B., Humenn, P., & Vajjhala, S. (2002). *OASIS eXtensible access control 2 markup language (XACML) 3. Tech. rep.* OASIS.

Goiri, I., Guitart, J., & Torres, J. (2010). Characterizing cloud federation for enhancing providers' profit.*Proceedings of the 3rd International Conference on Cloud Computing (CLOUD),*Miami, FL, USA (pp. 123–130). IEEE Computer Society. doi:10.1109/CLOUD.2010.32

Goiri, I., Guitart, J., & Torres, J. (2012). Economic Model of a Cloud Provider Operating in a Federated Cloud. *Information Systems Frontiers, 14*(4), 827–843. doi:10.1007/s10796-011-9325-x

Gomes, A. T., Bastos, B. F., Medeiros, V., & Moreira, V. M. (2015). Experiences of the Brazilian national high-performance computing network on the rapid prototyping of science gateways. *Concurrency and Computation, 27*(2), 271–289. doi:10.1002/cpe.3258

Gomes, E. R., Vo, Q. B., & Kowalczyk, R. (2012). Pure exchange markets for resource sharing in federated clouds. *Concurrency and Computation, 24*(9), 977–991. doi:10.1002/cpe.1659

Goodale, T., Jha, S., Kaiser, H., Kielmann, T., Kleijer, P., Von Laszewski, G., & Shalf, J. (2006). SAGA: A Simple API for Grid Applications. High-level application programming on the Grid. *Computational Methods in Science and Technology, 12*(1), 7–20. doi:10.12921/cmst.2006.12.01.07-20

Goodner, M., & Nadalin, T. (2009). Web Services Federation Language (WS-Federation) Version 1.2. OASIS Web Services Federation (WSFED) TC.

Google App Engine. (2015, May). *Google.* Retrieved from https://cloud.google.com/appengine/

Google apps for works. (2015). *Google Apps.* Retrieved from https://www.google.com/intx/pt-BR/work/apps/business/

Google Compute Engine. (2015). *Google.* Retrieved from https://cloud.google.com/products/compute-engine/

Google Endpoints. (2015, May). Retrieved from https://cloud.google.com/mobile/endpoints/

Google Mobile Cloud Platform. (2015, May). *Google.* Retrieved from https://cloud.google.com/solutions/mobile/

Gorton, I., Liu, Y., & Yin, J. (2010). Exploring architecture options for a federated, cloud-based system biology knowledge-base. Proceedings of theIEEE Intl. Conf. on Cloud Computing Technology and Science. doi:10.1109/CloudCom.2010.79

Greenleaf, G. (2012). Global Data Privacy Laws: 89 Countries, and Accelerating. *Privacy Laws & Business International Report,* Issue 115 (Special Supplement).

Grozev, N., & Buyya, R. (2012). Inter-Cloud Architectures and Application Brokering: Taxonomy and Survey. ACM Computing Surveys, 47(1), 7:1–7:47.

Grozev, N., & Buyya, R. (2012). Inter-Cloud Architectures and Application Brokering: Taxonomy and Survey. doi:10.1002/ spe

Grozev, N., & Buyya, R. (2014) Multi-Cloud Provisioning and Load Distribution for Three-Tier Applications. ACM Transactions on Autonomous and Adaptive Systems, 9(3), 13:1-13:21. New York, USA: ACM.

Gunjan, K., Sahoo, G., & Tiwari, R. K. (2012, June). Identity management in cloud computing–a review. International Journal of Engineering Research and Technology, 1(4).

Gupta, V., Gavrilovska, A., Schwan, K., Kharche, H., Tolia, N., Talwar, V., & Ranganathan, P. (2009). GViM: GPU-accelerated Virtual Machines. *Proceedings of the 3rd ACM Workshop on System-level Virtualization for High Performance Computing HPCVirt '09* (pp. 17-24). ACM. Retrieved from https://github.com/esnet/iperf

Hadji, M., & Zeghlache, D. (2015). Mathematical Programming Approach for Revenue Maximization in Cloud Federations. Proceedings of theIEEE Transactions on Cloud Computing.

Hardt, D. (2012). *The OAuth 2.0 Authorization Framework.*

Harsh, P., Jegou, Y., Cascella, R. G., & Morin, C. (2011, October 26-28). Contrail virtual execution platform challenges in being part of a cloud federation - (invited paper). In Abramowicz, W., Llorente, I. M., Surridge, M., Zisman, A., and Vayssière, J., (Eds.), *Towards a Service-Based Internet – Proceedings of the4th European Conference, ServiceWave 2011*, Poznan, Poland, LNCS (V*ol. 6994,* pp. 50–61). Springer.

Hassan, M. M., Abdullah-Al-Wadud, M., & Fortino, G. (2015). A socially optimal resource and revenue sharing mechanism in cloud federations. *Proceedings of the 19th IEEE International Conference on Computer Supported Cooperative Work in Design (CSCWD),* Calabria, Italy (pp. 620–625). IEEE Computer Society. doi:10.1109/CSCWD.2015.7231029

He, Q., Yan, J., Kowalczyk, R., Jin, H., & Yang, Y. (2007). An agent-based framework for service level agreement management. *Proceedings of the 11th International Conference on Computer Supported Cooperative Work in Design CSCWD '07* (pp. 412-417). IEEE. doi:10.1109/CSCWD.2007.4281471

He, S., Guo, L., Guo, Y., Wu, C., Ghanem, M., & Han, R. (2012, March). Elastic application container: A lightweight approach for Cloud resource provisioning. *Proceedings of the 2012 IEEE 26th international conference on Advanced information networking and applications (AINA)* (pp. 15-22). IEEE. doi:10.1109/AINA.2012.74

Helios. (2015, May). Retrieved from http://helios.io/

Herbst, N. R., Kounev, S., & Reussner, R. (2013). Elasticity in cloud computing: What it is, and what it is not. *Proceedings of the 10th International Conference on Autonomic Computing (ICAC),* San Jose, CA, USA (pp. 23–27). USENIX.

Heroku hosted Redis. (2015, May). *Heroku.* Retrieved from https://addons.heroku.com/heroku-redis

Heroku. (2015, May). Retrieved from https://www.heroku.com/

Hey, T. (2009). *The Fourth Paradigm: Data-Intensive Scientific Discovery.* Microsoft Research.

Hiden, H., Woodman, S., Watson, P., & Cala, J. (2013). Developing cloud applications using the e-Science Central platform. *Philosophical Transactions of the Royal Society A: Mathematical, Physical and Engineering Sciences, 371* (1983).

High Availability. (n. d.). *Wikipedia.* Retrieved from http://en.wikipedia.org/wiki/High_availability

Hochstein, L. (2014). *Ansible: Up and Running.* O'Reilly Media.

Hoefer, C., & Karagiannis, G. (2010). Taxonomy of cloud computing services. Proceedings of the 2010 IEEE GLOBE-COM Workshops (GC Wkshps), Miami, FL, USA (pp. 1345 - 1350).

Hovav, A., & Berger, R. (2009). Tutorial: Identity management systems and secured access control. *Communications of the Association for Information Systems, 25*(1), 42.

HP Openview. (2015). *HP*. Retrieved http://www.hp.com/

Huebscher, M. C., & McCann, J. A. (2008). A survey of autonomic computing—degrees, models, and applications. *ACM Computing Surveys*, *40*(3), 7. doi:10.1145/1380584.1380585

Hu, V. C., Ferraiolo, D., & Kuhn, D. R. (2006). *Assessment of access control systems*. US Department of Commerce, National Institute of Standards and Technology.

Huynh, T. D., Jennings, N. R., & Shadbolt, N. R. (2006). An integrated trust and reputation model for open multi-agent systems. *Autonomous Agents and Multi-Agent Systems*, *13*(2), 119–154. doi:10.1007/s10458-005-6825-4

Hyper-V. (n. d.). Microsoft. Retrieved from https://technet.microsoft.com/en-us/magazine/hh127064.aspx

I am Google Cloud. (2015). Retrieved from https://cloud.google.com/iam/

Identity in the cloud use cases version 1.0. (2012). *OASIS*. Retrieved from http://docs.oasis-open.org/id-cloud/IDCloud-usecases/v1.0/cn01/IDCloud-usecases-v1.0-cn01.pdf

ImageMagick. (2015, May). Retrieved from http://www.imagemagick.org/script/index.php

Impact Assessment SEC(2012) 72 final (Staff Working Paper). (2012, January 25). European Commission, Brussels.

IMS Fast Path Solutions Guide. (1997). *IBM*. Retrieved from http://www.redbooks.ibm.com/: http://www.redbooks.ibm.com/redbooks/pdfs/sg244301.pdf

Information Society and Media Directorate-General, Converged Networks and Services, Software & Service Architectures and Infrastructures, Cloud Computing: *Public Consultation Report*, European Commission. Brussels. (2011, 5th December). Retrieved from http://ec.europa.eu/information_society/activities/cloudcomputing/docs/ccconsultationfinalreport.pdf

Interoperable Global Trust Federation. (2015). Retrieved from http://www.igtf.net

Jaiswal, C., & Kumar, V. (2015). IGOD - Identifying Geolocation of Cloud Datacenter Hosting Mobile User's Data. *Proceedings of the16th IEEE International Conference on Mobile Data Management (MDM)* (pp. 34-37). Pittsburgh, USA: IEEE. doi:10.1109/MDM.2015.20

Jaiswal, C., & Kumar, V. (2015). IGOD: Identification of Geolocation Of Cloud Datacenters. *Proceedings of the 40th IEEE Conference on Local Computer Networks (LCN)*, Clearwater Beach, Florida, USA. IEEE.

Jaiswal, C., & Kumar, V. (2015, May). *Two-sce-doctoral-students-win-best-papermultimedia-presentation-awards*. Retrieved from sce.umkc.edu

Jaiswal, C., Nath, M., & Kumar, V. (2014). A Location-Based Security Framework for Cloud Perimeter. *IEEE Cloud Computing* (pp. 56-64).

Java Native Interface. (n. d.). Retrieved from http://java.sun.com/javase/6/docs/technotes/guides/jni/index.html

Javascript object notation. (2015). *JSON*. Retrieved from http://www.json.org/

Jayaram, K. R., Peng, C., Zhang, Z., Kim, M., Chen, H., & Lei, H. (2011, December). An empirical analysis of similarity in virtual machine images.*Proceedings of the Middleware 2011 Industry Track Workshop* (p. 6). ACM. doi:10.1145/2090181.2090187

Jebessa, N. D., van't Noordende, G., & de Laat, C. (2013, February). Towards Purpose-Driven Virtual Machines. *Proceedings of theESSoS Doctoral Symposium*.

Jeffery, K., & Neidecker-Lutz, B. (Eds.), (2010). The future of cloud computing: Opportunities for European cloud computing beyond 2010 (Tech. Rep). European Commission, Information Society and Media.

Jin, K., & Miller, E. L. (2009, May). The effectiveness of deduplication on virtual machine disk images.*Proceedings of SYSTOR 2009: The Israeli Experimental Systems Conference* (p. 7). ACM. doi:10.1145/1534530.1534540

Jo, H., Jeong, J., Lee, M., & Choi, D. H. (2013). *Exploiting GPUs in Virtual Machine for BioCloud*. BioMed Research International.

Juve, G., & Deelman, E. (2011). Automating Application Deployment in Infrastructure Clouds. In I. C. Society (Ed.), *Proceedings of theIEEE Third International Conference on Cloud Computing Technology and Science (CLOUDCOM '11)* (pp. 658–665). Washington, DC: IEEE Computer Society. doi:10.1109/CloudCom.2011.102

Keahey, K., & Freeman, T. (2008). Contextualization: Providing One-Click Virtual Clusters. *Proceedings of theFourth IEEE International Conference on eScience* (pp. 301–308).

Keahey, K., & Freeman, T. (2008). Science Clouds: Early Experiences in Cloud Computing for Scientific Applications. *Cloud Computing and Its Applications (CCA-08)*.

Keahey, K., Tsugawa, M., Matsunaga, A., & Fortes, J. (2009). Sky computing. *IEEE Internet Computing*, *13*(5), 43–51. doi:10.1109/MIC.2009.94

Kecskemeti, G., Kertesz, A., Marosi, A., & Kacsuk, P. (2012). Interoperable Resource Management for Establishing Federated Clouds. In M. Villari, I. Brandic, & F. Tusa (Eds.), *Achieving Federated and Self-Manageable Cloud Infrastructures: Theory and Practice* (pp. 18–35). Hershey, PA, USA: Business Science Reference. doi:10.4018/978-1-4666-1631-8.ch002

Keller, A., & Ludwig, H. (2003). The WSLA framework: Specifying and monitoring service level agreements for web services. *Network and System Management*, *11*(1), 57–81. doi:10.1023/A:1022445108617

Kertész, A., Kecskemeti, G., & Brandic, I. (2014). An interoperable and self-adaptive approach for SLA-based service virtualization in heterogeneous Cloud environments. *Future Generation Computer Systems*, *32*, 54–68. doi:10.1016/j.future.2012.05.016

Khan, K. M., & Malluhi, Q. (2010). Establishing trust in cloud computing. *IT Professional*, *12*(5), 20–27. doi:10.1109/MITP.2010.128

King, N. J., & Raja, V. T. (2012). Protecting the privacy and security of sensitive customer data in the cloud. *Computer Law & Security Report*, *28*(3), 308–319. doi:10.1016/j.clsr.2012.03.003

Kivity, A., Kamay, Y., Laor, D., Lublin, U., & Liguori, A. (2007). KVM: the Linux virtual machine monitor.*Proceedings of the Linux Symposium* (Vol. 1, pp. 225–230).

Klasky, S., Ludaescher, B., & Parashar, M. (2006). The Center for Plasma Edge Simulation Workflow Requirements. *Proceedings of the22nd Int. Conf. on Data Engineering Workshops (ICDEW'06)*. doi:10.1109/ICDEW.2006.143

Klyne, G., & Carroll, J.J. (2006). Resource description framework (RDF): Concepts and abstract syntax.

Kochut, A., & Karve, A. (2012, April). Leveraging local image redundancy for efficient virtual machine provisioning. *Proceedings of theNetwork Operations and Management Symposium (NOMS)* (pp. 179-187). IEEE. doi:10.1109/NOMS.2012.6211897

Kolb, S. W. G. (2014). Towards Application Portability in Platform as a Service. *Proceedings of the 2014 IEEE 8th International Symposium on Service Oriented System Engineering (SOSE)* (pp. 218 - 229).

Kovatsch, M. (n. d.). *Erbium REST Engine and CoAP implementation of Contiki*. Retrieved from http://people.inf.ethz.ch/mkovatsc/erbium.php

Kroes, N. (2012, January). *Setting up the European Cloud Partnership*. Davos, Switzerland, World Economic Forum.

Kumaraswamy, S., Lakshminarayanan, S., Stein, M. R. J., & Wilson, Y. (2010). Domain 12: Guidance for identity & access management v2. 1. Cloud Security Alliance. Retrieved from http://www.cloudsecurityalliance.org/guidance/csaguide-dom12-v2,10

Kumar, R., Gupta, N., Charu, S., Jain, K., & Jangir, S. K. (2014). Open Source Solution for Cloud Computing Platform Using OpenStack. *International Journal of Computer Science and Mobile Computing, 3*(5), 89–98.

Kumar, S., & Cohen, P. R. (2000, June). Towards a fault-tolerant multi-agent system architecture.*Proceedings of the fourth international conference on Autonomous agents* (pp. 459-466). ACM. doi:10.1145/336595.337570

Kurschl, W., & Beer, W. (2009). Combining Cloud Computing and Wireless Sensor Networks. In Proc. of iiWAS'09.

Kurze, T., Klems, M., Bermbach, D., Lenk, A., Tai, S., & Kunze, M. (2011). Cloud federation. *Proceedings of the 2nd International Conference on Cloud Computing, Grids, and Virtualization (Cloud Computing 2011)*, Rome, Italy (pp. 32–38). International Academy, Research, and Industry Association.

KVM Home page. (2015). *KVM*. Retrieved from http://www.linux-kvm.org/page/Main_Page

Kyriazis, D. e. (2013). *Data Intensive Storage Services for Cloud Environments*. Hershey: IGI Global. doi:10.4018/978-1-4666-3934-8

Lammps molecular dynamics simulator. (2013). *Sandia National Laboratories*. Retrieved from http://lammps.sandia.gov/

Lang, B., Wang, Z., & Wang, Q. (2007, July). Trust representation and reasoning for access control in large scale distributed systems. *Proceedings of the 2nd International Conference on Pervasive Computing and Applications ICPCA '07* (pp. 436-441). IEEE. doi:10.1109/ICPCA.2007.4365483

Lawton, K. P. (1996). Bochs: A portable pc emulator for Unix. *Linux Journal, 1996*(29), 7.

Lázaro, D., Kondo, D., & Marquès, J. M. (2012). Long-term availability prediction for groups of volunteer resources. *Journal of Parallel and Distributed Computing, 72*(2), 281–296. doi:10.1016/j.jpdc.2011.10.007

Le, D.-H., Truong, H.-L., Copil, G., Nastic, S., & Dustdar, S. (2014). SALSA: A Framework for Dynamic Configuration of Cloud Services. *Proceedings of the6th International Conference on Cloud Computing Technology and Science (CloudCom)* (pp. 146-153). Singapore: IEEE. doi:10.1109/CloudCom.2014.99

Lee, C. C., Li, L. H., & Hwang, M. S. (2002). A remote user authentication scheme using hash functions. *Operating Systems Review, 36*(4), 23–29. doi:10.1145/583800.583803

Lei, Z., Li, Z., Lei, Y., Bi, Y., Hu, L., & Shen, W. (2014, September). An Improved Image File Storage Method Using Data Deduplication. *Proceedings of the 2014 IEEE 13th International Conference on Trust, Security and Privacy in Computing and Communications (TrustCom)* (pp. 638-643). IEEE. doi:10.1109/TrustCom.2014.82

Le, K., Bianchini, R., Zhang, J., Jaluria, Y., Meng, J., & Nguyen, T. D. (2011). Reducing electricity cost through virtual machine placement in high performance computing clouds.*Proceedings of 2011 International Conference for High Performance Computing, Networking, Storage and Analysis,*Seattle, Washington (pp. 22:1–22:12). ACM. doi:10.1145/2063384.2063413

Li, A., Yang, X., Kandula, S., & Zhang, M. (2010). CloudCmp: Comparing public cloud providers.*Proceedings of the 10th ACM SIGCOMM Conference on Internet Measurement,*Melbourne, Australia (pp. 1–14). ACM.

Liang, T., & Chang, Y. (2011). GridCuda: A Grid-Enabled CUDA Programming Toolkit.*Proceedings of 2011 IEEE Workshops of International Conference on Advanced Information Networking and Applications* (pp. 141-146). IEEE Computer Society. doi:10.1109/WAINA.2011.82

Li, K., Zheng, H., & Wu, J. (2013). Migration-based virtual machine placement in cloud systems.*Proceedings of the IEEE 2nd International Conference on Cloud Networking (CloudNet)* (pp. 83-90). IEEE Computer Society. doi:10.1109/CloudNet.2013.6710561

Linstrom, P. J., & Mallard, W. G. (2003, March). National Institute of Standards and Technology: Gaithersburg. MD, USA.

Liu, Y. (2015). *Cuda-meme*. Retrieved from https://sites.google.com/site/yongchaosoftware/mcuda-meme

Liu, Y., Schmidt, B., Liu, W., & Maskell, D. L. (2010). CUDA–MEME: Accelerating motif discovery in biological sequences using CUDA-enabled graphics processing units. *Pattern Recognition Letters*, *31*(14), 2170–2177. doi:10.1016/j.patrec.2009.10.009

Liu, Y., Wirawan, A., & Schmidt, B. (2013). CUDASW++ 3.0: Accelerating smith-waterman protein database search by coupling CPU and GPU SIMD instructions. *BMC Bioinformatics*, *14*(1), 1–10. doi:10.1186/1471-2105-14-117 PMID:23557111

Li, Z., & Parashar, M. (2007). A computational infrastructure for grid-based asynchronous parallel applications.*Proceedings of the 16th International Symposium on High Performance Distributed Computing,*Monterey, California, USA (pp. 229– 230). ACM. doi:10.1145/1272366.1272404

Lomet, D., Fekete, A., Weikum, G., & Zwilling, M. (2009). Unbundling transaction services in the cloud. *Proceedings of the4th Biennial Conference on Innovative Data Systems Research (CIDR)*, Asilomar, California, USA.

Loopback. (2015, May). Retrieved from http://loopback.io/

Luis Rodero-Merinoa, L. M. (2012). *Building safe PaaS clouds: A survey on security in multitenant software platforms* (pp. 96–108). Computers & Security.

Luo, G., Huang, S., Chang, Y., & Yuan, S. (2014). A parallel Bees Algorithm implementation on GPU. *Journal of Systems Architecture*, *60*(3), 271–279. doi:10.1016/j.sysarc.2013.09.007

Luo, T., Ma, S., Lee, R., Zhang, X., Liu, D., & Zhou, L. (2013, October). S-cave: Effective ssd caching to improve virtual machine storage performance.*Proceedings of the 22nd international conference on Parallel architectures and compilation techniques* (pp. 103-112). IEEE Press.

LXC. (2015). *Linux container*. Retrivied from https://linuxcontainer.org/

Mahbub, K., & Spanoudakis, G. (2010). Proactive SLA negotiation for service based systems. *Proceedings of the 2010 6th World Congress on Services (SERVICES-1)* (pp. 519-526). IEEE. doi:10.1109/SERVICES.2010.15

Makkes, M. X., Ngo, C., Demchenko, Y., Stijkers, R., Meijer, R., & Laat, C. d. (2013). Defining intercloud federation framework for multi-provider cloud services integration. *Proceeding of the 4th International Conference on Cloud Computing, Grids, and Virtualization (CLOUD COMPUTING 2013),* Valencia, Spain (pp. 185–190). International Academy, Research, and Industry Association.

Malhotra, A., & Somani, G. (2013, September). VMCloner: A Fast and Flexible Virtual Machine Cloner. *Proceedings of the 2013 Third International Conference on Cloud and Green Computing (CGC)* (pp. 181-187). IEEE. doi:10.1109/CGC.2013.34

Manno, G., Smari, W. W., & Spalazzi, L. (2012). FCFA: A semantic-based federated cloud framework architecture. *Proceedings of the International Conference on High Performance Computing & Simulation (HPCS)*, Madrid, Spain (p. 42-52). IEEE Computer Society. doi:10.1109/HPCSim.2012.6266889

Marosi, A. C., Gombás, G., Balaton, Z., Kacsuk, P., & Kiss, T. (2008). SZTAKI Desktop Grid: Building a Scalable, Secure Platform for Desktop Grid Computing. In Making Grids Work (pp. 363–374). Springer.

Marosi, A. C., Kacsuk, P., Fedak, G., & Lodygensky, O. (2010). Sandboxing for Desktop Grids Using Virtualization. *Proceedings of the 2010 18th Euromicro Conference on Parallel, Distributed and Network-based Processing* (pp. 559–566). IEEE. doi:10.1109/PDP.2010.90

Marosi, A., Balaton, Z., & Kacsuk, P. (2009). GenWrapper: A generic wrapper for running legacy applications on desktop grids. *Proceedings of the2009 IEEE International Symposium on Parallel & Distributed Processing* (pp. 1–6). IEEE. doi:10.1109/IPDPS.2009.5161136

Marosi, A., Kecskemeti, G., Kertesz, A., & Kacsuk, P. (2011). FCM: An architecture for integrating iaas cloud systems. *Proceedings of the 2th International Conference on Cloud Computing, Grids, and Virtualization (CLOUD COMPUTING 2011)*, Rome, Italy (pp. 7–12). International Academy, Research, and Industry Association.

Marosi, A., Kovács, J., & Kacsuk, P. (2012). Towards a volunteer cloud system. *Future Generation Computer Systems*. doi:10.1016/j.future.2012.03.013

Marosi, A., Gombás, G., Balaton, Z., & Kacsuk, P. (2008). Enabling Java applications for BOINC with DC-API. In P. Kacsuk, R. Lovas, & Z. Németh (Eds.), *Distributed and Parallel Systems SE - 1* (pp. 3–12). Springer, US; doi:10.1007/978-0-387-79448-8_1

Marshall, P., Tufo, H., Keahey, K., LaBissoniere, D., & Woitaszek, M. (2012). Architecting a Large-Scale Elastic Environment: Recontextualization and Adaptive Cloud Services for Scientific Computing. *Proceedings of the7th International Conference on Software Paradigm Trends (ICSOFT)* (pp. 409–418). Rome.

Marshall, P., Keahey, K., & Freeman, T. (2010). Elastic site: Using clouds to elastically extend site resources.*Proceedings of the 10th IEEE/ACM International Conference on Cluster, Cloud and Grid Computing (CCGrid)*,Washington, DC, USA (pp. 43–52). IEEE Computer Society. doi:10.1109/CCGRID.2010.80

Marston, S., Li, Z., Bandyopadhyay, S., Zhang, J., & Ghalsasi, A. (2011). Cloud computing—The business perspective. *Decision Support Systems*, *51*(1), 176–189. doi:10.1016/j.dss.2010.12.006

Mashayekhy, L., Nejad, M., & Grosu, D. (2015). *Cloud federations in the sky: formation game and mechanism*. IEEE Transactions on Cloud Computing.

Massachusetts open cloud. (2015). *MOC*. Retrieved from http://www.bu.edu/hic/research/massachusetts-open-cloud

Mather, T., Kumaraswamy, S., & Latif, S. (2009). *Cloud security and privacy: an enterprise perspective on risks and compliance*. O'Reilly.

MBaaS. (2015, May 8). *Wikipedia*. Retrieved from http://en.wikipedia.org/wiki/Mobile_Backend_as_a_service

McGuinness, D. L., & Van Harmelen, F. (2004). OWL web ontology language overview. *W3C recommendation*, 10(10), 2004.

Meireles, F., & Malheiro, B. (2014). Integrated Management of IaaS Resources. In L. Lopes et al. (Eds.), Proceedings of the Euro-Par 2014: Parallel Processing Workshops (pp. 73-84). Cham, Switzerland: Springer International Publishing. doi:10.1007/978-3-319-14313-2_7

Mell, P., & Grance, T. (2011). *The NIST Definition of Cloud Computing*. Gaithersburg, MD. Retrieved from http://csrc. nist.gov/publications/nistpubs/800-145/SP800-145.pdf

Mellanox OFED for Linux User Manual. (2015). *Mellanox* Retrieved from http://www.mellanox.com/related-docs/ prod_software/Mellanox_OFED_Linux_User_Manual_v2.0-2.0.5.pdf

Mell, P., & Grance, T. (2011).*The NIST definition of cloud computing (Technical Report)*. National Institute of Standards and Technology.

Memcache. (2015, May). Retrieved from http://memcached.org/

Mendix. (2015, May). Retrieved from https://www.mendix.com/

Menzel, M., Klems, M., Le, H. A., & Tai, S. (2013, March). A configuration crawler for virtual appliances in compute Clouds. *Proceedings of the 2013 IEEE International Conference on Cloud Engineering (IC2E)* (pp. 201-209). IEEE. doi:10.1109/IC2E.2013.12

Mercosur. (2015). Retrieved from http://www.mercosur.int/

Merritt, A. M., Gupta, V., Verma, A., Gavrilovska, A., & Schwan, K. (2011). Shadowfax: Scaling in Heterogeneous Cluster Systems via GPGPU Assemblies.*Proceedings of the 5th International Workshop on Virtualization Technologies in Distributed Computing* (pp. 3-10). ACM. doi:10.1145/1996121.1996124

Michael Armbrust, A. F. (2009). *Above the Clouds: A Berkeley View of Cloud.*

Microsoft Active Directory. (2009). Retrieved from http://www.microsoft.com/windowsserver2003/technologies/direc-tory/activedirectory/default.mspx

Microsoft Azure cloud computing platform and services. (2015). *Azure*. Retrieved from https://azure.microsoft.com/

Microsoft Azure. (2015). Retrieved from http://azure.microsoft.com/en- in/documentation/infographics/cloud-identity-and-access/

Microsoft Azure. (2015, May). *Microsoft*. Retrieved from http://azure.microsoft.com/

Microsoft Identity Manager. (2015). Retrieved from http://www.microsoft.com/en-in/server-cloud/products/microsoft-identity-manager/

Mihailescu, M., & Teo, Y. M. (2010). Dynamic resource pricing on federated clouds.*Proceedings of the 10th IEEE/ ACEM International Conference on Cluster, Cloud and Grid Computing (CCGrid),*Washington, DC, USA (pp. 513–517). IEEE Computer Society.

Minhas, U. F., Rajagopalan, S., Cully, B., Aboulnaga, A., Salem, K., & Warfield, A. (2013). Remusdb: Transparent high availability for database systems. *The VLDB Journal, 22*(1), 29–45. doi:10.1007/s00778-012-0294-6

Mongo, D. *B.* (2015, May). Retrieved from https://www.mongodb.org/

More Than A Programming Model. (2015). *NVidia*. Retrieved from https://developer.nvidia.com/about-cuda

MySQL table deletion workaround. (2015, May). Retrieved from http://stackoverflow.com/questions/2300396/force-drop-mysql-bypassing-foreign-key-constraint

National security agency. (2015). Retrieved from https://www.google.com/intx/pt-BR/work/apps/business/

Navarro, T. (n. d.). What Is The Relationship Between Hybrid Clouds And Federated Clouds? *Computenext.com*. Re-trieved from https://www.computenext.com/blog/what-is-the-relationship-between-hybrid-clouds-and-federated-clouds/

Neumann, D., Bodenstein, C., Rana, O. F., & Krishnaswamy, R. (2011). STACEE: Enhancing Storage Clouds using Edge Devices.*Proceedings of the ACM/IEEE workshop on Autonomic Computing in Economics (ACE).* doi:10.1145/1998561.1998567

Ng, C. H., Ma, M., Wong, T. Y., Lee, P. P., & Lui, J. (2011, December). Live deduplication storage of virtual machine images in an open-source Cloud. *Proceedings of the 12th International Middleware Conference* (pp. 80-99). International Federation for Information Processing. doi:10.1007/978-3-642-25821-3_5

Nguyen, M. B., Tran, V., & Hluchy, L. (2013). A generic development and deployment framework for Cloud computing and distributed applications. *Computing and Informatics*, *32*(3), 461–485.

Nicolae, B., Kochut, A., & Karve, A. Discovering and Leveraging Content Similarity to Optimize Collective On-Demand Data Access to IaaS Cloud Storage. *Proceedings of theCCGrid'15: 15th IEEE/ACM International Symposium on Cluster, Cloud and Grid Computing*. doi:10.1109/CCGrid.2015.156

NIST US Government Cloud Computing Technology Roadmap. (2011) *NIST.* Retrieved from http://www.nist.gov/itl/cloud/upload/SP_500_293_volumeI-2.pdf

Node.js HTTP module. (2015, May). Node.js. Retrieved from https://nodejs.org/api/http.html

Node.js. (2015, May). Retrieved from https://nodejs.org/

node-redis. (2015, May). *Github.* Retrieved from https://github.com/mranney/node_redis

Núñez, D., Agudo, I., Drogkaris, P., & Gritzalis, S. (2011). Identity management challenges for intercloud applications. In Secure and Trust Computing, Data Management, and Applications (pp. 198-204). Springer Berlin Heidelberg.

NVIDIA GRID Technology. (2013). *NVIDIA.* Retrieved from http://www.nvidia.com/content/grid/pdf/GRID_K1_BD-06633-001_v02.pdf

NVIDIA Popular GPU-Accelerated Applications Catalog. (2014). *NVIDIA-app.* Retrieved http://www.nvidia.es/content/tesla/pdf/gpu-accelerated-applications-for-hpc.pdf

Nyréen, R., Edmonds, A., Papaspyrou, A., & Metsch, T. (2011). *Open cloud computing interface (OCCI) – core.* Retrieved from http://www.ogf.org/documents/GFD

OASIS Standard. (2003). Service Provisioning Markup Language (SPML) Version 1

OCCI. (n. d.). Retrieved from http://occi-wg.org/

Oikawa, M., Kawai, A., Nomura, K., Yasuoka, K., Yoshikawa, K., & Narumi, T. (2012). DS-CUDA: A Middleware to Use Many GPUs in the Cloud Environment. Proceedings of the 2012 SC Companion: High Performance Computing, Networking, Storage and Analysis (SCC) (pp. 1207-1214). IEEE Computer Society. doi:10.1109/SC.Companion.2012.146

Open computing infrastructure for elastic service. (2015). *Contrail.* Retrieved from http://www.contrail-project.eu/

Open standard for authorization. (2015). *oAuth.* Retrieved from http://oauth.net/

Open virtualization format. (2015). *OVF.* Retrieved from http://www.dmtf.org/standards/ovf

OpenId. (2015). Retrieved from http://openid.net/

OpenShift. (2015, May). Retrieved from https://www.openshift.com/

OpenStack. (2015). Retrieved from http://www.openstack.org/

Opinion 1/2010 on the concepts of "controller" and "processor" (Ref. WP 169). (2010, February). *Data Protection Working Party*. Retrieved from http://ec.europa.eu/justice/policies/privacy/docs/wp-docs/2010/wp169_en.pdf

Opinion 8/2010 on applicable law (Ref. WP 179). (2010, December). *Data Protection Working Party*. Retrieved from http://ec.europa.eu/justice/policies/privacy/docs/wp-docs/2010/wp179_en.pdf

Opscode. (2015). *Chef*. From http://ww.opscode.com

OPTIMIS FP7 project deliverable no. D7.2.1.1, Cloud Legal Guidelines. (n. d.). Retrieved from http://www.optimis-project.eu/sites/default/files/D7.2.1.1~OPTIMIS~Cloud~Legal~Guidelines.pdf

Oracle VM VirtualBox User Manual. (2015). *Oracle*. Retrieved from http://download.virtualbox.org/virtualbox/User-Manual.pdf

Oracle: SunOpenSSO Enterprise 8.0 TechnicalOverview. (2015). Retrieved from http://docs.sun.com/doc/820-3740

Oracle's Federation Manager. (2015). Retrieved from http://www.oracle.com/identity

Ostermann, S., Prodan, R., & Fahringer, T. (2009). Extending grids with Cloud resource management for scientific computing. *IEEE/ACM Grid*.

P2302 interoperability and federation (SIIF). (2015). *P2302*. Retrieved from https://standards.ieee.org/develop/project/2302.html

Padhy, R. P., Patra, M. R., & Satapathy, S. C. (2012). Design and implementation of a cloud based rural healthcare information system model.[VPN tunneling]. *Univers J Appl Comput Sci Technol, 2*(1), 149–157.

Pan, L. (2011). Towards a framework for automated service negotiation in cloud computing. *Proceedings of the 2011 IEEE International Conference on Cloud Computing and Intelligence Systems (CCIS)* (pp. 364-367). IEEE.

Parashar, M., AbdelBaky, M., Rodero, I., & Devarakonda, A. (2013). Cloud Paradigms and Practices for Computational and Data-Enabled Science and Engineering. *Computing in Science & Engineering, 15*(4), 10–18. doi:10.1109/MCSE.2013.49

Parashar, M., & Zhen, L. (2007). *A computational infrastructure for grid-based asynchronous parallel applications* (pp. 229–230). HPDC.

Parse. (2015, May). Retrieved from www.parse.com

Patel, P., Ranabahu, A., & Sheth, A. (2009). Service level agreement in cloud computing.*Proceedings of the Conference on Object Oriented Programming Systems Languages and Applications (OOPSLA)*, Orlando, FL, USA.

Pathan, M., Buyya, R., & Vakali, A. (2008). Content delivery networks: State of the art, insights, and imperatives. In R. Buyya, M. Pathan, & A. Vakali (Eds.), *Content Delivery Networks* (Vol. 9, pp. 3–32). Springer Berlin Heidelberg. doi:10.1007/978-3-540-77887-5_1

Pawar, P. S., Rajarajan, M., Dimitrakos, T., & Zisman, A. (2014). Trust Assessment Using Cloud Broker. In J. Zhou et al. (Eds.), *Trust Management VIII* (pp. 237–244). Berlin, Germany: Springer.

Pawluk, P., Simmons, B., Smit, M., Litoiu, M., & Mankovski, S. (2012). Introducing STRATOS: A cloud broker service. *Proceedings of the2012 IEEE Fifth International Conference on Cloud Computing* (pp. 891-898). IEEE. doi:10.1109/CLOUD.2012.24

Peña, A. J., Reaño, C., Silla, F., Mayo, R., Quintana-Ortí, E. S., & Duato, J. (2014). A complete and efficient CUDA-sharing solution for HPC clusters. *Parallel Computing, 40*(10), 574–588. doi:10.1016/j.parco.2014.09.011

Peng, C., Kim, M., Zhang, Z., & Lei, H. (2012, March). VDN: Virtual machine image distribution network for Cloud data centers. Proceedings of INFOCOM '12 (pp. 181-189). IEEE.

Perens, B. (n. d.). BusyBox: The Swiss Army Knife of Embedded Linux. Retrieved from http://www.busybox.net

Perez-Lombard, L., Ortiz, J., & Pout, C. (2010). A review on buildings energy consumption information. In *Energy and Buildings* (pp. 394-398).

Petcu, D. (2011). Portability and interoperability between clouds: Challenges and case study. *Proceedings of the 4th European Conference on Towards a Service-based Internet,* Poznan, Poland (pp. 62–74). Springer Berlin Heidelberg. doi:10.1007/978-3-642-24755-2_6

Petcu, D., Craciun, C., & Rak, M. (2011). Towards a cross platform cloud API.*Proceedings of the International Conference on Cloud Computing and Services Science (CLOSER),*Noordwijkerhout, The Netherlands (pp. 166–169).

Petcu, D., Di Martino, B., Venticinque, S., Rak, M., Máhr, T., Lopez, G. E., & Stankovski, V. et al. (2013). Experiences in building a mOSAIC of clouds. *Journal of Cloud Computing, 2*(1), 1–22.

Petri, I., Beach, T., Zou, M., Montes, J., Rana, O., & Parashar, M. (2014). Exploring models and mechanisms for exchanging resources in a federated cloud. *Proceedings of the IEEE International Conference on Cloud Engineering (IC2E),* Boston, Massachusetts (pp. 215–224). USA: IEEE Computer Society. doi:10.1109/IC2E.2014.9

Petri, I., Rana, O., Rezgui, Y., Li, H., Beach, T., Zou, M., ... (2014). Cloud Supported Building Data Analytics. *Proceedings of the14th IEEE/ACM International Symposium on Cluster, Cloud and Grid Computing (CCGrid),* (pp. 641-650).

Petri, I., Diaz-Montes, J., Rana, O., Punceva, M., Rodero, I., & Parashar, M. (2015). *Modelling and Implementing Social Community Clouds.* IEEE Transactions on Services Computing.

Petri, I., Li, H., Rezgui, Y., Chunfeng, Y., Yuce, B., & Jayan, B. (2014). A modular optimisation model for reducing energy consumption in large scale building facilities, Renewable and Sustainable Energy Reviews. *Renewable & Sustainable Energy Reviews, 38,* 990–1002. doi:10.1016/j.rser.2014.07.044

Petri, I., Montes, J. D., Zou, M., Beach, T., Rana, O. F., & Parashar, M. (2015). Market models for federated clouds. *IEEE Transactions on Cloud Computing, 3*(3), 398–410. doi:10.1109/TCC.2015.2415792

Philip, B., & Eric, N. (2009). *Principles of transaction processing* (2nd ed.). Burlington: Morgan Kaufmann.

phpMyAdmin. (2015, May). Retrieved from http://www.phpmyadmin.net/home_page/index.php

Pillow. (2015, May). Retrieved from https://python-pillow.github.io/

PingIdentity. (2015). *Ping Identity.* Retrieved from http://www.pingidentity.com

Pivotal. (2014, August). PaaS comparison. Retrieved from http://www.slideshare.net/Pivotal/paa-s-comparison2014v08

Playne, D. P., & Hawick, K. A. (2009). Data Parallel Three-Dimensional Cahn-Hilliard Field Equation Simulation on GPUs with CUDA.*Proceedings of the International Conference on Parallel and Distributed Processing Techniques and Applications* (pp. 104-110). CSREA Press.

Postgre, S. Q. L. (2015, May). Retrieved from http://www.postgresql.org/

Practical guide to cloud service level agreements version 1.0 (Tech. Rep.). (2012Cloud Standards Customer Council Workgroup. CSCC.

Privacy in a Connected World A European Data Protection Framework for the 21st Century, COM (2012) 09 final. (2012, January 25). (2012). Communication from the Commission to the European Parliament, the Council, the European Economic and Social Committee and the Committee of the Regions Safeguarding.

Prodan, R., & Ostermann, S. (2009, October). A survey and taxonomy of infrastructure as a service and web hosting Cloud providers. *Proceedings of the 2009 10th IEEE/ACM International Conference on Grid Computing* (pp. 17-25). IEEE. doi:10.1109/GRID.2009.5353074

Proposal for a Directive of the European Parliament and of the Council on the protection of individuals with regard to the processing of personal data by competent authorities for the purposes of prevention, investigation, detection or prosecution of criminal offences or the execution of criminal penalties, and the free movement of such data COM (2012) 10 final. (2012, January 25). Brussels.

Proposal for a Regulation of the European Parliament and of the Council on the protection of individuals with regard to the processing of personal data and on the free movement of such data (General Data Protection Regulation) COM (2012) 11 final. (2012, January 25). Brussels.

Protocol Buffer. (2015, May). Retrieved from https://github.com/google/protobuf/

Public Consultation on Cloud Computing by the European Commission. (n. d.). Retrieved from http://ec.europa.eu/your-voice/ipm/forms/dispatch?form=cloudcomputing&lang=en

Puppet Labs: IT Automation Software for System Administrators. (2015). Retrieved from http://puppetlabs.com/

PyMongo. (2015, May). Retrieved from http://api.mongodb.org/python/current/

Python. (2015, May). Retrieved from https://www.python.org/

Quinton, C., Haderer, N., Rouvoy, R., & Duchien, L. (2013). Towards multi-cloud configurations using feature models and ontologies. *Proceedings of the1st International Workshop on Multi-Cloud Applications and Federated Clouds,* Prague (pp. 21-26). ACM. doi:10.1145/2462326.2462332

Rackspace open cloud. (2015). *Rackspace.* Retrieved from http://www.rackspace.com/cloud/

Radha, V., & Reddy, D. H. (2012). A Survey on single sign-on techniques. *Procedia Technology, 4,* 134–139. doi:10.1016/j.protcy.2012.05.019

Rajkumar Buyyaa, C. S. (2009). Cloud computing and emerging IT platforms: Vision, hype, and reality for delivering computing as the 5th utility. In Future Generation Computer Systems (pp. 599–616).

Razavi, K., Razorea, L. M., & Kielmann, T. (2014, January). Reducing VM Startup Time and Storage Costs by VM Image Content Consolidation. In Euro-Par 2013: Parallel Processing Workshops (pp. 75-84). Springer Berlin Heidelberg. doi:10.1007/978-3-642-54420-0_8

Razavi, K., & Kielmann, T. (2013, November). Scalable virtual machine deployment using VM image caches.*Proceedings of the International Conference on High Performance Computing, Networking, Storage and Analysis* (p. 65). ACM. doi:10.1145/2503210.2503274

Reaño, C., Mayo, R., Quintana-Orti, E. S., Silla, F., Duato, J., & Peña, A. J. (2013). Influence of InfiniBand FDR on the performance of remote GPU virtualization.*Proceedings of the 2013 IEEE International Conference on Cluster Computing* (pp. 23-27). IEEE Computer Society. doi:10.1109/CLUSTER.2013.6702662

Rebai, S., Hadji, M., & Zeghlache, D. (2015). Improving profit through cloud federation.*Proceedings of the 12th Annual IEEE Consumer Communications and Networking Conference (CCNC),*Las Vegas, Nevada, USA (pp. 732–739). IEEE Computer Society. doi:10.1109/CCNC.2015.7158069

Recordon, D., & Reed, D. (2006, November). OpenID 2.0: a platform for user-centric identity management. *Proceedings of the second ACM workshop on Digital identity management* (pp. 11-16). ACM.

Redis4You. (2015, May). Retrieved from http://redis4you.com/

Reference architecture for an SLA management framework (Standard). (2011). EU FP7 project SLA@SOI.

Reich, J., Laadan, O., Brosh, E., Sherman, A., Misra, V., Nieh, J., & Rubenstein, D. (2012, December). VMTorrent: scalable P2P virtual machine streaming. In CoNEXT (pp. 289-300).

Reimer, D., Thomas, A., Ammons, G., Mummert, T., Alpern, B., & Bala, V. (2008, March). Opening black boxes: using semantic information to combat virtual machine image sprawl.*Proceedings of the fourth ACM SIGPLAN/SIGOPS international conference on Virtual execution environments* (pp. 111-120). ACM. doi:10.1145/1346256.1346272

Ren, X., & Wu, X. W. (2012, October). A novel dynamic user authentication scheme. *Proceedings of the 2012 International Symposium on Communications and Information Technologies (ISCIT)* (pp. 713-717). IEEE.

RFC 4158. (2015). *Request for comment.* Retrieved from http://tools.ietf.org/html/rfc4158

RFC 5280. (2015). *Request for comment.* Retrieved from http://tools.ietf.org/html/rfc5280

Rhoton, J. Discover OpenStack: the identity component keystone. Retrieved from http://www.ibm.com/developerworks/cloud/library/cl-openstack-keystone/

Rimal, B. P., Choi, E., & Lumb, I. (2009, August). A taxonomy and survey of cloud computing systems. Proceedings of the Fifth International Joint Conference on INC, IMS and IDC, NCM '09 (pp. 44-51). IEEE. (2013). doi:10.1109/NCM.2009.218

Rimal, B., Choi, E., & Lumb, I. (2009). A Taxonomy and Survey of Cloud Computing Systems. *Proceedings of the Fifth International Joint Conference on INC, IMS and IDC, NCM '09*, Seoul (pp. 44 - 51).

Riteau, P., Tsugawa, M., Matsunaga, A., Fortes, J., & Keahey, K. (2010). *Large-Scale Cloud Computing Research: Sky Computing on FutureGrid and Grid'5000.* ERCIM News.

Rochwerger, B., Breitgand, D., Levy, E., Galis, A., & others. (2009). The Reservoir model and architecture for open federated cloud computing.

Rochwerger, B., Breitgand, D., Levy, E., Galis, A., Nagin, K., Llorente, I. M., & Galán, F. et al. (2009). The RESERVOIR model and architecture for open federated cloud computing. *IBM Journal of Research and Development, 53*(4), 535–545. doi:10.1147/JRD.2009.5429058

Rosenblum, M., & Garfinkel, T. (2005). Virtual machine monitors: Current technology and future trends. *Computer, 38*(5), 39–47. doi:10.1109/MC.2005.176

Running Commands on Your Linux Instance at Launch. (2015). *Amazon.* Retrieved from http://docs.aws.amazon.com/AWSEC2/latest/UserGuide/user-data.html

Safe Harbor website of export.gov. Retrieved from https://safeharbor.export.gov

Sakimura, D. N., Bradley, J., Jones, M., de Medeiros, B., & Jay, E. (2011). OpenID Connect Standard 1.0-draft 20.

Samaan, N. (2014). A Novel Economic Sharing Model in a Federation of Selfish Cloud Providers. *IEEE Transactions on Parallel and Distributed Systems*, 25(1), 12–21. doi:10.1109/TPDS.2013.23

Sanchez, C. A., Blomer, J., Buncic, P., Chen, G., Ellis, J., Quintas, D. G., & Yadav, R. (2011). Volunteer Clouds and Citizen Cyberscience for LHC Physics. *Journal of Physics: Conference Series*, 331(6), 62022. http://stacks.iop.org/1742-6596/331/i=6/a=062022 doi:10.1088/1742-6596/331/6/062022

Sapuntzakis, C., Brumley, D., Chandra, R., Zeldovich, N., Chow, J., Lam, M. S., & Rosenblum, M. (2003). Virtual appliances for deploying and maintaining software.*Proceedings of the 17th USENIX Conference on System Administration,*Berkeley, CA, USA (pp. 181–194). USENIX Association.

Schmidt, M., Fallenbeck, N., Smith, M., & Freisleben, B. (2010, February). Efficient distribution of virtual machines for Cloud computing. *Proceedings of the 2010 18th Euromicro International Conference on Parallel, Distributed and Network-Based Processing (PDP)* (pp. 567-574). IEEE. doi:10.1109/PDP.2010.39

Security guidance for critical areas of focus in cloud computing v3. 0. (2011). Cloud Security Alliance.

Sellami, M. Y. S. (2013). PaaS-Independent Provisioning and Management of Applications in the Cloud. *Proceedings of the 2013 IEEE Sixth International Conference on Cloud Computing (CLOUD)*, Santa Clara, CA, USA (pp. 693 - 700).

Sellami, M., Yangui, S., Mohamed, M., & Tata, S. (2013). PaaS-Independent Provisioning and Management of Applications in the Cloud. *Proceedings of the 2013 IEEE Sixth International Conference on Cloud Computing (CLOUD)*, Santa Clara, CA, USA (pp. 693 - 700).

Semnanian, A. A., Pham, J., Englert, B., & Wu, X. (2011). Virtualization Technology and its Impact on Computer Hardware Architecture.*Proceedings of Eighth International Conference on Information Technology: New Generations (ITNG)* (pp. 719-724). IEEE. doi:10.1109/ITNG.2011.127

Seo, S., Kim, M., Cui, Y., Seo, S., & Lee, H. (2015). SFA-based cloud federation monitoring system for integrating physical resources.*Proceedings of the International Conference on Big Data and Smart Computing (BIGCOMP)*Jeju Island, Korea (pp. 55–58). IEEE Computer Society. doi:10.1109/35021BIGCOMP.2015.7072851

Sequelize. (2015, May). Retrieved from http://docs.sequelizejs.com/en/latest/

Seventh framework programmer. (2015). Retrieved from http://ec.europa.eu/research/fp7/index/

Shadowfax II - scalable implementation of GPGPU assemblies. (2015). Keeneland. Retrieved from http://keeneland.gatech.edu/software/keeneland/kidron

Shelby, Z., Hartke, K., & Bormann, C. (n. d.). Constrained Application Protocol (CoAP). Retrieved from https://datatracker.ietf.org/doc/draft-ietf-core-coap/

Shi, L., Chen, H., & Sun, J. (2009). vCUDA: GPU accelerated high performance computing in virtual machines.*Proceedings of IEEE International Symposium on Parallel & Distributed Processing* (pp. 23-29). IEEE Computer Society.

Sim, K. M. (2012). Agent-based cloud computing. *IEEE Transactions on* Services Computing, 5(4), 564–577.

Sipos, G., Turilli, M., Newhouse, S., & Kacsuk, P. (2013, April). A European Federated Cloud: Innovative distributed computing solutions by EGI. Proceedings of the EGU General Assembly Conference Abstracts (Vol. 15, p. 8690).

Smith, D. (2008). The challenge of federated identity management. *Network Security*, 2008(4), 7–9. doi:10.1016/S1353-4858(08)70051-5

SOA source book. (2009). *The Open Group*. Retrieved from http://books.google.com.br/books?id=SbZfhkdqbagC

Socket.io. (2015, May). Retrieved from http://socket.io/

Softlayer cloud built to perform. (2015). *Softlayer*. Retrieved from http://www.softlayer.com/

Song, J., Lv, Z., & Tian, K. (2015). *KVMGT: a Full GPU Virtualization Solution*. Retrieved from http://www.linux-kvm.org/images/f/f3/01x08b-KVMGT-a.pdf

Sood, S. K. (2012). A combined approach to ensure data security in cloud computing. *Journal of Network and Computer Applications*, *35*(6), 1831–1838. doi:10.1016/j.jnca.2012.07.007

SportE2 EU FP7 project. (n. d.). Retrieved from http://www.sporte2.eu/

SQLAlchemy. (2015, May). Retrieved from http://www.sqlalchemy.org/

Stantchev, V., & Schröpfer, C. (2009). Negotiating and enforcing QoS and SLAs in grid and cloud computing. In N. Abdennadher & D. Petcu (Eds.), *Advances in grid and pervasive computing (LNCS)* (Vol. 5529, pp. 25–35). Berlin, Germany: Springer. doi:10.1007/978-3-642-01671-4_3

Stihler, M., Santin, A. O., Marcon, A. L., & Fraga, J. S. (2012, May). Integral federated identity management for cloud computing. *Proceedings of the 2012 5th International Conference on New Technologies, Mobility and Security (NTMS)* (pp. 1-5). IEEE. doi:10.1109/NTMS.2012.6208751

Strand, R. K. (2001). Modularization and simulation techniques for heat balance based energy and load calculation programs: the experience of the ASHRAE Loads Toolkits and EnergyPlus. Proceedings of Building Simulation, (pp. 747-753).

Sturm, M., Bertsch, A., Gröpl, C., Hildebrandt, A., Hussong, R., Lange, E., & Kohlbacher, O. et al. (2008). OpenMS - an open-source software framework for mass spectrometry. *BMC Bioinformatics*, *9*(163). PMID:18366760

Subashini, S., & Kavitha, V. (2011). A survey on security issues in service delivery models of cloud computing. *Journal of Network and Computer Applications*, *34*(1), 1–11. doi:10.1016/j.jnca.2010.07.006

Suhendra, V. (2011). A survey on access control deployment. In *Security Technology* (pp. 11–20). Springer Berlin Heidelberg. doi:10.1007/978-3-642-27189-2_2

Summary of the Amazon EC2 and Amazon RDS service disruption. (2011). *Amazon*. Retrieved from http://aws.amazon.com/message/65648/

Summary of the aws service event in the US east region. (2012). *Amazon*. Retrieved from http://aws.amazon.com/message/67457/

Supervisord. (2015, May). Retrieved from http://supervisord.org/

Surkov, V. (2010). Parallel option pricing with Fourier space time-stepping method on graphics processing units. *Parallel Computing*, *36*(7), 372–380. doi:10.1016/j.parco.2010.02.006

Svantesson, D., & Clarke, R. (2010). Privacy and consumer risks in cloud computing. *Computer Law & Security Report*, *26*(4), 391–397. doi:10.1016/j.clsr.2010.05.005

Symplified. (2015). Retrieved from http://www.symplified.com-Symplified

Tang, C. (2011, June). FVD: A High-Performance Virtual Machine Image Format for Cloud. *Proceedings of the USENIX Annual Technical Conference*.

Teacy, W. L., Patel, J., Jennings, N. R., & Luck, M. (2006). Travos: Trust and reputation in the context of inaccurate information sources. *Autonomous Agents and Multi-Agent Systems*, *12*(2), 183–198. doi:10.1007/s10458-006-5952-x

Thain, D., Tannenbaum, T., & Livny, M. (2008). Distributed Computing in Practice: The Condor Experience. *Concurrency and Computation*, 2008, 323–356.

The enterprise-class monitoring solution for everyone. (2015). *Zabbix*. Retrieved from http://www.zabbix.com/

The Madrid Resolution: International Standards on the Protection of Personal Data and Privacy, Adopted by the International Conference of Data Protection and Privacy Commissioners. (2009, November 5). *U.S. Department of Justice*. Retrieved from http://www.justice.gov/opcl/privacyactoverview2012/1974intro.htm

The NVIDIA GPU Computing SDK Version 6.5. (2014). *NVIDIA*. Retrieved from https://developer.nvidia.com/cuda-toolkit

The R Project for Statistical Computing. (n. d.). Retrieved from http://www.r-project.org/

The Xen Project. (2015). *Xen*. Retrieved from http://www.xenproject.org/

Thomas, M. V., Dhole, A., & Chandrasekaran, K. (2015). Single sign-on in cloud federation using cloudsim. *International Journal of Computer Network and Information Security*, 7(6), 50–58. doi:10.5815/ijcnis.2015.06.06

Tolosana-Calasanz, R., Bañares, J. A., & Colom, J.-M. (2015). On autonomic platform-as-a-service: Characterisation and conceptual model. *Proceedings of the Agent and Multi-Agent Systems: Technologies and Applications – 9th KES International Conference (KES-AMSTA),* Sorrento, Italy (Vol.. 38. pp. 217–226).

Toosi, A. N., Calheiros, R. N., & Buyya, R. (2014, May). Interconnected cloud computing environments: Challenges, taxonomy and survey. *ACM Computing Surveys*, 47(1), 7:1–7:47.

Toosi, A. N., Calheiros, R. N., Thulasiram, R. K., & Buyya, R. (2011). Resource provisioning policies to increase IaaS provider's profit in a federated cloud environment.*Proceedings of the 13th IEEE International Conference on High Performance Computing and Communications (HPCC),*Washington, DC, USA (pp. 279–287). IEEE Computer Society.

Topology and orchestration specification for cloud applications (TOSCA) version 1.0. (2013). *TOSCA*. Retrieved from http://docs.oasis-open.org/tosca/TOSCA/v1.0/os/TOSCA-v1.0-os.pdf

Tordsson, J., Montero, R. S., Moreno-Vozmediano, R., & Llorente, I. M. (2012). Cloud brokering mechanisms for optimized placement of virtual machines across multiple providers. *Future Generation Computer Systems*, 28(2), 358–367. doi:10.1016/j.future.2011.07.003

TriCipher. (2015). Retrieved from http://www.tricipher.com

Tröger, P., Rajic, H., Haas, A., & Domagalski, P. (2007). Standardization of an API for distributed resource management systems. *Proceedings of the Seventh IEEE International Symposium on Cluster Computing and the Grid CCGRID '07* (pp. 619–626). doi:10.1109/CCGRID.2007.109

Tusa, F., Celesti, A., Paone, M., Villari, M., & Puliafito, A. (2011, June). How clever-based clouds conceive horizontal and vertical federations. *Proceedings of the 2011 IEEE Symposium on Computers and Communications (ISCC)* (pp. 167-172). IEEE. doi:10.1109/ISCC.2011.5984011

Twelve-Factor app. (2015, May). Retrieved from http://12factor.net/

Uhlig, R., Neiger, G., Rodgers, D., Santoni, A. L., Martins, F. C. M., Anderson, A. V., & Smith, L. (2005). Intel virtualization technology. *Computer*, 38(5), 48–56. doi:10.1109/MC.2005.163

UNIFY EU FP7 project. (n. d.). Retrieved from http://www.fp7-unify.eu/

Unleashing the Potential of Cloud Computing in Europe. COM(2012) 529 final. (2012, September 27). Brussels: Communication from the Commission to the European Parliament, the Council, the European Economic and Social Committee and the Committee of the Regions.

US Patriotic Act. (2001). Retrieved from http://www.gpo.gov/fdsys/pkg/PLAW-107publ56/pdf/PLAW-107publ56.pdf

Use cases and functional requirements for inter-cloud computing (Tech. Rep.). (2010). Global Inter-Cloud Technology Forum.

Use Cases and Functional Requirements for Inter-Cloud Computing. (2010). *Global Inter-cloud Technology Forum.* Retrieved from http://www.gictf.jp/doc/GICTF_Whitepaper_20100809.pdf

UserGrid. (2015, May). Retrieved from http://usergrid.incubator.apache.org/

Vaquero, L. M., Rodero-Merino, L., Caceres, J., & Lindner, M. (2008, December). A break in the clouds: Towards a cloud definition. *SIGCOMM Computer Communication Review, 39*(1), 50–55. doi:10.1145/1496091.1496100

Vazquez, C., Huedo, E., Montero, R., & Llorente, I. (2009). Dynamic provision of computing resources from grid infrastructures and Cloud providers. *Proceedings of theGrid and Pervasive Computing Conf.*

Vecchiola, C., Pandey, S., & Buyya, R. (2009). High-Performance Cloud Computing: A View of Scientific Applications. *Proceedings of the10th Intl. Symposium on Pervasive Systems, Algorithms, and Networks*, (pp. 4--16). doi:10.1109/I-SPAN.2009.150

Velasco, J. L., Bustos, A., Castejón, F., Fernández, L. A., Martin-Mayor, V., & Tarancón, A. (2012). ISDEP: Integrator of stochastic differential equations for plasmas. *Computer Physics Communications, 183*(9), 1877–1883. doi:10.1016/j.cpc.2012.04.005

Veloso, B., Malheiro, B., & Burguillo, J. C. (2015). Media Brokerage: Agent-Based SLA Negotiation. In A. Rocha, A. M. Correia, S. Costanzo, & L. P. Reis (Eds.), *New Contributions in Information Systems and Technologies (Advances in Intelligent Systems and Computing)* (Vol. 353, pp. 575–584). Cham, Switzerland: Springer International Publishing.

Venticinque, S., Aversa, R., Di Martino, B., Rak, M., & Petcu, D. (2011). A cloud agency for SLA negotiation and management. In M. R, Guarracino et al. (Eds), Proceedings of the Euro-Par 2010 Parallel Processing Workshops, LNCS (Vol. 6585, pp. 587-594). Berlin, Germany: Springer. doi:10.1007/978-3-642-21878-1_72

Villegas, D., Bobroff, N., Rodero, I., Delgado, J., Liu, Y., Devarakonda, A., & Parashar, M. et al. (2012). Cloud federation in a layered service model. *Journal of Computer and System Sciences, 78*(5), 1330–1344. doi:10.1016/j.jcss.2011.12.017

Vincent, A. (2005). AMD64 Virtualization Reference Manual. Retrieved from http://www.mimuw.edu.pl/~vincent/lecture6/sources/amd-pacifica-specification.pdf

Vockler, J.-S., Juve, G., Deelman, E., & Rynge, M. (2011). Experiences using cloud computing for a scientific workflow application. *Proceedings of the2nd Workshop on Scientific Cloud Computing in conjunction with ACM HPDC.* doi:10.1145/1996109.1996114

Vouzis, P. D., & Sahinidis, N. V. (2010). GPU-BLAST: Using graphics processors to accelerate protein sequence alignment. *Bioinformatics (Oxford, England).* PMID:21088027

vSphere 6.0 Datasheet. (2015). *VMware.* Retrieved from http://www.vmware.com/files/pdf/vsphere/VMW-vSPHR-Datasheet-6-0.pdf

vSphere. (n. d.). *VMware journal.* Retrieved from http://www.vmware.com/products/vsphere/features/availability

Wahl, M., Howes, T., & Kille, S. (1997). Lightweight directory access protocol (v3).

Walters, J. P., Younge, A. J., Dong, I. K., Ke, T. Y., Mikyung, K., Crago, S. P., & Fox, G. C. (2014). GPU Passthrough Performance: A Comparison of KVM, Xen, VMWare ESXi, and LXC for CUDA and OpenCL Applications.*Proceedings of the IEEE 7th International Conference on Cloud Computing (CLOUD)* (pp 636-643). IEEE Computer Society. doi:10.1109/CLOUD.2014.90

Wand. (2015, May). Retrieved from http://docs.wand-py.org/en/0.4.0/

Wang, C., Wang, Q., Ren, K., & Lou, W. (2010, March). Privacy-preserving public auditing for data storage security in cloud computing. Proceedings of the '10 INFOCOM '10 (pp. 1-9). IEEE. doi:10.1109/INFCOM.2010.5462173

Wang, J., Li, D., Li, Q., & Xi, B. (2007, September). Constructing Role-Based Access Control and Delegation Based on Hierarchical IBS. *Proceedings of the NPC Workshops IFIP International Conference on Network and Parallel Computing Workshops.* (pp. 112-118). IEEE. doi:10.1109/NPC.2007.106

Wang, G., Yu, J., & Xie, Q. (2013). Security analysis of a single sign-on mechanism for distributed computer networks. . *IEEE Transactions on* Industrial Informatics, *9*(1), 294–302.

Wang, W., Zhang, Y., Lin, B., Wu, X., & Miao, K. (2010). Secured and reliable VM migration in personal cloud.*Proceedings of the 2nd International Conference on Computing Engineering and Technology (ICCET)* (pp. 705-709). IEEE Computer Society. doi:10.1109/ICCET.2010.5485376

Watson, J. (2008). VirtualBox: Bits and Bytes Masquerading As Machines. *Linux J., 2008*(166). Retrieved from http://dl.acm.org/citation.cfm?id=1344209.1344210

Watson, P., Lord, P., Gibson, F., Periorellis, P., & Pitsilis, G. (2008). Cloud computing for e-science with CARMEN. *Proceedings of the 2nd IBERIAN Grid Infrastructure Conference,* Porto, Portugal (pp. 3–14). NETBIBLO.

Web ontology language. (2015). *OWL.* Retrieved from http://www.w3.org/TR/owl-ref/

Wei, Y., Shi, C., & Shao, W. (2010, May). An attribute and role based access control model for service-oriented environment. *Proceedings of the 2010 Chinese Control and Decision Conference* (CCDC) (pp. 4451-4455). IEEE.

What is EU Data Protection Directive 95/46/EC? (n. d.). *Whatis.com.* Retrieved from http://searchsecurity.techtarget.co.uk/definition/EU-Data-Protection-Directive

Whittaker, Z. (2011). *Safe Harbor: Why EU data needs "protecting" from US law.* Retrieved from http://www.zdnet.com/blog/igeneration/safe-harbor-why-eu-data-needs-protecting-from-us-law/8801

Wong, R. (2011). Data protection: The future of privacy. *Computer Law & Security Report, 27*(1), 53–57. doi:10.1016/j.clsr.2010.11.004

Wu, H., Diamos, G., Sheard, T., Aref, M., Baxter, S., Garland, M., & Yalamanchili, S. (2014). Red Fox: An Execution Environment for Relational Query Processing on GPUs.*Proceedings of Annual IEEE/ACM International Symposium on Code Generation and Optimization* (pp. 44-54). ACM. doi:10.1145/2581122.2544166

Xu, H., & Li, B. (2011). Egalitarian stable matching for VM migration in cloud computing. *Proceedings of the IEEE Conference on Computer CommunicationsWorkshops (INFOCOM WKSHPS)* (pp. 631-636). IEEE Computer Society. doi:10.1109/INFCOMW.2011.5928889

Xu, J., Zhang, W., Ye, S., Wei, J., & Huang, T. (2014, July). A lightweight virtual machine image deduplication backup approach in Cloud environment. *Proceedings of the 2014 IEEE 38th Annual Computer Software and Applications Conference (COMPSAC)* (pp. 503-508). IEEE. doi:10.1109/COMPSAC.2014.73

Xu, X., Jin, H., Wu, S., & Wang, Y. (2014). Rethink the storage of virtual machine images in Clouds. *Future Generation Computer Systems*.

Yamazaki, I., Dong, T., Solcà, R., Tomov, S., Dongarra, J., & Schulthess, T. (2014). Tridiagonalization of a dense symmetric matrix on multiple GPUs and its application to symmetric eigenvalue problems. *Concurrency and Computation*, *26*(16), 2652–2666. doi:10.1002/cpe.3152

Yangui, S., Marshall, I. J., Laisne, J. P., & Tata, S. (2014). CompatibleOne: The open source cloud broker. *Journal of Grid Computing*, *12*(1), 93–109. doi:10.1007/s10723-013-9285-0

Yang, X., Wallom, D., Waddington, S., Wang, J., Shaon, A., Matthews, B., & Kershaw, P. et al. (2014). Cloud Computing in e-Science: Research Challenges and Opportunities. *The Journal of Supercomputing*, *70*(1), 408–464. doi:10.1007/s11227-014-1251-5 PMID:25309040

Yan, L., Rong, C., & Zhao, G. (2009). Strengthen cloud computing security with federal identity management using hierarchical identity-based cryptography. In *Cloud Computing* (pp. 167–177). Springer Berlin Heidelberg. doi:10.1007/978-3-642-10665-1_15

Yanpei Chen, V. P. (2010). *What's New About Cloud Computing Security? EECS Department,* University of California, Berkeley, CA, USA.

Yuancheng, L., & Duraiswami, R. (2008). Canny edge detection on NVIDIA CUDA.*Proceedings of IEEE Computer Society Conference on Computer Vision and Pattern Recognition Workshops.* (pp. 1-8). IEEE.

Yuriyama, M., & Kushida, T. (2010). Sensor-Cloud Infrastructure-Physical Sensor Management with Virtualized Sensors on Cloud Computing.*Proc. of NBiS'10.* doi:10.1109/NBiS.2010.32

ZeroMQ enterprise messaging broker. (2015). *ZeroMQ.* Retrieved from http://zeromq.org/

Zhang, Q., Cheng, L., & Boutaba, R. (2010). Cloud computing: State-of-the-art and research challenges. *Journal of Internet Services and Applications*, *1*(1), 7–18. doi:10.1007/s13174-010-0007-6

Zhang, Y., Li, Y., & Zheng, W. (2013). Automatic software deployment using user-level virtualization for Cloud-computing. *Future Generation Computer Systems*, *29*(1), 323–329. doi:10.1016/j.future.2011.08.012

Zhao, X., Zhang, Y., Wu, Y., Chen, K., Jiang, J., & Li, K. (2014). Liquid: A scalable deduplication file system for virtual machine images. . *IEEE Transactions on* Parallel and Distributed Systems, *25*(5), 1257–1266.

Zhou, R., Liu, F., Li, C., & Li, T. (2013, March). Optimizing virtual machine live storage migration in heterogeneous storage environment. In ACM SIGPLAN Notices, 48(7), 73-84. ACM. doi:10.1145/2451512.2451529

Zillians GPU Virtualization Middleware (vGPU). (2015). *Zillians.* Retrieved from https://github.com/zillians/platform_manifest_vgpu

Zulkernine, F., Martin, P., Craddock, C., & Wilson, K. (2009, July). A policy-based middleware for web services SLA negotiation. *Proceedings of the IEEE International Conference on Web Services ICWS '09.* (pp. 1043-1050). IEEE. doi:10.1109/ICWS.2009.157

About the Contributors

Gabor Kecskemeti (M.Sc., University of Miskolc, 2004; Ph.D., University of Westminster, 2011) is a research fellow at the Laboratory of Parallel and Distributed Systems (LPDS) of MTA SZTAKI. In, 2013, he was a postdoctoral researcher at the University of Innsbruck, Austria. He has got involved in several successful Grid and SOA research projects (e.g., ePerSpace, EDGeS, S-Cube) as well as in the recently funded ENTICE project (focusing on cloud computing), financed by the EU's Horizon2020 framework program. He coordinated the Cloud research group of LPDS in 2011–2012. He was member or chair of the program committees of several European conferences and workshops. He was guest editor for the Journal of Grid Computing for a special issue on Cloud federations. He has published over 50 scientific papers (incl. 9 journal articles and 3 edited volumes) about cloud and grid computing, particularly from the field of virtual appliance delivery in IaaS clouds.

Attila Kertesz (MSc, University of Szeged, 2004; PhD, University of Szeged, 2011) is a research fellow at the University of Szeged, and at the Laboratory of Parallel and Distributed Systems of MTA SZTAKI, Hungary. His research work covers interoperability aspects of Cloud federations. He is a management committee member of the ICT COST Action IC1304 and has participated in several successful European projects including COST IC0805, SHIWA, S-Cube EU FP7 and the CoreGRID EU FP6 Network of Excellence projects. He has been a member of the program committees for European conferences and workshops, and has published over 60 scientific papers, having more than 350 independent citations.

Zsolt Nemeth received a MSc degree from the Technical University of Budapest, Budapest, Hungary, in 1994, and a PhD degree from the Budapest University of Technology and Economics, Budapest, Hungary, in 2001. He is a Senior Researcher at the Laboratory of Parallel and Distributed Systems, MTA SZTAKI, Budapest, Hungary. His research work has covered various aspects of parallel and distributed computing, formal modeling, grid computing, and unconventional programming paradigms. His work on semantic modeling of grid computing has met a reception. He has been a visiting researcher at Emory University and an ERCIM Fellow at IRISA-INRIA and FORTH.

* * *

Giovanni Aloisio is a full professor of Information Processing Systems at the Dept. of Innovation Engineering of the University of Salento, Lecce-Italy and Director of the CMCC Supercomputing Center. He is a member of the CMCC Strategic Council and the ENES HPC Task Force. He has contributed to the IESP and EESI exascale roadmaps. He is the author of more than 100 papers in referred journals on HPC, grid & cloud computing and distributed data management.

Marcio R. M. Assis is a computing lover and networks enthusiast. Master in Informatics at the Federal University of Paraná (Brasil) and Doctoral student at the University of Campinas (Brasil), researching multiple clouds organizations (Inter-Clouds). Currently investigating cloud federations, acting in characterizing architectures and the definition of functional and behavioral properties from federations.

Rosa M. Badia holds a PhD on Computer Science (1994) from the Technical University of Catalonia (UPC). She is a Scientific Researcher from the Consejo Superior de Investigaciones Científicas (CSIC) and team leader of the Workflows and Distributed Computing research group at the Barcelona Supercomputing Center (BSC). She was involved in teaching and research activities at the UPC from 1989 to 2008, where she was an Associated Professor since 1997. From 1999 to 2005, she was involved in research and development activities at the European Center of Parallelism of Barcelona (CEPBA). Her current research interests are programming models for complex platforms (from multicore, GPUs to Grid/Cloud). The group led by Dr. Badia has been developing StarSs programming model for more than 10 years, with a high success in adoption by application developers. Currently the group focuses its efforts in two instances of StarSs: OmpSs for heterogeneous platforms and COMPSs/PyCOMPSs for distributed computing including Cloud. For this last case, the group has been doing efforts on interoperability through standards, for example using OCCI to enable COMPSs to interact with several Cloud providers at a time. Dr Badia has published more than 150 papers in international conferences and journals in the topics of her research. She has participated in several European projects, for example: BEinGRID, Brein, CoreGRID, OGF-Europe, SIENA, TEXT and VENUS-C. Currently, she is participating in the project Severo Ochoa (at Spanish level), ASCETIC, Euroserver, The Human Brain Project, EU-Brazil CloudConnect, the BioExcel CoE, NEXTGenIO, and trasnPLANT and is a member of HiPEAC2 NoE.

Abmar Barros is a developer and researcher at the Federal University of Campina Grande. He obtained a B.S. degree in Computer Science from the Federal University of Campina Grande in 2009 and an M.S. degree from the same University in 2012. His interests involve the architecture and development of mobile applications, web-based systems and distributed systems in general. He was deeply involved in the development of Buddycloud, an open-source solution for federated social networks. He was also one of the main contributors of OurGrid, a grid middleware based on a peer-to-peer architecture. He now leads the development of the Fogbow middleware and holds the CTO title at Coddy, a mobile development company.

Tom Beach is a lecturer in Construction Informatics. He holds a PhD in Computer Science from Cardiff University. He specializes in High Performance, Distributed, and Cloud Computing. His recent work focuses on applications in the Architecture Engineering and Construction domain. This work has included the use of cloud computing for the storage, security, management, coordination and processing of building data and the development of rule checking methodologies to allow this data to be tested against current building regulations and performance requirements.

Luiz Fernando Bittencourt is an Assistant Professor of Computer Science at the University of Campinas, Brazil. He received his Ph.D. in 2010 from the University of Campinas, and his research interests involve aspects of resource allocation and management in heterogeneous distributed systems, focusing on algorithms for scheduling in hybrid clouds. He is the recipient of the 2013 IEEE ComSoc Latin America Young Professional Award.

Ignacio Blanquer (Ph.D.) is an associate professor of the Computer System Department at UPV since 1999, has been a member of the Research Group for Grid and High Performance Computing since 1993. He is currently the person responsible for this research group. He has been involved in Parallel Computation and Medical Image processing, participating in more than 55 national and European Research Projects, has authored and co-authored 32 articles in indexed journals and book chapters and in more than 80 papers in national and international journals and conference proceedings. He has served as coordinator of the application area in the Spanish Network for e-Science, including his role in the managerial board, participates in the user support of the Spanish National Grid Initiative and was Community Manager in VENUS-C, where he collected and evaluated user requirements and provided hands-on support for migration to the cloud. He is currently the project coordinator of the European Projects EUBrazilCloudConnect and EU-Bra BIGSEA and co-principal investigator in the CLUVIEM national research project.

Francisco Brasileiro is a full Professor at the Federal University of Campina Grande, Brazil. He received a BS degree in Computer Science from the Federal University of Paraíba, Brazil, in 1988, a MSc degree from the same University in 1989, and a PhD degree in Computer Science from the University of Newcastle upon Tyne, UK, in 1995. His research interests are focused in distributed systems, with emphasis in on-demand computing and collaborative systems. He is a member of the Brazilian Computer Society, the ACM, and the IEEE Computer Society.

Juan Carlos Burguillo holds a M.Sc. degree in Telecommunications and a Ph.D. degree in Telematics from the University of Vigo, Spain. He is currently an associate professor at the Department of Telematic Engineering at the same university. He has directed several R&D projects, and has published more than one hundred papers in international journals and conferences. His research interests include multi-agent systems, evolutionary algorithms, game theory and telematic services.

Jacek Cała is a Research Associate in the School of Computing Science at Newcastle University. He works on the e-Science Central workflow management system and its application to large scientific problems. His main interests include cloud-based, component-based and distributed solutions driving workflows and e-Science. Previously, Jacek worked as a Teaching and Research Assistant at AGH-University of Science and Technology in Kraków, Poland where he was one of the architects and key developers of TeleDICOM, a system which supports medical teleconsultations in over 20 hospitals and medical centres in the South of Poland.

Fernando Campos is a computer Science Engineer (Universidad Autónoma de Madrid) and Master of Parallel and Distributed Computing (Technical University of Valencia).

K. Chandrasekaran is currently a Professor in the Department of Computer Science and Engineering, National Institute of Technology Karnataka, with 26 years of experience. He has more than 120 research papers published in various reputed International journals, conferences which include IEEE,

ACM, Springer, etc. He has received best paper awards and best teacher awards. He serves as a member of various reputed societies, including IEEE (Senior member), ACM (Senior Member), CSI, ISTE and Association of British Scholars (ABS). He is also a member in IEEE Computer Society's Cloud Computing STC (Special Technical Community). His areas of interest include Computer Networks, Distributed Computing (includes Cloud Computing and Security) and Business Computing and Information Systems Management.

Thomas Fahringer is a Professor of Computer Science at the University of Innsbruck in Austria. He is leading a research group in the area of distributed and parallel processing which develops the ASKALON programming environment to support researchers worldwide in various fields of science and engineering to develop, analyse, optimize and run distributed applications for Cloud systems. Furthermore, he leads a research team that created the Insieme parallelizing and optimizing compiler for heterogeneous multicore parallel computers ranging from mobile systems to high end supercomputers. Before joining the University of Innsbruck, Fahringer worked as an assistant and associate professor at the University of Vienna in Austria where his research focused on compiler technology and tools for high performance applications. Fahringer is a graduate of the Technical University of Vienna with a doctorate in computer science. Fahringer was involved in numerous national and international research projects including 12 EU funded projects, three of which were coordinated by him. Fahringer has published 5 books, 35 journal and magazine articles and more than 180 reviewed conference papers including 4 best/ distinguished IEEE/ACM/Springer papers.

Sandro Fiore, Ph.D., Data Scientist and Director of the Advanced Scientific Computing at the Euro-Mediterranean Center on Climate Change (CMCC). His research activities focus on parallel, distributed, grid and cloud computing, in particular on distributed data management, data analytics/mining and high performance database management. Since 2004, he has been involved into several national and international projects like: EGEE, EGI-InSPIRE, IS-ENES1, IS-ENES2, EUBRAZILCC, EXARCH, ORIENTGATE, TESSA, CLIP-C. Since 2010, he has been the Principal Investigator of the Ophidia project (www.ophidia.cmcc.it), a research project on high performance data analytics and mining for eScience. Since 2011, he has been Visiting Scientist at Lawrence Livermore National Laboratory – LLNL (Livermore, CA, USA) working on proactive distributed monitoring systems in P2P environments. He is also member of the ENES Data Task Force and the INDIGO-DataCloud Technical Board. He is author and co-author of more than 50 papers in refereed books/journals/proceedings on distributed and grid computing and holds a patent on data management topics. He is editor of the book "Grid and Cloud Database Management" (Springer, 2011). He is an ACM Member.

Francisco Germano received a B.Sc. degree in Information Systems from the Faculty of Social Sciences (FACISA) at Campina Grande, Brazil, in 2013. He is an MBA candidate in Project Management at the Getúlio Vargas Foundation. Currently, he acts as a researcher and developer in the Fogbow project (fogbowcloud.org). Since the beginning of his professional career he has been involved in projects on software quality, distributed software, cloud computing, and web applications.

Ákos Zoltán Gorácz got his bachelor's degree in Computer Science from the University of Szeged in 2013. He's currently working as a programmer at the Department of Software Engineering and at the Student Union of the University of Szeged.

Antônio Tadeu A. Gomes is a researcher at the National Laboratory for Scientific Computing (LNCC), Brazil. He is head of the Mechanisms and Architectures for Tele-informatics Research Group (MARTIN), and the executive officer of the Brazilian National System for High-Performance Computing (SINAPAD). He received his Ph.D. in Computer Science from the Pontifical Catholic University of Rio de Janeiro (PUC-Rio), Brazil, in 2005. His main research areas are in computer networks, distributed systems, and software architecture, as well as in their application to e-Science, e-Gov and e-Health. He is a member of the Association for Computing Machinery (ACM) and the Brazilian Computer Society (SBC). He is recipient of the productivity research award PQ-2 from the Brazilian Research Council (CNPq).

Chetan Jaiswal is a PhD Scholar at University of Missouri-Kansas City. Chetan's research interest lies in Cloud Computing, Mobile/WSN/Cloud Security, Privacy in Cloud via geographic location of datacenters and Cloud based database transaction systems. He is also passionate about programming, learning new concepts and teaching.

Peter Kacsuk is the Director of the Laboratory of the Parallel and Distributed Systems in the Computer and Automation Research Institute of the Hungarian Academy of Sciences. He received his MSc and university doctorate degrees from the Technical University of Budapest in 1976 and 1984, respectively. He received the kandidat degree (equivalent to PhD) from the Hungarian Academy in 1989. He habilitated at the University of Vienna in 1997. He received his professor title from the Hungarian President in 1999 and the Doctor of Academy degree (DSc) from the Hungarian Academy of Sciences in 2001. He served as full professor at the University of Miskolc and at the Eötvös Lóránd University of Science Budapest. He has been a part-time full professor at the Cavendish School of Computer Science of the University of Westminster since 2001. He has published two books, two lecture notes and more than 300 scientific papers on parallel computer architectures, parallel software engineering, Grid and Cloud computing. He is editor-in-chief of the Journal of Grid Computing published by Springer.

Gabor Kecskemeti (M.Sc., University of Miskolc, 2004; Ph.D., University of Westminster, 2011) is a research fellow at the Laboratory of Parallel and Distributed Systems (LPDS) of MTA SZTAKI. In, 2013, he was a postdoctoral researcher at the University of Innsbruck, Austria. He has been involved in several successful Grid and SOA research projects (e.g., ePerSpace, EDGeS, S-Cube) as well as in the recently funded ENTICE project (focusing on cloud computing) financed by the EU's Horizon2020 framework program. He coordinated the Cloud research group of LPDS in 2011–2012. He was member or chair of the program committees of several European conferences and workshops. He was a guest editor at the Journal of Grid Computing for a special issue on Cloud federations. He has published over 50 scientific papers (incl. 9 journal articles and 3 edited volumes) about cloud and grid computing, particularly from the field of virtual appliance delivery in IaaS clouds.

Attila Kertesz (MSc, University of Szeged, 2004; PhD, University of Szeged, 2011) is a research fellow at the University of Szeged, and at the Laboratory of Parallel and Distributed Systems of MTA SZTAKI, Hungary. His research work covers interoperability aspects of Cloud federations. He is a Management Committee member of the ICT COST Action IC1304 and has participated in several successful European projects including COST IC0805, SHIWA, S-Cube EU FP7 and the CoreGRID EU FP6 Network of Excellence projects. He was member of program committees for European conferences and workshops, and has published over 60 scientific papers having more than 350 independent citations.

Vijay Kumar is the Curator's Professor at Computer Science, University of Missouri Kansas City. Vijay's research area includes information security, wireless and mobile computing and database systems with a particular emphasis related to cyber security and wireless data dissemination.

Craig A. Lee is a Senior Scientist in the Computer Systems Research Department of the Aerospace Corporation. He has worked in high-performance parallel and distributed computing for the last thirty years. This work has led to Dr. Lee's involvement in the Open Grid Forum (OGF) where he served as President from 2007 to 2010. Dr. Lee served as the main liaison between OGF and the DMTF, SNIA, TMF, the Open Cloud Consortium, Cloud Security Alliance, OMG, and OASIS. Dr. Lee is now on the OGF Board of Directors and is heavily involved with NIST, having contributed significantly to the NIST Cloud Standards Roadmap and supporting the NIST Cloud Technology Roadmap. He has served on the program committee for many conferences and workshops, as a panelist for the NSF, NASA, DOE, and as an international evaluator for INRIA. He is an associate editor of Future Generation Computing Systems (Elsevier) and on the editorial board of the International Journal of Cloud Computing (Inderscience). Dr. Lee has published over 75 technical works, including four book chapters and seven edited volumes and issues. He holds a Ph.D. in Computer Science from the University of California, Irvine.

Daniele Lezzi received a B.Sc. degree in computer engineering in 2002 and a Ph.D. in Information Technology Engineering in 2007 from the University of Salento, Italy. From 2002 to 2006, he has been a team member of the Center for Advanced Computing Technologies division of the National Nanotechnology Laboratory of the University of Salento and has been also been lecturing on computer science fundamentals. From 2006 to June 2008, he was a researcher in the Euro-Mediterranean Centre for Climate Changes (Italy) and involved in the design of the computational infrastructure and worked as a consultant of the SPACI (Southern Partnership for Advanced Computing Infrastructure) consortium, Italy. Since 2008, he has been a researcher in the Computer Sciences department of Barcelona Supercomputing Center. His research interests cover high performance, distributed, grid and Cloud computing and programming models. In particular this research addresses the design of programming frameworks for the porting and execution of scientific applications on distributed computing infrastructures like Grid and Clouds with special emphasis on interoperability. He participated in several EC funded projects like GridLab, CoreGRID, BEinGRID, OGF-Europe, SIENA, VENUS-C, IS-ENES, OPTIMIS and EU-Brazil OpenBio, and he is currently involved in the EU-Brazil Cloud Connect project. He is also contributing to the EGI Federated Cloud Task Force, whose goal is to deliver a blueprint that—targeted at both resource providers and user communities—defines how federated virtualized environments can be implemented; the Task Force is also producing a proof-of-concept workable test bed.

Maria Julia Dias de Lima is a Senior Researcher at Tecgraf Institute/PUC-Rio. She holds a D.Sc. in Computer Science from the Pontifical Catholic University of Rio de Janeiro, Brazil (2002). She co-ordinates research and development projects spanning technological solutions for the construction of distributed systems and transferring these solutions to partners from industry and academia. Her research interests include distributed computing, integration middleware, component-based architecture and grid and cloud computing.

Benedita Malheiro holds a Ph.D. and a M.Sc. in Electrical and Computers Engineering from the University of Porto (Faculty of Engineering). She is an Adjunct Professor at the Polytechnic Institute of Porto (School of Engineering) and a senior researcher at INESC TEC (Centre of Robotics and Intelligent Systems). Her research interests include multi-agent systems, conflict resolution, belief revision, personalisation, location-based, context-aware systems and engineering education.

Attila Csaba Marosi is a research fellow at the Laboratory of Parallel and Distributed Systems in MTA SZTAKI. He received his MSc. from the Budapest University of Technology and Economics in 2006. He is involved with Crowd Computing since the start of the BOINC-based SZTAKI Desktop Grid project in 2004. He performed research and development on the topic of cloud federations resulting in the Federated Cloud Management (FCM) architecture that provides a PaaS platform by federating IaaS clouds. He is currently focusing on distributed data processing ("big data"), especially on sensor related data. He was and is involved in many national (HAGRID, Web2Grid, AgroDAT, etc.) and international (EGEE, CoreGrid, EDGeS, EDGI, IDGF-SP, etc.) R&D projects. He is the coauthor of more than 40 scientific papers.

Fernando Meireles holds a M.Sc. in Electrical and Computers Engineering, Majoring in Telecommunications and a three year graduation degree in Electrical and Computer Engineering from the Polytechnic Institute of Porto (School of Engineering). He was a researcher at the INESC TEC (Centre of Robotics and Intelligent Systems) and at the Polytechnic Institute of Porto (School of Engineering. Currently, he is at CERN. His interests include cloud computing, interoperability and abstraction.

Javier Diaz-Montes is currently an Assistant Research Professor at Rutgers University and a member of the Rutgers Discovery Informatics Institute (RDI2) and the US National Science Foundation (NSF) Cloud and Autonomic Computing Center. He received his PhD degree in Computer Science from the Universidad de Castilla-La Mancha (UCLM), Spain (Doctor Europeus, Feb. 2010). Before joining Rutgers, he was Postdoctoral Fellow of the Pervasive Technology Institute at Indiana University. His research interests are in the area of parallel and distributed computing and include autonomic computing, cloud computing, grid computing, virtualization, and scheduling. He is a member of IEEE and ACM.

Marcos Nóbrega Jr is a researcher and developer at LSD-UFCG.

Simon Ostermann received his Dipl.-Ing. and Dr. Techn. degrees from the University of Innsbruck, Austria in 2008 and 2012, respectively. He is currently an Assistant Professor at the Institute of Computer Science, University of Innsbruck, Austria. His work for the Distributed and Parallel Systems Group focuses on the areas of Cloud computing, resource management, energy saving and scheduling. He is the author of over 25 journal and conference publications and won the National Award of Excellence for his PhD thesis.

Manish Parashar is a Professor of Electrical and Computer Engineering at Rutgers University. He is also the founding Director of the Rutgers Discovery Informatics Institute (RDI2), the NSF Cloud and Autonomic Computing Center (CAC) at Rutgers and the Applied Software Systems Laboratory (TASSL), and is an Associate Director of the Rutgers Center for Information Assurance (RUCIA). Manish received the IBM Faculty Award in 2008 and 2010, the Tewkesbury Fellowship from University of Melbourne, Australia (2006), and the Enrico Fermi Scholarship, Argonne National Laboratory (1996). He is a Fellow of AAAS, Fellow of IEEE / IEEE Computer Society, and Senior Member of ACM.

Ioan Petri is a Research Associate in School of Computer Science & Informatics at Cardiff University. He holds a PhD in 'Cybernetics and Statistics' and he has worked in the industry, as a software developer at Cybercom Plenware and then as a research assistant on several research projects. Starting in 2009, he collaborated with the School of Computer Science & Informatics, Cardiff University, as an internship researcher in Distributed and Parallel Computing. He also worked as a research associate in the School of Engineering as an Information Communication technology specialist. Currently, he is working in the School of Computer Science and Informatics as an associate researcher in Cloud Computing. His research interests are cloud computing, peer-to-peer economics and information communication technologies.

Tamas Pflanzner got his bachelor's degree in 2011 and his master's degree in 2013 in Computer Science, specialized in Software Development from the University of Szeged. He worked for the CAS Software AG in Szeged for 2 years as a mobile application developer and researcher. He's currently working as a researcher at the Department of Software Engineering at the University of Szeged. He started his PhD studies in 2015 at the University of Szeged in cloud computing.

Javier Prades obtained a MS degree in Computer Engineering from the Technical University of Valencia, Spain, in 2015. He is currently pursuing his PhD studies in Computer Science and performs research tasks in the Parallel Architectures Group of the University. His areas of interest include distributed systems, parallel programming, virtualization solutions, interconnection networks, and cluster architectures.

Radu Prodan is an Associate Professor at the Institute of Computer Science, University of Innsbruck, Austria. He has over 15 years of research experience in the parallel and 16 distributed computing areas. He earned his Ph.D. in 2004 from the Vienna University of Technology and completed his Habilitation in 2009 from the University of Innsbruck. Prodan coordinated and participated in numerous national and European projects and is currently scientific coordinator of the H2020 project ENTICE. He authored over 100 conference and journal publications (including one IEEE best 23 paper award) and one book in the areas of parallel and distributed computing.

Omer F. Rana is a Professor of Performance Engineering in School of Computer Science & Informatics at Cardiff University and Deputy Director of the Welsh e-Science Centre. He holds a Ph.D. in "Neural Computing and Parallel Architectures" from Imperial College (University of London). He has worked in the industry, as a software developer at Marshall BioTechnology Limited and then as an advisor to Grid Technology Partners. His research interests extend to three main areas within computer science: problem solving environments, high performance agent systems and novel algorithms for data analysis and management.

Carlos Reaño received a BS degree in Computer Engineering from the University of Valencia, Spain, in 2008. He also holds a MS degree in Software Engineering, Formal Methods and Information Systems from the Technical University of Valencia, Spain, since 2012. He is currently doing his PhD in virtualization of remote GPUs at the Department of Computer Engineering (DISCA) of that university, where he is working in the rCUDA project (www.rcuda.net). He has published several papers in peer-reviewed conferences and journals, and has also participated as a reviewer in some conferences and journals.

Yacine Rezgui, School of Engineering, Cardiff University, UK.

Federico Silla received MS and PhD degrees from Technical University of Valencia (UPV), Spain. He is currently an associate professor at the Department of Computer Engineering (DISCA) at that university. His research is mainly performed within the Parallel Architectures Group of Technical University of Valencia, although he is also an external contributor of the Advanced Computer Architecture research group at the Department of Computer Engineering at the University of Heidelberg. Furthermore, he worked for two years at Intel Corporation, developing on-chip networks. His research addresses high performance on-chip and off-chip interconnection networks as well as distributed memory systems and remote GPU virtualization mechanisms. The different papers he has published so far provide an H-index impact factor equal to 23 according to Google Scholar. Currently, he is coordinating the rCUDA remote GPU virtualization project since it began in 2008. Additionally, he is also leading the development of other virtualization technologies. With respect to his teaching activity, he teaches Computer Networks as well as High Performance Interconnects courses at the Computer Engineering School of the Technical University of Valencia.

Giovanni Silva currently acts as a researcher and developer in the Fogbow project (fogbow cloud. or) and as a Computer Science teacher in Software Engineering, Software Quality, Software Testing, and Agile Software Development. Since the beginning of his professional career, he has been involved in projects about Software Quality, Distributed Software and Cloud Computing. He holds a Master's degree in Computer Science and is specialized in public administration.

Vlado Stankovski, Eng.Comp.Sc., M.Sc., Ph.D. is an Associate Professor of Computer Science at the University of Ljubljana, Slovenia. He began his career in 1995 as consultant and later as project manager with the Fujitsu-ICL Corporation in Prague. From 1998-2002, he worked as a researcher at the University Medical Centre in Ljubljana. From 2003 on, he has been with the Department of Construction Informatics at the University of Ljubljana. He lectures in undergraduate computer science subjects. Vlado Stankovski's research interests are in semantic and distributed-computing technologies. He has been the technical manager of the FP6 DataMiningGrid project, financial manager of the FP6 InteliGrid project and took part in the FP7 mOSAIC Cloud project. He is currently taking part in the H2020 SWITCH and ENTICE projects in software engineering for Big Data and advanced Cloud computing. He has also participated in several Slovene national grid related projects. His past experience is in applications of machine learning techniques to engineering and medical problems.

Salman Taherizadeh has a 6-year experience of teaching undergraduate courses including "Web-based Programming" and "Computer Networks". He has published works in IJISM and IET IEEE (ISI) journals. He also has professional experiences in the fields of data mining and knowledge discovery, statistical modelling and computational statistics and object-oriented programming. He is currently employed as researcher at the University of Ljubljana, Slovenia where he works on the topics of monitoring federated Cloud systems and semantic modelling for Cloud interoperability and federation.

Manoj V. Thomas is currently pursuing Ph.D in the Department of Computer Science and Engineering, National Institute of Technology Karnataka, Surathkal, Mangalore, India. He obtained his Bachelor of Technology from RIT, Kottayam, Kerala and Master of Technology from NITK, Surathkal with First

Rank and Gold Medal. He has more than 10 years of teaching experience and he is a Life Member of Computer Society of India. His areas of interests include Computer Networks, Cloud Computing and Cloud Security.

Rafael Tolosana-Calasanz received his BEng and MEng in Informatics from the University of Zaragoza, Spain. He currently works as an Associate Professor at the Department of Computer Science and Systems Engineering of the University of Zaragoza. His research interests lie in the intersection of distributed and parallel systems, cloud computing, autonomic computing and problem solving environments.

Roland Tornyai got his bachelor's degree in 2012 and his master's degree in 2014 in Computer Science, specialized in Software Development from the University of Szeged. His master's thesis is about interoperability of cloud systems. Currently, he is working as a software developer at Ericsson Hungary and as a researcher with the Department of Software Engineering at the University of Szeged.

Erik Torres is a researcher in the Institute of Instrumentation for Molecular Imaging (I3M) since 2010. He received the Ph.D. degree in Computer Science from the Universitat Politècnica de València (UPVLC) in 2010. He has been involved in Grid Technologies, Cloud Computing and Biomedical Informatics, participating in 9 National and European Research Projects. He has authored and co-authored 5 publications in indexed journals and books chapters and more than 10 communications in conference proceedings.

Cristina Ururahy is a Senior Researcher at Tecgraf/PUC-Rio, since 2003. She has been participating in several R&D projects with partners from industry and academia, such as PETROBRAS, National Laboratory for Scientific Computing (LNCC), and Federal University of Campina Grande (UFCG). Currently, she leads the development of the BR-SiOP system, which aims to support the engineers' decisions, helping them in the process of optimizing oil and gas production. The BR-SiOP system leverages the CSBase framework to manage distributed computational resources and control the execution of the different simulators. Prior to Tecgraf, she was a researcher staff member of the Formal Methods Laboratory at PUC-Rio. She holds a D.Sc. in Computer Science from the Pontifical Catholic University of Rio de Janeiro, Brazil (2003). During 2001, she was a Visiting Researcher at the University of Illinois at Urbana-Champaign, working with Prof. Roy Campbell on middleware technologies for Ubiquitous Computing. Her research interests include: distributed computing, integration middleware, component-based architecture and cloud computing.

Szilvia Varadi is a senior lecturer in the Department of International and European Law, University of Szeged, Hungary. She graduated as a lawyer, and defended her PhD thesis at the University of Szeged, Hungary. Her research interests include the legal aspects of enlargement of the European Union, and European and international data protection legislation.

Bruno Veloso holds a M.Sc. in Electrical and Computers Engineering, Major in Telecommunications and a three year graduation degree in Electrical and Computers Engineering from the Polytechnic Institute of Porto (School of Engineering). He is a researcher at the INESC TEC (Centre of Robotics and Intelligent Systems) and a PhD student at University of Vigo. His interests include distributed artificial intelligence, multi-agent systems, personalisation and recommendation systems.

José Luis Vivas received a M.Sc. in Computer Science in 1996 from the Stockholm University, Sweden, and a Ph.D. in Computer Science in 2001 from the Royal School of Technology — KTH, Sweden. From 2002 until 2004, he worked as senior researcher at Hewlett-Packard Laboratories in Bristol, UK, and thereafter as researcher at the Computer Science Department of the University of Málaga, Spain, until 2014. Currently working as a researcher at the Federal University of Campina Grande, Brazil. Research activities are focused on formal methods, security engineering, assurance, and cloud computing.

Ali Reza Zamani is currently a PhD student of Computer Science Department of Rutgers University, and also a member of the Rutgers Discovery Informatics Institute (RDI2) and the US National Science Foundation (NSF) Cloud and Autonomic Computing Center. He received his Bachelor's degree in Electrical Engineering from Sharif University of Technology, Iran in June 2013. His research interests are in the area cloud computing, computer networks, software defined networking (SDN) and network functions virtualization (NFV).

Mengsong Zou is currently a PhD student of Computer Science Department of Rutgers University, and also a member of the Rutgers Discovery Informatics Institute (RDI2) and the US National Science Foundation (NSF) Cloud and Autonomic Computing Center. He received both of his Bachelor and Master degrees in Computer Science from Huazhong University of Science and Technology, China in June 2008, June 2011. His current research interest lies in parallel and distributed computing, cloud computing and scientific workflow management.

Index

Information Resources Management Association

Become an IRMA Member

Members of the **Information Resources Management Association (IRMA)** understand the importance of community within their field of study. The Information Resources Management Association is an ideal venue through which professionals, students, and academicians can convene and share the latest industry innovations and scholarly research that is changing the field of information science and technology. Become a member today and enjoy the benefits of membership as well as the opportunity to collaborate and network with fellow experts in the field.

IRMA Membership Benefits:

- **One FREE Journal Subscription**

- **30% Off Additional Journal Subscriptions**

- **20% Off Book Purchases**

- Updates on the latest events and research on Information Resources Management through the IRMA-L listserv.

- Updates on new open access and downloadable content added to Research IRM.

- A copy of the Information Technology Management Newsletter twice a year.

- A certificate of membership.

IRMA Membership $195

Scan code to visit irma-international.org and begin by selecting your free journal subscription.

Membership is good for one full year.

Printed in the United States
By Bookmasters